Morris Migration

MORRIS MIGRATION

A Saga of Forebears and Descendants

The "Morris Family Tree"

Anne Morris Mertz

HERITAGE BOOKS
2007

HERITAGE BOOKS
AN IMPRINT OF HERITAGE BOOKS, INC.

Books, CDs, and more—Worldwide

For our listing of thousands of titles see our website
at
www.HeritageBooks.com

Published 2007 by
HERITAGE BOOKS, INC.
Publishing Division
65 East Main Street
Westminster, Maryland 21157-5026

Copyright © 1996 Anne Morris Mertz

Library of Congress Catalog Number 95-80377

Library of Congress Cataloging-in-Publication Data
Mertz, Anne Morris
    Morris Migration: A Saga of Forebears and Descendants
1. Historical narrative, descendants of John Morris, born c.1677 in Wales; *Mayflower* antecedents of Sarah Cushman (1766-1842); descendants of Sarah Cushman and Morris Morris (1761-1809); descendants of Rachel Morris (1786-1863) and Morris Morris (1780-1864). 2. History: Pilgrims, Wales, Virginia, West Virginia, Indiana; Civil War, Gen. Thomas A. Morris. 3. Annotated genealogy; allied families of Cushman, Frazee, and others. Includes two bibliographies and index of the genealogy.
486 pages.

Cover illustration: Line drawing of reconstructed Fort Prickett, located near Interstate 79 on Route 3 not far from Fairmont, West Virginia. The original fort was built in 1774, the same year as Fort Morris, and about forty miles southwest.

All rights reserved. No part of this book may be reproduced or transmitted in any form or by any means, electronic or mechanical, including photocopying, recording or by any information storage and retrieval system without written permission from the author, except for the inclusion of brief quotations in a review.

International Standard Book Number: 978-0-7884-0550-0

THIS BOOK IS DEDICATED TO
all our adventurous ancestors who bravely explored,
suffered, and persevered in order to settle new land in our
great country—sometimes to discover, to battle, or to
conceive and create—leading the way for others to follow.

Genealogical Beatitudes

*Blessed are the great-grandfathers who saved embarkation and citizenship papers,
For those show when they came.*

*Blessed are great-grandmothers who hoarded newspaper clippings and old letters,
For they tell the story of their time.*

*Blessed are all grandfathers who filed every document,
For this provided the proof.*

*Blessed are grandmothers who preserved family Bibles and diaries,
For this is our heritage.*

*Blessed are fathers who elect officials that answer letters of inquiry,
For to some they are the only link to the past.*

*Blessed are mothers who relate family tradition and legend to the family,
For one of the children will surely remember.*

*Blessed are relatives who fill in family sheets with extra data,
For to them we owe the family history.*

*Blessed is any family whose members strive for the preservation of records,
For theirs is a labor of love.*

— Anonymous

MORRIS MIGRATION
—♦—
A Saga of Forebears and Descendants

A True Historical Narrative with an Extensive Genealogy of a Morris Family Who Came to America from England and Wales in the Seventeenth Century

Part One
Chapters I – V
Early Welsh Pioneers Unite with Descendants of English Pilgrims to Settle in America

Part Two
Chapters VI – XXIII
The Remarkable Accomplishments of One Morris Branch Which Migrated to Indianapolis, Indiana

Part Three
Genealogy of Our Morris Family
An Annotated Tabulation of Eleven Generations, from the Patriarch to the Present, Finally Assembled in One Book and Indexed

Allied Families: Cushman, Frazee, Friend, Robinett, Spurgeon, Worley, and Worrall
A Brief Record of Families Linked to the Morrises by Marriage or Locality

The Morris "Family Tree" has a sturdy trunk which bears many branches.

> # MORRIS MIGRATION
> ## ─◆─
> ## A Saga of Forebears and Descendants

A True Historical Narrative with an Extensive Genealogy of a Morris Family Who Came to America from England and Wales in the Seventeenth Century

The allied families of Cushman, Frazee, Friend, Robinett, Spurgeon, Worley, and Worral are mentioned in the text and documented in Part Three.

Contents

Acknowledgements and Credits...xii
Introduction...1

Part One
Early Welsh Pioneers Unite with Descendants of English Pilgrims to Settle in America

I   Earliest Accounts of Our Morris Forebears: Seven *Mayflower* Antecedents...7
Mayflower Relationships (Chart)...14
Howland Explorers...15
The Society of Mayflower Descendants...16

II   Beginnings of the Large Morris Family in Wales: Still Called "Cymru" — a Comradeship...17
The Morris Family of Tintern...33

III   Our Early Welsh Morrises: A Heritage to Hold, a Future to Fulfill...39
Morris Family Descent (Chart)...56
Early Intermarriage of the Morris, Cushman, and Frazee Families (Chart)...58
Endnotes...59

| IV | Beyond the Blue Ridge: A Hunter's Paradise...63
Indian Treatment...84 |
|---|---|
| V | Two Morris Morrises—First-Cousins: Trekking Westward Together...87
"Emigrant Woman"...103 |

Part Two
The Remarkable Accomplishments of One Morris Branch Which Migrated to Indianapolis, Indiana

| VI | Morris Morris II and Rachael Morris: Pioneer Sweethearts...109
Morris Parishioners at Cane Ridge Meeting...131 |
|---|---|
| VII | Thomas Armstrong Morris and Elizabeth Rachel Irwin: Their Early Years...135 |
| VIII | Thomas Armstrong Morris: The Railroad Era...147 |
| IX | Thomas Armstrong Morris: Civil War Years...161 |
| X | Thomas Armstrong Morris: Ending a Full Life...179
Selected Bibliography...195 |
| XI | Children of Thomas A. and Rachel Morris: John, Harry, Thomas, Eleanor, and Milton...199 |
| XII | Thomas O'Neil Morris and Estelle Jane Goodale: Middle Son of Thomas and Rachel...203 |
| XIII | Children of Tom and Estelle Morris: Morris III, Harold, Donald, Stanley, Theodore, and Fred...209 |
| XIV | Theodore Hatfield Morris: Early Years...215 |
| XV | Theodore Hatfield Morris and Lisette Susanna Krauss: Maturing...221 |
| XVI | Austin W. Morris and Jane Maria Peppard: Firstborn of Morris and Rachael...235 |

XVII	Milton Morris and Abigail Thayer: Second Child of Morris and Rachael...249
XVIII	John D. Morris and Martha Wiles: Fourth Son of Morris and Rachael...253
XIX	Amanda Melvina Morris and Dr. John Leland Mothershead: Fifth Child of Morris and Rachael...265
XX	Julia Ann Morris and Norman Ross: Sixth Child of Morris and Rachael...271
XXI	Elizabeth Mitchell Morris and John D. Defrees: Seventh Child and Lincoln's Friends...273
XXII	William Little Morris and Nicholas McCarty Morris: Eighth and Ninth Children of Morris and Rachael...285
XXIII	Conclusions...287

Part Three
An Annotated Tabulation of Eleven Generations, from the Patriot to the Present, Finally Assembled in One Book, and a Brief Record of Families Linked to the Morrises

GENEALOGY OF OUR MORRIS FAMILY
   Section I Generations One, Two, Three, and Partial Four: The
      Patriarch and Early Progeny...293
   Index, Section I...303
   Section II Generations Four to the Present: Descendants of Morris I
      and Sarah Cushman Morris...305
   Index, Section II...407

ALLIED FAMILIES: Cushman, Frazee, Friend, Robinett, Spurgeon, Worley, and Worral...443

GENERAL BIBLIOGRAPHY...457
About the Author...467

Acknowledgements

IF IT WERE NOT for the preserved records of a few deceased family members and the help of many wonderful and interested cousins living all around our United States, too numerous to mention here, this book could never have been written nor the extensive genealogy compiled. I do wish to give special accolades to my very good friend and editor, Polly Bowen, who has been tireless and most generous with her time and talents; to Wallace Thompson for editorial assistance and proofreading the narrative; to my librarian daughter, Sandy Smalley, for permissions research; and to my dear husband, Walter, for his patience and cooperation.

Sincere thanks also to Rick Toothman for professional assistance with research on the early Morrises in America, and to Amy Lawrence for the cover drawing on the paperback edition, the title page of both editions, three maps, and advice.

There are bound to be some inaccuracies and omissions in a book of this kind in spite of our efforts; please forgive them.

Credits

Photographs and illustrations not credited below or in the text are from the author's archives.

PERMISSION TO QUOTE copyright material follows: Pictures of Chepstow Castle, Cadw: Welsh Historic Monuments, Crown Copyright; pictures of a Welsh house, Museum of Welsh Life (formerly Welsh Folk Museum), Cardiff; "Builders of Destiny," the Jesse Stuart Foundation, P.O. Box 391, Ashland, KY 41114; sketches by Christian Schrader, Indiana Historical Bureau; "Ode on the Battle of Corrick's Ford," McClain Printing/Publishing Company, Books of Continuing Interest, © 1962, P.O. Box 403, Parsons, WV 26287; portraits, Morris-Butler House, a museum property of the Historic Landmarks Foundation of Indiana, permission from the foundation; photographs, Morris-Butler House exterior and parlor, McGuire Photography, Indianapolis, IN.

INTRODUCTION

In grateful remembrance of our ancestors who, through ... loss of fortune, suffering, and death, maintained stout hearts, and laid the foundation of our country, we [should] give our efforts to preserve that which is worthy in our nation's past ... and to build a worthy heritage for the future."
— From a salute and prayer of the
Colonial Dames of America

A PEOPLE MUST, from time to time, refresh themselves at the well-spring of their origin. When the past and its meanings are remote, it is not simple or easy to know how and why we came to be where we are. Historic preservation, therefore, becomes important to our store of knowledge. We should have interest, appreciation, and even pride in our heritage. We must cherish what our forebears have done before us, should reflect upon their struggles and preserve our knowledge of their beginnings, for they did leave us a legacy.

Each of us had four grandparents, eight great-grandparents, sixteen great-great-grandparents, and on into the past. I believe we should become aware of the significance of who, where, and what they were. By looking at our beginnings with affectionate contemplation we can better realize the contributions which our family has made to the life of this country, with their high standards of human dignity and freedom; of diligence and honesty; of effort, endurance, and physical strength. It should instill in us pride, humility, and a desire to live up to the expectations of our ancestors. By learning something of their past we will have a better feeling for and knowledge of what has already taken place.

Men are not literally created equal. Some are born with great potential, and only some of these achieve the momentum to make the most of that potential. Our progenitors, through their genes and their family traditions, have passed down to us the sacredness of family and the importance of community. There are strong family characteristics in successive generations; there *is* a heritage. We must admire and appreciate the qualities of those who do achieve success and prominence, and be proud and grateful that our heritage continues in the family line.

Too many fine people and happenings have gone unremembered, unrecorded. Unfortunately, the kind and wonderful deeds, the resourceful, heroic coping of our womenfolk have seldom been recorded or even remembered. In earlier times, without our modern facilities and medicines, the pain of bearing so many babies, and the anxieties and labors of nurturing very large families surely taxed their strengths to the utmost. Enduring hardships, pain, sometimes even danger and chaos, were facts of life. We can only imagine the supportive roles they played, in the background, while their menfolk rose to prominence in civil and military life.

This is a saga of *two* Morris Morrises—of those who preceded them and of those who followed. One was my great-great-great-grandfather; the other was his first-cousin and, later, his son-in-law, my great-great-grandfather. This unusual relationship is due to the marriage of two first-cousins-once-removed, both of whom had the same surname of Morris.

* * * * *

There came into my possession in December 1975 a folder and two notebooks containing family memorabilia collected over numerous years by my father, Theodore Hatfield Morris, and by his older brother, Donald Seymour Morris. They were both interested in and truly proud of their heritage. Donald, a lawyer, lived in Indianapolis, Indiana, and therefore had access to local resources, while my father lived in the East. Notes and papers, correspondence, newspaper clippings, and a few old history books of Indiana and the Civil War were all collected but never compiled and excerpted in an orderly fashion. So this material could never be used for reference or as an interesting and true *family* tale.

Desiring to accomplish something worth leaving for posterity, both tangible and meaningful, I believed that all the known achievements, activities, and movements of our ancestors should be assembled and recorded into one source, for our family's future generations. I hope that my family will thus have a sense of what they have come from, and what has brought them to be who they are. This belief—this hope—entailed, eventually, a great deal of research, for genealogy soon becomes a never-ending task. It is my hope that this resulting compilation will add to the knowledge of those who undertake to "unravel" later generations, and benefit all who are interested.

My original intention was to compile and record *all* that I could assemble of the available known material on the early members of my immediate Morris family. It very soon became apparent that this would be cumbersome if not impossible, for there was too much published material about some of the men to record verbatim, namely, that concerning one of the Morris Morrises, two of his sons, Austin and Thomas, and two of his sons-in-law, Dr. Leland Mothershead and John Defrees. Stated somewhat differently, this would have been a tremendous repetition of facts.

Instead, I have attempted to select and quote parts of most of it, giving references. In the case of General Thomas Armstrong Morris, there was entirely too much published material for even this procedure, therefore a bibliography is given at the conclusion of the four chapters concerning him. My undertaking became more challenging and extensive than I had anticipated, and each succeeding phase of study revealed more puzzles.

With some of the earliest research it became necessary to seek professional assistance, working first with a genealogist in Utah and finally with one in West Virginia, both of whom helped me get "unstuck." Correspondence with several third- and fourth-cousins was interesting and rewarding.

This chronological assemblage of facts, quotations, and existing fragments of our ancestors' lives does not necessarily make a fine narrative; an absorbing story, however, was not my primary intent. Rather, it was intended to be a chronological *documentation* of facts, so that a myriad of details, some quite trivial but interesting, would not become lost in time. Such details, moreover, provide a subtle insight into personalities and a way of life. Very probably, additional material is in other old history books not yet discovered.

It also seemed useful to include background information about contemporaneous times and places in order that we could put our forebears in better perspective. We can be proud of this family, some of whose members are mentioned frequently in published histories and newspapers. As they moved out across the land seeking a better life, they contributed much of their strengths and talents to a young nation, helping to expand American culture and the American way of life. *We* have been the beneficiaries of their courage and leadership.

In writing this chronology of our family, *for* my family, my purpose was not only to identify and date its members but also to relive, in a way, the family experience, to become part of something enormous and personal at the same time, something larger than one life, yet intimately connected with it. It is a way of discovering all the past people who have died, yet live on in us; a way to feel a kind of personal immortality. Perhaps that is the magic of genealogy.

Keeping records of our *present* is also important, for the present very soon becomes the past. But it should not be lost or forgotten. The pride and sense of continuity can enrich our existence and create a stronger identity. There can be a personal exhilaration in feeling a part of a living chain—reaching back into the past and looking forward into the future, of being a link between that which has been, what is, and what will be. We all must know and claim our past as we move forward, with points of reference to which we can return in order to compare and measure change and growth. The past was prologue to the present. We then become the link that is prologue to the future.

I hope this work will be useful to members of our extended family as well as a contribution to the genealogical literature in America. I shall leave this legacy of effort and hope. At some future time, may another Morris descendant be interested in delving further into specific bits of reality and care enough to carry this chronology forward—when *this* present has become the past.

Part One
Chapters I - V
Early Welsh Pioneers Unite withDescendants of English Pilgrims to Settle in America

Do not go where the pathway leads. Go, instead, where there is no path—and leave a trail.

— Anonymous

Chapter I

EARLIEST ACCOUNTS OF OUR MORRIS FOREBEARS
Seven *Mayflower* Antecedents

They would be one in building for tomorrow
A nobler world than they had in their day.
They would be one in searching for that meaning
Which bound their hearts to point them on their way
. . . with love and justice strove to make all free
To show mankind a new community.
— Samuel A. Wright

VERY EARLY records of our Morris family are rather meager. It is always hoped that further research will eventually reveal more substantial information. Specific facts stated herein are from research by the author and others, and some from old family notes which have been corrected, where possible, and documented. Because it should be interesting and helpful to have some historical background and knowledge of the life and conditions in which our forefathers lived, that too becomes part of this family history.

Since the very earliest records of the forebears of this Morris family (of which we are presently aware) go back to England, this saga will begin with those ancestors. The other half, the Morrises, hail from Wales —later.

Long before the *Mayflower* voyage of 1620, a female line with the names Tilley, Hurst, Cushman, Howland, and Allerton (but not Morris) is known. Certified genealogists have been able to trace some antecedents of twenty-six *Mayflower* passengers. It has now been definitely proven and genealogically accepted that Rachael Morris, daughter of one Morris Morris and wife of another Morris Morris, was a direct descendant of seven *Mayflower* passengers. Her progeny are therefore eligible for membership in the prestigious International Society of *Mayflower* Descendants—widely considered a privilege and an honor.

A summary of our earliest known ancestors follows. Some of their descendants came to America on the *Mayflower* and became the ancestors of Rachael Morris through her mother, Sarah Cushman.

Henry and Johan Tilley, c. 1465, of Henlow, England, were great-great-grandparents of John Tilley. The parents of his wife, Joan Hurst, have been traced to William and Rose Hurst, c. 1530, of Henlow. John and Joan Hurst Tilley and their daughter, Elizabeth, were *Mayflower* passengers. Elizabeth Tilley married John Howland, another *Mayflower* passenger whose parents have been traced to about 1567 in London. Thomas and Elynor Hubbard Cushman, c. 1550, of Kent, England, were grandparents of Thomas Cushman II, who married a *Mayflower* passenger, Mary Allerton. The Allertons can be traced back to Mary's father, Isaac, born about 1586. His son, Thomas Cushman III, married Ruth Howland, daughter of John and Elizabeth Tilley Howland. These forebears of our *Mayflower* ancestors are our earliest known *documented* ancestors.

The lives of the families in Plymouth will be dealt with in more detail later in this chapter, along with a chart showing the *Mayflower* relationships and descent through Cushman intermarriages.

Our earliest "known" Morris is probably John Morris of Wales, who came to America about 1697, more than a half century later than the *Mayflower* families. Chapter II begins the story of his descendants, one of whom, Morris Morris I, married Sarah Cushman and united the two lines.

But first a synopsis of our Pilgrim ancestors and their reasons for leaving their homeland, followed by more detail on our *Mayflower* families in Plymouth.

*   *   *   *   *

Our Pilgrim ancestors are worth our study, for they showed what can be accomplished by faith, determination, and hard work, with fearless devotion to the loftiest ideals of freedom—unique among the nations of the world. The Pilgrims of Plymouth made *all* men equal before the law, extended their jury system to include *all* men (not just the nobility), established the division of inheritance by *all* children (not only the oldest son), set up the public recording of births, marriages, and deaths by towns, set up the recording of deeds and mortgages and the probation of wills for *all* people, and made the most liberal laws of any society known

Chapter I. Earliest Accounts of Our Morris Forebears ♦ 9

in their time.[1] Their laws and practices were an excellent beginning of democracy, pre-dating by more than a century our Declaration of Independence as well as our American Constitution.

We can agree with Maurice Thatcher, who said so rightly: "We must be proud of the struggles and sacrifices of the Pilgrims, should emulate their spirit and character, [should] *preserve* and *deserve* their heritage."

These Pilgrims were not aristocrats but, generally, a group of intelligent, educated, cultured, devout people, primarily farmers, who had left a fertile and prosperous England. Much has been written about these people. It is very important for us to know the difference between *Pilgrims* and *Puritans*. Briefly, the Pilgrims were Separatists; the Puritans were reformers or "purifiers."

After King Henry VIII took over the Roman Catholic Church in England, no church was permitted in that country except the King's choice, the Church of England, with His Majesty as the supreme head. This resulted in many forms of protest. About 1600 two different groups were secretly organizing. The *Separatists* demanded complete separation from the Church of England, and later were called Pilgrims, for they moved about after 1600. They went first to Amsterdam, where there was true religious freedom, then to smaller, quieter Leyden, Holland, where they established their own community. After some years, wishing not to be absorbed by the Dutch, they finally decided on colonization in America. Although the Dutch offered them free transportation, land, cattle, and even a convoy to settle in New Amsterdam (New York), the Pilgrims declined. Yet they were unable to get a simple charter from their own English king! Eventually, in 1620, they settled in Plymouth, Massachusetts, where they were very friendly with the Indians. These Pilgrims had freedom and governed themselves with good and fair elected leaders, John Carver and William Bradford.

The *Puritans* wanted to reform the church from within. Ten years after the Pilgrims came to America, the Puritans formed the Massachusetts Bay Colony near Boston, which was soon larger than Plymouth. This colony included Salem, where the infamous witchcraft trials were held. It had very many Indian problems, and was governed by the domineering, dictatorial John Winthrop. There was not freedom here in this community, established for profit.

---

[1] *The Mayflower Story*, p. 1.

Our Pilgrims' story began with misfortunes. A poor ship called the *Speedwell* was purchased in 1620 by the Separatists for the voyage to America, where it was to remain. Another ship, the *Mayflower,* was chartered by the group in England to sail at the same time; it was to return to England. The fittest people of the Leyden group—only seventy—sailed from Holland on the *Speedwell* to join the *Mayflower* in England. There were other passengers recruited by the London Merchant Adventurers, who were financing the enterprise. The two ships left Southampton together, in mid-July, and returned to port twice because of the leaking *Speedwell*. It was finally declared unseaworthy, so some of its passengers crowded onto the *Mayflower,* making a total of 104 in all, while the rest returned home with Robert Cushman as their temporary leader. It was intended that other Pilgrims should come on a later ship, that eventually all the Separatists would come to America. Before their landing, forty-one men wrote and signed the *Mayflower* Compact, which became the foundation of most all American democratic institutions. It was simple, brief, comprehensive, and fundamental.

Aboardship, disease had attacked some of the passengers. How many tears were shed into pillows as pain and suffering increased, for the aid of real medicine was nonexistent, with nothing to cure the sickness and relieve the pain. Soon, scurvy, pneumonia, and quick consumption were to claim the lives of many. How extremely discouraging for those brave people who had left their warm homes to venture into an unknown place. A better life loomed more and more impossible. By spring, fifty-two had died; only fifty-two remained. Instead of the planned eighteen dwellings, only seven were needed. The crew of the *Mayflower* was also greatly reduced by sickness although the ship and its crew were to return to England in April. Would the few remaining weakened Pilgrims return with them? It was then that these stalwart souls—the men, women, and children who had survived—made a remarkable and unanimous choice to remain in America, to face together the wilderness, famine, and a terrible unknown. Not one soul voted to return; they all remained steadfast! One member of the crew also stayed in America.

We have all read of their adversities and hardships, of their struggles and strengths, of their first Thanksgiving, which probably occurred in October after the harvest. This was followed in November by the landing of the next ship-full of Pilgrims. Alas, the *Fortune* did not bring the promised provisions or supplies; it *did* bring thirty-five more beings who had to be fed and housed all winter.

There is no loftier example in our nation's history than that of the Pilgrims of Plymouth. Of all our colonies, theirs established the only

Chapter I. Earliest Accounts of Our Morris Forebears ♦ 11

system in which people actually governed themselves. For their time and for generations later, this was to give evidence and hope to great masses of people. Persons determined to be free would somehow find a way.[2]

* * * * *

Two of the families aboard the *Mayflower* particularly concern our Morris family. These were the *Allertons:* Isaac, a tailor, probably from County Suffolk and residing in London; his wife Mary; and their young daughter Mary. Also on board were the *Tilleys* of Henlow, Bedfordshire: John; his wife, Joan Hurst; and their daughter Elizabeth, the youngest of their five children and the only one who came to America with them. (They surely planned to send for the others after they were settled in their new and better life, but deaths would very soon change those plans.) There was also a young single man, *John Howland* of Fenstanton, Huntingdonshire, living in London. He came as a bond servant to the first elected governor, John Carver. These "servants" were not indentured (with written contracts). They were more likely people lacking money who agreed to accompany a friend or relative and work for them for a stated time. After Governor Carver's death, during the first year, John Howland succeeded to be the head of Carver's family group.[3] On the voyage to America, Howland had been washed overboard but he hung onto the topsail halyards and was saved by a boathook.

Seven of the people just named above (excluding Carver) are all direct ancestors of our Morris family, so we should know something of them. There is no evidence that the Tilleys were ever in Leyden, so they must have been part of the original *Mayflower* group from England. Both John Tilley and his wife Joan were dead within the first year. When their daughter Elizabeth was about sixteen, she married John Howland, who inherited Governor Carver's estate and soon afterwards purchased his freedom. He became successively an assistant, a deputy, and for eight years the commander of a trading post; he was deemed "a valuable citizen." John and Elizabeth Tilley Howland had ten children. The youngest of these was a daughter, Ruth, who married Thomas Cushman III.

Mary Norris Allerton also died early but her husband, Isaac Allerton, who had been a burgess and a tailor in Leyden, became Plymouth Colony's business manager. In this capacity he made seven return trips to England. The founder of the coasting trade and the fishing industry, he

---

[2] Ibid., p. 14.
[3] Frank B. Stoddard, *The Truth About the Pilgrims,* p. 140.

was at one time Plymouth's wealthiest citizen. After Governor Carver died in April 1621, Isaac Allerton was chosen as the only assistant to the new governor, William Bradford. In September 1621 he was one of ten men who explored Boston Harbor. The first headland at Nantasket was named Point Allerton in his honor. His daughter Mary married Thomas Cushman II, who arrived at Plymouth on the second ship, the *Fortune*, with his father, Robert (the man who had stayed in Holland to govern those left behind by the leaking *Speedwell*).

Robert Cushman was a wool comber and church deacon in Leyden. He and John Carver had worked together for these Pilgrims, had effected their migration from England to Holland, had chartered the *Mayflower* and bought the unseaworthy *Speedwell*, on which he had embarked at the start. He acted as agent for the Pilgrims in New England, so he left Plymouth to return to England to work on obtaining charters. Son Thomas was left in the home of William Bradford, who adopted him. In manhood Thomas became the governor's confidential advisor and friend. When Elder Brewster died, Thomas Cushman replaced him as ruling elder of the First Church of Plymouth.

There is a Cushman monument at Plymouth erected to the memory of Robert Cushman, the ancestor of all Cushmans in America. One side of the monument memorializes Elder Thomas and his wife, Mary Allerton Cushman, who was "the last survivor of the first comers in the *Mayflower*." Their son was Thomas Cushman III. He married Ruth Howland, the daughter of John and Elizabeth Tilley Howland, mentioned above. So it is through these two Cushman marriages that we Morrises claim seven ancestors who came over on the *Mayflower*.

The Cushman family continued to name their sons Thomas, eventually moving southward to Lebanon, Connecticut, and thence to Essex County, New Jersey. The sixth Thomas Cushman married into the very prolific Frazee family. At New Providence, New Jersey, in 1764 he took for his wife Mary Frazee, daughter of the Ephraim who sired eighteen children.[4]

It is certified that Thomas Cushman VI served as a private during the Revolution, in Bull's Troop, Second Regiment, Dragoons, Continental Army, enlisting March 2, 1777, in New Jersey. This was after thirteen years of marriage. He was discharged August 9, 1780.[5] When the war was over, attracted by the great possibilities of the new country west-

---

[4] "Early Bourbon Families," *The Kentucky Citizen*, cited hereafter as *Ky. Cit.*, p. 3.
[5] *Ky. Cit.*, from Adj. Gen.'s Off., Trenton, N.J.

Chapter I. Earliest Accounts of Our Morris Forebears ♦ 13

ward, Thomas and Mary Frazee Cushman migrated with their family to Monongalia County, Virginia, now West Virginia.[6] They purchased lands adjoining his brother, Isaac Cushman, in Pennsylvania, which were also next to the land of Mary's brothers, David and Ephraim Frazee, in Virginia.[7] This was real wilderness country.

Mary Frazee and Thomas Cushman had three known children. Their daughter Sarah married Morris Morris. Sarah and Morris had twelve children, all of whom were carefully recorded in a family Bible.[8] They are also all recorded in the Genealogy in this book with their families down to the present, as much as was possible. Second of their twelve children was Rachael Morris, who married another Morris Morris, her first-cousin-once-removed. These two Morris Morrises, sons of the brothers Richard and John, therefore first-cousins although nineteen years apart in age, will be designated henceforth as Morris Morris I and Morris Morris II, when distinction is needed. Please be aware that this is not the more familiar father-and-son designation.

Thus it is *up* through a line from Sarah Cushman, through two Thomas Cushmans in America, that our Morris family traces our *Mayflower* ancestry: to Isaac and Mary Norris Allerton and their daughter Mary, and to John and Joan Hurst Tilley and their daughter Elizabeth, who married John Howland. A chart to make this clearer follows this page.

But to make you smile, a bit of whimsy comes before it—with tongue in cheek, of course.

> The DAR-lings chatter like starlings
> Telling their ancestors' names,
> While grimly aloof with looks of reproof,
> Sit the Colonial Dames.
>
> And the Cincinnati, all merry and chatty
> Dangle their badges and pendants.
> But haughty and proud, disdaining the crowd
> Brood the *Mayflower* Descendants.
>   — Arthur Guiterman, 1936

---

[6] Alvah W. Burt, *Cushman Genealogy and General History*, p. 251.
[7] *Ky. Cit.*, from Off. of Co. Clerk, Monongalia Co., W.Va., Entry Bk. 2, pp. 8, 36, 129, 168.
[8] *Ky. Cit.*, from Bible listing, *Ky. Gen. Recs. 1934-1939*, vol. 3, in D.A.R. Library.

Mayflower Relationships
and Descent Through Cushman Intermarriage

Note: Seven *Mayflower* passengers' names, ancestors of the author, are in italics and boldface.

Cushman	Allerton	Tilley — Howland
		Henry Tilley (b. c. 1465) m. Johan *
		Thomas Tilley (b. c. 1490) m. Margaret*
		William Tylle (b. c. 1515) m. Agnes*
Thomas Cushman I (b. c. 1552) m. Elynor Hubbard		Robert Tilley (b. 1540) m. Elizabeth*
Robert Cushman (b. 1577) m. Sarah Reeder	*Isaac Allerton* (c. 1586-1658) m. *Mary Norris*	**John Tilley** (1571-1621) m. **Joan Hurst**
Thomas Cushman II (bef. 1607-1691) c. 1636 m. - - - - - - - - ->	*Mary Allerton* (c. 1616-1699)	*Elizabeth Tilley* (1607-1687) m. ***John Howland*** (1592-1672)
Thomas Cushman III - -> (1637-1726)	married - - - - - ->	Ruth Howland (d. 1672/9)
Thomas Cushman IV (1670-1727) m. Sarah Strong		
Thomas Cushman V (b. 1705) m. Mary*		
Thomas Cushman VI (1739-aft. 4/11/1787) m. Mary Frazee		
Sarah Cushman (1766-1842) m. Morris Morris I (1761-1809), son of Richard		
Rachael Morris (1786-1863) m. Morris Morris II (1780-1864), son of John II		
Thomas Armstrong Morris (1811-1904) m. Elizabeth Rachel Irwin		
Thomas O'Neil Morris (1846-1916) m. Estelle Jane Goodale		
Theodore Hatfield Morris (1883-1965) m. Lisette Susanna Krauss		
Anne Estelle Morris (b. 1913) m. 1937 Walter Day Mertz		

*Last name unknown

Chapter I. Earliest Accounts of Our Morris Forebears ♦ 15

HOWLAND EXPLORERS

BECAUSE the Howland name will not be mentioned later in this saga of exploration and pioneers, it is appropriate to tell here of two brave, pioneering descendants of John and Elizabeth (Tilley) Howland.[1]

They came from Isaac, John and Elizabeth's tenth and last child, down through eight generations to the mid-1800s, to Oramel Howland (c. 1833-1869) and Seneca B. Howland (1843-1869). These two half-brothers were members of the exploration party of Major John Wesley Powell in 1869. Backed by Senator Ulysses S. Grant, it was the first official group of Americans to explore the Colorado River and the Grand Canyon by boat. Beautiful Lake Powell was eventually named for their indomitable, one-armed leader.

Although these Howland brothers traveled more than two centuries after their Pilgrim ancestors, they were real explorers nonetheless, mountain men who encountered for ninety days and almost a thousand miles very real hardships, great dangers, and treacherous rapids. They, too, were some of our many wonderful ancestors who, like the Pilgrims, were pioneering heroes, with a spirit of courage and adventure inherited in their genes.

---

[1] R. A. Whitney, "In Search of Oramel and Seneca Howland," *The Mayflower Quarterly* (Plymouth, Mass., Aug. 1994).

THE SOCIETY OF MAYFLOWER DESCENDANTS
An International Organization

There is a Mayflower State Society in every state and in Canada. Some of the larger states have organized Colonies (branches) so distances are not too great for attendance at meetings.

The headquarters of the International Society of Mayflower Descendants is the large, handsome Winslow House, the former home of passenger Edward Winslow's grandson, in Plymouth, Massachusetts. Another building at the rear of the property houses the executive offices, the archives, and an excellent, newly-designed, well-staffed research library.

The Society is publishing the lineages, down through the first five generations, of all the twenty-six men of the *Mayflower* voyage who survived to have descendants. These volumes can be found in most historical libraries as well as in Plymouth, where they may be purchased. These new, professionally researched publications greatly assist those wishing to become members. Inquiries may be addressed to the Historian General, P.O. Box 3297, Plymouth, MA 02361.

Headquarters of The General Society of Mayflower Descendants
4 Winslow Street, Plymouth, Massachusetts

Chapter II

BEGINNINGS OF THE LARGE MORRIS FAMILY IN WALES
Still Called "Cymru" — a Comradeship

Lift up your heads in pride, O Men.
Recall the story, page by page,
Of whence you came, and once again
Acclaim your priceless heritage.
Lift up your heads.
— Rev. John MacKinnon

A PROJECTION OF BRITAIN with its three sides on the sea is the remote little country, the nation of Wales, which still retains the very same boundaries that were established in the Dark Ages. Celtic origins and a "spell of the landscape" have kept it always a separate entity—proud, defiant, individual. The Cymros (Welshmen) have a special holy feeling for kinship, for a pacifist tradition of Welsh non-conformity, for folklore and mystery, for poetic strength, a special feeling for their own Cymraig, the oldest *living* literary language in Europe. But not until about 1725 was there a Welsh Bible. Then their language became a written tongue.

Wales used to be a land of small, independent states composed of feudal lords residing in various-size castles, with a pastoral following in walled villages. Each had its own Welsh culture and folklore, located invariably at the base of the castle hill.

In ancient times the great Rys, later the Mauwr Rys, still later the larger Morris Family, resided in southern Wales, which was not an extensive area yet in a small country. Surely they were all related. As time passed they multiplied and spread out across Gwent, throughout Glamorgan, and even farther. Some remained noblemen, warriors, aristocrats; some became yeomen (freeholders owning their own land) and peasants, and eventually a middle class grew up. This multiplying occurred throughout most of Europe over a very long period of time. So the early Morris history of southern Wales is *our* history, *our* background, even though we cannot prove descent directly for the past nine hundred years. Our immediate family comes from the very same locale as the Morrises discussed in this and the next chapter. They are our antecedents, a part of our roots.

Even before the year 1100, European people adopted a second name to aid in distinguishing an ever-increasing population. Often "son" ("ap" in Welsh) was used, or a personal characteristic, such as "strongbow," or an occupation, such as "baker," was added. The knights needed identification in battle as their faces were covered with helmets, so they painted patterns on their helmets. Thus evolved the coats of arms. Records were kept, particular patterns being granted to knights and their families for valor, hence the beginning of heraldry.

At the southern "gate" of Wales, guarding the Wye River crossing near its mouth, set atop an enormous mass of grey, triangular rock was a huge feudal castle and below it a walled village, both called "Chepstow." Today the village, no longer walled, is a thriving small town. The castle, one of the first and possibly the greatest, still stands as a wondrous ruin, now approaching 940 years old. Its location between a high cliff and a ravine was of strategic importance from Roman times onward. Here the Wye produces the highest tides in the British Isles. Chepstow is worth our time and interest because it is "our" Morris castle.

This great structure was built in 1067 to 1071, just after the Norman Conquest. It was the first *stone* castle built in Britain where no earlier wooden castle had been constructed before. Its builder was William Fitz Osbern of Normandy, the great Earl of Hereford, a boyhood friend and companion as well as a political colleague and companion-in-arms of William the Conqueror. It was the first castle constructed, designed to be a secure base for pushing westward to conquer the Welsh kingdom of Ghent and to defend his newly acquired second home, England. Chepstow Castle was one of a chain of forts that included nearby Monmouth Castle, which Osbern also erected.[1] These massive buildings were powerful reminders of Norman influence and strength.

Chepstow Castle, alias "Striguil," was privately owned during its 929-year lifetime except for about four different times when it was held by the Crown. Built in four successive stages, it was altered in Tudor times and remodeled again after the Civil War for defense with cannon and musketeers.

The fourth owner, Walter Fitz Richard of Clare, founded nearby, in 1138, the beautiful and now famous Tintern Abbey, a monastery of the

---

[1] John C. Perks, *Chepstow Castle*, p. 5; *Castles & Historic Places*, p. 93.

Chapter II. Beginnings of the Large Morris Family in Wales ♦ 19

Cisterian Order, today a starkly beautiful ruin in the lovely, lazy countryside. Its broken tracery windows reveal the splendor which used to be there long ago. Henry I gave de Clare the lordship of Striguil about 1114. He also began the lordship called Marcher of Striguil, which lasted for centuries, until Henry VIII incorporated the marchers into the realm. Marcher lords (from "mark," dividing line) were border warriors. Striguil is an old Welsh name derived from Ystraigyl meaning "bend-in-the-river."[2]

De Clare's successor as owner of Chepstow Castle was his nephew of the same title and name but also better known as "Strongbow," one of the two conquerors of Ireland. The other was Rhys Fitzgerald (son of Gerald), the brother of the prince of Gwentland in southern Wales. Together these two warriors, Strongbow and Rhys Fitzgerald, led an expedition to conquer the Irish and accomplished "the Norman Conquest of Ireland" a century after that of England in 1066.

The *Morris* coat of arms was bestowed in 1171 to the *Rhys* family of Wales during that invasion of Ireland. King Henry I of England awarded to Rhys Fitzgerald the title of "Mawr," signifying in Welsh "great, warlike, powerful"; thus the name became *Mawr Rhys*.[3]

This large Rhys (or Rys) family continued to use proudly the name of Mawr Rys, which eventually, over a very long period of time, became *Morris*. This family multiplied greatly over the centuries, moving into other parts of Wales, especially the southern shires of Glamorgan and Carmarthen.

Let us go back in time to the earlier *Rys* family to find a Welsh hero, Lord Rys ap Tewdwr (1078-1093), the King of Deheubarth, in a very dominant position in South Wales.[4] There was a prestigious and famous Rys ap Gruffydd (1155-1197) who became the leading prince who won a pact from Henry II in 1171. He was master of most of south Wales, which then consisted of the two small principalities of Monmouth (or Gwent) and Glamorgan, and the larger Kingdom of Dehoubarth. "As the twelfth century drew to a close, much of Wales was still subject to the authority of native rulers. The most powerful was [another] Lord Rys of Dehoubarth.... Bard and chronicler alike sounded the praises of 'The Lord

---

[2] Perks, pp. 5-6, 44.
[3] Morris Bros., *The Morris Family & Its Coat of Arms*.
[4] *Encyclopedia Britannica (1957)*, vol. 23, p. 292.

Rys.'"[5] He ruled from his stronghold, Dinefwr, standing alone high on the edge of a precipice. Today it is haunting. Nearby are Llandeilo, Trapp, and the ruins of Castle Carreg Cennen, built by a marcher lord. It, too, was held for a time by Lord Rys.

A large Rys family was residing in the area of the walled villages of Chepstow and nearby Monmouth, birthplace of Henry II (1387), whose entrance is still guarded by the famous Monnow Gate, built in the middle of a bridge, the only fortified bridge in Britain. Here the wandering Wye River with steep sides and water meadows was surrounded by royal forest, where wild boar and deer were hunted by the king and the marcher lords. It is still said to be the most beautiful valley in Britain. (A couple of centuries later, in 1492, the name Mawr Rys had changed; a Robert *Morris* was bailiff [sheriff] of Monmouth.)

By 1283, Edward I, King of England, was determined to bridle the warring Welsh barons, to subdue the Welsh princes, and to rule Wales as part of England. He systematically built a colossal chain of immense fortress-castles on the edges of Wales, great symbols of glory and despair. Beaumaris, Caernarfon, Conway, Harlech, Aberstwyth, and Flint all stand as monuments to his determination to subdue the barons. He also conquered and greatly enlarged some existing castles, including Chepstow. Edward I then set up an administrator in each castle to control and dominate the surrounding Welsh people.

But the Welsh were perpetually unwilling and generally unruly subjects, with the marcher lords continually resisting and battling to maintain their baronial preserves, their prestige, and their power.

In an attempt to appease the angry Welsh, Edward finally promised them a *Welsh* king. So he forced his pregnant wife to move to the great castle of Caernarfon, prime symbol of English authority, where his son was born. Then Edward called the populace together and said that he would show them their next king, born in Wales—a Welshman! Before an anxious crowd, he held up the infant, his new English son, for them to see. Thus it was that the Welsh people were cheated by Edward, whom they now hated more than ever. (The English Prince of Wales is *still* invested with extravagant pomp in this same Castle of Caernarfon.)

All through the next 178 years, through the reign of seven kings of England, the willful defiance of the Welsh continued. We read of a revolt

---

[5] Ibid.

Chapter II. Beginnings of the Large Morris Family in Wales ♦ 21

led by Rys ap Meredydd of Dryslwn in 1287.[6] A Rys served Richard II as Captain of Archers. His younger brother, Meredydd ap Tudwr (but also a Rys), fathered the handsome Owen ap Meredydd, commonly called Owen Tudor.[7] This Owen Glendower (Owain Gllyndwr), was a Welsh nobleman, a Prince of Wales who, through his mother, claimed Lord Rys lands on the banks of the Dee and the Teify and for a time won the castles of Harlech and Aberystwyth in the early 1400s.

By 1440, Owen Glendower, ruling from Harlech Castle, continually attacked the enemy.[8] He was determined that his Welsh people should have a country which they could call their own. Ruling under the flag of the Red Dragon (still in modern times the symbol of Wales), Glendower finally achieved a princedom. He had united Wales. Now Wales was a state of Europe! The years of this golden age of dignity were brief, only about ten, but were a kind of climax in his country.

Owen Tudor became clerk to the beautiful French Catherine, widow of Henry V. They soon lived together and had five children who were legitimized by the courts. One of their sons, Edmund, made a similarly advantageous match with Lady Margaret Beaufort, who had Lancasterian connections to the Tudors.

The only son of Edmund and Margaret was Hari (later Henry). He was born at a time of strife between Lancastrians and Yorkists, rival claimants to the English throne. Yorkist Richard was on the throne in 1485. *Hari Tudwr,* who posed a threat, had been exiled to Brittany, where he plotted to return to wrest the crown from the Yorkist king. Hiring a personal guard of 200 men, Hari uniformed them in red, like the Welsh symbol of the red dragon. (Later these men were called buffetiers, as one of their duties was to watch over the king's plate. Today their lineal descendants are the beefeaters, dressed in red at the Tower of London.)[9]

Hari returned to England from Brittany with two thousand French mercenaries. He landed in the little cove at Mill Bay near Dale Village, then a smugglers' haunt near St. Ann's Head. This is not far from "Dewi

---

[6] Ibid., p. 293.
[7] Ibid., vol. 22, p. 536.
[8] This warrior hero Glendower, along with Llwelyn ap Gruffud, continually attacked from their mountain strongholds. Castles Raglan, White, Skenfrith, and Grosmont are still relics of those days of hope and glory. The latter is today in one of the prettiest backwaters in Britain.
[9] Pamela Dalton, *In Britain,* p. 26.

Saint," the magnificent cathedral of St. David's, one of Britain's first centers of Christianity. It was August 4, 1485, at sunset when Hari arrived, and here he added three thousand more supporters. Hari Tudwr was on his way to battle at Bosworth Field. There Richard III was waiting with eight or nine thousand men in his army. In the fifteenth century it was the custom for the king to ride into battle in full armor before his followers. Bosworth was the very last occasion on which an English king personally led his army.

The battle was furious. A knight of the Rys family, Sir Rys ap Thomas, led his troops to Hari's side and, so the legend goes, slew King Richard, knocked off his crown, which fell into a hawthorn bush, and placed it on Hari's head.[10] Hari triumphed. At the age of twenty-eight he became Henry VII, King of England *and* Wales!

This Hari Tudwr began the Tudor line, which gave sovereigns to England. So it was a Welshman who ended the longtime Wars of the Roses, the battles between Lancaster and York, and at last brought peace to England and Wales alike. The year 1485 is usually considered the founding of the Tudor dynasty, which lasted for 118 years.

Two years after he was crowned, Henry VII arranged a canny marriage to Elizabeth of York, thus uniting the Red and White Roses and assuring their children an indisputable right to the throne. (Their larger-than-life son was to be the famous Henry VIII, and they would have a remarkable granddaughter, Elizabeth I.)

Henry VII (Hari Tudor) was a cautious spender and money was the foundation of much of his success. He built St. Peter's Church at Ruthin in north Wales, with a roof of five hundred oak panels, as a gift to the Welshmen who helped him gain the throne.[11] He also built much of King's College Chapel in Cambridge, and also the Henry VII Chapel in Westminister Abbey, London. Here a stained glass window shows the crown of England on a hawthorn bush (Remember the Battle of Bosworth Field?), surmounted by a Tudor rose. Carved effigies of the couple adorn the tombs of Henry VII and Elizabeth.[12]

When Hari Tudor had taken the throne of England, the Welsh people thought that at last Wales would be equal, or perhaps even supreme, in Britain. They were wrong. Welsh lords, of course, had followed Hari Tudor to London. Being English became fashionable among their upper

---

[10] *National Geographic*, vol. 1, July 1993, pp. 50-57.
[11] Dalton, p. 28.
[12] Ibid.

Chapter II. Beginnings of the Large Morris Family in Wales ♦ 23

classes. But the peasant folk and literati back home in Wales kept the faith of loyalty and Welshness. Then domineering, self-centered Henry VIII came to the throne, declared there would be no country of Wales, no marcher lords, and, alas, even forbade the speaking of Welsh. Disbanding the monasteries to take their riches for himself, he withdrew from Catholicism and proclaimed himself head of the Church of England.

* * * * *

Having mentioned the names of the Rys family so very many times in this tale of the Welsh, perhaps now is the time to suggest, *with tongue in cheek, of course,* that the *Morris* family might possibly claim a *distant* relationship to English royalty through the *Rys* family, and thereby to the Tudor Line! We remember that *Rys Fitzgerald,* in the mid-1100s, won the honored title of "Great" and became *Mawr Rys.* Later the name changed to *Morris.*

* * * * *

In 1542, only fifty-seven years after the Battle of Bosworth Field, Wales, containing thirteen shires, was incorporated into the realm of England. One hundred fifty years after that, England had two civil wars. Then the magnificent and greatly enlarged Chepstow Castle, at that time six hundred years old, experienced the stormiest period of its long history. And the Morris family was still involved! Raids and skirmishes in and around Chepstow were frequent; however, the Parliamentarian general, William Waller, in 1643 was unable to reduce Chepstow and other Gwent castles for Cromwell. Then in 1645 Parliament's artillery forced the surrender of Chepstow's sixty-four men and seventeen cannon.

During the Second Civil War, in 1648, Chepstow was seized for the king by the Royalist Sir Nicholas Kemeys (Kemmis), the king's general. But soon Cromwell's forces under Colonel Ewer besieged and breached the walls. *Lewis Morris* (born 1601) of Tintern in neighboring Monmouth was second in command. He cut off a water supply which ran through Pearcefield, the adjoining estate of his son-in-law, John Walters. (Chepstow did have its own well, however.) Lewis Morris then set Chepstow Castle afire, probably at Marten's Tower (built so long ago in 1285 by Roger Bigod III), for that seems to have been the easiest place to attack by land. Charred places still show there today amid the ruins. For this strategic feat Lewis Morris was awarded a motto and a crest to be added to his coat of arms, as described below.

There are today several different coats of arms for different Morris families. The one in the front of this book represents the families of southern Wales: of Carmarthen, of Glamorgan, and of Monmouth, the area in which our family was rooted. As mentioned above, our family's coat of arms was bestowed in 1171 by King Henry of England to the Rys family of Wales during the invasion of Ireland, a century after the Norman Conquest. At that time the title of "Mawr," signifying great and powerful, was awarded to Rys Fitzgerald, and from then on he used "Mawr Rys" for his name.

The original coat of arms comprised a red and silver shield with gold lions and red dots surrounded by gold and red leaves, topped with a silver helmet trimmed in red. Below the shield was a banner of gold and red.

Four hundred and seventy-seven years later, in 1648, Chepstow Castle, then held by the king, was again besieged by Welshmen. As described above, Lewis Morris of Tintern (friend of William Penn) cut off the water supply from the adjoining estate, then set fire to that aged castle! For this action Lewis Morris was awarded a motto *added to* the banner in his coat of arms: "Tandem Vincitur," signifying "He Will Conquer in the End." Also added above the shield was a silver stone tower ablaze with red and golden flames. (See the Morris coat of arms at the front of this book.)

During its more than six-hundred-year-long, battle-scarred life, Chepstow Castle passed through many different hands, on many different sides of many causes. What a collection of tales it must hide beneath its crumbled walls!

After the war, the lands of the Marquess of Worcester were declared forfeit, and Chepstow, a "fairy-tale castle," was granted to Cromwell[13] until Charles II restored it to its rightful owner, Lord Herbert of the Beaufort family. It was held by them from 1468 until 1914. Multiple uses filled those years. It was a garrison until 1619, then used as warehouses, workshops, and meeting rooms, next a glass factory, then a smithy. How sad and demeaning were the fates of a giant, too big and too old. The castle was partially dismantled in 1690 and after that it was left to decay, although parts were still roofed and floored in the early nineteenth century. Chepstow was sold in 1914 to an individual, Mr. D. R. Lysaght. Eleven years later the owner's son gave it to the Department of the Envi-

---

[13] Jeremy K. Knight, *Chepstow Castle, Welsh Historic Monuments*, p. 14.

Chepstow Castle, near the mouth of the Wye River, Wales. Built in 1067–1071, it was the first stone castle in England.

ronment for Preservation, in perpetuity.[14] Striguil, or Chepstow, "can still be studied as the epitome of Marcher history and architecture."[15]

Chepstow Castle was still being preserved by the government in 1983 when this author was there, open for the public to climb all over (dangerously), to marvel, and to appreciate. It was then 916 years old! Chepstow, although in ruins, is still truly majestic, stretched out beside a bend in the Wye, on cliffs sheer to the river. Altered and enlarged numerous times, it contains various kinds of stone, stonework, and architecture. All the roofs and main floors are gone but it is possible to climb the towers and some walls. After approaching through the three-story gatehouse, which once had a portcullis, the lower bailey (courtyard) is entered between two round towers with slits for shooting arrows through. These towers used to contain a prison, a guardroom, and a fireplace.[16] There are still vestiges of beautiful tracery windows, of elaborate details of molding and carving, of existing latrines which extend over the river far, far below. Even some bands of very ancient, dark, reused reddish Roman tiles are on the lower walls, probably robbed from the ruins of the town of Caerwent, a few miles to the west.[17] Banding was a late-Roman technique. Remarkable preservation is there in a small sculptured panel of human figures—reused Roman sculpture. The middle bailey still has an ornate red plaster design.

In the first bailey were domestic buildings, a Lesser Hall, and the four-story Marten's Tower, which had a basement and a decorated chapel. Long, long ago the wealthy nobleman Roger Bigod III, third owner of Chepstow Castle who had inherited it and became Earl Marshall of England under Henry III, had elegant living quarters in here.[18] This, "the Great Tower," was named Marten after a prisoner who spent twenty years there in captivity.[19]

---

[14] Ibid., p. 32.

[15] Charles W. C. Oman, *British Castles*, pp. 153, 156.

[16] John Burke, *The Castle in Medieval England*. Windsor Castle has the most famous round towers. The advantages were military: no corners for attackers, and no "blind spots" which defenders could not cover. William Marshall, Earl of Chepstow and tutor to King Henry's son, emulated Windsor's technique by inserting circular towers into the walls of Chepstow.

[17] Knight, p. 32.

[18] Burke, pp. 25, 84. Like his predecessors in the unruly Bigod family, Roger deserted his king, then passed his inheritance to his nephew, who also turned against the Crown. The barons were all perpetually rebellious.

[19] Marten's Tower was called a "keep" because men lived and were kept there. It was square, could be built higher than the earlier wooden towers of Europe, and was easier to

Continued...

Chapter II. Beginnings of the Large Morris Family in Wales ♦ 27

Bailies, barbican, and walls divided the castle into separate sections; this aided in its defense, for each compartment could be defended separately if necessary.[20] The entire complex is a marvel of skillful architecture. The labors of the builders were amazing when one realizes that each stone was dug from the ground, cut by hand, dressed, hauled, hoisted, and fitted together with care, all without the aid of machinery.

The medieval village of Chepstow once had a wall one thousand yards long of unmortared stones which enclosed about 130 acres, with village houses huddled inside the fortress walls. There were towers and a gatehouse, which used to have a portcullis. This, the access into Chepstow from the landside in medieval times, was all built about 1272 by Roger Bigod III, then owner of Chepstow Castle. This nobleman also rebuilt, enlarged, and greatly beautified nearby Tintern Abbey during his lifetime.

Today, with steep cliffs behind it, the haunting ruin of Tintern Abbey nestles in the Wye Valley in Gwent. A delicate shell, it is a lovely sight despite the plunder of the Reformation. The original Abbey, built long ago in 1138 by the fourth owner of Chepstow, Richard de Clare, was on a smaller scale than the later thirteenth-century design of grandeur, rebuilt in 1288 by Chepstow's sixth owner, the nobleman Roger Bigod III, who beautified it. This was a Cisterian house of fine craftsmanship with stone-vaulted ceilings and massive tracery windows.

William Wordsworth was inspired to write a poem of several pages about this area of the wandering Wye, "Lines composed a few miles above Tintern Abbey, on revisiting the banks of the Wye during a tour. July 13, 1798." A few of his immortal "Lines" follow.

Once again I see
These hedge-rows, hardly hedge-rows, little lines
Of sportive wood run wild: these pastoral farms
Green to the very door, and wreaths of smoke
Sent up, in silence, from among the trees!...
Oh sylvan Wye! thou wanderer thro' the woods,
How often has my spirit turned to thee!

---

defend with fewer soldiers. There was also a two-story Great Hall with many passages and rooms, storage, a buttery, a pantry, a porch, and four stairways.

[20] The middle bailey contained a corner tower, a gallery, and another tower of many rooms. Although there were never buildings in the next upper bailey, there was a tower. Beyond this was a fourth and last enclosure, the barbican, more towers, and an upper gate. The stone walls, called curtains, were twelve to twenty feet thick, so they withstood most medieval siege artillery except the bore and the battering ram. Beyond the back gatehouse, a deep ditch extending from the castle to the cliff was cut right through solid rock.

The ruins of Tintern Abbey, in the Wye Valley near Chepstow Castle, Gwent, Wales. The original Abbey was built in 1138 and rebuilt in 1288. The detail shows one of its massive tracery windows.

About four hundred years after Roger Bigod, a prominent *William Morris* lived in the mid-1600s on that same "Tintern" estate mentioned earlier, in Monmouthshire near Chepstow. He had five children: Lewis, a colonel under Cromwell who set Chepstow on fire, thereby adding to the coat of arms; William; Mary; Richard, a captain under his brother Lewis; and perhaps Thomas. At least four, possibly all, of these children of William Morris came to Barbados and later, in the mid-1600s, some moved to New York. From this family are descended many distinguished Americans including one signer of the Declaration of Independence, one signer of the U.S. Constitution, two state governors, and several state chief justices. The *English* Robert Morris who was a signer of the Declaration of Independence and "financed the Revolution" was not a relative.

A separate addendum concerning this family follows this chapter, although these Morrises are not our *direct* relatives. All Morrises of southern Wales were "cousins" in *early* Welsh times. But our branch came to America a few decades later, in the *late* 1600s, and directly from Wales to Philadelphia, not via Barbados. It behooves us, then, to know about this illustrious Tintern family so we will not confuse them with our

Chapter II. Beginnings of the Large Morris Family in Wales ♦ 29

own less aristocratic Morris ancestors. We should not make false claims of relationship to the signers of the Declaration of Independence and the U.S. Constitution, or the Revolution's financier, if we are asked.

The earliest Morrises of *Wales* rooted wide and deep, intermarried, and became a large part of the Welsh populace. Our Morris family was probably of less affluent stock than the earlier aristocracy of Tintern. By the eighteenth century Wales was generally a poor country. The few exceptions were the large landholders and the wealthy coal and slate mine owners. Only ninety miles wide, forty at its narrowest point, and one hundred thirty-six miles north to south, Wales contains only eight thousand square miles. It is about the size of New Jersey and is smaller than Massachusetts. Wales' great northern mountains provide little fertile land.

In the south, the vale of Glamorgan still has small, fertile farms, just north of which are the coal fields. In the eighteenth century mining conditions were extremely poor, always done by candlelight.

Housing was meager. A small-holder's hut, called a tyddyn, was often of native stone, built into a hill, with a flagstone entrance. It was usually long and low, with a low door used by the people as well as their animals. Each group had a room on either side and provided heat for each other. Sometimes a kitchen and second story were added. To quote a contemporary observer of the 1700s, "The situation of farm houses ... is frequently very bad. They are in instances built in the Low Bottoms [on the very bank of a stream, hence a damp area], and in others at the extremity of the farm ... many of them constructed of large stakes and wattle [corn husks and rubble], then plastered over with a mixture of loam and cow dung, some of them whitewashed."[21]

Without exception the roofs were of straw thatch, with broom, heather, and fern forming the under-thatch. The houses or cottages were dark, the only light being admitted through the door, but in some instances there were lattices for admission of light, formed by interwoven sticks, which might or might not be shuttered. This lack of windows was attributed by some writers to the window tax.[22]

Some Welshman, however, were well-to-do and had money enough to be frivolous, with no thought of leaving their homeland. We read of a

---

[21] Edward Williams, alias Iolo Morganwg, ref. 13115 B.
[22] Peate Iowerth, *The Welsh Home*.

Welsh Folk Museum, Saint Fagans, near Cardiff. *Above:* Typical stone house with slate roof. *Below:* Interior, showing enclosed bed, for warmth, and "corn dollies," above the gun, for good luck.

Chapter II. Beginnings of the Large Morris Family in Wales ♦ 31

Valentine Morris, who was one of the most spectacular of the eighteenth-century squires. He made his seat in the town of Chepstow a showplace of the "Picturesque," a fashionable thing to do at the time. This meant the transformation of one's abode into the quaint and pretty, giving it an artistic, delightful, pastoral feeling.[23]

New schools were just beginning to produce a literate populace. Strict Methodism was overtaking the Church of England among the literati and peasant people alike. Some non-conformists resisted that very strict Methodisim for a free form of religion. This was quite typical of the Welsh temperament: to be individual, intellectual, to be free thinkers.

There were many Quakers and Unitarians among the Welsh. Edward Williams of Flemingston (see footnote 21), who called himself "Iolo of Glamorgan," was the primary founder of the Unitarian faith in Wales. The most learned Welsh scholar of his time, he was a pacifist, an opponent of slavery, a poet, a writer of hymns, and a strong nationalist. He was devoted to Welsh culture, especially that of Glamorgan.

William Penn's father was a Welshman and friend of William of Tintern. Penn's son, also named William, was a Quaker and a friend of William of Tintern's son, Lewis Morris (who set Chepstow Castle afire in 1648), also a Quaker. Because of political reasons Lewis eventually went to Barbados, then later to New York.

In fact, many people left Wales for political reasons. In the 1690s, 1740s, and 1750s England went to war against France and fought in both Europe and America, the Protestants against the Catholic "Pretenders." Other Welshmen came to the new America to escape religious prejudices, the mandatory tithes, and Englishmen. Some hoped to create a new Welsh homeland.

When William Penn came to the tract of land King Charles had given him in 1681, he suggested naming it "Sylvania," meaning woodland. The king added "Penn" as a prefix, hence "Pennsylvania," meaning Penn's woods. It included the "three lower counties," which later became the state of Delaware. The Pennsylvania Quakers settled in beautiful countryside near Philadelphia, leaving many very Welsh place names: Bryn Mawr, Bryn Athen, Tredyffrin, Radnor, Saint Davids, Berwyn, Narberth, Bala Cynwyd—the area where the author spent her growing-up

---

[23] Iowerth, p. 218. It was Valentine Morris and his kind, particularly, who could afford to use the greeting "Vos Hail" (to your health), which is the original of "Wassail," of Welsh origin. Today "wassail" is used as both a verb and a noun. This fermentation of apples, spices, ale, and sugar is usually associated with Christmas.

years. There was a Welsh Tract in Delaware, granted in 1664. Welsh Baptists settled Swanzey in Connecticut.

We think *our* Morris ancestors came to America in the very late 1600s "to be free," as several old Welsh folk songs sadly relate—free of the life and the conditions in their homeland.

Above: Interior of the Unitarian Chapel, the only church that was moved to the village at the Welsh Folk Museum. This chapel represents the liberal free-thinkers of Wales, so typical of their national personality.

Chapter II. Beginnings of the Large Morris Family in Wales ♦ 33

THE MORRIS FAMILY OF TINTERN

Note: This document concerns the prominent William Morris family of Tintern, Wales, who came to America in the mid-1600s, more than a half century before our own Morris family emigrated. It is important for us to be cognizant of this information, so we will know which Morrises were signers of the Declaration of Independence and the Constitution, and also about other well-known American leaders bearing the name.

WILLIAM MORRIS, rooted in his own acres, chieftain of his countryside, was living in the 1600s on an estate called "Tintern" in Monmouthshire, Wales, near the lovely Tintern Abbey. Along the Wye River were farms with pretty pastures, water meadows, rabbit warrens, fishponds, and quiet woods. William Morris was a Quaker and a friend of William Penn's father. He had five children: 1) Lewis, 2) William, 3) Mary, 4) Richard, and 5) Thomas.

This family sided actively with Cromwell's Parliamentary Party during the Rebellion. About 1656 William was seized of his estates Tintern, Denham, and Ponterey. Eventually each of these grown children considered it prudent to cross the ocean until the "storm blew over." Brief accounts of these descendants follow, with Richard taken out of chronological order for reasons explained later.

I. LEWIS MORRIS (1601-1691), the eldest and the daring one who set Chepstow Castle on fire and cut off its water supply in 1648, was a strong Quaker and a good friend of William Penn. Penn's father was a Welshman and an admiral under Cromwell. Lewis Morris was made a colonel in 1655 and then was advised by Cromwell to make himself "master of the West Indies." The Restoration made Lewis deem it expedient to remain at Barbados. Col. Lewis Morris is listed in 1679 (by Hotten) as having four hundred acres and two horses. He acquired the island of Saint Lucia and married Elizabeth Almy, daughter of Chris Almy of England, who went to Boston in 1635. Before Lewis died he left property to his nephew Lewis, son of Thomas (V, below), by deed, in 1689. All the rest he left by his will to another nephew, also named

Lewis, son of Richard (IV, below). His wife, Elizabeth, was executor of his will, in 1695.

II. WILLIAM MORRIS JR. (born 1612), second son of William of Tintern, was lost at sea but his son John (died 1688) owned plantation lands in Barbados.

III. MARY MORRIS of Tintern (born 1614), possibly married William Webly, came to America and held lands in New York next to her younger brother, Richard the merchant.

V. THOMAS MORRIS (born c. 1633?) the probable fifth child of William of Tintern, possibly never came to America but stayed in Barbados where he was in charge of two rascals at St. Michaels in 1680. He married Sarah (last name unknown), who was living in 1680 when Thomas owned 144 acres and 100 slaves. They had four children:

    A. LEWIS (c. 1655–1694 or '95), of Passage Point, Shrewsbury, New Jersey, was the sheriff in 1692 of Monmouth County, N. J. (which was most certainly named for Monmouth in Wales whence this Morris family came). This Lewis owned three hundred acres in Middletown, 1670–1678, and was also judge of Sessions Court in 1695. He became known as "Lewis of Passage Point" to distinguish him from other Lewis Morrises. Lewis had received property by deed in 1689 from his uncle, Col. Lewis Morris, before the latter's death.

    B. ROBERT, born c. 1660, married Frances Staley.

    C. THOMAS (twin), born 16 February 1678 in Barbados.

    D. DOROTHY (twin), born 16 February 1678 in Barbados.

IV. RICHARD MORRIS (1616 or '36, died 1672), the fourth child and third son of William of Tintern, became the main progenitor of the American Morris family, hence this author has taken him out of chronological order and listed him last. Richard had served with distinction as captain in his older brother Lewis's regiment under Cromwell, after which he also went to Barbados in 1654. A Richard is listed in 1679 as owning two horses. Mormon Church records on film (not always reliable) listing American Morris immigrants show that he was married in Barbados to Sarah Poole (born c. 1643 at Barbados). But Richard left that island to become a merchant in New York. In 1650 he purchased 2,000 acres, although another account says that in 1670 he purchased a 500-acre plantation known as Bronxland, just over the Harlem River in Westches-

Chapter II. Beginnings of the Large Morris Family in Wales ♦ 35

ter County, of which he owned a third. His brother, Colonel Lewis Morris, owned two-thirds. This estate became known as "Morrisania" (pronounced Morris*ay*nia), in what is now the city of New York. Captain Richard Morris also held a grant from Phillip Carteret of 1,000 acres of land on the Delaware River next to New Castle, Delaware. After only two years in New York, Captain Richard Morris the merchant died at Morrisania, leaving a son.

A. LEWIS MORRIS (1671-1746) was the progenitor of many outstanding descendants. Inheriting the properties of both his father and his uncle, Colonel Lewis Morris, he became an extremely wealthy and landed gentleman and owner of Tintern Falls Iron Works. He resided at both Tintern Manor, Shrewsbury, N.J., and later the Westchester plantation Morrisania. He was a judge of the Superior Court of New York-New Jersey in 1692, New York chief justice in 1715, and was appointed in 1738 the first governor of New Jersey when it was first separated from New York, serving for eight years until his death. He became known as Governor Lewis Morris to distinguish him from his uncle, Colonel Lewis Morris of Chepstow fires and of Barbados. He was a Tory. In 1702 he requested from Queen Anne an Anglican church. The present building of 1769, in Shrewsbury, Monmouth County, N.J., has a gilded crown on its spire. He is buried there. Morris County, N.J., and its county seat, Morristown, as well as the New Jersey National Historical Park are named for him. Two of his sons were Lewis and Robert.

1. LEWIS MORRIS (1698-1769) became judge of the Court of Admiralty in 1738 and speaker of the New York Assembly in 1737-1746. He had four sons.

   a. LEWIS MORRIS (1726--1798) was a Yale graduate, a New York representative in the Continental Congress, a signer of the Declaration of Independence, and third lord of the manor of Morrisania. It is interesting to note that this "Lewis the signer" was the great-grandson of Captain Richard of Tintern, the immigrant to New York, the merchant. This same Lewis the signer was a friend of William Penn's father, also a member of the Continental Congress, 1775-1777, was an aide to General Nathaniel Greene, and eventually became a major general in the Revolution. He married Mary Walton of New York and had four daughters and six sons. At least three of these served as officers in the Revolution and received the special thanks of Congress for their services.

b. STAATS LONG MORRIS (born 1728) married an English girl and served in the British Army during the Revolution.

c. RICHARD MORRIS (1730-1810) was a framer of the first state constitution of New York, the second chief justice of New York, and judge of the Admiralty.

d. GOUVERNEUR MORRIS (1752-1816) (son by a second marriage; his mother's maiden name was Gouverneur), was a graduate of Columbia University. An intimate friend of George Washington, he served in the Continental Congress, was a member of the committee that wrote the Constitution of the fledgling United States in its final form, and was one of its signers. As assistant to Superintendent of Finance Robert Morris, no relation, he helped devise the U.S. coinage system, using "dollar" and "cent" and decimals. He served for two years as minister to France during the French Revolution.

2. ROBERT HUNTER MORRIS (brother of 1 Lewis 1698-1769, judge and speaker) was the governor of Pennsylvania. His son:

a. ROBERT MORRIS Jr. was a chief justice of New Jersey.

The above members of this complicated Morris family, who have been selected from a large genealogy with many repetitive names and mentioned here for their special achievements, are but a small part of forty-eight pages of Morris genealogy, researched and published in Stillwell's *Historical and Genealogical Miscellany* (see References, below). Only a portion of it is given here, primarily to show something of the Morris family that was illustrious in early American political, military, and judicial history, about which we frequently read but of which we are not a direct part.

This should make it clearer for us to know who are *not* our direct ancestors when we read about the "signers" and other well-known Morris men of the East in our country's early history.

* * * * *

Two other Lewis Morrises are mentioned here because they were from Carmarthen and were sufficiently well-known to be in the *Britannica*. Lewis Morris (1700-1765) was born just after our ancestor John had departed for America. He became an important Welsh poet and antiquarian.

Chapter II. Beginnings of the Large Morris Family in Wales ♦ 37

His great-grandson, Lewis Morris (1833-1907), born in Carmarthen, graduated from Oxford, became a lawyer, was knighted, and published many books of fine poetry.[24]

There was also a Morris Morris (no descendants) from Melbourne, Australia, living in New York City in 1933 who came from a line of Welsh Morris Morrises, from Penrhyndnedrooth near Port Madoc, Wales. Twin brothers, sea captains David and Morris Morris (born 1819), settled in Melbourne, Australia, and sired a line of Morris Morrises. In 1933 Donald Morris of Indianapolis, who met Morris, remarked, "He has the Morris nose and eyes like Uncle Milton A. Morris."

We must not be confused by the *English* Robert Morris (1734-1806), born in Liverpool of humble parentage, son of Robert and Murphet Morris, whose antecedents are said to have come from North Wales. Robert, the son, came to Philadelphia with his parents as a young lad of thirteen. He became the superintendent of finance for Pennsylvania with Gouverneur Morris (above, but no relation) as his assistant. Robert was a member of the Continental Congress and a signer of the Declaration of Independence, and came to be known as "the Financier of the Revolution," contributing considerably from his personal resources. In 1871 he set up the Bank of North America.

In the new America, out of fifty-six signers of the Declaration of Independence, eighteen were of Welsh descent, as were fourteen generals in the American Revolutionary Army.

Thomas Jefferson's ancestors are said to have come from Snowdonia in Wales, where a plaque honoring Jefferson was erected in 1933.

Henry Adams of Dyfed came to America in 1636. His great-grandson, John Adams, was the second president of the new United States.

One of the greatest American architects, Frank Lloyd Wright, named both of his complexes "Taliesin" in honor of his ancient family's home in Wales.

Today, branches of the Morris family can be found in every state of the Union. They are well represented in the arts, sciences, and professions, as well as in the world of commerce and government. In our own immediate family we find many military leaders as well as professional writers, both men and women.

---

[24] *Encyclopaedia Britannica*, 1957 ed., vol. 15, p. 821.

References

Church of Jesus Christ of Latter Day Saints, Salt Lake City, Utah.
Encyclopedia Britannica. Vol. 15. Chicago: Encyclopedia Britannica Co., 1957.
Mertz, Anne Morris. 726 Loveville Road #904, Hockessin, Delaware 19707-1513.
Morris, Jan. *The Matter of Wales*. Oxford: Oxford University Press, Walton Street, OX2 6DP, 1984.
Philadelphia Inquirer, The. July 1969.
Seaver, J. Montgomery. *Morris Family Records*. Philadelphia: American Historical and Genealogical Society, 1924.
Spofford, Ernest. *Armorial Families of America*. Philadelphia: Bailey Banks & Biddle, 1929.
Spooner, Walter W. *Historic Families of America*. Vol. 3. New York: Historic Families Publishing Assoc., 1907.
Stillwell, John M. *Historical and Genealogical Miscellany, Early Settlers of New Jersey and Their Descendants*. Vol. 4. Baltimore: Baltimore General Publishing Co., 1970.
Virkus, Frederick A., ed. *Abridged Compendium of American Genealogy*. 7 vols. Chicago: The Virkus Co., 1925-1943.

Chapter III

OUR EARLY WELSH MORRISES
A Heritage to Hold, a Future to Fulfill

Roots hold me close; wings set me free.
Spirit of life, come to me, come to me.
— Unitarian hymn

CYMRAEG, THE WELSH LANGUAGE, was spoken quite generally in Wales through the 1800s. In the seventeenth and eighteenth centuries both the surname and the given name of Morris were very common, and even the double name of Morris Morris was occasionally bestowed. To complicate matters further, before 1813 a patronymic system of naming children was frequently used. (This was the custom also in the Netherlands and in Scandinavia before 1900.)

An added prefix or suffix to a proper name, such as Fitzhugh, son of Hugh, or Morrison, son of Morris, is a true patronym. There was also the frustrating Welsh patronymic naming system of having the surname change with each generation by dropping the second name. For example, David Jones's son John became John David, whose son Jenkin became Jenkin John, whose sons Richard and James became Richard Jenkin and James Jenkin. This ancient system was used extensively but not entirely, so research in early Wales is truly confusing and challenging, and the results questionable.

In spite of all this, the author has made a serious attempt to tie into one logical story line all the available *corrected* family notes in addition to the result of research from many sources, although records do differ. All evidence must be examined and sorted before any deductions can be made, in order to make reasonable inferences consistent with available facts.

All our family tales have said that brothers came from Wales. Some say the towns of Swansea and Glamorgan, near Cardiff, the capital, was the source of our Welsh forebears. This is an area of Wales where the Morris family was quite prolific. Glamorganshire (the county of Glamorgan), formed in 1536, contains 660 square miles and is on the southern coast of Wales, on the Bristol Channel. The vale of Glamorgan is still called the genial "Bro Morgannwg." Carmarthen County adjoins Glamorganshire on the west.

Fishing, agriculture, and the manufacture of fine woolens are important industries today, but one mostly thinks of coal mining. In addition to coal, there is also still some copper, iron, lead, and slate to be mined. The old hamlet of Morris Mawr (Great Morris) is buried beneath the steelworks of Port Talbot in Glamorgan.

The port towns of Swansea, Llanelly, and Kidwelly, and inland Carmarthen are all very close together within an area of about twenty-one miles. Llanelly (pronounced Klan-*eth*-ly—between the teeth) is situated between both counties.

Carmarthen's gentle, undulating farming countryside belies its ancient origins, for the ruins of a Roman fort are there and some remaining medieval streets. Scattered over the green hills are impressive remnants of several Norman castles: Kidwelly, Llanstephan, Dynevwrand, and Carreg Cennen. The modern National Library and a University College are now in Carmarthen, whose people still speak the old Welsh language lovingly.

Not far away is Chepstow, a little town on the winding Wye, reigned over by the enormous castle in ruins. Here also is St. Mary's Church and a sixteenth-century town gate containing a small museum. Only four miles away stands the once-elegant thirteenth-century Tintern Abbey, whose lovely, delicate tracery windows still remain, mid-air, to beguile today's admirers. This whole beautiful area is part of our Welsh heritage.

The Latter Day Saints of Utah (Mormons), noted for their vast genealogical efforts and extensive library, provide long lists of early Welsh Morrises, a few even in the 1600s. The author carefully studied all their recorded Morrises, with particular emphasis on the counties of Glamorgan and Carmarthen. Our family names and appropriate dates were concentrated in one area and are recorded in the LDS library. The puzzle seemed to piece together. There is still no definite proof, however; therefore the relationships are not published here.

Some Morris family branches possess notes and old charts, often undocumented and incorrect, yet some of our forebears did care enough about their roots to attempt to keep old records. They had few published materials to research, no indexes, no microfilm, microfiche, or computers. We must not be too critical, only grateful that they had memories, and that they tried.

There is variance and disagreement. How many brothers actually came to America? Did one or some remain in the East? And how many of

Chapter III. Our Early Welsh Morrises ♦ 41

them did pioneer over the mountains into present West Virginia and beyond? Only *two* brothers have been definitely documented, after disproving a great deal of false "tradition," incorrect "research," and even some old published history books of Indiana. So this book will deal primarily with the two proven brothers, with some careful reconstruction added as "probable." It is my hope that future careful and correct research will add to this account.

* * * * *

Times had not been good in Wales in the late 1600s and early 1700s; economic, intellectual and religious conditions were all restricted. Most people existed with few comforts and worked very hard for a meager living. The freeholder was no longer free. There was a spirit of revolt in some people against the conditions of life; in others there was a spirit of adventure to win greater opportunity. Many Welshmen, Englishmen, Germans, and some Irishmen and Scots considered emigration to that new and uncharted land of America, where there were acres of virgin soil for all, religious tolerance, and no barriers of class distinction. There was a promise of future betterment and a kind of adventure. On the other hand, there was not the security of a long-established community.

Some Morrises emigrated to America in the very late 1600s, and many more came during the early-to-middle 1700s. About sixty years after our English Pilgrim forebears—the Tilleys, Allertons, and a Howland —arrived in 1620, some of *our* Morris family came from Wales to pioneer in America. They surely came in a small sailing vessel, very probably leaving from "the County Borough of Carmarthen,"[1] or possibly from Swansea or Llanelly of Glamorgan country on the southern coast of Wales, to land and disembark in Philadelphia.

Many early passenger lists have been studied. The most logical one found to date begins with a document of "... ffreightment, 1697-1698 between Owen Thomas of the County burrough of Carmathen [Carmarthen], mercer [dealer in woven fabrics and small wares], owner of the good ship called the *William Galley,* now riding in the river of Towy, of the one part, and David Powell, of the parish of Nantmell, in the county of Radnor, and John Morris of the parish of Karbadamfyneth, in the county of Radnor, yeomen, of the other part ... being desirous to goe beyond seas for Pensilvania ... with the next good wind ... after the tenth day of May next ... and directly sail for Philadelphia in Pensilva-

---

[1] "An Old Charter Party," *Welsh Emigration to Pennsylvania,* pp. 30-2. Nancy Haines' file also mentions Philadelphia.

nia." David Powell, eleven passengers, is the first named on a list of sixty-two, and three other Powell families. John Morris, six passengers, is second on the list. The cost was five pounds and thirty shillings for those "twelve years and upward," thirty shillings if under twelve except "sucklings," who were free. Below this account of "a charter party" is the reassuring notation that "... *the passengers named were in Philadelphia by March, 1699*" (two to three years later).[2] Listed in Filby's *Passenger and Immigration Lists Index* (near the end of the first of three pages of Morrises) is "Morris, Jno. 20, Maryland and/or Virginia 1699, *9151 p. 195.*" (Numbers in italics denote the dated book source and its page number.)[3] Could this be the same John Morris?

It should be mentioned here that there was a Thomas Morris, born in 1691, who is frequently mentioned in early Maryland records[4] and living at the same time in the area of Point of Rocks, Maryland, near the area of our documented Morris family; however, no proven connection has yet been found. It would seem logical that he was a relative; if so, perhaps a younger brother of the John just mentioned above, possibly being one of the six passengers listed in John's group.

Immigrants coming to America were rarely recorded because people were simply moving from one part of the British Empire to another, so the English government kept little track of it, very unlike the German situation. Did this family of Morrises remain in Philadelphia, or perhaps in "Upland," now called Chester? Many with that surname were already in Philadelphia, those who had come mostly from Barbados during the earlier 1600s. (See Endnotes to this chapter.)

Welsh families settled just west of Philadelphia in great numbers, also southwest in William Penn's Welsh Tract in what is now Delaware. Indications would make us think the Morrises were not Quakers, for they didn't remain in Pennsylvania. Instead, they, along with other families (some who came with Penn in 1683), eventually moved on westward

---

[2] "An Old Charter Party," pp. 30-2. Emphasis added. The double ff, as in ffreightment, was used before the capital F was invented.

[3] P. William Filby, ed., with Mary K. Meyer, *Passenger and Immigration Lists Index,* vol. 2, p. 1494.

[4] Thomas Morris signed a petition in 1742, Grace L. Tracey and John P. Dern, *Pioneers of Old Monocracy, Early Settlement of Frederick County, Md., 1721-1743;* another in 1748 (for road from Nelson's Ferry to Fredericktown). In 1749 he was allowed money by the March Court of Frederick Co., Md., (Tracey and Dern, p. 389) for burying a poor woman, and an additional sum to care for her orphaned child. Two years later, at the June Court 1751, he petitioned to be set levy free, as he was sixty, poor, and very infirm.

Chapter III. Our Early Welsh Morrises ♦ 43

across northern Maryland, usually about the distance of a day's walk, before settling once again.

It has been impossible to find any complete account of early settlements, for their residents kept no commonplace books. Paper was very scarce; there was no time for diaries. Even the dead were not always marked or recorded, resulting in sparse records of the wilderness. Of these, few were kept; many have been lost or destroyed.

The American story has been one of movement, dangerous and costly, but a story of challenge and bravery. Our family was indeed a part of this movement. John Morris, who arrived in America with his party of six on the good ship *William Galley,* sired a family; we know, surely, of only two sons. There is a definite pattern over a period of many years of migration for our two Morris brothers, Richard and John, and likely their father John (until he died) moving westward in a straight line directly below and very close to the present east-west southern boundary of Pennsylvania, over a period of many years. This border was not settled when they purchased the land, lived on it for a while, and then moved on. Today we call the land they lived on Maryland and West Virginia. Border disputes had raged for years. Not until 1787 did Francis Deacon survey Maryland's military lots, and in so doing he located what is now the state line. Seventy-six years later, in 1863 during the Civil War, *West* Virginia's boundary lines were settled.

Land transactions and tax lists have been found in Maryland which enable us to be specific as early as 1748. Richard Morris (son of John I, the emigrant) of Frederick County, Maryland, purchased "a parcel of land and plantation," fifty acres for forty pounds, called "Swedeland" near Toms Creek in northern Frederick County, near Emmitsburg, Maryland, from Elizabeth and John Friend.[5] Friend was a Swede of Lancaster County, Pennsylvania. This was our Richard; there were no other Morrises listed or found in or near this area, and records indicate that the Morrises were acquainted with the Friends and other area families who started out in Philadelphia.

Just a year after this land purchase by young Richard Morris, we find that in the same area in 1749 one John Morris, very probably Richard's emigrant father, was appointed constable of Sugarloaf Hundred by the justices of the March Court of Frederick County, Maryland.[6] (Sugarloaf was the name of their mountain.)

---

[5] State Archives, Annapolis, Md., Hall of Land Records, Land Book 21.
[6] Millard Milburn Rice, *This Was the Life,* p. 252.

The Swedes and Finns had first come to America in 1638, landing in what later became Wilmington, Delaware. Having lived in a forested land, they brought to America their practice of forest clearance, shifting cultivation, dispersed farms, and the construction of log houses and mills. Very soon other colonists adopted their ways.

John Friend had earlier "patented" Morris land in 1741,[7] meaning he had secured a government grant of bounded territory. The purchase of the land which Morris acquired was not absolute. The Lords Baltimore required annual rent, even on purchased lands, and property could revert to the proprietary for failure to pay the rent. No recorded conveyance of this land by Richard Morris was found, and the next roll indexes never show Morris as being charged with annual rent at Swedeland.[8] The 1783 statewide assessment for Frederick County is not preserved, otherwise it might have been possible to have backtracked to Swedeland.

After living in Swedeland about seven years and then selling to Richard Morris, John Friend moved on westward, crossing the North Ridge, "the Devil's Backbone," into Virginia, which shows on a 1780 Maryland map. Then Friend retraced a bit to Maryland, where he and other Friends settled, in 1765, in a former Indian camp in old western Garrett County, very near the present West Virginia line.[9] The Friend family called their settlement "Friendsville, in Sandy Creek Glades," although Sandy Creek did not run through there.

This community of mostly Swedish Friends had connections with the very large family of Frazees who settled close by at Frazee Ridge, Buffalo Run, and at Blooming Rose, along with most of the Spurgeons. Both of these families will become in-laws of the Morrises later. We will find some Friends, Frazees and some Spurgeons together twenty-six years later in Fort Morris during Indian raids!

Richard Morris remained back in Swedeland, Maryland, on Toms Creek for about twelve years. Then he too moved directly westward only about sixty-three miles (a good day's walk) further (toward Friendsville) to Oldtown, Maryland, where he purchased, on 31 July 1759, one hundred acres for fifty pounds on Town Creek in present Allegheny County, east of Martins Mountain. This land was already called "Morris

---

[7] Annapolis, Index 54. Friend later patented at least two parcels in present Washington County which he called "Chestnut Level" in 1744 and "Brandywine Level," n.d.

[8] Annapolis, Index 56, 58.

[9] John Friend was a chain carrier for George Washington, which meant that he held the chain as his job in Washington's surveying party. There is a helpful library in Friendsville.

Chapter III. Our Early Welsh Morrises ♦ 45

Chase," also referred to as "Morris Choice."[10] It was about six miles from the mouth of Town Creek,[11] and had also been patented by Joseph Flint and his wife, Charity, in 1753.[12] This implies that Richard (or some Morris) was in the area (living there?) as early as 1753, as we cannot find any other Morrises before him. Or, possibly, could Joseph Flint have foreseen a wedding for his daughter with Richard? This is a wild guess for we know not Rebecca's last name; it might have been Flint. The same day in 1759 Richard also bought, for twenty-five pounds, a second tract called "Morgans Chance" nine miles from the mouth, also patented by Flint in 1753.[13]

We can feel very sure that this is our Richard Morris (there were many others) because the Robinett and Spurgeon families were also there. Later, they appear on the land and marriage records as neighbors, as well as family. We have often read of friends and whole families traveling together as they migrated. Knowledge of this practice is an aid in research.

Here in Oldtown, called that by the Indians, five feeder Indian trails still exist as roads to the meeting place of the Shawnees, their trading post and campsites. Maryland State Road Commission signs say that it was the "fording place for the 'Great Warriors Path' of the 'Five Nations' from New York to the south." It was one of the longest Indian trails in America.

The Indians left no dates or deeds; only the white men's writings mention them. Charles Calvert of England granted a patent in 1739 through Governor Ogle to J. Charlton for the old, abandoned Indian village on the Potomac already called Oldtown. This was sold in 1746 to Thomas Cresap, the first white person in Allegany County, Maryland, who then added more land to his property[14] and built a shelter at his home in connection with his Indian trading. Lots were eventually laid out in 1763. (Richard Morris had come in 1759 and was constable in 1764.) The Ohio Company took over the shelter, establishing a larger warehouse. Now "violent but not vicious" Tom Cresap was Maryland's most important and notable frontiersman and a deputy surveyor for the province, a patronage position. Very likely it was he who created the Ohio

---

[10] Annapolis Index, pp. 770-1.
[11] Old Town Creek empties into the Potomac River southeast of the Town Creek bridge, which crosses Route 51 near the C&O Canal dam.
[12] Annapolis Land Rec. 54.
[13] Annapolis Index, pp. 772-3. Following the recording of the second deed, the clerk inserted a notice of a stray horse that Richard had apprehended.
[14] Irvin G. Allen, *Historic Oldtown, Maryland*. The Shunto Indians moved on to the Ohio Valley.

Company (in 1748), although he and son Daniel were the only non-investors. Wealthy men such as Governor Dinwiddie of Virginia, George Fairfax, Thomas Lee, and Lawrence and Augustine Washington (brothers of George) were the influential investors, having requested 500,000 acres along the Ohio River from the king.

A whole book has been written about this large fur-trading Ohio Company. Although it never mentions a Morris, eventually one feels pretty sure that our Richard must have known the Cresaps well and traded with or for them. We begin to see the emergence of Richard's character as an enterprising, eager frontiersman, making the most of his very early pioneering situation.

"Hundreds" were judicial divisions, similar to townships, generally thought an area large enough to provide a hundred men. This term was eliminated in Maryland in the very late 1700s but is still used in Delaware.

The 1761 tax assessment for Oldtown Hundred, Frederick County, is apparently the only surviving tax list for this portion of the county. The constable, one Providence Mounts, returned a list of taxables—males of sixteen and upwards—in the hundred. Quite a few of these tax names turn up later in Monongalia County, (West) Virginia, and in Fayette County, Pennsylvania.

There are no Morgans on this tax list who might have named Richard Morris's Morgans Chance. It was probably named by David Morgan (1721-1813), originally from Berkeley County, Virginia, later from Monongalia County. Morgan's son Evan's pension records stated that he was born in Oldtown.

James Spurgeon Sr. is taxed with four tithables. This is probably the same James who was in the Antietam Creek area as early as 1733.[15] Listed also are Wm., Jno., and James Spurgeon Jr., each with one tithable. Richard Morris is listed immediately ahead of the three younger Spurgeons. John Morris, Richard's brother, is listed immediately following the Spurgeons on the same list. (Both of these Morris brothers are direct antecedents of the author in two different lines, because, as we shall see later, a Morris married a Morris first-cousin-once-removed.) Richard and John are the two brothers whose migration we will continue to follow and document.

---

[15] Annapolis 19839-16.

Chapter III. Our Early Welsh Morrises ♦ 47

Maryland's government was unique among the North American colonies because it had proprietary status. Only officers and His Majesty's custom service were appointed directly by the Crown. Their patronage became a mainstay of political power; patronage supported several successive Lords Baltimore with large sums. Even county clerks were part of this patronage system. Personal revenues included quit rents and fees for land sales, as well as customs duties, license fees, fines, and forfeitures. Taxes were higher in Maryland than in any other colony.[16] It was in this system that Richard Morris was "appointed" constable of Oldtown Hundred in 1764.[17] One must wonder if he paid for the job!

Thomas Cresap built a stockade fort here in 1771 which was used as a refuge during the French and Indian War after General Edward Braddock's defeat, because the Maryland and Pennsylvania frontiers were constantly exposed to the ravages of the Indians.[18]

An interesting house, built on the main street of Oldtown in the 1700s by Michael Cresap (1742-1773), son of Thomas, is now a museum. It still has the original cupboards and fireplace. Surely Richard and his brother John knew Michael Cresap and likely were in this house, as this was the time when Richard was constable of Oldtown Hundred. Michael, a trader, had cleared wilderness, fought in Cresap's War in Ohio, and brought his bride here in 1764. A captain in 1774, he led riflemen painted Indian style to Boston.

The Cresaps once owned more than 2,000 acres around Oldtown, so either Flint had bought some of the land in 1753, or the Morris property joined Cresap's further south, down the creek. Backwoods record-keeping is often confusing.

The same year that Richard Morris was appointed constable, in 1764[19] to replace James Crabtree, he resold his fifty-acre Morgans Chance to Flint for twenty-nine pounds, only four more pounds than he had paid for it. Rebecca, his wife, "was privately examined," as the law required, and agreed to the conveyance of her dower in the land.[20] This suggests that Richard married Rebecca about 1764 because it mentions her dower. Two years later, on 23 September 1766, he added eighty acres

---

[16] Tracey and Dern, *Pioneers of Old Monocacy*, pp. 87, 225.
[17] James Haw, "Patronage, Politics, and Ideology 1753-1762"; Millard Milburn Rice, *This Was the Life*, p. 252.
[18] George Washington was also here on his first visit to Maryland in 1748, and often after that.
[19] Rice, p. 254.
[20] Annapolis, Land Bk. J, p. 835.

called "Morris Luck," adjoining Morris Chase.[21] This fact also suggests that Rebecca was the daughter of Joseph Flint, since Flint was so accommodating and also had previously named Morris Chase and Morris Luck. A certificate of survey located the land. The name usually stuck as the land was transferred, therefore the name might give a clue to its former owner, although not necessarily.

Richard's younger brother, John, born about 1737, must have been in the Maryland militia, although this has not yet been proved. When he was taxed in 1761, he was recorded as head of household, so we can assume he was already married to Eleanor. The recorded birth of Dorcas Morris (who later married David Cushman) was 1765. She was very probably the second daughter of John and Eleanor, judging from a family count and a family will. So Dorcas must have been born in Flintstone as was her older sister, because their parents, John and Eleanor, lived there at least four years. This, so far, is conjecture, as no parentage can surely be assigned to Dorcas.

Four years was time enough to save money to buy land, which John II did in 1765. The record shows that John Morris, "farmer," bought a fifty-acre tract for forty-four pounds and ten shillings called "Johnsons Folly," also referred to as "Johnstons."[22] It was on the east side of Martin's Mountain near "the head of the draught" of Flintstone Creek, a branch of Town Creek. This was probably a minor draught in Maryland since the document didn't bother to name it. Patented in Maryland, it was also sold in Maryland by a Maryland deed, well after the Pennsylvania-Maryland line was established. So, although the "big draught" is north in Pennsylvania near Cheneysville, there is no doubt that John's land was not there. His land was in or somewhere very near the village of Flintstone, probably not far from the two tracts of land owned by Richard Morris, about nine miles from the Potomac River. The Morris brothers probably lived much nearer Flintstone than Oldtown. (Flintstone is about fifteen miles east of Cumberland on Route 40, and Flintstone Creek flows into Town Creek.)

A curious reference to a John Morris was recorded in the March 1769 session of the court: "Ordered by the Court that John Morris be set levy free for the future."[23] However, no petition requesting exemption from taxes was found. In this period the court generally rejected such

---

[21] Annapolis, Land BC & GS 31, p. 52.
[22] Annapolis, Land BC & GS 28, pp. 292-3. There was a "Johnson's Hollow" in the area, on Warrior's Mountain.
[23] Annapolis, Judgements Bk. P, p. 467.

Chapter III. Our Early Welsh Morrises ♦ 49

petitions, even some from persons on the county support list who requested extension of their payments. Normally, reasons for exemption were age or infirmity. So probably this John who was set levy free was aged, infirm, and unlisted, and was the old father, John Morris I, emigrant from Wales who was living with his son, wife Eleanor, and their children. The family notes of Nancy Haines, great-granddaughter of John Morris II, mention his father John. Only one John Morris was listed in Frederick County at this time. By 1782 there were eleven persons in John II's household, which would account for his old father John, for Dorcas, and for her sister (name unknown).

Also curious is a record of 1771 which tells of the beating and assaulting of Eleanor Morris, presumably John II's wife, by one Patrick Daugherty. The indictment in a Frederick County Court was "quashed," recorded in a marginal note.[24]

* * * * *

The author made a pilgrimage to Maryland in June of 1990 to the area of Oldtown and Flintstone. She found Oldtown a rather sleepy village with one main street, a population of about 2500, three churches, one school of 240 pupils from kindergarten through twelfth grade, one general store, and a small post office. There were some very nice brick and stone houses, outlying "mobile" (but stationary) homes, and farms with big barns, cornfields, and black Angus cattle. Nearly in the center of town is the old Chesapeake and Ohio Canal, which runs from Cumberland through Harper's Ferry to Washington, D.C., with its wooden locks in disrepair. A rustic towpath runs beside the canal, where now only ducks and geese ply the water. Fishermen and children were enjoying picnics in this pictorial scene. Here, a one-lane-wide-no-railings bridge with a quaint, privately owned toll gate (probably few exist) crosses the Potomac. This is used quite a bit by the local folks and costs "fifty cents to cross unless you want to come back for a dollar." There used to be a ferry here over to Green Spring, West Virginia.

Flintstone is about fifteen miles east of Cumberland on the four-lane Interstate Route 68, which is designated on maps and road signs as a scenic route. Scenic it surely is, the hillsides generously planted with daisies and pink vetch. Visible through tremendous modern cuts in the red-rock mountains are miles of vistas which are truly magnificent, and a splendid lookout at Martin's Mountain. Just barely off this highway on

---

[24] Annapolis, Bk. Q, p. 382.

old Route 40 is the quiet village of our ancestors, now with a population of 3500, a small post office, one store, three churches, and neat but simple homes on one street. In the schoolyard is a sign telling of the time when Flintstone was on "The Warrior's Path."

Just behind the school is Flintstone Creek, which soon flows into Town Creek. Its banks, overgrown with elderberry and wild roses, are filled with layered rocks which could be easily split into thin slabs, good for flints and arrows. In the mid-1700s this was all in the district of Oldtown Hundred, and under the aegis of Constable Richard Morris.

Flintstone is only about fifteen miles north of Oldtown; however, the roads between the two villages are not direct. They wind and wind among woods, fields of Queen Anne's lace and butterfly weed, through lovely, thick forest. These roads must surely be the remains of curvy, ancient Indian footpaths. They cross and recross Oldtown Creek, which in places is about seventy-five feet wide. It is fine farmland, beautiful terrain. Why, then, did they want to leave it after only a few years?

Some pioneers did strip the land, never replanting trees or nourishing the soil, so they thought *their* land was used up but that America's land and trees were endless.

Another reason must have been that in Maryland people had to pay annual rent to the Lords Baltimore although they had already bought and paid for their land. In the West they were promised free land by means of settlement rights. The future looked brighter there. So the Morrises, the Spurgeons, some of the Robinetts, and others moved on. Their migration pattern moved westward about another forty-five miles into Virginia—"beyond the Blueridge."

Distances From	To	Approx. Miles
Wilmington, Del. (a port city)	Emmitsburg, Md.	75
Baltimore, Md. (a port city)	Emmitsburg, Md.	40
Emmitsburg, Md.	Flintstone, Md.	63
Flintstone, Md.	Glade Farms, W.Va.	45
Oldtown, Md.	Flintstone, Md.	15 directly; however, the only road is very winding.

Chapter III. Our Early Welsh Morrises ♦ 51

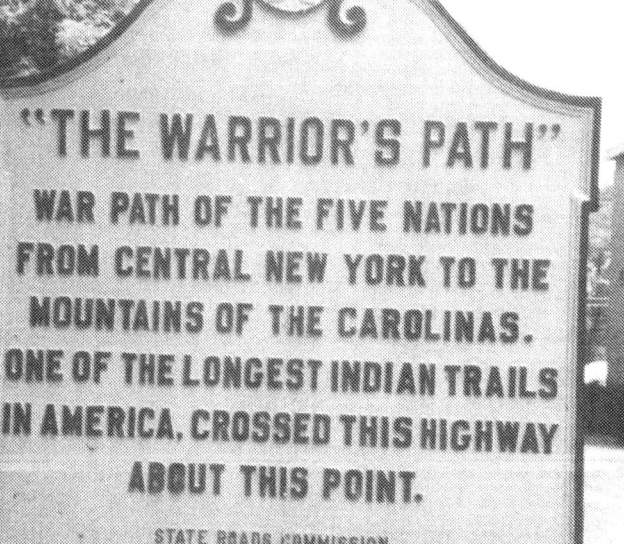

Before this saga leaves the Flintstone area, it should be recorded here that Richard Morris retained his 180 acres of Morris Chance and Morris Luck for nine years longer, even after moving to (West) Virginia in 1770. He sold them in 1779 for 900 pounds to Charles Parril (Pevril),[25] having paid seventy-five pounds for them thirty-one years before. The deed and the endorsement were both signed by Richard Maurice Morris, which was his usual way. No wife is mentioned, so it is likely Rebecca had died and he was between wives.

John and "Elandor" Morris held their Johnsons Folly land for less than five years after they left it, before 1780. John does not appear on the 1778 oaths-of-fidelity listings or on its militia rolls during the Revolution. They probably stayed behind in Maryland longer than his elder brother Richard because of younger children, possibly because of that aged father. In 1785 they sold their fifty-acre tract,[26] although the buyer, Jonathan Bishop, was assessed for the taxes in 1773.[27] It is probable that John and Eleanor did not live in Maryland during this period but had already gone to the Sandy Creek Glades to join his brother about 1774.

Very many of the prolific Robinett family remained in Flintstone into the late 1800s and never did emigrate into Virginia,[28] although a few brothers did go, along with the Morrises and Spurgeons. George Robinett was one of four men appointed as late as 1791 to survey and locate the road from Hancock to Fort Cumberland.[29] Before this, land to the west was accessible only by horse trail over Martins Mountain into Dickerson Hollow, just west of Flintstone. This was the very horse trail, before it was a road, which our ancestors traveled. Richard and his grown sons, John III and Morris Morris I, left Flintstone before 1770—some of the very earliest pioneers in an immense region. Not for a few more years were John and Eleanor and their family of younger children to follow this same path to Virginia, over the Alleghenies, then known also as "the Endless Mountains."

The year 1770, when settlement was finally recorded, was at that time considered a time of peace. The French and Indian War was over, even Pontiac's War, which was the last part of it. Then for about six years the Indians had been rather quiet, had not bothered the white men much. It seemed to the Morrises and their friends to be a good time to

---

[25] Annapolis Hall of Records, Land B, p. 120; Western 2, 1986.
[26] Annapolis Land D, p. 562.
[27] Annapolis Index, p. 66.
[28] Hilary F. Willison, *History of the Pioneer Settlers of Flintstone*.
[29] *Rocky Gap State Park* (Flintstone, Md., 1990).

Chapter III. Our Early Welsh Morrises ♦ 53

move westward, a pretty safe time. Little did they know what was ahead in less than four years.

* * * * *

Very great and important Indian troubles at the Virginia frontier had *preceded* these pioneers' decision to move on and should indeed be told, although the Morrises were not yet in Virginia and so were not as cognizant or involved as were those few settlers across the mountains. What follows is a brief tale of a dangerous, cheerless twenty-year period *leading up to 1770*, when those preceding several years of quiet encouraged Richard Morris, sons John III and Morris I, and some of their friends to move on over the mountains into Virginia, seeking free land. Word-of-mouth reports had been their only source of information, their only knowledge of the "West."

Christopher Gist and John Frazer (Frazee) had made a survey of Virginia as early as 1749. Gist had a store by 1752. John Frazer, who had a gunsmith shop on the Allegheny River, was driven by the French to Washington County, Pennsylvania. After that he had a trading place on the Monongahela River. In 1753, because of Indian trouble, he was "commanded to build four strong houses."[30]

The Dunkards were the first white men of whom we have any account in what is now Preston County, once part of Augusta County. In 1753, these German Baptists, seeking peace and freedom of religion, attempted settlement but were soon murdered by the Indians.[31] Now only the local place names for Dunkard Creek and Dunkard Bottom memorialize their sect.

Ruthless Indians had long been allies of the French, who intended to make the British remain east of the mountains. They planned to join French Canada to Louisiana, with a line of forts to back up French territory. As early as 1753 young George Washington had been sent by the Virginia government to Fort LeBoeuf to warn the French off "English" soil, but the French would not leave. This led to the French and Indian War. In the opening battle Washington surrendered Fort Necessity, fifty miles west of Fort Cumberland in Maryland. The fort, which he had built at the confluence of the Monongahela and Allegheny Rivers (now Pittsburgh, Pennsylvania), was promptly recaptured, rebuilt, and renamed Fort Pitt.

---

[30] Boyd Crumrine, ed., *History of Washington County, Pennsylvania*, pp. 18-31.
[31] Oren F. Morton, *History of Preston County, West Virginia*.

Braddock's defeat in 1755 had left the whole western frontier exposed to both the French and the Indians. Then followed a destructive and cruel period for all western pioneers, even as far west as our families in western Maryland. It was a dangerous time. After nine long, terrifying years, in 1761 an Indian treaty finally ended this war, the longest of any period of frontier warfare. Pontiac was an excellent organizer who formed a secret Indian confederation, captured a line of nine forts, had a furious battle at Fort Pitt, and was finally defeated by the British in 1763. Although King George III had issued the Proclamation Line of 1763 and Indian treaties covered the land west of this, the Indians' treachery and harassment did not stop instantly. But gradually there followed a period of about ten years of relative peace. It was toward the end of this stretch of "peace" that our family decided to move on once again.

* * * * *

Charles Mason and Jeremiah Dixon and their surveying party had axed out of the wilderness a twenty-four-foot-wide lane through primeval forest in 1764 which was gladly used as a roadway by western-bound settlers. In the summer and fall of 1767 the northern end of Preston County in Maryland was cleared,[32] so it was not yet choked with saplings and undergrowth when Richard and sons traveled with other frontiersmen to check out land. Richard's family were settled by 1770, the year their coming was first recorded, along with a very few others. Our people settled on the backwaters of inland rivers in a wilderness. Richard with his three grown sons and three daughters, as well as John and wife Eleanor with their nine children, were among the earliest of what eventually proved to be one of the largest immigrant treks ever.[33]

How extremely different were the ways, the life, the homes, the culture, and the politics of these people—different from the planter society of Tidewater Virginia with its large plantations, great mansions, and lavish furnishings. Monongalia County seemed a world away from these and from elegant Williamsburg, yet they existed in the same time span and the same state of Virginia. This early difference in people, their ideals and goals was already planting the seeds for a separate state of West Virginia a hundred years later. Foremost among these differences was the policy regarding slavery.

---

[32] Ibid, p. 53.
[33] Charles Henry Ambler, "West Virginia, the Mountain State" (1940), in *Enc. Brit.* (1957 ed.), vol. 23, p. 547.

Chapter III. Our Early Welsh Morrises ♦ 55

* * * * *

Following are two charts, entitled Morris Family Descent, and Early Intermarriage of the Morris, Cushman, and Frazee Families.

One must remember that, in early genealogy, first and subsequent wives' names were often unrecorded, and large families produced over a long period of time were common. Also unrecorded were miscarriages, stillbirths, and deaths in infancy which occurred between the recorded births, resulting in space-years among the survivors. Genealogists consider those possibilities and other circumstances, as well as the names of wives and children listed in wills and enumerated in censuses, to help determine early pedigrees.

Morris Family Descent

Note: Direct ancestors of the author in Generations 1 through 5 are in boldface.

Generation 1

John Morris I (b. in Wales c. 1677; to Philadelphia c. 1697-9; d. c. 1774)	Probably Thomas Morris (1691-c. 1760) (Md. records) Possibly William and Morris Morris (Md. records)

Generation 2. Children of John I

Richard Morris I (c. 1722-5 Pa. or Md. -1803, Mason Co., Ky.). 1st m. Rebecca (Flint?, died c. 1759, Md.), six children; 2nd m. Mary (m. bef. 1761. Md. deed)	John Morris II (c. 1737-c. 1797, Georges Creek, Pa.), m. Eleanor (d. Mason Co., Ky.); probably nine children (unsure of order)

Generation 3. Children of Richard I

a. John III (1758?, Georgetown, Md. [record] - bef. 1800); five children
b. Rachel (b. c. 1750) m. Joseph Robinett (b. 1751)
c. Thomas (1751-bef. 1807) m. Mary "Polly"
d. Mary (b. c. 1756) 1st m. c. 1776 Daniel Greathouse (d. 1777); 2nd m. Andrew McCreary
e. Catherine (b. c. 1758) m. Samuel Spurgeon
f. **Morris I** (1761-1809) m. c. 1781 Sarah Cushman; twelve children, below

Generation 3. Children of John II (will)

a. ?Daughter
b. Joseph (b. ?1760) (minister) m. ?Mary Overfield (L.D.S.)
c. Dorcas (b. 1765) m. David Cushman (1764-1788)
d. Richard II (Revolution) m. ?Mary Watts
e. James, unmarried, remained in Virginia
f. John IV
g. Morris II (1780-1864), m. **Rachael Morris** (1786-1863, Gen. 4, letter b, below left), daughter of Morris I and Sarah (Gen. 3, letter f, left column); ?nine children, below, Gen. 5
h. Elizabeth (b. bef. Nov. 1784), 2nd wife of Moses Frazee (b. 1770)
i. Eleanor (b. bef. 1793)

Generation 4. Children of Morris I and Sarah (Cushman) Morris

a. Thomas (b. 1783) m. Sophia Talbot, Mary Parker, and Lucinda Fruit
b. Rachael (1786-1863) m. 1803 Morris Morris II (Gen. 3, letter g, above right)
c. Daniel (1788-1853) m. Anna Minnick/Meenack
d. Mary "Polly" (1791-1822) m. Ezekial McIntyre
e. John (1793-1870-1) m. 1827 Elizabeth (Bowles) Payne and Katherine Turney
f. Rebecca (1794-?1881) m. Jessie Turney and Henry Parker
g. Nancy (1796-1876) m. Thomas Bowles, John Thomas, and Jessie Turney
h. Elizabeth (1798-bef. 1835-6) m. Samuel William Brown
i. Horatio (1800-1881) m. Polly Hughs and Malinda Fruit
j. Preston (1802-1869) m. Adaliza Miller
k. Albert (1804-1869) m. Mary Summers
l. Beauford (1807-1849) m. Elizabeth (Bowles) (Payne) Morris and Jane Dobson

Generation 5. Children of Morris II and Rachael (Morris) Morris
(First-cousins-once-removed)

a. Austin (1804-1877) m. Jane Maria Peppard
b. Milton (1808-1835) m. Abigail Thayer
c. Thomas Armstrong (1811-1904)
   m. Rachel Elizabeth Irwin (1822-1893)
d. John V (1815-1904) m. Martha Wiles
e. Amanda Melvina (1817-1851) m. John Mothershead
f. Julia Ann (1820-1885) m. Norman Morris Ross
g. Elizabeth Mitchell (1824-1904)
   m. John D. Defrees
h. William Little (1828-1853) m. Ann Morrison
i. Nicholas McCarty (b. 1830, d. 1830)

Descent from Thomas Armstrong (c, above) and Rachel (Irwin) Morris

Gen. 6. Thomas O'Neil Morris (1846-1916) m. Estelle Jane Goodale (1850-1938)
Gen. 7. Theodore Hatfield Morris (1883-1974) m. Lisette Susanna Krauss (1883-1965)
Gen. 8. Anne Estelle Morris (b. 1913) m. Walter Day Mertz (b. 1914)

Early Intermarriage of the Morris, Cushman, and Frazee Families

Morris			Cushman		Frazee		
Richard					Ephraim*		
	John I		Thomas VI		Mary (by 1st wife)	Samuel (by 2nd wife)	Moses (by 3rd wife)
		John II		David			
Morris I	Elizabeth	Morris II	Dorcas				
			Sarah	Ann (by 2nd wife)			
Rachael							

Marriages
- Morris Morris I married Sarah Cushman.
- Rachael Morris married Morris Morris II.
- Elizabeth Morris married Moses Frazee.
- Dorcas Morris married David Cushman.
- Thomas Cushman VI married Mary Frazee.
- Ann Cushman married Samuel Frazee

*Because Ephraim Frazee had eighteen children by three wives over a period that exceeded one generation, his children do not fit tidily into a single generation.

References (See the Bibliography for publication data.)

Burt, Alvah W. *Cushman Genealogy and General History*. This book is in the libraries of Congress, Washington, D.C.; The Mayflower Society, Plymouth, Massachusetts; and Daughters of the American Revolution, Washington, D.C.

Hamilton, Frances Frazee. *Ancestral Lines of Doniphan, Frazee, and Hamilton*. This volume is in the Library of Congress; Michigan State University Library, Lansing, Michigan; and the La Crosse Public Library, La Crosse, Wisconsin.

Both of the above books contain Morris family genealogy. The book on the Frazee family is incorrect in showing Sarah *Frazee*, rather than Sarah *Cushman*, married to Morris Morris I. The probable reason for the error is the similarity of their birth dates: Sarah Cushman was born 10 September 1766, and Sarah Frazee exactly three months later, 10 *December* 1766. Sarah *Cushman's* birth is recorded in the family Bible along with eleven other siblings. Her birth date is accepted by the Mayflower Society and the DAR, as is her marriage to Morris Morris I.

Chapter III. Our Early Welsh Morrises ♦ 59

ENDNOTES

Note: Part of the following research and written statements were made by a certified West Virginia genealogist. The author possesses copies of all proofs mentioned.

MANY "TRADITIONAL" FAMILY NOTES passed down and even some published Indiana information, incorrectly remembered, tell of a Welsh brother James who migrated west with two brothers (John and Morris), and of his son, James Jr., who fathered Morris Morris (the one who married his cousin Rachael Morris in 1803). These sources hold that Rachael was the daughter of John Morris. She was *not*, as has been proven many times in many ways, and proof is now always accepted that her father was Morris (not John) and her grandfather was Richard Morris. (Also established is that Richard did have two sons named John and Morris.)

There is *no* tangible trace of the called-for James Morris in Monongalia County at the time he should have been there fathering a second Morris Morris. Faulty memories have caused incorrect records.

Family tales mentioned a James Jr. who served in the Revolution in the First Pennsylvania Battalion, was appointed an ensign by General Gates, and served at Ticonderoga. The author spent many years unsuccessfully hunting for proof of James, then she employed three different professional genealogists to do the same, one from Utah, one from West Virginia, and one from Kentucky. All three concluded, independently, that there was no James (or James Jr.) in our family, as one of the three migrating brothers. A few scattered Jameses did exist. None were found to patent land in Pennsylvania, Maryland, West Virginia, or Kentucky near the rest of the family, nor was a James Morris listed on tax lists near them or with the family and neighbors on the petition of 1782, a copy of which, listed by neighborhood groupings, is in the author's possession.

At a compatible *later* time and place a James Morris, plausibly son of John II, does appear, grown up as an adult. There seems to be nothing relevant to this family in the Pennsylvania counties of Greene, Westmoreland, Washington, or Fayette, with one exception in the latter. Possibly the matured James, son of John II (who died in 1796) mentioned just above, came back up the Potomac River in his late middle age and bought the old stone house in Geneva, Maryland, in 1824, and sold it to James Dougherty (or Daugherty) in 1831.

Lyman C. Draper's account of the James Morris of Mays Lick, Mason County, Kentucky, interviewed by the Reverend John D. Shane, determines (proves?) that *that* James Morris was one of a group of Morrises who came to Monongalia County in 1788 *directly* from New Jersey.

Army records were thoroughly checked. Only two men belonging to the First Pennsylvania Battalion were from Monongalia County, neither of our family. One had moved there later and was pensioned from that county; the other was born in Old Town, Maryland, and served with Cresap. Five companies were recruited from Philadelphia, two from nearby Berks County and one from nearby Bucks County. The First Pennsylvania Battalion existed for only one year, in 1776, then became the Second Pennsylvania Regiment, which had no recruits west of the Alleghenies. The Eighth Pennsylvania Regiment was the only Pennsylvania regiment raised on the western frontier for the state; there were no Morrises and none of our Morris neighbors' names appear on that listing.

The *single* instance when a James Morris is recorded, as being promoted to ensign in the First Pennsylvania Battalion on 31 November 1776, to January 1777 (a very brief time), is thought to be a *clerical error;* the last name, Jones, was mistakenly omitted. Never again does the name appear for service, promotion, or dismissal. However, a *James Morris Jones* was appointed by Gates on the same day, the same year, the same rank, from the same state. This name appears many times for promotions and service in the Second Regiment, the Third Battalion, etc., until the war's end in 1783 (Heitman). The successor of this battalion is definite (Stille). The conclusion is that the word "Jones" was mistakenly omitted one time, "Morris" has a single reference in a spot that should have been "Jones," and the name James Morris is never recorded again.

Family tradition was probably the result of someone's research and mistaken discovery some time during the past 100 years. Data in the Pennsylvania Archives, Vol. 2, have been available since the mid-1880s. Modern research has proven, without a doubt, that our family tradition was not all correct.

Chapter III. Our Early Welsh Morrises ♦ 61

References

Note: See the General Bibliography for publication data of the following volumes:

Draper, Lyman C. Manuscript-interview, MSS13CC, pp. 202-5.

Heitman, Francis Bernard. *Historical Register of Officers of the Continental Army, April 1775 to December 1783*, pp. 39-51, 229-31; 237-41.

Montgomery, Thomas Lynch. *Pennsylvania Archives*. Vol. 2, pp. 56-7, 68-9, 74-9, 630-3, 773, 781-5.

Stille, Charles J. *Anthony Wayne and the Pennsylvania Line*, pp. 376-385.

Trussel, John B. B., Jr. *The Pennsylvania Line, Regimental Organization and Operations, 1776-1783*, pp. 39-51, 227-31, 237-41.

The "Morris Family Tree"

Chapter IV

BEYOND THE BLUE RIDGE
A Hunter's Paradise

*A freedom that reveres the past
But trusts the dawning future more,
And bids the soul in search of truth
[To] venture boldly and explore.*
—"Singing the Living Tradition"

OUR WELSHMEN made their way through the Cumberland Narrows, a thousand-foot-deep natural gap with sheer rock cliffs on one side, carved by Wills Creek and named for the well-liked Indian Chief Wills. This was a few miles upstream from its confluence with the Potomac River. As early as 1748 there had been McCullough's Packhorse Path, formerly an old Indian trail. A good bit later, in 1772, and two years after Richard Morris and his sons went westward, a couple of log-wheel wagons of wide tread and extra length were drawn by oxen and cows over the rough trail. General Braddock and his men further improved and extended it to the mouth of Wills Creek. Here was Caiuctucucu, an Indian village, later a trading post. Then Michael Cresap, who worked for the Ohio Company, built a stockade called Fort Ohio as a defense against the Indians and the French. This became Fort Cumberland by 1750, where George Washington had begun his military career as an aide to General Braddock.

Christopher Gist, also of the Ohio Company of Virginia, helped by Indians, soldiers, and young George Washington, widened and enlarged the way westward. Michael Cresap blazed a trail toward the Ohio River, later to become "Braddock's Trail." By 1773 Teagarden Road became the first public road west of the Monongahela River. This gradual improvement was an encouragement to all pioneers, and our John Morris II must have had an easier transport than Richard by waiting just a few years. (More than three decades later, in 1806, the National Pike, once an Indian trail, was finally authorized as a transport system to connect the East and West. It was the first federally-funded highway in the United States.)

Early transient families planted some of the very first seeds of society and civilization in their new land; our own hardy and self-reliant ancestors were some of them. They were able to endure and overcome the hardships of a rugged, perilous wilderness in order to conquer and cultivate the soil. At a time when our eastern colonial cities and plantations were providing a refined social order, these pioneers made great sacrifices of comfort, of culture, and of blood.

Political, religious, and social freedoms of this frontier society and the prospects of free land were great attractions. Tales of rich, fertile ground just waiting to be homesteaded were extremely tempting. Considering the probable hardships and possible dangers from Indian warfare, it is almost surprising that they went at all, that they did not abandon this harsh country of unbroken forests. Apparently they thought the advantages seemed greater for them than the disadvantages. For many men it must have been an adventure, a masculine challenge; their women never had a choice: they simply *had* to go along to care for their families, to hold them together. They couldn't possibly stay behind—there was nowhere else to go.

These families traveled mostly with packhorses or mules, with packsaddles, cattle, and meager baggage. They had little money, iron, or salt. Food, clothes, and implements were great treasures; all were difficult to obtain. Furs and peltry for barter over the mountains were their only resources. How perceptive was the fine writer, Ayn Rand, who once said, "Throughout the centuries there [have been] men who took first steps, armed with nothing but their own vision."

These very first pioneers eeked out a hard and simple living on a dangerous frontier, but they thought it was "the prettiest country in the world." It was heavily inhabited by deer, bears, turkeys, pheasants, partridges, and bees, and the streams teemed with fish. Men were delighted; the few women were not as fond of these wild woods, where there were also panthers, wolves, wildcats, cougars, and lynxes to frighten them and the children from straying.

In the beginning there were no mills to grind or to saw, no schools to teach, few books, no mail. There were no churches to comfort, no roads to travel, only bridle and footpaths—Indian trails. There were no nails or glass, and very seldom pewter. In their shelters, only a little daylight came from slitted holes, for shooting, or from windows too small to crawl through, covered only with greased paper or animal tissue. Wooden plates and furniture made of sticks were crude. Corn was the staff of their lives—lives so grim, and often frightening, a sorry existence for many. General privation was unavoidable, yet in spite of all the obstacles there

Chapter IV. Beyond the Blue Ridge ♦ 65

was a sense of liberty, and a looking forward to better times. What else was there to work for?

The region of Virginia to which the Morrises, Spurgeons, Robinetts, and Frazees went is difficult to define both geographically and historically. At first it had no name except "Territory—west of the Blue Ridge." In 1720 it was called "Spotsylvania" and by 1734, "Orange County." Four years later the counties Frederick and Augusta (named for the wife of the Prince of Wales and mother of King George III) were laid off by the colonial legislators. These two counties included all the land west of the Blue Ridge Mountains to the Mississippi River. A mixture of English, Welsh, Scotch, Irish, German, and Dutch would eventually come to settle here—an amalgamation of people. The early comers from the north seem to have been almost entirely from Pennsylvania and Maryland.

By October of 1776 the "District of West Augusta" was laid off as a subdivision by the Virginia General Assembly and could send two delegates to the General Convention of Virginia. From this "territory" of about nine thousand square miles three counties were later organized, namely Ohio, Yogohania, and the largest, Monongalia. The latter was intended to be Monongahela after the river, an Indian name meaning "River of Caving Banks." The incorrect spelling is said to be due to an unschooled clerk.[1] It is unfortunate that the wrong name was retained. The large Monongalia County now included part of Greene and Fayette Counties from Pennsylvania, and western Virginia's whole of Monongalia and Preston Counties as well as parts of six other counties.

A very early map of West Augusta shows Monongalia County existing in both of the present states of Pennsylvania and Virginia.[2] Eventually there was an extension of the western boundary and the dispute was not finally settled until 1784, according to historian Oren Morton; however, Earl Core says western Pennsylvania was claimed by Virginia until 1789.

Four old consecutive maps specifically show how the General Assembly established boundaries in 1776, enlarged them in 1779 and 1780, and then decreased the size of Virginia a little by straightening its northern boundary.[3] Finally only the land in Virginia was called "Monongalia County," which was later split up to become several counties. In 1818 Preston County was formed from part of it. Much later, on 20 June 1863,

---

[1] Oren F. Morton, *History of Preston County, West Virginia*, p. 52.
[2] West Virginia Archives, Dept. Culture and History, Charleston.
[3] Earl L. Core, *The Monongahela Story: A Bicentennial History*, pp. 160, 171, 181, 183.

this whole section of "western Virginia" became a separate state and was then called "West Virginia."

Needless to say, research in this geographically mixed-up area involving the records of numerous counties and states is extremely confusing. To compound matters, the Monongalia Courthouse, with twenty years of accumulated papers, was burned in 1796. Some of our old family notes which state "Monongalia County" must have included part of Pennsylvania Colony.

A small town called Mount Morris, on Dunkard Creek in Pennsylvania south of Pittsburgh but only fifteen miles west of Morgantown, West Virginia, was founded by one Levi Morris in 1765, according to a Pennsylvania state sign. However, these signs are not always accurate. Less than ten miles east of Mount Morris is Morris Crossroads, in Pennsylvania. To the west of these villages, on the Pennsylvania state line, is Morris Run, a tributary of Dunkard Creek, which snakes in and out of both Pennsylvania and West Virginia. Many Morris families came to live in this area, even in the early 1700s. Richard Morris's younger brother John and wife Eleanor lived on Georges Creek in Georges or Wharton Township in Fayette County, Pennsylvania, when he made his will in 1796. He was living just north of the Pennsylvania border and Morris Crossroads.

In 1770 or just before, Richard Morris and two of his sons went directly to find and check out the land they would later settle on. They first came to Friendsville in Sandy Creek Glades Hundred, where the Friend family had established a village of sorts and had put up some block houses. There is no Sandy Creek in western Maryland, but Little Sandy heads near the Maryland-West Virginia line to unite with Big Sandy to flow from Pennsylvania through northern West Virginia into Cheat River. This area, although now in Maryland, was known then as a part of the Sandy Creek settlement.

Richard Morris and sons John III and Morris I, in 1770 grown to manhood, only visited the Friends, the Frazees, and some Spurgeons living there. It was important to catch up on the latest reports, to learn all they could about the "West." But they soon traveled on, penetrating forests on the Braddock Road, but not for long. They left it to take the trail opened up by the Mason and Dixon party not long before. They came to a flatter area with streams and low, marshy, treeless places which the first settlers called "glades." Surrounding these glades were gentle contours of rich soil inviting cultivation. Soon there would be many place names named by the settlers using "glade."

Chapter IV. Beyond the Blue Ridge ♦ 67

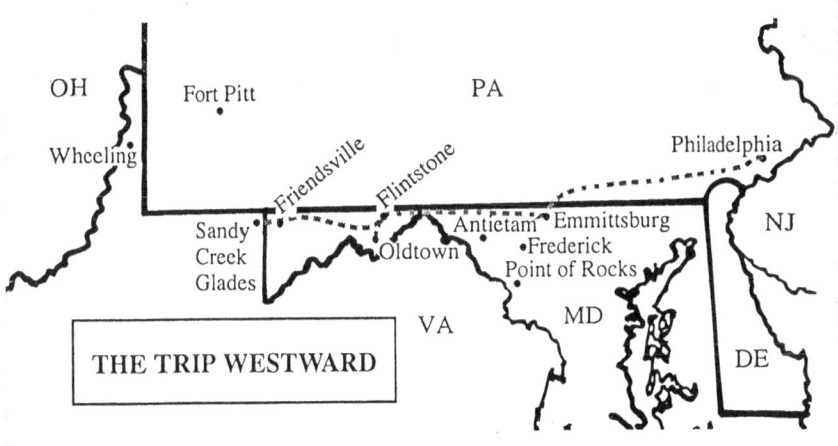

Since the early 1900s—possibly 1904—this particular area has been called "Glade Farms" and sometimes "Twin Churches."[4] It is in the farthermost, northwest corner of West Virginia where Route 26 now crosses Route 5. Now there are very small churches on two corners, surrounded entirely by farmland.

Having found this unused, unclaimed land, and, pleased with his find, Richard went back to his Morris Choice in Maryland to get the rest of his family and then returned to Sandy Glades. They became one of the very first families in this area, in 1770 taking up their land by settlement rights.

The first pioneers took up their large tracts about five miles from the new Braddock Road, which ran from Fort Cumberland to Fort Necessity. Here the Richard Morris family settled in a territory quite famous at the time as a hunting ground. We know there were three sons: Thomas, John III and Morris I; and four daughters: Mary, Rachel, Catherine, and Rebecca. It is written that these very early settlers were under the impression that they were settling within the boundaries of Pennsylvania. People really had no titles to their land. They had heard that clearing the land, building a cabin, and planting a crop made it a legal claim with the Virginia government. This claim included 400 acres and a preemption right to 1,000 acres more at $1.67 for each 100 acres, and forty cents for the

---

[4] Hamill Kenny, *West Virginia Place Names.*

certificate. Another way to claim land was by "tomahawk rights"—a way of slashing trees to mark and identify choice tracts. This was neither legal nor safe.

Richard was not the first, but nearly. Jacob Judy with 400 acres and David Frazee with 346 acres are credited as the very first recorded permanent settlers of this area of Monongalia County, in 1769, and also John Cuppett "on the waters of Sandy Creek."[5] By the very next year, 1770, our Richard Morris is recorded claiming 400 acres. (In 1986 a member of the Frazee family still owned the farmland adjacent to the old Richard Morris property.)

In that same year of 1770 came Zebulon Hogue (Hoge, Hog) as well as Daniel Greathouse, who soon married Richard Morris's daughter Mary. Samuel Worral, his son, Samuel Worral Jr., Joshua and Anthony Worley, and John Scott were there.

Also settling in that same year of 1770 was Thomas Cushman V and his son Thomas VI, our direct ancestors from the second Thomas Cushman who married Mary Allerton of the *Mayflower*. The younger Thomas returned to Connecticut before March 1777 to enlist there in the army to fight in the Revolution. After discharge in 1780, he came back to Sandy Glades with his wife, Mary Frazee, whom he had married in New Jersey. She was a daughter of Ephraim Frazee. The Cushmans' daughter Sarah married Richard Morris's son Morris I. Quite naturally the young adults began to marry their neighbors—the only ones they knew.

By 1773, three Morgans and Robert Butler had settled on the Cheat River. The "newcomers" kept coming to these lovely glades, these white-oak groves, in spite of more Indian problems. Hostility was further aroused by this advance on their lands, and, alas, the ten years of peace were coming to an end. Another problem: There were not enough crops to feed everyone who came, so 1773 became "pinching times," known as "the starving year." Clearing the land was hard work, made even more difficult by real danger. The long-suffering women struggled and coped in crude housing, quite unprotected. The men planted crops and worried. Many times our Morrises must have wished they had never left Maryland. In the wild Muddy Creek section these pioneers discovered almost pure lead, which they used for molding bullets.[6]

East of Big Sandy Creek were Ephraim Frazee and his brother David, holding adjoining lands although one brother's parcel was in Virginia and the other's in Pennsylvania. Here also were the two Thomas

---

[5] Evelyn Guard Olsen, *Indian Blood*, p. 46.
[6] Ibid., p. 49.

Chapter IV. Beyond the Blue Ridge ♦ 69

Cushmans, father V and son VI, of a long line of Thomas Cushmans. The Frazees' sister, Mary Frazee Cushman, wife of Thomas VI, claimed acres in her own name (an enterprising family!). These surveys are in the earliest Augusta County records.

Actual title to the lands of the pioneers wasn't legal until 1774, when Augusta County sent its deputy surveyor, James Trimble. Working rapidly, he surveyed sixteen locations in nine days, all in Grant District. These sixteen men for whom surveys were made had already cleared 336 acres. Three commissioners gave certificates of settlement rights for the land on which they had already been living for years; some had even taken up additional tracts. A later August record shows Thomas Cushman, 140 acres, 15 cleared (joining David Frazee's land); Thomas Cushman Jr., 400 acres, 30 cleared; Ephraim Frazee, 324 acres, 10 cleared; Richard Maurice (Morris), 730 acres, 40 cleared; John Maurice (Richard's son), 500 acres, 26 cleared; Sam Worral, 550 acres, 30 cleared; Anthony Wordley (Worley), 300 acres, 18 cleared. The glades were already partly open ground, so these men were not felling acres of solid woodland.

In 1774 Thomas Cushman VI and Morris Morris I, son of Richard, each had 400 acres adjoining Richard's. Old Ephraim Frazee had joined his sons by 1775 and was on the Cheat River. John Morris Jr. is recorded in 1775 as having 1,000 acres in the forks of Cheat River and Sandy Creek. This was very probably Richard's brother John, son of their emigrant father, John of Wales, who had arrived at the Glades by 1774.

By then, Richard's brother John and his wife Eleanor were able to leave Flintstone, Maryland, as tales of wonderful hunting and settlement rights continued. Their delayed move west was probably due to the aged father, who, we think, lived with them (tax count), and many dependent children, younger than those of his older brother, Richard. It was about four years after Richard had moved west that John and Eleanor and their large, younger family also crossed the Blue Ridge Mountains—on a slightly improved trail, in 1774. Probably by this time his aged father had died and moving had become possible.

The following must be said *here* because of the geography and the time—1770-1775. A revelation came to the author as she recorded these settlers, a realization of genealogy, history, and geography remarkably coming together which apparently no one else has ever comprehended, because never before have the myriad threads of this Morris family been researched and then pieced together to make a continuous story:

Four special men, all of the same generation, came to settle in this wilderness where few white men had ever been. Among the very first were *Thomas Cushman V,* from New Jersey (1770); *Ephraim Frazee* (by 1775), also from New Jersey; *Richard Morris* (1770), from Maryland; and his brother, *John Morris* (1774), also from Maryland. There were very few people there altogether, so they all must have known each other well. All four of those men—Thomas Cushman, Ephraim Frazee, Richard Morris, and John Morris—were the author's great-great-great-great-grandfathers! What a genealogical coincidence of inheritance this is—descent from four adventurous pioneers, all in the very same place in a wilderness!

There are records showing Hezikiah Frazee on the site of Rowlesburg by 1776, and our direct antecedent, John Morris II (Richard's brother), owning 600 acres on Sovereign Run the same year. This waterway doesn't appear on our maps by name, only as a wiggly line; however, the 1786-1788 tax lists show four families of "Severns" in the area.[7] Streams were frequently named for families who settled on them, and this was probably a misspelling. Evan Jenkins (a good Welsh name!) and David Graham ran a powder mill on this creek in a building only about eighteen feet square; the powder was "course and unglazed."[8] This mill was near Cheat River, south of the present Bruceton Mills on Route 26.

On Little Sandy Creek were Ephraim Frazee (Jr.?) and also Joseph Robinett, who married Rachel Morris, Richard's daughter. James Spurgeon was there, too; his son Samuel married Catherine, another daughter of Richard Morris. Richard's second daughter, Mary, had already married a neighbor, Daniel Greathouse, but he died of measles, after which she married Andrew McCreary. Samuel and John Robinett and John's wife, Catherine, are mentioned in records by 1781.

The few recorded families are enough to account for a scattered population of about 250 people in 1776. Yet these were not all the settlers living in the glades. "Some others who patented land during the decade of the '80s were doubtless already here, although the date of the settlement is not recorded in the land books. And as [at] other frontier communities of that day, there were unquestionably a few other men in the settlements who were not land holders at all."[9] Even Thomas Jefferson was overlooked in the very first tax lists.

---

[7] Nettie Schreiner-Yantis and Florence Speakman Love, *Personal Property Tax Lists for the Years 1786, 1787 (Partial), and 1788 for Monongalia County, Virginia.*
[8] Morton, pp. 1, 78.
[9] Ibid., p. 57.

Chapter IV. Beyond the Blue Ridge ♦ 71

No records were ever found for Richard's oldest son, Thomas, of a stakeout land claim in Virginia, although he must have been there. There *is* a record of his wife, Polly, as sole administratrix of his estate in Kentucky in 1818.

One of the earliest surveys of Garrett County, Maryland, in April 1774, was on Sandy Creek on an old Indian trail (later the Morgantown Road). It was for a community Baptist Church to which traveling backwoods preachers came, and a school for the Sandy Creek settlement, on James Spurgeon's land less than a mile from Fort Morris. A record of a very old man, Ephraim Frazee, shows him attending church there in 1775. He rejoiced at the preaching of the Reverend John Taylor and bragged of having eighteen children, and of his father having more! At this time Indians still lived nearby and sometimes came back to their family graves.

In 1774 Lord Baltimore opened his lands "westward of Fort Cumberland" to settlement, and many tracts in what is now Garrett County, Maryland, were surveyed for land speculators "down east" the same year Virginia sent John Trimble to survey lands on Sandy Creek.

John Murray, the thirteenth Lord Dunmore of Scotland, was the last British governor of the Virginia Colony. Evidence exists that he issued land grants to many Tory Loyalists in the 1770s in order to cloud the titles of settlers with claims lesser than military grants. Realizing that war with the Colonies was inevitable, he despoiled the land ownership situation by tying up titles to lands claimed by Virginia but also by the Pennsylvania Colony, the British, the French, and the Shawnees. The British neither supported nor defended these lands.

This Lord Dunmore, Virginia's evil British governor, gave a land grant of some 28,000 acres, covering the waters of both the Cheat and Kanawha Rivers, to a British soldier named Richard Morris, to his principal sergeants and soldiers, and to a British regular army officer named Savage. A Virginia lawsuit ensued in which for many years our Richard Morris was a defendant and deposee. Savage claimed the land our Richard had settled on in 1770. Complicating this matter was that one of the plaintiffs with Savage was the British soldier named Richard Morris.[10]

Dunmore was cruel to the pioneers, who hated him. He paid a ransom for scalps—of men, women, children—it didn't matter. He stole and murdered, hoping to win back Americans. He also sent an emissary to

---

[10] Lyman Chalkley, *Records of West Augusta County, Virginia*.

stir up the Indians in order to assist a regiment of Tories—to burn, plunder, rape, scalp, massacre—all in the name of the British.

This was "Lord Dunmore's War."

Sometimes the settlements were deserted in panic from torch and tomahawk. "The frontiers suffered greatly, scarcely a lone and exposed household escaping attack. Most of the settlers fled to a line of seventeen forts which had been established under Benjamin Franklin's direction in the mountain gaps."[11]

The magazine at Winchester, Virginia, was fortified. Butler's Fort was built at the mouth of Roaring Creek, near the Cheat River. Then occurred in April of 1774 the horrible murder by drunken white men, renegades, of the defenseless wife and children of the Indian Chief Logan, "peaceable, inoffensive Indians at Captiva and Yellow Creek, [which] brought on the [despicable, terrifying war of Lord Dunmore] in the spring of 1774."[12] Records say the men were led by Daniel Greathouse, a neighbor of Richard Morris, whose daughter he had married. The chief of the Mingoes returned with thirty-one white scalps, and Logan never again forgave or agreed to peace terms.

These pioneers who had settled beyond the beautiful Blue Ridge watched each night the blue deepen into purple, saw the darkness slowly cover the mountains and trees, and finally the cabins. Each simple, rustic abode became a lonely, separated, darkened island in the night. Only the noises of the wildlife disturbed the silence. They seldom slept very soundly, and an uneasiness must have been ever-present until first light came through chinks in the shuttered windows.

Very soon after this horrifying massacre of Logan's family so near the Morris family, they had even more reason than others to be fearful, since Richard's violent, uncouth son-in-law was the known leader of the drunken "party." With the help of the entire community, the settlers felled trees and erected a fort on Richard's land in 1774, raising log walls with a communal room, laying puncheon floors, and building a protective barricade. Richard Morris was said to have the most cleared land at this time; a forty-acre plot was recorded. It was a great advantage to have a wide clearing for preventing a foe from getting within good range. This Fort Morris on Hogue's Run and Butler's Fort were two safety zones in Preston County. Ashby's and Friend's Forts in western Maryland added

---

[11] Samuel Kercheval, *A History of the Valley of Virginia, 1883*.

[12] The Rev. Dr. Joseph Doddridge, "Memoir," in *Notes on the Settlement and Indian Wars*, p. 82.

Chapter IV. Beyond the Blue Ridge ♦ 73

to the settlers' line of defense. Open glades became empty; the woods again belonged to the Indians, with the trees their barricades.

Not surprisingly, "No Indian alarms disturbed [our Morris] settlers until the Shawnee War of 1774 when Fort Morris ... was built for the protection of the tri-state area."[13] Because the fort was in the northwest corner of Virginia, near the boundaries of both Pennsylvania and Maryland, it served as a link with militia activities of all three colonies. Curiously, no Morrises or their neighbors seem to have been on the payrolls for Dunmore's War. But many, many records have been lost.

Maryland's *Mountain Democrat* described "Fort Morris in the open glade on Hog Run ... built in time for the Sandy Creek settlement and [for] others including the Friends, Frazees, and Halls of Maryland to take refuge during the Battle of Point Pleasant."[14] Our Frazee "cousin" Samuel was twenty-one and served as a scout under General Lewis for this fierce battle, which took place on the tenth of October 1774, when recruited settlers defeated the Indians.

Hog Run was a tributary of Little Sandy, called this several times in old records. Other records show that Zebulon Hogue (Hoguemeyer), from Hagerstown, Maryland, was one of the very first settlers here in 1770. In 1986, however, the local farmer, seemingly amused, called it "Hog Run." The latter name seems to be the one that prevailed.

A year after Fort Morris was built, a company of "Rangers" was organized by the settlers of the Sandy Creek area and was headquartered at Fort Morris. This company protected the settlement until the close of the Revolutionary War, according to "West Virginia History," which lists the officers as Captain Augustine Friend, Lieutenant Gabriel Friend, and Sergeant Abija Herrington.

This fort was used until after the war. In 1784, ten years after it was built, George Washington and his nephew, Bushrod Washington, stopped there on their return from Washington's last exploratory trip across northwestern Virginia. Coming eastward from Ice's Ferry and Bruceton Mills, they passed through the old Quaker settlement of Brandonville and asked for lodging at the house of James Spurgeon, which was right beside Fort Morris and Richard Morris's home. The next night they camped on the ground, sleeping on their overcoats, then traveled southward to the house of Charles Friend to get porridge (corn or mush) for their horses. They traveled the old McCullough Path, then over the Allegheny table-

---

[13] Charles E. Hoye, "The Cuppett Family," quoted in *Maryland Mountain Democrat* (1935), p. 8.
[14] Ibid., p. 250.

lands and home to Mount Vernon on the Potomac. This trip is described in "West Virginia History," which provides a map and reveals the detailed notes that Washington kept. (Bushrod Washington, the nephew, became an associate justice of the U.S. Supreme Court.)[15]

Accounts state that Fort Morris could accommodate many families, and they stress its great importance. Several of these forts and blockhouses were erected during the terror and panic of the spring and summer of 1774. By affording shelter and protection, even the smaller forts served their purpose and prevented abandoning entirely this section of the country at the time of Dunmore's War. The Indians had no artillery so they seldom attacked or scarcely ever took a fort. Sometimes additional cabins outside the fort were erected for temporary living. Then the occupants could retreat into the fort in case of attack. These cabins were not only a range of defense, but also formed a neighborhood group.[16]

"An assemblage of cabins ... built of sapling logs standing eight or ten feet above the ground [were] sunk about three feet into the black alluvial earth.... Here the families of the Sandy Creek Glades fled for shelter at the rumor of an Indian incursion.... Within a stockade the people were fairly secure, since the natives did not like to storm a fort which they could not reduce by stratagem."[17]

"The people in the vicinity ... fled across the Monongahela River to the shelter of Morris's fort ... southeast of Uniontown ... one of the first grade ... was much resorted to by the old settlers on the upper Monongahela and Cheat [Rivers] and from Ten Mile."[18] (Ten Mile country covered an area of today's Greene and Washington Counties of Pennsylvania, settlements of the Ohio Valley and of Ten Mile River and its tributaries in West Virginia and Maryland, according to Hilda Chance in *Ten Mile Country*.)

Fort Morris was "... a stockade fort enclosing about an acre. The settlers of Washington County [Pennsylvania] and Morgantown [West Virginia] repaired over the Old Sandy Creek Road [earliest road on record and within a mile of Fort Morris] for protection.... The settlers forted during the summer, but were not molested."[19] It was also written that the settlers got the ague from the bad water.

---

[15] Charles Henry Ambler, "West Virginia History," *Encyclopedia Britannica*, vol. 23.
[16] Boyd Crumrine, ed., *History of Washington County, Pennsylvania*, p. 73.
[17] Core, p. 358.
[18] Franklin Ellis, *History of Fayette County, Pennsylvania*, pp. 68-70.
[19] Richard T. Wiley, *The Monongahela: the River and the Regions*, pp. 367-8.

Fort Morris "was the nucleus of the Sandy Creek settlement ... thither flocked the families from a considerable radius. As soon as an immediate danger was over, the men went back to their homes, the women and children remaining in the little stockade. From considerations of health the spot was objectionable. It was low and damp and the 'forters' were made ill by drinking the impure water of the mucky glade."[20] "... Logs [were] laid end to end ... inside a sloping place where men could lie and shoot through gunholes.... In the center [was] a meat-block where the venison and bear were butchered. [There was] a three-way entrance, a way-laying entrance, where an enemy had to turn three corners before he gained admission to the fort's interior."[21]

* * * *

This fort-place has been memorialized. The author had read about it in history books. To get there the first time, she found the West Virginia crossroads with two small corner churches, then found the resident farmer of the 300-acre dairy farm, Chester Earl Metheny. Mr. Metheny was gently persuaded to drive her party over a very bumpy, plowed cornfield. It was a hilarious, jiggly ride for the five of them and her son's very large dog, all squatting beside a load of farm implements in the back of a dirty pickup truck. It was marshy land and, remembering what she had read about the ague, she asked, "So where is Hog Run?" "Ma'am, you just crossed it! It used to be crooked and winding. Now it's only a trickle because it has been drained and straightened. The strip-miners partly filled it in." Of course then she thought, "If only our early Welsh ancestors had known there was soft coal under their soggy land!" This small stream was a tributary of Little Sandy, which was a tributary of the larger Big Sandy. Indeed, their kind driver was patient with his laughing riders, who wished to take lots of pictures.

They took photographs of the monument marking the site of Richard Morris's Fort Morris of 1794. Standing beside it were three very proud direct descendants: the author, Anne Morris Mertz, seventh generation from "the Patriot"; her son, Theodore Morris Mertz, of the eighth generation; and his young son, Gregory Morris Mertz, of the ninth generation.

They were surprised by the size of this lonely stone monument. From the ground it is six feet tall, seven feet deep, and ten feet wide at the base

---

[20] Core, pp. 341-3.
[21] Olsen, p. 58.

—now standing on the site of Fort Morris, far, far from any road or path. The impressively large stone states simply:

THIS TABLET MARKS THE
SITE OF
OLD FORT MORRIS
1774
UNVEILED AUG. 23, 1915
IN MEMORY OF
THE EARLY PIONEERS OF
THE SANDY CREEK GLADES
(VA.) W.VA.

At the base of the large stone are the remains of a more recent emblem, placed there in 1975 by the Women's Historical Society of Pennsylvania. Also on the base, marked on each front corner, were two arrows, one pointing toward "Fort Necessity 1754" and the other toward "Point Pleasant." The arrow markers were not securely attached. Two years later when the author again visited this place with her younger daughter and *her* two daughters, alas, the arrows were gone.

On the first trip, in May of 1980, they also located a second farmer, Glen Barnes, who was the grandson of the 1915 farmer, Flemming C. Barnes. Glen thought that his grandfather had donated the monument. He remembered that this patriotic man had hauled the stone tablet on "Mud Pike" (Braddock's March) in a wagon pulled by four horses, from Great Crossing at Summerville, Pennsylvania, about fifty miles northeast of Pittsburgh. He said that when his father, James, was a boy, he had found lots of Indian arrowheads in the vicinity of the monument. Mr. Barnes vividly recalled the ceremony for the erection of the monument when he was twelve years old.

On the second trip, in 1982, they found that the Metheny farm had been sold and abandoned; the field was weed-grown and impassable except in a strong jeep. Strip-mining continued, however. Their farmer-driver on this second visit made quite a point of showing them "the old moccasin footstep of olden times" imprinted in a very large stone by the roadside. He approached it with reverence as though it really *was* the imprint of an Indian, instead of the natural indentation it appeared to be.

Chapter IV. Beyond the Blue Ridge ♦ 77

Later, an account was found in the *Preston County Journal* of 26 August 1915 headlined "PIONEER FORT TO BE MARKED BY A MONUMENT." There was to be a ceremony and an address by a pastor from Connellsville, Pennsylvania, on 28 August 1915. An unveiling of a six-foot-tall monument would take place at 2:00 P.M., with music. All were invited to bring their dinner and spend the day. "There will also be a bronze tablet in the form of a Keystone donated by the Women's Historical Society of Pennsylvania through its President ... of Pittsburgh, Pa. The base will contain stones from Fort Necessity, Gist's Plantation, Crawford's Spring at Stewart's Crossing, and from Doddridge's Farm.... [Rev.] Dr. [Joseph] Doddridge[22] coming from Washington County, Pa., in the spring of 1774, leaving the women and children at the Fort and the men returning to put out the crops." So farmer Glen Barnes of Glade Farms, at sixty-eight, had remembered correctly!

Many of us are not truly aware of the hazards and very real dangers which the Native Americans, Indians of many tribes, caused frontier people. The Indian nations fought a different kind of war from that which the civilized white man was used to. There was never an exchange of prisoners. The savages killed indiscriminately—women and children too. Redmen had a barbarous thirst for human blood; they resolved to have the total extermination of the white people. So the tomahawk and scalping knife were dreaded weapons of horror around our defenseless frontier settlements. In Preston County there were only two "feeble" stockades, Morris's Fort and Butler's Fort, to withstand invasions by the Indians, who were always a vicious threat. Sustaining American morale during the tribulations of a young nation must have been a challenge for every family.

An interesting and enlightening *first-hand* recollection, published in 1883, is worth quoting.

> My father and a few neighbors settled in the spring of 1773 across the mountains.... There was peace until the Indians came at Captiva and Yellow Creek.... Our little settlement then broke up. The women and children were removed to Morris's fort in Sandy Creek Glade, some distance to the east of Uniontown. [This was not the

---

[22] Rev. Doddridge and wife, Mary Biggs, lived on "Antietam Level" close to the Spurgeons and the Maryland-Pennsylvania line on the current Frederick-Washington County boundary. The Doddridge family often came to Fort Morris for safety and were good friends of the Morrises, though not close neighbors.

modern-day Captiva, about seventy miles south of Wheeling, West Virginia, on the Ohio River.]

The fort consisted of an assemblage of small hovels, situated on the margin of a large and noxious marsh, the effluvia of which gave most of the women and children the fever and ague. The men were compelled by necessity to return home, risking the tomahawk and scalping knife of the Indians, to raise corn to keep their families from starvation the succeeding winter. These sufferings, danger, and losses were the tribute we had to pay to that thirst for blood which actuated those veteran murderers who brought war upon us![23]

Samuel Kercheval, the narrator quoted above, vividly recalls numerous occasions when as a small child he was awakened in the night and removed quietly to the fort from a cabin some distance away, because of warnings of Indians in the area. Even small children understood the importance of complete silence; their very lives depended upon it. He recalls long hours in Fort Morris with many ill people.

* * * * *

It seems appropriate to relate here the origin of the expression "Indian summer," which we today think of only as a spell of warm weather in the fall, a rather pleasant connotation for us. Not so for those pioneers. The original meaning of the expression was quite different. During the long Indian wars endured by our Morris men and their hardy women, there was peace in the winter season. During severe weather the Indians did not make incursions into the settlements. It was a grim and horrible Indian custom, however, to burn to death the first person caught in the early spring as a celebration, a time for entertainment and merriment. Therefore, it was a necessity for the safety of all families to be cooped up spring, summer, and fall in small, uncomfortable forts. Confinement usually meant that the rails, clapboards, fences, and cabins were left unfinished. Sometimes men became too restless being confined, then were captured or lost their lives. When men went out to their gardens, it was imperative that they be accompanied by a watchman or watchwoman, with a gun. Horses were belled so any sensing of danger could be relayed quickly. Inside the fort, buffalo fat was often thrown on the fire to make spying eyes see that the fort was full and busy.

"The approach of winter, in spite of gloomy days, was greeted with pleasure. All the farmers, except the owner of the fort, returned to their

---

[23] Kercheval, p. 242.

Chapter IV. Beyond the Blue Ridge ♦ 79

own cabins to repair them. This release from confinement was a real joy. Thus began the harvesting of their crops and a bustling preparation for winter. But if the sun melted the snow, their hearts were chilled. If the weather became warm again this meant the Indians had another opportunity to maraud and plunder the settlement."[24] Surprise attacks did occur often. The very words "Indian summer" brought horror to our frontier forebears and not pleasure, as it does to us today.

* * * * *

Although the French had succumbed to the British in 1763, this did not stop the harassment or treachery of the Indians; now they were no longer under the control of the French. And yet, "... following the French and Indian War, *present West Virginia became the center of one of the largest and most important immigrant movements in world history.* ... Ambitious and resourceful pioneers, following the example of George Washington, possessed themselves of strategic locations along and near the inland river.... Here leaders among them resolved to adjust themselves to a new economic order motivated by ideals of liberty, justice, and equality. Pursuit of these purposes soon brought ... conflict"[25] with the eastern, aristocratic, slave-holding settlers. These accounts remind us that Richard and John Morris and their brave families were truly early pioneers for they were at the beginning of this large westward migration. They were not just some recorded names we read about; they were *our* real people, our very own family.

During the decade of 1770 to 1780 there was strong feeling between Virginia and Pennsylvania about the rightful ownership of the lands between the Laurel Hills and the west as far as the Ohio River. Meanwhile, the vertical boundary between Lord Baltimore's land and Penn's land was also disputed. The Maryland-Virginia boundary lines were not settled until later, with Deaken's survey in 1787.

Before this, in 1782, many citizens presented a Virginia legislative petition to the Continental Congress. The pioneers wished this territory to be organized into a new state of "Westsylvania." Numerous copies of this petition were circulated for signature throughout the countryside. One of these petitions was found in the Library of Congress in 1945, and a five-year study failed to show up a single faked name of anyone who did not

---

[24] Kercheval, p. 211; Core, pp. 52-3; Wiley, pp. 42-3.
[25] Ambler, "West Virginia History."

exist; the names are entirely authentic.[26] The signers included many Morrises—ours and others.

There were also petitions signed for a request that the government of Virginia officially inform the citizens whether part of the region had been given to Pennsylvania.[27] One list is in alphabetical order, with Frazees, Morrises, Robinetts, Spurgeons, Worleys, and Worrals all signed up.[28] The author possesses another copy—more important because all the signers are listed by neighborhood. Since we have records of most of our Morris neighbors, the signers' names help to determine which are our Morrises. It appears that probably at least five members of the combined two Morris brothers' families were old enough to be signers.

The big revolt against England had been brewing in coastal towns for some time. It soon became a duty for seaboard people to stay in the East in order to help resist the invading enemy; emigration across the mountains nearly ended. So now there was little opportunity for the pioneers to trade for tools, salt, and weapons.

Frontier people had to be self-sufficient in every way and had to defend alone their homes from the savages turned loose by the British. Backwoods Indian hostility grew fierce as liquor-peddling traders brought poverty and debility to the unknowing natives, and their vengeance had no limits. This "second front" of the colonies has been much neglected by historians. It has been said, however, that frontier battles were as much a part of the revolutionary conflict as the battles of Trenton and Monmouth. Border life seemed a "ceaseless patrol."

Now called to fight for their rights and fair taxation, frontiersmen also answered the call for independence with great ardor. Accounts reveal that practically all Virginia settlers served sometime during the Revolution, although many, many records no longer exist to prove it. As an incentive to enlistment, Virginia, Maryland, and Connecticut promised bounty land to everyone who lived in those sections of the Northwest Territory which their charters included. A former serviceman's land warrant was a license to find land anywhere in the public domain. Maryland, on the other hand, appropriated all the vacant lands west of Fort Cumberland to fulfill service obligations and issued numbered lots of fifty acres each. Rank determined the number of lots a man received. This was not like the Virginia and Federal systems. All this free bounty land was a

---

[26] Howard L. Leckey, *The Ten Mile Country and Its Pioneer Families*, pp. 142, 144-6, 148, 152.
[27] Archives of the Virginia State Library, Richmond.
[28] *Virginia Genealogist*, vol. 17 (1973), pp. 216-223.

great inducement to join the Continental Army—a powerful one but life-risking.

During the Revolutionary War, the Sandy Creek settlers maintained a company of "Rangers" for the protection of the country between the Yougheny and Cheat Rivers. Captain Augustine was thirty-nine when he was given command of the Rangers in 1775. Gabriel Friend was only fourteen but served as a Ranger spy.[29] Some men even returned to Oldtown, Maryland, to serve as militiamen in that "Skipton" District.

It is truly remarkable that an attempt by the U.S. Government was made to take a population count of the citizens soon after the Revolution. It is even more remarkable that a census in this wilderness area was largely accomplished as early as 1782. In those days and in those places few pioneers could read and write.

In Virginia's large Monongalia County in that first 1782 count are listed our Morris brothers, who had settled there much earlier, Richard in 1770 and John about 1774. Richard, who had altogether six known children, is, by this time, recorded as having three in his household, probably himself; his second wife, Mary, who was stepmother to those children;[30] and one unmarried daughter. He lived next to his youngest son, Morris Morris I, who had matured to age twenty-one and had only two in his household. Morris had just married Sarah Cushman (of the *Mayflower* ancestral line), the daughter of their neighbor, Thomas Cushman VI, whose first child, Thomas VII, was born in 1783, after the population count.

Also adjoining Richard Morris was his oldest son, John III, who is recorded as having "4 white." This included his wife, Martha, and probably two unmarried children. Another John Morris, not adjoining, is listed as having eleven in his household. This was surely Richard's younger brother, John, who had come from Flintstone, Maryland, with his wife, Eleanor, to Sandy Creek with a "passel" of children.

Guided by the will of this John Morris written twenty-two years later,[31] it figures that probably these nine were, first, a daughter, name unknown; second, oldest son, Joseph; third child, Dorcas (born 1765 in Flintstone and later, in 1788, married her neighbor, David Cushman,

---

[29] Olsen, p. 59.
[30] Kentucky Archives, File Box 282 (Morgantown, W.Va.). Mary is mentioned as stepmother of Morris Morris.
[31] *Monongalia County Deeds*, OS 052: 347; Monongalia County Will Bk. 1, pp. 302-3. Admitted to record 20 Oct. 1766. Witnesses: Job Bacorn, Samuel Woodbridge, and Dunham Martin. There was an early town called Bacorn near Glades Farms, the current name for the Sandy Glades settlement.

brother of the above-mentioned Sarah); then Richard, James, John IV, Morris II, Elizabeth, and Eleanor. This would account for the five sons and two daughters mentioned in John's will. The two oldest daughters, not mentioned in the will, were married long before the will was written, had established homes, and probably had received a dowry earlier, which was often the custom. Married daughters were frequently not mentioned in these early wills.

Families pretty much stuck together in clusters of small cabins in the clearings, dangerous in the daytime when all must be watchful for the red men, and lonely in the silent nights with only the sounds of whistling winds, hooting owls, and howling wolves to break the quiet of the darkness.

By 1788 quite a few families lived in the Sandy Creek settlement, although some folks had already left the Glades and moved westward. Again the tax lists tell us that the aged Richard Morris was still there with his two sons, John and Morris. Richard's brother John also had two sons who were old enough to be taxed, named Richard and John. Joseph, the oldest brother, was a minister and probably owned no land to be taxed, or else had already gone to Ohio.

Also living in the Sandy Creek settlement were three Robinetts: Joseph, John, and Samuel, who had married Catherine Morris, daughter of Richard. There was David Cushman (Sarah Cushman Morris's younger brother), who married Dorcas Morris, John II's second daughter. Also there were the Frazees: David, Squire, Samuel, and Moses, who married Elizabeth Morris, John II's younger daughter. Near neighbors, the Severns: Joseph, Joseph Jr., Daniel, and Absolam were living along the stream (misspelled "Sovereign" Run) on which John Morris II had staked his claim and also lived. Other neighbors were the Spurgeons: Samuel, William, James, Jeremiah, and Zephaniah, living near Anthony Worley. Also in the area were the Martin Judys, Sr. and Jr., and John Judy.

By 1788 the aged Richard Morris was no longer tithable. But the two Welsh brothers, Richard and John, who had come from Maryland, still worked the land, and grew older along with their offspring and their neighbors; all produced big families.

Now if you have this untangled, you are remarkable! It took this author a *long* time. To better comprehend the mixed-up relations of these three families who lived and loved together, refer back to the Intermarriage chart on page 58 in Chapter III.

Chapter IV. Beyond the Blue Ridge ♦ 83

Peace had been made with England in 1783, but not with the Indians. Fort Morris was used for twenty years as a place of security (even after the Morrises left it). A lasting peace was finally secured by Anthony Wayne's victory on the Maumee River as late as 1794. Not until after the Battle of the Fallen Timbers in August of that year were the forts dismantled. The Indians were driven back from the Ohio, and left their lands forever. Gradually the settlements had increased; clearings were transformed into sizable farms. It was—and still is—beautiful country.

For our clearer understanding, boundary disputes and changes affecting Richard and John have been recorded in a chronological time frame in the Genealogy.

The Virginia-Maryland border was well established long before the Revolution. The boundary line was drawn due north from the headspring of the Potomac River. In the 1740s it was decided that the north branch of the Potomac was the main fork. Lord Halifax's surveyors marked the headspring with a stone, a replacement of which now marks the spot near Blackwater Falls in Tucker County, West Virginia.

The border between Virginia and Pennsylvania was an entirely different matter and has caused genealogists many a difficult problem. Until 1769 Pennsylvania claimed the Allegheny Mountains as its western boundary. Virginia had claimed that its West Augusta District was bounded on the west by the Ohio River. In 1782 to 1783 the borders were settled but deeds conveyed only interest, not absolute title. In 1787, after much immigration, it was agreed that a survey boundary would be established east of the Ohio. In this agreement between Pennsylvania and Virginia on the extension of the Mason-Dixon Line, Virginia gave up all claim to the counties of Greene, Washington, Fayette, Bedford, Westmoreland, and parts of others in western Pennsylvania. Two years later, in 1789, when the nation was ratifying its Constitution, a formal concession by the Virginia Assembly was made in the final resolution of the land boundary fixes. To compound the confusion that existed for many years, all Pennsylvania boundary records were lost in 1796!

The narrow neck of land between the western edge of Pennsylvania and the Ohio River has been *West* Virginia since 1863, when the state of West Virginia was established, even *before* the War Between the States was concluded.

INDIAN TREATMENT

WE CAN UNDERSTAND the very real hatred of the emigrants for the Indians who killed with a vengeance and completely wiped out many families, even whole villages. They were treacherous, mean, frightful. Their kind of warfare was entirely different from any other, with a different sense of rules and values. These barbarians scalped with pleasure, bought and bartered for scalps, performed all sorts of atrocities; women and children were no different from men. They never exchanged prisoners, and seemed to have no feelings for life or people. They even fought their own kind, other tribes, with this same lack of decency. They had never known our Christian teachings of values and kindness. It is no wonder the white people were unforgiving.

We know of a few individual Indians who showed a strain of kindness, of nurturing, of helpfulness, but generally they were the exception. One thinks of Pocahontas, also Sacajawea, who guided the Lewis and Clark expedition, cared for the men for many months, and loved the experience.

The Indians were a terrible hindrance to the settlers, who seemed to think the land was theirs for the taking. After all, their Colonial government had either sold, awarded, or given it to them. For centuries the tradition of Europeans had been to conquer by force, to take, and therefore to own. The Pilgrims (although not the Puritans), and the Quakers of William Penn did buy their land from the Indians and made treaties but most confiscated by force. There are, however, two sides to everything, and it's only fair to mention the Indians' side of a bad and sad situation.

At the beginning of the Europeans' arrival in America there were between 600,000 and 900,000 Indians inhabiting what has become the continental United States. Explorers, traders, and settlers were generally friendly, but white men eventually came in large numbers, which caused resentment and hostilities. So in 1773 the British established the Proclamation Line along the Appalachian Mountains, prohibiting whites to settle beyond it without tribal or royal approval. *This was often ignored; the Richard Morrises were settled in (West) Virginia in 1770 with others!*

Chapter IV. Beyond the Blue Ridge ♦ 85

After the Revolution the United States began forming new states west of the line proclaimed by the British. The following events chronicle the Indians' containment:

1825 A separate Indian country was declared west of the Mississippi.
1830 The Relocation Act required *all* Indians to live there. Ulysses S. Grant's Peace Policy made reservations inviolate, but they rapidly shrank and were not improved.
1850 Indian population was two-thirds smaller, largely from diseases brought by the white man.
1870 Indian lands were now shrunk to a space smaller than Minnesota.
1890 Indian Wars ended with the massacre of the Sioux at Wounded Knee, South Dakota.

Today the National Park System is attempting to trace the 400-year struggle between American Indians and the U.S. Government by documenting some of the most significant events of the wars. The struggle was most intense between 1860 and 1890. These events still convey a sense of what was at stake in the struggle and the passion with which it was fought:

At Horseshoe Bend in Alabama in 1814 Andrew Jackson's troops defeated the Creeks, who lost 23 million acres of land.

The historic homelands of the Cherokees included West Virginia, Kentucky, Tennessee, and Alabama, in addition to the valleys of the southern Appalachians from Virginia to Georgia. Gold was discovered in Georgia.

In 1830 President Jackson signed the Indian Removal Act, forcing Indians to the Indian territory west of the Mississippi. The Trail of Tears, an 800-mile trip for the Cherokees and Creeks, killed an estimated 4,000 to 8,000 Indians.

Gold was discovered in California in 1848. Most Indians soon migrated elsewhere, but one tribe in northern California, the Modocs, resisted at their ancient sanctuary, the Lava Beds, and were wiped out.

In 1868 gold was found in the Black Hills, which had been guaranteed to the Sioux by treaty—their sacred land, the center of the world. General George Custer was defeated and killed at the Battle of Little Bighorn, but in the end, after their Indian leaders were eliminated, the Sioux were forced onto reservations, which changed their way of life forever—a roving life of hunting buffalo.

Other sites preserved by the National Park System include Big Hole National Battlefield, Wisdom, Montana; and Nez Perce National Historic Trail and National Park, Spalding, Idaho.

This fact is worth telling: Some southeastern tribes reacted differently to white settlement. Some "Cherokees took on elements of white culture while retaining their culture. [They] added to their already highly developed culture an elected government and learned new methods of business and farming. A Cherokee named Sequoyah developed a written language, and by the 1820s the tribe had a written constitution and began publishing a newspaper."[32]

Author Julia Davis has articulated so very well both sides of the tragic dilemma which faced both Native Americans and white men for many years of warfare and suffering. No one has expressed it more beautifully nor more compassionately.

The Indians had a music, a deep breathing harmony with nature and the forest, but the whites could not hear it. *Their* tune was different, an epic of striving, of heroic determination that would eventually become an anthem of Manifest Destiny, and *that* the Indians, in their time, could not hear. Lost in their mutual deafness, the two peoples found no alternative to a struggle for survival that lunged on across the continent through new scenes, new men and women, new battles, until the whites prevailed, and the Native Americans vanished as a potent entity.[33]

---

[32] Elizabeth E. Hedstrom, "Scenes From the Indian Wars," in *National Parks Magazine,* Jan./Feb. 1995. The author has borrowed heavily from this excellent, informative article, written by the former news editor of the publication.
[33] Julia A. Davis, *Shenandoah, Daughter of the Stars,* p. 52. Emphasis in the original.

Chapter V

TWO MORRIS MORRISES — FIRST-COUSINS
Trekking Westward Together

Builders of Destiny
They lie, our pioneers, where highways run.
They lie where railroads go and cities stand.
Their brittle bones have been exposed in sun and wind.
Their bones are restless in this land.

What does it matter if their bones do lie
Beneath the turning wheels where millions pass,
Builders and dreamers born to live and die
Like white plum petals on the April grass?

What does it matter if their bones turn stone,
Their flesh be richer dust our plowshares turn,
Builders who made America our own,
Whose blood has fed the roots of grass and fern?

Dreamers and builders of our destiny,
They left their epitaph for all to read:
A land of dream and wealth and energy,
A land where freedom is the greatest greed.

— Jesse Stuart

DANIEL BOONE was hired to blaze a southern route, "the Wilderness Road," through Tennessee to Kentucky. While hunting and fighting Indians, he and his men opened the lands beyond the Blue Ridge. At the southeastern corner of Kentucky, where that state converges with Tennessee and Virginia, is Cumberland Gap, named in 1750 by Dr. Thomas Walker. This is not to be confused with the gap at Cumberland, Maryland, on the northern Old Braddock Road, which our Morrises had traversed in the earlier 1770s to reach Monongalia County.

Boone and his men, a group of thirty, threaded a trace through dense thickets of beautiful rhododendron and laurel at the base of Cumberland Mountain, named for the Duke of Cumberland. They were ambushed by

Indians but by 1769 had established a "Station Camp." (There is a good reconstruction of that early fort built by Boone and James Harrod at what is now Irvine, Kentucky.) The very first permanent white settlement, however, was Harrodstown, later called Harrodsburg, built in 1774, the same year Fort Morris was built farther east. Fort Boonesborro, north of Franklin, was formed a year later by Daniel Boone.

Boone and his trusting wife, Rebecca Bryan Boone, some of their ten children, and a few follower families were among the first to use the new southern route to Kentucky. The settlers who followed on this Wilderness Road were mostly from the Carolinas and Virginia, but not our Morris families, who eventually arrived at the same destination by a northern route.

By 1787, a U.S. ordinance established the Northwest Territory, a commonwealth, the first in the world whose organic law recognized every man as free and equal, including slaves and Indians. This document was unique, providing religious freedom, trial by jury, and habeas corpus. This Territory was to be three or five states, and included all the land north and west of the Ohio River to the Canadian border, and west to the Mississippi River.

Our Morris story is now to change locale from the Monongalia County, Virginia, area. Pioneers were receiving free bounty lands in the new west, which was described in glowing terms. These acres were payment by the government to soldiers who had risked their lives fighting in the war, for which they had spent long times away from their families whom they had left behind to farm, and sometimes to fight the Indians. Some thought their cleared land had been depleted; it would be much richer farther on; it seemed smarter to go west. This became a time of great migration. The Morrises, like many others, were about to get caught up in this fever of movement.

But these "western" lands needed investigating. Richard's son, the first Morris Morris (the elder Morris whose daughter Rachael married her cousin Morris), made three trips from the West Augusta District prior to 1790, on business for his father. (He deposed, meaning testified under oath, in 1804.) He was primarily investigating warrants for purchase of land in Kentucky. Richard, while still in the Sandy Creek Glades, bought pre-emption rights of a Revolutionary War soldier, Thomas Clark, two warrants for 400 acres each on Licking Run in Bourbon County.[1] But Richard and son Morris could not locate these acres. Richard also bought

---

[1] Land Grant records show that Thomas Clark was entitled to these.

Chapter V. Two Morris Morrises—First-Cousins ♦ 89

other land including one-tenth of a 200-acre military pre-emption granted to Thomas Gist in Bourbon County, Kentucky. The Gist purchase ended up in the courts, for Gist was a scoundrel, and the suit was not settled until after Richard's death.[2] We must conclude that Richard probably did not serve in the Revolutionary War or he would have exercised his right to establish a claim to land in Kentucky for military service. He was probably infirm or too old.

Only a year after the federal Constitution was adopted, in the early spring of 1788 Richard and his second wife, Mary, and their married sons John III and Morris I, both with young children, joined Richard's brother John II and wife Eleanor and their young ones to take to the trail. After working so hard, they left their beautiful mountain vistas and cleared lands, their settled homes, their Sandy Creek Glades community with school, church, and protective fort, to wend their way westward. Women and children traveled in wagons, the men on horseback. They became part of the early migration.

Once a man had made up his mind, the wife must go too: the choice was not really hers. Even pregnant wives were expected to travel, to cope, to cook, to nurse, and to care for all the other little ones. Usually reluctant to move on but with no other alternative, tragically, their hearts were often broken at leaving behind aged parents, the graves of their dead children, and the safety of a community. The author's three-greats-grandmother, Sarah Cushman Morris, was one of the pregnant ones.

Along with the Morrises were the Spurgeons, the Robinetts, and the Frazees, all going west to encounter another wilderness. By now these pioneer people had intermarried. "Families tended to move west within a kinship network.... They drew together from neighboring counties and states so that the extended family with all its households [was] transplanted."[3]

Was there a primal urge to move? It is difficult for us to understand this extensive migration. For some the woods had been stripped, the pastures used up. There were tales of huge buffalo herds feeding on great stands of cane, deer at every salt lick, and lush land, even into Indiana

---

[2] The Monongalia County Land Records show that Richard was involved in another lawsuit, this one with Henry Hazzle, to whom he agreed to sell his Virginia land. He made three bonds in 1788 and two in 1789 plus 1,000 pounds, committing himself to give Hazzle a deed, but apparently he never got around to it before moving to Kentucky. Hazzle did take possession of the land and eventually sued to gain a degree of ownership, and of course won the case. In 1804, after Richard's death, his widow and children gave a quitclaim for 540 acres to Hazzle for five shillings, as a result of the decree, thereby clearing up the paperwork.
[3] Lillian Schlissel, *Women's Diaries of the Westward Journey*, p. 31.

Territory. And best of all, there was all that free bounty land, the government's war payment! Nearly all the adult settlers of Kentucky had seen service in the Revolutionary War; this was especially true of the settlers from Virginia.[4] They didn't *have* to go; they chose to go, chose to toil again for fruitful fields, and again risk dealing with Indians, who proved to be much more numerous and fierce in Kentucky than they had been in the glades of Virginia.

Traveling by a northern route, our people went in wagons up to the little frontier town of Wheeling, Virginia. Long, harsh days must have drained their vitality and spirits. There they either had to arrange passage on an open or shanty-topped flatboat, or cut or buy wood to make one themselves, hoping to use the lumber in building their eventual next house. Flatboats were floating boxes attached to cut logs, sometimes 100 feet long altogether, and were the primary mode of transportation for these pioneers. Then they began a difficult, frightening ride, floating down the Ohio River, all the way to Cincinnati. The spring of 1788 was early for migration by this route, fifteen years before Ohio was admitted to the Union as a state. Marietta, right on the Ohio, was the river's first permanent settlement, founded in 1788, the same year the Morris families began their westward migration.

"Moving down the river on a flatboat." Drawing by Christian Schrader.

---

[4] Anderson Chenault Quinsbury, *Revolutionary Soldiers in Kentucky*.

Chapter V. Two Morris Morrises—First-Cousins ♦ 91

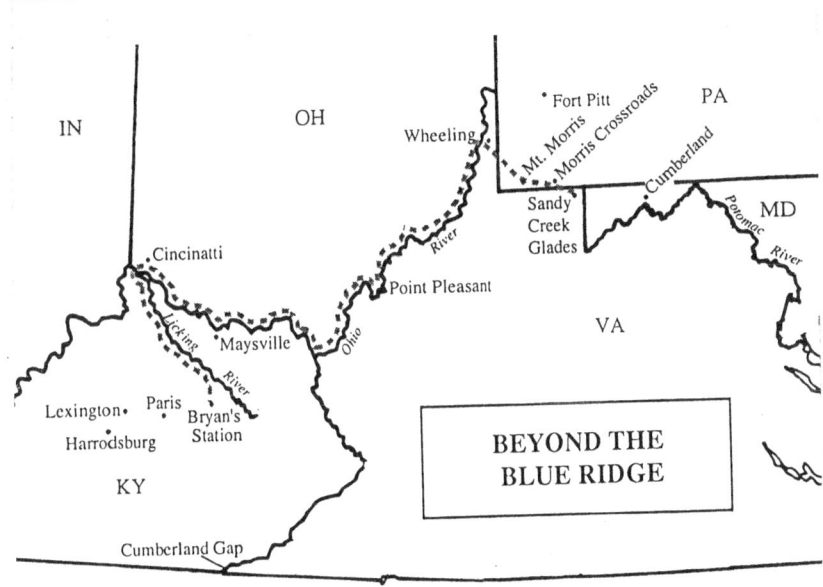

It is written that surprise Indian attacks occurred frequently. The flatboats were often plundered for salt, gunpowder, tools, lead, livestock, clothing, and scalps! Unspeakable Indian atrocities were common: disemboweling, dismembering, burning alive, hanging, and scalping live victims. It was estimated that in seven years more than fifteen hundred settlers had been killed and scalped on the Ohio River alone.[5]

Although the Revolutionary War had allegedly ended in 1782, it hadn't ended in the Ohio Territory or the Kentucky District even by 1790. The settlers and the army still had skirmishes with the Indians, who were constantly supplied with guns and ammunition by the British in Detroit and in their northern Ohio forts, which they called "trading posts." The British still paid for every prisoner and white scalp. Not until 1796 did they give up Detroit and Fort Miami to General Wayne's army.

Our Morris families were some of the lucky ones who survived these horrible, nerve-shattering dangers. From Cincinnati they left the great Ohio River to head southward probably on the Licking River, then took the South Fork, then down Stoner Creek, disembarking at the river-road junction. This route would bring them toward the same south-central area

---

[5] Allan W. Eckert, *The Frontiersmen*, p. 357.

of Kentucky where Boonesborough (1775), Boone's Station, and Bryan's Station were located, a little southwest of the present city of Paris in Bourbon County. Just north of here was Blue Licks, where in 1782, only six years before the Morris migration, the settlers were badly defeated by Indians and British officers together. This fierce Blue Licks attack is still called "the last battle of the Revolution," for word of Cornwallis's defeat had not yet reached Kentucky nearly a year later. Our band of Morrises probably didn't know this or else they were mighty brave, perhaps foolish.

Bryan's Station, named for another pioneer family, that of Daniel Boone's wife, Rebecca Bryan Boone, had forty-three men living in it, some of whom were too old to fight, thirty-two women, and sixty-two children. Here the Morrises lived for some time in the fort. "The men took turns standing as sentinels."[6] "Mary Frazee Morris made bullets for the men to fight the Indians."[7] The latter quotation is from Maria Frazee Browning, who surely meant Mary Frazee *Cushman,* then a grandmother in her forties. Memory just mixed up the names a bit.

Both the author's great-great-grandmother Rachael Morris (a granddaughter of the bullet maker) and her great-great-grandfather Morris Morris II (son of Richard's brother John) were small children and cousins, part of this pioneer group who traveled together in wagons and on the flatboat down the rivers into Kentucky.

(Perhaps the reader is already questioning the spelling of "little Rachael's" name, so the explanation should be near the beginning of Rachael's appearance in this narrative. The author possesses some deeds signed by Rachael herself in her middle years in which she used "Rachael" instead of the more common Rachel. Therefore we can only assume that was the way she wished her name spelled. It does help to distinguish her from Richard Morris's daughter Rachel, her great-aunt, and also from her daughter-in-law Rachel Morris, wife of Thomas O'Neil Morris, of the generation following her own.)

John II and his wife, Eleanor, traveled with a large family of children, probably nine including eight-year-old Morris Morris, who eventually married his cousin Rachael.[8]

Also traveling in this large family group were the elder Morris Morris (nineteen years older than his first-cousin of the same name) and his

---

[6] Nancy Haines' files, in possession of Reily Adams; *Enc. Brit.*(1957 ed.) vol. 23, p. 333.

[7] Browning letter, in possession of the author.

[8] Haines' files.

Chapter V. Two Morris Morrises—First-Cousins ♦ 93

wife, Sarah Cushman Morris, with their two children: Thomas, age five, and little Rachael, who was only two. Sarah was pregnant and soon to deliver her third child. We do know from many recorded family stories that young Morris and his little cousin Rachael played and traveled together with their families during this westward trek. Nancy Haines, who recorded fragments of her family's history from memory, knew her grandparents Rachael and Morris well, but she was only nine or ten years old when they died. These two children were not *first*-cousins but were first-cousins-once-removed, because they were in different generations, Morris in the third generation and Rachael in the fourth. However, they were only six years apart in age.

These two families must have been very close, for they had planned, shared, worked, farmed, hunted, and played together for much of their lives. It was said that a single piece of slate was passed around so each student might do sums and practice handwriting. "The children had only three months' schooling. *The Book of the World* passed from neighbor to neighbor and was the first geography they ever saw."[9] "Readin', writin', 'n' cipherin'" were seldom accomplished.

Sarah Cushman Morris (wife of Morris Morris I and daughter-in-law of old Richard) was the daughter of Mary Frazee and Thomas Cushman VI, who had come to the west from New Jersey. Sarah had endured this arduous trip from Virginia to Kentucky in the later stage of pregnancy, and gave birth to her third child, David Cushman Morris, at Bryan's Station in Kentucky in April of 1788.[10] The birth date and place are recorded on his tombstone, and it is said that his cradle was a sugar tub. (Sarah's first child, Thomas, had been born when she was but seventeen; now she was twenty-two.)

How extremely *dreadful* that these unsung, brave pioneer mothers had to give birth in a fort! Can we possibly imagine their plight: coping in wagons and flatboats with vomiting and disease, with bleeding and birthing, with diarrhea, diapers, and death? Stalwart and brave, these women knew how to skin a deer, use a flintlock and powder horn, knew how to mold bullets; they *had* to know. And they surely were frightened and exhausted much of the time, both psychologically and physically.

Medicines and remedies were pitifully few. Laudanum (tincture of opium), physicking pills, quinine, camphor, and peppermint essence were all very precious. Some knew about hartshorn for snakebites, and citrus

---

[9] Ibid.
[10] *Kentucky Citizen*, p. 3.

for scurvy. Whiskey and rum were used as medicines. Herbs and water baths were more common. But mostly they used nothing at all. Their many children endured a variety of hurtful experiences, such as teething, earaches, tummy pains, coughing, constipation, diarrhea, awful mosquito and snake bites, with little to ease the pain. We cannot really imagine a parent's helpless anguish and frustration. They *needed* to be resilient, resourceful, and strong.

The women themselves endured exposure, dysentery, and menstruation while lacking sufficient cloth and water, to say nothing of privacy. They suffered exposure and the very frightening uncertainty and panic of childbirth and possible death. Miscarriages, stillbirths, and infant and very early childhood deaths were common and largely unrecorded. One must suspect that most women "went on their journeys with obedience and considerable courage, but not by the acquiescence of their spirits."[11]

The frontiers*men,* buoyed by an expansive future and confident in their own strength, were usually large, burly, whiskered, and brusque, even uncouth. They often made decisions alone to move, to travel, to go on, generating a natural resentment between husbands and wives. These women were used to a "patriarchal deference." They had no choice but to follow and cooperate, pregnant or not. Nearly always it was the women who kept the family records, who wrote the diaries. While the men were sometimes far away exploring, hunting, building, or fighting Indians, the women found comfort in the company of other women. There was a bonding among those who shared their tasks, their skills, their fears, their friendships, their food, patterns, and recipes, who taught the children and kept the family a unit. "Their legacy to history was the survival of the family on the westward journey."[12]

Sarah Cushman Morris, the mother who had given birth to her third baby in a fort while *her* mother was making bullets, was the author's great-great-great-grandmother and the direct descendant of seven *Mayflower* passengers. Sarah's first daughter, Rachael, was the author's great-great-grandmother. Both Sarah and Rachael had in them the genes and the stamina of their Pilgrim ancestors. Like them, strong in body and spirit, they too were *survivors,* producing and rearing twelve and nine offspring, respectively. The author is truly proud to be descended from such strong, wonderful women, about whom, unfortunately, we know too little.

---

[11] Schlissel, p. 150.
[12] Ibid.

Chapter V. Two Morris Morrises—First-Cousins

Here, with a few words pluralized, is a paraphrase of Jane Parker's cherished poem from "Women," so appropriate for our "great-greats."

Their hands had never scorned their humble deeds.
They ministered to life and human needs,
And watched by loved ones' beds with bated breath
The simple dramas—birth, and love, and death.
Blessed wives and mothers, this their fate.
How they would smile—if we should call them great.

* * * * *

One event we do know about. A terrible tragedy in Sarah's life occurred when she was a young woman in her early twenties. A horrible tale is written about her maternal grandfather, who caused the death of her father, Thomas Cushman (the sixth in a direct line to bear that name).[13] It happened sometime after 1787, probably either just preceding or during their trek to Kentucky. Thomas was shot dead by his own father-in-law, Ephraim Frazee, who mistook Thomas for an Indian. Imagine the remorse and anguish of that family! This must be the reason no Thomas Cushman is recorded in early Bourbon County, Kentucky, only David Cushman (Sarah's brother), much later, in 1796.

In the beginning, living in Kentucky was never simple or safe. Throughout the summer, fall, and even into winter Indian raiding parties burned isolated cabins, killed cattle, stole horses, took prisoners and scalps. Guards had to be posted when field work was in progress. Danger was ever-present; children grew up rapidly.

Our family surely must have known Daniel Boone and his large, extended family who lived here too until October 1788, when Daniel decided to go farther west. Boone had lost his tomahawk claims, as he had several times before, so he moved on. Sharp land grabbers preyed on the ignorance and illiteracy of the frontiersmen who had opened up this land. Boone must have been too trusting or too careless.

* * * * *

Several records indicate that Richard Morris's youngest son, Morris I, was the closest to him of all the children, for Morris went three times exploring in the west to buy land for his father, since Richard had not fought in the war and was not allotted any free land. In 1783, Richard is recorded with three persons in his house. Then, later, he states that he and Mary went to live with son Morris.

---

[13] Alvah W. Burt, *Cushman Genealogy and Family History*.

Always eager to be among the first and have the most, Richard was a wise man and he knew he was getting old. Now he was ready to give his entire estate to son Morris in payment for lifetime care for himself and Mary. Fortunately, he had put this in writing, which explains why he died intestate. (Long ago Rebecca had been his first wife, mother of his children back in Maryland. Then he had married Mary, probably in Virginia, making her stepmother to his six children. They had all moved westward as a family, finally settling in Kentucky. Richard outlived two of his sons.)

That deed was signed in August 1799, saying that "*Richard* hath *transferred* to said *Maurice* all his interest in the following property.... Maurice hath for some time past supported said Richard Morris and hath given bond for maintaining him the rest of his natural life...."[14] So we know that Richard and Mary eventually lived with Morris and Sarah, who cared for them in their old age. That was the agreement. And Sarah had already reared twelve children. Richard died in 1798, judging from tax records. However, he had no taxes to pay and might have lived until 1803.[15]

In 1805 "Maurice Morris and heirs [were] asserting their right to moity" (a half portion).[16] That *grandson* of Richard, Maurice III (or Morris Morris III), was trying to get what he thought was his share of his grandfather's estate. The children of Richard's son John III were Maurice Jr.; Richard; William; Rebecca, who married Edward McConnell; and Drucilla, who would later marry John Sidwell. This court case dragged on for six years, until 1811, when the case was dismissed. Richard's foresight in putting in writing his lifetime care by Sarah and Morris had proven both wise on Richard's part and legally valuable. Thus many, many years later, a cousin's greediness is revealed in old records.

* * * * *

Morris I, who had cared for his parents, died in 1809, not many years after his aged father (and before the cousin's lawsuit was dismissed). He was only forty-eight years old and left twelve children, one of whom was a baby. All are recorded in the family Bible. His wife, Sarah, and eldest son, Thomas, were administrators of his estate. It was considerable for those times, even included two slave girls, Dice and Mary. At settlement Dice was sold by the sheriff for $415 and Mary, for $245. But Mary was bought back by widow Sarah. The original account of estate and ap-

---

[14] Bourbon County, Ky., Deed Bk. E, p. 185.
[15] *Kentucky Citizen*, p. 3.
[16] "Morris Morris Heirs vs. Morris Morris Heirs," Bourbon County, Ky., deed.

Chapter V. Two Morris Morrises—First-Cousins ♦ 97

praisement of the estate of Morris Morris of the September Court of 1809 are in the possession of the author, all written in longhand. Incidentally, it mentions whiskey at fifty cents a gallon!

Later, Sarah married Gresham Forrest. Either he died or the second marriage didn't work out, for she returned to her children and used both surnames, Morris and Forrest. Widows could call themselves anything they wished during widowhood, in those days.

Sarah Cushman Morris Forrest made her will in 1839 in Bourbon County. Less than three years later, in 1842 when she was seventy-five years old, she died of a "paralytick stroke" at the home of her daughter Rebecca and her son-in-law Henry Parker, Esq. So she survived her husband Morris by thirty-three years—a long, long time. They were both buried in Kentucky. Sarah had been the epitome of the pioneer woman, a strong individual typifying a whole group of wives and mothers in a period of dangerous and strenuous endeavor.

Morris and Sarah Cushman Morris produced twelve living children in their twenty-seven years of marriage. All but two were born in Kentucky. With great diligence it has been possible to trace the descending lines of most of these twelve offspring right down to present times. Remarkably, all twelve married and raised families. Some of their men fought in the Civil War. It appears that only two, Thomas, the oldest of the seven sons, and John eventually remained in Kentucky. John was a Mississippi River boat captain, an attorney who owned ten slaves, and a proud Confederate soldier. He remained in the same Kentucky area of his parents and became a devoted member of the old Cane Ridge Meeting near Paris, as did many of his family. Some of his descendants still live there. John and his wife's photographs are on the next page.

Four sons of Morris and Sarah emigrated to Illinois: Horatio, Preston, Albert, and Beauford; one of these, Preston, went on to Oregon by way of the Oregon Trail. Lawyer Horatio also left Illinois for Iowa. Daniel, born in a sugar trough, migrated from Kentucky to Indiana; his sister Rachael, about whom we will read in much more detail later, also went to Indiana with her husband Morris II, also a lawyer. Little is known of the other four daughters, but two stayed in Kentucky and one possibly went to Illinois. Most of the twelve children had large families, producing many Morris descendants who spread across the land, to Missouri, Wisconsin, Nebraska, Montana, Washington, and California. These are well recorded in the Genealogy in Part Three of this book. The records have come to the author from family members. America's West was being populated rapidly!

Captain John and Mrs. Katherine (Turney) Morris

Although John Morris II (the author's great-great-great-grandfather) was younger than his brother Richard, he too was getting old and was prescient enough to make a will. He died a year later, in 1797, when he was probably about sixty-five. That will was *finally* found, and solved several huge "puzzlements" in placing our family members. He wrote that he "was of Campbell County, Kentucky [once part of Bourbon], now residing in Pennsylvania on Georges Creek."[17] This was in Georges or Wharton Township, Fayette County, Pennsylvania, not very far northwest from the old Fort Morris where he had once lived in Sandy Creek Glades.

He named as executor his eldest son, Joseph the minister. The two eldest daughters, a probable sister (but name unknown) and Dorcas Morris Frazee (married c. 1787), were not mentioned, probably because they had already received their dowries, as was often the practice then.

To Joseph he gave 100 acres which he still owned back in Monongalia County, Virginia. He left money to his wife "Elanor,"[18] his two

---

[17] Monongalia County Will Bk. 1, pp. 302-3; Ross B. Johnston, comp., *West Virginia Estate Settlements*, p. 80.

[18] Notes of John Graves Morris, Albuquerque, N.M. Widow Eleanor was living in Cynthiana, Ky., in 1810 and 1820. She returned to Mason County after the death of her second husband, whose name is unrecorded. Her will is filed in Staunton, Va.

Chapter V. Two Morris Morrises—First-Cousins ♦ 99

daughters Eleanor and Elizabeth, and his other four sons. John's children were grown at the time of his death.

His oldest son, Joseph, was in the Rangers and the militia for Monongalia County, as every man had to be. Then he became a minister and is mentioned for non-military services during the Revolutionary War,[19] was a Baptist preacher in Kentucky and later in Ohio, probably married Mary Overton in 1813 in Kentucky.[20] Here he performed the marriage ceremony for his younger brother Morris to their cousin Rachael, at Cane Ridge Meeting near Paris, Kentucky.

If the will lists the sons in the usual descending order of age, the next son was John IV (born *after* his cousin John III, son of Morris II), probably a merchant at Mays Lick, Mason County, in 1810. He probably wed Malinda Ward, married by his brother, Reverend Joseph Morris, in Kentucky in 1815.[21]

Son Richard was in the Revolution, received bounty land, and probably married c. 1803 a young Mary Watts.[22]

Another son was James, who seems not to have migrated west with his family but remained unmarried, living in Monongalia County, Virginia, where he was involved between 1791 and 1816 with land transactions.[23] By 1816 James was in Adams County, Ohio.

The elder mentioned daughter, Elizabeth, was married to Moses Frazee in 1805, also by her preacher brother Joseph. She was Moses' second wife. He had come to Kentucky from New Jersey in 1784 as a carpenter four years before the Morrises had arrived. Intermarriage among the Frazee, Cushman, and Morris families continued in Kentucky into this generation. Elizabeth and Moses had four offspring. It is interesting to know that their first son was named for his father, Moses Frazee, that their second son was named for his grandfather, John Morris

---

[19] A. W. Reddy, *West Virginia Revolutionary Ancestors*.
[20] University of West Virginia Library.
[21] *Kentucky Ancestors*, V19-3 (1984), Brides Index to Bourbon County, p. 136.
[22] Mary Watts was a widow in 1807 and is recorded requesting bounty land for her husband's services (not Richard Sr., who was not in the war); Bayless E. Hardin, "Dr. Preston W. Brown, 1775-1826, His Family and Descendants," *Genealogies of Kentucky Families*, in *The Filson Club Quarterly*, vol. 106, p. 136. Mary Watts was the daughter of Col. William and Mary (Scott) Watts of Campbell County, Ky. She is buried in Cynthania, Ky., where her widowed mother-in-law, Eleanor Morris, lived.
[23] Monongalia Court Records, Env. 57A: To David Collum, sale of ninety acres on Muddy Creek, Va., to H. Hardesty–Deeds OS 1:299; to E. Hardesty–OS 6:496; to C. Clester–OS 2:433. George Sipolt appears fairly often in the transactions. (This James, son of John, was not the James who, with wife Margaret, moved into the county after buying land on Scotts Mill Run clear across the county. Monongalia Deeds OS 1:555 and OS 2:203.)

II, and the third son for the other grandfather, David Cushman. Alas, their little daughter Dorcas, named for her aunt, "died young." This family eventually migrated to Indianapolis.

Morris Morris II, the third from the youngest of John and Eleanor's nine children, was only about thirteen years old when his father died. How sad it is that his father never lived to know what an outstanding citizen and leader his baby boy was to become. In the 1810 Kentucky census we find Morris II in Nicholas County (once part of Bourbon). By then he was thirty, married, a father, and a self-taught, practicing lawyer[24]. Seven years later, in 1817, his legal services were needed by his older brother Joseph, executor of their father's will, who had sold his father's farm back in Virginia and was having legal problems. (There is much more information about Morris II in a later chapter.)

Youngest of this large family was Eleanor, but nothing has been found about her. Unrecorded maiden names became a disaster for genealogy.

Of the nine children of John II, only two, Dorcas and Morris II, have descendants known to the author; the other cousins are still not located.

* * * * *

A newly found fourth-cousin once casually said to the author that he had heard they had a relative who had been on the Lewis and Clark Expedition. She investigated the published list of members[25] and recognized the name Robert Frazer, recalling a statement by Frances Frazee Hamilton in her researched book, *Ancestral Lines of Doniphan, Frazee, Hamilton.* The name Frazee has been spelled many ways in early records, but all derivations in America, such as Fraze, Frazer, Frazier, Frasure, are from the original immigrant to New Jersey, Ephraim Frazee. We can consider any Frazee a "cousin," some much more distant than others.

It was logical that a Kentucky pioneer would be selected for this expedition that became the most important exploration in American history. Robert Frazer, born in Augusta County, Virginia, originally with Warfington's detachment, enlisted in 1804 in the permanent party of forty men of the Meriwether Lewis and William Clark expedition, ordered by President Thomas Jefferson. A private, he stayed until the end of this dangerous and difficult trip from St. Louis, Missouri, through Idaho, Washington, and Oregon via the Snake River and Hells Canyon, through the deep, deep Columbia River Gorge, down the great, wide Columbia River all the way to the Pacific Ocean—and back again. Like the others,

---

[24] Haines.
[25] Charles G. Clarke, *The Men of the Lewis and Clark Expedition.*

Chapter V. Two Morris Morrises—First-Cousins ♦ 101

he was rewarded with 320 acres of land in 1807.[26] Frazier Creek at South Boulder was named for him. Later, some time after the expedition was over, he was a witness at the trial of Aaron Burr.

No real effort has been made to find a family connection with Robert; there are *so many* Frazees and Fraziers! The days aren't long enough.

In 1994, the author and her husband took the trip in the wake of Lewis and Clark through the beautiful volcanic Cascade Mountains, into the tremendous Columbia Gorge and Hell's Canyon on the Snake River, then into the gentle Polous River in a zodiac. They traveled back down the great Columbia to the Pacific Ocean, just the reverse of the explorers' trip. Today there are more than a hundred dams and eight locks built by the United States Government to control those very dangerous rapids around which Lewis and Clark's men had to navigate or portage with heavy dugout canoes. Their admiration of their stamina and patience was very great and the scenery was spectacular. Sacajawea, the Shoshone Indian mentioned in Chapter IV, had been a mighty brave woman to travel with this expedition as guide and interpreter, carrying her very young baby all the way.

So another documented explorer was a "cousin" on that first, dangerous expedition, which encountered hostile Indians.

* * * * *

The "bluegrass land" with delicate bluish-purple buds on the spring grass was beautiful and good to these venturesome people, if they could survive the Indians. Our imaginations must supply a great deal of the story of these early generations, as only fragments survive for us to read about. Children grew up to see the land around them develop from a wilderness into a new territory, governed by the Virginia Assembly, then, in 1792, to become a new state at Danville, just south of Lexington. Later, Frankfurt was the chosen capital. The Indian problem was finally settled in 1794, when General Anthony Wayne won a decisive victory.

In only twenty years Kentucky expanded into a settled, organized society, with a set of values and a gentry class. Lexington would develop into the cultural center of the "West." The slave problem was becoming a burning question and would affect the future locale of the author's family.

The early, stalwart pioneers were being replaced by a younger, hardy generation who began to spread out across the land over the treacherous Oregon Trail, to populate and develop our expanding country, always

---

[26] Clarke, p. 325.

seeking a better life. They contributed much to American culture and our way of living. We are in their debt for their courage, their strengths, and for their labors.

We recall that Morris Morris II married his cousin, Rachael Morris, at the Cane Ridge Meeting House near Paris, Kentucky.[27] This young couple, who as children had traveled on a flatboat, played, and grown up together, would become part of another generation of Midwestern pioneers. Like both their grandparents and their parents, they too would again move on.

* * * * *

The two Morris Morrises about whom this book is written have been traced and recorded here, sometimes briefly but with more details in the complete Genealogy in Part Three. The double name is rather unusual, and it is a strange coincidence that one was the father of the bride and the other was his first-cousin who became his son-in-law. Because of a marriage, both of these lines are those of the author. Her closer line is of Morris Morris II. This line has been traced very completely to the present, with much factual material of historic interest. The lives and remarkable achievements of this descent are related with pride in the stories following this chapter. Included are a Civil War general who was a close friend of President Benjamin Harrison, the first woman to be recorded in the Indiana history books, a personal friend of Abraham Lincoln who founded our National Bureau of Engraving and Printing, an inventor, and more!

---

[27] Bourbon County, Ky., Reg. 2, p. 14; copy of original marriage document in possession of the author.

Chapter V. Two Morris Morrises—First-Cousins

> **EMIGRANT WOMAN**
> By
> **Sylvester Osmer Morris**

This poignant description of pathos and sufferance seems appropriate to add here as we think of the Morris, Cushman, and Frazee families just described who left Virginia for Kentucky. Sylvester Morris was writing about his great-grandmother, Lucinda (Powell) Probst, who later became an ancestor of Morrises. She traveled on the Oregon trail with the Powell wagon train as a young bride of only seventeen—pregnant, frail, and pathetic.

The author, Sylvester Osmer Morris, was a great-great-great-grandson of Sarah Cushman and Morris Morris I and a descendant of Preston (their tenth child of twelve), who was Rachael's little brother.

Sylvester Morris was born in the cabin of a Nez Perce Indian, in Lewis County, Idaho, in 1898 and pioneered in Oregon. He became a commercial artist, served in World War I, and died in Dayton, Washington, in 1987.

Sylvester located the grave of his great-grandmother. She was buried near Pendleton at the crossing of Butter Creek, Oregon, then "a regular campsite for emigrants [for] there would be grass, water, and probably cottonwood for fuel.... The whole wagon train drove over the grave to conceal it from the Indians.... There is little remaining to remind the traveler of the toil and hardship that was the common lot of Lucinda and her people."

THE MEN TALKED IT OVER, day in, day out. W'y, they say the soil is so rich, you can take two crops in a single season. Rains every month of the year, but lots of sun, and the winters are so mild, some of the trees never lose their verdure. And timber, for building, right on your own land. That was it, the land! Free for the taking. A man can have his own place to work. He said he was tired of hiring out, he wanted land of his own. She had her say, too; she was a woman grown, eighteen—well, near eighteen. She would be, before the baby came. She couldn't say how she knew, but it would be a little girl. A little girl would be company, and you could teach her things, too.

But of course she'd go, she'd promised, time they stood up in front of Preacher. They were better off than most. The wagon was almost new, and the oxen young, and his father had given him his share. And she had things too, bedding, and the red heifer, Sookey. Ma gave her the little keg of vinegar to take. They said it was good to sweeten the bad water, and good for things, and to season. She had some pieces of ribbon in the trunk; a little girl would need ribbons. She hoped there would be a lilac at the new place.

The old man was the first. He turned yellow and weakened, and one morning Preacher felt and said he was burning up. They used her vinegar to wipe his face and set his tongue and lips. But it didn't help much. They buried him where others had been left and Preacher read, and led in a song. "I am the resurrection and the life, whosoever believeth in Me ...." Had the old man believed? She wondered.

She lost the red heifer. Indians tried to make off with the livestock one night and there was shooting, and Sookey got bad hurt.

The men had it hardest, they claimed. But even a stout man needed looking after. Meals and the bedding aired, and clothes washed and patched. He sided with Preacher, most times. He was past nineteen, and most were older, but they listened to him.

Grass got scarce, and water, and wood, and the dust got into everything, seemed like. But a day came they quit following up the stream, and the stream ran ahead of them, West.

On a harsh, cold grade of the Blues, almost in sight of the river, they laid over a day, and they made a grave for the little girl. She'd only lived a week, and was early. Preacher said it was all the walking, and they'd had to pitch in and help the oxen, times. She looked back once, but she couldn't be sure she could make it out. The sun was in her eyes and her eyes blurred.

But they made it, most of them, and he had his land. He still had to hire out for a while, and it was some years before they had much cleared. By then the boys were beginning to be some help. She never got the lilac bush, but he planted wild currant around the privy, and the trapper's dark wife showed her how to move the wild flags that grew in the low ground below the spring.

... A body gets tired.... He was gone, maybe he still needed looking after. And the girl, w'y she'd be a grown woman now. She wanted to see them again [her man, and their first-born little girl], and she was glad she had a place to rest, there at the foot of the orchard.

Chapter V. Two Morris Morrises—First-Cousins ♦ 105

The story above was excerpted from *Powell History,* a book written by James Madison Powell, M.D. The excerpt is used by permission of Jean Morris Laws.

The Powells were connected to the Morris family through marriage in the 1800s. Margaret Probst, a daughter of Lucinda (Powell) Probst, married Nathaniel Morris in 1862, and Margaret's nephew married Nathaniel Morris's sister the same year. Although the Morris and the Powell families were in Virginia, Kentucky, and Oregon, they didn't know each other until the 1850s.

Jean Morris Laws, a daughter of the author of "Emigrant Woman," is now a grandmother living in Olympia, Washington. She is one of those many interested distant cousins who have aided considerably with research for this book and has given permission for including the above excerpt. Jean and her husband, Keith Laws, recently visited Castle Madoc in Brecon, Wales, the ancestral estate of the ancient Powell family, situated just south of the county of Radnor and about twenty-five miles northwest of Chepstow Castle of Morris fame. They discovered that Castle Madoc had been demolished completely. Alas, there was nothing to see but lovely countryside.

Remember that in 1697 a David Powell of the county of Radnor of Carmarthen, Wales, came to Philadelphia in a charter party on the ship *William Galley* (Chapter III). He was listed first as head of a group of eleven people. Three other Powell families (no names) were also aboard among the sixty-two passengers. Listed second, and also from the county of Radnor, was our ancestor John Morris as the named head of his group of six.

Here is a tantalizing question: Were the several marriages between Morrises and Powells in the 1800s descendants of those families who came to Philadelphia together on the *William Galley?* We probably will never know.

Keith Laws, mentioned above, has had a colorful and productive life. He was in a Navy submarine at Pearl Harbor and became a scholar and educator with many awards and honors including Fulbright professorships to Israel and India.

Professor Keith Laws

See the Genealogy for more details of this contemporary family and their Morris ancestors.

Part Two
Chapters VI – XXIII
The Remarkable Accomplishments of One Morris Branch Which Migrated to Indianapolis, Indiana

It's a lovely thing to live with courage, and die leaving an everlasting flame.
— Alexander the Great

Chapter VI

MORRIS MORRIS II and RACHAEL MORRIS
Pioneer Sweethearts

From all the rich resources of our earth
[They] wrought, by honest toil of hand and brain,
The complex pattern needed to sustain
[Their] lives, and make them worthy of [their] birth.
— Rev. John MacKinnon, from "Astonishing Grace"

A SMALL BAND of pioneers had camped at a large sinking spring in 1786 in Kentucky County, later to be known as Bourbon County. This area grew to become Paris, the county seat. Meanwhile a small cluster of Presbyterian ministers arrived to give support. One of them, the Rev. Andrew McClure, nurtured a group seven miles from Paris, the first Presbyterian congregation in central Kentucky, on the highest ridge in the county, with vistas of woodlands, limestone streams, and green pastures. Daniel Boone had recommended this location and named it "Cane Ridge" for its extensive, fifteen-mile-long cane brake. Soon, in 1791, the Reverend Finley arrived to build a log church there. Then, in 1801, Barton Stone organized the Cane Ridge Revival, lasting six days and drawing 30,000 worshipers! Rev. Stone became a distinguished reformer of the nineteenth century and made Cane Ridge a center of religious freedom. During this time it played an important role in the Morris families who lived in this area.

Meanwhile, two young people, first-cousins-once-removed with the same surname of Morris who had started life together in western Virginia, had traveled across the mountains in the early spring of 1788 to survive unfriendly Indians and all the other vicissitudes of pioneer life. Rachael was a brave and helpful little girl, the second oldest in a family that eventually included twelve children. A handsome fellow was young Morris, serious and smart, who read a lot, later studied law alone, and became well-informed. He was surely ambitious in a climate of rough surroundings and simple living. These cousins soon developed a great respect and love for each other in their brand new state of Kentucky.

Rachael Morris and Morris Morris II were married on 7 August 1803 in the Cane Ridge Meeting House near Paris. She was only seventeen and he was not yet twenty-three. The original marriage contract still exists, signed the day before the ceremony by both of the Morris Morrises, father (in-law) and bridegroom.[1] The sum of "fifty pounds, current money of Kentucky" was paid as a binding fee, and the minister was Joseph Morris, older brother of the bridegroom. The interesting but already famous thirty-by-fifty-foot log church, then only twelve years old, built of rough-hewn virgin, barkless logs and wooden pins, had seating-in-the-round, with a pulpit on one of the long walls instead of at the end. A freestanding gallery, reached by ladder, was for slaves.

Less than a year after this marriage, the movement in American Protestantism known as the Christian Church, or the Disciples of Christ, was founded here by Barton Stone. This historic church, on the National Register, still stands today, well preserved, a physical reminder for us of this union of two Morrises. Their pictures are there in the museum with a copy of their 1803 marriage bond, sent by this author. There are also Morrises buried in its graveyard.

Cane Ridge Meeting House, near Paris, Kentucky

---

[1] Author's file.

Chapter VI. Morris Morris II and Rachael Morris ♦ 111

Enlarged and improved in 1829 and again in 1882, Cane Ridge Meeting House was finally restored to its primitive appearance in 1932. To prevent decay and disintegration, the "Cane Ridge Shrine," a stone and steel superstructure costing over $100,000, was erected to encase and shelter the original building. A historic cemetery and an annual Cane Ridge Day every June was supplemented in 1991 by a bicentennial celebration.

During the era of 1812, very popular large revivals took place regularly at this church. Morris surely was a part of these for he was a deeply religious man of very strong convictions—as we shall see. The deeds of his later life proved the influence of these Cane Ridge revivals. A serious person, he was self-taught, "read law," and practiced law in Kentucky before and after his marriage.

It is possible that Morris had the middle name of Austin, the name they gave their first son, as some heirloom tablespoons of his still extant in Indianapolis bear the initials "M. A. M." However, no other reference to this middle initial has yet been found elsewhere, nor has the name Austin.

Morris and his families surely spent time in Duncan Tavern on the public square of Paris for much business was carried on there. It had been built by Major Joseph Duncan in 1788, the same year the Morris families had arrived in Kentucky. Here, Daniel Boone, Simon Kenton, and other famous frontiersmen had often gathered. Today the tavern is nicely restored.

Rachael and Morris lived in Bourbon County for at least a year, as the birth of their first child, Austin, is recorded there exactly a year after their marriage. They probably moved about some, although settlements become confusing. A family might have remained on the same land for many years, but the county name could change one or more times in a relatively short span of time as population increased and the large counties were divided for administrative purposes. Old counties kept their records, while newly-formed counties started their own. For example, Mason County was formed from Bourbon in 1788, Campbell from Bourbon in 1794, and Nicholas in 1799. All of these county names appear in our family records.

When Morris was twenty-seven, his older brother Joseph, the executor of their father's will, retained him to act as attorney to resolve their father's long-lasting lawsuit. Originally, back in Virginia, their father had left a tract of more than 600 acres, 100 of which Joseph had inherited outright and later sold to William Griffin.[2] The remainder of the farm was to be sold and divided among the other four sons. David Gundy (Gunty) had contracted to buy from executor Joseph Morris the bulk of John Morris II's remaining property, over 490 acres, but seems never to have finished paying for it. No deed was ever made to Gundy. In 1807 Morris Morris II went to Monongalia County to wrap up the business on this land and obtain a property attachment. However, the value was not nearly sufficient. Gundy was jailed, the case died in court in 1811, and in 1814 Morris sold the land to John Fike.[3]

The author carefully compared several signatures of Morris Morris on the deeds with other signatures in her possession known to be his. They were the same. There is no doubt that our Morris Morris II was attorney for Joseph, son of John Morris II of Maryland, later of Monongalia County, Virginia, and still later of Campbell County, Kentucky.

Morris's name appears on the Nicholas County tax lists from 1811 through 1819. He owned thirty acres in 1814, fifty acres in 1815, seventy in 1816, and sold fifteen acres that year for one dollar. He and his family lived in the environs of Ellisville[4] and later owned a town lot in Carlisle, in 1818 and 1819. In 1817 he was a magistrate,[5] lived in Ellisville and practiced law in Carlisle, the county seat.

His associates were important men and he helped his townsmen politically. Thomas Metcaffe, not a lawyer but a stonemason, was soon to become the tenth governor of Kentucky. Another friend was John Jordan Crittendon, who practiced law in Russellville but moved to Frankfort in 1819. Crittendon, too, became a governor of Kentucky after serving as U.S. attorney general in the cabinets of Presidents W. H. Harrison, John Tyler, and Millard Fillmore.[6] Also, there was lawyer Henry Clay (1777-1852), "the great pacificator" and popular orator, whose office was in Lexington. From time to time Clay was hired as defense attorney in trials in other counties requiring his ability to defend a murderer. Henry Clay became a great American statesman, spent many years in both the Kentucky Senate and the House of Representatives, eventually serving as the United States secretary of state (from 1825 to 1829, only four years after Morris left Kentucky). It was said by many that Morris resembled Henry Clay.[7]

---

[2] Monongalia Co. Deeds D, p. 1479.
[3] Monongalia Co. Deeds OS6, p. 179.
[4] Nicholas Co. Rec. DRE 11.
[5] Rec. 5, 392.
[6] *Encyclopedia Britannica*, 1959 ed., vol. 6, p. 729.
[7] Maria Frazee Browning, Indianapolis, Ind., personal letter in author's file.

Chapter VI. Morris Morris II and Rachael Morris ♦ 113

These three well-known associates, Metcalfe, Crittendon, and Clay, were good friends of Morris and of each other. It is said that Clay suggested the name "Forest Retreat" for Metcalfe's home, still called that today. There is no doubt that Morris was in very good company. One cannot help but wonder what he would have become if he had remained in Kentucky.

By 1820, Morris was an established lawyer and a landowner with a family of six children. He was already forty years old, which in those days was considered past middle age. A pious and good man, he was both reverent and devout, but willful, according to all accounts. He had a *very* strong belief that he did not want to rear his family in a state that condoned slavery. More than one history book mentions this.[8] In Kentucky slavery was legal, and there were many slaves in that state. Thus his uncompromising integrity spurred on the urge to move *again;* this began to haunt him.

In 1821 a brand new capital was about to be established in a very new and neighboring state called Indiana, which had recently been admitted to the United States, in 1816. Morris and others believed that Indiana would not condone or legalize slavery because a 1787 ordinance for Indiana Territory had actually prohibited slavery but did not abolish that which was in existence. The new state constitution of 1816 pronounced strongly against it. Almost all of the slaves had been liberated or moved to Kentucky.[9] This was due primarily to the action of the upright Quakers who had already settled in the southeastern section of Indiana Territory.[10]

This area of Indiana was just north of where Morris was living and working, in the northeastern part of Kentucky. It is understandable how a righteous, moral lawyer could get very caught up in the antislavery movement, so near to him geographically, so dear to him ethically and politically. He was indeed "passionately seeking truth."

But how could he leave a lifetime of study, work, and achievement, the law firm, and those prestigious men with whom he worked and associated? How could he ask Rachael and six children to leave their home,

---

[8] B. R. Sulgrove, *History of Indianapolis and Marion County* ; Haines' files.

[9] As early as 1681 LaSalle had made a treaty in South Bend, in northern Indiana, with the Miami and Illinois Indian tribes, and the French built a post the next year. A hundred years later Anthony Wayne built a fort just south of there. In 1811, farther south, General William Henry Harrison (later president of the United States) defeated the Shawnee Confederacy at the Battle of Tippecanoe.

[10] *Encyclopedia Britannica*, vol. 12, p. 212.

their friends and family, their community? These questions must have tormented his conscience.

It is easy for us to admire in hindsight but truly difficult for us to comprehend fully the convictions of people who felt strongly enough to tear up their roots again, to unsettle a whole family, to start anew in an undeveloped, roadless wilderness. Such remarkable conviction, determination, sacrifice, strength, vigor, tenacity, and courage we can only reflect upon with real respect and admiration. Our Morris surely was one of those who had, as Jane Adams once said of our pioneers, "faith in new possibilities, and courage to advocate them."

* * * * *

The United States Congress had appointed a committee of five men to determine the location of the newly planned capital of the new state of Indiana, admitted to the Union in 1816 and the nineteenth state to be formed, after being carved out of part of Indiana Territory. (This was the same year that Abraham Lincoln and his family moved to Spencer County, Indiana.)

The seat of government had been established at Vincennes (the oldest town, founded in 1702), then was moved temporarily to Corydon. Seven years later it was moved to a *central* site which was then dense forest at the junction of Fall Creek and White River. Soon its name was selected: "Indianapolis," meaning "the city of Indiana" from the Greek "polis," which means "city of." At this period in our nation there was a lofty, often-expressed sentiment that Americans were the spiritual descendants of ancient Greece, with its democratic ideals. This feeling became evident in many names of new towns in the West and Midwest, such as Athens, Sparta, Ithaca.

This new Indianapolis was a roadless, trackless, uninhabited forest, supporting Indians, deer, bear, rattlesnakes, wild turkeys, ducks, geese, swans, and pigeons. Some fifteen families already lived there when the land was surveyed in April 1821. A small trading post was located not far away. By an 1820 Act of Congress, White River and certain other streams were declared public highways, the only exception being the erection of dams by persons who had purchased the river bed from the government. Flatboats began arriving from Kentucky with families and supplies. Newcomers lived in tents. Gradually primitive shelters and rustic dwellings were erected, and people shared their lodgings.

In 1821 Alexander Ralston and Elias Fordham surveyed the city of Indianapolis. Ralston was a Scotsman who had already helped L'Enfant design Washington, D.C. An integral part of his plan was a mile-square

Chapter VI. Morris Morris II and Rachael Morris ♦ 115

town with a circle, which was intended to be the center. He was hired by the legislature to lay out the city, survey White River, and evaluate the expense of making it navigable.[11] "To this land he [Morris Morris] moved his family about the first of October, and a few days before the sale of lots."[12] It is said he drove a small cattle herd from Kentucky.

It was to a real frontier that Rachael and Morris Morris came, in 1821, across rivers and through the wilderness, with six children ranging in age from only one year to seventeen. They were one of the earliest families. They are the *first named* in a list of fifteen in an old history book which includes three doctors.[13] A similar list of eighteen also names Morris first.[14] Still another list names eleven arrivals in 1820, and fifty-one in 1821 including "Morris Morris—October."[15] It also gives many occupations but not one for him.

"Prior to this change of residence he abandoned the practice of law, giving as a reason the fact that the pursuit of his profession interfered with the Christian life he desired to lead. He did not judge others by the same rule, but believed it, in his own case, to be the only course in harmony with his convictions. This incident might be taken as a key to his character. He was conscientious to a rare degree, and could not be swerved from his idea of right. At the same time he never arraigned others at the bar of his own judgment. His standard was for himself only." This excerpt is from a full-page biography, with a full-page picture, in the best and most complete of all the early histories of Indianapolis.[16]

During the sale of lots, 314 were sold for $200 to $500. The city lots were inside the mile square, and there were out-lots for farms. Ten years later the state still owned three-fourths of the city lots and nearly all of the out-lots, but they were finally disposed of by 1842.[17] "On his arrival in Indianapolis, ... [Morris] bought land largely within and without its limits, and was among the most active in advancing the growth of the new settlement."[18] In 1821 this new wilderness capital seems to have at-

---

[11] Christian Schrader, *Indianapolis Remembered: Christian Schrader's Sketches of Indianapolis*, p. 84.
[12] John H. B. Nowland, *Early Reminiscences of Indianapolis*.
[13] *Logan's History of Indianapolis from 1818*, p. 2.
[14] A. C. Howard, publisher, *Historical Sketch of Indianapolis* (Indianapolis, 1857), p. 4.
[15] Jacob Piat Dunn, *Greater Indianapolis*, vol. 1, p. 46.
[16] Sulgrove, pp. 216-217. The same engraving was previously published, with a different biography, in *A Biographical History of Eminent and Self-made Men of the State of Indiana*, p. 258.
[17] Max R. Hyman, ed., *The Journal Handbook of Indianapolis*, p. 8.
[18] Sulgrove, p. 216.

tracted men who wanted to build a town with roots, a solid, law-abiding town. Their city was not to be a "jumble of cowpath streets."

The "Tract Book" in the County Auditor's Office gave a list of entries of land from July 1821 to 1826. Morris Morris is the twenty-seventh name in a list of approximately 1,020 entries.[19] In July 1821 the Morrises purchased two eighty-acre plots in section 15 from the United States Government "according to the Act of Congress of the 24th of April 1830," signed by President Monroe. Morris's land was west of White River bounded by streets later known as *Morris*, Harding, and Minnesota, and on the west by Belmont Avenue.[20]

For many years there was much flooding of the rivers, often ruining the cultivated bottom lands, covering fertile fields with sand and gravel and washing away fences. Indianapolis had great ravines where water stood and malaria ("the ague") was abundant, so there was a great deal of sickness in the beginning. In 1821 the ague was rampant but became less common as the land was cleared, although this problem continued for many years, especially in the wet seasons.

"Soon after [Morris] settled in his new home his whole family were taken sick with chills and fever. This discouraged him very much, so much so that he wished to return to Kentucky, and would have done so had not Mrs. Morris opposed it, and to her Indianapolis is indebted for what afterwards turned out to be several of its most valuable citizens."[21] One can easily imagine the weariness of a mother of six (one a baby) who had moved many times before, now desiring to settle once and for all in spite of disease, floods, and uncleared land!

The Morrises had just recently arrived "in that memorable year of sickness and death, 1821.... The doctor [Isaac Coe] had brought a large supply of Peruvian bark [quinine-in-the-rough] and wine, which was the only thing with which he could conquer the fever and ague.... He could be seen at almost any time of night dodging through the woods [no roads] in his gig, and by the light of his lantern, from one cabin to another administering to the sick in other ways as well as giving medicine."[22] This ailment, resulting from undrained swamps and newly turned soil, affected nearly everyone in the small community.

Dr. William Wishard records that "There was a small frame house on the east side of the street, near the small stream [Pogue's Run] occupied

---

[19] Ibid., p. 60.
[20] Donald S. Morris handwritten document in author's file; Recorder's Office of Marion Co., Ind., deed record EE 481.
[21] Nowland, p. 105; 1850 census of Indianapolis.
[22] Ibid., p. 104.

Chapter VI. Morris Morris II and Rachael Morris ♦ 117

"Indianapolis in 1820," by Alois E. Sinks. Scene near Morris Morris's first home in Indianapolis, depicting a typical log cabin and Pogue's Run.

by Morris Morris ... then there was a one-room log house on the west side occupied by Hiram Brown, lawyer. A log house on the east side occupied by a widow [name forgotten], ... on the corner occupied by a colored woman who took in washing ... [another corner] a grocery by Jerry Collins, who sold whiskey, gingerbread, and root beer." Nearby were Nowland's boarding house, a little shanty doctor's office, and Hawkin's Tavern opposite Higgen's Tavern.[23]

"Mr. and Mrs. Morris had been neighbors of the Wishard family in Kentucky, and their new home in Indianapolis was always open to their friends with the hospitality that was a conspicuous feature of pioneer life. ... Father had the misfortune to fall from his horse while fording a stream ... he sought the kindly ministrations of Mrs. Morris, who gave him clothes in exchange for those he wore ... frozen stiff ... [later, in 1832 during the Black Hawk War] father [colonel of the 57th Regiment] wore his military coat but decided uniforms would be a menace in fighting redskins, thereupon discarded his bright-colored military clothes and bor-

---

[23] Elizabeth Moreland Wishard, *William Henry Wishard, A Doctor of the Old School*, pp. 33-4.

rowed a coat of Morris Morris. He left his own coat here and went to war in the borrowed coat."[24]

These first settlers united in making a common field, with a fence of underbrush, to keep out the cattle. This was cultivated for several years while the settlers cleared the land. Crops were well started in this common plot before the sickness became prevalent; this probably saved the pioneers from starvation. "Mr. Morris brought the corn he had raised at the bluffs to within a mile of his house in a boat."[25] *He* had been foresighted to plant corn in July with the help of his oldest son, Austin, and then he and the family all came to Indianapolis together in October. Corn, always the main crop, was made into johnnycake, corn pone, mush, and hominy, and it also fattened the hogs. In this family it was never used to make whiskey.

With the help of their children, Morris and Rachael cleared their 160 acres, plowed with a "jumping-shovel-plow" to cut the roots, perhaps borrowed a "sod plow" for tree roots, then harrowed, planted, and eventually developed a real farm. Here they lived at least two years. This land was bounded on one side by what soon became Morris Street.

The well-known Indianapolis artist Jacob Cox made a large painting about 1850 named "The Morris Farm." Donald S. Morris gave this painting to the Heron Institute of Indianapolis and it is now owned by the Morris-Butler House Museum. The building in the painting is typical of the homes built in Indianapolis from 1821 to 1840.[26]

Jacob Cox lived in Indianapolis from 1833, starting as a stove and tin dealer with his brother, before his first announcement as a portrait painter appeared in December of 1841: "Has removed to the room over the store of Morris and Brother adjoining the Post Office." Cox later became the town's most revered and prominent portrait and landscape artist. A neighbor and friend of Morris and Rachael, he painted portraits of both of them which are quite valuable and now hang in the Morris-Butler House Museum. (This couple were parents of the museum's builder, John Morris IV.)

"When Mr. Morris first came to Indianapolis [they] were known only as 'dad and mam,' or 'pap and mammy,' but they were soon called 'pa and ma,' learned from Mr. M.'s children. They were called [that] by both old and young from time immemorial. [They were probably among

---

[24] Ibid., pp. 34, 105.
[25] Ibid., p. 106.
[26] Donald S. Morris letter in author's file.

Chapter VI. Morris Morris II and Rachael Morris ♦ 119

the oldest of the group.] ... His house was ever the home of ministers of all denominations."[27]

The first formal religious service in Indianapolis was held in 1813 where the capitol now stands. A Methodist, Resin Hammond, conducted the first real service under a walnut tree. In 1821 the first church was organized by the Reverend William Gravens in the log-cabin home of Isaac Wilson. We can feel very sure that Morris and Rachael were there, for they were a truly pious and devout couple and were among the founders of this *first* Methodist Church.

The first log schoolhouse was also built in 1821, at the corner of Kentucky Avenue and Washington Street. Five years later Ebenezer Sharp opened a school in the back part of the Presbyterian Church, located at the corner of Alabama and North Streets.[28] Not surprising is that the Morrises' oldest, Austin, now twenty-two, was a teacher there, and sons Thomas and John were students.

Morris soon became identified with the general progress of Indianapolis, whose history showed "for the first score of years few events of public concern in which he was not prominent."[29]

The town builders were men of varying backgrounds, some uncouth, some sensitive and articulate. For these latter men, holding public office must have been a form of self-expression, so politics was important from the beginning. In 1822 the very first elections were held, for two associate judges, a clerk, a recorder, and three commissioners for the new county.

Clerk was considered to be the most important office at the time. Our self-taught pioneer, who had "read law" and then practiced it for years in Kentucky, ran for this office, along with four other candidates. The field was eventually narrowed and the community divided naturally into two geographical factions. Part of the people had reached the New Purchase by way of the "Whitewater country," and the rest had come up from Kentucky. The Kentucky contingent had chosen Morris Morris as their chief and leading candidate. He was a "strong and able man who fired the first gun by issuing a campaign pamphlet on January 30, the first literary product of the city outside the newspaper."[30]

Morris was using his skill with a pen to shape public opinion; a skirmish of words followed. This pamphlet was answered by the opposi-

---

[27] Nowland, p. 108.
[28] Ibid., p. 119.
[29] Sulgrove, p. 216.
[30] Dunn, pp. 49-50; Howard, p. 15; *Indianapolis News,* 1 Nov. 1948 and 4 Oct. 1965, n.p.; Sulgrove, p. 38; Logan, p. 9; Nowland, p. 89; Howe, p. 326.

tion, and Morris issued a second handbill—"an effective weapon." But he did not win. He was defeated by the "'in yonder on Whitewater' vote, which outnumbered that of the Kentuckians. [Morris did] represent his county several years in the legislature and ... made a very efficient and popular officer."[31] The winner was James Ray, who, three years later, in 1825, went on to become Indiana's first governor and held that position until 1831.[32] How very different this story might have been if the Kentuckians had outnumbered the Whitewater contingent!

"The first roll of grand jurors, selected from among the taxpayers of the county at the May session, 1822, and numbering fifty-four discrete house-holders" included Morris Morris, listed tenth.[33]

Active in Jacksonian Democratic politics, Morris was reported to be active also in various religious and social organizations. We next read of Morris Morris, Esquire, in 1823 delivering an oration, followed by a prayer, a banquet, and a "ball" at the Fourth of July celebration at the cabin of Wilkes Reagan, who lived next door in the woods near Pogue's Run. Reagan was the first auctioneer and the first butcher. He served a barbecue to the assembly![34]

The following year the annual election contest was mainly for sheriff, with Morris Morris one of the principal opposing candidates, and again he was not the winner.[35] But *Water Runs Downhill,* the modern history of the Indianapolis Water Company, mentions him as "civic-minded Morris Morris ... [who] soon exercised a steady hand in most public events of the times."[36]

In 1824 Morris, along with a judge, a general, a governor, and two others listed as "older citizens" joined a very popular and influential organization, "the Indianapolis Legislature," to discuss legislative matters in depth. It had been started earlier by a group of younger men including two of Morris's full-grown sons, Austin and Thomas, and their first cousin John Frazee.[37] (This will be covered more fully in a later chapter on son Thomas Armstrong Morris.)

---

[31] Nowland, p. 106.

[32] James M. Ray married Marie Coe, the doctor's daughter. Both had their portraits painted in 1828 by Richard Terrell, who was the second portrait painter to arrive in Indianapolis, after Jacob Cox. These portraits hung in the Senate Chamber.

[33] Sulgrove, p. 112.

[34] W. R. Holloway, *Indianapolis, Railroad City,* pp. 25, 27; Dunn, p. 89; Howard, p. 22; Sulgrove, p. 57.

[35] Howard, p. 117; Sulgrove, p. 57; Holloway, p. 27.

[36] Marjie Gates Giffin, *Water Runs Downhill.*

[37] Dunn, p. 81; Nathaniel Bolton, *Early History of Indianapolis and Central Indiana,* p. 170.

Chapter VI. Morris Morris II and Rachael Morris ♦ 121

Although Morris is never mentioned by name in any of the accounts of "the massacre of Fall Creek," he must have been involved in the excitement, the settlers' fears, the legal arguments, and the moral discussions which occurred in March of the year 1824. It was only three years after his arrival in this new and sparsely populated state. Because he was a deeply religious leader with a legal background, he must have had a part at this momentous time. Among his friends and associates were Governor James Ray (from 1825 to 1831), who had defeated him only three years before for the office of county clerk; General James Noble, a U.S. senator; and Calvin Fletcher, a leading Indianapolis lawyer.

The alarming incident of a massacre so close to Indianapolis, near Pendleton, resulted in a historic trial, so it seems important to mention the facts here. We can feel very sure our Morris ancestor was indeed concerned, probably involved, as were all leading citizens of the locality.

Briefly, in 1824, four white men were formally charged with the premeditated killing of nine Indians—two braves, three squaws, and four children. These white men were indicted, tried by jury, found guilty, and sentenced to die. A fifth white man, the ringleader, was never apprehended. Three of the condemned men were hanged. The fourth, a youth, was saved from the gallows by a last-minute reprieve by Governor James Ray, who arrived melodramatically on a sweated horse. General James Noble, then a U.S. senator, was employed by the secretary of war, John C. Calhoun, to prosecute. Calvin Fletcher was the regular prosecuting attorney.

The killing of Indians had been a persistent part of the westward thrust of this nation up to this time. It had always been "necessary and acceptable." Indians had not been considered as humans but as animals. They had a very different culture and fought inhumanely, according to the white man's set of standards. This trial in 1824, here in the new city of Indianapolis, was the first time in the history of the United States that white men were tried, convicted, and executed for the killing of Indians. Their tribes were then pacified here, and this was the last ever seen of Indians in Marion County (except for migrating tribes in 1832).

This historic event of the first U.S. execution of men by due process of law for killing Indians is described in some detail twice in Sulgrove's *History of Indianapolis and Marion County,* on pages 9 and 10, and 54 and 56. A stimulating book by Jessamyn West, *The Massacre at Fall Creek,*[38] has turned the bare facts into a good novel, depicting the tor-

---

[38] Jessamyn West, *The Massacre at Fall Creek* (New York and London: Harcourt Brace Jovanovich, 1975).

tured relationship with the Indians and life in Indiana in 1824. It opens moral questions so difficult to solve in those early times. Although Ms. West claims that most of the characters are her own invention, one can read the history and find counterparts in the novel. One of the leading men, "Caleb Cape," reminds the author *very* much of Morris Morris. Caleb's personality and character—good, religious, wise, stalwart, brave, always a leader—seem to parallel the traits of our ancestor. Jessamyn West's novel aptly reveals the rough and dangerous times, the simple backwoods living of an era we tend to forget. Morris had chosen this life for his family, had left behind an established profession in Kentucky because of very strong convictions about humanity, about black men and slavery. The outright, intentional killing of nearby red men and women who were harming no one surely concerned this good man also.

By 1828 Morris had given up the practice of law completely and was elected auditor of the state of Indiana. This very important position he held for fifteen successive years, from 1829 to 1844,[39] discharging his duties in a responsible and trustworthy manner. Morris was "one of the most esteemed citizens of any period.... During his administration pretty much all of the scrip issued at all was put out and into the currency of the State."[40] This was a real responsibility. The auditor's office was a red brick home on the southwest corner of Senate and Washington Streets, also the office and residence of the state treasurer. There was a fireproof vault in the basement with a double-locked iron door at the top of the stairs.[41]

Three years after coming to Indianapolis with a one-year-old and five other offspring, Rachael Morris gave birth to a seventh child. By March of 1830 she had borne nine children. The last, a boy, lived only seven months but all the other eight survived to grow to adulthood. The 1830s proved difficult financially for many people, but Morris expanded his city holdings by buying lots from owners who could no longer make the payments. In addition to his position as state auditor, he built and oversaw the operation of a grist mill along Pogue's Run. Mills were a necessity in early communities, therefore a smart investment.

Another recorded vignette of their lives concerned Morris as a leader in the new town. Up until 1831, only a few large boats had attempted to navigate White River. Governor Noble wished to encourage navigation,

---

[39] Sulgrove, p. 58, 103, 494; O. H. Smith, "Distinguished Pioneers," *Early Indiana Trials and Sketches*, p. 173.
[40] Sulgrove, p. 216.
[41] Schrader, p. 114.

Chapter VI. Morris Morris II and Rachael Morris ♦ 123

and so offered a generous $200 prize. A loaded boat did arrive in Indianapolis by April. This event was hailed with joy, so a parade was planned. Morris was one of a committee of fourteen to arrange the celebration.[42]

A strange piece of information, which should be recorded, came to me in November 1987 from Ruth Dorrel, who in 1983 compiled *Pioneer Ancestors of Men of the Society of Indiana Pioneers* and was the society's inspector of applicants-data. She said there were *two* Morris Morrises who have been accepted as pioneer ancestors. One, sometimes recorded as Maurice, was also born in Virginia, date unknown, came to Harrison County, then to Floyd County, Indiana, in 1824 or 1825, and married Rebecca Wilkison. In all this author's (Anne Mertz) research, she has never encountered this Morris; however, he was not of Indianapolis.

Another John Morris (III) descending from Richard *was* encountered who was born in 1752, probably in Maryland; he was Richard's second son. A grown young man in his thirties, he went to Sandy Glades, in Virginia, with his father and brother, claimed land there next to his father Richard, and married Mary "Polly" Cummins, daughter of Jacob Cummins (born 1789). They moved on to Bourbon County, Kentucky, with their family and are recorded in the 1820 census, again near father Richard and brother Morris I. They had started what would become a large family of thirteen children (all Richard's grandchildren; see the Genealogy in Part Three). John and Polly migrated to Indiana in 1834, settling southeast of Rushville, then lived in Hancock County for nine years, returning to Rush County in 1866. This adds another Morris family who migrated to Indiana, but later, not as "pioneers," and not to Indianapolis. The pattern of families moving together and living near each other seems to have repeated itself frequently. It does help to find and identify relatives, in this case solving a "puzzlement," about *another* John Morris whom we found in Indiana.

Backing up a bit, Indianapolis, situated in the new state's geographic center, had become the capital in 1816. Land had been set aside at the time of the survey of the city in 1820 for the use of public buildings. The plan was that monies received from the sale of lots would provide the funds for erection of these public structures.

In 1832 three commissioners were appointed to superintend the building of a new state capitol edifice, the first real state capitol building in Indiana. These were the governor, Noah Noble; the state treasurer,

---

[42] Dunn, pp. 18, 19.

Samuel Merrill; and the state auditor, Morris Morris.[43] It was to be completed by 1838 but was finished by 1836, two years ahead of schedule! The cost of $60,000 was derived from the sale of lots in the town, as planned.

How fortunate that Thomas Morris, a son of Morris, was an engineering student at West Point. He surveyed and laid out the grounds.[44] Today we would call this nepotism, but here in this pioneer place and era there was no other trained engineer in all of Indiana.

The capitol building followed the style of the Parthenon except for the crowning dome. It had eight large, lovely statues carved from Italian marble, which represented the attributes of law, oratory, justice, agriculture, art, commerce, liberty, and history. Perhaps this was rather erudite and impressive for a wilderness town in a new state, but these three commissioners were all men of letters, refinement, and wisdom. The building was used for forty-one years, until it was outgrown in 1877.

A visitor to Indianapolis in 1833 wrote, "Nothing had been done to the streets except to remove the stumps from two or three.... There were no sidewalks, and the streets most in use, after every rain, and for a good part of the year, were knee deep with mud ... utterly forlorn ... in the spring.... The town was difficult to reach, but the soil was fertile.[45] Historian Sulgrove described Meridian Street as an awful mass of rails and saplings and chunks of swamp-slush, bordered by a willow-fringed cow pasture and a cornfield. This was a far cry from Kentucky's flourishing towns they had left behind. Those early resettlers *had* to be hopeful and patient.

The 1830 census shows Morris with ten individuals in his household, still residing next to Wilkes Reagan, the butcher. Close by lived Moses Frazee, who in 1805 had married, in Kentucky, Elizabeth, an older sister of Morris. Moses (born 1770) was the son of Ephraim Frazee by his third wife. Ephraim had eighteen children by three wives spanning forty-one years.

Joseph Frazee, Ephriam's grandson by the second wife and fourteen years younger than his cousin Morris, was also one of the first settlers of

---

[43] Ibid., p. 105; Howard, n.p.; author's file, newspaper article, n.d., n.p.
[44] Sulgrove, p. 103; author's file, Indianapolis newspaper, obituary of Thomas Morris, n.p., 1904.
[45] W. D. Peat, *Pioneer Painters of Indiana* (1954), p. 152.

Chapter VI. Morris Morris II and Rachael Morris ♦ 125

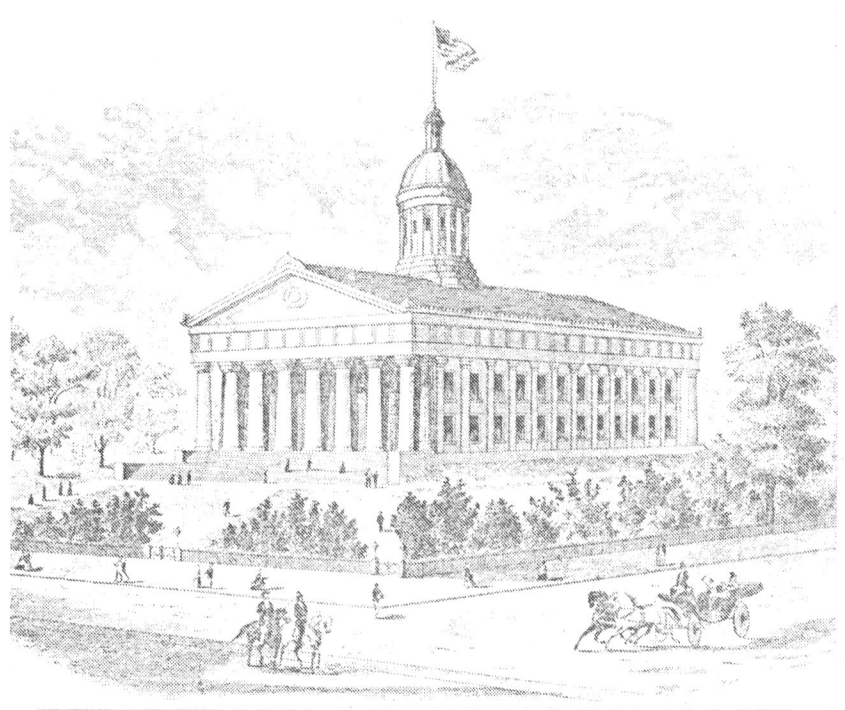

Old State Capitol

Indianapolis. His purchase was the second listed when land was first offered in July 1821. He and Jessie McKay together bought fifty-nine acres in section three. Joseph Frazee's second marriage was to Ann Cushman, daughter of David and Dorcas (Morris) Cushman. So the Morris family did not emigrate alone to the wilderness of Indianapolis. To have family nearby was comforting, throughout all the early disease, sacrifice, and hardship, while raising their large families.

Nancy Haines must have remembered the number of years incorrectly, for her memoir states that Morris lived on the farm only two years and "in 1823 grandfather concluded to practice law, so rented in a more convenient location, a house at the corner of Tennessee Street [now Capital Avenue] and West Washington, lived there a short time until he built his home on Louisiana and Meridian Streets."[46] The farm must have been rented some of the time. We know that by 1833 Morris and Rachael

---

[46] Haines' file.

had sold their 160 acres to Andrew Wilson for six thousand dollars. The original deeds of sale were photostatted.[47]

Tragedy struck Rachael and Morris about 1839 when they lost their second son, Milton, who died in a flatboat accident in the bayous of Louisiana. Married, with a wife and a four-year-old daughter, Caroline, he worked for a hardware company in Covington, Indiana, and transported goods, often via the Mississippi River.

"A roster of city officials for 1847-1909 under City Common Council shows Morris Morris, for 1847-48, "filled Harrison's vacancy."[48] Then the 1850 census shows Morris, age seventy-two, holding real estate to be worth $10,000, and his occupation is listed "milling business." It also lists Caroline, age fifteen, in his household. This was their granddaughter Caroline, the daughter of their deceased son Milton. Also living in his household was an eighteen-year-old girl, Obie Shelton, and a German teamster, Henry Berry. These two were probably servants.

In the General Assembly directory, Morris is described as "House 1826-27, Methodist, Indiana Militia, colonel, lawyer, real estate agent, anti-Jackson, Whig."[49] The chief swimming holes in the creek were on the property of Governor Noble and just south of Morris Morris's house on South Meridian Street.

Working long and hard, this large pioneer Morris family prospered. Like the new capital, they had become quite substantial, and had also greatly increased their worldly goods.

A granddaughter, Julia Ann Defrees Sample, daughter of Rachael's youngest daughter, Bettie, wrote some delightful recollections when she was an old lady. Julia mentioned that her grandparents were the first citizens in Indianapolis to have a bathroom in their house. "The tub was a great lumbering tin affair, with the water tank on the roof which was filled by a little hand pump in the garden. Of course in the winter months we had to resort to the old round tub, brought to the bedroom and filled from fancy flowered pitchers." When the bathroom was brand new, can't you picture the grandchildren all competing to have a bath at Grandma's house!

Morris had purchased a full city square in Indianapolis, dividing it into large lots—five for himself and one for each of his living children. The deed for the land from Morris and Rachael to son Thomas is dated 20 April 1849. It was given "in consideration of parental affection and good will, and in consideration of one dollar." This deed is signed by

---

[47] Author's file, Recorder's Office of Marion County, Ind.
[48] Dunn, p. 638; Sulgrove, p. 490.
[49] *A Biographical Directory of the Indiana General Assembly, 1816-1899*, vol. 1.

Chapter VI. Morris Morris II and Rachael Morris ♦ 127

both Thomas and his wife.[50] (On this deed as well as several others, Rachael signed her name with an "ae," here in three different places, writing clearly and unmistakably, hence there is no doubt that is the way she spelled it, unlike other Rachels of her family and time.) By the 1850s Morris had sold off most of his holdings for profit, or sold to his children "for $1.00 and Christian consideration due an aged parent."

This entire square, block No. 87, was bounded by Georgia, Meridian, Louisiana, and Illinois Streets, with two twelve-foot "private alleys" crossing in the middle. Situated close to the State Capitol Building, this square eventually became the center of the city's business section, increasing greatly in value. So the Morris family reaped the profits. (It is almost the exact location of the present Union Station, later built by son Thomas in 1853. He conceived the idea and built the very first union "depot" in the United States.)

A colorful and personal quotation is here excerpted from a chapter called "Some Old Time Religion," by Mrs. Anna C. Baggs, daughter of one of the very earliest settlers. It is printed in full in Dunn's *History of Greater Indianapolis*.

> I rather liked the early arrival at the church for I could watch the people as they entered. Fathers and mothers, brothers and sisters could walk to the church together [Wesley Chapel, built in 1829] but at the door they must be separated, the boys with the father on one side of the aisle, and the girls with the mother on the other side.
>
> Among the very first to enter, in a very stately, dignified manner, were Morris Morris, wife, boys, and girls. The father, a tall, angular man, accompanied by sons Austin [Milton is not mentioned: deceased], Thomas, and John; the mother, a stout lady, always dressed in soft dresses, wool in winter, silk in summer, her daughters Amanda, Julia, and the little girl Bettie. Mrs. Morris occupied a chair in the "amen corner" and the girls sat near her. Mrs. Morris carried a large white feather fan, which was the admiration of my young life. I resolved that when I grew up to be a big lady I would have a fan like hers.[51]

In another account, Morris, described as "a fiery abolitionist," and Rachael were said to be devoted friends of the well-known minister, Henry Ward Beecher, who came to the new Presbyterian Church in 1839 and lived on East Market Street. It can therefore be assumed that the fa-

---

[50] Author's file, original deed with drawing showing lots and streets.
[51] Dunn, p. 179.

Rachael Morris
1786-1863

Morris Morris II
1780-1864

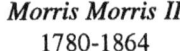

The photographs of Rachael and Morris were made from oil paintings hanging in the parlor of the Morris-Butler House Museum in Indianapolis.

Left: Morris Morris II in later life.

Chapter VI. Morris Morris II and Rachael Morris ♦ 129

mous author, his daughter Harriet Beecher Stowe, was also known to the Morris family. *Uncle Tom's Cabin*, published in 1851, immediately became the most popular book in the state. Incidentally, Mrs. Stowe drew her characters from a real Uncle Tom, a real Louisa, and others residing in Indianapolis.[52]

Reverend Beecher baptized the Morrises' fully grown son Thomas on the banks of White River and also, at the same time, the infant Matilda Vandergrift, who much later became the wife of Robert Louis Stevenson.[53]

An Old Settlers meeting was held at the home of Morris and Rachael on 6 June 1854 to organize an association limited to those who were in Indianapolis prior to 1826. This group was to meet annually on the first Tuesday in June.[54]

These anecdotes and notes all help to give us a pretty good idea of the stature of this pioneer family; personalities begin to emerge.

After his career as auditor of the state had ended [in 1864], Mr. Morris retired to private life [at age sixty-four] and engaged in no business other than the care of his property, which had in the growth of the town become a large estate. In his mature years he became a member of the Methodist Episcopal Church, and until his later life was active in the advancement of its interests.... Mr. Morris was a man of commanding presence, and in his prime exceedingly robust and active. He was noted for clearness of judgement and the union of remarkable decision of character with rare gentleness.[55]

By now the Morris children had reached adulthood and had married and raised families. Several of the sons became prominent Indianapolis leaders, and their daughters all married leading citizens. Their names, their activities, even some of their pictures appear many times in Indianapolis history books and will be considered in later chapters. The Morris tradition of civic leadership was continuing in their offspring, in time for the parents to recognize the good qualities they had instilled in their children. This must have been gratifying to them in their later years. They also had the satisfaction of having participated in the growth of a capital, of the rather rapid transition in forty years of a trackless woods and swampy area into a real city with good government, culture, and large, beautiful Victorian homes.

---

[52] Ibid., pp. 242-244.
[53] *Indianapolis Sunday Star*, July 1979.
[54] Dunn, p. 44.
[55] Sulgrove, p. 217.

The Honorable O. H. Smith wrote an interesting description of our ancestor on Christmas Day in 1857:

> Morris Morris was one of the prominent early emigrants from Kentucky that settled in the woods where the Capitol now stands. The first time the court was held at Indianapolis I became acquainted with Mr. Morris, then residing in a small cabin on Pogue's Run. In person, Mr. Morris was tall, over six feet high, fine form, dark complexion, good eye, fine features. Mr. Morris was many years [eighteen] auditor of the State and discharged the duties with great fidelity. He was an ardent Methodist, and his door was ever hospitably open to the itinerant ministers who called upon him. Mr. Morris is the father of Austin W. Morris, Col. Thomas A. Morris, and John Morris of Indianapolis. [Also of daughters Amanda Melvina, Julia Ann, and Elizabeth Mitchell—all married, and Milton, William Little, and Nicholas McCarty—all deceased.] I saw him yesterday, venerable and aged, trembling, as it were, on the brink of the grave."[56]

However, Morris lived six and a half more years! Mr. and Mrs. Morris lived the last years of their lives in deserved comfort in the large home on the estate of their son, Thomas Armstrong Morris, one of the city's finest.

Rachael, sturdy pioneer with the genes of her *Mayflower* ancestors and mother of nine children, lived to be seventy-seven—in spite of the hardships of early days and the rigors of middle life. Morris, six years older than his wife, died a year later at age eighty-four. One marvels at their fortitude and convictions. Both were buried in Indianapolis. When the new, expansive cemetery, Crown Hill, was opened in 1884, their graves were moved to the large Morris plot. A tall monument now appropriately marks their resting place.

After sixty years of marriage, they "left a rich heritage of service to the community, having been some of the most active in promoting the progress and development of [their] community and new capital."[57]

Indiana was growing in many ways because of "... political liberty, the general diffusion of knowledge, the prevalence of sound moral and religious principles which [give] force and sustained energy to the character of a people."[58]

---

[56] Smith.

[57] Wayne Guthrie, newspaper article, second in a series on Indianapolis pioneers, n.d., n.p., in author's file.

[58] Washington Irving, "English Writers in America," in *The Sketch Book*.

Chapter VI. Morris Morris II and Rachael Morris ♦ 131

Morris Parishioners at Cane Ridge Meeting Paris, Kentucky

IN THE SPRING OF 1991, the author corresponded with the Reverend Franklin R. McGuire, who very kindly read old church lists and gravestones for her. The attempt to learn if Morris I and Sarah (Cushman) Morris were buried there was unsuccessful. Many gravestones are weathered beyond reading. It is very probable that both Morris and Sarah are resting there with others of this Morris family. It is absolutely certain that his son-in-law, Morris Morris II, was *married* there.

The following has been compiled from Reverend McGuire's notes, with dates and marriages supplied by the author.

1829	Included in the list of contributors for repair of the Meeting House: John Morris, b. 10 Feb. 1793, Paris, Ky., son of Morris I and Sarah (Cushman) Morris; merchant and captain on a Mississippi River boat, lived at Cane Ridge, farmer, owned at least ten slaves before his death on 22 Aug. 1867/70/71, bur. Millersburg, Ky.; m. three times: 1st, unknown, two children; 2nd, 4 Oct. 1827, Bourbon Co., Ky., to Elizabeth (Bowles) Payne (widow of John Payne), 2 children; 3rd, Katherine Turney, seven children. *Note*: The contribution mentioned above occurred during the period of John's second marriage, to Elizabeth.
1832	Notes: Sarah A(nn) (Sally) Morris, child of Captain John and 2nd wife, Elizabeth.
1838	On the roster of members: Morris Henry Morris, child of Captain John and 2nd wife, Elizabeth.

Table continued next page→

1848	Roster of members, continued: John Morris, probably the same Captain John. John Morris, apparently a different person, probably John Graves Morris, 8th child of Capt. John, b. 25 April 1839, Bourbon Co., m. 1 Aug. 1865 Hepsibaugh Ricketts, thirteen children, in Kentucky. Mounted Infantry, captured, escaped, then in Morgan's Raiders, promoted to 4th corporal in 1864; d. 10 Sept. 1918, Lexington. Rebecca Morris, possibly sister of Captain John, *dau. of Sarah and Morris I*, b. 17 Oct. 1794. M(orris) Henry Morris, above, 3rd child of Captain John. Katherine (Turney) Morris, 3rd wife of Captain John, b. 1 April or 29 March 1803, Bourbon Co., d. 25 March 1885, Bourbon Co., seven children. Lucinda Morris, 5th child of Captain John and 1st child by Katherine, b. c. 1832; m. James Sconce, issue. Nancy G. Morris, 7th child of Captain John; m. 21 Sept. 1854, John L. Soper (Bourbon Co. Records). Susan A. Morris, m. Robert Soper, issue. Kitty Morris, b. 1873, probably dau. of John Graves Morris. She m. 1890 Albert Collins. Elizabeth Morris, "married Cottingham"; probably 2nd child of 1st wife of Captain John. "Lizzie" was said to have gone to California with her husband, who was a thief.
1852	Among the list of church members: John Morris, "Captain John." John Shumate Morris (affiliation unknown). Rebecca Morris, perhaps Captain John's sister. Morris H. Morris, 3rd child of John. Catharan (Katherine?) Morris, possibly Kitty, above. Lucinda Morris, 5th child of Captain John, 1st child by Katherine. Nancy Morris (Nancy G., above); married John L. Soper in 1854, two years after this list was made. Susan A. Morris, m. Robert Soper.

Continued next page →

Chapter VI. Morris Morris II and Rachael Morris ♦ 133

1860	Lizzie Morris, joined 19 Nov. 1860. Rebecca Morris, d. 1860, sister of Captain John (maiden name although a widow).
1881	**Marked graves** Rebecca D. Morris, b. 9 May 1809, m. John R. Morris, d. 18 Feb. 1881, all recorded on gravestone; wife of John R. Morris, "aged 76 yrs." (b. c. 1805), m. Rebecca D. Morris (above), d. 22 Oct. 1881. Probably the nephew of Morris Morris II (m. 1803 in the Cane Ridge Meeting House who had older brothers Richard and John). So the birth date is logical, the name (John R.) is appropriate, and the location is possible. The author could find no other John Morris appropriate to this place and this time in all of the Morris family tree, which is virtually complete. Therefore, the above John R. Morris was most likely a son of John III or Richard IV (both sons of Eleanor and John II of Campbell County). The names of both John and Richard appear in the 1820 census of Bourbon County. **Note:** Rev. McGuire reported that this, the only fenced-in plot behind the Meeting House, is the "most striking monument in the cemetery," made in four parts: a base, then two engravings in stone, two columns on bases, an arched top with missing finial, altogether five and one-half feet tall, now partially fallen over, with a broken column.

The "Morris Family Tree"

Chapter VII

THOMAS ARMSTRONG MORRIS and RACHEL IRWIN
Their Early Years

Destiny is not a matter of chance;
It is a matter of choice.
It is not a thing to be waited for;
It is a thing to be achieved.
— William Jennings Bryan

GENERALLY, one would tell of a family's children in chronological order. The author has decided, however, to start with the third offspring of Rachael and Morris because he was undoubtedly the most illustrious of all their nine children. Following the remarkable story of his many, many achievements will be chapters about his siblings, who in their different ways also contributed very much to their new city of Indianapolis.

So much has been written of Thomas A. Morris that it would be extremely repetitious to quote it in this account. However, a selected bibliography follows Chapter VIII, for readers wishing more details on his life. It is impressive to find in *many* history books accounts of a relative and to see two full-page pictures of both Thomas and his father, Morris, in the best old history book of Indianapolis,[1] as well as a fine full-page photographic portrait in a recent modern Indianapolis history.[2]

Born in Nicholas County (originally Bourbon), Kentucky, Thomas Armstrong Morris was the third child of Morris and Rachael Morris. As a lad not quite ten years old, Tom traveled with his parents, along with three brothers and two sisters, to Indiana in 1821. They were some of the very earliest pioneers to come to this new state.

All of the family were surely put to work at the start, helping to clear their newly purchased land so it could be drained and farmed. They lived

---

[1] B. R. Sulgrove, *History of Indianapolis and Marion County*, pp. 216-217, 301-302; also steel engravings in *Biographical History of Eminent and Self-made Men of the State of Indiana*, pp. 258-60; Thomas A. Morris in Civil War uniform, in *Indiana and Indiananans*, p. 598; *National Cyclopaedia of American Biography*, vol. 10, p. 124.

[2] Marjie Gates Giffin, *Water Runs Downhill*.

in a log cabin near Pogue's Run for several years. Fragments of published trivia remain today to help reveal the character of a young boy.

At age twelve Tom "began to learn the printer's trade and found employment on a newspaper called *The Western Censor and Emigrant's Guide.* "[3] "The boy continued at his trade for three years and became an excellent printer, which in those days included theory and practice of hand press work as well as type-setting."[4]

Three years afterwards he entered a private school conducted by Ebenezer Sharpe at the Indianapolis Academy.[5] Mr. Sharpe had two assistants, Miss Isabella and Thomas H. Sharpe, who was only eighteen. A fee of $2.00 a quarter was charged for spelling and reading, $2.50 for writing and arithmetic, and the even greater sum of $3.00 for geography, English grammar, mathematics, philosophy, and the languages.[6]

The first printed mention of Thomas participating in school is an account in the *Journal,* 6 October 1827 of the school's first public exhibition, at the court house, declaring "The original pieces that were spoken on the occasion were of character well deserving commendation.... Tom Morris enacted the part of a miser so well in his recitation that old farmer McDowell, who had the reputation of being a little near, took offense and left the room with audible denunciations of the whole performance. In fact, this may almost be called the beginning of amateur theatricals, for Thomas appeared in costume, with knee britches and a wig which he had himself constructed of cow tails."[7]

There are several detailed accounts of early Fourth of July celebrations. The *Journal* mentioned the artillery commanded by Captain Morris in 1827 when Tom was sixteen.[8] Boys did grow to manhood fast in those days.

In anticipation of the moving of the capital from Corydon to center-state Indianapolis, a number of young men met at the land office one evening in the fall of 1824 and organized a private organization called "the Indianapolis Legislature." Among the early members were brothers Austin and Tom Morris, and John Frazee, their first cousin. Popular from the first, it grew to include some of the "older citizens" such as the governor, a judge, and Morris Morris II, father of Austin and Tom. This

---

[3] Ibid., p. 238; *The Indianapolis News,* 24 March 1904 obituary, n.p.
[4] Sulgrove, p. 301.
[5] Christopher B. Coleman, "Thomas Armstrong Morris," in Dumas Malone, ed., *Dictionary of American Biography,* vol. 8, p. 227. Only those who have made a significant contribution to American life are included.
[6] Jacob Piatt Dunn, *Greater Indianapolis,* p. 91.
[7] Ibid., p. 92.
[8] Ibid., p. 89.

Chapter VII. Thomas A. Morris and E. Rachel Irwin ♦ 137

group met weekly, winter and summer, for more than ten years; some ladies of the town also became quite regular attendants. It had jurisdiction over all known subjects, especially those which came before the real legislature. It was generally attended by the members of the state legislature, and it is said that many of the problems of the real legislature were settled by its debates.[9]

Thomas, one of its earliest members, was then attending school. He also served as an apprentice in the *Journal* office.[10] Tom then worked in the office of the secretary of state of Indiana for two years, which is revealed in a letter of recommendation.[11] By this time this young man had the determination and desire to go to West Point in an era when very few boys ever went on for a higher education. Doctors and ministers went away to college for training, while lawyers were mostly "self read" and apprenticed. But Tom wanted to be an engineer. There were very few in the whole country. He needed to apply officially and he needed an official appointment.

These were both accomplished when Thomas was seventeen. He was accepted, he thought—he was told. But there was a mix-up, for a Mr. Dewey received the appointment, then a Mr. Vanderburgh, who didn't even go. By this time it was too late to enter that year. Very determined, Tom reapplied for the next session, when he was eighteen, to the secretary of war, Thomas Eaton. Enclosed with his application were several letters of recommendation: from his teacher, Mr. Ebenezer Sharp, who had been tutoring him in Latin; from the governor of Indiana; the secretary of state; the speaker of the house; and two letters signed by *all* the members of both branches of the legislature, for a total of fifty-seven signatures.[12] Excellent recommendations they were, from an impressive group of important men. Tom's father, Morris Morris II, probably knew all of these people well for he had been elected state auditor for many years and had been, before this, a practicing lawyer. Morris was also a popular and respected leading citizen of this far away, little-known western town.

So, after only four years of real schooling, at age eighteen "the boy, gifted with a sturdy physique and singularly strong and self-reliant nature,"[13] was "appointed to a cadetship at West Point, for which place he started on horseback to Cincinnati when the route east was by way of the

---

[9] Ibid., p. 81.
[10] Sulgrove, p. 238.
[11] West Point Archives, copies in author's file.
[12] Ibid.
[13] Obituary "General Morris," unknown newspaper, n.d., n.p., in author's file.

Ohio River."[14] What a journey! What an undertaking to go to college from the backwoods frontier of Indiana all the way across the mountains to New York State, probably alone! Ambition, determination, courage and stamina already appear strong in this lad of eighteen with apparent real potential. On 1 July 1830, Thomas entered the United States Military Academy after the required signed consent by his father—for five years.

Of the ninety-one of Tom's classmates who entered with him, only thirty-six graduated; fifty-five did not, including Edgar Allan Poe (who later went to West Virginia for one year).[15]

While still enrolled as a student there, about 1832 (perhaps during a vacation) he was given the task, as a trained engineer, of surveying the site and supervising the grading for Indiana's first real state house, the construction of which was under the supervision of his father, Morris Morris II, and two other appointed commissioners. "The site, previously a dead level, was plowed and scraped into an elevation in the center...."[16]

On 30 June 1834, four years after entering West Point, he graduated *fourth* in a class of *thirty-six* men.[17] (Remember, he had had only four years of formal schooling.) Only two were engineers. "His education as an engineer, and in those days the best education that an engineer in this country could have, equipped him for the supreme needs of a young community, the new capital of a young state."[18] On 1 July 1834, he was breveted second lieutenant of the First Artillery in the regular army[19] and was commissioned second lieutenant on 25 February 1835.[20] After a brief time at Fortress Monroe in Virginia, he was sent to Fort King in northern Florida, about sixty miles south of the present Tampa near Ocala, where the land had been virtually untouched by humans.

Why would a young man, a newly commissioned second lieutenant, be sent so far away to the outskirts of our country, to swampy, unpopulated Florida? When the United States received Florida by cession from Spain in 1819, they also acquired the Seminole Indians living there. Pres-

---

[14] Sulgrove, p. 301.

[15] Henry Algernon du Pont, father of Henry Francis du Pont of Winterthur, now an internationally known museum near Wilmington, Delaware, graduated from West Point in the class of 1831 ("Register of Officers and Cadets of U.S. Military Academy June 1831"), so he was there at the same time as Thomas A. Morris (graduated 1834).They must have known each other, since classes were so small.

[16] Sulgrove, p. 103; author's file.

[17] Sulgrove; Coleman; *Indianapolis News;* F. B. Heitman, *Historical Register and Dictionary of the U.S. Army.* This was the thirty-third graduating class, the first being in 1802. There had been only fifty-three graduate engineers until 1834.

[18] Author's file.

[19] Sulgrove.

[20] U.S. Military Academy Records.

Chapter VII. Thomas A. Morris and E. Rachel Irwin ♦ 139

sure was brought to bear on Congress to have them removed entirely so the country could be thrown open to settlement. "Seminole" means "runaway," or "he who separates." They were the descendants of the Creek Indians, who in the mid-1700s had migrated from Georgia southward because white men had taken their land there, attempting to enslave them. The Seminoles became a huge problem for the United States Government because of the duplicity of government action, unjust treaties, and the slavery situation. Runaway black men were aided by red men, then intermarried and were infused into the tribe. For many years cruel fighting and much politics resulted in a Seminole War in 1817-1818 and the building of about ten forts in northern and central Florida. The second Seminole War (1834-1842) was flourishing when Thomas Morris was sent to Fort King.

This was the fiercest of all American Indian wars. Awful heat, snake-infested swamps, vicious alligators, terrible mosquitoes, and malaria all contributed to real hardship for our army. Four United States generals and 200,000 troops used desperate measures, because the Seminoles fought a guerrilla war. More than 1,500 soldiers, uncounted civilians, and an unknown number of Indians died. Our federal government spent over twenty million dollars in this conflict. The Seminoles were the only Indian tribe in America that never officially made peace with the United States Government.

Eventually, 38,000 Seminoles were removed to Oklahoma, while only 1,000 remained in Florida. These now have only a few thousand descendants, who are darker than other tribes because of their mixed heritage.

Before all this occurred, just 500 infantrymen and artillery men in Florida had constituted the nation's only safeguard in a country of 52,000 square miles "infested" with thousands of Creek and Seminole Indians, who then began to feel their power. In December 1835, as three groups of U.S. soldiers were marching peacefully from Fort Brook to Fort King, 107 officers and regular men were attacked and killed. This horrendous "Dade Massacre" at Fort King is now memorialized with a park near Ocala, north of Tampa. This massacre began the second Seminole War, which lasted for seven years.

The author was very glad to learn from the West Point records that her great-grandfather was not present at the time of this massacre. Lieutenant Tom Morris was truly a very, very lucky man, for only part of a year did he have to encounter these Seminoles and endure Florida's accompanying awful heat, swamps, alligators, and insects. Fortunately, a trained engineer was desperately needed in his own state. He was back in

Indiana by March 1835! But how did he get back? He may have had to slug northward (alone?) through palmetto thickets and snake-infested swamps, and walk or ride a horse many, many miles through nearly impenetrable tangles of woody brush known as "dog-hair thicket," for there were still no railroads to Tampa, not until 1884, and no roads, only a few dangerous Indian trails.

Very luckily, Tom was sent by the War Department to assist Major Monroe of the Engineer Corps in constructing the National Road in Indiana and Illinois.[21] George Washington and Albert Gallatin had proposed a national highway in 1784. This army assignment brought him home, where a wonderful future was in store for him. Constructing the first highway in Indiana was the first of many firsts for our to-be-great ancestor, Thomas Armstrong Morris.

President Thomas Jefferson had signed the National Road Act in 1806. Construction began in 1811 in Cumberland, Maryland, and proceeded westward, built piecemeal over the Allegheny Mountains, across Ohio and Indiana, then to Vandalia, Illinois, some 800 miles from Cumberland. Morris was "detailed ... to assist Major Ogden ... and had charge of the division between Richmond and Indianapolis. This was the first turnpike in the state."[22] It was reputed to be the first highway ever wholly constructed by the federal government.

In the beginning this "National Pike," a plank "corduroy" road, was built for the pioneers traveling westward. For farmers it was a cheap, dependable route to market their produce and meant less isolation for their families. The "Plank Road," as the Pike was also known, built up a dependency between country and town and became an east-west route. In Indiana it was surveyed and constructed between 1827 and 1839. But the National Road was not always maintained, and by 1849 it was turned over to the Central Plank Road Company.

Throughout the years the fame of the National Road spread. Some of our greatest statesmen and diplomats often traversed its rugged terrain. General Lafayette, James K. Polk, Andrew "Old Hickory" Jackson, and President Ulysses S. Grant were some who frequently traveled on "the Pike." Today it is U.S. Route 40.

After a year with the United States Army (required by West Point), Tom resigned on 13 April 1836 and settled in Indianapolis, where he had already been working on the National Road. A civil engineer, he soon became the first resident engineer in the service of the state of Indiana,

---

[21] *Indianapolis News.*
[22] Sulgrove.

Chapter VII. Thomas A. Morris and E. Rachel Irwin ♦ 141

and was put in charge of building the twenty-two-mile Central Canal (linking Broad Ripple, Indianapolis, and Waverly), Indiana's first canal.[23] It was thought that a system of internal waterways would soon supersede the stagecoach and covered wagon for moving people and freight. Propaganda was sweeping inland communities. At this time the Mammoth Improvement Bill was passed and a program of building was begun. Indiana made an outlay of a million dollars to create a link connecting the Wabash and Erie Canal from Toledo with Evansville on the Ohio via Indianapolis, a distance of 476 miles—the longest canal in the United States. Waterpower derived from the Indianapolis canal was used to operate at least ten mills. One of these was Tom's father's grist mill at the corner of Pennsylvania and South Street.

Part of the 476-mile canal was slack-water navigation on the Maumee and Wabash Rivers. The locks were made of limestone, brought from Putnam County by ox teams. Through this flat land the canal had to be built *up* rather than down. The banks were mostly artificial, and they were constantly undermined by muskrats, grass, and debris.

Before only nine miles of the canal were completed, the program collapsed and the state was near bankruptcy. Indiana had planned to build 857 miles of canal but only 472 miles were built. The canal *was* completed from St. Joseph River at Huntington in 1835, opened to Lafayette in 1843, and abandoned in the 1860s. So Indiana's canal was not a success, and eventually the state sold it to private enterprise at a great loss. Canals failed as a means of transportation because railroads soon flourished: railroads were faster.

The author has an old, undated clipping headlined "General T. A. Morris Tells of the Early System of Improvements by Canal" and quotes him in a long article, only part of which is given here.

> The Central Canal, of which the piece from here to Broad Ripple was the only completed portion ... a part of the system adopted by the Indiana Board of Improvements in 1836 [with] work begun 1837 and prosecuted [for a few years].... The Board failed and repudiated its debt ... no money ... issue of scrip ... to contractors ... later ... sale to outside parties. Alexander Morrison and myself were appointed commissioners to value the property which was to be sold at our evaluation ... sold to parties in New York ... [then] to a company formed here.... I located the line of this canal, laid it off, and superintended the construction. I surveyed the line from Wabashtown to Martinsville. It went through a rather rough country. I camped out

---

[23] Ibid.

for six months, but came in town for Christmas. Many a morning we had to shake the snow off ourselves when we got up.

There were forests and thickets and a great deal of swampy ground ... a great feeding place for wild ducks ... have had some good sport shooting snipe and ducks there ... noted for its big pickerel .... The surveyor had to be an expert in jumping as he made his way by springing from hummock to hummock.[24]

At one place the engineers anticipated difficulty in uniting two streams, but they found that beavers had long before built a dam at the very spot and had already accomplished what the engineers had in view.

As late as 1837 swamps and lowlands still plagued the city, so the legislature finally provided for drainage. As chief engineer in the state's service, Tom Morris was given the job of constructing the *first* "State Ditch." In flood times the water would "swim a horse" and the city was "almost an island," for there were no bridges but many great ravines.[25] Thomas is "credited with the suggestion and execution of the State Ditch, which saved Indianapolis from recurrent floods and greatly lessened the prevalence of fever incidental to its early settlement."[26] "The building of this ditch physically made Indianapolis possible."[27]

For some of Indiana's early years a militia was maintained requiring all able-bodied men to serve. Even though the danger of Indian wars was over, the military spirit of the people did not die out, so in February 1837 a military company was organized. They wore showy grey uniforms and carried armed muskets. The second year, in 1838, Thomas A. Morris was commissioned captain of the "Marion Guards" and recommissioned in 1842. The Guards were assigned to the Fortieth Regiment. "Captain ... Morris was a fine drill master, and brought his company to a high state of efficiency, it being the crack company of the state. Its imposing appearance on parade awakened other military ardor."[28] The Marion Riflemen were organized in 1842, and there was great rivalry and even a sham battle between the Guards—called the "Greys" (Captain Morris's militia)—and the "Rifles." The Greys were "solid men, verging, many of them, upon middle life; ... the uniform [was] of rich cloth, ... [they] carried

---

[24] Newspaper clipping, n.d., n.p., in author's file.
[25] Dunn, pp. 22, 13.
[26] Coleman.
[27] Obituary, "General Morris."
[28] Dunn, p. 136; Max R. Hyman, ed., *The Journal Handbook of Indianapolis*, p. 24; Max R. Hyman, *Indianapolis*, p. 22; Sulgrove, pp. 121, 300; W. R. Holloway, *Indianapolis, Railroad City*, p. 59.

Chapter VII. Thomas A. Morris and E. Rachel Irwin ♦ 143

muskets with bayonets; ... timed their steps to sonorous music of a brass band."[29] A. C. Howard's 1857 city directory said of this company, "... commanded by Captain T. A. Morris, was for a long time a very excellent, disciplined, efficient corps, and when on parade attracted universal admiration. It included many of our best citizens." This group became the National Guards in 1856 and eventually went into the Civil War in the Eleventh Regiment.[30]

For several years, from about 1835 on, prospects seemed very good for Indianapolis. Work on the National Road, the canal, and the ditch, all of which were under Thomas's supervision, brought laborers to the vicinity and stimulated trade. In 1839 the population count was established at 4,000.

There was a general financial panic in 1837, however, which began to affect the prosperity and industry of Indianapolis. Internal improvement work was stopped, and even the National Road work was abandoned in 1839. There are two references to Morris at this time concerning labor disturbances. He was one of two men who prevented real trouble at a camp meeting by controlling a drunken leader of the "chain gang," a lawless crowd brought to work on the National Road and the Central Canal.

Between 1840 and 1847 (when the railroad came), the life of the town was quiet and the town grew at a slower pace. We can only wonder what part Thomas Morris took in the decisions during this time of the work stoppage of both the National Road and Indiana's canal, for both were under his direct supervision. By this time he was also involved in the new railroad business, as we shall see in the next chapter. It was a great time in history to be an engineer!

The Reverend Henry Ward Beecher came to Indianapolis to be the first pastor of the new Presbyterian Church in 1834. Although his great prominence came later, he made himself and his church known throughout Indiana. He left such an impression that for years that church was known as "Beecher's Church."

He became a close friend of the whole Morris family, particularly of Thomas's father, Morris Morris II. Tom was baptized by the Reverend Beecher during a group baptismal ceremony on the banks of White River. "It is told by a citizen of good memory that when Mr. Morris became a member ... he wished to be baptized by immersion ... by Henry Ward Beecher. They went to the river, followed by crowds. Some small boys

---

[29] Dunn, p. 136.
[30] Sulgrove, p. 303.

144 ♦ MORRIS MIGRATION

who climbed a convenient sycamore 'for to see' observed from their advantageous position that Mr. Morris ... had not been completely immersed, his head not having been wholly under water. They spread the news, and for a long time afterward there were people who expected that the ceremony would be repeated, as the repentant sinner was a very thorough man. But it never was."[31]

An interesting anecdote appeared in a clipping about "A Thallan's Last Song,"a rhyme of eight stanzas printed on satin cloth and written to the refrain of "Old Rosin the Bow," a favorite melody in the Harrison campaign of 1840. The Thallans were a club of that day, and the song was written by Thomas A. Morris in honor of the wedding of his friends, the Davidsons, which took place on 19 May 1840. A copy was given to each wedding guest.[32]

* * * * *

By 1840, Thomas had become a highly respected young man of twenty-nine with large responsibilities. His sweetheart, Elizabeth Rachel Irwin, lived in Madison, Indiana, and was only nineteen when they were married in that year. Tom was ten years older than his bride. After nearly two years, their first child was born. John Irwin Morris, named for his paternal grandfather, John II, was to be the oldest of a family of five, all boys but one. The second child, Harry, died in infancy. Alas, we know very little of their mother, Rachel, although two pictures show a buxom lady with beautiful eyes. This was a time when the husband was dominant in the family. The men were the ones who were mentioned in the history books, scarcely ever their wives. It is as though they were not there to share in the work and responsibilities. Tom was a city leader, frequently in the newspapers and in the public's eye because of his many, many civic projects, yet nothing was ever mentioned about Rachel, "behind the scenes."

Rachel raised a big family, had nine grandchildren, and managed a large and active household. She eventually lived on an estate in a fine mansion with carriage house, barn, servants, gardens, orchards, and stables. For fifty-two and one-half years she was the wife of a busy, prominent, and enterprising civic leader. We must again *imagine* the role she played in an era when women were expected to run things smoothly while quietly remaining in the background. We only know from a

---

[31] Anna Nicholas, *The Story of Crown Hill*, pp. 76-7.
[32] "Little Stories of Daily Life," printed in the *Journal*, n.d., n.p.

Chapter VII. Thomas A. Morris and E. Rachel Irwin ♦ 145

newspaper article that toward the end of her life of seventy-one years she was a very ill lady. We must not forget her or her part in their very full life together. Surely Rachel could not have foreseen at the time of her marriage, when only nineteen, the role she would play in a large family. How sad that the numerous activities and uncounted good deeds of our early, gentle women went unrecorded, while only their menfolk attained the limelight.

Rachel was my great-grandmother. I wish I had known her.

The "Morris Family Tree"

Chapter VIII

THOMAS ARMSTRONG MORRIS
The Railroad Era

*The real lesson of the past is that it shows us
what can be done for the future.*
— Margaret Sanger

THE ADVENT OF THE RAILROAD in Indiana followed very soon upon the heels of canal building, so that the state was investing enormous monies in both projects simultaneously without putting one enterprise on a paying basis before starting another. They undertook so much that the Hoosier State nearly became bankrupt because of it, but also because of the 1837 panic. Yet eventually Indiana did come very close to accomplishing what they undertook.

"Indiana has not, like Illinois and some other states, received the patronage of the General Government in the shape of lands, to aid in the construction of her railroads.... Much ... had been done for the state ... by private capital and enterprise."[1]

The location of the Indianapolis and Lafayette Railroad bed was begun, but only eighteen miles of railroad had been built under the Internal Improvements Program when the state had to abandon the project. Because it was financially unable to carry on itself, it sold its share in the Madison and Indianapolis Railroad to a private company, and Thomas Morris joined this company. He was smart to get out of the canal business at the right time! And he had real self-confidence. From 1841 to 1847 he was chief engineer of the Madison and Indianapolis Railroad and finished the project which the state had given up. He built the road from North Vernon to Indianapolis. This was the first railroad in the state[2] and ultimately supplanted all the canals.

Because the private company was underfinanced, Thomas Morris conceived "and carried through"[3] the then unorthodox plan "of taking

---
[1] Hon. O. H. Smith, *Early Indiana Trials and Sketches*, p. 423.
[2] B. R. Sulgrove, *History of Indianapolis and Marion County*, p. 301.
[3] Christopher B. Coleman, "Thomas Armstrong Morris," in Dumas Malone, ed., *Dictionary of American Biography*, vol. 13, p. 228.

land for subscriptions [from the farmers] to build the road at an appraised value. Upon these lands scrip was issued to the amount of the appraisement. The scrip of the company was used to pay for the construction of the road, redeeming the scrip with lands on presentation. This is the first instance where land was used as the basis of railroad construction."[4] The entire financing idea was Tom Morris's. At that time railroad building was only beginning; much was experimental, and Thomas successfully executed an ingenious experiment with scrip.

But here were endless problems. One of them was iron nails, mostly made in England. They were very expensive, costing $60 to $80 a ton by the time they were laid in Indiana. Slowly the rails were inched overland to reach Columbus in 1844.

Finally, three years later, the rails extended to the capital. The Madison and Indianapolis Railroad was completed to Indianapolis! Brief excerpts here may give some of that exuberant feeling of success.

> Of course the railroad increased in usefulness to the town as it approached, ... whetting public desire to have it completed. October 1, 1847 was a "red letter day" ... thronged with people. The last rail was laid at nine o'clock in the morning. At ten the circus entered ... mounted volunteers ... artillery company. At three o'clock, ... the belching forth of the loud mouthed cannon announced ... the approach of the cars from Madison.... People thronged there by acres ... shrill whistle of the locomotive ... two iron steeds puffing and snorting majestically ... followed by two long trains of passengers and freight cars, completely filled with human beings, the ladies waving their white handkerchiefs.... The men ... huzzas ... speech from the Governor....
>
> Confusion ... confounded by a snort from a locomotive, and the chime of its bell, which signified a pleasure ride to Greenwood and back for fifteen cents a head. La me! what a scampering among the novices of railroad riding.... And away went about five hundred as happy, uproarious fellows as was ever mixed up.... Fireworks after dark, the illumination of many buildings, and a performance.... Thus the day ended at ten o'clock ... excitement satiated.[5]

When the last track was laid ... Mr. [John Peter] Frenzel Sr. [a construction engineer] drove the locomotive on the first run.[6] (His daughter-in-law was a sister of the author's grandmother.)[7]

---

[4] Sulgrove, p. 302.
[5] Jacob Piatt Dunn, *Greater Indianapolis*, pp. 148-9.
[6] Helen R. Jarvis, ed., *The City and the Bank* (priv. pr., 1965), p. 10.

Chapter VIII. Thomas A. Morris: The Railroad Era ♦ 149

Another account tells of rejoicing natives, many of whom saw a locomotive for the *first* time there and ran in fright.[8] "It must have been a proud day for those ... energetic managers of the affairs of the company. The immense throng, the enthusiasm ..., the receipts...."[9]

Because that was the *first* railroad in the entire state of Indiana, and into Indianapolis, Thomas Armstrong Morris was surely a hero, and very greatly admired. He was then only thirty-six years old. The completion of the Madison Railroad to Indianapolis was "the most significant single event in the early history of the capital."[10]

Abandoned by the state, this project had been financed and built almost single-handedly by the "dogged determination" of Tom Morris. He had had courage and confidence. This accomplishment ended forever the isolation of his city. It started Indianapolis on its way toward becoming a major industrial center.

Railroading was now definitely the right business to be in, and Thomas was surely in the right place at the right time. There were soon several chartered railroads. Meanwhile, there was expansion, competition, and mergers; there were consolidations and changes of names. Four separate depots were built. Indianapolis became known as "the railroad city," and its location was soon the crossroads of the country.

From 1847 to 1852 Thomas Morris was chief engineer of the Terre Haute and Richmond Railroad, later called the Vandalia, connecting Terre Haute and Indianapolis. During that same time he was also chief engineer of the Indianapolis and Bellefontaine Ohio Railroad, later part of the Big Four. Early in this period he prepared estimates and reports on the Peru and Indianapolis Railroad.[11]

Another venture for Thomas at this time was a milling business with his brothers Austin and John. Dunn records that in 1848 the Morris grist mill was built on South Pennsylvania Street. It burned in 1851.[12] Sulgrove differs a bit: "In 1848 Gen. T. A. Morris built a flouring-mill on the northeast corner of Meridian Street and the Union tracks, at the

---

[7] John Peter Frenzel Sr. was the father of ten children including Otto Sr., who founded the Merchants Bank. This began a dynasty of family bankers and a wealthy family of Frenzels. Otto Sr. married in 1880 Caroline Goepper, sister of Anna Marie Goepper, the author's maternal grandmother.
[8] Wylie J. Daniels, *The Village at the End of the Road—A Chapter in Early Railroad History*, Indiana Historical Society Publications, vol. 8, p. 37.
[9] Ibid., p. 62.
[10] Ibid., p. 17.
[11] Coleman, p. 3.
[12] Dunn, p. 344; W. R. Holloway, *Indianapolis, Railroad City*, p. 314.

east end of the Union Depot site and carried on merchant milling there successfully, but the mill burned in 1853. In this establishment was first used the automatic or machine packing apparatus, which steadily and regularly kept the flour, as it entered the barrels, from the bolting cloths, pressed smoothly down."[13]

Morris Grist Mill

The semi-weekly *Sentinel* on 28 February 1849 contained the following: "Morris and Co. have lately erected a large and fine Steam Flouring Mill, adjoining their capacious warehouse on Meridian Street. The Morrises have made many and extensive improvements in the city within a few years; and none of more utility than the Steam Sawmill, Flouring Mill, etc. connecting with the Madison and Indianapolis Railroad by a branch built by themselves."[14] A sketch of the Morris mill by Christian Schrader is one of more than ninety sketches now in the Indiana division of the Indiana State Library.[15]

"The property on which the new circular street was laid off (on which track was laid) belonged to the Morrises, sarcastically referred to by Chapman as 'the Royal Family.'"[16] (Chapman was a Democrat newspaper editor opposing the "Whig Junto.")

When Tom was thirty-eight, in 1849, a year after his marriage, he was deeded a lot 70' x 205', a twelfth of city plot No. 87, which his father had purchased long ago, about 1821. Morris and Rachael had divided this into twelve parcels, one for each of their living children, and they retained five for themselves. In this area the family all built homes. Eventually some lots were exchanged or added to others. Each of the living Morris offspring had become the head of a very prominent Indianapolis family.

Austin W., Thomas Armstrong, and John D. Morris; Amanda Morris Mothershead; Bettie Morris Defrees; and Julia Ann Morris (about to be married to Norman Ross, on 5 July 1849) all lived across from or beside each other, with a twelve-foot "private alley" crossing their city

---

[13] Sulgrove, p. 449. The 1850 census records a Morris milling business.
[14] Daniels, p. 35; Office of Recorder, Marion County, Ind., plat of Austin W. Morris, 1 April 1846, rec. 7 May 1846, in Deed Rec. Q, p. 264.
[15] *Indianapolis Times*, 1 Dec. 1964, n.p., in author's file.
[16] Daniels, p. 35.

Chapter VIII. Thomas A. Morris: The Railroad Era ♦ 151

square both north-south and east-west. Morris and Rachael built on two of these lots and lived on the corner of Meridian and Georgia Streets.

Jacob Cox, Indiana's first good artist and painter, was a very near neighbor. Also a few houses away was Richard Gatling, inventor of many agricultural machines but best known for his rapid-fire machine gun.[17]

The 1850 census shows Thomas A. Morris holding real estate property worth $10,000 and his wife owning $21,500. It was rare to see a woman listed as owning a large amount of property in those days, unless she was a widow. Six other people, a family, were living on their property. These were servants. His estate was large and valuable.[18]

At this time another venture of enterprising Thomas was the banking business. In 1853 the Indianapolis Insurance Company, authorized to do both banking and insurance business, was revived by Thomas, John D. Defrees (his brother-in-law and owner-editor of the *State Journal*), and others.[19] It had been chartered in 1836, suspended in 1840, revived in 1853, and after six years of "moderate operations" was suspended again until 1865.

When the railroads were first built in Indianapolis, each line had its own depot and its own track. This required the passengers to travel throughout the city in order to change lines. "With the increase in the number of railroads centering in Indianapolis, ... Morris conceived the idea of a system of union tracks and a union depot."[20] "His services on these [many] different roads suggested to Morris the idea of a *union depot* for Indianapolis, which he planned and built."[21] At a meeting in 1849 of four railroad lines then serving Indianapolis, the resolution was adopted. "Such was the origin of the *first union track and Union Station in the United States,* an arrangement which has proved equally advantageous to Indianapolis and to the railroads."[22] Again Thomas Armstrong Morris had had a novel idea—a central system with simplicity and convenience and a true innovation for the whole country! Other cities would soon use the idea.

"The railroads ended Indianapolis's isolation from the rest of the nation. The city's population doubled after the completion of the first railroad. In 1847 approximately 4,000 more had moved to the city. By 1860

---

[17] "South Meridian Street was Noted for Its Residences," unidentified newspaper, 23 Feb. 1916, n.p., in author's file.
[18] Author's file, old deeds.
[19] *National Cyclopaedia of American Biography*, p. 124.
[20] Sulgrove, p. 301; Coleman, p. 3.
[21] Coleman, p. 228; emphasis in the original.
[22] Daniels, p. 99; emphasis in the original.

Indianapolis had grown to 18,000. The railroads provided jobs, made goods from other cities more readily available and cheaper, and made travel to other parts of the country faster and less expensive."[23]

President of the Bellefontaine Railroad at this time was the Hon. O. H. Smith, with Austin W. Morris (Thomas's older brother) as treasurer. Men named Brough and Rose were presidents of the Madison and Terre Haute Railroads, with "Thomas A. Morris being the Chief Engineer in the construction of the track and buildings. The other railroads subsequently came into the central arrangement, which is found to work admirably."[24] "The Union Railway Company, wholly confined to the city, was organized in 1849, mainly by ... Thomas A. Morris, ... Smith, ... Rose and Peck. The Union tracks were laid in 1850, and the depot, upon ... Morris's plans in 1853."[25]

Several references to his work on this are given in Daniel's account of railroad building. Started in 1852, costing $30,000, with five passenger tracks inside the building and two freight tracks outside, the station had "Colonel T. A. Morris ... [as] engineer in charge of the work."[26] "Old records of Colonel Morris on the original Union track show that T rails" were used.[27]

"The method of construction in use at that period is shown very clearly by ... an engineering report made by Colonel Thomas A. Morris to the Terre Haute and Richmond Board of Directors which appears in full in the weekly *Sentinel* of March 30, 1848.... The plan I would recommend to your Board.... As Colonel Morris was the leading engineer of Indiana at that time, we may assume that the above type of construction was in general use in the state."[28]

The *Journal* reported on 29 September 1853: "The inauguration of the Union Passenger Station was attended by a goodly array ... drawn there by the novelty of the scene. 'Twas a lively sight ... one that did the

---

[23] Christian Schrader, *Indianapolis Remembered*, p. 146.
[24] Smith, p. 424.
[25] Sulgrove, p. 136; Holloway, pp. 258, 328, 334.
[26] Daniels, p. 100.
[27] Ibid., p. 105.
[28] Ibid., p. 107.

Chapter VIII. Thomas A. Morris: The Railroad Era ♦ 153

Above: Union Depot, passenger entrance, and Morris Hotel, 1854.
Below: Union Depot, south side of Louisiana Street from Illinois to Meridian Streets, looking west. *Sketches by Christian Schrader.*

eyes good." Six passenger trains left for all parts of the country, one with 240 passengers![29]

The new station, handsomely lit up with gas by night, eventually became the prototype for all the later stations around the country. This building was considered adequate for several years, but railroad traffic increased very rapidly, so it was enlarged in 1866, and then a new and bigger Union Station was constructed in 1888. As recently as 1975 the 1888 building was designated a historic landmark. This great structure with a tall tower clock has now been restored to an attractive complex of shops and restaurants and is again full of happy people—not travelers but, instead, eager shoppers and gourmet diners.

Back when tracks and stations were being built in the Midwest, the East still claimed the *manufacturing* of the giant trains which pulled both freight and people. Their transport west is of interest.

> The parts of the locomotives are put in ... sections of boats at the machine shop in Philadelphia. From thence they are floated along the canal to Hollidaysburg, where a car [pulled by horses] is run under them, which takes them over the mountains to Johnstown. Here they are again put in the canal and floated to Pittsburgh, [then through the locks] into the Ohio River, and put in tow of a steamboat for [Indianapolis]. Not a single article is moved from the place it was put in by the Philadelphia machinist until it is put in charge of the railroad agent here. Nothing is broken, nothing damaged, and a vast deal of heavy lifting is entirely dispensed with. *Courier,* May 19, 1849.[30]

The foregoing account from the *Courier,* quoted by Daniels, makes us realize how much the mountains isolated the Midwest, which was always struggling to grow and prosper.

The Madison and Indianapolis Railroad was completed during the "prosperity" of the Mexican War. Other roads were built in the boom period following the discovery of gold in California. By 1857 Indianapolis had eight railroads. Then the depression of 1857 stopped work on several lines, and construction resumed only after the Civil War. "In the ten years preceding the War Between the States, Indiana, Illinois, Wisconsin, and Iowa together had 7,000 miles of road ... far in advance of the country's needs. But this proved indeed a great preparation for the unforeseen

---

[29] Smith, p. 424.
[30] Daniels, p. 52.

MAP OF INDIANAPOLIS AND HER RAILROAD CONNECTIONS

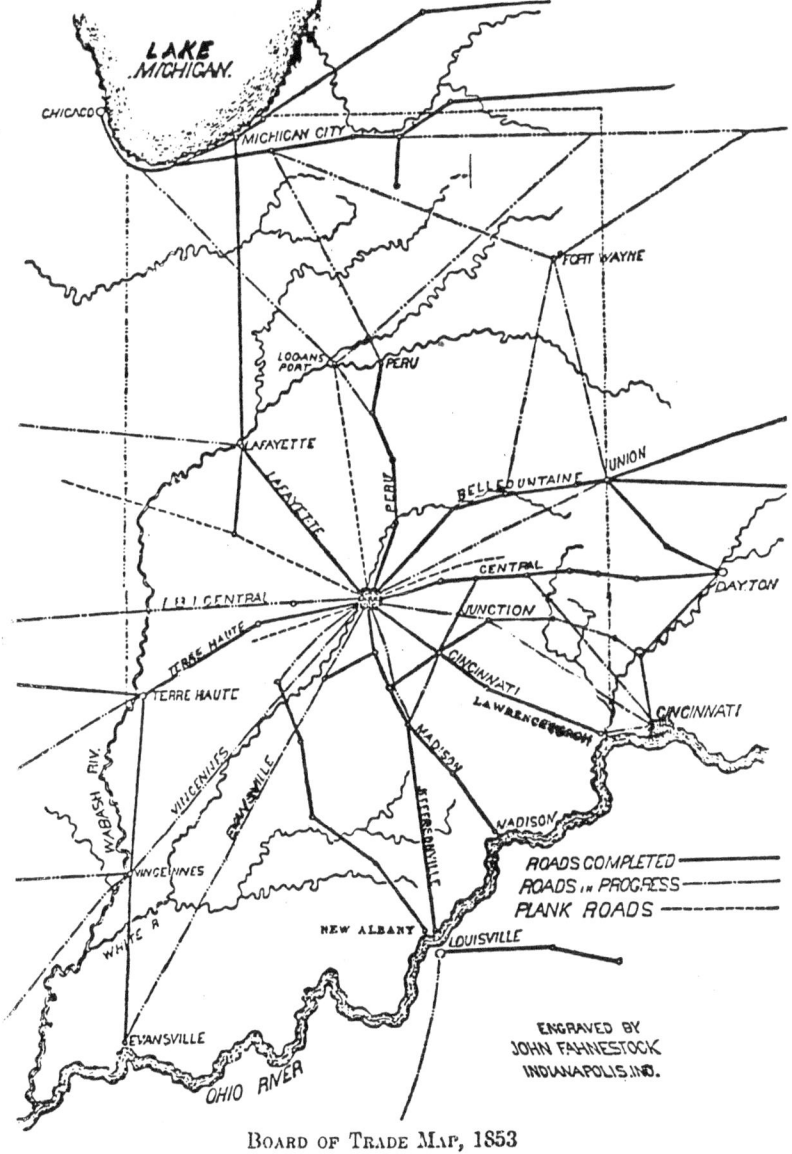

BOARD OF TRADE MAP, 1853

needs of war. When the Mississippi River, formerly an outlet for marketable goods, was closed, there was no outlet except the railroads. There are some who think those midwestern states might otherwise have followed their market into secession, so it is possible that the Union was saved by the railroads."[31]

Preceding these war years we find Thomas a man of boundless energy and enterprises. In addition to railroading, milling, and banking, he entered still another field of business. "In 1852-3 while the building of the Union tracks and depot was under discussion and in progress, ... T. A. Morris built a three-story brick hotel, subsequently made four stories, on the north side of Louisiana Street, opposite the Union Depot."[32] First it was called the "Morris House." It changed names several times although it was owned by Morris for about twenty years.

At this same time Thomas was also chief engineer of the Indianapolis and Cincinnati Railroad, from 1852 to 1854. He moved up to president in 1854 and served in that capacity for three years.

Meanwhile, Thomas and Rachel, very successful and also very prosperous, planned and built a large, twenty-seven-acre estate just outside the northern city limit, which at that time was Tenth Street. This extensive property, then called "the outback," lay between Tenth and Thirtieth Streets. It was bounded on the east by Central Avenue (then called Fall Creek Grave Road) and on the west by a line between Delaware and Pennsylvania Streets. Their large, handsome, grey-brick mansion, facing Central was situated on what later became the corner of Twelfth and New Jersey Streets. It was completed in 1854. "The old neighbors on the Fall Creek Gravel Road were few ... Judge Morrison, General Morrison, ... Ovid Butler."[33]

This elegant Victorian house, made of hard-burned brick, was three stories high, with two asymmetrical side wings and an ample central veranda on both the first and second floors, both with clustered columns. It had overhanging eaves, decorative brackets, and very tall shuttered windows, some of which were arched at the top with hood moldings.[34] It was a spacious, wonderful house for living, a play house for hide and seek, for castle climbing, for exploring gables, nooks, and turrets, a house for a big family to cherish. The grandchildren loved to go there,

---

[31] Daniels, p. 103.
[32] Sulgrove, pp. 270-271.
[33] Unidentified newspaper clipping in author's file.
[34] Old picture, in author's file.

Chapter VIII. Thomas A. Morris: The Railroad Era ♦ 157

"Turkey Castle"
and
the Master of the
House

and they adored their grandparents. There were outbuildings for the servants, stables for the livery, and kennels for the hunting dogs.

The old Morris homestead ... was in its day one of the largest and best residences in Indianapolis and so much a part of this community that novelist Meredith Nicholson [in 1905] gave it a setting in his book *The House of a Thousand Candles*. It was the home for half a century of ... Thomas A. Morris ... stood near the center of twenty-seven acres and was outside the city limits.... The grounds leading up to the front door ... were entered by a long driveway.... North of the house was a large orchard while south and west of the house was a vineyard noted for its rare grapes, a well cultivated garden.... When the General first built there and for several years he raised a good many turkeys on his place. His mother [Rachael, who also eventually lived there with her husband, Morris Morris II] took much comfort in caring for these birds, and the neighbors gave the place the name of "Turkey Castle."[35]

Running a large Victorian household was a real task, usually managed from a second-floor sitting room-office where paperwork was done, the domestic staff reported, and the children were handled. Educating and rearing the children, planning social events, supervising the servants, corresponding, sewing, and other domestic tasks was truly a full-time job for those matriarchs of big families in large mansions.

This fine home was the scene of many a grand party. Important meetings and decisions took place within its rooms. Numerous prominent people came to this mansion, which was the delight and joy of Thomas and Rachel, who were known for their hospitality and cordiality.

Among those important guests was a very close friend, Benjamin Harrison, who was a United States senator in 1881 and in 1888 became the twenty-third U.S. president. President Harrison and Tom often went hunting together, even up until their very last days (see page 190). Although the president was a good bit younger than the general, they both enjoyed the outdoors and each other's company.

Also frequenting this home were many relatives. In Tom's own family there were three prominent brothers-in-law and a very distinguished elder brother. This was Austin, a well-known "city father," active civic leader, and one of the wealthiest and most benevolent men in Indianapolis. (He was the young lad who had come from Kentucky with his father, Morris Morris II, back in 1821 to plant corn even before they could buy land in the new city, the serious boy who was an early school teacher.)

---

[35] Unidentified newspaper clipping with picture, in author's file.

Chapter VIII. Thomas A. Morris: The Railroad Era ♦ 159

Although ladies were virtually never mentioned in the first historical accounts of Indiana, Mrs. Austin W. Morris was the exception as the founder and president of the city's first orphanage, forerunner of the present Childen's Bureau.

John Defrees, husband of Thomas's youngest sister, Bettie, was owner and editor of the city newspaper, an active Whig, a personal friend of Abraham Lincoln, and became the founder of the U.S. Bureau of Printing and Engraving in Washington.

Dr. Leland Mothershead, husband of another sister, Amanda, was a highly respected Indiana pioneer physician and druggist.

Another brother-in-law, Norman Ross, married sister Julia Ann, was superintendent of the Cincinnati Railroad, and later worked in Washington. All these siblings had children and grandchildren who loved to come to Turkey Castle. Imagine this big home at Christmas!

Among the neighbors and friends who frequented this hospitable mansion were two neighbor families of Morrisons, one headed by a judge and the other, a doctor; and Ovid Butler, who eventually bought bankrupt brother John D. Morris's home and was distantly connected to the Butler University family (see Chapter XVII).

Other close friends of Rachel and Tom who spent happy times at Turkey Castle were the beloved Reverend Henry Ward Beecher, father of Harriet Beecher Stowe, who wrote *Uncle Tom's Cabin;* artist Jacob Cox, who painted several family portraits; author Meredith Nicholson; and inventor Richard Gatling. And there were others, including military and government personnel. It was a very busy, active household.

An interesting, tattered newspaper clipping describes a bit of the life of dearly loved old black "Mun" Richman, whom the author's own father fondly remembered from his childhood days at his grandparents' estate. "The most cherished event in Richman's career was his association many years ago with the family of the late General Thomas Morris where he served as first servant, stableman, and trainer.... General Morris was a lover of horses and Mun was the official trainer. The Morris estate was virtually an orchard. Mun's reputation as guard over the Morris orchard was widely known on the North Side...."[36]

The Morris children and grandchildren lovingly remembered this spacious, comfortable home with genuine fondness and pride. In later years, living there also were Tom's parents, Morris and Rachael, that pair who, long before, had started out on Pogue's Run in a log cabin. These Morrises all labored hard for their families and for their city.

---

[36] Ibid., n.d., n.p.

Fortunately, they lived long enough to reap the rewards of their labors. Turkey Castle provided a full life for fifty-six years, until it went under the hands of the wreckers in 1910, although all those acres of city land had already been divided about 1890.

By 1856 Thomas had become president of yet another railroad, the Indianapolis and Bellefontaine, remaining for two years. Then from 1859 to 1861 he was needed again as chief engineer of the Indianapolis and Cincinnati Railroad.[37] He was president and chief engineer of the Indianapolis and St. Louis Railroad and acted as receiver for others and advisor to still others. "All in all, Morris's contributions to life in the Hoosier capital via the railroads were lasting ones. Perhaps in no other line of work could he or any other man have so stamped the city for progress."[38]

---

[37] Coleman, p. 228.
[38] Marjie Gates Giffin, *Water Runs Downhill*, p. 32.

Chapter IX

THOMAS ARMSTRONG MORRIS
Civil War Years

Go placidly amid the noise and haste, remembering what peace there may be in silence. As far as possible, without surrender, be on good terms with all persons. Speak your truth quietly and clearly.
— Desiderata. Found in
Old Saint Paul's Church, Baltimore, 1692

ABRAHAM LINCOLN called for troops in April 1861. Indiana's quota was six regiments. The military spirit had begun to pervade all classes, and more than a regiment of well-drilled men were presently prepared. The City Greys, the Riflemen, and the National Guards were already organized. On 22 March 1861, "at the beginning of the war Thomas A. Morris [one of Indiana's few mature West Point graduates] was appointed quartermaster general of the state by Governor Oliver P. Morton and as such had charge of the equipment of Indiana's first regiments, which were so promptly in the field."[1] This appointment was logical, even though Thomas Morris was nearly fifty years old, for he was a respected West Point graduate and a good friend of the governor.

Morris had occupied this office only eleven days when, on 27 April 1861, President Lincoln commissioned him brigadier general of the Indiana Volunteers. In less than a month, toward the last of May, he was ordered into the western part of Virginia by General George B. McClellan, who was then in command of the Department of the Ohio.

McClellan was also a West Point graduate but a good bit younger than Thomas Morris, who had graduated twenty-seven years ago, was already well into his forty-ninth year, and had fathered five children. Now he, a busy, established engineer and a beloved city leader, must leave his active civic life to go to war for his country. Although not a young man,

---

[1] B. R. Sulgrove, *History of Indianapolis and Marion County*, p. 301; Christopher B. Coleman, "Thomas Armstrong Morris," *The Dictionary of American Biography*, vol. 8, p. 228; Max R. Hyman, *The Journal Handbook of Indianapolis*, p. 36.

[161]

he was trained, seasoned, mature, and patriotic, and, most important, he firmly believed in the cause of the northern states.

Very ironically, this place to which Thomas was sent was the very area of the country in which his earlier family had pioneered and settled. His grandfather, great-uncle, at least two uncles, and an older cousin—from the two combined Morris Morris families—had wished for and signed the 1782 Virginia legislative petition for a separate, new state of "Westsylvania." His mother and father, Rachael and Morris Morris II, were both born right there in Monongalia County, then called "Western Virginia," although his closest kinfolk had already migrated to Kentucky. He was destined to fight some of his own kinfolk and their friends. The tragedy of family members and friends fighting each other was to occur frequently in the border territories; it was a sad and heart-rending confusion of divided loyalties. Fate and circumstances, as well as geographical position, made what we now know as West Virginia a buffer between western Pennsylvania and land held by the Confederacy.

"Morris [had] insisted on mustering volunteer regiments of the Western Virginia Unionists (official records, ser. II, 673) ... and the troops did good service."[2] McClellan actually sent Indiana troops into the Northwest without orders from the War Department![3] This was typical of an arrogant man who would eventually test the patience of our ancestor to the extreme. "As General, he [Morris] commanded the first brigade of troops from the State. He was in the West Virginia Campaign and commanded the battles of Philippi, Laurel Hill, and Carrick's [Corrick's] Ford, *all of which he won*. His first battle, that of Philippi, was *the first conflict [of the first land campaign]*, of the War of the Rebellion."[4] "... [H]istorians credit him with drawing up the plans of the West Virginia Campaign. His planning and handling ... [were] brilliant."[5]

A political revolution midway in the war years, the success of this first land battle, and the success of the *first sustained campaign* were followed by Federal control of its territory, and then later the formation of a new state. West Virginia was admitted to the Union on 20 June 1863.[6] This was something the pioneer ancestors of Thomas Morris had

---

[2] Jacob Piatt Dunn, *Indiana and Indianans*, vol 1, p. 598.
[3] Eva Margaret Carnes, *The Tygarts Valley Line, June–July 1861*, p. 79.
[4] Sulgrove, p. 301. Emphasis in the original.
[5] E. L. Leary, "Morris Brought First Railroad Here," *Indianapolis Star*, 1 Jan. 1971.
[6] Charles Henry Ambler, "West Virginia History," *Enc. Brit.* (1957), vol. 23, p. 547: "It was admitted to the Union conditionally on Dec. 31, 1862. The condition having been met by an amendment to the state constitution providing for the gradual abolition of Negro slavery, West Virginia was proclaimed a separate state on April 20, 1863, effective sixty days later."

Chapter IX. Thomas Armstrong Morris: Civil War Years ♦ 163

wished for nearly a century before, in the latter 1770s. *Now* we realize that these first victories of Thomas Morris in the War Between the States played a major part in the formation of the state of West Virginia. This, then, was another "star in his crown."

Covered bridge at Grafton, West Virginia

Let us back up—to learn details of the first land battle of the Civil War. The Battle of Philippi (pronounced *Fil*-i-pee) took place about 110 miles directly south of Pittsburgh and sixteen miles south of Grafton[7] (then Virginia, now West Virginia) on the Tygarts Valley River, a tributary of the Monongahela. Spanning the river, in the town, there was then and still exists the original wooden covered bridge built in 1852 by Lemuel Chenowith of Beverly and used by both the North and the South during the Civil War. This was the first bridge captured by the Union forces and is most unusual. Built entirely of wood except for the iron bolts holding the segments together, it is an example of the best in covered-bridge architecture. A partition down the center reaches to the roof, completely dividing the bridge and enclosing each center side. The

---

[7] Ross D. Johnston, comp., *West Virginia Estate Settlements*, p. 80. This river was named for David Tygart, who was a very early settler of the upper waters of the Monongahela, in 1754.

outer sides are also boarded closed. It has a wooden footpath with a railing on the *outside* of its wall, but under cover. Enormous curved, solid beams hold up the span. After a 1934 strengthening, it is today part of U.S. 250 and the only divided, two-lane covered bridge on a federal highway.

Colonel Porterfield of the Confederate forces, after burning two railroad bridges, had left Grafton. He withdrew to Philippi to reorganize and await reinforcements. Newly appointed to command, General McClellan, nowhere in or anywhere near this area, eagerly assumed the bridge burnings were an act of war and took matters into his own hands. He ordered, long distance by telegraph, that the bridges be hastily rebuilt.

Meanwhile, General Morris and his troops had been sent by railroad from Indianapolis to Grafton. Supervision of the rebuilding of those bridges was probably one of the first jobs of engineer Morris, who then directed Colonel B. F. Kelly and his men to go by the Baltimore and Ohio Railroad from Grafton to East Thornton, then on foot to Philippi, to arrive at 4:00 A.M. He directed Colonel Ebenezer Dumont to take his men by railroad southwest to Webster, to be joined by two other colonels, Steedman and Crittenden, who were also to arrive at 4:00 A.M. at Philippi with more troops. Morris's plan was to direct the attack so that all means of escape would be cut off for the Confederates, now at Philippi, and they would be captured.

Orders were followed. The march was carried out on a dark, rain-drenched night. Regrettably, a shot by a farmer's wife was mistaken for the opening battle signal and this started activities too soon. The shot warned the Confederates. Meanwhile the Union's Colonel Kelly and his troops were misled by a guide and arrived moments too late. So the Confederates, leaving stores and baggage behind, escaped on horseback, by only a margin of minutes.

General Morris attributed the failure of the pursuing Union forces to capture the enemy to the fact that the Union soldiers were without horses and were physically exhausted from the night-long march through the pouring rain. So one unfortunate shot by a civilian denied them their capture of the enemy troops.

Another account relates: "When Morris arrived at Grafton he learned that Colonel Porterfield was at Philippi, a few miles away, with 1,200 rebel troops, 500 of whom were cavalry. He planned a surprise, divided his forces into two parties, marched twelve miles through rain and mud on the night of June 2, and struck Porterfield's camp at dawn of June 3.

Chapter IX. Thomas Armstrong Morris: Civil War Years ♦ 165

The rebels fled at the first fire [of that first mistaken shot], leaving their baggage, 380 stand of arms, and one flag."[8]

It was said that the significance of the Battle of Philippi was not in the fighting but in the effect upon the preservation of the Union. It strengthened the hold of the Union upon western Virginia and discouraged secessionist movements. The Baltimore and Ohio Railroad was saved!

During all this time McClellan chose to remain in Ohio, not to join his troops in the first skirmishes. Upon serious reflection of his (cowardly?) behavior, one must conclude that McClellan deliberately stayed away to save his own life for future, grander events, since he had so recently been given a command. There had been adequate time for him to get there. He did send his aide-de-camp, who *did* participate in that first battle. Instead, McClellan had wired the newspapers of *his* battles, never mentioning that he was far away in Ohio.

Finally, the flamboyant General McClellan came himself to western Virginia and to Grafton—a huge surprise to the Eastern newspaper editors, who thought that he had been there all the time! This was at the beginning of the war, so, although the battles were not large, they were the first land battles. They were big news for the newspapers, and McClellan, who had provided all the reporting, was suddenly a hero.

The acclaim that General McClellan received in the papers for "his" movements of the forces in western Virginia resulted in his being given command of the Army of the Potomac. "He had made headlines at a time when Mr. Lincoln and his cabinet were in daily dread of an invasion of Washington.... He was the hero of the day and most [people] believed he was actually present at the Philippi action. So the General [McClellan] at his telegraph key in ... Ohio mounted the first rung of that sometimes rickety ladder to fame."[9] McClellan had had the gall and the effrontery to take credit for a success in which he had had no part personally. He was not even there, should have been, but sent others instead to do the fighting.

Today we would call him an opportunist of the worst kind, perhaps a deceitful "whippersnapper." But that is *not* what the troops from Indiana called him—that wouldn't be fit to print! For the rest of the war McClellan was a problem to most everyone and arrogantly continued to steal the glory and the limelight from others. Unfortunately, since historians fre-

---

[8] Jacob Piatt Dunn, *Greater Indianapolis,* vol. 1, p. 598.
[9] Carnes, p. 60.

quently get their material from the newspapers of the day, many histories are still incorrect and glorify this haughty man.

Today a monument on the crest of a hill overlooking old Philippi commemorates the battle. This site is now part of the campus of Alderson Broadus College, founded in 1871. A tall cross is implanted in a stone base, in front of which is a metal plate on a marble base that gives the details, below.

* FIRST LAND BATTLE OF THE CIVIL WAR *

From this spot on the morning of June 3rd, 1861, was fired the first cannon after Fort Sumter. About 3,000 Union Troops marched in two columns, one from Webster, the other from Thornton, in mud, darkness and rain to attack 1,200 Confederate Troops encamped in the valley below. A pistol shot by Mrs. Thomas Humphreys was misinterpreted as the planned signal for the cannoning to begin. Col. Kelley was to close the exit on the Beverly-Fairmont Road, but failed to do so, and the Confederates retreated to Beverly 30 miles south. Col. Lander, who had supervised placing of the cannons, saw the Confederates escaping and, spurring his horse, made a daring ride straight down the hill, crossed the covered bridge, and joined Col. Kelley.

Chapter IX. Thomas Armstrong Morris: Civil War Years ♦ 167

CASUALTIES

Col. Kelley was severely wounded in the chest. James E. Hanger of Churchville, Va., was wounded in the leg by a cannonball and his leg was amputated by Dr. Robinson of the 16th Ohio Inf. This was the first casualty of the war. Capt. Fauntleroy Dangerfield of Hot Springs, Va., was wounded in the knee by a rifle ball, and the consequent amputation performed at Beverly the following day by Dr. John T. Huff was the first by a Confederate surgeon.

OFFICERS AND TROOPS ENGAGED

Federal Troops under the direction of General George B. McClellan *and under the direct command of General Thomas A. Morris,** 9th Indiana Inf.; Col. Benjamin F. Kelley, 1st Va. Regt.; Col. James Irvine, 16th Ohio Inf.; Col. R. H. Milroy, 16th Ohio Inf.; Col. James B. Steedman, 14th and 18th Ohio Vols.; Col. Thomas T. Crittenden, 6th Indiana Inf.; Col. Ebenezer Dumont, 7th Indiana Vols.; Col. Frederick Lander, Aide-de-Camp to Gen. McClellan. Confederate Troops consisting of Virginia Militia under active command of Col. George A. Porterfield.

This marker placed by the Philippi Battlefield Commission, August 1952

*   *   *   *   *

General Morris had been sent to Philippi, where he encamped for the rest of June and into July, with his men itching to be active. "The regiments lay [on Talbot Hill] five weeks ... idly waiting, while the rebel troops continued to fortify ... they burned with desire for action ... they raged against McClellan ... his orders were always to wait."[10] This waiting is mentioned repeatedly; McClellan obviously was an annoying procrastinator. "He dilly-dallied ... puttered around ... became a target for ... none too respectful comments."[11]

At last General Morris received orders to leave Philippi. He was to march on the encampment of General Robert S. Garnett, the southern leader who was gaining a stronger and stronger position as time passed,

---

* Emphasis added.
[10] Carnes, p. 65.
[11] Ibid., p. 83.

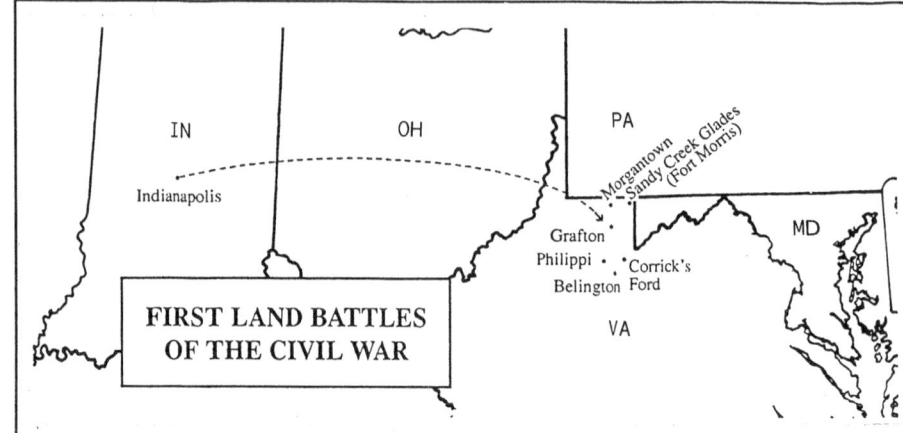

The map shows the tri-state area where Virginia, Maryland, and Pennsylvania converge, also the sites of pre-Revolution Fort Morris and Civil War Battles of Grafton, Philippi, Corrick's Ford, and Belington.

at Laurel Hill. Garnett was there attempting to secure Virginia for the Confederacy. Twelve miles south of Philippi, General Morris engaged about 6,000 rebel troops in a six-day skirmish in the Battle of Belington. Garnett slipped away from Laurel Hill but was followed by Morris, who then defeated him at Corrick's Ford on 13 July 1861. Garnett was killed in the engagement two days later fighting a rear-guard action. A former commandant at West Point, he was the first general officer to die in the war. Confederate General George Pegram was hemmed in at Rich Mountain and surrendered to Morris.[12]

"In this brief campaign western Virginia was cleared of rebel troops; five guns, twelve flags, and 1,500 stands of arms, and 1,000 prisoners were taken."[13]

It seems to have been the custom in earlier days for the leader of a war effort to commandeer one of the larger houses in the area to be his headquarters, to appropriate its temporary use from which to direct operations, and sometimes even to use as a hospital. Such a building was often that of the enemy, but not always. General Morris also used this

---

[12] West Point records reveal that George Herbert Pegram graduated from West Point in 1833, the year before General Morris. He was born in Virginia and served in Florida from 1840 to 1841, five years after Thomas had left Fort King. Can we possibly imagine the drama, the chagrin, the humiliation twenty-eight years after graduation from West Point of one good man surrendering to another—his own collegemate?

[13] Dunn, p. 598.

Chapter IX. Thomas Armstrong Morris: Civil War Years ♦ 169

procedure, for we read that while in Belington he made the house of a Mr. Elliot his headquarters before moving four miles from Kalars to the farmhouse of William Corrick, which was also used as a hospital. Later he returned to the Belington headquarters. (See Epilogue at end of this chapter.)

During this bloody Battle of Belington, the Confederate soldiers panicked and left their wounded General Garnett lying on the battlefield with the dead, so he fell into the hands of the Union Army. From the writings of Hu Maxwell we can surmise that he was a strong southern sympathizer. Noble and kind was Mr. Maxwell, however, because not very long after his South's defeat, he described with appreciation the story of General Garnett's death. The mortally wounded general was lying in the house of William Corrick. "Morris came to visit him. He and Morris had been classmates at West Point. The hatred that existed between the North and the South was forgotten by them, and after Morris had done all that could be done for the wounded officer, Garnett died in the General's arms. The generous and magnanimous Morris showed every respect and kindness in his power to [Robert Beldon] Garnett, and when he was dead, he dressed him in his own blue uniform and sent him to his people in the south."[14] Garnett's body was transported in a canoe to Rowelsburg (situated on the Baltimore and Ohio Railroad on Cheat River), in charge of Whitelaw Reid, who was on General Morris's staff. It was sent to Governor Letcher at Richmond.

Maxwell erred, however, in his statement about West Point, for these two generals were not classmates, as he stated. This point has been checked with West Point. There was almost eight years difference in their birth years: Morris, 1811-1904 and Garnett, 1819-1861.

In Homer Fansler's later history of Tucker County are a photograph of General Morris in his uniform and three sketches entitled "The Battle of Corrick's Ford, July 13, 1861," "Finding General Garnett Wounded and Private Chaplet Dead," and "Corrick's Ford and the Corrick House Where General Garnett Died as They Appear in 1961."[15] In that same publication there is also a poem written by Karl Myers. The fourth of six verses of "Ode on the Battle of Corrick's Ford" reads:

> Long be the decades ere we forget
> Noble Morris and brave Garnett
> Classmates of other days;
> Here in their final parting met,

---

[14] Hu Maxwell, *The History of Tucker County, West Virginia.*
[15] Homer Floyd Fansler, *History of Tucker County, West Virginia.*

> One to die gloriously, one victoriously
> Go his ways.

Eva M. Carnes gives the following account of this campaign:

Due to the fact that General Morris made only two reports [and one has not been found] on the Belington action, this battle has been largely overlooked and historians who have mentioned it are under the impression that it lasted only one or two days. Actually it was the longest battle fought in the entire Tygarts Valley campaign, and General Garnett's guns threw a lot of heavy ammunition. The skirmishing began on July 7th and continued through July 11th, and the men who had had "too little to do in Philippi" were out every day against the enemy. So, from these two reports, and from local tradition with some help from the regimental histories, which do not always agree, the story has been compiled.

Chapter IX. Thomas Armstrong Morris: Civil War Years ♦ 171

There can be no doubt that a definite feud had been started between Generals McClellan and Morris when the former sent his scorching letter to General Morris in relation to the supposed Confederate attack on Philippi. In fact, General McClellan was definitely "off" General Morris.[16]

At the conclusion of a long letter, in print, dated 13 July from General Morris to McClellan there is a note by this same author, Carnes: "Morris was accused of asking ... for more troops and received a severe reprimand from McClellan for asking for them. Of course, as shown (in the above-printed letter), Morris asked only for supplies."[17] So we read many times in published books of this feud between two West Point graduates of very different character. Several such accounts follow.

General Morris in 1861

"Morris possessed the general qualities of a military commander, developed by a thorough course of instruction at West Point, and when the Civil War broke out they made him of inestimable value to Governor Morton's [of Indiana] irrepressible but inexperienced energy. He was commander of all the Indiana regiments in the three months' service, and thus in command of the first West Virginia campaign, where all were sent, which he planned and won before General McClellan knew more of it than he could learn from the papers. The latter absorbed the credit of it, and became commander in chief by luckily reaching the field about a week before the end of it and proved ... that his glory was a secondhand acquisition...."[18]

"General Thomas A. Morris [was] the real victor in the first West Virginia campaign...."[19]

---

[16] Carnes, p. 91.
[17] Ibid., pp. 101, 102.
[18] Sulgrove, p. 301.
[19] Ibid., pp. 38, 238.

"[General Morris] was the hero of the West Virginia campaign, the credit of which McClellan absorbed."[20]

"He drove the Confederate forces back from Philippi on June 3, and was well started in the task of driving them out of western Virginia when McClellan took command in person of the campaign.... On July 3, McClellan harshly refused reinforcements which Morris had requested ... and on July 14, in his report, criticized him for not pursuing the Confederates more vigorously at Laurel Hill."[21]

"He was promised appointment as Major General ... but failed to receive it, due, it was charged, to the hostility of General McClellan."[22]

"He distinguished himself ... by really doing all the planning and work that made so brilliant a success. General McClellan was still in the East, and arrived just in time to see the completion of General Morris's work, and appropriate all the credit of it."[23]

An extremely specific description of the entire war is written from official sources by Thomas P. Kettell in *History of the Great Rebellion*. Three pages, too long and detailed to repeat here, describe the battles previously mentioned and use General Morris's name seven times. The entire account is favorable to Morris.[24]

A clear analysis of the reasons for and execution of this first Western Virginia campaign is detailed in *The Tygarts Valley Line*, in which E. M. Carnes "tells it like it was," with no holds barred. General Morris is mentioned forty-one times, and pictures of him and his battles are in the book.[25]

David Stevenson devotes two chapters comprising eighty-four pages to a very detailed account of "The Western Virginia Campaign" in his *Indiana's Roll of Honor*. General Morris is quoted twice, is listed in the table of contents, and is mentioned by name forty-four times. Random selections follow. "General Morris faithfully carried out the instructions given him ... cool and cautious ... carefully watched over his little army ... will show how careful he was to recognize the supremacy of the civil authorities...."[26]

Kenneth Williams, probably one of the best-known Civil War authorities, has taken his sources from the official records, letters, and

---

[20] Ibid., p. 49; W. R. Holloway, *Indianapolis Railroad City*, p. 117.
[21] Coleman, p. 228.
[22] Dunn, p. 598.
[23] Sulgrove, p. 121.
[24] Thomas P. Kettell, *History of the Great Rebellion*, pp. 110-113.
[25] Carnes, p. 102.
[26] David Stevenson, *Indiana's Roll of Honor*.

Chapter IX. Thomas Armstrong Morris: Civil War Years ♦ 173

accounts of McClellan, Morris, and others. There is no doubt of Williams' opinion of McClellan as a delayer, an arrogant, self-centered, poor general, and of the unfortunate treatment of General Morris,

> ... a cool and deliberate man ... most creditable to himself, his soldiers, and their officers ... a trained soldier ... Morris had no men killed.... This looks like an effort to hit Morris below the belt.... As a matter of fact, Morris pursued Garnett quite effectively over difficult roads toward St. George, through rain and with little food for his men.... [McClellan was] successful because of the good troop leading by brigadiers he openly affronted.... Miles away he himself heard no discharge of cannon, no roll of musketry ... gave Morris the smaller half of his forces ... while he took the larger half.... After lecturing his subordinate in a lofty tone, the man who had not yet heard the noise of battle said to the man who had, "I propose taking the really difficult and dangerous part of this work on my own hands.... Do not ask for further reinforcements. If you do I shall take it as a request to be relieved from your command and to return to Indiana.... I speak officially.... I must have generals under me who are willing to risk their lives and reputation.... Let this be the last of it."

So wrote the general who a few months later began pressing his own superiors for reinforcements. A man who could write like that, who had no military achievement to his credit—except the invention of an uncomfortable saddle—was not likely to prove fit for high command.... Again McClellan failed to carry out ... and allowed the enemy to escape with valuable supplies....

As one studies McClellan's future career it is to be remembered that he was completely unseated.... Forgetting what Morris and Rosencrans had done, he asked Scott "in heaven's name" to give him general officers who understood their profession; he wrote the untrue and ungracious sentence, "Unless I command every picket and lead every column I cannot be sure of success." McClellan's failure to follow up.... [etc.][27]

An interesting sideline and result of this campaign: J. E. Hanger, a Confederate soldier listed on the Battle of Philippi monument, had his leg shattered by a cannonball the day after he joined up. His leg was necessarily amputated, by a Union doctor, and it was the first amputation of the war. Hanger experimented throughout the war with his own and others' artificial legs and eventually became one of the largest manufacturers of artificial limbs in the world.

---

[27] Kenneth P. Williams, *Lincoln Finds A General*, vol. 1, pp. 105-113.

The original term of enlistment of Morris and his regiments was for only three months, for no one anticipated that the war would last long. Their term expired in July and these regiments came home. "He was honorably mustered out on July 27, 1861. He expected another commission, but none came for more than a year. Believing his services were not really wanted, he declined a commission as Brigadier General on September 20, 1862, and another as Junior Major General in October of that year."[28] The West Point records of the Association of Graduates refer to his conducting the campaign with "marked ability, ... assurance that he would be made a Major General, ... and advancement withheld fourteen months."[29]

The biographical sketch of Morris in *Appleton's Cyclopaedia* says he was offered and declined an appointment. The historian Barry Sulgrove states that he believed his services to have been worthy of a more speedy recognition.[30]

President Abraham Lincoln wrote a note to Simon Cameron, secretary of war (the political Mayor Daley of his time), "Today, Sept. 28, 1861, Hon. Messrs. Dunn, Mitchell, and Porter, and John D. Defrees, Mr. Donohue, Fletcher, and Jones, all of Indiana, call and ask that Thomas A. Morris of that state be a *Major General* of Volunteers, and they say such is the wish of the entire delegation in Congress."[31] This information appears in Bassler's well-respected *The Collected Works of Abraham Lincoln*. These notes were held by Lincoln's grandson and not released for publication until seventy-five years after Lincoln's death. How very sad that General Morris never knew this—at least he did not see it in print. This note, "autograph endorsement signed," is now in the Illinois State Historical Library in Springfield, Illinois. The editor's footnote says, "William M. Dunn, William Mitchell, and Albert G. Porter were United States Representatives, and John D. Defrees was Superintendent of Public Printing [appointed by the president]. The other men named were probably D. C. Donohue of New Castle, Calvin Fletcher of Indianapolis, and Aquilla Jones of Greencastle."[32]

(John Defrees was a personal friend of Lincoln, as well as brother-in-law of Thomas Morris. See Chapter XVII on Tom Morris's sister, Elizabeth Mitchell Morris.)

---

[28] Coleman, p. 228.
[29] Author's file, copied records.
[30] Sulgrove, p. 301.
[31] Roy P. Bassler, ed., *The Collected Works of Abraham Lincoln* (New Brunswick, N.J.: Rutgers University Press, 1953), vol. 4, p. 539. Emphasis added.
[32] Ibid.

Chapter IX. Thomas Armstrong Morris: Civil War Years ♦ 175

Thomas A. Morris received no appointment as major general. The president was a busy man; perhaps the letter got lost in the confusion of war. But one cannot help but wonder about the grip of influence that McClellan must have had on the president, who was so dependent on him.

"McClellan not only denied Morris credit for his victories, but he also apparently blocked Morris's promised appointment as major general at the close of the three months of service. The promise of this appointment had been confirmed by President Lincoln himself (Morris spent an evening with Mr. Lincoln following the West Virginia campaign) but Morris never received it. In fact, after a long delay, he was tendered only another brigadier generalship. After a yet longer delay, he was offered only a junior commission as a major general. Morris, disenchanted with the whole experience, never accepted either appointment."[33]

If circumstances had been quite different and if there had been no General McClellan and political cohorts, General Morris might have gone on to major victories to become one of the great generals of the Civil War. On the other hand, he might have been killed, never to achieve his many accomplishments *after* the war. Indianapolis would have been the great loser.

The only known war records of General Thomas A. Morris are in the *Order Book of the First Indiana Brigade of Volunteers,* only an outline of a unit history which contains little or no commentary. It lists the posts, camps, and stations as well as the action in which units or individuals participated. There are no personal or private papers relating to the action in western Virginia in June and July 1861. We may conclude that the general, who declined to discuss the events in western Virginia, decided never to write his personal memoirs, perhaps in disgust or disappointment. Because of the absence of commentary or narration of what took place on a given date—detailing of the western Virginia campaign—there is reason to believe that it was destroyed or removed after the First Brigade ceased to exist.[34] When we read of his continuing very active civic life after the army years, we can readily believe that he was too busy, if not reluctant, to write his memoirs.

A very long, dear, and complimentary obituary, with a large picture, ends with the following:

Army Promotion Promise Unkept. It was always felt that General Morris had been ill-used, that the promotion he deserved had been

---

[33] Marjie Gates Giffin, *Water Runs Downhill,* p. 31.
[34] John Graves Morris's notes, Albuquerque, N.M., 87108.

delayed until he could not in justice to himself accept, and that his service during the years of the Civil War following the three months' campaign had been lost to the country through promotions to those who were less able and less deserving but who made themselves felt at court. On this subject Morris Morris Ross of *The News* (writer and managing editor), nephew of General Morris, said: "On Sunday, May 1, 1898, Uncle Thomas said to me, in speaking of the war, that the reasons he had been silent were many. He had fought the West Virginia Campaign, had met an army the size of his own, had broken it up and scattered it utterly in three months, and would have done it in less time if McClellan had let him. The soldiers who were with him and the officers thought he had made a success. He himself thought he had. In view of this an appointment was promised him. He spent an evening with Mr. Lincoln, who promised him an appointment.

"He went home and waited a year, and then an appointment of the grade he had given up in the three months' service, a brigadier generalship, was tendered him. This he felt he could not accept. A long time after that a major-generalship was tendered him, but it was a junior commission and he had lost his chance during the time he had been waiting. He felt that it was not meant he should accept either one.

"During all this time he never opened his mouth to anyone, never asked anyone to get him an appointment. He carried himself thus because he wanted to feel that if it was meant that he should go into the army, it would come in such a way as to demonstrate itself. His wife was sorely afflicted; his children were young; his father and mother who lived with him were old, and much was depending on him in life. He felt that God had meant him to recognize his obligations in life, and he did not know whether that same power meant he should serve the country first or the family in which he found himself.

"And so he allowed himself to drift in the hope that they would assert themselves in such a way as to make his duty clear. For this reason he made no effort, feeling that God would guide matters so as to make his duty plain. He believes influences at Washington and here worked against him, but he did not assert himself or try to combat them for the reasons named."[35]

---

[35] *Indianapolis News*, 24 March 1904, p. 2, in author's file.

Chapter IX. Thomas Armstrong Morris: Civil War Years ♦ 177

From many accounts, including letters from President Lincoln reprimanding McClellan,[36] it appears very obvious that McClellan was disliked, distrusted, and finally dismissed. McClellan was relieved from his command on 9 November 1862 by order of the secretary of war.[37]

Later, Lincoln, always an easy, forgiving man, and very, very desperate for a general, asked McClellan to come back. Still later, the president fired him again. The historian Fansler says that Lincoln released McClellan *seven* times from the command of the General Army of the Potomac! Finally, President Lincoln found a good leader in Ulysses S. Grant.

Still later, McClellan ran for president of the United States on the Democratic Party ticket against Abraham Lincoln. He won a majority in only three of the then-existing thirty-six states. Those three were Delaware, New Jersey, and Kentucky. So Lincoln defeated this man by a landslide. In spite of all this, McClellan was elected governor of New Jersey in 1877.

The author had the opportunity to meet and talk with the well-known historian Kenneth Burns right after she had seen the production of his wonderful, very long and ostensibly complete television documentary on the Civil War, released to the public in 1989. His story does not specifically mention General Morris or the first land battles in western Virginia (nor do most of the maps and history books). She thought at least *he* would have gotten it right, with all his research, so she questioned him. Burns admitted that she was correct but said he and his advisors had decided to use that period as a logical introduction of General McClellan. He promised to write her about it. Some time later, she did receive a letter from Burns saying essentially the same thing he had told her in person. She was disappointed that a historian of his caliber would stoop to a conscious error, actually a falsification, in a historical documentary, simply to provide a dramatic introduction. Such poetic license has no place in a documentary.

* * * * *

And so we began this chapter of a kind man with the quotation, "Go placidly amid the noise and haste, remembering what peace there may be in silence." History did not reward him with the credit he deserved. Perhaps he was too silent, but he was a gentleman—who lived to go on to greater things.

---

[36] Kettell, pp. 242, 386.
[37] Ibid., p. 390.

EPILOGUE: Corrick's Ford Revisited

IN THE LATE 1980s, the author made a most interesting discovery about Corrick's Ford. Through their mutual interest in genealogy, she and a newly-found fourth-cousin-once-removed realized they both had a close tie to the old stone house used as headquarters by General Thomas Morris in 1861.

The cousin, Frances Gibson Poulos of Potter Valley, California, is the great-great-great-granddaughter of Preston Morris, a younger brother of Rachael Morris, the general's mother, making Frances also the three-greats-grandniece of Rachael and Morris II.

Frances's husband, Dr. Paul Poulos Jr., is the great-great-grandson of William Corrick, owner of the house appropriated by the author's great-great-grandfather.

Their daughter, Paige Poulos, thus has ties to the Corrick house through both parents. Below are photographs of Paul and Paige, outstanding *contemporary* members of our Morris family.

See Preston's line in the Genealogy for details of their many accomplishments.

Dr. Paul Poulos Jr. Internationally known Ph.D. in veterinary medicine	*Paige Poulos* Public relations expert and wine specialist

Chapter X

THOMAS ARMSTRONG MORRIS
Ending a Full Life

Behold the wonder you have wrought
Within your little time,
The projects won, the battles fought,
The noble goals of rhyme.
— Old Hymn, St. Anne

THINKING THAT the war was to be for only a short duration, the Indiana Brigade returned from West Virginia, amid great accolades of cheering, after their three months' enlistment was up. This is the term all the Indiana men had signed up for, although many were now eager to reenlist. Rachel Morris's husband returned to Indianapolis, receiving a great acclamation for battles well won. Now he would again resume his important place in a community which was lacking men and needed leadership. Thomas, "the stalwart Morris," went back to the business he knew best: railroad construction. From 1862 to 1866 he was chief engineer of the Indianapolis and Cincinnati Railroad, and during that time he built the road from Lawrenceburg to Cincinnati.[1] The railroads were to play an ever-increasing part in the campaigns of the Civil War.

During the turmoil of these war years the city transit system of Indianapolis was born. Benefiting from "Morris's boundless attention ... on June 5, 1863, the Indiana Street Railroad Company was incorporated under the general law, with Thomas A. Morris as President."[2] This was to be the first transit trolley car system in the city. Two companies applied for the charter; Morris's company received it but later decided it was expedient to decline. So the other company was eventually chartered, and by 1866 about seven miles of track had been completed.

---

[1] B. R. Sulgrove, *History of Indianapolis and Marion County*, p. 301; Christopher S. Coleman, "Thomas Armstrong Morris," in *The Dictionary of American Biography*, vol. xiii, p. 223.

[2] Jacob Piat Dunn, *Indiana and Indianapolis*, vol. ii, p. 336; "The Indianapolis Story," *The Indianapolis Star*, 27 Sept. 1953, p. 144; *Logan's History of Indianapolis from 1818;* W. R. Holloway, *Indianapolis, The Railroad* City.

Gothic gateway, Crown Hill Cemetery. Another view on facing page.

Although Alexander Ralston had provided for a cemetery in his original city plan, it became apparent that it would soon be inadequate for the fast-growing town. Also, many war casualties were helping to fill up this old city burying ground, called "Greenlawn" and located on Kentucky Avenue southwest of the capitol. So in October of 1863 a group of prominent citizens organized to find land for a new cemetery. They purchased a large farm and tree nursery and other adjacent farms on the outskirts of the city, 246 acres of rolling land three miles north of downtown. In less than two years the area, cleared and landscaped, was named "Crown Hill" and formally dedicated in June 1864. Many Civil War soldiers were soon reburied there, and families removed their loved ones from Greenlawn to the new Crown Hill.

Thomas Morris had been one of the ten prominent citizens to organize the Association of Crown Hill and now became one of the thirty original trustees, who were designated "corporators." The board was self-perpetuating, with preference to nearest male relatives or close associates.

Chapter X. Thomas Armstrong Morris: Ending a Full Life ♦ 181

In later years, Donald Morris, grandson of Thomas, became a corporator, as did Wilson Mothershead, great-grandson of Amanda Morris, sister of Thomas. Reily Adams, husband of the great-granddaughter of Thomas's brother John, was one until his death. His son, Reily Morris Adams, is now secretary of the larger board of corporators, as well as secretary of the active board of managers.

Because of the "great distance" by horse and carriage of the new cemetery from the city, the Crown Hill Railroad Company was organized under the laws of Indiana, with General Thomas A. Morris as president. It was opened for travel in 1867. Later, but during the lifetime of the original corporators, an impressive Gothic gateway and a waiting station were built in 1888. Now these are National Historic Landmarks. A Gothic chapel was added in 1975, and by 1987 there were twenty-three miles of paved roadways and seven miles of fencing. Nearly 173,000 members of Hoosier families were resting in Crown Hill by 1991. One United States president, two United States vice presidents, ten Indiana governors, fourteen mayors of Indianapolis, more than 2,000 soldiers, and more than 1,600 Confederate prisoners of war are buried there.

It has been "increased and embellished" since those early days, but "the true treasure ... is the people buried there, the rich and the poor, the known and the unknown who blended their lives with the history of Indianapolis."[3] "The men who founded Crown Hill were visionaries ... who managed somehow to look hundreds of years into the future and establish a non-sectarian cemetery of far greater dimensions than called for by their times."[4] So for one more reason our Morris family can be proud of our ancestor Thomas Armstrong, for he was one of those "visionaries."

Thomas and Rachel, and probably his two living sisters and a brother, altogether purchased lot No. 1 in Section 6 "containing 7,363 superficial feet" for $1,840 on 26 May 1871 for the "heirs of Morris Morris."[5] This large area, on a corner and bounded by two roads, is a beautiful knoll with tall trees. In the center of a bent-V shape is the Morris Morris section, the largest part. It has a tall spire monument, which was very probably erected by the children of Rachael and Morris II, who are memorialized upon it and are buried there.

On one side of this area is a section for Julia Morris Ross and heirs. Beside it is one for Amanda Morris Mothershead, then one for Thomas Armstrong Morris. On the other side of their parents is a section for Austin W. Morris, then one for John D. Morris, and one for Elizabeth Morris Defrees.[6]

In December 1864 thirteen bodies were removed from the old Greenlawn Cemetery to this burial lot, including Rachael and Morris II, three of their children, and many grandchildren. (This is puzzling, for Crown Hill records show interment of thirteen individuals on 15 December 1854 and one in April 1870, yet the actual purchase of the property did not occur until May 1871—possibly an error.)

By 1976 there were seventy-two Morris family members resting there on this quiet knoll. *Any direct descendant or spouse of one may be buried in this Morris lot at no cost for the space.* The grounds are well cared for, in perpetuity.

* * * * *

On the day of Lincoln's death, a group of Army and Navy officers of the Union forces who had been appointed Honor Guard of his funeral cortege met at the Union League of Philadelphia and decided to form the Military Order of the Loyal Legion. Its principle was, briefly, true allegiance to

---

[3] Crown Hill Cemetery publication, in author's file.
[4] *Indianapolis Star*, 26 June 1977, sec. 5, 1-4; "Board of Corporators," publication of Crown Hill Cemetery, author's file.
[5] Crown Hill Cemetery office.
[6] Ibid.

Chapter X. Thomas Armstrong Morris: Ending a Full Life ♦ 183

the United States of America and a deep sense of patriotic obligation. Membership was open to commissioned officers who served in the Union forces from 1861 to 1865, and to their descendants.[7]

It has been impossible, thus far, to determine if General Morris was actually part of Lincoln's Honor Guard, which traveled with the funeral cortege. It is probable, since he was a railroad man and surely had easy access to immediate transportation. On the other hand, he may have been bitter over his lack of promotion because of McClellan, or he might not have been part of the cortege, as he did not become a member of the Loyal Legion until 1890, two years after its founding, although in the records he is considered an original member.[8] Some other family men who have been members of the Loyal Legion since then were the general's sons Thomas O'Neil and Milton A. Morris, his nephew Lewis Thompson Morris, his grandsons Donald Seymour and Theodore Hatfield Morris, and his great-grandson Morris Morris, all deceased. Wives and daughters are now also eligible for the Dames of the Loyal Legion. The author's father, Theodore Hatfield Morris, was very proud of his membership in that organization, wore a buttonhole rosette, and attended meetings in Philadelphia. On a few occasions he took the author and her mother along on day trips.

Surely General Morris was an important part of the proceedings as Lincoln lay in state in Indianapolis inside the State House which Thomas's father, Morris Morris II, had designed, built, and supervised, years ago (with two other commissioners). After all, Thomas Morris had been one of Lincoln's generals and they had once spent an evening together. "April 30, 1865, ... Governor Morton, ... staff ... legislature ... council went to Richmond to meet the train and escort it to the city ... congregated around the Union Depot ... conveying the body to the State House ... under the dome of the Capitol.... Citizens marched through the great hall ... to gaze upon the face of the man they had learned to love."[9]

One hundred thousand people came, many from other parts of the state. "Army officers and a group of Indianapolis's most eminent citizens were a guard of honor, watching until midnight, until the doors of the State House closed and the coffin was conveyed again to the train."[10] No specific names are mentioned, but surely Thomas Morris, Indiana's West Point general, was one of the dignitaries accompanying Governor Morton

---

[7] Loyal Legion booklet, author's file.
[8] Loyal Legion records.
[9] Max R. Hyman, ed., *The Journal Handbook of Indianapolis*, pp. 41-2.
[10] W. R. Holloway, *Indianapolis, the Railroad City*, p. 126. The author investigated every possible source to determine positively if T. A. Morris was in the guard of honor, but to no avail.

and participating in that day's sad ceremonies as the slain president lay in state.

* * * * *

According to the historian W. R. Holloway, the decade of the 1860s was very important for Indianapolis. The city rose from "a mere flourishing inland town and prominent railroad station to ... a manufacturing and commercial center, increasing ... population 130 percent."[11] After the Civil War it changed greatly from "a quiet, neighborly village ... [to] a noisy, bustling city, with expanding cultural and artistic activities."[12]

Railroading continued to develop and expand, and with it Tom Morris's activities and responsibilities. From 1868 to 1869 he was president of the Indianapolis and St. Louis Railroad, building the road from Terre Haute to Indianapolis. He resigned to become the receiver of the Indianapolis, Cincinnati, and Lafayette Railroad, an important task of reorganizing and saving it.[13] This enormous contribution concluded Morris's railroad activities, for now he was called upon to supervise still another civic enterprise, another responsible undertaking. "The indefatigable Morris was at the height of his public career. His name was recognized throughout the city and the state, and his abilities had withstood the test of time. This was the year then [1877] that allowed history to repeat itself in the Morris family."[14]

Indiana's first state house, built half a century before by a commission of three including Tom's pioneer father, State Auditor Morris Morris II, was by this time in bad repair, overcrowded, and outgrown. Although a ceiling that had fallen in 1867 had been repaired, Indiana was very much in need of a new capitol building.

Ten years passed. In March 1877 a board of four commissioners, two from each party, was appointed by the governor to select plans and to superintend the construction of a new state house. This was to cost no more than $2 million.[15] Funds were raised by an assessment of one cent upon each $100 worth of taxable property in the state.

General Thomas Morris, of the Republican Party and by this time the most respected engineer in the state, was made president of the board of commissioners. The membership of the commission changed frequently and two resigned soon, so that General Morris bore the greatest share of

---

[11] Ibid.
[12] Jeanette Covert Nowland, *Hoosier City, The Story of Indianapolis*, p. 173.
[13] Sulgrove, p. 301; Coleman, p. 228.
[14] Marjie Gates Giffin, *Water Runs Downhill*, p. 31.
[15] Sulgrove, pp. 352-2; *The Indianapolis News*, 10 Oct. 1949; Hyman, p. 70, Dunn, vol ii, p. 709.

Chapter X. Thomas Armstrong Morris: Ending a Full Life ♦ 185

responsibility during the whole of its planning and construction. Unlike today's tales of padded expense accounts, with graft, cheating, and politics, there are stories which have been passed down in our family telling of the general's many personal contributions, numerous times, in bearing some of the expenses "right out of his own pocket," as the author's father used to say. He was concerned and determined, in spite of enormous difficulties and frequent problems, to see the project through on time and for the specified amount. He was a good man and a responsible one.

Morris and the other commissioners visited the capitols of Illinois, Connecticut, and Michigan, and other public buildings throughout the country. They finally selected the drawings from twenty-four submitted plans. The Modern Renaissance structure was to stand on nine acres of land where the old building had stood. The state bought a square and a part of Market Street to add to the property.[16]

First, the old capitol had to be demolished so the new one could be started. The old building was razed in 1877 and the new edifice begun in September 1880. It was completed in only eight years, in 1888, and, as my father often said, is one of the few and probably the only structure in the entire country ever built with public monies to stay within its allotted budget. Indeed, it was slightly under, at a cost of $1,980,969.

The new capitol was made of Indiana limestone with a marble interior and had a handsome, blue stained-glass inner dome, 105 feet above the floor with 130 more feet to the top of the rotunda. Thomas Morris and his committee wanted to have the very finest and most beautiful for their capitol; they had great vision.

Ever mindful of the state's money, and using again the best of the old first capitol in Corydon, they put the eight original beautiful statues of Carrara marble around this rotunda.

A grand atrium sixty-eight feet wide extends the length of the building, lighted from the attic to the main floor for three stories by translucent skylights. It is a marble tiered corridor. "The halls are set at regular intervals with [eight] polished marble columns ... and extend the entire length of the building ... forming the finest colonnade in any public building in the Union, except those of the national capitol at Washington."[17] Eighty-one enormous doors on the main floor are carved from white oak.

---

[16] Christian Schrader, *Indianapolis Remembered*, p. 50. "The West Market, financed by the state, had been built in 1839 facing Ohio Street between Mississippi (Senate) and Tennessee (Capitol) Streets. Beside it was a vacant space used by traveling circuses in the 1840s. Beside that were two residences. The state bought this square and a part of Market Street to build the new capitol."
[17] Sulgrove, p. 253.

The Supreme Court room is still as it was in 1888, with its original oak woodwork, brass chandelier, highly decorated ceiling, stained-glass window, and furniture lending a certain grandeur and graciousness.

The fourth-floor chandeliers are all the originals from the old building. It is interesting to know that when the state house was two-thirds completed, provision had not yet been made for electric lights. Because the state house board was fearful that the added cost of an electric plant would exceed the budget, it postponed the purchase, leaving the decision to the legislature. The building, upon completion, was lighted by gas; however, it was wired throughout for electric lights.[18] Our Thomas Morris was a far-sighted individual. This state of Indiana a century ago built for itself a splendid edifice still elegant today, little changed, and still in constant use well over a hundred years later.

A large plaque in the rotunda lists the board of the state house commissioners. It reads "... Thomas A. Morris ... May 24, 1877, to Jan. 29, 1881." However, much more time than that was involved in its building. "His knowledge as an engineer, his thorough mastery of any subject that engaged his mind made him specially valuable as the President of the Board of Commissioners.... All these commissioners deserved and received praise, but to the domination of General Morris is due the result, a State House built in accordance with all the requirements of the board and within the appropriation made by the State."[19] "Still used today, it stands as a monument to one man's tenacity and engineering skills, and integrity."[20]

Morris Morris Defrees, a civil engineer and nephew of Thomas and grandson of Morris Morris II, landscaped the grounds in 1879. Although this might be considered nepotism today, it must have been acceptable then or it surely wouldn't have occurred under the supervision of Thomas Armstrong Morris. This landscaping was a definite "repeat," because Tom, as a West Point engineering student, had landscaped the grounds of his father's first Indiana capitol. (Corydon's building had been considered temporary because it was not near the state's center.) Now a Morris of the next generation was landscaping the new state house grounds. So history did repeat itself.

Opposite: Indiana State Capitol, exterior and interior

---

[18] *Indianapolis News,* 10 Oct. 1949.
[19] *Indianapolis News,* obituary, 24 March 1904, p. 2.
[20] Theodore H. Morris, note in author's file.

Chapter X. Thomas Armstrong Morris: Ending a Full Life ♦ 187

"Outside this majestic capitol was a gravel walk, and near it a wooden pump. This supplied all the drinking water for the building as well as for all other purposes of the house. There was a fence and wooden gate with a ball and chain, in front of steps that led up to great Doric columns."[21]

In 1975 a writer for the Indiana Architectural Foundation penned a very complimentary piece describing the state capitol; this was eighty-seven years after it was built. It is so enthusiastically descriptive that it must be included here, even though it may be a bit repetitive.

> Soaring like an eagle, a focal point for the western portion of the Mile Square, the Statehouse is a feast for the eyes, a gargantuan assemblage of the best that nineteenth century art and architecture could create. The limestone facade, executed in the classical and more lavish Corinthian styles, is but a delicious prelude to the splendor that awaits within. The interior basks in a French Renaissance atmosphere of rich woods, gleaming stonework, and ornamental brass and bronze. The rotunda with the dome dancing 250 feet above the marble floor contains large, blue glass windows diffusing light on eight marble sculptures representing Law, Agriculture, Art, Oratory, History, Commerce, Justice, and Liberty. North and south of the rotunda are open colonnades rising an impressive three stories to translucent skylights. The Statehouse displays a richness and beauty unique to the city.[22]

This elegant edifice will instill pride in any relative, and should be seen!

*　　*　　*　　*　　*

Once again General Thomas Morris was to be in the forefront of another progressive enterprise for his city. Natural gas had been discovered in Indiana in 1886. "The Indianapolis Natural Gas Company was then formed by local men of means to supply gas to the city.... When the new trust was organized, all the stock was assigned to five trustees to be held and managed for the common good"[23] and "General Morris was made one of the Life Trustees of the Consumers Gas Trust Company,"[24] organized in 1887. It saved millions of dollars by using natural gas in the vicinity. "No other agency ... has done as much to stimulate the growth of

---

[21] Schrader, p. 65.
[22] *Indianapolis Architecture*, 1975 guidebook, Indiana Architectural Foundation.
[23] William Willard Howard, "The City of Indianapolis," supplement of *Harper's Weekly*, 11 Aug. 1888, p. 1.
[24] Obituary.

Chapter X. Thomas Armstrong Morris: Ending a Full Life ♦ 189

the city."[25] However, when it first sought to get into Indianapolis, the Standard Oil Company had met with unexpected opposition, for the citizens had been strongly opposed.

The following year, 1888, at a time in life when other men would have retired or expired, General Morris became president of the Indiana Water Company. This position he held until his retirement at the age of ninety-two.[26] Indianapolis's system of waterworks cost $1 million to build but was said to be worth the money.[27] It supplied a large part of the domestic and manufacturing service of the city and all of its fire service.

With his experience and leadership, Morris tackled the troubles of the new company and gradually resolved its problems. He was truly a "welcomed presence ... and it has been under his experience and wise direction that the great new 'gallery,' and an inexhaustible supply of pure water have been secured."[28] As president he was also a director. "M. A. Morris" was listed as secretary.[29] This was the youngest son of Thomas, Milton Aspden Morris, then in his late thirties.

For several more years the aged Thomas continued to be a busy, active civic leader. A great sadness arrived, however, on 6 January 1893 when he became a widower. Elizabeth Rachel, mother of his five children, died "of disease" at the age of seventy-one, when Thomas was eighty-two. An earlier newspaper mentioned that she had been very ill for a long time. Crown Hill records show that her interment didn't take place until 4 June 1893, six months later. (This may have been due to frozen ground in the winter months, or perhaps an error in the dates.)

"Even after [Thomas] had passed his eighty-fifth year he continued to hunt and fish. He was a thorough sportsman, his knowledge of woodcraft having been received when Indiana was covered with thick forests, and redmen were yet in the woods and [were] frequent visitors to the little town of Indianapolis."[30] He is quoted in Sulgrove's old history as saying, "It was just like camping out in a forest on a hunting expedition when he came here with Father in 1821, except that the camping places were cabins instead of tents or brush houses."[31]

On the general's ninetieth birthday, in 1901, he was photographed in a boat, duck shooting on the Illinois River with two guides and his very

---

[25] Hyman, p. 140.
[26] Howard, p. 4.
[27] Sulgrove, p. 140.
[28] Ibid., p. 312.
[29] Hyman, p. 144.
[30] "In Memoriam," a publication of The Military Order of the Loyal Legion of the United States, in author's file.
[31] Sulgrove, p. 36.

good friend, a former president of the United States, Benjamin Harrison of Indianapolis.³² On that day, remarkably, Tom shot a record 110 ducks! An old photograph of this outing is reproduced below.

President Harrison passed away in March of that year but Thomas lived for three more years. An undated newspaper article with a large picture is headlined "General Thomas A. Morris Retires as President of Water Company." The text notes: "He will spend the remainder of his life in and around California.... General Morris left at once for his new home near San Diego ... in an effort to recuperate his health. General

---

³² This friend, Benjamin Harrison (1833-1901), twenty-third U.S. president, was the second in a direct line in his family to be president of the United States. This distinction is shared only with the Adams family of Massachusetts. Pres. Benjamin Harrison's great-grandfather, also named Benjamin (1740-1791), was a close friend of George Washington; lived in the beautiful James River Plantation "Berkeley," built in 1726; was a member of the Continental Congress and a signer of the Declaration of Independence, and thrice governor of Virginia. His younger son, William Henry Harrison (1773-1841), born at Berkeley, was a noted Indian fighter and the first secretary of the Northwest Territory. Known as "Old Tippecanoe," William Henry Harrison became the ninth U.S. president in 1841 but died of pneumonia after one month in office. Gen. Morris's friend, Benjamin Harrison, a grandson of William Henry Harrison, was born at North Bend, Ohio, near Cincinnati; admitted to the bar in 1853; moved to Indianapolis in 1854; was brigadier general in the Civil War; served one term as president, from 1889-1893; returned to private law practice; and died at Indianapolis, 13 March 1901. See *Encyclopedia Britannica* (1959), vol. 2, pp. 218-19. Mrs. Benjamin Harrison was the first president general of the Daughters of the American Revolution. See NSDAR 1995 calendar, August, published by NSDAR, 1994. The Harrison home in Indianapolis, near the Morris-Butler House Museum, is also open to the public as a museum.

Chapter X. Thomas Armstrong Morris: Ending a Full Life ♦ 191

Thomas Armstrong Morris in 1903, age ninety-two

Morris carries his ninety-two years lightly, but enfeebled legs prevent him from following his favorite pastime, hunting."

Over the years Indianapolis grew up around Turkey Run until it was surrounded and was the only open space in the area. Thomas held his twenty-three-acre estate together until after the death of his ill wife in 1883. Then the land was sold off as suburban building lots; large homes replaced the last open ground. Turkey Hill was finally knocked down, alas, by wreckers in 1898. Had this not happened it would surely have been restored by now and today would be an open museum.

Unfortunately, the author possesses not a single heirloom from that wonderful home of Thomas and Rachel—only memories passed down. What *happened* to everything? Where could it all have gone? There must have been numerous certificates, awards, honors, medals perhaps. She knows of no one in the family who has a single thing—a chair, a painting, or a piece of silver. And there must have been so many beautiful things which should be our treasures today. It is puzzling.

For several years this author tried very hard to find an oil portrait of General Morris, perhaps painted by Jacob Cox, because she had located portraits of some of his siblings and owns two of those. She has written to the Indianapolis Art Institute, the library, and the historical society and asked them to look around, but with no success. Because Thomas was the most famous of the family, it would seem logical that there is a portrait somewhere. On the other hand, he may have been one of those who couldn't be bothered with such foolishness.

Thomas died 22 March 1904 of "senile debility," having lived his last years in California with his daughter Eleanor, whose husband, Dr. John M. Chambers, had been deceased for twelve years. Although Thomas's peers were all gone, he was still greatly admired and respected. Quite naturally, there was a large attendance at his funeral service in Indianapolis, on 1 April 1904. He was buried beside Rachel in the Morris family plot in beautiful Crown Hill Cemetery, which he had helped to establish.

He was the oldest member of the Second Presbyterian Church. It was during Henry Ward Beecher's ministry that he became a member of that church, as well as Reverend Beecher's close friend.

Thomas was the oldest living graduate of the United States Military Academy. Obituaries at West Point and of the Order of the Loyal Legion and in several newspapers are all long and complimentary.

> His technical work had demonstrated the rare qualities of his mind, its logic, executive powers and prescience which made him sought after as head and manager of enterprises.... He never traveled beyond brief business visits to the east. His recreation was hunting and fishing.... His integrity was so absolute, his honesty not merely of heart, which is common, [but] of mind, which is uncommon, was so absolute [that] he not merely meant right, but knew right ... peerless quality of character.... Tom Morris's approval or disapproval of a proposition, his appearance at the head of a scheme was decisive.... It might be said that truth was his god. The lives of few men have been more the living truth than his was ... keenest possible

Chapter X. Thomas Armstrong Morris: Ending a Full Life ♦ 193

sense of humor ... deeply religious, but as in all things he expressed himself rather by deeds than words.[33]

So we come to the close of a long and productive life of a good and great man, of a "celebrated pathfinder, ... stalwart, ... indefatigable, ... a man of many talents. A respectful city mourned a near-centenarian's passing."[34]

Thomas Armstrong Morris, after only four years of schooling, as a boy of eighteen climbed onto a horse, rode to New York State to enter and, four years later, to graduate third in his class from our nation's West Point Military Academy.

Soon he was employed as the new state of Indiana's first engineer. He was conceiver and builder of Indiana's great "drainage ditch" in order to purify the land and water, then builder of the first turnpike in Indiana and builder of its first canal.

While still a cadet at West Point, Morris was surveyor of grounds of the first real state capitol of Indiana, and much later chairman of the commission, builder, and engineer of the second, which is still in use today. He was chief engineer and builder of the first railroad in Indiana and of the first railroad into its capital city. He was president of three railroads and chief engineer of five. Later, by necessity, he was appropriately appointed by the courts receiver of another, to save it.

An outstanding national accomplishment was conceiving and building the first union station in the United States. He was also builder and owner of a large flouring mill and a big city hotel. Thomas Morris was one of a group of early planners and trustees of the city's very beautiful cemetery, now a National Historic Landmark. He was president of a bank and an insurance company, builder and president of Indianapolis's first streetcar company, life trustee of the city's first gas company, and president of the city's water company. As a general in the United States Army, he was victor in the very first *land* battles of the Civil War, which took place in West Virginia.

Most appropriately, one of his obituaries said, "It has been many times remarked that no man in Indiana has had a life of so long-continued activity, and that it has fallen to his lot to be the first in more enterprises of different kinds, and all of public importance, than usually falls to the lot of any one person."[35]

---

[33] Obituary in author's file, n.d., n.p.
[34] Giffin, p. 46.
[35] Association of Graduates, U.S. Military Academy Annual Reunion, 14 June 1904, p. 187; Loyal Legion publication, "In Memoriam," p. 2.

Thomas Armstrong Morris will forever stand very tall in the history and the legend of the "new West."

Chapter X. Thomas A. Morris: Bibliography ♦ 195

SELECTED BIBLIOGRAPHY
Thomas Armstrong Morris

Bassler, Roy, ed. *The Collected Works of Abraham Lincoln.* Vol. 4. New Brunswick, N.J.: University Press, 1953.

Battle of Corrick's Ford, The. Booklet. Philippi, W.Va.: The First Land Battle Centennial, 1961.

Biographical History of Eminent and Self-made Men of the State of Indiana, A. Vol. 2. Arranged by Congressional districts. Cincinnati: Western Biographical Publishing Co., 1880.

Boatner, Mark Mayo, III. *The Civil War Dictionary.* New York: David McKay, 1959.

Bolton, Nathaniel. *Early History of Indianapolis and Central Indiana.* Indianapolis: Austin H. Brown, Printer, 1853.

Burt, Alvah Walford. *Cushman Genealogy and General History.* Greenfield, Ind.: Wm. Mitchell Printing Co., 1942.

Butterworth, Hezekiah. *In the Boyhood of Lincoln.* New York: D. Appleton & Co., 1898.

Carnes, Eva Margaret. *The Tygarts Valley Line, June - July 1861.* Philippi, W.Va.: First Land Battle of the Civil War Centennial Commemoration, Inc., 1961.

Coleman, Christopher B. "Thomas Armstrong Morris." *Dictionary of American Biography,* Dumas Malone, ed. New York: Charles Scribner & Sons, 1934.

Concise Dictionary of American Biography. New York: Charles Scribner & Sons, 1990.

Cullum, George W. *Biographies of Regular Officers and Graduates of the U. S. Military Academy at West Point, N.Y., from Its Establishment in 1802 to 1890.* Vol. 1, 3rd ed. Boston: Houghton, Mifflin, 1891.

Daniels, Wylie J. *The Village at the End of the Road: A Chapter in Early Indiana Railroad History.* Indianapolis: Indiana Historical Society, 1938.

Darrell, Ruth. *Pioneer Ancestors of Members of the Society of Indiana Pioneers.* Indianapolis, 1983.

Dayton, Ruth Woods. *The Beginning: Philippi 1861*. Booklet. Philippi, W.Va., n.d. First publication in *West Virginia History Magazine*, 1952.

Dunn, Jacob Piatt. *Greater Indianapolis: The History, the Industries, the Institutions, and the People of a City of Homes*. Vol. 1. Chicago: The Lewis Publishing Co., 1910.

———. *Indiana and Indianans*. Vol. 2. Chicago and New York: American Historical Society, 1919.

Fansler, Homer Floyd. *History of Tucker County, West Virginia*. Parsons, W.Va.: McClain Printing Co., 1962.

Giffin, Marjie Gates. *Water Runs Downhill*. Indianapolis: privately published by the Indianapolis Water Co., 1981.

Grayson, Andrew J. *Spirit of 1861, History of the Sixth Indiana Regiment in the Three Months' Campaign in West Virginia*. Madison, Ind.

Heitman, Francis Bernard. *Historical Register and Dictionary of the U.S. Army*. Vol. 1. Washington, D.C.: Government Printing Office, 1903.

Hoge, Mary R. *A House Divided*. Booklet. Philippi, W.Va., 1961.

Holloway, W. R. *Indianapolis, The Railroad City*. Indianapolis: Journal Print, 1870.

Howard, A. C. *Directory for the City of Indianapolis*. Indianapolis, 1857.

———. *Historical Sketch of Indianapolis*. Indianapolis: publisher not given, no date. Pamphlet published before *any* other written history of Indianapolis. In author's file.

Hyman, Max R. *The Journal Handbook of Indianapolis*. Indianapolis: Indianapolis Journal Newspaper Co., 1902.

———. *Indianapolis*. Indianapolis: News Journal Co., 1916.

———. *Indianapolis, An Outline History and Description of the Hoosier Capital*. Published in Commemoration of the Centennial Celebration of Indiana at Indianapolis, October Two to Fifteen. Indianapolis: Max R. Hyman, 1916.

(Indianapolis) *Journal*. May 1840, March 1904.

Indianapolis News. March 1904, 1965.

Indiana Roll of Honor. Charles Scribner & Sons.

Indianapolis Times. Dec. 1964.

Kettell, Thomas Prentice. *History of the Great Rebellion, from Its Commencement to Its Close, Giving an Account of Its Origin, the Secession of the Southern States and the Formation of the Confederate Government, the Concentration of the Military and Financial Resources of the Federal Government*. New York: N. C. Miller, 1862.

Chapter X. Thomas A. Morris: Bibliography ♦ 197

Leary, E. L. "Morris Brought First Railroad Here," in *Indianapolis Star*. 1 Jan. 1971.

Maxwell, Hu. *History of Tucker County, West Virginia*. Kingswood, W.Va.: Journal Printing House, Preston Publishing Co., 1884. Reprint, Parsons, W.Va.: McClain Printing Co., 1971.

Maxwell, Hu, and H. L. Swisher. *History of Hampshire County, West Virginia*. 1897. Reprint, Parsons, W.Va.: McClain Printing Co., 1972.

McCormick, David Isaac. Indiana Battlefield Commission. *Battleflags and Organizations of Indiana Regiments*. Indianapolis: Indiana Battle Flag Commission, 1928.

Merrill, Catherine. *The Soldier of Indiana in the War for the Union*. Vols. 1 and 2. Indianapolis: Merrill & Co., 1866-69.

Military Order of the Loyal Legion, The. *In Memoriam: Thomas Armstrong Morris*. Headquarters Commandery of Indiana, 1904.

National Cyclopaedia of American Biography, The. Vol. 10. New York: James T. White & Co., 1900.

Nicholas, Anna. *The Story of Crown Hill*. Indianapolis: privately printed by Crown Hill Association, 1928.

Nowland, Jeanette Covert. *Hoosier City: The Story of Indianapolis*. New York: Julian Messner, Inc., 1943.

Nowland, John H. B. *Early Reminiscences of Indianapolis with Short Biographical Sketches of Its Early Citizens and a Few Prominent Business Men of the Present Day*. Indianapolis: Sentinel Book and Job Printing House, 1870.

Reminiscences of West Point in the Olden Times. East Saginaw, Mich.: Evening News Printing and Binding House, 1886.

Derived from various sources, this publication is also a register of graduates of the U.S. Military Academy corrected to 1 Sept. 1886. The *Reminiscences* cover the eighteenth-century days at West Point before the U.S. Military Academy was established and ends in 1818 before Thomas A. Morris entered in 1830. A copy of this rare book is owned by Capt. Gordon Campbell of Durham, N.C., a descendant of the general's brother John.

Report of the Adjutant General of the State of Indiana, 1861-1865. Vol. 2.

Representative Men of Indiana. Vol. 2. 1889.

Seaver, J. Montgomery. *Morris Family Records*. Philadelphia: American Historical-Genealogical Society, 1924.

Smith, O. H. *Early Indiana Trials and Sketches*. Cincinnati: Moore, Wilstack, Keys, 1858.

Sons of Indiana: Stories of Indiana's Famous Sons. From series of newspaper messages entitled "Sons of Indiana." Indiana Bell Telephone Company, 1966.

Stevenson, David. *Indiana Roll of Honor.* Vol. 1. Indianapolis: A. D. Streight, 1864.

Sulgrove, B. R. *History of Indianapolis and Marion County, Indiana.* Philadelphia: L. H. Everts & Co., 1884. Reprint, Evansville, Ind: Unigraphic, 1974.

Thayer, William M. *The Pioneer Boy and How He Became President.* Cambridge: University Press, Welch, Bigelow & Co., 1864.

U.S. Military Academy. *Annual Reunion.* "June 14, 1904, No. 753, Class of 1834." *Thirty-fifth Annual Association of Graduates.* West Point: U.S. Military Academy, 1904.

U.S. Military Academy. Records of Association of Graduates. West Point, N.Y.

U.S. Military Academy. "Register of Officers and Cadets of the U.S. Military Academy, June 1831." West Point, N.Y

U. S. Official Army Records. *The War of the Rebellion.* Vol. 2, series 1. Washington: Government Printing Office, 1899. Includes record of all orders and correspondence of Gen. T. A. Morris in the West Virginia campaign.

Williams, Kenneth P. *Lincoln Finds a General: A Military Study of the Civil War.* Vols. 1 and 2. New York: Macmillan & Co., 1949. Reprint on p. 173 by permission of Simon & Schuster.

Wilson, James Grant, and John Fiske, eds. *Cyclopaedia of American Biography.* Vol. 4. New York: D. Appleton & Co., 1888.

Microfilm

T. A. Morris Records. One reel of film (one volume), Manuscripts and Archives in the West Virginia Collection, West Virginia University Library, Morgantown. Original in the possession of the Wells Memorial Library, Lafayette, Ind., 1961.

Copies of general orders, circulars, and letters issued and received by Brigadier General Morris of the First Brigade, Indiana Volunteers, from May through July 1861. Correspondents include Gen. George B. McClellan and Gen. Charles W. Hill. Most of the orders and letters pertain to the military operations of the U.S. Volunteers in Western Virginia under the command of Gen. McClellan during June and July. Morris was at Grafton, Philippi, Laurel Hill, Corrick's Ford, Belington, and Cheat Mountain.

Chapter XI

CHILDREN OF THOMAS A. and RACHEL MORRIS
John, Harry, Thomas, Eleanor, and Milton

To keep a lamp burning, we have to keep putting oil in it.
— Mother Theresa

ACCOUNTS FOLLOWING those of Thomas Armstrong Morris are bound to be an anticlimax. As is true in every family, some members distinguish themselves more than others. Yet it is the intent of this writer to document, as much as possible, all of the existing facts in her possession which concern our Morris family.

First, the direct line of descendants of Thomas Armstrong Morris will be discussed, because we have just described his illustrious life. Then, by returning to his pioneer parents, Rachael and Morris Morris II, their other eight children will be documented in chronological order.

* * * * *

As mentioned earlier in Chapter V, Thomas and Rachel had five children. Yet that great, important man unfortunately had but one son who produced a line of descendants—about whom we know.

After two years of marriage, a son was born and was named for his paternal (West) Virginia grandfather, John Morris II, with a middle name of Irwin, his mother's maiden name. What became of this boy who grew up in a great big house in the center of twenty-three acres? We know very little—only that he "served through the Civil War as a Lieutenant in the twentieth Indiana Battery."[1] There seems to be no record of his marriage or of his wife, only of two children, John and Helen I(rwin?), who might have married a Mr. Sould. John Irwin Morris died at age fifty-five of apoplexy. We know nothing more of this line, which seems very strange.

---

[1] Annual Reunion, "Thomas A. Morris," U.S. Military Academy, p. 189. The article mentions John as the oldest of Thomas's children and gives his war service.

Tom and Rachel's second child, Harry, was born two years after his brother and died at age two, so this young couple were very soon bereaved. There is no record of the cause of death.

Their only daughter, Eleanor Irwin, probably named for her great-grandmother, John II's wife, married an eminent physician, Dr. John M. Chambers. Dr. Chambers was born in Belfast, Ireland, but was also from Liverpool, England, and came to Indianapolis to begin a new practice in that small Midwestern town. It must have been a true love match aboard ship, followed by an elegant wedding in that huge Victorian house on the general's estate. Eleanor was twenty-six years old when she married.

For many years Dr. Chambers had been employed by the Cunard Line as ship surgeon.

In this way he met his future wife, Miss Nellie Morris, daughter of General Thomas A. Morris, when the father and daughter were making a trip abroad. He was a distinguished surgeon and one of the most popular teachers with medical students. During the active period of his professional career in Indianapolis [from 1875 to 1890], he was generally regarded by the profession as having almost encyclopedic knowledge of all departments of medicine. In the Medical College of Indiana he successively held the positions of demonstrator of anatomy, professor of anatomy, professor of theory and practice of medicine, and later professor of diseases of women. He is given credit for being the first to introduce antiseptic methods in the treating of wounds in the city of Indianapolis and the City Hospital.[2]

This account mentions only the father and daughter traveling abroad together. Other indications and notes lead this author to believe that Rachel was ill during the latter part of her life, although she lived to be seventy-one years old and probably suffered greatly without our modern pain relievers.

Sadly, Eleanor and John Chambers had no children to provide descendants. As wife of a very respected doctor and teacher and the daughter of General Morris, we must suppose that she was mistress of another fine household within the dictates of Victorian society. Without the responsibilities of child-rearing, Eleanor probably did a great deal of useful charity work. Her aged father spent his last years with her, when she was a widow living in California, until he died at age ninety-two.

---

[2] Anna Nicholas, *The Story of Crown Hill,* p. 232.

Chapter XI. Children of Thomas A. and Rachel Morris ♦ 201

The fifth and last child of Thomas and Rachel was Milton Aspden Morris, who married Emma Kennedy. They had one daughter, Gladys, who lived to be only eleven years old. "Milt" was married a second time, to Sarah Hurst, but had no other offspring. He was a member of the Loyal Legion, like his father, because of direct descendancy from a Civil War general. He was secretary of the Indiana Water Company in 1888 when his father was president,[3] but resigned the same day his father died.[4] This is also curious.

In 1898, when Turkey Hill, the old Thomas A. Morris homestead, was demolished by wreckers, Milton, who then lived in New York City, was one of the owners, along with his older brother, Thomas O'Neil Morris, who lived in Colorado. Milton also lived in Buffalo, New York, and Philadelphia, Pennsylvania.

* * * * *

This accounts for four of Thomas and Rachel's five children. None of these four left descendants. Only one of their five, the middle child, Thomas O'Neil Morris, carried on the family line. An account of him and his offspring follows in the next four chapters. How unfortunate that we know so little about these other siblings.

The Indianapolis newspapers' archives may contain more information, but the author did not have the opportunity to peruse this source.

---

[3] May R. Hyman, ed., *The Journal Handbook of Indianapolis*, p. 144.
[4] "General Thomas A. Morris Retires as President of Water Company," newspaper article, n.d., n.p., in author's file.

The "Morris Family Tree"

Chapter XII

> **THOMAS O'NEIL MORRIS and
> ESTELLE JANE GOODALE
> Middle Son of Thomas and Rachel**

*A nurtured strength of spirit to shield one in misfortune
.... No matter how full,... our lives must inevitably
remain, in some respects, random and incomplete.*
— New Horizons

THOMAS O'NEIL MORRIS, born in May 1846 in one of the largest homes in Indiana, grew up in an affluent, influential family as the son of a very prominent citizen and Civil War general. Like his elder brother John, four years his senior, he too served in the Civil War but only briefly. He enlisted in the army when he was eighteen, at the very end of the conflict. He "prepared in Major James M. Whittemore's ordinance corps ... "[1] and was a corporal in the 132d Indiana in 1864. Then, with the war over, in 1867 Tom entered Rensselaer Polytechnic Institute in Troy, New York, following in his father's footsteps in engineering. He graduated in 1870 as a civil engineer, like his father, then went to work at once for the Indianapolis and St. Louis Railroad as assistant engineer, a position he held for three years.

In November 1871, nearly two years after graduation, he married his sweetheart, Estelle Jane Goodale, one of two sisters in a well-to-do Rochester family. They were married in Christ Church in Rochester.[2] We may suppose that he had known her during his college years, for Rensselaer is not a great distance from Rochester and Vassar, where she had attended college for only a year but four years before their marriage. We find this happy, prosperous couple had first lived on Western Avenue in Indianapolis. In a little more than a year they had their first of six sons. "Stella" was petite, very feminine, and extremely artistic. *(My grandmother surely should have had some girls! She once confided that having only boys was a disappointment.)*

---

[1] Alumni Records, Rensselaer Polytechnic Institute, p. 409.
[2] "At home" announcement, in author's file.

Their first child was born at Turkey Hill, the homestead of his grandparents. He became a third Morris Morris but was never called that. He always used his middle name, Chester, a proud name in his mother's New England Goodale family since colonial times.

After three years as assistant engineer, Tom became general contractor of public works for another three years, then chief engineer of the Indianapolis, Cincinnati, and Lafayette Railroad, until 1884.[3] His father had been chief engineer long before, from 1852 to 1854, and then was president for three years. Much later, it became necessary for General Morris to take over as receiver of that same line from 1869 to 1872, to reorganize and save it.

Now son Tom was there, fifteen years later, as chief engineer holding the same position his father had once had. It must have made the general very proud to watch his son follow in his footsteps, assuming responsibility and leadership with a similar training and aptitude for civil engineering. The son, however, had many advantages, with a ready-made wealthy and social background to begin with.

Sometime before 1878, when Estelle's second son, Harold Chambers, was born, she and Tom moved into their own large Victorian mansion on a corner, at 52 Central Avenue, later renumbered 1108. It was a twelve-room, three-story brick building with tall, ceiling-high windows, a vine-covered front porch, a side porch, a gate, and a picket fence. It had *two* bathrooms and running water and gas in each bedroom, a "dummy elevator," stable, servants' quarters, "beautiful trees and lawn,... one of the finest homes."[4] This house rang with the activities of boys. An old photograph shows a backyard with nine boys of varying ages (two are black), mostly barefoot, in knee britches with suspenders, and all nine are wearing hats! Two of the boys are sitting high on bicycles with very large front wheels.

The boys also played a great deal in their grandfather's expansive grounds, in the orchards, and with the sons of the hired men. They felt close to and took great pride in their important grandfather, "the General," who encouraged their enterprises and helped finance bicycles and perhaps college.

The Tom Morrises lived well. They entertained a great deal and elegantly, with lovely furnishings and fine things. Stella really enjoyed being a grand lady. She dressed fashionably and was a handsome, talented woman who attended Christ Episcopal Church and saw that her sons went to Sunday School.

---

[3] Author's file.

[4] Unidentified newspaper article with picture, n.d., n.p., in author's file.

Chapter XII. Thomas O. Morris and Estelle Jane Goodale

But tragedy entered this busy household in July 1883, only a very few months after the author's father, the fifth son, was born. Young Harry (Harold Chambers), almost eight years old, was brought home, held out to his mother's arms dripping wet, and dead. He had drowned in the river. "Oma" once described to the author this horrible shock. Just five years later the family was saddened again when the youngest son, Frederick Davis, died at age two. He pushed and tipped himself over in his high chair to receive a fatal blow on his head from the sideboard, which probably was marble-topped.

In 1884, father Tom became engineer/maintenance-of-way for the Cincinnati, St. Louis, and Chicago Railway and branches,[5] a position he held for many years. Like his brothers, he too became a member of the Loyal Legion, that honorary society for descendants of Civil War officers. This could have been due to the influence of his wife, for Estelle was always very interested and proud of both sides of their families' ancestors, and joined the Daughters of the American Revolution.

Estelle Jane Goodale Morris was born in Mount Morris, New York, and lived in Rochester for about four years before her marriage. Vassar College, not very far away, opened in 1865. Stella attended at the beginning but only for a year, in 1866-1867. Had she stayed she would have been in the first graduating class. The author recalls her tale of helping to select Vassar's colors, rose and gray. All her life, like her mother, she did beautiful needlework and crocheting. It became fashionable to do wood burning, at which she was very adept. Her mind and her fingers were truly creative. Eventually she studied wood carving at Purdue University. Wood carving was in their curriculum at that time, although there exist no attendance records for those years.[6]

About 1893 (when the author's father was ten years old and could remember), Stella hired a carpenter or cabinet maker to build a heavy, solid desk and accompanying bench. Both of these she carved expertly, covering them with graceful, delicate flowers, butterflies, ivy, and designs, each representing some attribute. Her initials are carved on the bench. The set is quite an unusual and beautiful creation. The author's middle name is Estelle and the desk and bench were willed to her.

Educating the children, planning social events, managing the servants, sewing, and corresponding made a full-time job for most matriarchs of those large Victorian homes. Some well-to-do ladies of her period had leisure time while servants tended the large home and, to some

---

[5] Rensselaer records.
[6] Vassar College records.

extent, the family. Stella seemed to have managed also to pursue her artistic talents to a high degree of accomplishment.

* * * * *

The four living sons were growing up, but the good life they had all enjoyed together was fast disappearing. Tom was "away" more and more and evidently "took up the life of a railroad man—gambling, wine, and women" (the author's father's only words on this matter—ever). The family fortune was fast depleted. One uncle said of him that he had always had too much given to him all of his life, that he was spoiled by his parents' affluence, as are many sons of wealthy families.

Stella was left to cope with four developing sons, a big house, mounting bills, disgrace, and heartbreak. The third son, Stanley, left home for California when the house was gone. (His maternal grandparents lived in California.) He was sixteen; he never returned. This broken marriage of Tom and Stella resulted in divorce, a rather unusual occurrence in those days. Very little of all this tragic "disgrace" was ever mentioned in the author's family. They were ashamed and embarrassed. The author just remembers the sadness of Stella's life and her vivid descriptions of the glorious past; those recollections would rejuvenate her temporarily.

Stella remarried in 1897, but it was not to be a happy marriage for long. Tom remarried a year later but that alliance was also very brief.

In 1898 a newspaper article appeared with headlines:

T. O. MORRIS HAS RESIGNED.... Thomas O. Morris, chief engineer of the Chicago division of the Big Four, yesterday resigned.... The resignation of Mr. Morris caused great surprise among railroad men here, and will create surprise all over the country, for he is one of the best-known civil engineers in the railroad business. He has been with the Big Four for thirty-two years, and his father at one time was president of the road. The west end of the division was built under his direction and supervision. He took great pride in his work and frequently said he would leave it as a monument to himself. For several months Mr. Morris has not been in good health, and the duties of his office have been wearing on him, and he decided to take a long rest. He may return to railroad work after a while, but on that point he is undecided.[7]

---

[7] Unidentified newspaper article, 6 July 1898, n.p., in author's file.

Chapter XII. Thomas O. Morris and Estelle Jane Goodale ♦ 207

An undated clipping indicates somewhat the sad situation:

MANY ARTICLES OF FURNITURE TAKEN FROM THE MORRIS HOME.... The family moved from the house some time ago, and most of the furniture had been removed ... two women, police ... under the supposition that the family of Mr. Morris had deserted it, and that the things left were not wanted ... many others in the neighborhood had ... helped themselves ... abandoned since last July ... commonly understood the contents had been abandoned by the owners.... Mr. Morris said he valued the property and his son, M. C. Morris [Chester, in California], had a quantity of things there ... involves a number of respectable families in the neighborhood.[8]

Still another undated clipping gives a complete description of the Tom Morris home with a photograph of it, and an announcement of an auction of "this beautiful home."

Tom left Indiana and was in Colorado by 1898, for he is mentioned in an article concerning the large old homestead of his father, the beloved general, "in the hands of the wreckers.... It is owned by two sons of General Morris, Thomas O. of Colorado Springs, and Milton A. Morris of New York City."[9] Leaving the value of his house to two "less fortunate" sons must have been his way of trying to help them to the last. So Tom was not *then* destitute, but he was to end up a poor and broken man. He died at only sixty-eight, in 1916 in Denver at the home of his eldest son, Chester, who, like his father, had nothing. It was up to brothers Donald and Theodore to have his ashes brought to the Morris plot in Indianapolis.

Stella held a lifetime pass on the railroad, so she was able to make trips to California to visit her parents, who had moved from Rochester because of better weather for her father's failing health. (This is the same reason her father-in-law, Thomas Armstrong Morris, had gone to California to live with his daughter Eleanor. Florida, with its warm weather, although closer, had not yet been developed as a desirable attraction.) Stella also traveled by train to the East to visit son "Theo" and family.

She spent her remaining years in a small apartment in Indianapolis living very frugally. Whatever happened to all their beautiful things, to her jewels and the finery she loved so much? The Morris money was *all* gone. There was no inheritance. Both Donald and Theo had to borrow and work for small wages in order to finance their own college education

---

[8] Unidentified newspaper article, n.p., n.d., in author's file.
[9] Ibid.

while continuing to support their mother, financially and otherwise, until the end of her long, lonely later years.

It had been a life that began so splendidly but ended so sadly. Pride in the achievements of her three living sons kept her buoyed, however. Donald and Theo and their families were her lifeline to the end of her ninety years. Stanley was little help, for he lived in California and Honolulu, which in those times without airplane travel was very far away. But he did keep in touch, and gave her much to be proud of.

* * * * *

How dreadful that the evils of alcoholism, excessive gambling, and infidelity could conquer one fine, educated man, and eventually disgrace and destroy a whole family, their splendid home, and their happy, wholesome life together. It was somewhat the downfall of a dynasty, with only Donald, out of six sons, to remain in that city to restore a respected family name. And he did—in his own way!

Chapter XIII

**CHILDREN OF TOM and ESTELLE MORRIS
Morris III, Harold, Donald, Stanley, Theodore, and
Frederick**

> *One ship drives east and another drives west
> With the selfsame winds that blow,
> 'Tis the set of the sails
> And not the gales
> Which tell us the way to go.*
>
> — Ella Wheeler Wilcox

ALTHOUGH he was always called "Ches," Tom and Estelle Morris's firstborn bore the illustrious family name of Morris Chester Morris. But unfortunately he left no legacy of any kind, for he did not inherit the leadership qualities of his great ancestors. We only know that he left home but not when, and that he married twice and had a son, "Billy" Patterson Morris, who was born in 1909 in Colorado. Very late in life Ches took in his neglectful, rundown father, who soon died there. Then he wired his two brothers, Donald and Theo: "No funds available," and they took over the responsibility of having their father's ashes brought back to Crown Hill. Thirteen years later Chester himself died in a state institution in Pueblo, almost blind, at only fifty-seven, unlike his long-lived family. Again his brothers had to take over and bring their brother's ashes back to the family plot. Son Billy has never been located.

We know already of Tom and Estelle's second son, Harold, and little Harry's tragic drowning at age seven.

Very, very different was the third son, Donald Seymour Morris, who became a brilliant, successful, and well-loved man. Comparing the portrait of Morris Morris II to a good photograph of Donald, we can readily see that the latter had the strong Morris face and a remarkable resemblance to his great-grandfather. It seems that Donald emulated him as well in his attributes of moral leadership and community outreach.

Having been active in all athletics and captain of the football team, he graduated from Shortridge High School in Indianapolis in 1897. Then he chose the profession of that great-grandfather, graduating first in his class from Indiana Law School to become a fine attorney. His final averages for ten subjects each year were 97.8 and 97.4! The records, signed by Dean Fishback, still exist. An old photograph shows him in uniform as a member of the National Guard in 1918.

Donald practiced law for fifteen years. In 1915 he was made an assistant trust officer of the large Fletcher Savings Trust Company of Indianapolis, with whom he was associated for thirty-nine years, eventually becoming chief counsel, vice president, and trust officer. (During this time the bank's name was changed.) After leaving the bank, he remained on the board of directors and resumed private practice.

George Bernard Shaw once said, "I am of the opinion that my life belongs to the whole community, and as long as I live, it is my privilege to do for it whatever I can." This also seems to have been the philosophy, belief, and practice of Donald. A list of his activities found among his papers gives credence to a published remark: "... [T]he enthusiasm shown by Donald S. Morris, not only for his business but for his community, is truly inspirational!"[1]

Donald S. Morris, Esq.

When one reads a curriculum vitae like his, one knows it represents years of dedication to rise to the top leadership. It involves the commitment of countless hours of time—for meetings, responsibilities, and work—for a city that may never realize the effort expended. Donald was director of the Boys Club of Indianapolis and of the Marion County Tuberculosis Association; very active in the work of the United Fund; the Republican member of the Indianapolis Board of Safety for nine years; twice appointed by the mayor to have jurisdiction over the police and fire departments; treasurer of the Indianapolis Bar Association; on the board of managers of Crown Hill Cemetery (from June 1926, as a descendant of an original trustee); and leader for many years, with his wife, of the Great Books Club. He was a member of the Indiana Bar Association, the Masons, Oriental Lodge No. 500, the Lawyers' Club, the Chamber of Commerce, the Gentlemen's Literary Club, the Society of Indiana Pioneers (as a descendant of one

---

[1] *The Teller,* bank publication, n.d., p. 6, in author's file.

Chapter XIII. Children of Tom and Estelle Morris ♦ 211

before 1830), the Loyal Legion (as a descendant of a Civil War officer), the Woodstock Club, the Athletic Club, and the Indianapolis Country Club.

Blessed with an unusual amount of vigor and energy, very like his grandfather and great-grandfather, his favorite hobbies were fishing and hunting. Donald played seventy-two holes of golf on his seventy-second birthday!

He married Lucy MacDaniel (daughter of his mother's second husband) and had two children. They divorced much later and Donald married again.

Donald died in 1964 at age eighty-six. He was a respected, successful person, kindly, generous to a fault, proud of his heritage, and interested in genealogy. He never traveled, except when, late in life, he and his second wife, Mary (Wildhack), took an extensive automobile trip through the southern United States—and another to Mexico—with his brother Theodore and wife Lisette. These two brothers were always close and kept in touch with each other more than any of the rest of the family.

Donald and Lucy's first child, Josephine, attended Barnard College but left it to study law, like her father, and graduated from law school at a time when few women did. She married Robert McKee twice. They had only one son, a fine, handsome young man with great promise who graduated from Harvard Medical School. After begetting four children, he met a tragic death by automobile in 1964, a shocking loss to the family. Of those four children, both boys have died; daughters Katherine and Josephine McKee were last known living in Bennington, Vermont, but did not communicate.

Donald's only son, Morris Morris IV, was not at all like his father and was a great disappointment to a traditional family, although he did attend college briefly and served in World War II. He married an English girl; had twin sons in 1949, Steven and Andrew; divorced; lived a solitary life; and died at age sixty-six.

Steven graduated from Purdue, married, and was last known, in 1983, to be living in Glen Ellyn, Illinois, working as a programmer for the Fermi National Accelerator Laboratory in Batavia. Contact has since been lost. Andrew was living in Indianapolis but did not respond to the author's letter. These twins are the only two males with the name Morris descending from Donald's line.

The next two sons of Tom and Estelle Morris, Stanley and Theodore, tended to be much more like their father and grandfather, inheriting their talents and interests in engineering, constructing, and creating.

Stanley Sherwood Morris, the fourth son, had a career which was sometimes daring and adventurous, if not profitable. He apparently never finished school, yet became a good electrical engineer and held very responsible positions in spite of his lack of advanced technical training. Self-taught, he had a fine mind and a knack for engineering.

Stanley went to California in 1897 as a young boy of sixteen when his family's home in Indianapolis was broken up. His maternal grandparents, the Goodales, had moved there from New York State in 1896, which may have been part of the reason for his going there. Apparently he never returned. He was a volunteer in the Spanish American War and served for its duration with the Seventh California Volunteers.[2] After marriage at age twenty-one, he sired a son and a daughter.

"The list of his executive electrical jobs—installation and maintenance —would read something like a footnote to the history of California's industrial expansion during the decades since the turn of the century.

"... Just some of his major electrical construction jobs [were] Fort Mason, California, the San Francisco Federal Reserve Bank (a three-year task), the Otis Elevator Plant there, the Clift Hotel, the Alameda Tube, the Sears Roebuck Building, and not a few others...."[3] In early 1900 he installed and was in charge of the electrical part of the Tower of Jewels, a magnificent, sparkling, electrically-lighted building at the San Francisco World's Fair. In the early 1930s, he went prospecting for gold in northern California but that proved unsuccessful.

Stanley "put in considerable pioneer service for Uncle Sam, directly in the interests of national defense and expansion ... rehabilitation of several navy destroyers ... [and] the great Sunnyvale airbase."[4]

In 1935 he was the electrical chief of the very first constructional expedition to Midway Island for Pan American Airlines. A group of forty-four technicians and many workmen went by ship, with much cargo, stopping first in Hawaii, then on to Midway, Wake, and Guam, in the vanguard of a gigantic aviation project. These islands had been isolated for centuries, being off the course of regular trans-Pacific shipping. One was uninhabited. Construction of airbases involved the establishment of operating facilities. This was to be the "first *aerial* causeway across the Pacific."[5] Later, he went to Wake Island and made another trip to Samoa, when Pan American's facilities were being established there.

Electrifying and building airbases on these outer islands made it possible for Pan American Airlines to fly to the Orient, and thus began

---

[2] Documents in author's file.
[3] *Ka Hoku o Red Hill*, p. 2.
[4] Ibid.
[5] Ibid., emphasis added.

Chapter XIII. Children of Tom and Estelle Morris ♦ 213

long-distance air travel to far-off places previously reached only by ship. It also made it possible, not much later, for the United States to win World War II, for its chain of islands became links to Japan. If Pan Am had not developed these islands, there would have been no already-in-place airbases. These were vital to the United States.

Stanley had many experiences which he thoughtfully shared in his letters, sending gifts of beautiful tapa cloth, dolls, and oil paintings he himself created and framed in bamboo, having inherited some of his mother's artistic talent.

More than a year before World War II, he served his country in Hawaii as electrical superintendent of Camp Red Hill, concerned with "defense projects in Hawaii and other Pacific Islands, but not affiliated financially with either the Navy Yard or any of the various contractors of defense projects."[6] He was in Pearl Harbor during its bombing and continued working there during the war.

"Here where a vital national defense project has taken shape literally under the hands that shaped and wove the mesh of electrical wiring to make it run, Morris has brought out of a barren hilltop a vast and complicated organization whose every spurt of power must depend upon his skill to keep the essential current alive.... There flows ... into Red Hill some 10,000 horsepower of electric power which is ingeniously diverted through a system of substations into its several functions.... He has done that job well and may walk with considerable respect among his fellow men."[7]

Stanley S. Morris

A photograph labeled "Controller of the Current" shows a "bland, wise craftsman, Stanley S. Morris, Red Hill's electrical superintendent."[8] We can detect the inventive mind of the grandfather, General Morris, but, alas, without the West Point education. Stanley was sixty at the be-

---

[6] "Science and Invention," *Literary Digest*, 23, March 1935, p. 162; *Honolulu Star Bulletin*, 4 April 1935, p. 1.
[7] *Ka Hoku o Red Mill* (a newspaper), Honolulu, Hawaii, 13 Dec. 1941.
[8] Ibid.

ginning of World War II. He died at seventy-two, back home in California, not rich but worldly.

Stanley's daughter, Estelle, called "Pat," married three times, losing her last husband in the war. She bore no children.

Stanley Jr. was another self-made man. He owned and managed the Merchants Credit Association in San Francisco, was an ardent outdoorsman, very civic-minded, active in youth projects and in the Chinese community. Married twice, he provided many descendants for this Morris family. His first child, Mary Louise, married Charles Friley in North Dakota. They had Susan; Stanley Sherwood Morris III, who lived only three days; William; and Timothy.

Stanley Jr.'s second marriage was a long and happy one, resulting in a son whom he also named Stanley Sherwood Morris III. Stanley Jr. had altogether four children who lived and eight grandchildren, all listed in detail in the Genealogy at the back of this book.

Continuing the chronology of the six sons of Tom and Estelle Morris, the fifth was Theodore Hatfield Morris, the author's father, whose life will be narrated in the following two chapters.

So we come to the sixth and last of these Morris brothers: little Frederick Davis Morris, who was born two years after Theo and lived but two and one-half years. He died of spinal fever resulting from tipping himself over in his highchair to strike his head against the sideboard. This became the second lost child for poor Stella, in despair, not many years before her home life was to deteriorate completely. (Stella was Estelle, wife of Thomas O'Neil Morris. This same accident had happened in the previous generation to a child who would have been this baby's uncle had they both lived.)

There are at present six male Morrises from Stanley's line. Adding the twin cousins from Donald's Indianapolis line gives a total of only eight *male* descendants of General Thomas Morris to carry on the family name—a bit surprising in view of the fact that earlier families were so large. See the indexed Genealogy for many more details.

Chapter XIV

THEODORE HATFIELD MORRIS
Early Years

Those who sought to strive,
To sense the wonder there
Were glad to be alive
To live more free and fair.
— Anonymous

THE FIFTH MORRIS SON was "Theo," my father. "*Another* boy," my grandmother must have groaned inwardly!*

Daddy and I were always very close. He lived nine years longer than my mother, quite near to us in a lovely retirement home, so my husband and I saw him often all that time he was a widower. We were able to know him very well. As the years passed, I was freer of other duties and had more time to be with him. Also, I was more mature and better able to appreciate him. Aging for both of us had a mellowing effect. He delighted our friends with his natural humor and interesting stories, and he was very often included in social gatherings. There was a fine rapport and compatibility between us. I became aware of the fact that there must be more Morris genes in me than those of my dear, gentle mother's family. My father and I were a lot alike. How I wish now that I had asked more questions!

Although Theo always greatly admired his grandfather ("the General") and also became an engineer, unlike him, he did not become a community leader, a great conceiver and builder. Instead, he spent his free time designing, drawing to scale, crafting and making things, in addition to spending many, many hours in the yard and his extensive gardens. He loved to grow things—trees, bushes, fruit, vegetables, rare plants, and flowers. He was also a collector, a historian, and a saver, hence many clippings are now in my files.

---

* Because of the very personal nature of this and the following chapter, the first person singular has been used.

But not until after his death did I find his collection of early Indiana books, photographs, old clippings, and pages of handwritten notes. I'm glad they still exist. Because they give insight into a late-nineteenth-century boyhood, I have chosen several of his anecdotes to relate—trivial perhaps, but revealing.

Theodore Hatfield was named for the doctor who either attempted to rescue or assisted after the drowning of his older brother, Harold Chambers. The drowning occurred only a month and a half after Theo was born. That tragedy for a young nursing mother must have been almost unbearable.

Theo grew up with three older brothers in a large Victorian city home with a carriage house at the rear, part of a bustling household with servants, bicycles, pets, and all the usual activities of a social, well-to-do, influential family in Indianapolis. Only two years after the arrival of Theo, the sixth and last son, Frederick, arrived. Petite, artistic Estelle was frustrated, having wished so long for a girl.

A charming photograph of the six boys shows five alive and a framed picture of Harold, the second son who had drowned. Each boy is very dressed up—for the picture, of course. The older ones are wearing large, stiff white collars and big neck bows. Theo, beside the baby all decked out in white frills, looks about four years old. He is wearing high button shoes, long dark stockings, a velvet dress and hat, and a bib collar and cuffs, each trimmed with ermine fur. Long, very blond curls hang below his shoulders, and the face is cherubic.

Those long curls remind me of the way he finally managed to get his mother to cut them off. Playing in the fields of tall grasses with his older brothers, he easily persuaded them to fill his hair with cockleburs—lots and lots of burs. They clung persistently, as he had planned, and became more and more tangled and impossible to remove. The curls were shorn! But his mother always did win the weekly battle of wearing shoes to Sunday School. The boys' feet grew bigger and wider all summer long as they went barefoot, so of course wearing shoes was torture.

Theo had a pet billy goat who, daily, stood on the roof of his tiny house eating the grass that grew on it while he waited for his adoring master to return from school. Then away they went, the billy goat pulling Theo in a little cart! Also, he often rode around on his big high bicycle, perched up in the air on a seat behind an enormous wheel. This was the design of that day. Grandfather Morris's extensive grounds and orchards played a great part in their lives, as did the "crick" for swimming, boating, and canoeing. James Whitcomb Riley and Booth Tarkington were older playmates—actually good friends of Theo's (and my mother's)

Chapter XIV. Theodore Hatfield Morris: Early Years ♦ 217

brothers. This was a time long before Cub Scouts, Little League, and organized school activities that now keep boys busy. They made their own fun in the woods and fields. The black sons of the servants were their good friends and very much a part of their gang.

According to a newspaper clipping, one of them, "James Brown ... without a rabbit foot ... was 'jonered.' A few weeks ago he made an aerial flight on the cover of a manhole leading to a junction of gas mains, into which he had intentionally dropped a match. He ascended amid a scene of flames considerably burned.... The black skin had not yet grown over the white, his friends said, when he was again the victim of another painful accident. Supporting himself on the step of another boy's bicycle [this was Theo's!], he turned his foot, which was bare [of course], into the chain of the bicycle. The big toe was carried onto the sprocket and almost entirely torn off. His companions carried him to Dr. Malone's home where the physician put him under chloroform and amputated the toe."[1] Can you imagine this story in today's newspaper?

Stanley, Theo's older brother, was nearly blinded for a while and bore a partially disfigured face for life because of the lack of laws and restraints for hazardous fireworks. The boys were behind the barn when he, carefree, lighted one firecracker and the entire bundle of hundreds exploded in his face all at once.

Another undated clipping is different and interesting. "Captures Alleged Thief—Passerby Takes Up Chase—Bold Prowler Surprised in Dwelling ... is Overtaken — an exciting chase.... Theodore Morris of 128 East 32nd Street was the captor.... While [the servant in the entered home] was getting the revolver, Morris, who was passing the house, took up the chase, and after covering two squares, caught up with the negro. Not daunted by Johnson's action in reaching for his hip pocket, as though he had a weapon and intended to use it, Morris caught the man and held him until Edmunds arrived with his revolver. [An officer] from police headquarters relieved Morris of the prisoner and sent him to the City Prison."[2]

I guess if you were a proud young hero and a saver too, you might very well have kept this clipping for many years.

* * * * *

The dedication of the World's Columbian Exposition took place in October of 1892 in Chicago, in celebration of the four hundred years follow-

---

[1] Unidentified newspaper, n.p., n.d., in author's files.
[2] Ibid.

ing Columbus's discovery of America. Actually, this magnificent World's Fair was not ready and didn't open until the next May, in 1893. This was the first time in history that such a worldwide assembly of peoples and the developments of civilization were brought together. A colonnaded park, a lagoon with real gondolas, and elaborate buildings of foreign architecture brimming with exhibits created a memorable feeling of brotherhood. Theo attended this wondrous event with his mother when he was only ten and very impressionable. They were proud too, for his mother's mother, Elizabeth Jane (Davis) Goodale of Rochester, New York, had won a prestigious citation and a blue ribbon in the international competition of women's handwork for her creation of a gossamer, hand-knit lace wedding dress, which took sixteen months of steady application to make. (Today this heirloom is treasured by the great-great-great-granddaughter who wore it last, in 1993.) Theo often talked of that World's Fair although he was later to attend several others with more and more new wonders.

There is a fine old-fashioned, formal photograph of Theo at fourteen which shows a very handsome face, a tight-fitting new suit, shirt with a wing collar, knee britches with long black stockings, shiny high-button shoes, and a boutonniere in his lapel. The flower suggests that this picture was probably taken at the time of his mother's second marriage, which occurred that same year.

An attractive printed program still exists within a handmade cover tied with black and gold ribbon of the graduating exercise of the June Class of 1899, Room No. 12, School No. 3, 16 June 1899. The Class Roll contains thirty-three names including Theodore Morris, who had just reached sixteen. Accompanying this is a diploma, certified and signed from the Indianapolis School District Schools. Who else in the world would have saved all this memorabilia but my father, who savored his childhood memories.

The next educational step was Manual Training High School, "one high school where girls are not in the majority, an attraction to boys because the training is regarded as a preparation for business studies, and practical work."[3] In 1899-1900 it had 927 enrolled of whom 476 were boys. The mechanical course required both freehand and mechanical drawing, and advanced work in science and mechanics. There was a year of woodworking—bench working and turning, a year of forging, one in foundry and pattern work, and one in mechanic fitting—all this in high school!

---

[3] Article in author's files.

Chapter XIV. Theodore Hatfield Morris: Early Years ♦ 219

All his friends were going to college so he left high school a year early and entered Purdue University without having graduated from high school, probably an impossibility today. But he had to spend five years instead of the usual four to finish college, which he never regretted. During these he was an active member of the Tippicanoe Club and the Sigma Kappa Fraternity, which provided many good friends, youthful pranks, and long-lasting happy memories. His college "vacations" were spent working in Baltimore at special apprenticeships in machine shops of the Baltimore and Ohio Railroad, and at the Atlas Engineering and Boiler Works in Indianapolis—for $1.00 a week.

No alumnus was ever more proud of or loyal to his alma mater than Theodore Morris. He never ceased to be amazed at new discoveries. In later years the earliest astronauts who were at Purdue were a source of prideful conversation for Theo. Theo graduated as one of 216 seniors in Fowler Hall (no longer standing) in June 1906 with a bachelor of science degree in mechanical engineering, one of "73 mechanicals." Among his memorabilia is his graduation thesis, titled "A Combined Test of a Stirling Boiler and a Chandler and Taylor Engine Direct-Connected to a 75 KW Bullock Generator in Purdue University Power Plant."[4]

(After my mother's death, my father, long retired, finally attended a class reunion, his sixtieth, which he truly enjoyed. I recall his remarking that there wasn't a single building standing which was there when he was in college.)

"My first job on graduating from Purdue ... was with the Buffalo Forge Company performing supervision, design, testing, and installation of heating and ventilating machinery, at a salary of $40.00 a month. Willis Carrier was the chief engineer with a salary of $40.00 a week. I had the privilege of working for him on some of his first experiments in air conditioning."[5] *Time Magazine* said of Willis Carrier "... In 1902 his corporate heirs [said he was] air conditioning's Edison [who] designed his first system for a Brooklyn printing plant. [Muggy air was wrinkling the paper for *Judge Magazine*.]."[6]

Two years later Theodore worked for the Indianapolis Water Company as a machinist doing maintenance work, where his grandfather had been president until his death five years prior to this. During this period in Indianapolis Theo belonged to the Maennerchor, a large German singing club. He had a fine voice but never learned to read music. In

---

[4] Theodore Hatfield Morris college thesis, in author's file.
[5] Theodore Hatfield Morris manuscript, in author's file.
[6] *Time Magazine*, 27 July 1962, p. 42.

1909 he returned to Buffalo as a salesman for the Barber Asphalt Company and was later promoted to sales manager of the machinery division.

Back in 1911 the Masons were an important part of many men's lives; the members felt a strong loyalty and sense of fraternity. Theo was initiated into Austin Lodge No. 850 AF and AM in Chicago. Masonic activities held his interest for many years following.

Next we see newspaper headlines "... Theodore Morris Battles Against Death." Three separate articles and a drawing concern a perilous yachting accident in July 1910. This occurred during the Columbia Yacht Club races on Lake Michigan, which ended in "disaster, danger, and spectacular rescues for several of the craft contesting for the Sir Thomas Lipton Trophy. Battles 40-mile gale over an hour ... ten miles out the 21-foot sloop Bilposter capsized ... four sailors were thrown into the water ... clung to sides of their slippery, bobbing craft ... another yacht went ... mast cracked in the gale ... another went ... too windy to go alongside .... cast a line ... one by one they crept along the rope to the Evanston ... cut line ... rescued from death by another yacht ... left Bilposter bottom side up ... another yacht, a steamship, and wireless had a part in the rescue ... race continued ... only two finished in the 21-foot class."[7]

Naturally those sailors never forgot this. *I'm* glad they were saved!

*   *   *   *   *

Having written this chapter years ago, it seems now very different from the preceding ones, composed as it is of selected trivia. I reflect, however, that these accounts were originally written only for my family, when I was intent on recording a few of the many tales my Dad had told to me. For my family, at least, they seemed precious, interesting, some amusing. Now they seem to reveal a more carefree, less cautious, less supervised childhood in those days.

---

[7] Unidenified newspaper in author's file, n.p., n.d.

Chapter XV

THEODORE HATFIELD MORRIS and LISETTE SUSANNA KRAUSS
Maturing

With love we celebrate
Their works of heart and hand and mind,
Their graceful gifts of life to humankind.
We gratefully bless their noblest dreams.
— Anonymous

ALTHOUGH A RESIDENT of Chicago in 1911, Theo's trips by train back to Indianapolis became very frequent, for he was in love with a beautiful girl, Lisette Susanna Krauss, with whom he had played as a small child but more often with her three brothers. The Morris home and the Krauss home were on parallel streets, so for years there was a family joke about who lived behind the other. Once when "Settie" was a very little child, Theo took her for a ride in his billy-goat cart and dumped her onto the road. He was never allowed to forget it!

When Settie was only eight and again at thirteen she broke her arm. She was always an active, athletic girl.

But as the teen years passed these two young people had seen little of each other, and each became engaged to marry someone else. Subsequently each of them broke their engagements. Settie was often beau-ed by her two older brothers and she had a happy social life. Growing up in a solid, hardworking German family which prospered, she often traveled with her parents. Her father frequently cruised to Europe just to get away from the telephone and his businesses: a thriving haberdashery, a large shirt factory, and a big-city mechanized laundry which occupied a whole city block and maintained a large barn full of delivery horses and wagons.

For several summers the Krauss entourage traveled to the Rocky Mountains and rode into Estes Park on a buckboard. At that time there was no national park and Estes was only a crossroad in the woods. Settie's health was not very hearty, although she had always been athletic and was a fine swimmer. As a precaution against tuberculosis, the western mountains were a good place to vacation, away from scorching Indiana summers. Lisette went to Germany for three summers and had some serious beaus there. She often pondered the fate of her German friends and family during World War I.

Settie's plans had been made to enter Vassar, along with good friends and two very close cousins, the Frenzel sisters; even her room had been assigned. But poor health prevented her going to college, and she unhappily remained behind, to teach Sunday School to "her" special favorite little five-year-old boys. Missing college was a great disappointment. She was an excellent horsewoman, had her own horse which she rode sidesaddle, took fencing lessons, and drove the Krauss automobile, one of the first in Indianapolis. In those days it was rather brave and unusual for a girl to drive.

At twenty-eight, then a beautiful lady, Lisette married my father, who was also twenty-eight and handsome in his maturing years. (Remember, they had both been previously engaged.) Their wedding was in the Krauss's huge Victorian house on North Park Avenue, where she and her four siblings were all born. The wedding took place on an April evening, followed by a gala seated dinner served to a very large gathering in the parlor, music room, dining room, and the spacious library.

Lisette Susanna Krauss
and
Theodore H. Morris

Chapter XV. Theodore H. and Lisette K. Morris ♦ 223

They traveled on no honeymoon but went straight to their little house in Indianapolis. Theo went to work as usual the next day. He had left the Chicago company in February and by now had set up a new business to sell Chase trucks, the "Morris Motor Sales Company," with his brother, three brothers-in-law, and his father-in-law, all incorporators. (Presumably this occurred so Settie could remain in Indianapolis.) This arrangement was short-lived, however, and nineteen months later Theo was back in Chicago with the Barber Asphalt Company, with wife and new baby of two months.

Like many another daughter, Settie went "home" to have her first child, and a little girl was born in 1913, a year and a half after the wedding. This baby was often transported in a basket specially built for her which just fit in the Pullman seat on the train from Chicago to Indianapolis. Before she was quite three she was taken along on a Great Lakes Shriners' cruise, Indianapolis to Buffalo, wearing a miniature fez, for her grandfather, Paul Krauss, was then the grand potentate of the Indianapolis Shriners. That same year, 1916, she posed for a photograph taken beside the very *first* airplane about to fly from Chicago to New York. That was then a wonderful occasion and a remarkable feat.

Theo was made director of the Barber Asphalt Company's manufacturing division, the Iroquois Iron Works, which produced steam rollers, tanks, asphalt mixing plants, and machinery—in Buffalo. This meant a move to that cold and windy city. But always there were Christmases and Easters back in Indianapolis for both sides of the family lived there. Summers were generally at Elkhart Lake in Wisconsin with the Krausses.

A promotion for Theo in April 1917 meant a move to Philadelphia, and this family of three prepared to drive the long journey in their open "Tin Lizzy." The little four-year-old girl (the author), all dressed to leave in her new winter coat, accidentally fell into the neighbor's sandbox, which was three feet deep with stagnant and muddy rainwater. Ugh! What was Mother to do? The child traveled in borrowed clothes. From Buffalo to St. Davids, a suburb on the Philadelphia Main Line, took five long, grueling driving days. Roads, maps, directions, and cars were quite different in May 1917, when there were no such things as route numbers.

Almost immediately, Theo contracted influenza and for three weeks was in the hospital near death. They didn't even know a doctor. Poor Settie, a stranger to the neighborhood and the area, had much to cope with during those first months in the East.

I dimly recall a few attempts at camping, for my father was enthusiastic and purchased tent, utensils, cots, and netting at the Army-Navy

Store, surplus from World War I, but camping was not my mother's "cup of tea," although she enjoyed picnicking a great deal.

In the spring of 1918 a son was born to Theo and Lisette. Like both his parents, he was very blonde with beautiful curls. No two people ever loved children more, and their joy was complete. *He could carry on the Morris name!*

About 1919, Theo started his own business, a partnership of Staley and Morris in Philadelphia, which handled contractors' and municipal equipment, employing eight salesmen and several mechanics. This company grew and prospered for quite a few years.

Sometimes grandparents came from the "West" to visit. But always at Christmas, for years, there were overnight Pullman trips "back home" to Indianapolis to stay with generous and loving grandparents and to play with many cousins.

One day tragedy struck. A strange man arrived at the front door, which Settie opened. He was holding a limp, dead little body and said brusquely, "Is this your child?" The shock was terrible. Teddy, who would have been three years old in another month, had been playing with a neighbor's child and was under the care of the neighbor. The little boys were pulling toys on the sidewalk; Teddy ran into the street. An automobile ran over him, dragging the wagon also under the car. The driver was not at fault and was later exonerated.

The long train ride to Indianapolis for burial was horrible. My family just *couldn't* come back to live in that house for over a year, so shaken were they by this accident. We went to live in a very nice boarding house in Devon, a nearby suburb, while they slowly recovered from their loss.

It was here that ingenious Theo put together first one and then two of the very first crystal radio sets. He had one ready for the first public broadcast, where there was intense excitement in that parlor, disbelief when the first sounds came from that little box, and great admiration for Mr. Morris by the assemblage!

Finally back in their own home, it was several years before they were really cheerful. I recall very long afternoon walks "trying to get strong."

One afternoon I jumped off the school bus, as usual, and ran toward the opposite sidewalk—just one block from where my brother was killed. There were no bus-stop laws then. A car knocked me down, ran over my leg and stopped. The chauffeur was as shaken as I, but saw that I was not hurt and he drove off! It was many months before I could bring myself to tell my parents of this incident, this near miss. It preyed on my con-

Chapter XV. Theodore H. and Lisette K. Morris ♦ 225

science desperately, but, though only a little girl, I thought I should not upset them further with my careless mishap. How close I had come to being a second tragedy for them! So I was never allowed to have a two-wheeler—I never asked for one.

Settie and Theo wanted so very much—expected for years—to have more children, but they didn't. If only today's knowledge had been available then, for of all the people in the world, *they* should have raised a large family. Feeling sorry for their only child, thoughtfully, generously, they often took one of my friends along on weekend trips to take the place of the sister and brother I didn't have.

Settie was burdened many years with serious foot trouble and even worse with her eyes. Innumerable long, all-day trips to doctors in Philadelphia didn't seem to help the glaucoma enough and she eventually lost the sight in her left eye completely, in spite of the fact that she was a patient of the very well-known Dr. George L. deSchweinitz. Could the aching heart, the nervous disorder caused by loss of a child have led to these disabilities? They developed close on the heels of Teddy's accident.

In 1925 they bought a larger, more spacious home in Wayne, an adjoining suburb, and proceeded to develop their bare half-acre into a beautiful yard with large perennial beds, rock garden, fish pool, rose garden, and very extensive vegetable and fruit gardens. This was done entirely by themselves over the years. In 1949, they received the Wayne Saturday Club Flower Show's coveted blue ribbon, first prize for "A Complete Garden—of great charm, with exceptionally beautiful beech and dogwood trees."[1] They raised gooseberries, currants, boysenberries, rhubarb, strawberries, quince, celery, asparagus, and fine herbs, as well as the usual vegetables.

Lisette Krauss Morris

Lisette won many awards in flower shows for specimen blossoms and arrangements. She had a "feel" for the artistic, loved beautiful things, possessed a treasure trove of family heirlooms and exquisite wedding presents. Entertaining was a real pleasure. One of her delights was parlor games, of which she had an endless collection. Her joy was in pleasing

---

[1] Author's file, 1976.

others. Her loves were children and flowers. Her generosity was boundless.

In the twenties the Wayne Men's Club sponsored an annual minstrel show which evolved into the Merrimen Minstrels. The chorus, in which Theo sang for several years, was always excellent. A newspaper article of 1937 mentions Theo Morris being added as a new "End Man."[2] He was always good at jokes, at whistling in a variety of different ways, and at harmonizing. Although he never had a music lesson in his life, he played the mandolin well and could pick up just about any instrument, string or horn, and make a tune.

In a similar way he could pick up any tool and use it. Although trained in mechanics, he was a fine electrician, carpenter and plumber, all hobbies, and could fix just about anything, often with a hairpin!

The early automobiles were a real joy to him, and once he completely took apart our beloved Overland "American Beauty," every single solitary part of its engine and body, every screw, bolt, pin, fender, running board—everything! This he did for sheer pleasure, much to Mother's consternation. And he put it all back together again with only one nut left over. In his later years he remarked that that feat would be impossible now, for the automobiles were so much more complicated.

His jokes and sense of humor were a joy throughout all our lives.

Theo eventually sold his share of the Staley and Morris Company, with the agreement that he would not enter the machinery business for a certain period of years. So real estate became a new field to explore and learn. It was a pleasant challenge which gave him a knowledge of the beautiful rolling countryside of eastern Pennsylvania, which he never ceased to admire, after a boyhood in flat Indiana.

Always a history buff, he delighted in seeking out local spots of historical interest and tripping to historical places. Philadelphia and Valley Forge provided much material for all the visiting Midwestern relatives. A nephew wrote: "I was always shy of adults as a child but felt a great affection and instant communication with Uncle Theo. I still cherish our infrequent but super times together: the trips to the Philadelphia houses, the visit to the little Revolutionary Church, and his descriptions and stories about the battlefields and historic points of interest around Wayne."[3]

Unfortunately, his ex-partner, Mr. Staley, did not make good his payments; court proceedings took place, resulting in a judgment against him, and not until many years later was the debt finally paid.

---

[2] "In Retrospect," *The Suburban and Wayne Times,* 23 April 1937, n.p.
[3] Letter in author's file.

Chapter XV. Theodore H. and Lisette K. Morris ♦ 227

Settie and Theo bought a charming farm site on which stood a colonial stone farmhouse much in need of repair. They had dreams of restoring and developing this as a country place and damming the stream for a pond. But times began to grow difficult and the Great Depression was soon upon them as well as all their associates. There was a rapid demise of many dreams, of good living, and eventually of security. Only those who can remember the scrimping, the jobless, men selling apples on street corners can realize the strength required of the adult population to bear those difficult years.

This was the time when I was to enter college, in 1931, the autumn when the bank failed, when everyone's savings were *lost*. In spite of this, they were wise, dear, self-sacrificing and farseeing. They somehow made it possible for me to remain in college, even when there was absolutely no work, no income, for years. In those hard times ingenuity and imagination came in very handy; endurance, kindliness, sympathy and patience were essential traits for well-being. Everybody saved everything; it became our way of life.

These were also lonely years with their only child away at college. Vacations were spent in Vermont, rather simply, or at the Krauss's rustic family lodge in very northern Wisconsin. We could be gone for long stretches of time, for there was no business, no work to come home for.

Again Settie had a serious illness: shingles so severe she was unable to attend my college graduation, for which they had sacrificed so much, and so painful she suffered continually and never fully recovered. Today's wonderful medicines and pain killers had not yet been discovered.

Then there was a small home wedding, simple but lovely in our beautiful garden, under a copper beech tree, and so appropriate near the end of the Depression. Anne came back from Virginia to marry the boy who lived up the hill—next door.

Finally, the clouds of the Depression began to lift, and both the Theodore H. Morris Company and his Bituminous Road Machinery Company in Wayne, Pennsylvania, began to pick up financially, as did the nation. "Design, production, and sale of municipal and contractors' plants and equipment"[4] filled his days. Later he also had general supervision of the design and production of asphalt mixing plants and machinery, of sand and stone dryers of his own patent.[5] Then for over ten years he was a very successful district representative for the Elgin Corporation,

---

[4] Document in author's file.

[5] "Aggregate Treating Apparatus, Asphalt Dryer. Combination hot and cold dryer for the production of mineral aggregates at predetermined temperatures." U.S. Patent Office, 11 December 1934; received many contracts in 1945 for production..

selling municipal sanitation machinery, mainly street sweepers and enclosed garbage collection units. He also represented Nicholas Engineering and Research Corporation of New York City, who made municipal incinerator plants and the road machinery patented by Theo.

In the winter of 1940, with neighbors who were dear friends, Settie and Theo took a Caribbean cruise on the *S.S. New Amsterdam* to St. Thomas, Cuba, Curaçao, and Venezuela. That fall they enjoyed a 6,000-mile Pullman tour of the West in an American Express special train. They went to Colorado, Yosemite, Santa Fe, the Grand Canyon, the Pacific Coast from Los Angeles to Seattle, and returned via Vancouver, Lake Louise, and Banff. Travel had become easier; trips were better planned.

When World War II came, it meant all kinds of sacrifices for everyone. Settie and Theo took into their home *all* the furniture and belongings of another entire household, as there was no longer any rentable storage space available. And along with the furniture came their daughter, with a four-year-old, a two-year-old, and a two-weeks-old baby. Settie and Theo unselfishly provided a haven and security for this little family for two whole years, while their son-in-law was overseas in the far Pacific, not heard from for months at a time.

Notwithstanding the turmoil of three very young children, they did everything in their power to provide a normal, happy home life during those distressful months. They truly enjoyed the children. My father made a sandbox, a seesaw, scooters, and a bunny cage. He put up the tent for them to play in and provided imaginative activities, for we could go nowhere. Even a trip to the grocery was an expedition in those gas-rationed days. These loving parents also supplied an endless amount of moral support so necessary to me as a young mother.

Theo's patriotism motivated an unselfish desire to serve his country even further, and he soon applied to the Civil Service Commission in Washington for federal employment. Then he volunteered for the brand new Port Security Force of the U.S. Coast Guard Reserve, first established in Philadelphia and eventually in every principal port city in the United States.[6] The required age limits were twenty-five to fifty. Theo was sixty, ten years over age, but he was determined. So it was necessary for him to persuade and then get special dispensation to enlist. All members were in for the duration, serving without pay, subject to strict Coast Guard discipline, even to courtmartial. They became known as the Watchdogs of the War Who Watched the Waterfront. Eventually there were about 2,600 Philadelphia businessmen to replace the regular Coast Guard, most of whom were then released for sea duty. Working three

---

[6] Documents and articles, 1 October 1943, in author's file.

Chapter XV. Theodore H. and Lisette K. Morris ◆ 229

Theodore H. Morris

eight-hour watches around the clock every fifth day or night, they safeguarded about ten miles of piers and warehouses, and the loading of ships for the war front. It was dreary work, often freezing cold, always dangerous and strenuous, with the same responsibilities, authority, and risks as a regular Coast Guardsman under military discipline.

Training was tough and included "anti-sabotage, anti-espionage, ship and dock knowledge, loading explosives, general fire prevention, airraid instruction, jujitsu,... how to use truncheons (clubs which they carried on duty),... and how to shoot."[7] Performing the real job was hazardous, and not a sinecure. This was "the first time Americans have been privileged to serve in this type of organization since the founding of our Republic."[8] This Reserve Force of busines men from all walks of life was "superimposed upon the ordinary civilian life of the volunteers, for only in that way could it aid the sore manpower problems."[9] These tireless men continued to carry on their regular businesses as well. This operation then "materially facilitated the safe and uninterrupted flow of our country's manpower and materials to the battle fronts of the world."[10]

One highlight of Theo's two years of patriotic endeavor, often under adverse conditions, was on Thanksgiving Day in 1944 when he was in charge of the Coast Guard detail responsible for the security of the Swedish Red Cross Mercy Ship *Saivo* in the Port of Philadelphia. It was loaded with food and clothing for the 49,000 American prisoners of war in Germany. This ship had come over loaded with Christmas bundles for the 281,344 German prisoners of war in this country. "The American Red Cross sends packages regularly ... the Germans do not send any of this collective relief for their men over here. The Christmas bundles were

---

[7] Warner Oliver, "They Cover the Waterfront," in *The Saturday Evening Post*, 31 July 1943, pp. 62-3.
[8] "Information, U.S. Coast Guard Volunteer Port Security Force," Philadelphia, Pa., 18 August 1943, p. 4., in author's file.
[9] Ibid.
[10] Citation from the Commandant of the U.S. Coast Guard, Washington, 4 August 1944, in author's file.

the only thing along that line that they have done for prisoners in America."[11]

It was a time of joy when, many months after the conclusion of the war in the Pacific, their son-in-law was able to return. Serious illness had struck this crowded household. So it surely was a time of relief when the family of five was finally able to move out, into their own house. Then generous Settie and Theo could again call their home their own. But they missed us.

Theo was a charter member of the Philadelphia Athletic Club, a thirty-second degree Mason, and a Shriner, member of Lulu Temple in Philadelphia.[12] He seemed most proud of his membership in the Military Order of the Loyal Legion,[13] his membership derived through descent from his Civil War grandfather, General Thomas A. Morris. Particularly in later years, genealogy became more of a consuming hobby; he was genuinely proud of his heritage, and rightfully. Once in a letter to his brother he wrote, "Talk about the marvelous happenings over the years—I cannot realize that we had and knew a grandfather born in 1811 before there was a railroad in this or any other country, when Jefferson and many other famous boys were still on deck, and George Washington had been dead only twelve years!"[14]

After the war clouds had cleared, in 1947 the Morrises took an extensive automobile trip to Yellowstone and came back through the magnificent Canadian Rockies. In the winter of 1949 they returned to Cuba, this time by plane with Settie's sister and her husband. The next winter they went to Yucatan in Mexico and to Guatemala, driving back with friends through New Orleans and the Deep South. That summer they enjoyed a St. Lawrence cruise from Montreal to Quebec, the Saguenay River, and Murray Bay.

The next year, 1951, a Caribbean cruise to Puerto Rico, the Dominican Republic, Haiti, and Jamaica provided more colorful subjects for Theo to photograph. He was an excellent photographer and often entertained with fine slide shows.

In August 1953 they flew to Europe, taking an extensive Grand Tour. It was Theo's first trip to the Continent and the first for Settie since her girlhood.

---

[11] "Mercy Ship Laden with Cheer for War Prisoners," *The Evening Bulletin*, 2 December 1944.
[12] Document dated 21 May 1926, in author's file.
[13] Document dated 14 May 1953, in author's file.
[14] Theodore H. Morris to Donald Morris, in author's file.

Chapter XV. Theodore H. and Lisette K. Morris ♦ 231

Theo had experienced one severe heart attack before this trip and had had to be hospitalized. After that he was always very careful but never had a serious recurrence. Generally he was a very healthy gentleman.

In September 1954 when he was over seventy-one, Theo finally retired from business. They had saved for many years toward their future in retirement but had lost *all* their savings in the Depression. Now, with ample time and means for travel, they drove in 1955 to Mexico, with Theo's brother Donald and his wife, the former Mary Wildback, as traveling companions. This trip resulted in many unusual experiences in the back country with the natives.

From that time on they spent their winters in a cottage in Hollywood, Florida, then a small town with only one hotel, occasionally taking along some family. Each of their four grandchildren, individually, had the opportunity of enjoying a long, educational, sightseeing automobile trip to Florida. They each had a summer vacation in Wisconsin and even a "Grand Tour" of Europe. These grandparents' generosity and thoughtfulness were immeasurable.

The most impressive trip of all for Theo and Settie was in 1958: their three-month Mediterranean cruise on the Greek ship *Olympia*. For this their enthusiasm was boundless, because of their interest in and appreciation of all other cultures and history.

By 1956 the big house and extensive gardens were becoming a burden to this active but aging couple, and they found a smaller home just a few blocks away. It, too, had a patio and a lovely yard with a grape arbor and smaller garden, which delighted them for quite a few years.

In the last years, pleasure and interest in their grandchildren was uppermost. They lived for others, always. While on a trip to Virginia taking the oldest grandchild to college, Settie experienced her first stroke, and then began the deterioration which resulted in a fatal stroke three years later, in 1965. She was exactly eighty-two, a small and gentle *lady,* a brave and loving noble woman.

The loss was severe, a poignant separation especially for her husband, for they were a most devoted couple who shared a full measure of true affection and understanding. Theo lived alone only a year, during which he took a Caribbean cruise and attended his sixtieth class reunion at Purdue University. Then he moved into a fine retirement home[15] near his daughter's house, where he made friends easily and was well-liked. A trip alone—that is, with no family member but with a tour group—to Scandinavia and Lapland was interesting. For nearly ten years he carried on a useful and contented life before passing on at age ninety-one and a

---

[15] Methodist Country House, 4830 Kennett Pike, Wilmington, Delaware.

half. He was alert, humorous, interested and interesting up until the very end, beloved by all who knew him. He danced with a nurse the week before he died!

* * * * *

A prophet once said, "Your old men shall dream dreams, your young men shall see visions."[16] Looking back, it seems to me that this loving couple, who had their share of tribulations, were fortunate enough to experience both visions and dreams. Born into the late nineteenth century with its gaslights and buggies, they lived through a remarkable period in history. They were able to experience the development of electricity and the many advances made possible because of it; of sound transmitted via telephone and radio; the wonders of television; of movement by motors into the air and across oceans, and by rockets even up into outer space.

They witnessed the enlarging of man's thoughts and comprehension, of greater freedom and democracy encompassing not just a single people or country but the whole world. Lisette and Theo, wise enough to realize this great change in the lifestyle of people all over the world, often marveled and appreciated as they observed and participated. Forthright, morally excellent and strong, their principles always remained high.

They gave joy, wisdom, and fun, displayed patience and endurance. "Heaven sent" and blessed with love and caring, they possessed a genuine love of life. Both of them were dearly loved in return by all who knew them—very special people of their time. They epitomized the aphorism, "Love is the strongest force in the world, one of the few things to give away and still have more than ever left over."

* * * * *

In order to be consistent and trace the descendants of each family line, it should be recorded here that Theodore and Lisette Morris had only one child who lived to adulthood, a daughter, Anne Estelle Morris, born in 1913. She married Walter Day Mertz. They had four children and eleven grandchildren.[17]

Their first child, Suzanne Day (Mertz) Smalley of Nashville, Tennessee, is an art history researcher and librarian and has three daughters: Anna (Smalley) Flanagan, Sallie Smalley, and Martha Smalley. The second daughter, Elizabeth Morris (Mertz) O'Brien of New Jersey, is a special education teacher of English-as-a-second-language to young foreign children, and mother of two daughters: Kathleen (O'Brien) Rose and

---

[16] *The Holy Bible,* Book of Joel, Chapter 2, Verse 28.
[17] As of August 1995.

Chapter XV. Theodore H. and Lisette K. Morris ♦ 233

Tracy Morris (O'Brien) Boullé. Their older son, Walter Day Mertz Jr. of Fort Valley, Virginia, is a mediator and father of three sons: Walter D. Mertz III, Jonathan Frederick Mertz, and Andrew Mackay Mertz. Their second son, Theodore Morris Mertz of Foxboro, Massachusetts, is a banker and father of three sons: Gregory Morris Mertz, Peter Tyler Mertz, and David Allerton Mertz.

Grandchildren are the glue that holds the generations together. See the complete Genealogy in Part Three of this book for more details of this family as well as for other branches of the Morris family.

Because "Teddy," the second child and only son of Theodore and Lisette Susanna Morris (of this chapter), was killed in early childhood, they have no descendants with the surname of Morris. Their descendants comprise their daughter, Anne Morris Mertz; and her four children and eleven grandchildren: eight male Mertzes and seven females, five of whom (the two Mertz daughters and three granddaughters) have already changed their name through marriage.

The "Morris Family Tree"

Chapter XVI

AUSTIN W. MORRIS and JANE MARIA PEPPARD
Firstborn of Morris and Rachael

Uncompromising integrity,
Sharing themselves and their beliefs
With their whole community.

HAVING WRITTEN of only one line of descent from the Indiana pioneers, Morris and Rachael Morris, it is appropriate to return now to that same generation and tell of the other eight children. All but one grew to adulthood. Thomas Armstrong Morris was taken out of chronological order because he was by far the most illustrious. Nearly all the others became a special leader or married one, and are mentioned in published history books. "The Royal Family," as they were sometimes called, all living for a time together in a city square block, a family complex, was possibly an appropriate name for this second generation—an influential, well-to-do group of good citizens of Indianapolis.

* * * * *

Austin W.* was the first of Morris and Rachael's nine children. Born in Bourbon County, Kentucky, on 8 August 1804,[1] Austin grew up in the "western" wilderness. As a child he lived first in Ellisville, then in Carlisle, both in Nicholas County, Kentucky. He was a young lad of seventeen when his pious forty-year-old father, reluctant to raise his family amid slavery, decided to move once again, this time northward into the brand new, to-be-slave-free state of Indiana. Austin accompanied his father on their first trip to Indianapolis, in early spring, to purchase land and plant corn on the bluffs of White River.[2] Then they returned to Kentucky for the rest of the family, who came up in the autumn of 1821. We can imagine that because he was the oldest of (then) six children and

---

* No record has been found of what W. represented.
[1] 1880 census of Indianapolis; family records.
[2] John H. B. Nowland, *Early Reminiscences of Indianapolis*, p. 105; 1850 census of Indianapolis.

having just reached his seventeenth birthday the month before, he necessarily shouldered much responsibility and shared a great deal of the physical work for his family in this roadless, forested, swampy settlement. They farmed in the early years, but the land had to be cleared first. Big, strong sons were a real asset.

The earliest recorded mention of Austin is in the fall of 1824 when he was one of the organizers of the "Indianapolis Legislature," a group which existed for about ten years and has already been described, meeting weekly to discuss and debate important issues to come before the real state legislature. It was an important and influential group, whose membership also included Austin's father, Morris, his brother Thomas Armstrong, and his cousin John Frazee.

Austin is one of eight men listed as an early teacher in the "pay school" (there were no others in the early days of Indianapolis) of Mr. Ebenezer Sharp, which his younger brother Thomas attended.[3]

Austin is mentioned as a deputy state auditor and principal clerk, from 1828 until 1844. (His father held the *elected* position of state auditor during those exact same years.)[4]

By 1830 Austin was a very active Mason and was elected for five consecutive years grand secretary of the Grand Lodge of Indiana Masons. In Dunn's account of fraternal organizations, he says, "Austin W. Morris had been re-elected Grand Secretary in 1831, and, in that capacity, he was directed to take charge of the property of Center Lodge, which had failed to pay its annual dues, and to hold it until the lodge was reorganized and the debt paid. This was accomplished in 1835. From that time its condition was prosperous, and there was a general revival of Masonry throughout the state from the same time.... Austin W. Morris of Center Lodge in 1833 took an active part in the Grand Lodge meetings."[5] Again in 1839 he was elected grand secretary of the Grand Lodge and held that office continuously until his death in 1851.[6]

Jane Maria Peppard, born in New Jersey, had by now become an important part of Austin's life. They were married in March 1831, just a few days before Jane became nineteen; Austin was twenty-seven. She was the daughter of Francis Whitaker Peppard, the granddaughter of Nathaniel and Maria (Greer) Peppard, and the great-granddaughter of Joseph Greer, an Irishman born about 1740 who was the founder of the Greer family in America.

---

[3] Jacob Piatt Dunn, *Greater Indianapolis*, p. 81; Nathaniel Bolton, *Early History of Indianapolis and Central Indiana*, p. 169.
[4] *Indiana Freemason*, p. 372-3.
[5] B. R. Sulgrove, *History of Indianapolis and Marion County*, p. 368.
[6] *Indiana Freemason*, p. 373.

Chapter XVI. Austin W. Morris and Jane Maria Peppard ♦ 237

Austin was a lieutenant colonel in the Fortieth Regiment of the Indiana Militia in 1833. Probably nearly every able-bodied man in early Indianapolis served in this militia, a body of men enrolled and trained for emergency military service. Austin's father, Morris, was a colonel in the same organization. Indians had been an early danger, and could be again.

Jacob Dunn tells of Austin acting as secretary at a meeting of citizens held to discuss cooperation with the state in building and manning a firehouse to protect the new state capitol. His father and two other commissioners had been in charge of building it. Another mention of Austin relates his winning a prize for vegetables and eggs at a fair in the fall of 1836. He was then thirty-two. These fairs were the forerunners of the Indiana State Fair, established in 1852.

Described in early Indiana histories as a leading man in the community, a successful Whig, politician and legislator, Austin became a trustee of the Indianapolis Female Seminary, a trustee of Indiana Asbury University (later DePauw University), and clerk to the Indiana State Board of Canal Commissioners. Always interested in the politics of his new state, Austin Morris was elected a member of the Indiana State House of Representatives and served from 1836 to 1839 as clerk. He ran for state senator in 1833 and again in 1837, but lost both times, and for representative in 1841 and lost. He finally won an election, however, and became secretary of the state senate. He was also a presidential elector in 1836.[7]

Austin must have also been in the milling business with his brother Tom (mentioned in Chapter VIII) because Daniel's account not only mentions "the Royal Family" but also notes that the plot of land for the mill was in Austin's name.[8]

In 1846 he served on a vigilance committee organized to combat the increase of gambling in Indianapolis.[9] Another insight into this gentleman's character is revealed with the account of the Union Literary Society of 1846. They "had a few lectures delivered in churches by ... Henry Ward Beecher, Rev. Theodore Parker, and others, to considerable free audiences, the expense being paid by contributions from old citizens like ... Mr. Austin W. Morris ..." and six others mentioned.[10] Even Horace Greeley spoke to this society, on "Henry Clay." Austin at age forty-two was called "old"!

---

[7] *A Biographical Directory of the Indiana General Assembly 1816-1899*, vol. 1.

[8] Platt of Austin W. Morris dated 1 April 1846, recorded 7 May 1846, in Deed Record Q, p. 264, Office of Recorder of Marion County, from Wylie J. Daniels, *The Village at the End of the Road*, p. 35.

[9] Dunn, p. 155.

[10] Sulgrove, pp. 201-2.

Austin W. Morris   *Jane (Peppard) Morris*

Jane Maria (Peppard) Morris is the only one of the early Morris women to "make" the history books. She obviously was a doer, along with her well-to-do, "establishment," solid-citizen husband. Jane did more than raise a big family and manage a large household. She was the first president of the Widows' and Orphans' Asylum, chartered in 1851 dedicated to "affording relief to widows in distress, or procuring employment, and educating their children...." Jane was thirty-nine and already the mother of five living children. She was still president six years later when the Senate Act of Incorporation was signed in 1857 for the Indianapolis Orphans' Asylum, encouraging adoption as a solution to a growing child-care problem. This organization became the forerunner of the present Children's Bureau of Indianapolis.[11] Sulgrove gives the dates as formed in 1849 and chartered in 1850. "... oldest of local asylums of the city, uniformly well managed.... Largely dependent on the contribu-

---

[11] Letter from the Bureau's executive director, 1976, in author's file; W. R. Holloway, *Indianapolis, Railroad City*, p. 197; and recent Children's Bureau quarterly publication, vol. 1, no. 1, 1994.

Chapter XVI. Austin W. Morris and Jane Maria Peppard ♦ 239

tions of the charitable, the indefatigable zeal of its managers has succeeded in keeping it always in effective condition."[12]

This present organization celebrated 125 years of continual existence and uninterrupted service to children in February 1976 and has grown considerably since then. It has maintained a "Morris House," the first of several group homes in Indianapolis (1974) used first for disturbed young boys and today for girls fifteen to twenty-one, preparing young women for independent living. This home was named in honor of their founder and first president, Jane Maria (Peppard) Morris (Mrs. Austin W.). Her framed picture hangs there, a gift of the author.

Austin was an active member of the Indiana Historical Society. His name appears near the beginning of the list of signers of the constitution (prior to 1860) and three times as recording secretary in the early minutes.

It was in April 1849 that Morris and Rachael Morris gave to each of their children a large city lot, as described in previous chapters. According to the drawing on the original deed, A. W. Morris was assigned *two* plots on Illinois Street, Nos. 9 and 11, but not adjoining, and a plot for Morris Morris with a twelve-foot-wide alley between them. Later there was some buying and selling of land among the Morris children.[13]

A 1916 newspaper article describing residents in the once-fashionable residential section names the Morris Morris children and their lots. "Across from him [John D. Morris] was the Austin W. Morris mansion."[14] They lived on the southwest corner of Georgia and Meridian Streets in a very large Victorian house. A photograph taken in Civil War times shows the homestead with a gate, a white picket fence, and a large buckeye tree, a survivor of the original forest.[15] An article describes it as "... a big white frame house which occupied nearly a whole square."[16]

The 1850 census lists Austin W. Morris as "clerk," with two German servants. The value of his real estate was $40,000, a goodly sum for those days. He was a clerk in the government land office and also treasurer of the Indianapolis and Bellefontaine Railroad[17] (of which his

---

[12] Sulgrove, p. 382.
[13] Deeds of sale, in author's file.
[14] Unidentified newspaper article, 13 February 1916, n.p.
[15] *Indianapolis News*, 10 March 1909. Reily Morris Adams of Indianapolis owns a painting of this home.
[16] "Many Notable Names in Maryland Street's History," vol. 22, no. 276, n.d.
[17] *Indiana Freemason*.

brother Thomas was chief engineer and later president). When the central railroad system was organized, Austin was treasurer.[18]

Still active in the Grand Lodge, Austin helped plan a much-needed hall. The building committee consisted of three men, one being Gov. James Whitcomb, and another, Austin Morris.[19] Completed in the spring of 1851, the hall served as the scene of concerts, lectures, and most of the cultural life of the city.

Austin was named by the legislature as one of the incorporators of the Gaslight and Coke Utility, in 1851.[20] He and his family were members of Wesley Chapel of the Methodist Church.

The activities of this man, oldest son of a devoted, church-going community builder, indicate many of the same characteristics which were in his father, Morris Morris II. Austin, too, was generous and very civic minded, as was his wife. He also became a leading citizen with a leaning toward books and culture, from the time he was an early school teacher until his very last years, when he helped build a Masonic cultural hall and actively contributed his talents. He worked for many years in public service and was a well-respected community leader and the pride of his parents.

At the time of his death in 1851, when he was only forty-seven, there were many tributes. "One of the few men who leave their impress upon everything to which they direct their attention."[21] "He brought to the discharge of his duties a high degree of intelligence, an untiring industry, and unquestioned integrity.... [He was] one of the most highly respected Masons in Indiana."[22]

Jane was pregnant with their last child, Austin W. Jr., at the time of her husband's death. That same year a list of nineteen "large tax payers" was published, giving descending amounts. "According to the new assessment, the following persons own over $20,000 worth of taxables in the corporate limits of this city: ... [third from the top] Austin W. Morris's Heirs, $43,555...."[23] This throws some light on their relative wealth in 1851, the results of a conscientious, hard worker.

Ten years later the 1861 city directory listed Jane Morris as "widow," still residing at 53 South Meridian Street. Living with her was her son, age twenty-one, Lt. Louis Thompson Morris. "Mrs. Morris sold the house in 1865. It was used as a boarding house until 1874, when it

---

[18] O. H. Smith, *Early Indiana Trials and Sketches*, p. 424.
[19] Dunn, p. 374.
[20] Letter in author's file.
[21] *Indiana State Journal.*
[22] *Masonic Review.*
[23] Daniels, p. 93.

was torn down to meet the growing demands of the wholesale district along Meridian Street."[24] Jane died in New York City in 1877 of paralysis.[25]

> **Children of Austin W. and Jane Maria (Peppard) Morris and Their Offspring**

The author has attempted to trace these descendants, and the others of Morris and Rachael Morris, down to the present day, with the kind cooperation of living relatives.

Austin and Jane's first child, Gabrielle, died in infancy.

Their second, Josephine B., married her second-cousin, George Greer of New York City. This cousin relationship was through the Peppard-Greer line. Both Josephine and George were great-grandchildren of the Irish Joseph Greer who founded the Greer family in America.[26] Married in 1857, they lived in Rye, New York. George Greer had a partnership in his father's New York firm of Greer, Turner and Company, but soon after the death of his father in 1870 he sold his interest in this firm and retired from active business. He maintained directorships in the West Shore Railroad and other corporations. He was keenly interested in outdoor sports, especially fishing and hunting. Josephine and George had five children.

George Morris Greer was their first child. Born in New York City, he attended school there until he was fifteen, then tried the wholesale grocery business. Fascinated with the great outdoors, he became a cowboy at age twenty and moved to Cheyenne, Wyoming. There he pursued the cattle business and bought a ranch in 1877 in San Luis Valley, Colorado. This was the year he married Lena Dell, daughter of Mary (Campbell) and Benjamin Reuben Dell (originally the German Diehl). Mr. Dell was an early pioneer to Nebraska and a peripatetic miner, eventually settling down in Cripple Creek.

The George Morris Greers maintained their ranch until 1908, when they went to live in Denver. They had two sons: Theodore Morris Greer, who had no issue; and George Bates Greer, who had two children: George Bates Greer Jr. and Marjorie Isabella Greer, who married Charles Appell. There is George Bates III, also Michael Daly, Gregory Patrick,

---

[24] *Indianapolis News.*
[25] Crown Hill Cemetery records.
[26] *Greer,* family history belonging to George Bates Greer Jr. of Denver, privately printed 1977, pp. 5, 12.

and two girls, all Greers, in Denver. Their cousins are Christopher, Charles, Mark, Joseph, and two girls, all Appells, also in Denver.

To return chronologically to the family of Josephine (Morris) and George Greer: Following their first child, George Morris, came the second child, Austin Morris Greer. Very different from his older brother, he became a city man, a stock broker who for many years was a member of the New York Stock Exchange. Among his social affiliations were the Larchmont Yacht Club and the Seventh Regiment Veterans Club. He married Ida Northrup; there were no children.

Of the third offspring of Josephine (Morris) and George Greer, we know only his name, Theodore Morris Greer, also born in New York City. He lived to be only eighteen.

The fourth child was Louis Morris Greer, who attended the Kellogg School and graduated from Harvard University in 1891. He then attended Columbia Law School and subsequently embarked upon a business career. When he was only twenty-four years old, he acquired a seat on the New York Stock Exchange which he held from 1892 to 1900. He became a director of the Consolidated Gas Company and of the New York Carbide and Acetylene Company.

At age twenty-three Louis joined the New York National Guard. In the war with Spain he served as second lieutenant in the Fourteenth Regiment of the New York Volunteers. When he was thirty, he was commissioned major in the New York National Guard, served for fourteen years in the reserves, and then returned to active duty as zone supervisor of Manhattan and Westchester County under the compulsory Military Training Law of New York. Louis Greer was affiliated with Delta Phi and the following clubs: Piping Rock, Riding, Ardsley, Racquet and Tennis, Garden City Golf, University, and Down Town.

Just a month before he became forty, in 1908, Louis married Mabel Adele Seymour, who, it was said, was twelve years younger, "a perfectly proportioned figure ... alabaster skin ... a profusion of chestnut hair in a regal coil ... a soft English accent ... the girl who came from nowhere and snatched the prize."[27] She had been born in Manchester, England, the daughter of James and Charlotte (Barnes) Seymour, and came to the United States as a very young girl. Eventually Mabel Seymour became an actress, then a nurse, with a rather unknown background. She was strikingly beautiful.

---

[27] David W. Peck, *The Greer Case*, p. 4. David Peck was a judge of the Appellate Division of the New York State Supreme Court and for many years a partner in the eminent New York law firm of Sullivan and Cromwell.

Chapter XVI. Austin W. Morris and Jane Maria Peppard ♦ 243

These two, Louis—handsome, charming, rather dashing, and very, very rich, and enchanting Mabel—became members of "The 400" and for many years were a vital part of the social world. This was the era of pre-World War I elegance and postwar prosperity. Theirs was a very affluent lifestyle, with everything money could buy while Louis continued to amass a still larger fortune. They frequented the Fifth Avenue mansions and the estates in Newport, Bar Harbor and the Berkshire Hills. They had no children. There is a most unusual tale concerning them, following:

About these two David Peck has written a fascinating book, *The Greer Case, A True Court Drama*. A best seller published after they were both dead, the book is still available in libraries. Mr. Peck claimed to have written the book because the case was by far the most interesting and unusual he had ever encountered, "more drama, mystery, conflict, pathos, irony ... than one could dream up."[28]

Of Louis Morris Greer (Austin's grandson), Peck wrote, "Members of the present generation remember him as a leader in the realm of finance, an executive of the giant utility company which supplies the city of New York with gas and electricity.... An older generation remembered him as the exemplar of the elegant age, one of the manor born,"[29] remembered with his high hat, neat suit and walking stick. This "scion of one of America's first families," Louis died shortly before his wife, in 1946, leaving an estate valued at possibly $500,000—a fortune in 1946— and leaving Mabel, a strikingly beautiful young dowager who could "command the world" with her fortune and her beauty. But this was to be for only a very brief time. "Just before her death, Mrs. Greer had acknowledged that an illegitimate son had been born to her and Dr. Willard B. Segur of Ware, Massachusetts, when they were very young, and that Dr. Segur had adopted the child."[30]

This "lady with a past,"[31] Mabel Seymour Greer, soon died (10 August 1946) and willed her fortune to Harvard, her husband's alma mater, but Harold A. Segur, the [putative] adopted son, brought legal action to upset Mrs. Greer's will. A very long, tense legal battle followed to determine the issue of heirship, because a legal son could contest the will. The judge eventually ruled that Harold was *not* her son. Then a curious and persistent lawyer, Joseph A. Cox, later a justice of the New York Supreme Court, determined to locate the *real* illegitimate son, for there must have been one or why would Mabel have admitted to having one?

---

[28] Peck, preface, p. ix. Mrs. Charles Farquar ("Nannie") Haines, on a ship to Europe, became acquainted with the Armbrewsters mentioned in the book.
[29] Peck, p. 4.
[30] Peck, pp. 5, 6. Dr. Segur was born in 1865 and died in 1939.
[31] Peck, p. 31.

Many more months of searching ensued and another long court battle. Finally Willard *Seymour* (Mabel's maiden name), born in 1894, was proved the real illegitimate son. Disowned by his father, eventually abandoned by his mother, he had led a derelict life.

When this unfortunate human who might have inherited $500,000 was finally discovered, he had just died an alcoholic in Boston City Hospital and had been buried in a pauper's grave in Mt. Hope. Because he had been a ward of the State Board of Charity, Massachusetts was entitled to contest the validity of Mrs. Greer's will and lay claim to her property. This would have entailed a third lawsuit. "There is a long-standing comity between the Commonwealth [of Massachusetts] and its leading educational institution [Harvard]. They did not wish to litigate it further, and in the end they divided the financial stake."[32]

All this really concerned not a Morris descendant but the wife of one, a woman who in death had given the family a notoriety long avoided. Another member of the Morris family is mentioned in the book: Louis Greer's first cousin was Mrs. Desdemona Morris Delgado, "a gentle lady and a member of a family which had always had a distaste for publicity."[33] She had come to live in New York in 1912, had a "long intimacy" with Mrs. Greer, and had been with the Greers almost constantly. She was called to testify in court. So ended two intense trials which lasted for many months and became a familiar topic in most American households of the time.

Again returning to the chronological delineation of Josephine and George Greer's children: Their fifth and last child was Desdemona Morris Greer, sister of Louis of the trial drama. Also born in New York City, she lived to be only forty-two and never married. This name, Desdemona, as well as the nickname "Dessie" are found often in the Morris family.

* * * * *

Now we must return two generations back to continue chronologically with Austin and Jane (Peppard) Morris's children, who are the original subjects of this part of this chapter.

We come to Theodore, their third child, brother of the deceased infant Gabrielle, mentioned earlier, and also of Josephine, whose progeny were Greers. Theodore was tragically killed in 1855 near Lawrenceburg, New Jersey, by a train at the young age of nineteen.

---

[32] Peck, p. 205.
[33] Peck, p. 154.

Chapter XVI. Austin W. Morris and Jane Maria Peppard ♦ 245

The fourth child, Louis Thompson Morris, the aforementioned infantry lieutenant of the Civil War, made the United States Army his career. He became a major of the Third Cavalry, in 1889; then, a lieutenant colonel of the First, and later of the Fourth Cavalry. At the beginning of his career, when he was a first lieutenant in the Nineteenth U.S. Infantry, he joined the Loyal Legion,[34] the society of direct descendants of officers of the Civil War, described in detail in Chapter VI. He also became a member of the Sons of the American Revolution from his great-great-grandfather James Morris, although this name has since been *proven* incorrect. (See Endnotes to Chapter III.)

During the Civil War, Lt. Morris was made "Brevet Captain in 1864 for gallant and meritorious service during the Atlanta Campaign, and Major ... 1864 for [same] in the Battle of Nashville."[35] After the Civil War he fought on the Western plains against hostile Indians. He served his country with honor and distinction for more than forty years.[36] He served at Fort Clark in Texas and Fort Ethan Allen in Burlington, Vermont, and was the commanding officer of the Presidio in San Francisco during the Spanish-American War. He retired in 1898, lost his home in the San Francisco earthquake of that same year, died in 1899, and was buried in Arlington Cemetery.

Lt. Col. Louis T. Morris

Louis sired seven children: Louis Thompson Morris Jr., who lived only four years; Desdemona of renowned beauty, who had a son but no

---

[34] Loyal Legion, Indiana records, in author's file.
[35] Francis B. Heitman, *Historical Register and Dictionary of the U.S. Army*, vol. 1, p. 728; *Army and Navy Journal*, 10 June 1899, p. 984.
[36] Obituary, 1899, unidentified newspaper, n.p., in author's file.

grandchildren; Anna, who at twenty-one was killed in a horse accident; twins, who died of diphtheria at age six; handsome Horace McKay Morris, who became a well-known actor in the 1930s and '40s, playing opposite such illustrious actresses as Catherine Cornell, Kay Francis, Jessie Royce Landis (in "Colonel Satan"), and Mary Martin (in "Lute Song"). He was an intimate friend of Catherine Cornell and of John Barrymore. McKay never married.

And there was Leland, the only one of the seven to produce descendants. Leland Burnette Morris was born in 1886 in Texas (where his father was stationed at the time) and graduated from the University of Pennsylvania. Embarking on a long diplomatic career, he was in the U.S. Consular Service in Iceland, Greece, Turkey, Germany, Egypt, and Austria. Stationed in Vienna in World War II, he had the unhappy distinction of handing Germany's declaration of war to the U.S. representative, and America's declaration of war to Germany's representative. In 1917 he married Marie de Zaba of Venetian and French descent, although she was born in Smyrna, Turkey. Later Leland Morris served as inspector general for all the U.S. Central and South American embassies.

A 1942 Philadelphia newspaper article with photograph is interesting. "... nominated by President Roosevelt ... to be U.S. Minister to Iceland ... was Charge d'Affaires at the American Embassy in Berlin when the U.S. entered the war ... studied law ... and Turkish 1904-1909 at the University of Pennsylvania ... student interpreter at the embassy in Turkey in 1910 ... 1912-1913 Deputy Consul at

Ambassador Leland B. Morris and the Shah of Iran, in 1944

Chapter XVI. Austin W. Morris and Jane Maria Peppard ♦ 247

Cologne, Jerusalem, Alexandria, Vienna, and Cairo ... to Berlin in 1940."[37]

In 1944 President Franklin D. Roosevelt appointed Leland Morris the first U.S. Ambassador to the Shah of Iran.

After more than forty years in the U.S. Foreign Service, the Honorable Leland Morris retired and was appointed the U.S. representative on the United Nations Commission to conduct the plebiscite in Greece, after which King Paul and Queen Frederika were recalled. He lived in Greece two more years.

Then he became the director of a Foreign Service course at the Liberian Embassy in Washington. This class was for the officers of the new Liberian State Department who had arrived in the United States in June 1950. "His longtime tenure in the Foreign Service ... enabled him to interlineate the entire course ... to the Liberian trainees, with recitations of personal experiences [and] personal knowledge."[38]

His biography is in "Prominent American Morrises of Today," *Morris Family Records,* published in 1924.[39]

The only child of Leland Burnette Morris is Kenneth Archbell Morris. He graduated from Lawrenceville and Princeton; served in World War II and the Korean War as a commander in the Navy, with citations; was technical manager of information systems for the General Electric Company; project manager for the U.S. Secretary of Health, Education, and Welfare in Washington, D.C.; and adjunct professor at the U.S. International University in San Diego.[40] His wife, Lois, a graduate of Western Reserve University, was a script writer.

Kenneth had five children: three sons and two daughters. Only two sons are living: Jonathan Morris (b. 1953) a television engineer; and Jeffrey Morris (b. 1955), a former tennis coach now in sales management in San Diego. Both daughters are married. The elder bears the family name of Desdemona but is called "Desda." Formerly a ballet dancer in Hollywood, she is now an early childhood counselor with an M.A. in psychology in Los Angeles, and mother of Christienne Metropole (b. 1964) and Sabrina Lundquist (b. 1978). Kenneth's other daughter is Alexandra, a teacher and artist in San Diego, and mother of Domingo Lizarraga (b. 1975) in Los Angeles.

*   *   *   *   *

---

[37] *Philadelphia Evening Bulletin,* August 1942.
[38] Obituary, *The Listener,* 5 July 1950, n.p.
[39] J. Montgomery Seaver, *Morris Family Records,* p. 46
[40] This is the cousin from whom the author purchased the two old oil portraits of his great-grandparents, Austin and Jane Morris.

Austin and Jane's fifth child, Desdemona, married Richard Corwin, whose daughter married Walter E. Wallace of the English Navy. Their son, Corwin Wallace (b. 1906 in England), and a daughter, name unknown, may have descendants. Unfortunately, they are still "lost" to the writer.

Chapter XVII

MILTON MORRIS and ABIGAIL THAYER
Second Child of Morris and Rachael

A family is like a river: Some of it has passed on and more is to come, and nothing is still, because we all move along, day by day, toward our destination.
— Dolores Garcia,
Twentieth-century Chicana grandmother

CHILDREN OF THE SAME PARENTS and background often seem to develop very different characters. After learning about eldest son, Austin, and middle son, Thomas Armstrong, there is little to say of Milton, although indeed his life was a lot shorter. Unlike the rest of his brothers, he is not ever mentioned in the early histories. He was born in 1808 in Kentucky, in Bourbon or Nicholas County, where his father practiced law in Ellisville and Carlisle, the county seat. In 1821, when Milton was thirteen years old, he came with his family to the wilderness capital of Indianapolis. Being a strong young boy, he too shared much of the burden of clearing the land in preparation for farming. The children had to help and work hard.

By the time he was twenty-four, Milton had married Abigail Thayer, on 1 May 1832. He "was for several years a clerk for the late Nicholas McCarty, who was a well-loved merchant with a large business who was once a candidate for governor.[1] Milton then engaged in the mercantile business at Covington, Indiana, in Fountain County and was quite successful. He died in the south many years since, where he had gone with several boats laden with produce."[2]

These flatboats usually carried flour, whiskey, salt-cured pork, tobacco, and hemp. They are often pictured as small, open, raft-like floating barges carrying two or three young men with poles. Some barges

---

[1] In 1830, Rachael and Morris Morris named their ninth child Nicholas McCarty, for this man, evidently their very good friend. This infant, their last child, lived only seven months.
[2] John H. B. Nowland, *Early Reminiscences of Indianapolis*, p. 106.

[249]

were larger and enclosed with flat rooftops on which there would be as many as seven fellows sitting, lying, singing, or dancing, so the term "the jolly flatboatmen" evolved.

Boatmen usually returned overland along the Natchez Trace. Abraham Lincoln, also a young man in his early twenties and also from Indiana, made two trips down to New Orleans on a flatboat as a hired man, one before and one after 1830.

As related earlier in another context, it appears that Milton went down the Mississippi River toward the port of New Orleans and died en route, at the early age of twenty-seven. The date was 1 May 1835, also his third wedding anniversary. The place of death was probably Bayou Sara[3] in West Feliciana Parish, near Baton Rouge, Louisiana. No details of the accident have been found. Abigail had given birth to their first child, Caroline, less than three months before. This son death's was another real tragedy for the Morris family.

Grandparents did the natural thing in this unhappy situation and took in the young family, for how long we do not know. We know from the 1850 census that when Caroline was fifteen years old, she was living with her grandparents, Rachael and Morris Morris. When she was over twenty, Caroline married, on 5 September 1855, Fabricus "Brish" McCalla Mothershead, son of Nathaniel and Sarene Threlkeld Mothershead, who were relatives of Dr. John Leland Mothershead. Milton's younger sister, Melvina Morris, had married Dr. John in 1836, the year following Caroline's birth on 12 February 1835, in Covington, Indiana.

It was not until years later, in 1849, that Milton's parents gave the large city lots to each of their children, all in one city block, on which to build a home. This explains why there was never a building lot recorded for Milton: He had been dead fourteen years. They did give a lot to Caroline, however, when she was married; the author possesses the deed.

Caroline (Milton's child) and Fabricus moved often, judging from their children's birthplaces. Their first child was born in Indianapolis, the next two in Vernon, and the last in Mitchell, Indiana. One must think that they felt a part of and kept in touch with the family, because that generation and the next were given the frequently-used family names of Milton, Leland, Katherine, Desdemona, and Morris. Fabricus died when he was only forty-seven.

---

[3] Family records show Bayou "Sayre" and Bayou "Sare." There is no known place in Louisiana by either name. The courthouse-recorded deaths of Bayou Sara in West Feliciana Parish in St. Francisville date from only 1940. Bayou Sayle in St. Mary Parish near Franklin does not have records for the 1800s. Word-of-mouth and a southern accent could easily have produced "Sayre" from "Sara," hence the error in old family records.

Chapter XVII. Milton Morris and Abigail Thayer ♦ 251

We know of descent from only Caroline's oldest child, Katherine Bullard Mothershead, born 21 July 1856. She married James W. Wallace on 9 June 1883 in Columbus, Indiana, and bore two sons: Harry Mothershead Wallace, born 7 October 1884 in Columbus, and Leland Morris Wallace, born 18 April 1888 in Garden City, Kansas. The latter, Leland, had two daughters: Harriet Marie Wallace and Rose Katherine Wallace. These only two descendants of Milton are still "lost" to us, and were the only possible means of continuing this line of descent, as the following information will show.

Caroline's other three children must be recorded here although they too were "lost" even a generation earlier. The second child, Milton Morris Mothershead, was born 14 June 1858 and died 15 October 1874 at Vernon, Indiana, unmarried. The third child, Leland Moses Mothershead, was born 15 October 1854 at Vernon, married 22 November 1907 Alvina Liese but had no children. The fourth child, Desdemona "Dessie" Morris Mothershead, was born 22 February 1867 at Mitchell, Indiana; she also had no issue.

The "Morris Family Tree"

Chapter XVIII

JOHN D. MORRIS and MARTHA WILES
Fourth Son of Morris and Rachael

Take kindly the counsel of the years. Nurture the strength of spirit to shield you in sudden misfortune.
— Desiderata. Found in
Saint Paul's Church, Baltimore, 1692

MORRIS WAS FORTUNATE to have four sons in a row. They would grow up to help work the land, raise food, and, if necessary, protect the family. Young pioneers worked hard; everybody helped. John D. Morris, the fourth son, was born in 1818 in Carlisle, Kentucky, the county seat, where his father practiced law. He was almost six when his parents left there for the wilderness of Indiana.

Ebenezer Sharp came to Indianapolis in 1826. Shortly after that "he opened a school in the back part ... of the Presbyterian Church."[1] "Among Mr. Sharp's pupils were Thomas A. and John D. Morris....The former has risen to distinction in his profession, that of civil engineer, the ... latter might [have] in theirs, had they paid the attention they should have to the example and precept of their worthy tutor."[2] John's older brother Austin taught in that school for a while, located at the corner of Alabama and North Streets.

When John was twenty-two, "[i]n 1840 an epoch was marked by the organization of the Indianapolis band."[3] Their uniform was green coats, black, tight-fitting pantaloons, and black velvet caps. John D. Morris was listed among the charter members, and for more than five years it was quite a feature in the life of the town.[4] Its first service, in its own bandwagon, was to meet Henry Clay at the state line in 1840. Surely John's father was also there, for these two lawyers had been associates

---
[1] John H. B. Nowland, *Early Reminiscences of Indianapolis*, p. 219.
[2] Jacob Piatt Dunn, *Greater Indianapolis*, p. 134.
[3] Ibid., p. 235.
[4] Ibid.

[253]

years ago in Kentucky. When not playing in the band, John participated in Masonic Lodge affairs.

An amusing insight into the times is revealed by a wedding performed in 1840 in which John Morris was a groomsman. It was the first church wedding in Indianapolis, and the bride's brother, "the Beau Brummel of the town ... was attired for the occasion in the first dress suit worn in Indianapolis.... It was evidently the usual custom to send cake with wedding notices to the newspapers. In fact, the editor of the *Indianapolis Journal* served notice that if no cake was received with the marriage announcement, it would be put in small type in an outlandish corner of the page ... and if the editor attended the ceremony and kissed the bride, the notice would be in very large type with 'the best poetry that can be ... borrowed or coined from the editorial brain.'"[5] Times and customs have changed!

When John was twenty-five, he married Martha Ann Wiles, the daughter of William McKinley Wiles (related to President McKinley) and Nancy (Ames) Wiles. The Wiles were some of the earliest landowners in Indianapolis, even a few months before Rachael and Morris. They had bought seventy-four acres in Center Township outside the city in July 1821. Old records show, however, that little Catherine, third child of the Wiles, was born in Lebanon, Ohio, in September 1821, revealing a wise decision to have the prospective mother remain behind for the birthing in preference to an undeveloped place.

Unlike his brothers and brothers-in-law, John's activities have gone almost unrecorded. His name appears in only a few early histories, so we know less of his character and his occupations than of the others.

He and Martha first lived on Illinois and Jackson Place between Forty-fourth and Forty-seventh Streets. They eventually had six children, four boys and two girls. Like many early, big families, this one too had its share of sorrow, for their fourth child, little Johnny, died of an accidental fall before he was five.

Older brother Thomas built a grist and flour mill on South Pennsylvania Street in 1848. The 1850 census lists John Morris as being in the milling business, possibly with Thomas, but the mill burned in 1851. According to that year's census, John owned property worth $2,500 and had an Irish girl, probably a servant, living in his home.

In 1849, when John was thirty-one, he received a fine building lot from his parents, as did all the other living children of Rachael and Mor-

---

[5] *The Veranda* (Indianapolis: publication of the Morris-Butler House Museum, May 1995), p. 4.

Chapter XVIII. John D. Morris and Martha Wiles ♦ 255

ris. As related in earlier chapters, this entire area of lots made up one whole city block with an alley down the middle. Here the family ("the Morris dynasty") built their lovely, large mansions.

Historian Nowland wrote of the Morris family in his *Early Reminiscences*, mentioning all the living children. "John D. Morris, the fourth son, has for several years been engaged [as a clerk and freight agent— 1855-1874] in the freight office of the Cincinnati and Indianapolis Railroad [brother Thomas was chief engineer and then president of that railroad], and to him the writer is indebted for having stood by him at a very trying time, and he takes this occasion to return him thanks, after twenty-nine years, for the prompt manner in which he performed his part. True, he made a slight mistake at the altar in handing the minister the money instead of the legal document."[6] This was no doubt a private joke, strangely made public in the print of a quaint history book. "Twenty-nine years ago" John would have been about forty-one and probably was best man in Nowland's wedding.

Writing on Christmas Day in 1857, the Hon. O. H. Smith described Morris Morris (II) as a venerable, fine old man and concluded "Mr. Morris is the father of Austin W. Morris, Col. Thomas A. Morris, and John Morris."[7] Milton, the second son of Morris, we remember, had died long before, in 1835 on a riverboat-business trip in Louisiana. So this published account only mentions John but sheds no further information about him.

Martha was active in the Second Presbyterian Church of the Rev. Henry Ward Beecher and made sure her family attended.

As early as 1862, a landowner named Ovid Butler planned a neighborhood of beautiful homes—a retreat from the overcrowded city of Indianapolis. He would subdivide a large piece of his property south of his home directly adjacent to the campus of Northern Christian University. The plot was nicknamed "College Corner." Such modern amenities as the streetcar and gas lighting would serve these homes. Cisterns would provide water for an interior tank allowing the house to be plumbed, although a well was to be used for drinking water. A new gravitational heating system and a servant-summoning system through the walls were also innovations. There would be a carriage house at the rear, and orchards and gardens.

---

[6] Nowland, p. 235.
[7] O. H. Smith, *Early Indiana Trials and Sketches*, p. 173.

In 1864 when the street-railroad (trolley car) system was begun by Thomas Morris, its builder and first president, much real estate changed hands. By then there was war and inflation. "John Morris sold his lot on the southwest corner of Meridian and Georgia Streets, 96 x 205 feet, at $200 per foot, for $19,200."[8] This lot, the lot his parents had given him in 1849 and on which he had lived for fifteen years, was beside that of Thomas and across the street from brother Austin.

In the author's file is a warranty deed dated 9 November 1857 which documents the transfer of Lot 7 from Morris and Rachael to their sons Thomas and John together, for $1.00 and "in further consideration of parental consideration."[9]

Another old contract of sale dated May 1865 shows John D. and Martha A. Morris selling this same lot of Morris Morris's subdivision (plat 87) to his brother Thomas for $7,980.[10]

Although the Civil War was straining many households' finances in 1864, John bought Lot 112 in Ovid Butler's subdivision for $2,000, then employed the noted architect Deitrich A. Bohlen and the builder John Clements to begin a spacious and stately new mansion in Second Empire-style brick, at 1204 North Park Avenue. A secondary kitchen with a laundry-washroom and two privies was a separate building but attached at the rear. There were servants' quarters and a stable. In less than a year it was practically finished, for an estimated cost of $22,000. John and family were living in it by the fall of 1865, according to the city directory.

The John Morrises had horses, an orchard, and gardens. This was the very first of all the grand Victorian homes that were to be built in Ovid Butler's beautiful new subdivision outside the noise and bustle of the city. Slowly but gradually it began to develop.

By 1868 John Morris was a clerk and partner in the merchandising firm of Wilson, Hazelett, and Morris.

Within six years the first naval wedding in Indianapolis was held in this new elegant Victorian mansion, in 1871; a gala affair it must have been. Their third child, "Kate" (the earlier-mentioned baby Caroline), married Commander George Brown, who later became an admiral and was a colorful figure during the Civil War.

Through his son James, John invested heavily in several firms including Roll and Morris, retailers in wallpaper, shades, and carpet, in 1773. It is believed that the funds for these ventures came from selling

---

[8] Warranty deed, in author's file.
[9] Contract, in author's file.
[10] Deed, in author's file.

Chapter XVIII. John D. Morris and Martha Wiles ♦ 257

his inherited lands. It is also possible that money was inherited from his wife's Wiles family. After five years son James, who ran the business, sold out to his partner, who then made it quite profitable.

"Mr. Morris was engaged in several business enterprises during the more than fifteen years that he and his family resided there."[11] This is not very specific; however, after employment as a railroad clerk, he later became vice president of Capital City Planing Mill in 1874. At this same time John was a partner in the firm of Glazier and Morris, dealers in coke, coal, lime, grain, flour, and feed. But his business ventures did not prosper, and this one folded after only a year.

The depression of the 1870s spoiled Butler's grand neighborhood vision and forced his large lots to be subdivided and more modest structures eventually built. Most of this occurred after John Morris's home was finished, or nearly finished.

The Morris family struggled to pay off debts during the panic of 1873 and all through the 1870s depression, but there was no money to complete all of the details. There are several indications in the house, now a museum, to suggest this, according to its administrator, Mrs. Tiffany Sallee. An example is lack of second-floor crown moldings.

This financial downturn forced many businessmen and investors to close up and declare bankruptcy. As the depression escalated Morris took out a loan, using the house as collateral. He could not meet the lump-sum payments of interest and principal. The city eventually sued for unpaid taxes and the loan was called. John Morris had no choice but to declare bankruptcy in 1878. Alas, the family had to leave their fine home. They moved with all their belongings, because they could legally keep them, to another house, in Woodruff Place.

The lot was subdivided. Noah Armstrong purchased the house for speculation, and nine months later sold it to Noble Chase Butler (no relation to Ovid Butler of the original suburban area) in 1881. This was a different family that moved in, with seven children. Members of this Butler family lived there consecutively for many, many years, until as late as 1958, when some very old maiden relatives were residing there. Never modernized and crudely electrified, it eventually fell into very great disrepair.

An important highway was to be built through the city, to be elevated right over the site of the subdivision, so many fine old neigh-

---

[11] Smith, p. 173.

Above: The Morris-Butler House Museum, built in 1865 by John D. Morris, *left*, whose portrait hangs in the Victorian parlor shown opposite.

Opposite, bottom: The German silver tea service used by the Morris family, on display in the dining room of the Museum.

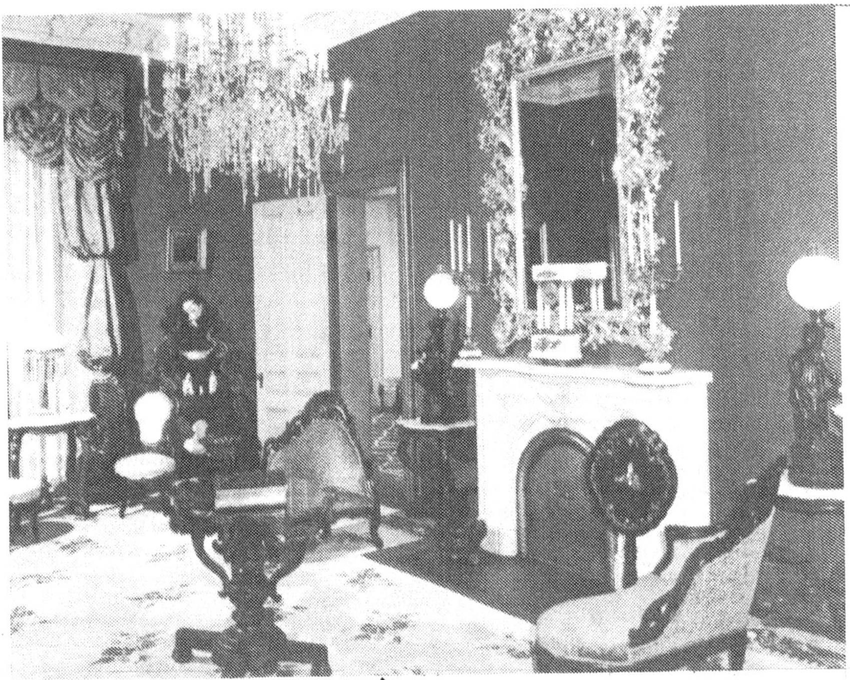

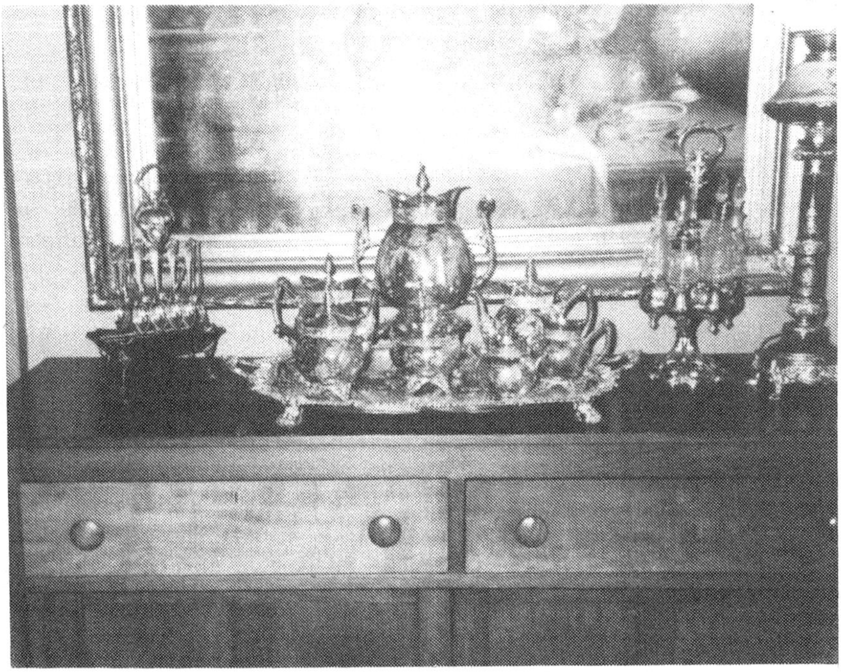

borhood houses were torn down. Very fortunately, this beautiful home was not demolished, as were many of its counterparts in a once-fine neighborhood. This house with its five-storied tower-entrance of the mid-Victorian era was rescued, barely saved from demolition and development, although the highway was indeed built very close beside it—much too close for an appropriate, attractive situation. But at least it was saved!

The late Mr. Eli Lilly, head of Indiana's large pharmaceutical company, was interested in preserving this elegant vintage home and others in the neighborhood. He purchased the venerable, decrepit, forlorn house, then established the Historical Landmarks Foundation of Indiana. Thanks to generous enthusiasm, effort, and fundraising, it has been beautifully restored and was opened in 1969 to the public as a museum of decorative arts of the mid-Victorian era. Now it is recorded in the National Register of Historical Places as the Morris-Butler House Museum of the Historic Landmarks Foundation. It was the first of the foundation's enterprises; more have followed.

Landscaped, refurbished, and appropriately decorated, "it is a fine example of the French mansard style"[12] and "a domestic version of the second Empire style. Its asymmetrical, towered plan is almost identical to the earlier Italianate villa plan"[13] and "typifies the ultimate in gracious living in Indianapolis a century ago."[14]

Entering the long entrance hall, one soon notices at the foot of the stairs an original painting of the first "Morris Farm," painted by Indiana's early artist, Jacob Cox. Donald Morris of Indianapolis, great-nephew of John Morris, gave the farm painting to the art museum, who has now appropriately given it to this museum. Two original portraits of Morris and Rachael, parents of the home's first owner, now hang in the Victorian parlor. They were also painted by Jacob Cox and were given to the museum by Morris Morris's great-great-grandchildren, the late Josephine Morris McKee and Morris Morris of Indianapolis, children of Donald.

At the other end of the parlor hangs a portrait of a very handsome John Morris, given by his great-grandson Morris Reily Adams. Unfortunately, there is no portrait of Martha. The "centerpiece" is a pair of extremely rare couches called meridiennes. A large matching set of fine furniture, carved by John Henry Belter, and an ornate crystal chandelier complement this Victorian parlor setting. In the dining room is a sideboard which was made for Mr. Morris by a local cabinet maker. A Ger-

---

[12] *Old Northside Historic District Preservation Plan 3.*
[13] John S. Peppliers and others, "What Style Is It? Part III," in *Historic Preservation.*
[14] Rita Reif, *Treasure Rooms of American Mansions, Manors, and Houses,* p. 141.

Chapter XVIII. John D. Morris and Martha Wiles ♦ 261

man silver tea service used by the Morris family is displayed on it. Nothing more is there from this family whose home it was originally.

How ironic that this beautiful home remains as a memorial to a couple who had serious financial reverses and about whom we know so little. John died in 1895 at age eighty. Martha lived three years longer; a son always lived with her.

It was their fifth child, Nancy Morris Haines (always called "Nannie"), who wrote family notes and who, obviously proud of her family, became the "Indianapolis family historian" of sorts and passed on much of the family lore that has been handed down. She could remember her grandparents, although she was only nine when her grandmother Rachael died and just ten when grandfather Morris passed away. Unfortunately, not all her "facts" were remembered correctly but were widely distributed. This has resulted in inaccuracies even in printed Indianapolis histories and caused genuine consternation and dismay on the part of a few family researchers.

The Children of John D. and Martha (Wiles) Morris

Charles Goodman Morris, John and Martha Morris's firstborn, worked as a druggist and later had a drug establishment with a partner named Hazlitt until the panic of 1873. Then he went into the fertilizer business. He lived with his parents until age thirty-two, when he married Juliet Nold and moved to Louisville. A son, John D. Jr., died in World War I; his son, John III, was born in 1899. There are no known records of any descendants.

The second child, James Wiles, lived at home until he was forty-five and worked in the retail carpet company of Roll and Morris, financed by his father. He married Maude Staub but had no children.

The third child, Catherine but known as "Kate" (1847-1915), attended Miss Catherine Merrill's School.[15] She was selected to assist in the decorative ceremonies at the first Memorial Day, generally called "Decoration Day," in May of 1868.[16] Kate Morris married Commander George Brown, who later became an admiral in the U.S. Navy. He was the son of William J. Brown, assistant postmaster general under President

---

[15] Obituaries, in author's file.
[16] Anna Nicholas, *Indianapolis*, p. 47.

Polk.[17] Their wedding, in October 1871 with all the accompanying ceremony including an arch of crossed sabers, was the first naval wedding ever celebrated in Indianapolis. We can imagine the lovely gala in her parents' spacious, beautiful home, and the pride of her family in having it there.

The Browns first went to Chicago, then lived in Annapolis, Maryland, and Washington, D.C., then Portsmouth and Norfolk, Virginia, where he was in command of the Navy Yard, and also in Honolulu. This was a peripatetic life but an important and busy social responsibility for an admiral's wife.

Rear Admiral Brown is said to have fired both the first and the last shots of the Navy during the war for the Union. "I commanded a division of guns on the *Powhatan* which fired the first shot. This was in Pensacola, Florida. I claim to have pulled the lock-string of the last gun fired on the part of the Navy at the end of the war. This was on the iron-clad *Cincinnati* at ... Cahaba, on the Alabama River, about fifteen miles below Selma, Alabama. Immediately after ... we met a boat flying a flag of truce.... An officer of General Sherman's staff ... announced to both armies the armistice.... After that date there was not a gun fired from a naval vessel."[18]

After the war was over Brown was detailed to deliver a ship to Japan by sailing it around Cape Horn, since in those days there was no Panama Canal. The *Stonewall,* built by the British for the Southern Confederacy, did not arrive until after Lee's surrender, so it became the property of the United States. As our government did not need the vessel, it was sold to Japan, and Captain Brown was to deliver it to the purchasers.

From a harbor on the coast of Patagonia, one of the most forbidding spots on earth, Brown spied a white man signaling him. The ship sent out a boat to bring him aboard. That person was George McDougal, who just happened to be known to Brown from boyhood and had been long missing from Indianapolis! McDougal was eager for news but did not wish to return to America. He was enjoying too much his position as king of a native tribe of tall men. Captain Brown wrote the Indianapolis newspaper of the incident, thus McDougal's family learned of his whereabouts in Patagonia.[19] This story seems unbelievable, but it was true!

Another newspaper article tells that George Brown was entitled to wear many insignia and he evidently overdid; it "would cover his coat as

---

[17] Unidentified Indianapolis newspaper, n.p., n.d., in author's file.
[18] Ibid.
[19] Unidentified Indianapolis newspaper, n.d., n.p.

Chapter XVIII. John D. Morris and Martha Wiles ♦ 263

thickly as currants on a cake."[20] One of those decorations, Grand Officer of the Order of Kalakana, was from the Hawaiian king. "I have been [in Hawaii] twenty times or more since 1852.... The longest period [was] six months when stationed there with my flagship. I speak a little Kanaka ... but my youngest boy went to school at Honolulu and learned to speak good Kanaka. English is taught in the schools there and it is just as high English as we get in the best schools here."

Upon Admiral Brown's retirement at age sixty-two, the Browns returned to Indianapolis to live in Woodruff Place with Catherine's mother and two servants, in the house where her father, John Morris, had last resided, "for it was undergoing extensive repairs."[21] Admiral Brown lived to be seventy-eight; Catherine Morris Brown survived her husband by only two years.

There were three Brown sons. The oldest, George Jr., graduated from the U.S. Naval Academy, married Anne Miller, served as paymaster with the Adriatic Fleet, also was in China and San Francisco, and had a daughter, Catherine, who married in 1925 Thomas Beattie of the U.S. Navy. We have no knowledge of their issue. The middle son, John Morris Brown, died as a small child. Hugh Brown also graduated from the U.S. Naval Academy, married Estelle Johnston, was commander of the USS *Virginia,* and had only Sara Brown (b. 1917).

The fifth child of Martha and John D. Morris was Nancy, always called "Nannie," who married Charles Haines. Proud of her family's pioneer heritage, she became the family historian, although apparently she did not record what her father did for a livelihood or for his community. She named her only son John Morris Haines, and he became a trustee of Crown Hill Cemetery. He had no sons but had two daughters: Mary Stuart Haines, and Barbara Carey Haines. The former married Reily Adams. Their only son, Morris Reily Adams, became a trustee of Crown Hill. He is also currently secretary of their board of managers

Barbara (Haines) Werbe in recent years has developed the old Haines family farm into a condominium complex, where she resides beside her older daughter. Her fourth child, Eleanor "Noni" Carey (Werbe) Krauss, has already achieved a lifetime goal of climbing spectacular Mount Kilimanjaro, the highest point in Africa, almost 20,000 feet up! (Having personally been at its very *bottom* and watched the exhausted climbers return, the author knows this is truly a remarkable feat for a young woman.) Noni's photograph is on the following page.

---

[20] Ibid.
[21] Ibid.

*Eleanor "Noni" (Werbe) Krauss
on Mount Kilimanjaro*

The sixth and last child of John D. and Martha Morris was David Corwine Morris, who never married. So again the Morris surname has become lost to the female lines.

This family is documented in detail in the Genealogy.

Chapter XIX

AMANDA MELVINA MORRIS and DR. JOHN LELAND MOTHERSHEAD
Fifth Child of Morris and Rachael

History is a mirror we hold up to ourselves, a way of redefining and re-examining ourselves.

— Ken Burns, Filmmaker

AS WAS GENERALLY true in earlier days, nothing is recorded, even remembered, of the female side of this early family. There is not even a known picture of Amanda. We know that she was born in 1817 in Nicholas County, Kentucky, and also came with her parents in 1821 to the new capital of Indianapolis as a very little girl only four years old. Amanda, the fifth child, grew up in a large, hard-working, church-going family which prospered and increased in prominence over the years. When she was not quite nineteen, she met and married a promising doctor from Kentucky who had just finished his education at Transylvania Medical College in Lexington. (That and Ohio Medical College were the only two in the West until 1837.) John was eight years older than Amanda, and, having come to Indianapolis in 1830,[1] he had already gained a place for himself in the fast-growing city he chose for his home—chosen because it would be an advantageous place to establish a practice.[2]

At age twenty-two he had been one of the earliest pioneer physicians. "Very soon Dr. Mothershead became distinguished for his skill and thorough medical training, and speedily attained the largest practice in the ... city.... His presence was frequently sought in consultation in the neighboring cities and towns."[3] "Dr. Mothershead formed a partnership with Dr. Mitchell for about a year, and then with Dr. Sanders ... a very popular and competent firm."[4]

---

[1] Jacob Piatt Dunn, *Greater Indianapolis*, vol. 1, p. 543.
[2] B. R. Sulgrove, *History of Indianapolis and Marion County*, p. 279.
[3] Ibid.
[4] Dunn, p. 543.

In 1832, after living in Indianapolis only two years, Dr. Mothershead was one of five men suggested by the newly incorporated voters to be a trustee of the city.[5]

At the beginning, in 1821, a bucket and ladder fire company had been organized, but a few years later, in 1835, a real fire engine, called "the Marion," was purchased and the fire department—the Marion Engine Company—was organized. A relief company and a second engine soon followed. "The members of both of these companies were among the leading citizens...." A few "leading citizens" were mentioned by name including Dr. John L. Mothershead, who was one of the fire department's earliest captains.[6]

"In connection with his profession he also engaged in business as a druggist.... The oldest drug house in the city, probably in the state, was established by Dr. Mothershead about the year 1840."[7] In 1848 he was elected treasurer of the first medical society of Indianapolis,[8] and two years later took in a Mr. Browning as a partner.

John and Amanda raised two sons and two daughters, and were active in the Baptist Church.

In 1849, when Amanda was thirty-two, she too was given a large city lot, part of block 87, by her parents. Amanda and John built a fine, big house there beside her brothers and sisters. The Mothersheads are referred to in an old newspaper article along with the other family members.[9] Another article, undated, reminisces: "Maryland Street ... has had its families who are identified with the splendid history of our city, families living in dignified, spacious mansions, flanked by orchards and gardens, gates opening upon the quiet, wide, tree-bordered street ... Morris, Defrees, [Jacob] Cox, ... Ross, ... Browning,... these were some of the well-known names of the Maryland Street neighborhood ... setting *[sic]* back in a very large yard was the home of Dr. Mothershead."[10] The 1850 census shows his real estate to be worth $15,000. Living in their home were two servants, a seventeen-year-old German girl and a seventeen-year-old laborer.

---

[5] Ibid., p. 113.
[6] Ibid., p. 169; Sulgrove, p. 148.
[7] Sulgrove, p. 279.
[8] Dunn, vol. 2, p. 805.
[9] "Old Resident Recalls the Days of Long Ago," in unidentified newspaper dated 23 Feb. 1916, n.p., in author's file.
[10] "Many Notable Names in Maryland Street's History," article in unidentified newspaper, n.d., n.p., in author's file.

Chapter XIX. Amanda Morris and Dr. J. L. Mothershead ♦ 267

"Dr. Mothershead was in politics a Whig, and although not an aspirant for office, filled the responsible position of first President of the Board of Health," from 1850 to 1855.[11]

Dr. John L. Mothershead

After his medical partner removed to Missouri in 1839, Dr. Mothershead "practiced alone for some time but for a period before his death [in 1854] he was associated with Dr. Bullard. These were the medical pioneers of Indianapolis ... quite as fearful that someone who was ignorant of correct principles might practice medicine."[12]

A full-page picture of Dr. John Mothershead, along with his biography, is in Sulgrove's 1884 *History of Indianapolis.*

Amanda died in 1851 at the early age of thirty-four, when her last-born was only eight years old. How sad that she was able to enjoy her large, beautiful, new home for less than two years. She is buried in Crown Hill.

John married again, perhaps so his young family would have a mother. He had a daughter by his second wife, Emmeline Grant, but Dr. John lived only three years longer than Amanda and died at age forty-six, "not less remembered for his professional attainments than for his many genial traits of character."[13] Emmeline lived twelve more years and cared for the family.

The well-loved doctor and dear Amanda had both lived a taxing and strenuous but good life. We can imagine that popular, young, busy doctor, trustee of the city, captain of the fire department, and president of the board of health, also trying to cope in a horse and buggy with many, many patients. He probably took care of all those Morris children in their whole city block "for free," because they were all family. Just think of the many cases of Morris mumps, chicken pox, measles, and whooping cough! No wonder they both "died young."

---

[11] Sulgrove, p. 279.
[12] Ibid., p. 279; W. R. Holloway, *Indianapolis, Railroad City,* p. 43.
[13] Sulgrove, p. 279; Dunn, p. 543.

Descendants of Amanda Morris and Dr. John Leland Mothershead

Amanda Morris and John Leland Mothershead had three children: 1) Alvin Mothershead, 2) Julia Mary Morris Mothershead, and 3) John Leland Mothershead Jr.

1. Alvin Mothershead, born 13 September 1838 in Indianapolis, became a lawyer in Omaha, Nebraska, and eventually went to Chicago. He married Louise Brackenbush in 1865 in Omaha and had three children. Neither of his daughters had offspring. The first, Amanda Morris Mothershead, became a teacher in Chicago and never married. Carlotta, the second daughter, married Henry Bernard Lusch. Their brother, Leland Mothershead, born 1882, lived in Montclair, New Jersey.

2. Julia Mary Morris Mothershead, born 19 April 1841, married 8 October 1868 David A. Burr of Washington, D.C., and also lived in Montclair. He was with the New York *Evening Post*. They had three children: first, a son, Leland Mothershead Burr (1869), who married Ruth Merritt and had four children: Helen, Ruth, Leland (1907), and David A. (1909) Mothershead, all in Montclair. No Burrs or Merritts have been located currently living in Montclair.

Second child, Desdemona Burr (1872), married in 1900 John S. Lichnor, lived in Capetown, South Africa, and had no children.

Her brother, David E. Burr (1880), was also in Montclair.

3. John Leland Mothershead Jr. (1842), second in a direct line of six generations bearing the same name, was prominent in Indianapolis Republican politics; treasurer of Marion County 1881-1883;[14] a member of the Columbia Club and the Second Presbyterian Church; and a Mason. A successful business man, John Jr. was also president of the Indiana Foundry Company,[15] owned a chemical company in the gas belt but sold it to work for Grasselli Chemical Company in Cleveland (now part of the DuPont Company). "He was a genial and kindly man, endowed with great capacity for friendship."[16] He married Anna Owen of Philadelphia, sired four children, and died of apoplexy in Cleveland in 1915 at age seventy-two.

---

[14] Sulgrove, p. 279; Holloway, p. 247.
[15] Sulgrove, p. 279.
[16] Obituary with picture, dated Aug. 1915, in unidentified newspaper, n.p., in author's file.

Chapter XIX. Amanda Morris and Dr. J. L. Mothershead ♦ 269

The first daughter, Julia Mothershead (1872-1945), never married. The second, Bessie Owen, died in infancy. The third child, Owen Morris Mothershead (1880-1957) of Indianapolis, married Mary Wilson of Welsh descent, had only one son, Wilson (1905-1990), who was chairman of the Indiana National Bank in Indianapolis, chairman of the Indiana National Corporation, on the board of directors of the Indianapolis Water Company, and a corporator of Crown Hill Cemetery (as a direct descendant of an original corporator, Thomas Armstrong Morris). His two children were adopted.

The fourth child of John L. Mothershead Jr. was John Leland Mothershead III (1882). Called "Lee," he was a Christian Science practitioner in Pasadena, California, and owned ACA Company, which made stained and leaded glass windows. John III first married Ethel Warner, daughter of the socially prominent family of the Ezra Warners of Lake Forest, Illinois. John III knew General Pershing, for there is a picture of them both in uniform (World War I) in Los Angeles, with John as the driver of the car. John III and Ethel had two sons:

John Leland Mothershead IV was a well-known educator in Stanford, California. *Who's Who* says of him, "b. Indianapolis Nov. 18, 1908, AB Stanford 1930, MA 1933, PhD Harvard 1938; ... instr. philosophy Syracuse U. 1939-41; mem. faculty Stanford, 1941- , successively asst. prof., assoc. prof., 1941- 55, prof. 1955. Recipient Lloyd W. Dinkelspiel award for outstanding service to undergraduate education 1964; mem. Amer. Philosophy Assn., Amer. Assn. for the Advancement of Science, Amer. Assn. U. Profs.; author, *Ethics: Modern Conception of the Principles of Right,* 1955. Home: 666 Mayfield Ave., Stanford, CA 94305."[17] He married, first, in 1932, Elizabeth Ashley Crossett; they had two children; Elizabeth died in 1976. His second marriage, in 1978, was to Diane Frazier Hefner; no issue. John IV died of a stroke in

John L. Mothershead IV

---

[17] *Who's Who in America*, 39th ed., p. 2256.

1991; his widow, Diane, lives in Portola Valley, California.

The two children of John IV and Elizabeth Crossett are John Leland Mothershead V and Ann Ashley Mothershead.

John V (1939) married Therese Petkelis and lives in San Marino, California. Their one child is John Leland Mothershead VI (1966), who married in July 1995 Malinda Marie Luthin and lives in Ojai, California.

Ann Ashley Mothershead (1944) was formerly an instructor, researcher, and manager of the Health Division at the Stanford Research Institute in Menlo Park, California, and is now a community volunteer. She is married to Peter Bjorklund, a statistician who has four married children and a grown adopted daughter. Ann Bjorklund has two of her own biological children: Peter and Ashley Bjorklund, living in Los Altos Hills, California.

The brother of John Leland IV, Morris Warner Mothershead (1915), deceased, was a travel agent living in Pasadena. He married Alice Bonzi of Milan, Italy. Their two children are 1) Warner, who is in the birdseed business in Oregon and has two children by a first marriage, Maria and Michael Anthony Mothershead; and 2) Maria, who married Professor Andrei Rogers and has four children, all born in the sixties: Michael, an engineer with NASA, Ames; Professor Christopher Rogers, an engineer at Tufts University; Kevin, in fisheries management, finishing his Ph.D.; and Laura, married to a city and regional planner. Maria Mothershead and Andrei Rogers have eight very young grandchildren: Steven, Kevin, and Brian Rogers; Peter, Mathew, and Kimberly Rogers; Kyle Rogers; and James Grayson Sweeney.

*   *   *   *   *

The descendants of Amanda Morris and pioneer Dr. John Leland Mothershead appear to have been in Montclair, New Jersey; one, deceased, in Indianapolis; many in California; and some in Oregon and the Boston area. The Burrs have not been found.

See the Genealogy in Part Three of this book for more details on this family.

Chapter XX

JULIA ANN MORRIS and NORMAN ROSS
Sixth Child of Morris and Rachael

*Real joy comes not from the praise of men
but from doing something worthwhile.*
— Sir Wilfred Grenfell

LITTLE JULIA ANN was just a toddler at the time of Morris and Rachael's migration to Indiana in September 1821. Born in February of the year before, she would have been about nineteen months old. What a care she must have been to her courageous mother, who had no zippered buntings, no disposable diapers, no jars of strained baby food, and little sanitation or convenience to aid in their travels on the long wagon journey from Kentucky.

Too young to remember the arduous trip, she grew up in a brand new settlement and witnessed its development from its earliest beginnings. She was fortunate to experience and to remember the better years, when prosperity had rewarded their large family. Julia was twenty-nine and about to be married when her industrious parents gave each of their children a plot of land in the spring of 1849. She was given Section 4 on Meridian Street next to her older brother John. That summer, in July, she married Norman M. Ross, who also had been born in Kentucky. They, too, built a fine home there in the Morrises' whole block of family homes. They are referred to in two old newspaper articles along with the rest of the family.[1]

Nothing is written, not even known, about this lady or of her motivations and accomplishments, yet she was a mother and a member of a large and important family.

Norman Ross was "formerly superintendent of the Cincinnati Railroad, but now [1870] is engaged in one of the departments in Washington."[2] (The reader will remember that Julia's older brother Thomas A.

---
[1] "Many Notable Names in Maryland Street's History," vol. 22, no. 176, n.d., n.p.; "Old Resident Recalls the Days of Long Ago," unidentified newspaper, 23 Feb. 1916.
[2] John H. B. Nowland, *Early Reminiscences of Indianapolis*, p. 107.

Morris was formerly chief engineer and then president of that same railroad. He helped many of the family with his various enterprises.) "One of the departments in Washington" implies that Ross had been appointed to a governmental position, perhaps through another brother-in-law, John Defrees.

The Child of Julia Ann and Norman Ross

Julia and Norman had only one child, born just a year after their marriage and named for his popular maternal grandfather. Morris Morris Ross graduated from Cornell University in 1870, much to the pride of all the family. (A cousin, Thomas O'Neil Morris, also attended college, unusual in an era when very few men had such an opportunity.) During the six years after Cornell, Morris spent his time "in newspaper work in Washington, Indianapolis, and New York."[3] It is also recorded that in 1873 he signed the constitution of the Historical Society of Indianapolis, presumably to join.

An appointment as secretary of the American Legation in Vienna was for one year. There Morris enjoyed the opportunities and pleasures of Europe. In 1876 he returned to Indianapolis, went to work for the *Indianapolis News*, and remained there until his death. At various times he was an editorial writer, a drama critic, and managing editor. Edwin Booth once said of him: "He was the best dramatic [sic] critic in the world."[4]

At that time the *News* had the largest daily circulation of any paper in the state. "For some eight years or so Mr. Morris Ross has done editorial writing and contributed largely to the establishment of the paper's reputation for wide and accurate information and literary ability."[5]

"Morris Ross was the first man in Indiana to advocate the building and owning of a labor temple by the unions, and he spent a great deal of time in working for this plan."[6]

Morris Morris Ross was thirty-two when he married Miss Frances McIntyre. They had no children, and he died at age sixty-five. So this is still another line from Morris and Rachael which produced no descendants with the surname Morris.

---

[3] Obituary with picture, dated 8 Oct. 1915, in unidentified newspaper, n.p.
[4] B. R. Sulgrove, *History of Indianapolis and Marion County*, p. 246.
[5] Ibid.
[6] Author's file.

Chapter XXI

ELIZABETH MITCHELL MORRIS and JOHN D. DEFREES
Seventh Child of Morris and Rachael

Large families are like quilts—
Lives pieced together,
Stitched with smiles and tears,
Colored with many memories,
Bound by enduring love.
— Betty Hober Massey

JUST TWO AND A HALF YEARS after Rachael and Morris arrived in the brand new settlement of Indianapolis, their seventh child was born, in 1824. She, also, was too young to remember the rigors and hardships of those earliest days in the small log cabin. Then it was a rough wilderness village, but the refinements of a more comfortable life came fairly rapidly.

Although her name was Elizabeth, she is referred to as "the little girl, Bettie" in an early description of the family attending church.[1] Since she was one of the youngest, her family had become well-to-do by the time she was growing up. Bettie soon became accustomed to nice things and important people.

In 1844, when Bettie was not quite twenty, she married John Dougherty Defrees, who at age thirty-four was nearly fourteen years her senior. In that same year, John, born in Sparta, Tennessee, had come from South Bend, Indiana, to Indianapolis, bought the *Indianapolis State Journal,* courted and married Bettie Morris—all in one year. He had been married before and had a daughter, Harriet, so from the very beginning of their marriage Bettie bore the responsibility of a stepdaughter just ten years younger than she. Census records show that Harriet lived with them.

---

[1] Jacob Piatt Dunn, *Greater Indianapolis,* p. 179.

That must have been an interesting relationship, preceded by the courtship of a determined suitor who had his mind set on marrying the beautiful and much younger Bettie. We can also imagine a popular girl of nineteen being swept off her feet by an older, brilliant, important newspaper man serving in the legislature, and wonder if her older brother Thomas, a close friend of John, had a part to play as matchmaker. Their honeymoon was a trip to South Bend in a covered wagon. Schuyler Colfax, another close friend, made this trip with them, visiting in the same town, which was also his home.

Five years later, in the spring of 1849, Bettie's parents, Rachael and Morris, gave them lot No. 8 between sister Julia and brother John in the Morris family complex, where they too built a fine home. Like those of her siblings, it is referred to in old newspaper articles. A sketch of the house by Indianapolis artist Christian Schrader is in the Indiana State Museum.

Their first offspring was named after Bettie's grandfather, Morris Morris, as were some of Bettie's nephews. This son followed in the footsteps of his uncle Thomas and became a civil engineer. Julia, the second child, married well, and, fortunately for her descending family, wrote a delightful memoir of Washington in the eventful 1860s. Baby Amanda, the third child, died in infancy.

Then followed twin boys, John Jr. and Anthony Colfax, born in 1855. The latter was named for John Sr.'s lifelong friend, Schuyler Colfax, to whom John gave his first newspaper job, that of reporter of the legislature. When John came to Indianapolis, he sold the South Bend newspaper to Colfax. Their friendship extended through many trying times in Washington. Colfax eventually served as vice president under President Ulysses S. Grant, from 1869-1873.

A fourth son, Thomas Morris Defrees, named for John's very good friend and brother-in-law, completed the large family. Five of these children lived to grow up on Meridian Street in a large, comfortable Victorian mansion until they all moved to Washington, D.C. The 1850 census showed their new property to be worth $2,000. Two German printers were also living in the household.

The father of these five children by Bettie, and of Harriet from his first marriage, was an important man, both in Indianapolis and in Washington. John Defrees; his father-in-law, Morris Morris; and his brothers-in-law, Thomas Armstrong Morris and Dr. Leland Mothershead, each have a full-page picture with biography in Barry Sulgrove's *History of*

Chapter XXI. Elizabeth M. Morris and John D. Defrees ♦ 275

Indianapolis.[2] A biography of Defrees is also in Appleton's *Cyclopaedia of American Biography*. This was no small honor, and the biographies provide us with many facts about their lives.

John Defrees was apprenticed at fourteen to the printers' trade, as was his brother-in-law Thomas Morris. He studied journalism under antislavery editor Horace Greeley, and then studied law. At only twenty-one he began the publication of a newspaper, the first in northern Indiana, with his younger brother in South Bend. When he sold it and bought the *Indiana State Journal* in 1844, it was "located in the 'Sander's Block,' one of the first three-story brick buildings in the city, on the north side of Washington Street."[3] Defrees edited the *Journal* for a decade and during the latter years mostly "confined himself to the business department."[4] Dunn mentions "the facile pen of John D. Defrees, more deadly than an Indian tomahawk."[5]

In 1853 a second attempt was made at forming a merchants' exchange—a board of trade—which was the forerunner of the Indianapolis Chamber of Commerce. A citizens' meeting appointed six men including Defrees to be "a committee to make a constitution, prepare a circular and map, and obtain money."[6] After the board was organized Defrees became a member of the executive committee. Also in 1853 John Defrees is mentioned along with "Gen. Morris and others" as reviving the Indianapolis Insurance Company, authorized to do both banking and insurance business.[7]

Defrees is mentioned again in the same year as taking part in the trial of Freeman, a free Negro of long-standing who was accused of being a runaway slave. Defrees "had some trouble in explaining that he was neither a free-soiler nor an abolitionist."[8]

The following year, at the death of Nicholas McCarty, a good Whig friend and prominent citizen, we read of Defrees on the committee to prepare a public resolution.[9] Also in 1854 John published a campaign sheet called "We the People."[10] Each bit of trivia, in a labyrinth of facts, further establishes his character and his early importance in the growing community.

---

[2] B. R. Sulgrove, *History of Indianapolis and Marion County*, pp. 239-43.
[3] Ibid., p. 243.
[4] Ibid., p. 240.
[5] Dunn, p. 135.
[6] Ibid., p. 346; Sulgrove, p. 141.
[7] Sulgrove, p. 218.
[8] Dunn, p. 247.
[9] Sulgrove, p. 100.
[10] Ibid., p. 243.

From 1855 the Central Bank was owned chiefly by Defrees and Ozias Bowen, its successive presidents. It was begun with a nominal capital and wound up with no serious loss.

Defrees is credited with still another enterprise in 1856, stave-making, "a very important industry of the city. The first machinery for making and dressing staves and barrel heads was brought here ... by ... John Defrees and his brother Anthony."[11]

W. R. Holloway lists him in *Indianapolis, Railroad City*, in 1870, along with four others, as having been president of the Peru and Indianapolis Railroad.

John sold *The Journal* in 1854,[12] published Whig campaign papers, and started *The Atlas* in 1859, merging with it *The Citizen*, which he had bought. This was printed with "an Ericson hot-air engine, the first one ever brought here, and the only one, probably."[13]

"Progress seemed to be his watchword. He was the first man in the State to use steam to drive a printing press, the first to use a caloric engine for the same purpose, the first to see the value of the Bullock printing press, and he encouraged the inventor. Defrees also was the first to use the metallic stretching machine for binding, and the first to use the Edison electric light except the inventor.... He never seemed to doubt the ability or genius of man.... [It] colored his whole life ... faith in progress ... restless energy ... classical student ... books were his delight ... political student ... courage ...."[14]

Much more was said of this fine man. It is recorded in the publications of the Indiana Historical Society that he was an early signer of its constitution.

Wylie Daniels mentions Defrees several times as being in an editorial battle[15] and advocating the sale of railroad stock in his *State Journal*.[16] He tells of a trip when Defrees "came down in the cars ... took the boat to Cincinnati, and may be, for aught we know, on his way to Washington to get an office."[17] Daniels said in his preface that Indiana was fortunate in having many outstanding men as editors of its leading papers in the forties and fifties, when John D. Defrees edited the Whig paper. Only three

---

[11] Ibid., p. 460.
[12] Ibid., p. 241.
[13] Ibid., p. 247.
[14] Ibid., p. 239; Dunn, p. 393.
[15] Wylie J. Daniels, *The Village at the End of the Road*, Indiana Historical Publications XIII, p. 83.
[16] Ibid., p. 85.
[17] Ibid., p. 95.

Chapter XXI. Elizabeth M. Morris and John D. Defrees ♦ 277

others are mentioned. S. C. Beeley, in his Pulitzer Prize-winning *The Old Northwest*, called Defrees Indiana's most distinguished ante-bellum journalist.

John kept his paper going until after the election of 1860 and sold it to *The Journal* in 1861,[18] because the whole Defrees family was about to make an exciting move to Washington. Having spent the first seventeen years of her marriage in Indianapolis, Bettie was now a capable and handsome young lady of thirty-six. There exists today in Durham, North Carolina, a pair of portraits of Bettie and John, painted by a fine but unknown artist. Of course she appears much younger looking than her considerably older husband. Bettie was black-haired and fine-featured, with a delicate, pretty face. Very petite and quite beautiful, she must have been a remarkable belle in the midst of Washington's society.

Elizabeth Morris Defrees

John D. Defrees

Of the Defrees family's move to Washington and some subsequent experiences, the oldest daughter, Julia, wrote the following revealing account from memory in 1904, sixty-seven years after the event, when she was eighty years old.

---

[18] Sulgrove, p. 247.

I was a little girl of thirteen when ... at the supper table my father said, "I had a letter from Washington to construct and direct a printing office for the government." Tragic day for us when he answered the President's urge and accepted the office.... Political people in those days did not get rich!

We started for Washington the 15th of April, 1860,[19] ... Mother, Father, five children and two German girls who adored my mother ... lunch baskets ... no dining cars in those days ... excited sleeping in little berths. Every man on board was armed, for Fort Sumter had [just] been fired upon ... neared Harper's Ferry ... excitement ... tense but silent ... children to hide under the hoop skirts of their mothers ... train passed through the town, the men uncovered their pistols ... got through without a shot. Our train was the last to get through for many a day. The next one was fired upon; the Civil War was on.

My father had leased Senator Rice's house [from Massachusetts] ... high-ceilinged parlors and libraries, great folding doors between the rooms, long gold mirrors to the floor and red damask curtains everywhere. Coloured servants were very cheap.... Old Martha as cook and Charles as house boy were attached to our house.... My little brother was frightened to death at first of these black people.... Charles was still a slave and mother rented him from his master.

We went to school every day when most of the streets were thick, yellow clayish mud. Little negro boys and girls would stand with planks for us to cross on and of course the expected pennies would be thrown to them.... Rainy days when my father had the carriage we would sometimes have to go on the street cars drawn by horses. The conductors would get off, close our umbrellas, assist us up the steps and go through the same courtesy when we reached our destination.

... One could scarcely get a block or two without running into a wandering cow or have one run into you. Once it happened to me while wearing a red dress and carrying a crimson sunshade ... rescued from the savage horns of a big yellow cow by two soldiers.

The unfinished capitol and [the] Washington Monument looked down on a straggling town of disorder and unpleasant perfumes, as there was only open sewage. Few of the streets were paved and those that were, of cobblestones, were badly cut to pieces by wheels of artillery and big wagons mired to the hub ... sound of bugle, drum and fife, together with the tramp, tramp of marching regiments every hour of the day and night. Many times we were in great peril.... July 1864 ... General Early's men were so close that we could hear the

---

[19] Mrs. Sample must have meant 1861. Fort Sumter was attacked 12 April 1861.

Chapter XXI. Elizabeth M. Morris and John D. Defrees ♦ 279

picket firing. Had the confederates been informed, there were two days following their arrival in which they could have marched into Washington without serious opposition ... sharp skirmish at nightfall, the Confederates decamped knowing their chance was gone.

The old Stephen Douglas house had been turned into a hospital. It was the overflow from this hospital which caused my mother and [some] neighbors to open their doors to the sick. My mother was a born nurse and always had one or two ill soldiers to care for.... [T]en or twelve of them ... promised letters ... not one word.

... [T]he streets were now filled with coloured people of all ages coming across the line ... this one crying, another laughing ... on their way to Contraband Camp on Meridian Hill....

On many occasions Lincoln sent for my father to talk over the grave situation of the country and it was way into the night that I would sometimes hear his step on the stair and into his room.... One morning at breakfast he appeared with the most obvious cold in the head.... "I am convinced," my mother said, "that you and the President allowed the fires to go out and continued sitting and talking in a cold room for hours." Stoves in the halls and open fires in the rooms were the only mode of heating the White House in those days. "I shall have to ... forbid you going to see Mr. Lincoln except in the daytime and even then you return filled with too many off-color stories. I shall have to inform Mrs. Lincoln of this during my next visit or else appoint a guard to watch over you two overgrown boys." They were both over six feet.... [My father] replied, "... [T]he President and I sat way into the night, and we did let the fire go out, but, you see, it was like this, the wood box is just outside the door and we took turns in fetching ... logs, and then we became so interested in our problems and decisions that we forgot whose turn it was. We got stubborn so neither of us would go, and along about two o'clock I became chilled and left for home."

Another time ... the President drove up to our house which was now across the street from the one we had rented.... Father bought [it] ... higher ceilings if possible, and more heavily carved black-walnut doors ... more gold mirrors ... lived in it for many years. The President arrived in a landau with a coloured driver ... stovepipe hat always brushed the wrong way ... very hot ... no coat or vest but the long linen duster of the mode.... They were off to inspect the army. Choice costume for the Commander in Chief![20]

There are other interesting stories fondly recalled in this memoir—thirteen typewritten pages—too many to duplicate here. However, one incident the author had heard before receiving Julia's paper warrants relating here. It reveals the close relationship that Lincoln and Defrees experienced for many years. As a journalist and able writer, John Defrees seems to have served his president and good friend as a "press secretary" as well as confidante.

The following is Julia Morris Defrees Sample's account. Written by the daughter of the man who said it, this is most likely a true tale.

> Of course my father always read over all of Mr. Lincoln's speeches and addresses before sending them to the press—correcting any slight error, and sometimes he would drive to the White House if he thought Mr. Lincoln should change or withdraw or reconsider some decision. There was one thing neither would ever resort to and that was slang....
>
> It has often been said that Mr. Lincoln wrote his great masterpiece of English on the train bearing him to Gettysburg, but this is a mistake. The President sent his carriage with his card to my father requesting him to come to the White House weeks before the ceremony at Gettysburg.... Handing him some papers, [the president] said "Defrees, I want you to read this and make any changes your judgement dictates.... After reading it, father said, "Mr. President, don't change a word of it. It's perfect."[21]
>
> ... [When] our troops occupied Richmond, our city went wild! Men who never touched anything were drunk ... noise deafening ... salvos of cannon ... windows illuminated everywhere ... fireworks in profusion ... [then] Lee's surrender. Washington was drunk again.

We of the Morris family can truthfully say that two of our cousins witnessed the assassination of Lincoln. The following is an eye-witness description of that tragic event written by one of them, Julia Morris Defrees Sample.

> On Good Friday it was announced in the papers that the Lincolns would attend Ford Theater, where Laura Keen's company was

---

[20] Julia Ann Morris Defrees Sample, "Washington in the Sixties," unpublished paper written in the spring of 1904. Sent to the author by Capt. Gordon Campbell, Mrs. Sample's great grandson, in May 1990.

[21] This account refutes the stories of scribble on the back of an envelope.

Chapter XXI. Elizabeth M. Morris and John D. Defrees

playing *Our American Cousin*.... My brother and I ... had chairs near the stage and it was during the third act a shot was fired. I had seen the play once before and said to my brother that I remembered no shooting in this play. Then Mrs. Lincoln screamed. I can still see plainly the dark, hatless man with the heavy black mustache jump from the President's box to the stage, gripping a shiny dagger, muttering and dragging his broken ankle across the stage until he was gone—behind the scenes. Everyone was on his feet and the excitement was tense. Some gentlemen firmly and tactfully ordered the crowd out. My brother and I had just one thought now, to gain home in safety....

The months have sped since I started to write these few recollections ... forsythia has shot its golden stars ... the great design of life goes on.

And so Julia Morris Defrees Sample closed her interesting personal remembrances of an important era of America's history. We are grateful she wrote them down.

* * * * *

It is interesting to imagine the wartime social life of these parents of six children in the 1860s. They surely were entertained by the Lincolns in the White House, by the Johnsons, the Hayes, possibly even by the Grants, and they knew the Colfaxes very well. The Civil War and post-war times were important. Bettie had been raised in a proper and prosperous Indianapolis family. Her parents and her brothers and brothers-in-law were nearly all wealthy and prestigious. She and her good husband, John, were indeed well able to handle themselves creditably in the political, financial, and social life of the capital.

John Defrees held the office of government printer for five years and developed the Bureau of Engraving and Printing, which still exists today as a very important entity of our government. Then, President Johnson, angered at some criticism by Defrees, removed him. Congress soon made it a Senate office, and he was reappointed within thirty days. Because he opposed Grant, Defrees was again out of office in 1869. He was a good man in every respect but rather outspoken for a politician. Both his removals were said to be due to criticisms of the Administration. But in 1877 when President Hayes came in, he was again appointed superintendent of that same Bureau of Engraving and Printing which he had established. Previous to this time all government printing had been contracted outside.

Th historian John Nowland wrote, "It is to John D. Defrees that the present [1870] Vice President of the United States is indebted for his high position, and as the New York *Tribune* remarked in regard to Grant and Rawlings, so with Colfax and Defrees: had there been no John Defrees there would have been no Vice President Colfax."[22]

Activity with the Whigs is referred to in still another history which tells of Defrees receiving and returning to Connecticut $5,000 which was intended for use in a state canvass. It was not needed.[23]

Defrees held this position until 1882, when declining health compelled his resignation. The responsibilities and distractions of six children added to a very busy political life would exhaust most people. Records of Crown Hill Cemetery reveal that he "died of exhaustion" in 1882, the year he resigned. He was seventy-two. Bettie lived twenty-two more years as the gracious and beloved matriarch of her family. She died in 1904 at age eighty. Neither John, Bettie, nor any of their family ever returned to live in Indianapolis.

A remark made by one of the Defrees-descendant cousins is so typical of our modern wish to recall but reveals our failure to preserve. The remark is truly regretful, while disclosing a small bit of family lore. "My dearest Mother, Julia Defrees Sample, dearly loved and often told about her grandmother.... She was of the 'old school' and part of her upbringing consisted of learning of family background. Mother spent a good deal of her growing years with her grandmother, Elizabeth Morris Defrees, who passed on to her a vast amount of information about our illustrious Morris and Defrees ancestors. It is a shame that none of us recorded the delightful tales of some of those experiences."[24]

Let *us,* the readers, *not* cause the same regrets!

Children and Descendants of Elizabeth Morris and John Defrees

Harriet Defrees, John Defrees' daughter by his first wife, became Mrs. Harriet Oakley, of New Orleans, Louisiana.[25]

---

[22] John H. B. Nowland, *Early Reminiscences of Indianapolis,* pp. 107-8.
[23] Dunn, p. 730.
[24] Col. Allan Campbell, letters to the author, 30 June 1978, and 1 December 1978, from Key Largo, Fla.
[25] Sulgrove, p. 240.

Chapter XXI. Elizabeth M. Morris and John D. Defrees ♦ 283

Elizabeth "Bettie" Morris and John DeFrees had six children, only five of whom lived to adulthood.

1. The first child, a son, was named Morris Morris Defrees for his maternal grandfather. He married Lydia Bradley and is mentioned three times in *The History of Indianapolis,* once as the son-in-law of John H. Bradley, a prominent banker, railroad operator, and member of the legislature.[26] More important to this saga, Morris was the civil engineer who laid out the surrounding grounds for the second and present state capitol.[27] His uncle Thomas A. Morris was in charge of its construction. Morris was also involved in building the monument in The Circle, and his name is at the base of the column. He is listed as head of the board of public works in 1892.[28]

Morris and Lydia Defrees had five children: Frederick Bradley Defrees, who was in the Spanish American War; Elizabeth; Lydia; Ellen; and Hugh. One great-grandson (descended from Hugh), Hugh Jackson Defrees Jr., is the only known member of the Morris family who died in World War II, in August 1942 aboard the *Quincy* in the Solomon Islands. See the Genealogy for further generations.

2. The second child was Julia Ann Morris Defrees, born in Indianapolis in 1848. She married James Anthony Sample, who became cashier of the U.S. Treasury and president of a Washington bank. They had four children: Morris, an engineer; Mary; Julia, who married a brigadier general and had ten children; and Amanda. One grandson, James A. Sample Jr. (descended from Morris), became chief of issues, U.S. Treasury Department. Among the very many great-grandchildren descending from Julia Defrees Sample were two brothers who graduated from West Point, Donald and Bruce Campbell. Their brother Gordon was an Annapolis graduate; Donald was in the U.S. Army Medical Corps and was awarded the Legion of Merit medal in 1968. A sister, Julie Campbell Tatham, must have inherited some of the genes of her great-grandfather, John D. Defrees the journalist, for she has published more than thirty books and is in three different *Who's Who*s.

A great-great-grandchild of Bettie and John DeFrees is a fine composer. Catherine MacDonald, daughter of Charmian who is a sister of the military men above, has already achieved a special niche among musical directors at New York's Lincoln Center and Washington's Folger, Carter

---

[26] Ibid., p. 214.
[27] Ibid., p. 216
[28] F. B. Heitman, *Historical Register and Dictionary of the U.S. Army,* vol. 1, p. 364.

Barron, and Lansburg Theaters, where she has contributed original scores.

3. The third child of Bettie Morris and John Defrees was Amanda, who lived less than a year.

4. The fourth child was John Dougherty Defrees Jr., 1855-1924, married, lived in Washington, and had no children. No more is known about him.

5. The fifth child, twin of John Jr., Anthony Colfax Defrees, died in 1903, unmarried, in Berkeley Springs, West Virginia.

6. Their sixth and last child was Thomas Morris Defrees, who, like the other five siblings, was born in Indianapolis. He entered the U.S. Army from West Virginia, 2nd Lt., Fifth Infantry in 1880, became 1st Lt. in 1885, and retired in 1897.[29] Thomas married Lydia Bradley Defrees, the widow of his eldest brother, Morris Morris Defrees, who had died at sixty-one. There were probably no children from this late marriage. Although named for his uncle the general, who was a very good friend of his parents, we know little of this last child of a large family, nor does the present generation of that family know more than is given here.

Catherine MacDonald

Bettie and John Defrees had six children, only nine grandchildren, and fifteen great-grandchildren. It is really surprising there were not more, and even more surprising that we have no records of any living descendants with the Defrees surname, although there could be some, unknown, from Morris Morris Defrees. There are only descendant records of the female lines, with married surnames other than Defrees.

See the detailed Genealogy of this entire family in Part Three of this book.

---

[29] Ibid.

Chapter XXII

WILLIAM LITTLE MORRIS and NICHOLAS McCARTY MORRIS
Eighth and Ninth Children of Morris and Rachael

> *We are the thousand winds that blow,*
> *The stars that shine at night,*
> *The diamond glints on snow,*
> *Great birds in circled flight.*
> *Our spirits live; we did not die.*
> — Anonymous

A BRIEF CHAPTER this must necessarily be. After telling of the seven children of Morris and Rachael, all of whom had eventful lives, we come to the eighth, William Little Morris. He was born in 1828, nearly seven years after the arrival of our pioneer family in Indianapolis. There are no records of his activities, but he died before he was twenty-five so he really didn't live very long to have anything recorded, unlike his siblings.

It seems a bit strange that he is not listed as one who was given a city building lot in April 1849 by his parents at the same time they gave one to each of his living brothers and sisters. There were several more lots left over. Morris had kept five for himself at the beginning, although we know that he later gave one to his granddaughter Caroline Mothershead and sold some to Thomas. But in 1849 William was only twenty and perhaps too immature. A curious fact: He is not listed with his parents in the 1850 census.

William married Ann E. Morrison in February 1850. They had a baby who died in infancy, no dates available. Cemetery records show a "Johnny Morris, born 1850, died 1855," who is probably that child. If so, the child died after his father.

William Little Morris died in 1853 and is buried at Crown Hill.

* * * * *

Nicholas McCarty Morris, the ninth and last child, was named for a family friend, Nicholas McCarty, an early pioneer and prominent Whig. Nicholas Morris was born in 1830, two years after William. Rachael, his mother, was forty-four. Nicholas lived only seven months and is buried at Crown Hill. (Small wonder the mother lived, back in those days of primitive medicines.)

This final child was born twenty-six years after Rachael gave birth to her first baby—indeed an extremely long span of childbearing even for a strong woman!

Both parents outlived five of their nine children. Their firstborn, Austin, died at forty-six, before the Civil War, after a very full and productive but short life, by our modern standards. Their second son, Milton, died in a tragic flatboat accident at twenty-seven, and William, their fifth son, died at twenty-four. Their lovely fifth child and oldest daughter, Amanda Mothershead, was deceased at thirty-four. And the last baby lived only seven months. Periodically, sadness seemed to penetrate the lives of these two pious, reverent, good people.

* * * * *

Thus ends this account of the six sons and three daughters of Rachael and Morris—an industrious, productive, important, and renowned family. Rachael died at age seventy-seven and Morris, at eighty-four. It was a long and eventful marriage which lasted sixty years.

Noted in numerous history books and articles over many decades, at last these people are *recorded together as a family* who contributed generously to the growth of Indianapolis and, in doing so, to the development of America. They left us a prideful heritage and a legacy to carry on.

An old Dartmouth College song affirms what we, too, must cherish: "Our heritage abides, miraculously remembered in our hearts."

Chapter XXIII

CONCLUSIONS

*It is good to have an end to journey towards,
But it is the journey that matters, in the end.*
— Ursala K. LeGuin

ALL NARRATIVES MUST HAVE AN ENDING, but family history is neverending. So the Morris lineage will continue in the genes, in the brains, in the lives of oncoming generations. A heritage to be passed on to the future is our immortality. All of us are wanderers, now-and-then pilgrims, explorers, adventurers. Across space and time we affirm and connect with one another, move in and out of one another's lives.

This tale of the Morris family has coalesced from a welter of names, dates, morsels of anecdotes, illuminating vignettes, and important historical facts into a narrative-history, yet often a plodding chronology, tedious at times, but factual.

Much more can be researched, blanks filled, dates verified. There are yet many truths to be discovered. The original intention was to compile and organize already-accumulated miscellany into a permanent, orderly and convenient form. It was my hope that in accomplishing this we might gain not only facts but *meanings* from the places, times, and happenings which we would encounter on the way. We might also gain some further knowledge of the settings and events during the eras in which successive generations of our family lived. We might better understand the religious, political, and economic aspects of our ancestors' lives.

There *are* hereditary influences which make up our ancestral life stream. And there are always the mavericks and the gifted. We must remember that those who wrote down family histories didn't always report everything. They usually failed to tell of the imperfections, failures, malfunctions, deformities, retardations, and personality quirks that could have caused some of the situations we do not comprehend today. In spite of this, certain physical features and character traits seem to emerge throughout the generations.

Setting Chepstow Castle's tallest tower ablaze; our Pilgrims' treacherous travels; the Welsh migrations in the late 1600s, some via Barbados and others directly to America—all of these events surely indicate real courage and a strong desire for adventure, to test the new and unknown. The odyssey of our forebears—men, women, and even children trudging through the wilds over miles of mountains and deserts, through dangerous country with no protection but ax and gun—was courageous. Their journeys from the East, through uncharted territory to western Virginia and eventually on to the far West, reveal a restlessness, a yearning, an optimism, a deep desire to improve, perhaps difficult for us today to imagine. Just a few generations later, two Howland brothers joined the party of John Wesley Powell to navigate the Grand Canyon on the dangerous Colorado River. Not long after this, a Frazee cousin was part of the Lewis and Clark expedition, exploring for President Jefferson the tremendous rapids of the great Columbia Gorge in Oregon. Their stories show the same adventurous courage, daring, and endurance of their predecessors. (I detected some of these same traits in my young son, so very determined to become a paratrooper in the jungles of Panama and Vietnam—and he did!)

In the early times of our country there was tremendous growth and opportunity for those with strength, health, intelligence, convictions, enthusiasm, and a propensity for *hard work*. They prospered at a rather rapid pace, with a sense of fulfillment and satisfaction. It is remarkable that some were able to accomplish so much in a relatively short life span. In 1776, life expectancy was only forty years for men.

This Morris family seems to have shown an early recognition of the importance of education. They manifested their genuine concern for other people's welfare by participation in community and civic affairs. The men are often recorded for their wisdom and leadership talents. We must assume that the women gave of themselves in supportive and nurturing ways. Lying fallow in these women was a greatness and a grace which they developed in spite of the early roughness of their lives.

The majority of our early men in America were farmers. Later, quite a few became engineers, and a great many served in the military, especially during our conflicts. Several were West Point graduates and one was an Annapolis graduate. A few were in the Revolutionary War, fewer in the War of 1812. Quite a lot were in the Civil War. One headed California's Presidio. Some were in World War I, even more in World War II, a couple in the Korean War, and more in the Vietnam War. As far as we know, only one brave son was lost in World War II. This noble young man was Hugh Jackson Defrees Jr., a great-great-great-grandson of Morris Morris II.

Some family names persist down through the generations, mainly John and Morris. There are also Leland, Louis/Lewis, Stanley, Julia/Julie, Ann/Anne/Anna, Amanda, Desdemona, and Elizabeth.

After locating and corresponding with very many of our Morris cousins, the fact emerges that the majority of the family are now in the western part of the country. The earlier Morris Morris remained in Kentucky. Many of his twelve offspring or *their* children eventually traveled farther west. Only one daughter, Rachael who married Morris Morris II, and one son, Daniel, migrated north to Indiana. One daughter, Bettie, moved to Washington, D.C., and now many of her peripatetic Army and Navy Campbell descendants are scattered in the East. Morris II's great-grandson, my father, came east in 1918 and has left descendants on the East Coast. I believe, however, that more of our Morris family are now living in California than in any other state.

This story has been about migration, which in the first decades was two-pronged. We must realize that our Pilgrim forebears left from the southeastern coast of England, sailing southwesterly to land in Massachusetts, then moving south to Connecticut and New Jersey. Only a few decades later our Welsh Morrises left their small country in southwest England to sail in the same direction and land in Philadelphia. They proceeded on foot westward across Maryland and into Virginia, where they connected with the descendants of our Pilgrims. Together, they all moved farther westward to Kentucky, some to remain there. But many, or their children, were to press on, mainly via the Oregon Trail, into Nebraska, South Dakota, Montana, Idaho, Oregon, California and Washington. Some of *their* descendants traveled even farther, partway across the Pacific Ocean, to settle in Hawaii.

Thus, these Morris forebears and their descendants have migrated across one ocean, the entire continental United States, and half-way across another ocean! This is "migration" in a very real sense.

*　　*　　*　　*　　*

Genealogy is a limitless pursuit of information about relatives, early as well as contemporary, for they too will become ancestors. So it behooves us to record, always being grateful to those who are kind enough to cooperate and respond. We should not fail our descendants! Nor should we fail, in the midst of comforts and modern medicine, to appreciate how we came by what we have and what we are.

And so I close with two thought-provoking metaphors, penned by a father and his daughter, perhaps appropriate to conclude an endless history.

The Metaphor of Coral

Life is a coral reef. We each leave behind the best, the strongest deposit we can, so that the reef can grow. But what's important is the reef.

— the late *Erwin Goodenough,*
Professor of Theology, Yale University

The Metaphor of the Circle

A human life is commonly perceived as a path from life to death, and most religious systems have sought to ameliorate this perception by offering such concepts as salvation or reincarnation. In its deepest sense, a credo of continuation perceives death as ultimately irrelevant and each life as immediately sacred. What's important is the circle.

— *Ursula Goodenough,*
Professor of Biology, Washington University, and
President, Institute for Religion in an Age of Science, 1995

Part Three

Genealogy of Our Morris Family

An Annotated Tabulation of Eleven Generations, From the Patriarch to the Present, Finally Assembled in One Book

Section I Generations One, Two, Three, and Partial Four: The Patriarch and Early Progeny
Index, Section I

Section II Generations Four to the Present: Descendants of Morris I and Sarah Cushman Morris
Index, Section II

—♦—

Allied Families: Cushman, Frazee, Friend, Robinett, Spurgeon, Worley, and Worral

A Brief Record of Families Linked to the Morrises by Marriage or Locality

There are but two lasting bequests we can give our children. The first is roots; the last is wings.
— Anonymous

> **GENEALOGY OF OUR MORRIS FAMILY**
> **Section I, Generations One, Two, Three, and Partial Four: The Patriarch and Early Progeny**

Here we are all gathered—in a bond of kinship from the past and of the present.

Notes: Generations are designated numerically: 1, 2, 3, etc. Individuals within each generation, alphabetically: 1a, 1b, 1c, etc.; 2a, 2b, 2c, etc. All known descendants of each individual, from his generation to the present, are listed before continuing with the next person in that generation.

Generation 1 names are flush with the left margin; succeeding generational names are indented incrementally across the page.

Direct ancestors of the author are in boldface type.

Using very limited available dates and information, and calculating from approximate generation and birth spans, the author has interlinked these very early Morris generations in a manner that appears reasonable.

Sources: Author; family tradition; Feather Davis, 5001 Wetheredsvale Road, Baltimore, MD 21207; Virginia Gray, 17833 Sixth Avenue SW, Seattle, WA; Gary W. Quincy, 7123 Angelsea Drive, West Jordan, UT 84084.

> **Generations One, Two, Three, and Partial Four: The Patriarch and Early Progeny**

1a John Morris I, born c. 1677 probably in parish of Karbadamfyneth, in the county of Radnor, Llanelly, borough of Carmarthen, Wales; yeoman; second on list of passengers as heading a group of six on a ship called the *William Galley* leaving 1697-8 for Philadelphia; a "document of ffreightment" drawn up by Owen Thomas of Carmarthen, owner of the ship, was among David Powell and John Morris, and three other Powell families. The "charter party," listed as sixty-two, was recorded as definitely being in Philadelphia by March 1699 ("An Old Charter Party," *Emigrants to Pennsylvania*).

Also listed together in P. William Filby's *Passenger and Immigration Lists Index* were a "Morris, Jno. 20" and a "Morris, Hugh 14," both "Maryland and/or Virginia 1699." Could these two also have been part of the "Charter Party"? No records of a Hugh have been found; he might not have survived.

After probably living in Philadelphia a short time, John and his party traveled westward into Maryland, where they eventually must have settled only a short distance apart. John became the constable of Sugar Loaf Hundred, Maryland, in 1749. (Sugarloaf was also the name of a nearby mountain.) John was the father of two known sons, (generation 2, below). In his later years he must have lived with his younger son, John II, for he appears with him in a 1768 Maryland record. An old man, he was "set Levy Free for the future," although no petition requesting exemption from taxes has been found. Records indicate that he died in Maryland before the family's postponed move to Virginia.

Note: The children of Richard Morris have heretofore been listed in published material naming the three sons first and the three girls last, no dates given. That order is herein proven incorrect; however, the order given below is still not definitive, as some dates are estimated from other known dates.

2a Richard Morris I born c. 1722-5 in Pennsylvania or Maryland, 1st m. to Rebecca (deed) ?Flint (d. c. 1759 Maryland [rec.]), six children; 2nd m. before 1761 to Mary —— (Archives, File Box 282, Morgantown, W.Va.) (she might have been Mary Watts I, the mother of Mary II and widow of Col. Wm. Watts of Campbell Co., Ky.; see 3d under John II); bought land in Frederick Co., Md., 1748, 1759, 1766; taxed in 1761 along with Spurgeons; constable of Old Town Hundred, where many Robinetts lived, in 1764; moved to Virginia before 1770, as did some Spurgeons and Robinetts; built Fort Morris in 1774; moved to Kentucky in 1788, died intestate in 1803 in Mason Co., Ky. (rec.), "far advanced in years." See Richard's Chronology at the end of this Section I for more details.

3a John Morris III, b. c. 1758 ?Georgetown, Md. (rec.), d. before 1800; five children:

4a Richard Morris II, b. c. 1782; m. 1807 Rebecca Todd (b. 1797; Rebecca was under age, so bonded by father, John Todd of Virginia [rec.]); nine children.

Genealogy of Our Morris Family, Section I ♦ 295

4b Maurice Morris III, b. 1787; m. 3 Aug. 1809 Polly Cummins (under 21 in 1811 so bondsman was Jacob Cummins) (Pendleton Co. marriages); 4 Oct. 1834 Maurice and Polly sell to Wm. Kenny for $1,695.75 56 acres and 4 poles in Bourbon Co. on Little Houston (Edw. McConnell's line); 1834, above, Maurice and Polly and John B. and Priscilla Cummins sell ... near Paris, etc.

4c William Harris Morris, b. ?1788 in Pendleton Co.; m. Jane Irvine.

4d Rebecca Morris, b. 1790, m. in 1824 Edward McConnell (rec.); Edw. McConnell sells to Maurice Morris, who becomes security for McConnell, etc. (rec.).

4e Drusilla Morris, b. c. 1792, m. 4 Nov. 1817 John Sidwell (1798-1873) (rec.); five children; ancestor of Gary Wayne Quincy of West Jordan, Utah, whose name-line follows:

    5 John Sidwell Jr. (1818-1895), m. Emiline McConnell (1823-1864).

    6 Nancy Jane Sidwell (1842-1922), m. William V. Buchanan (1840-1909).

    7 Mollie Mae Buchanan (1874-1938), m. Joseph M. Scranton (1868-1932).

    8 Robert Gerald Scranton (1910-1962), m. Lura Elvea Rowley (1906-1976).

    9 Marquiet M. Scranton (b. 1932), m. Arnold Wayne Quincy (1925-1961).

    10 Gary Wayne Quincy (b. 1949), m. Jane Ellen Hebertson (b. 1952).

3b Rachel Morris, b. c. 1790 (children's record); m. Joseph Robinett ([1751-1810] [rec.]; son of Ann —— and Samuel Robinett, who came to America with William Penn [see *Robinett Family*]; occupation was leathercraft); 1774 in Monongalia Co., Va.; 1790 in Bourbon Co., Ky.; ancestor of Gertrude Gray of Seattle, Wash., former teacher, professional genealogist who spent seven years abstracting entire series of Northern Neck of Virginia Land Grant books which were published in 1995; formed a genealogical group at the Seattle Public Library. Gertrude's name-line follows:

4 Richard Robinett, b. c. 1729, m. Ruth Collier.

5 Julia Ann Robinett (1800-1869), m. James Ritchey I (1822-1875); she was his 2nd wife.

6 James Ritchey II (1822-1875), m. Nathena Whitlock (1824-1892).
7 Nancy Jane Ritchey (1858-1929), m. Andrew Jackson Trotter (1875-1903).
8 Erie Blanche Trotter (1875-1903), m. William McCullah Mathews.
9 Viola Erie Mathews (1896-1991), m. Phillip Carl Entz (1889-1977).
10 Gertrude Viola Entz (b. 1919), m. William Lee Gray (b. Oklahoma, worked for Boeing Airplane Co.).

3c Thomas Morris, born 1751 (rec.), m. Mary —— , thirteen children; farmer, Democrat, member of the Church of Christ; eventually settled in Indiana; d. before 1807; deposition of brother Morris dated 1807 that he, Morris Morris I, was the only living son of Richard; Nov. 1800 estate appraisal in Bourbon Co., Ky., wife "Polly" the sole administratrix.

3d Mary Morris, b. c. 1756 (based on rec. of 1st child's birth); 1st m. c. 1776 Daniel Greathouse (said to be the leader of a treacherous act during Dunmore's War when several unarmed Indian men and three squaws were slaughtered after being enticed to Baker's cabin and plied with liquor; frightening reaction followed; Fort Morris was built; Greathouse d. 1777 of measles); 2nd m. Andrew McCreary.

3e Catherine Morris, b. c. 1758 (census: children); m. c. 1775/6 Samuel Spurgeon (possibly son of William); 1782 census, five in household, only one daughter, who died young.

3f **Morris Morris I**, b. 12 Feb. 1761 (rec.), m. c. 1781/2 **Sarah Cushman** (b. 10 Sept. 1766 [rec.]; 2nd m. 1820 Graham Forrest of Harrison Co.; later returned to Bourbon County to be with her children; d. 10 Jan. 1842); 1798 written covenant with Joseph Robinett, brother-in-law, for land and goods (1799 bond); Morris Morris II "supported and maintained" father Richard and wife Mary for the rest of their lives, in return received all Richard's property; 1800 William Conner sells Morris Morris horses, one Negro boy Harry, all furniture etc.; 1808 Morris Morris buys one Negro slave named Dice for $135.63; 1800 buys another female slave; d. 17 May 1807 in Bourbon Co., Ky. (record of estate settlement, Book A, p. 55); twelve children.

See Section II for individual generation four genealogies of the twelve children of Morris and Sarah Cushman.

2b John L. Morris II (brother of Richard I), b. c. 1737, m. Eleanor —— (d. Mason Co., Ky. [rec.]); lived near his brother Richard on Flintstone Creek, Md., where he bought land in 1765; wife Eleanor was beaten in 1771 (rec.); moved to Virginia in 1774 (after Richard; had aged father and young children); 1788 moved to Kentucky; still later to Pennsylvania on Georges Creek near Maryland border; died after 1793 (will), c. 1797 (rec.); nine children. See his Chronology at the end of this section for more details.

John's nine children, in probable order of birth:

    3a ?Daughter not named in will so assumed married by 1793.

    3b Joseph Morris, b. ?1760 (rec.); minister; m. ?Mary Overfield (LDS); executor of father's estate 1796; served in Revolution in Capt. John Whitsell's company of Rangers from Monongalia County when it exercised actual jurisdiction over much of present Fayette County; also in Monongalia County in militia under command of Gaddis, a militia officer before present boundaries were determined; stationed part of the time at Fort Morris; 1797 Joseph lived in Fayette County; the same year he was executor of his father's will; via attorney Morris Morris II (John II's youngest son) he sold 490 acres to David Gundy, followed by twenty-four lawsuits, as Gundy paid only half; case died for want of Gundy's security; lived in Bracken County, Ky., by 1807; same year, via lawyer brother Morris Morris II, sold 100 acres in Monongalia Co. which Joseph had inherited in his father's will; 1814 lived in Champaign Co., Ohio; 1814 sold, via Morris Morris II, remainder of the Monongalia land Gundy had tried to buy; minister Joseph conducted the marriage service for both his brother Morris and sister Elizabeth (rec.).

    3c Dorcas Morris, b. 15 Aug. 1765 (rec.); m. (before father's will; not named in will) 22 June 1788 David Cushman (b. 1764 [rec.], brother of Sarah); lived Mason Co., Ky.; at 85 living with daughter Ann (m. 1834 Joseph Frazee); d. 13 March 1854.

        4a Thomas Cushman, b. 16 Oct. 1796, d. 26 Jan. 1851.
        4b Ann Cushman, b. 12 Oct. 1798; 1st m. —— Holliway; 2nd m. Joseph Frazee; d. 11 Aug. 1851.

            5a Joseph T. Frazee

5b John Morris Frazee, b. c. 1792; m. Eliza J. Lusk; medical doctor; lived Maysville, Ky.

    6a Anna C. Frazee, m. Posey Dixon Ball; in Mayflower Index.
    6b Frances L. Frazee, m. Henry Lloyd; in Mayflower Index.

    7a Henry Lloyd Jr.

5c David Cushman Frazee, b. 17 Sept. 1842; Confederate army; m. Marie Lee; lived Maysville and Lexington, Ky.

4c Joseph Cushman
4d Mary Cushman
4e Eliza Cushman

3d Richard Morris II, in the Revolution, probably m. Mary Watts (daughter of Col. Wm. and Mary Watts of Campbell County, Ky.; as a veteran's widow, Mary applied for bounty land in 1808; lived in Cynthiana, Ky., near her mother-in-law).

3e James Morris, remained in Virginia, probably unmarried, as no wife's name appears on any deeds; 1798 sold 90 acres on Muddy Creek, Preston Co., Ky., to Henry Hardesty, land cornered by George Sipolt and Henry Criss; 1799 was sued for $500 debt with Sipolt co-signer; 1802 Muddy Creek tract of 185 acres deeded to James Morris by Christina Clester, conveyed to her by Criss and wife, adjoining lands of Sipolt. In 1816, James Morris of Adams Co., Ohio, conveyed land to Elijah Hardesty referred to as "part of G. Sipolt's old survey he sold to Henry Criss ..."; possibly in 1824 still no wife, coming back up the river in his late middle age, bought the old Stone House in New Geneva, Fayette County, and sold it to James Daugherty in 1831; in 1762 signed petition concerning division of Virginia and Pennsylvania; also signing the petition were Ezekiel, John, John Jr., and Jonathan (not ours) Morris.

3f John Morris IV (probably younger than his cousin-once-removed, Richard's son John III).

3g Morris Morris II, b. 1780, m. **Rachael Morris** (b. 1786, his first-cousin-once-removed, daughter of Morris Morris I).

3h Elizabeth Morris, b. before Nov. 1784; m. Moses Frazee (b. 1770, d. Indiana); 2nd wife; d. Indianapolis.

3i Eleanor Morris, a child at time father wrote his will so is named in his will. Her sisters probably received dowries.

*1b Thomas Morris I, b. c. 1691 (record); probably a younger relative, possibly a member of John I's charter party group, as he was residing near the same families as John I; 1749 in Maryland signed petition for a bridle road near Point of Rocks on the Potomac River (Judgement Recs. 1748-1765); same year for burying a poor woman (ibid., 35); 1750 for aiding an orphan (ibid.); a 1751 petition to be set levy free as he was sixty, poor, and infirm, was rejected in 1752; lived at Point of Rocks, Md. (Tracey and Derm's *Pioneers of Old Monocacy*), on the Potomac River not far from Oldtown where Richard lived, and nearer Antietam where old James Spurgeon had a ferry; d. c. 1760. (Many Spurgeons and Robinetts were in Antietam, as well as at Oldtown; some Robinetts never moved westward.)

*1c William Morris, recorded nearby in Maryland, was also probably a relative and possible passenger on the emigrant ship (rec.).

*1d Morris Morris (family name) also probably a relative and a possible member of this group of six; on a 1750 lawsuit judgment (Rec. A: 1748-1752, p. 303); also on a Georgetown, Montgomery Co., Md., 1777 tax roll.

*Note: These three men are shown in the same generation as John I of Wales but there is no proof that they were brothers. It is probable, however, that they were related to John, having the same surname.

Chronology of Generation Two
Brothers Richard I and John II Morris

Source: Rick Toothman, professional genealogist. References are noted in his report to the author and include photocopies of relevant documents.

Year	*Richard Morris, 2a, son of John I of Wales*
	Event
1748/9	Sale of land to Richard Morris of Frederick Co., from John and Elizabeth Friend (Swedish) of Lancaster Co., Pa., called "Swedeland," near Toms Creek in northern Frederick Co. near Emmitsburg, Md.
1755	Militia consisted of all able-bodied men from 16 to 60 excluding ministers, servants and slaves, providing themselves with firearms and ammunition. No Richard named.
1759	Bought 100 acres from Joseph and Charity Flint on Town Creek, Alleghany Co., already called "Morris Chase" (also referred to as "Morris Choice"), six miles from mouth of Town Creek. Flint had patented this in 1753. This implies that Richard or another Morris (or Flint) was in this area by 1753. Flint also patented, in 1753, 50 acres called Morgans Choice nine miles from mouth of Town Creek, Old Town Hundred. Richard also bought Morgans Choice in 1759 from Flint.
1761	No Morgans on 1761 tax list for Old Town but was probably David Morgan (1721-1813) originally from Berkeley Co., Va., later from Monongalia County. Son Evan (1754-1850) stated in pension that he was born in Old Town, Md.
1761	Tax assessment, listed immediately ahead of three Spurgeons, then John Morris following the Spurgeons.
1764	Appointed constable in Old Town Hundred, Frederick Co., Md. Maryland eliminated hundreds in the very late 1700s.
1764	Resold Morgans Choice to Flint. Wife Rebecca's name is on deed.
1766	Bought 80 acres called "Morris Luck," which adjoined Morris Chase.
1770	or earlier. Moved to Monongalia Co..
1774	Built Fort Morris in Grant District but no Morrises or neighbors were on payrolls of Dunmore's War; curious but perhaps records were lost.
1779	Sold the above two parcels, 180 acres, in Washington County, no wife mentioned, presumed dead.
1782	Signed petition concerning division of Virginia and Pennsylvania protesting the latter's annexation of territory north of Mason-Dixon Line.
1783	Taxes: 1 tithe (male over 16), 4 horses, 16 cattle.
1786	Taxes: 1 male, 3 horses, 3 cattle; in Daniel McCollum's district.

Genealogy of Our Morris Family, Section I

1787	Taxes: 1 male, 4 horses, 6 cattle, himself not tithable (shown in margin).
1788	Tax list: not tithable, no tithable males, 6 horses.
1788	Or earlier, moved to Kentucky.
1798	Living with son Morris I. Taxed for 400 acres. Henry Hazle is on the land and will sue to get title in another year or so; now no official conveyance of property.
1800	Lawsuit begun concerning three bonds in file of 1788, and two for 1789 where Richard promises a deed to Henry Hazle plus 1,000 pounds but does not oblige. Signs all bonds "Rich. Maurice."
1803	Died intestate. (Recorded in *Kentucky Citizen*.)
1804	Monongalia County deeds: Mary (widow), Jos., Rachel, Sam. and Catherine Spurgeon, Andrew and Mary McCreary, all of Bourbon County, release their interest in 540 acres for token sum of five shillings.

John L. Morris II, 2b, son of John I of Wales

c. 1737	John L. Morris born.
c. 1760-1761	Married Eleanor (last name unknown). She died in Mason Co., Ky. (record).
1755	All able-bodied men age 16 to 60 in militia. No John named, probably records lost. Maryland also recruited provincial troops for war service; few records extant.
c. 1760-1770	Lived near Flintstone Creek, Frederick (now Allegany) Co., Md.
1761	Taxed in Old Town Hundred, 1 tithable. Listed after Spurgeons.
1765	Bought 50 acres called "Johnsons (Johnstons) Folly," east side of Martins Mountain near head of draught of Flintstone Creek (probably a minor draught since the deed didn't bother to name it), in or near Flintstone, Md., on U.S. 40, near two tracts of Richard Morris, about nine miles from the Potomac River. This was patented in Maryland and sold in 1785 by a Maryland deed well after the Pennsylvania-Maryland line was established.
1771	Eleanor Morris beaten and assaulted by Patrick Daugherty, recorded in Frederick County Court; quashed.
1774	Went to Monongalia County. Not on payrolls for Dunmore's War, nor were other Morrises or neighbors; curious (records lost?).
1782	On list showing 11 in household.
1782	Also signed petition concerning annexation of Pennsylvania-Virginia territory.

1783	Jonathan Bishop had paid the Maryland taxes on Johnsons Folly, so he must have been living on it. John Morris had gone to Virginia. Later sold it.
1783	Monongalia Co., Va., tax list shows John Morris Sr. plus 1 tithable (male over 16, probably Joseph), 2 horses, 12 cattle.
1785	John Morris and wife "Elendor" sold Johnsons Folly, Washington Co., Md., to Bishop. John not living on it as not in Washington County fidelity listings or Maryland militia during Revolution.
1786	Tax list: 1 male, 3 horses, 9 cattle.
1788	Tax list: son Richard, 1 tithable, 7 horses.
1788	Moved to Kentucky (Campbell County).
1793	Wrote will in Georges Creek, Pa., recorded in Monongalia Co., Va. One of the witnesses was Sam Woodbridge, who lived near Woodbridge town on road from Ices Ferry (now Cheat Lake) to Uniontown, in Springhill Township. In 1796 this was Springhill.
1796	Lived on Georges Creek, in Georges or Wharton Township, Fayette Co., Pa.
1796-1797	Between 20 Oct. 1796 and 4 April 1797, John L. Morris died.
1798	Residence unknown (dead!), taxed with 600 acres still in John's name. Gundy has the bigger portion but will not be able to keep it (can't pay). Griffin has the rest but won't get a deed until 1807.

*   *   *   *   *

Following the Index to Section I is Section II, comprising the fourth generation *individual* genealogies of the twelve children of Morris I and Sarah Cushman Morris.

INDEX
Genealogy, Section I

Notes:
1. Chronologies are excluded.
2. Married women are indexed under married, not maiden, name(s).

Ball, Anna C. (Frazee), 298
Ball, Posey Dixon, 298
Buchanan, Nancy Jane (Sidwell), 295
Buchanan, William V., 295
Clester, Christina, 298
Conner, William, 296
Criss, Henry, 298
Cummins, Jacob, 295
Cummins, John B., 295
Cummins, Priscilla, 295
Cushman
    David, 297
    Dorcas (Morris), 297
    Eliza, 298
    Joseph, 298
    Mary, 298
    Thomas, 297
Daugherty, James, 298
Entz, Phillip Carl, 296
Entz, Viola Erie (Mathews), 296
Forrest, Graham, 296
Forrest, Sarah (Cushman) (Morris), 296
Frazee
    Ann (Cushman) (Holliway), 297
    David Cushman, 298
    Eliza J. (Lusk), 298
    Elizabeth (Morris), 298
    John Morris, 298
    Joseph, 297
    Joseph T., 297
    Marie (Lee), 298
    Moses, 298
Gaddis, 297
Gray, Gertrude, 295
Gray, Gertrude Viola (Entz), 296
Gray, William Lee, 296
Greathouse, Daniel, 296
Greathouse, Mary (Morris), 296
Gundy, David, 297
Hardesty, Elijah, 298
Hardesty, Henry, 298
Holliway, —, 297
Holliway, Ann (Cushman) (Frazee), 297
Kenny, Wm., 295
Lloyd, Frances L. (Frazee), 298
Lloyd, Henry, 298
Lloyd, Henry, Jr., 298
Mathews, Erie Blanche (Trotter), 296
Mathews, William McCullah, 296
McConnell, Edward, 295
McConnell, Rebecca (Morris), 295
McCreary, Andrew, 296
McCreary, Mary (Morris) (Greathouse), 296
Morris
    Eleanor, 299

Eleanor (———), 297
Ezekiel, 298
Hugh, 294
James, 298
Jane (Irvine), 295
Jno., 294
John, 298
John I, 293
John III, 294
John IV, 298
John, Jr., 298
John L. II, 297
Jonathan, 298
Joseph, 297
Mary, 296
Mary (———), 296
Mary (———), 294
Mary (Overfield), 297
Mary (Watts), 298
Maurice III, 295
Morris, 299
Morris I, 296
Morris II, 296, 298
Polly (Cummins), 295
Rachael (Morris), 298
Rebecca (?Flint), 294
Rebecca (Todd), 294
Richard, 294, 296
Richard I, 294
Richard II, 294, 298
Sarah (Cushman), 296
Thomas, 296
Thomas I, 299
William, 299
William Harris, 295
Powell, David, 293
Quincy, Arnold Wayne, 295
Quincy, Gary Wayne, 295
Quincy, Jane Ellen (Hebertson), 295
Quincy, Marquiet M. (Scranton), 295

Ritchey, James, 295
Ritchey, James II, 296
Ritchey, Julia Ann (Robinett), 295
Ritchey, Nathena (Whitlock), 296
Robinett, Ann (———), 295
Robinett, Joseph, 295, 296
Robinett, Rachel (Morris), 295
Robinett, Richard, 295
Robinett, Ruth (Collier), 295
Robinett, Samuel, 295
Scranton, Joseph M., 295
Scranton, Lura Elvea (Rowley), 295
Scranton, Mollie Mae (Buchanan), 295
Scranton, Robert Gerald, 295
Sidwell, Drusilla (Morris), 295
Sidwell, Emiline (McConnell), 295
Sidwell, John, 295
Sidwell, John, Jr., 295
Sipolt, George, 298
Spurgeon, Catherine (Morris), 296
Spurgeon, James, 299
Spurgeon, Samuel, 296
Spurgeon, William, 296
Thomas, Owen, 293
Todd, John, 294
Trotter, Andrew Jackson, 296
Trotter, Nancy Jane (Ritchey), 296
Watts, Mary, 298
Watts, Wm., Col., 298
Whitsell, John, Capt., 297

> # GENEALOGY OF OUR MORRIS FAMILY
> Section II, Generations Four to the Present:
> Descendants of Morris I and Sarah Cushman Morris

Note: The author, Anne Morris Mertz, is a descendant of Morris Morris I and Sarah Cushman, and Morris Morris II and Rachael Morris.

Generations:
    First   John Morris of Wales
    Second   Richard and Rebecca Morris of Maryland
                  Thomas Cushman VI of Connecticut and Mary Frazee of New Jersey
    Third   Morris Morris I and Sarah Cushman, both of Virginia (now West Virginia)
               John Morris II and Eleanor of Maryland

> **Generation 4: Thomas Morris, First Child of Morris I and Sarah ♦ Descendants and Court Records**

Sources: Author; *Cushman Genealogy and Family History,* by Alvah W. Burt; and Robert Thomas, 303 S. Harrison Street, Papillion, NE 68046, a descendant of Horatio Morris.

4a Thomas Morris, b. 3 May 1783; 1st m. 21 Dec. 1815 Sophia Talbot; 2nd m. 27 March 1818 Mary "Polly" Parker; 3rd m. Lucinda Fruit (d. 18 Sept. 1846, sister of Malinda Fruit, 2nd wife of younger brother Horatio Morris, bef. July 1837); seven children:

  5a Laura Morris, b. 25 May 1818, Kentucky.
  5b Edwin Talbot Morris, b. 2 Aug. 1819, Bourbon Co., Ky.; d. 13 Jan. 1846.
  5c Hyrum Bowles Morris Sr., b. 23 Dec. 1821, Boonsville, Bourbon Co., Ky.; m. Eleanor Roberts.
  5d Tallitha Thomas Morris, b. 1823.
  5e Nancy Beauford Morris, b. 3 Jan. 1828 Barbara, Ky.; m. John Lyle Riggs; d. 14 Aug. 1903.

5f John Preston Morris, b. 15 Jan. 1833 Barbara, Ky.; d. 8 Oct. 1833.

5g Rebecca Ann Morris, b. 15 Jan. 1838, Barbara, Ky.

Court Records, Thomas Morris

Sept. 1809: Thomas administrator with mother, Sarah Morris, of his father's estate. Bourbon Co. Order Book D, pp. 146, 391; June 1811, Book D, p. 404; Will Book D, pp. 13-16, sale; 4 Dec. 1815, Order Book E, p. 462.; 6 May 1816, Order Book E, p. 503, settlement.

12 June 1818: James Williams of Pike Co., Ohio, sells to Thomas Morris for $112 a lot on Main St. in Paris, Ky., No. 19, 66'-front and 214.5' to Pleasant Street. Book Q, p. 71.

22 Jan. 1824: "Robert Bowen and Delilah his wife sell to Thomas Morris for $750, 32 acres on Hinkson (Dimitt's line to Millersburgh Rd., a part of Samuel Nesbitt's settlement and preemption)." Book Q, p. 127.

22 Jan. 1824: Thomas Morris sells to [brothers] Horatio, Preston, Albert F., and Beauford Morris, all of Bourbon County, for $500, a Negro boy George about 5 years old, 1 sorrel mare, 1 bay mare, 7 beds and bedding and bedsteads, 1 cow and calf. Horatio has lent $300 in silver; there are several executions in the hands of Benjamin Todd, constable of Bourbon County, in favor of different persons against Thomas amounting to $100; Horatio has become security for Thomas in replevy bonds. Thomas, wishing to secure and indemnify, has executed this mortgage. If Thomas pays the mortgage in two years with interest, this to be void. Thomas is also to retain the use of said merchandise. Book R, p. 419.

22 Jan. 1825: Bourbon Co., Ky., Thomas borrowed $500 from brothers Horatio, Preston, Alfred, and Beauford. Security: all household and livestock, which Thomas may use in the meantime. Horatio (lawyer) will go his bond.

> **Generation 4: Rachael Morris**
> **Second Child of Morris I and Sarah Cushman Morris**

Notes: Rachael is an unusual spelling but is verified by her own signature on several deeds in the possession of the author. The more common spelling, Rachel, was used by her daughter-in-law and also by one of her aunts who married a Spurgeon. Rachael was a direct *Mayflower* descendant through her mother. The names of the twelve children of Rachael and Morris II are underlined. These children are the fifth generation, designated 5a, 5b, 5c, etc.

Sources of information: The author; and many of her cousins, particularly the following: Reily Gibson Adams of Indianapolis, deceased; R. Morris Adams, 15902 Farr Hills, Westfield, IN 46074; Ann Mothershead Bjorklund, 12784 Normandy Lane, Los Altos Hills, CA 94022; Captain Gordon Campbell, 3838 Somerset Drive, Durham, NC 27707; Julie Defrees Campbell, 1202 S. Washington Street, Alexandria, VA; and Mary Louise Morris Friley, Box 256, Minto, ND 58261. All are descendants of Rachael Morris and Morris Morris II.

4b Rachael Morris, b. 20 Jan. 1786 Monongalia Co., Va.; m. 8 Aug. 1803 Cane Ridge Meeting House, near Paris, Ky., her first-cousin-once-removed, Morris Morris II (b. 18 Dec. 1780, Monongalia Co., Va.; son of John Morris I; self-read lawyer; assoc. of Henry Clay; Ind. militia; real estate agent; anti-Jackson; Indianapolis city councilman 1847-1848; one of three commissioners appointed to plan and oversee building new Indiana State Capitol; elected state auditor 15 years; retired at age 64, a leading citizen; d. 16 Aug. 1864 Indianapolis; buried Crown Hill Cem., Indianapolis). Rachael, when two years old, traveled in wagons and then on a flatboat on the Ohio River with her family and those of her cousins, from Virginia to Kentucky, where she grew up and married at 17. After six children, in 1821, with very strong convictions, moved with her immediate family to the wilderness of the new state of Indiana because it was probably not going to condone slavery; Morris and Rachael purchased land which eventually became very valuable mid-city property. Rachael died 1 July 1863, Indianapolis; buried in Crown Hill Cemetery.

5a Austin W. Morris, first child of Morris and Rachael Morris, b. 9 Sept. 1804 Bourbon Co., Ky.; m. 3 March 1831 Jane Maria Peppard (b. 15 April 1812, first woman mentioned in Indiana history books, as founder and president of Indianapolis Widows and Orphans Society, today the Children's Bureau; great-granddaughter of Joseph Greer, b. c. 1740 in Ireland, founder of Greer family in America; d. New York 24 Oct. 1877 of paralysis); one of Indianapolis's first school teachers; Ind. militia, 40th Reg., lt. col., 1833; clerk, Ind. State Board of Canal Commissioners; presidential elector 1836; trustee Ind. Asbury (DePauw) Univ.; trustee Indianapolis Female Seminary; Freemason; leading citizen; prominent Whig; one of the wealthiest men in Indianapolis; d. 21 or 22 June 1861.

6a & b Gabrielle Morris and Milton Morris, died in infancy (twins?).

6c Josephine B. Morris, b. 1836, m. 18 Nov. 1857 her second-cousin, George Bates Greer (b. 26 June 1829, Greer Turner & Co., New York City; dir. North Shore Railroad and other corporations; d. 4 Sept. 1898); lived Rye, N.Y.; d. 3 July 1893; five children.

7a George Morris Greer, b. 19 April 1859 New York City; m. Lena Dell (b. 1 Feb. 1867, dau. of Benjamin R. and Mary Campbell Dell of Villa Grove, Colo.); cattle rancher to 1907, then lived in Denver.

8a Theodore Morris Greer, b. 26 Dec. 1888; d. 7 May 1968.

8b George Bates Greer, b. 5 Feb. 1897; m. 9 June 1920 Isabell Elizabeth McCarthy (b. 23 April 1899 Denver, dau. of Michael Joseph and Nannie Patrick McCarthy); d. 25 Aug. 1955.

9a George Bates Greer II, b. 2 Feb. 1922; m. 3 Aug. 1944, Denver, Mary Patricia Sarbach (b. 13 Oct. 1924 New York City).

10a George Bates Greer III, b. 23 Dec. 1947 Denver.

10b Michael Daly Greer, b. 20 April 1951 Denver.

10c Mary Janice Greer, b. 4 ? 1953 Denver.

10d Gregory Patrick Greer, b. 30 May 1955 Denver.

10e Mary Sharon Greer, b. 6 Feb. 1959 Denver.

9b Marjorie Isabelle Greer, b. 30 Nov. 1927; m. 19 June 1949 Evergreen, Colo., Charles Wilbur Appell (b. 30 Sept. 1919).

    10a Christopher Anthony Appell, b. 8 May 1950 Denver.
    10b Genevive Marjorie Appell, b. 14 Jan. 1952 Denver.
    10c Ruth Elizabeth Appell, b. 14 July 1953 Denver.
    10d Charles Wilbur Appell, b. 13 Oct. 1954 Denver.
    10e Mark Andrew Appell, b. 16 Sept. 1955.
    10f Joseph Patrick Appell, b. 27 March 1958 Denver.

7b Austin Morris Greer, b. 22 Nov. 1863 New York City; broker, mem. N.Y. Stock Exchange; m. N.Y., Ida Northrup; d. 18 Dec. 1920.

7c Theodore Morris Greer, b. 23 Aug. 1865 New York City; d. 17 April 1884.

7d Louis Morris Greer, b. 30 Dec. 1868 New York City; grad. Harvard, Columbia Law; m. 26 Nov. 1908 Mabel Adele Seymour (b. 28 Jan. 1881 Manchester, England; d. 10 Aug. 1946), mem. N.Y. Stock Exchange 1892-1900; dir. Consolidated Gas Co., N.Y. Carbide & Acetylene Co.; 2nd lt. Spanish Am. War, major N.Y. Nat. Guard; d. 10 Aug. 1946, just before wife Mabel; no issue.

7e Desdemona "Dessie" Morris Greer, b. 14 Feb. 1871, New York City; unmarried.

6d Louis Thompson Morris, b. 21 Dec. 1840; entered U.S. Army Infantry 1861, 1st lt. 1861, breveted capt. 1864 for gallantry and meritorious service during the Atlanta Campaign, to major 1864 for gallantry and meritorious service in the Battle of Nashville; twice decorated during Civil War; lt. col. 1897; commanding officer of the Presidio in San Francisco during the Spanish Am. War; transferred to cavalry 1889; retired 1898; m. in Baltimore, Md., Susan Frances Reece (d. 8 June 1899); member of Sons of American Revolution and the Loyal Legion; lost home in San Francisco earthquake; d. 7 June 1899, bur. Arlington, Va.; seven children.

    7a Louis Thompson Morris Jr., b. 1880; d. 11 Sept. 1884.

7b Desdemona Corwin Morris, b. 1881; m. 2 June 1902 Washington, Sherwood Delgado; d. 1962.

8a Louis Sherwood Delgado, b. 16 Feb. 1907 Ardmore, Pa.; no descendants.

7c Anna Morris, b. 1882; d. 1903 from horse accident; no issue.

7d Twin, b. 1884 ?, d. 1890 diphtheria.

7e Twin, b. 1884 ?, d. 1890 diphtheria.

7f Leland Burnette Morris, b. 1886 Texas; U.S. Consular Service, appt. by Pres. F. D. Roosevelt the first U.S. ambassador to Iran; minister to Iceland; had the unpleasant distinction of handing the U.S. declaration of war to the ambassador of Austria in W.W. I.; then taught protocol to foreign ambassadors in Washington; m. 1917 Marie de Zaba (of French and Polish heritage, from Smyrna, Turkey, b. 1 Jan. 1895; d. 6 June 1974); d. 2 July 1950, Washington, D.C.

8a Kenneth Archbell Morris, b. 24 April 1918 Washington, D.C.; grad. Lawrenceville and Princeton U., B.A.; Tufts, M.A.; USNR Naval Academy 1941; Navy commander of destroyers in Pacific, W.W. II 1941-1946 and Korean War 1951-1952; six campaigns with citations; tech. manager computer systems with General Electric, San Diego; senior staff OS/DHEW Washington, D.C.; adjunct prof. International Univ., San Diego; m. 2 Dec. 1941 Akron, Ohio, Lois Loomis (b. 2 June 1918 Los Angeles., grad. Flora Stone Mather College, the Women's College of Western Reserve U. in Cleveland; script writer); live Carlsbad, Calif.

9a Desdemona "Desda" Marie Morris, b. 17 Aug. 1942 San Francisco; UCLA, B.A., M.A. in dance and psychology; former Hollywood ballet dancer in San Francisco; marriage and child counselor specializing in early childhood education and therapy in Los Angeles; 1st m. Feb. 1963 James Metropole (b. New York City, promotion photography); one child; divorced; 2nd m. 17 Feb. 1977 Stephen Lundquist, psychotherapist, d. April 1979); one child; divorced; lives Agoura Hills, Calif.

10a Christienne Elene Metropole, b. 5 Feb. 1964 Athens, Greece; B.A. UCLA in theater arts; bilingual elementary school teacher, Los Angeles.
10b Sabrina Lundquist, b. 21 Jan. 1978 Calif.; high school senior, college bound.

9b Alexandra Morris, b. 17 Jan. 1947 Boston, Mass.; grad. U. of Md.; elementary school teacher and artist, San Diego; 1st m. 17 March 1974 Manuel Lizarraga (b. Mexico, construction, d. murdered 1980); one child; 2nd m. 18 Dec. 1983, San Diego, Stephen Ross Arnold; no issue; divorced 1985.

10a Domingo Gregory Lizarraga, b. 10 Feb. 1976 Los Angeles; college student in San Diego.

9c Leland Burnette Morris II, b. 1951 Winchester, Mass.; d. 1964, Silver Spring, Md.
9d Jonathan King Morris, b. 27 Sept. 1953 Frederick, Md.; grad. Ithaca Col.; television engineer, sound and editing technician in film industry; m. 2 Oct. 1982 Jennifer Grase of Oregon; divorced 1986; lives San Francisco.
9e Geoffrey McKay Morris, b. 25 Oct. 1955 Frederick, Md.; grad. U. of Ariz.; former swim and tennis coach; sales and management, San Diego.

7g Horace McKay Morris (seventh child of Louis Thompson Morris), b. San Antonio, Tex., c. 1888; d. c. 1957; well-known actor, unmarried.

6e Desdemona H. "Dessie" Morris, b. 1841; m. Richard Mortimer Corwin; lived Cincinnati and Washington, D.C.; d. 29 Aug. 1925 at Tadworth, near London.

7a Desdemona Morris Corwin, b. 1872 Indianapolis; m. 7 June 1905 Walter E. Wallace (English Navy paymaster); d. 8 Nov. 1906 in Kent, England.

8a Daughter
8b Corwin Wallace, b. 11 March 1906 in England.

6f Theodore W. Morris, b. 1843; d. 28 Sept. 1855, killed by a train at age 12.

6g Noah Noble Morris, b. 12 Oct. 1844 Indianapolis, named for Indiana governor, son of Dr. Noble of Virginia who moved in 1774 to Kentucky. Noah died of heart disease 26 Feb. 1874.

6h Austin W. Morris Jr., b. 1 March 1852; m. 17 Nov. 1875 Kate Tousey (prob. dau. of Geo. Tousey, one of the thirty original corporators of Crown Hill Cem.); no issue; d. 20 or 21 Aug. 1887, suicide.

5b Milton Morris, second child of Morris and Rachael Morris, b. 2 May 1808; m. 1 May 1832 Abigail C. Thayer; d. 1 May 1835 Bayou Sare, La., on his way down the Mississippi River on a flatboat with a load of produce. He was in the mercantile business in Covington, Ind.

6a Caroline "Carrie" Morris, b 12 Feb. 1835 Covington, Ind.; at age 15 was living with her grandparents, Rachael and Morris Morris (1850 census) in Indianapolis; 1st m, 5 Sept. 1855 Fabricus "Brish" McCalla Mothershead (b. c. 1830 Scott Co., Ky., son of Nathaniel and Serene Threlkeld Mothershead, distantly related to Dr. John Leland Mothershead whose wife was Amanda Melvina, dau. of Morris and Rachael Morris). Carrie's grandparents gave her, also, a lot in the family square-subdivision, probably at the time of her marriage in 1855, to which her Uncle Thomas Armstrong Morris added some more property. This whole piece was sold back to T. A. Morris two years later, on 7 April 1857, probably when the Fabricus Mothersheads moved away from Indianapolis. This deed of sale, in the possession of the author, was signed by F. M. Mothershead and Caroline M. Mothershead (which solved/proved their marriage). Possibly later Carrie married Dr. Bennet F. Mothershead (b. Scott Co., Ky., lived Earlington, Ky., nephew of Dr. John Leland Mothershead, from *The Mothershead Family* by Marie R. Davis, 1975, which said Fabricus also was married twice but gave no children's or wives' names). Caroline died 1886, Indianapolis, *or* 29 Oct. 1882, Columbus, Ind. (from old family notes). Four children of record; no known living descendants.

7a Katherine Bullard Mothershead, b. 21 July 1856 Indianapolis, m. 9 June 1883 Columbus, Ind., James Walter Wallace.

8a Harry Mothershead Wallace, b. 10 July 1884 Columbus.

8b Leland Morris Wallace, b. 18 March 1888 Garden City, Kansas.

9a Harriet Marie Wallace (of St. Louis?)
9b Rose Katherine Wallace

7b Milton Morris Mothershead, b. 14 June 1858, d. 15 Oct. 1874 Vernon, Ind., unmarried.
7c Leland Morris Mothershead, b. 15 Oct. 1864 Vernon, Ind., m. 22 Nov. 1907 Alvina Liese, no issue.
7d Desdemona Morris Mothershead, b. 22 Feb. 1867, Mitchell, Ind.; married, no issue.

5c Thomas Armstrong Morris, third child of Morris and Rachael. Born 26 Dec. 1811 Nicholas Co., Ky., m. 19 Nov. 1840 Elizabeth Rachel Irwin (b. 27 July 1822, Madison, Ind., d. 6 Jan. 1893, Indianapolis). Thomas had only four years of schooling in Indianapolis, grad. West Point 1834 fourth in a class of thirty-six; first Ind. state engineer; built first drainage "ditch," first canal, first turnpike, first trolley line, first railroad, first railroad to its capital; general in the U.S. Army, victor of the first land battle of the Civil War (Battle of Philippi, Va., 3 June 1861); surveyor of Indiana's first capitol, builder of the second (the present one), conceiver and builder of the first Union Station in the U.S.; president of three and chief engineer of five railroads; personal friend of Pres. Benjamin Harrison; one of original founders of Crown Hill, which is one of the largest cemeteries in the nation; died 22 March 1904 San Diego, Calif.; buried Crown Hill Cem., Indianapolis.

6a John Irwin Morris, b. 9 Oct. 1842 Indianapolis; served through the Civil War (West Point records), lt., 20th Indiana Battery; d. 13 Aug. 1899.

7a John Morris
7b Helen I. Morris, m. —— Sold ?

6b Harry Morris, b. 1844, Indianapolis, d. 22 July 1846.
6c Thomas O'Neil Morris, b. 30 May 1846 Indianapolis; corporal at age 18 at very end of Civil War, Co. D, Indiana Infantry, private for 100 days; Co. T, 10th Infantry, private for few weeks; grad. 1870 civil engineer Rensselear Polytechnic Institute, Rochester, N.Y.; worked for several years for Indiana railroads; lived Indianapolis, Delphos, Ohio, and Denver; 1st

m. 16 Nov. 1871, Rochester, to Estelle Jane Goodale (b. 13 Oct. 1850, Mt. Morris, N.Y.; attended Vassar Col.; very artistic—sewing and woodcarving; six sons; divorced; d. 3 Jan. 1938, Indianapolis, bur. Crown Hill Cem.); 2nd m. 1898 Margaret Smith, no issue; d. 1 Dec. 1916 Denver; buried Crown Hill Cem.

7a Morris Chester Morris, b. 27 Dec. 1872 Indianapolis; 1st m. Ethel Gibben; 2nd m. Molly Patterson; d. Pueblo, Colo.

   8a William Patterson Morris, b. 4 Aug. 1909 Denver?

7b Harold Chambers Morris, b. 7 Aug. 1876 Indianapolis; d. 22 July 1883, age 7, drowned.

7c Donald Seymour Morris, b. 27 Sept. 1878 Indianapolis, grad. 1st in class 1899 Indiana Law School; 1st m. 16 June 1906 Lucie MacDaniel (b. 13 May 188- Indianapolis; d. Sept. 1949 Indianapolis); two children, divorced; 2nd m. 30 June 1934 Mary Miller (Wildhack) Humes (b. 16 June 1888; d. Nov. 1971 Indianapolis); no issue; lawyer, trust officer, vice pres. and general counsel, American Fletcher Bank and Trust Co.; Mason; board of corporators Crown Hill Cem.; Indianapolis Board of Safety; director Boys Club; d. 3 Dec. 1954; bur. Crown Hill.

   8a Josephine Goodale Morris, b. 2 June 1909 Indianapolis, atten. Barnard Col., grad. law school in Indianapolis.; m. 16 May 1928 Robert G. McKee of Indianapolis (advertising bus.); m. him twice, div. twice; d. March 1983 Indianapolis; bur. Crown Hill.

      9a Donald Morris McKee, b. 18 Sept. 1929; grad. Harvard U; Boston Gen. Hospital, medical doctor; m. Lucie Mayer (lived Bennington, Vt., 1980s); d. 1964 automobile accident.

         10a John Douglas McKee, b. 1958, d. 1962.
         10b Kenneth Morris McKee, b. 18 Sept. 1959 Fort Sill, Okla.; d. 1973.
         10c Kathryn McKee, b. 1961.
         10d Josephine McKee, b. 1963.

   8b Morris Morris, b. 14 Oct. 1911 Indianapolis; attended Wabash Col.; U.S. Army W.W. II; m. 20 Sept. 1947

Margaret Mary Bond (b. 19 April 1914 Surrey, London; div. 1965; d. 19 March 1986 Calif.); d. 3 Aug. 1985 Indianapolis; bur. Crown Hill.

   9a Steven William Morris, b. 20 July 1949 Indianapolis (twin); grad. 1974 Purdue U.; m. 11 April 1981, Chicago, Sue Ann Christman; live Costa Mesa, Calif. (1986).

   9b Andrew Seymour Morris (twin), b. 20 July 1949, lived Indianapolis (1977).

7d Stanley Sherwood Morris, b. 20 Jan. 1881 Indianapolis; m. 27 Aug. 1903 Katherine Berry (b. 8 Jan. 1885, San Francisco; d. 7 Sept. 1967, San Francisco; family came from County Cork, Ireland, during the potato famine; called "Oma," which means grandmother in Irish); left his home in Indianapolis at about age 16 after his parents' divorce; went to California where his aged grandfather and aunt lived; self-taught, very fine electrical engineer; chief electrician for the Golden Gate Bridge and the World's Fair Tower of Lights on Treasure Island; electrical engineer for Pan Am's first installations on Midway Island and Samoa; was in Pearl Harbor when the Japanese attacked; d. 28 Oct. 1954, San Francisco.

   8a Stanley Sherwood Morris Jr., b. 25 May 1905, San Francisco; 1st m. May 1926, San Francisco or Redwood City, Lillian Nowlin (b. 18 Nov. 1906 Concord, Mass.; div. 1939; two children; d. 8 Oct. 1990, Grafton, N.Dak.); 2nd m. 14 Feb. 1941 San Francisco, Eileen Mae Spoon (b. 9 June 1917, Los Angeles, secretary of family business; four children; d. 30 March 1992, melanoma cancer); owner-manager Merchants Credit Assoc., San Francisco; active civic leader in Chinese community; d. 1 Aug. 1981, San Francisco.

   9a Mary Louise Morris, b. 28 May 1933 San Francisco; atten. S.F. State Col.; m. 14 Aug. 1953 Charles Edward Friley, Jr. (b. 20 Dec. 1928 Sennecaville, Ohio; bus driver; both active in Jehovah's Witnesses); live in Minto, N.Dak.

      10a Susan Dawn Friley, b. 20 April 1956 San Francisco; insurance agent; m. 21 May 1977

James Harrison Haworth (b. 12 April 1956 Fargo, N.Dak.); div. Dec. 1985.

11a Leah Ashley Haworth, b. 22 Oct. 1980 Fridley, Minn.

10b William "Billy" Arthur Friley, b. 30 Aug. 1957 San Francisco; profoundly retarded since birth, microcephalic cerebral palsied, nonverbal, can't walk, at home until age 12, 1995; lives N.Dak. State Development Center, occasionally brought home for visits. Note: No other known Morris family members with this affliction; if any are known, kindly notify the family at Box 256, Minto, ND 58261.

10c Timothy John "Butch" Friley, b. 16 Nov. 1964 San Francisco; bartender; m. Sherrie Gage.

11a Michael Gage Friley, b. June 1990, Grafton, Calif.

9b Stanley Sherwood Morris III, b. March 1936 San Francisco; d. June 1936, infancy.

9c Stanley Sherwood Morris III, child of 2nd m., b. 3 March 1942 Oakland, Calif.; named the same name as 9b, deceased half-brother, but fact not known by first wife or children for many years; m. 30 Oct. 1964 Gail Simpson; div. Feb. 1966; inhalation therapist in Pendleton, Oregon.

10a Kevin Morris, b. 5 May 1965 San Francisco; m. Ingrid Anton (b. 25 May 1948).

10b Antoinette Morris (twin), b. 15 May 1967 Los Angeles.

10c Deseriee Morris (twin), b. 15 May 1967 Los Angeles.

9d Laurine "Laurie" Mae Morris, child of 2nd m., b. 29 Sept. 1943 Palo Alto, Calif.; m. 28 April 1962 Joseph Krofcheck (b. 1941, d. 1974); live Redding, Calif.

10a Susan Marie Krofcheck, b. 20 Oct. 1963 San Francisco; m. Michael Haren (b. 30 Dec. 1960); no issue.

10b Debora Ann Krofcheck, b. 4 June 1965 Sunnyvale, Calif.; m. Michael G. Morris II (b. 15 April 1960, Redding, Calif.).

10c Julia Lynn Krofcheck, b. 4 May 1969 Sunnyvale, Calif.; B.S. Northwest Missouri Univ., M.A. phys. ed., Kansas State U; m. 5 Aug. 1995.

9e Michael Dennis Morris, child of 2nd marriage, b. 13 Feb. 1950 San Francisco; m. 15 April 1972 Donna Antoinette Piva (b. 14 Feb. 1950 S.F.); telephone company; live Novato, Calif., near San Francisco.

10a Stephen Michael Morris, b. 12 May 1976 San Francisco.

10b Michelle Denise Morris, b. 19 April 1979 San Francisco..

9f Judith Ann Morris, child of 2nd marriage, b. 1 May 1953 S.F.; lives Camptonville, Calif.

8b Estelle Patricia "Pat" Morris, b. 17 April 1910, San Francisco; 1st m. —— Topping; div.; 2nd m. —— Chism (d. W.W. II); 3rd m. 1959 John "Jack" Farnsworth (electrician; d. 28 Feb. 1969); d. 19 July 1974 San Francisco; no issue.

7e Theodore Hatfield Morris (fifth child of Estelle Goodale and Thomas O'Neil Morris), b. 20 May 1883 Indianapolis; B.S. 1906 Purdue U, Kappa Sigma fraternity; mechanical engineer, inventor; Mason, Shriner, active in Wayne Men's Club and minstrel shows; member Military Order of the Loyal Legion, for direct descendants of officers of the Civil War; U.S. Coast Guard volunteer W.W. II, guarding the Philadelphia docks at night, over age with special dispensation; m. 10 April 1912 Indianapolis, Lisette Susanna Krauss (b. 12 Oct. 1883 Indianapolis; a gentle lady, avid gardener and horticulturist, winning many prizes in flower shows; active in the Neighborhood League, the Saturday Club of Wayne, Pa.; board member and director of the Needlework Guild; d. of stroke at Bryn Mawr [Pa.] Hospital 30 Oct. 1965; bur. Crown Hill, Indianapolis); d. 8 Dec. 1974 Wilmington, Del.; bur. Crown Hill.

8a Anne Estelle Morris, b. 29 Sept. 1913 Indianapolis; B.A. cum laude 1935 Randolph-Macon Woman's Col., Va.; teacher, museum guide, writer, lecturer, researcher; elected to Nat. Soc. Amer. Pen Women; former governor Delaware Mayflower Soc.; Colonial Dames of Delaware; pres. Travelers Aid; honorary board, Family and Children's Services of Delaware—award; chair of trustees, American Association of University Women, honored with a named grant; in Marquis' *Who's Who of American Women;* m. 29 June 1937 Wayne, Pa., Walter Day Mertz (b. 27 Feb. 1914; B.A. 1936 Dartmouth Col., C.F.A. (certified financial analyst) Rutgers School of Banking; lt. U.S. Navy W.W. II, Pacific area; senior vice president and director, head of trust dept., Wilmington Trust Co.; retired May 1977); together they have traveled almost all over the world; lived in Wilmington, Del., until late 1995.

9a Susanne Day "Sandy" Mertz, b. 9 May 1940 Philadelphia, Pa., B.A. Randolph-Macon Woman's Col.; art researcher, Fogg Library, Harvard; librarian; m. in Wilmington, Del., 2 Sept. 1963 James Lee Smalley (b. 10 Nov. 1939 Augusta, Ga., B.A. U. North Carolina; B.D. Vanderbilt Theological Col.; attended Oxford Univ., England; teacher in Mass., counselor at UNC; minister); live Nashville, Tenn.

10a Anna Hamilton Smalley, b. 31 Oct. 1966 Nashville, Tenn., B.A. Wellesley Col., Phi Beta Kappa, Sigma Psi; M.A., Ph.D. in psychology, U. of Denver; teacher U. of Denver and Metropolitan State, Denver; m. 19 June 1993 Christopher John Flanagan (b. 12 Oct. 1964 Pittsburgh, Pa.; B.S. Bates Col., Me.; J.D. U. of Denver Col. of Law; attorney); live Denver.

10b Sallie Morris Smalley, b. 27 May 1969 Greenfield, Mass.; B.A. U.N.C.; bank officer in Philadelphia, Pa.; M.B.A. candidate Wharton School of Banking, U.Pa., Philadelphia.

10c Martha Day Smalley, b. 9 June 1972 Turners Falls, Mass., B.A. Trinity Col., Conn.; team re-

Genealogy, Section II ♦ 319

searcher, writer, and data analyst with international management consulting firm; lives Boston.

9b Elizabeth Morris "Betsy" Mertz, b. 4 Sept. 1942, Philadelphia, Pa.; B.A. Randolph-Macon Woman's Col.; special education certificate, Trenton College, N.J.; stewardess; teacher and tutor; m. Wilmington, Del., 27 Nov. 1965 Terence Becker O'Brien (b. 20 Feb. 1939, Philadelphia, Pa.; B.A. Muhlenberg Col.; marketing executive, Insurance Co. of North America; vice pres., Fed. Reserve Bank of Philadelphia; president and owner of Topsight, Inc., marketing); live Mount Laurel, N.J.

 10a Kathleen Becker "Katie" O'Brien, b. 27 Sept. 1968 Camden, N.J.; B.S. U. of Richmond; B.S.N. Johns Hopkins School of Nursing.; m. 28 Nov. 1992 in Richmond, Va., Robert Nelson "Rob" Rose (b. 24 Oct. 1969 Camden, N.J.; B.S.E. Claiborne Robins School of Business, U. of Richmond; M.B.A. candidate, U.Va. Colgate Darden School of Business).

 10b Tracy Morris O'Brien, b. 13 April 1970, Camden N.J.; B.A. Lynchburg Col., Va.; administrative marketing associate, Virginia Health Planning Agency, Richmond; m. Ewing, N.J., 16 July 1994 Robert "Bob" Patrick Boullé (b. 14 May 1970 New Brunswick, N.J.; B.S. Lynchburg Col.; M.B.A. candidate, Graduate School, William and Mary Col., Williamsburg, Va.); live Williamsburg.

9c Walter Day "Skip" Mertz Jr., b. 21 Sept. 1944 Philadelphia; B.A. Park Col., Kansas City; Vietnam War; 1st lt. U.S. Army Military Intelligence and paratrooper in 101st Airborne Div.; personnel for John Hancock Insurance Co., Boston; for Fed. Reserve, Washington; mediator, teacher for Mediate Tech, Front Royal, Va.; m. 17 Feb. 1967 Carol Mackay (b. 11 March 1947 Wilmington, Del.; B.A. Geo. Mason U., Va., magna cum laude; teacher, decorator; graphic artist; sculptor); live Fort Valley, Va.

10a Walter Day Mertz III, b. 16 Sept. 1968 Fort Bragg, N.C.; attended Davis Elkins Col., Elkins, W.Va.; nationwide trainer for Novawall Acoustical Systems and lead installer; wilderness back packer and rock climber.

10b Jonathan Frederick Mertz, b. 23 May 1978, Wash., D.C.; student, NCU School of the Arts.

10c Andrew Mackay Mertz, b. 31 Jan. 1980, Wash., D.C.

9d Theodore Morris Mertz, b. 11 July 1951 Wilmington, Del.; Eagle Scout and troop leader; experienced in rock mountain climbing, rappelling, and sea kayaking; B.A. Dartmouth Col., M.B.A. Tuck Grad. Sch.; senior v. pres. Mellon Bank, Pittsburgh, and Bank of Boston; dir. of product development; m. 16 Dec. 1972 Harrisonburg, Va., Deborah "Debbie" Elizabeth Smith (b. 7 Nov. 1949 Richmond, Va.; B.A. U.N.C., Greensboro, N.C.; psychiatric and neuropsychological test examiner; pres. Foxboro Garden Club); live in Foxboro, Mass.

10a Gregory Morris Mertz, b. 4 Oct. 1976 Pittsburgh; Eagle Scout; student at Allegheny Col., Meadville, Pa., Lambda Sigma honor society.

10b Peter Tyler Mertz, b. 6 Aug. 1980 Pittsburgh.

10c David Allerton Mertz, b. 25 Dec. 1983 Pittsburgh.

8b Theodore Hatfield Morris Jr., b. 6 April 1918 Bryn Mawr Hosp., Pa.; d. 21 March 1921, killed by an automobile.

7f Frederick Davis Morris (sixth child of Thomas O'N. and Estelle Morris) b. 20 July 1885; d. 13 April 1888 of spinal fever caused by head injury after tipping over in his high chair.

6d Eleanora I. Morris (dau. of Thomas A. and Rachel Morris) b. 1848, m. 7 May 1874 John M. Chambers of Liverpool, England (b. 26 Dec. 1846 Belfast, Ireland; in Co. A, 113rd Ind. Infantry, private for few weeks; beloved medical doctor, Indianapolis; d. 12 Sept. 1892), d. 24 Sept. 1904 at San Diego, bur. Crown Hill Cem., Indianapolis; no issue.

6e Milton Aspden Morris (son of Thomas A. and Rachel Morris), b. Indianapolis, 1st m. Emma Kennedy, one child; 2nd m. Sarah Herst, no issue.

7a Gladys Morris, b. 20 Jan. 1891, d. 11 May 1903.

5d John D. Morris, fourth child of Morris and Rachael Morris, b. 9 Sept. 1815 Carlisle, Nicholas Co., Ky.; m. 30 June 1841 Lebanon, Ohio, Martha A. McKinley Wiles (b. 8 Aug. 1821 Lebanon, Ohio, dau. of Nancy Ames and William McKinley Wiles, who were some of the first land owners in Indianapolis along with Morris Morris, said to be related to Pres. McKinley. Martha d. 2 Sept. 1904 Indianapolis); milling business; d. 30 May 1895 Indianapolis. His large, beautiful home, built c. 1862, was rescued from highway construction and is today the Morris-Butler House Museum on Park Avenue in Indianapolis, restored and handsomely furnished.

6a Charles Goodman Morris, b. 1 May 1842 Indianapolis, m. 9 April 1874 Juliet Ann Nold, lived Louisville, Ky.; d. 11 Feb. 1900.

7a John D. Morris Jr., b. 15 Oct. 1876; m. 12 July 1897 New Albany, Ind., Ora Henri Crawford; lived Louisville; d. W.W. I.

8a John D. Morris III, b. 4 March 1899.

6b James Wiles Morris, b. 28 April 1844; m. 22 Oct. 1899 Terre Haute, Ind., Maude Courtney Staub; lived Indianapolis; no issue, d. 23 July 1901.

6c Catherine Morris, b. 7 May 1848 Indianapolis; m. 4 Oct. 1871 in the first naval wedding in Indianapolis to Commander George Brown (b. 19 June 1835, son of William J. Brown, asst. postmaster general for Pres. Polk; grad. 1853 U.S. Naval Academy, later rear admiral; commanded Norfolk Navy Yard; d. 29 June 1913 of nephritis; bur. Crown Hill; lived Annapolis, Wash., D.C., Honolulu, and Indianapolis); d. 21 Aug. 1915 of cirrhosis of the liver, Indianapolis; bur. Crown Hill.

7a George Brown Jr., b. 12 Oct. 1875 Boston Navy Yard, grad. U.S. Naval Academy; m. 12 Oct. 1904 Berkeley,

Calif., Anne Maxwell Miller; U.S.N. pay inspector Adriatic Fleet, China, and San Francisco.

    8a Catherine Morris Brown, b. 10 July 1905 Annapolis; m. 3 Feb. 1925, San Francisco, Thomas Tyler Beattie, U.S.N.

7b John Morris Brown, b. 17 June 1878 Indianapolis; d. 12 Feb. 1882 Staten Island, N.Y., four years old.

7c Hugh Brown, b. 13 Aug. 1884 Thompkinsville, N.Y.; grad. U.S. Naval Academy, served on USS *Maryland* in Honolulu, commander of USS *Virginia;* m. Estelle Johnston; d. 26 July 1918.

    8a Sarah Elizabeth Brown, b. 14 Feb. 1917.

6d John Peck Morris, b. 27 Sept. 1850 Indianapolis; d. 23 Jan. 1855, four years old.

6e Nancy "Nannie" Maria Morris, b. 23 Nov. 1854 Indianapolis; m. 14 June 1876 Charles Farquar Haines (b. 1847, d. 9 July 1902 of bronchitis, bur. Crown Hill); d. 13 Aug. 1929 Indianapolis; bur. Crown Hill.

    7a John Morris Haines, b. 9 Dec. 1877 Indianapolis, m. 10 June 1911 Ruth Newman Carey (b. 18 Jan. 1878; d. 25 Sept. 1941 Indianapolis); v. pres. and gen. manager Stewart Carey Glass Co.; both buried Crown Hill.

        8a Mary Stewart Carey Haines, b. 17 Dec. 1912 Indianapolis; first-cousin of Booth Tarkington; m. 6 Aug. 1938 Reily Gibson Adams (b. 12 April 1911 Indianapolis; chairman Stewart Carey Haines, glass; corporator Crown Hill Cemetery; director Merchants National Bank & Trust Co.; d. 3 Oct. 1980 Indianapolis); d. 15 April 1975 Indianapolis.

            9a Ruth Carey Adams, b. 6 Sept. 1940; m. 4 April 1964 Douglas Franz Linsmith; live Indianapolis.

                10a Stewart May Linsmith, b. 27 Dec. 1965 Indianapolis; grad. Ball State U.; m. 17 June 1989 Denise Gay Adams (b. 18 Sept. 1965 Indianapolis; grad. Ball State U.; M.A. in sign language); live Portland, Me.

11a Miles Howard Linsmith, b. 4 May 1994, Portland, Me.

10b Eleanor Adams Linsmith, b. 3 Oct. 1968 Indianapolis; m. 1993 Stephen Patrick Troy (b. 16 Oct. 1966 Indianapolis); live Indianapolis.

10c Scott Culbertson Linsmith, b. 27 Sept. 1970 Indianapolis; lives Indianapolis.

9b Reily Morris "Morrie" Adams, b. 30 Sept. 1943; A.B. Wabash Col; M.B.A. Indiana U; m. Birmingham, Mich., 9 July 1966 Nancy Gay Gould (b. 16 Sept. 1943, Detroit, Mich.; B.S. Indiana U.; teacher Carmel, Ind.); before 1984 was chrm. of Stewart-Carey Inc., commodity distributors (sold 1984); pres. Monohippic Corp. (The Print Shop), member and secretary of the board of managers and secretary, board of incorporators, Crown Hill Cem.; lives Westfield, Ind.

10a Douglas Bruce Adams, b. 1 Oct. 1967, Royal Oak, Mich.; B.S. DePauw U.; m. 26 Oct. 1991 at Chagrin Falls, Ohio, Pamela H. Wakeman of Darien, Conn.; live Darien, Conn.

10b Julia Anne Adams, b. 7 May 1972 Indianapolis; grad. cum laude Taylor U.; m. Indianapolis 8 Oct. 1994 Douglas E. Browning of Ballwin, Mo.; live Almont, Mich.

9c Martha Morris Adams, b. 9 March 1949, twin; B.A. Christian College; grad. John Heron School of Art at Indiana U., Bachelor and Master of Art Education; lives in Indianapolis.

9d Mary Culbertson Adams, b. 9 March 1949, twin; grad. Christian College, Assoc. of Arts; Assoc. Business, Ivy Tech.; Indiana Weslyan U., B.S. and Master of Science-Management; participated in missionary trip to Haiti.

8b Barbara Carey Haines, b. 22 May 1916 Indianapolis; grad. Connecticut College, New London; m. 29 June 1940 Thomas Chandler Werbe Jr. (of Anderson, Ind.; grad. Princeton; investment banker and broker; lt.

(j.g.), W.W. II in Hawaii; d. 5 Feb. 1983 Indianapolis; bur. Crown Hill); she lives in Defiance, Ohio.

9a Ann Morris Werbe, "Mrs. A. W. Wallace," b. 31 Aug. 1941; grad. Park Tudor School; grad. Mount Vernon Junior College, Washington, D.C.; ran a retail shop, built a complex of condominiums on farmland of old Haines farm property; m. Michael Lee Wallace, divorced June 1975; lives Indianapolis.

10a Barbara Wallace, b. 27 July 1966 Indianapolis; grad. DePauw U.; m. 15 June 1991 Todd Connely Rumsey (b. 26 Jan. 1965, grad. DePauw U., Indiana Univ. Medical School; practicing obstetrician and gynecologist); live Fort Wayne, Ind.

11a Peter Connely Rumsey, b. 13 Dec. 1994, Columbus, Ohio.

10b Timothy Wallace, b. 21 May 1968 Indianapolis; B.A. DePauw U.; gen. manager, Bellepaints, lives Columbus, Ohio.

10c Michael Stewart Wallace, b. 2 July 1972 Springfield, Ill.; B.A. DePauw U.; works for Lilly Pulitzer; lives Philadelphia, Pa.

9b Thomas C. Werbe III, b. 25 June 1943; grad. Choate School, Wallingford, Conn; B.A. Wabash Col., Crawfordsville, Ind.; M.B.A. U. of Va., Charlottesville; runner; marketing research with Eli Lilly; with Elizabeth Arden; Hertz; vice pres. Chemical Bank of N.Y.; m. 5 Oct. 1968 Mary French Jackson (grad. Sweet Briar Col., Va., presently a student at Yale Divinity School, New Haven); live Greenwich, Conn.

10a Elizabeth French Werbe, b. 8 April 1975; student Haverford Col., Pa.

9c Daniel Stewart Werbe, b. 29 March 1947; grad. Park School; B.A. Wabash Col.; M.B.A. Butler U., Indianapolis; in sales for Eli Lilly; national sales manager for Leitz Cameras; currently with J. D.

Gould & Co.; m. 5 Oct. 1974 Catherine Frost Daggett; div. May 1989; he lives in Indianapolis.

10a Catherine "Kit" Chandler Werbe, b. 11 May 1980 Denver, Colo.; lives Indianapolis.

10b Barbara Stewart Wallace, b. 21 Sept. 1981 Denver, lives Indianapolis.

9d Eleanor Carey "Noni" Werbe, b. 6 Oct. 1949, Indianapolis; grad. Tudor Hall, Indianapolis; B.A. Connecticut Col., M.A. in Arctic and Alpine plant ecology U. of Colo, Boulder; thesis work in Alaska along the Pipeline "haul road" in a polar desert; worked for the Nature Conservancy in administration in Colorado; Indiana and Arkansas, director of development; July 1988 successfully climbed Mount Kilimanjaro in Tanzania, Africa (19,400 feet); m. Indianapolis, John Landers Krauss (b. East Orange, N.J., 20 Oct. 1948; grad. Park School; grad. with honors Colo. College with first-ever Ford Foundation Venture Grant; grad. Ind. U. Law School; formerly deputy mayor of Indianapolis 1982-90; presently a Senior Fellow in the School for Public and Environmental Affairs; assoc. dir., Center for Urban Policy and the Environment at Ind. U.; also serves as international consultant through nonprofit D.C. agencies on the role of local gov't in emerging democracies for Estonia, Russia, Turkey and Morocco); live Indianapolis.

6f David Corwine Morris (seventh child of Martha Wiles and John D. Morris), b. 28 Sept. 1860 Indianapolis; d. 25 July 1919 Indianapolis, unmarried.

5e Amanda Melvina Morris, fifth child of Morris and Rachael Morris, b. 2 Feb. 1817 in Nicholas or Fleming Co., Ky.; m. 17 Dec. 1836 Dr. John T. Mothershead (b. 6 Jan. 1808 Scott Co., Ky., the last of twelve children of Nathaniel Mothershead [1754-1834; see account below]; grad. Transylvania Medical College, Louisville, Ky., came to Indianapolis 1830 as a pioneer physician; also owned and ran a pharmacy; pres. board of health, second fire captain; d. 4 Nov. 1854 Indianapolis, bur. Crown Hill). Amanda d. 10 Feb. 1851 Indianapolis, only 34 years old; bur. Crown Hill.

The father of Dr. John Mothershead, Nathaniel Mothershead, was in the Revolutionary War; b. March 1754, Orange Co., Va.; m. 27 Aug. 1781 Ruth Burt (b. 2 Nov. 1763); entered Continental Army 1775, served twelve months, then enlisted for three years; was a private and sergeant in Battles of Trenton, Princeton, Brandywine (wounded), Germantown, Monmouth, Mud Island, and was present at the surrender of Cornwallis at Yorktown; lived in Virginia and later Scott Co., Ky.; applied for pension 1828 at age 70; d. 29 Dec. 1834. Meanwhile, his wife Ruth stayed home to bear and care for twelve children! Richmond, Va., records show a 1783 warrant for 200 acres for three years' service in the Continental Line, signed by Thomas Meriwether and Benjamin Harrison.

6a Alvin Morris Mothershead, b. 13 Sept. 1838 Indianapolis; m. Omaha, Nebr., to Carlotta Brackenbush; lived Chicago 1918; lawyer in Nebraska.

    7a Amanda "Amy" Morris Mothershead, b. 17 Jan. 1870 Indianapolis; teacher in Chicago; unmarried; d. 1916.
    7b Leland Mothershead, b. c. 1872 Montclair, N.J.
    7c Carlotta Mothershead, b. 30 Oct. 1873 Indianapolis; m. 25 Dec. 1895, Chicago, Henry Bernard Lusch; no issue; lived Chicago.

6b Julia Mary Morris Mothershead, b. 19 April 1841; m. 8 Oct. 1868 in Wash., D.C., David August Burr (b. 1 May 1838, Wash.; d. 20 May 1891 Montclair, N.J.).

    7a Leland Mothershead Burr, b. 25 Sept. 1869 Wash., D.C.; m. 20 Sept. 1898 Ruth Cooley Merritt; worked for the *New York Evening Post*.

        8a Helen Merritt Burr, b. 21 June 1899 Montclair, N.J.
        8b Ruth Winifred Burr, b. 13 July 1901 Montclair.
        8c Leland M. Burr Jr., b. 11 Nov. 1907 Montclair.
        8d David Augustus Burr, b. 17 Sept. 1909 Montclair.

    7b Desdemona Augustine Burr, b. 24 Aug. 1872. Charleston, W.Va.; m. 25 Oct. 1900 Montclair, N.J., John S. Lichnor; no issue; lived Cape Town, S. Africa.
    7c David (Shields ?) Eugene Burr, b. 23 March 1880 Montclair.

6c John Leland "Lee" Mothershead Jr. (son of Amanda and Dr. John L. Mothershead; every other generation is called "Lee"), b. 9 June 1842 Indianapolis; 1st m. 27 Oct. 1870 Anna Stockton Owen (b. 1845 Phila., Pa.; d. 13 Oct. 1928); 2nd m. ——— ; one child, Irene, d. infancy; prominent in Republican politics; member Columbia Club, Masons, Presby. Church; treas. Marion Co., Ind., 1881-83; owner-pres. Indiana Foundry Co., sold it to Grasselli Chem. Co. (later DuPont) in Cleveland, Ohio; d. 16 July 1915 of a cerebral hemorrhage in Cleveland; bur. Crown Hill.

7a Julia Mothershead, b. 14 Oct. 1872 Indianapolis, lived Cleveland; unmarried; d. 5 Feb. 1945.
7b Bessie Owen Mothershead, b. 4 Dec. 1874 Indianapolis; d. 9 July 1876, infant.
7c Owen Morris Mothershead, b. 17 Aug. 1880 Indianapolis; attended Cornell U.; partner in architectural and building firm, executive in the Packard Manufacturing Co.; W.W. I served with Army Ordnance in Europe although he was 40 years old; sports enthusiast, sailor, dramatist; m. 14 Oct. 1903 Mary Duncan Wilson (of Welsh descent, b. Lake Forest, Ill., 17 July 1880, d. 4 May 1962); d. 20 Nov. 1957 Indianapolis.

8a Wilson Mothershead, b. 24 Sept. 1905 Indianapolis; attended Cornell until the Depression; m. Indianapolis 29 Oct. 1936 Katharine Brown; lt. comdr. U.S. Navy; developed Indiana National Bank's branch banking system and became its president; pres. Central Indiana Council of Boy Scouts, pres. Navy League of Indianapolis, pres. Marion County's Bankers Assoc., treas. Visiting Nurse Assoc., dir. Indiana Chamber of Commerce, treas. United Fund, pres. Community Chest, dir. Indianapolis Water Co., Life Ins. Co. and Morgan Packing Co., chairman Ind. Nat. Corp., incorporator Crown Hill Cem., board Indianapolis Water Co.; d. 17 April 1990 Indianapolis, bur. Crown Hill. Katharine lives in Indianapolis.

9a John Wilson Mothershead, b. 2 July 1945 in Evanston, Ill., adopted; d. 19 Dec. 1992, kidney failure; bur. Crown Hill.

9b Katharine Mothershead, b. 9 Nov. 1947, Chicago, adopted; 1st m. 27 Nov. 1971 Stanley Lecy (d. 28 April 1973); 2nd m. Richard Kruse (b. 11 July 1942, Little River, Kans.); lives Indianapolis.

    10a Mathew Wilson Lecy, b. 2 Oct. 1972, Indianapolis; not a Morris descendant.

    10b Katharine Marie Kruse, b. 29 April 1982 Indianapolis.

    10c Anne Elizabeth Kruse, b. 15 May 1986 Indianapolis.

7d John Leland "Lee" Mothershead III, b. 3 Jan. 1882 Indianapolis; m. 7 Jan. 1908 Lake Forest, Ill., Ethel Warner (dau. of socially prominent family of Ezra J. Warner; d. 20 July 1950 Pasadena, Calif.); Christian Science practitioner in Pasadena; owned a company which manufactured stained and leaded glass windows; knew Gen. Pershing during W.W. I, drove him around Pasadena; d. Pasadena 15 Dec. 1958.

    8a John Leland Mothershead IV, b. 18 Nov. 1908 in Pasadena, Calif.; m. 9 Aug. 1932 Cape Cod, Mass., Elizabeth Ashley Crossett (b. 10 Jan. 1910 Davenport, Iowa; active community volunteer; d. 18 Feb. 1976 Stanford, Calif.); two children; 2nd m. 21 Jan. 1978, Stanford, Diane Frazier Heffner; no issue. John was an educator, author, philosophy prof. at Stanford U., in *Who's Who;* d. 30 Jan. 1991 of a stroke.

        9a John Leland "Lee" Mothershead V, b. 10 Jan. 1939, Boston; m. 23 June 1963 Brockton, Mass., Therese Petkelis (b. 22 Feb. 1938 in Lithuania); dean and teacher at Southwestern Academy, San Marino, Calif.

            10a John Leland Mothershead VI, b. 2 Feb. 1966 Torrence, Calif.; m. 5 Aug. 1995 Ojai, Calif., Melinda Marie Luthin; computer consultant and installer for his own company; live San Marino.

        9b Ann Ashley Mothershead, b. 23 June 1944 Stanford, Calif.; B.A. Cornell U., attended George Washington Univ., M.P.H. School of Public Health at

UCLA; health research at Stanford Research Inst., Menlo Park, Calif.; four stepchildren (three are married); m. 28 May 1977, Stanford, to Peter B. Bjorklund (b. 6 June 1938, Murray, Utah; independent consultant, mathematician and computer specialist); live Los Altos Hills, Calif.

10a Peter Burton Bjorklund Jr., b. 11 Sept. 1980, Stanford, Calif.

10b Ashley Elizabeth Bjorklund, b. 24 June 1985, Stanford.

8b Morris Warner Mothershead, b. 13 Feb. 1915; m. Alice Maria Bonzi (b. 5 Dec. 1914, Milan, Italy); travel agent in Pasadena, Calif.; d. April 1981, Pasadena.

9a Warner Bonzi Mothershead, b. 30 Oct. 1936; 1st m. 14 July 1958, Pat —— , two chil.; 2nd m. 30 July 1977, Mary —— ; no issue; birdseed supply business, Gladstone, Ore.

10a Maria Christy Mothershead, b. 18 Oct. 1958, m. —— Sandhagen.

11a Dusty (male) Sandhagen.

10b Michael Anthony "Tony" Mothershead, b. 21 June 1961.

9b Maria Mothershead, m. Andrei Rogers, professor; live Boulder, Colo.

10a Michael Mothershead Rogers, b. 3 Dec. 1961; mechanical engineer, NASA, Ames; m. 1985 Walden, Colo., Linda Lee Walden.

11a Steven Lee Rogers, b. 1987.
11b Kevin Lee Rogers, b. 1990.
11c Brian Lee Rogers, b. 1992.

10b Christopher Buergin Rogers, b. 17 May 1963; m. 1988, Missouri, Catherine Hunter McDonnell; mechanical engineer; prof. Tufts U., Boston.

11a Peter McDonnell Rogers, b. 1991.

11b Matthew Marbury Rogers, b. 1992.
11c Kimberly Buergin Rogers, b. 1995.

10c Kevin Bonzi Rogers, b. 15 June 1966; Ph.D., fisheries management; m. 1990 in N.J., Emilie Adele Falls.

11a Kyle Andrew Rogers, b. 1994.

10d Laura Lynn Rogers, b. 15 April 1968; m. 1991 in Colo. Stuart Howard Sweeney (city and regional planner).

11a James Grayson Sweeney, b. 1994.

5f Julia Ann "Lulie" Morris, sixth child of Morris and Rachael Morris, b. Carlisle, Ky., 1 Feb. 1820; m. 5 July 1849 Norman Ross (b. 1817 Ky.; d. 12 Feb. 1885); d. "of old age" 7 Aug. 1897 Indianapolis, bur. Crown Hill.

6a Morris Morris Ross, b. 1 Aug. 1850 Indianapolis, grad. 1870 Cornell U., sec. of the Am. Legation in Vienna for one year, mng. editor *Indianapolis News,* well-known dramatic critic, m. Jan. 1882 Frances McIntyre (b. 1856, d. 21 April 1940); no issue, d. 7 Oct. 1915.

5g Elizabeth Mitchell "Bettie" Morris, seventh child of Morris and Rachael Morris, b. 17 March 1824 Indianapolis; m. 17 Jan. 1844 John Dougherty Defrees (b. 8 Nov. 1810 Sparta, Tenn.; member, state legislature; owner and editor *Indiana State Journal,* merged 1904 with *Indianapolis Star;* prominent Whig and very close friend of Abraham Lincoln; appointed by Lincoln government printer 1861-1866; established the U.S. Bureau of Engraving and Printing; reappointed by Pres. Hayes 1877-1882; d. 19 Oct. 1882 in W.Va. of exhaustion; bur. Crown Hill); d. 2 Nov. 1904 of senility, in Washington; bur. Crown Hill.

6a Morris Morris Defrees, b. 16 Nov. 1846 Indianapolis; civil engineer, laid out grounds for Indiana's second (and present) capitol in 1879, Spanish Am. War 1898, 161st Ind., 3rd Div.; head, board of Indianapolis Public Works 1892-1893; m. Lydia Ellen "Nellie" Bradley (b. 20 April 1853, dau. of John H. Bradley, noted banker and railroad operator; d. 8 Aug. 1928 Indianapolis); d. 17 Oct. 1912 of cardiac arrest, age 66.

7a Frederick Bradley Defrees, b. 31 Jan. 1875 Indianapolis; m. 28 June 1905 Aurora, Ind., Ethel Held (b. Aug. 1878; d. Nov. 1928); lived Indianapolis and Toledo, Ohio; d. 28 April 1936.

    8a Bradley C. Defrees, b. 21 Feb. 1911 Toledo, Ohio.

7b Elizabeth Morris "Bessie" Defrees, b. 26 June 1882 Indianapolis, d. 9 March 1958, Toledo; unmarried.

7c Lydia Ellen Defrees, b. 20 April 1883; d. 8 Aug. 1883, infant.

7d Hugh Jackson Defrees, b. 21 July 1886 Indianapolis, m. 1920 Beatrice Fay Johnson (b. W.Va. 22 Aug. 1893; d. 20 May 1950 Lucas Co., Ohio); d. 17 April 1953.

    8a Lou Ellen Defrees, b. 12 March 1921 Baltimore, Md.; m. 1940 Norman C. Sass (b. 18 May 1917); live in Temperance, Mich.

        9a Nancy Lee Sass, b. 27 March 1942; m. 28 Oct. 1961 Thomas Christopher Soules; live Holland, Ohio.

            10a Thomas Christopher Soules Jr., b. 19 Dec. 1962; m. Julia Cranston (b. 11 Feb. 1963).

                11a Megan Lynn Soules, b. 26 Feb. 1989.
                11b Justin Thomas Soules, b. 16 Oct. 1991.

            10b Tracey Lee Soules, b. 11 Aug. 1964; m. 16 June 1962 Russell Ryan (b. 14 June 1962).
            10c Darren Thomas Soules, b. 30 Aug. 1965; m. 11 July 1963 Jackie Cieslwicz (b. 11 July 1963).

                11a Ashley Rose Soules, b. 23 Aug. 1994.

        9b Dale Lynn Sass, b. 2 July 1944; m. 12 Sept. 1964 Rosemary Curtis; two children; 2nd m. Janet A. Lietaert (b. 19 May 1942); four stepchildren; live in Toledo.

            10a Daniel Warren Sass, b. 31 Jan. 1965.
            10b David Norman Sass, b. 23 Aug. 1968; m. Kristy Stachak.

                11a Tobis Thomas Sass, b. 22 May 1988.
                11b Nicole Elizabeth Sass, b. 9 Sept. 1989.
                11c Jacob Isaac Sass, b. 31 March 1994.

9c Carol Anne Sass, b. 1 Oct. 1945, m. 2 Dec. 1966 Frederick Ernest Hall (b. 18 Jan. 1942); live in Toledo.

10a Frederick Ernest Hall Jr., b. 18 Feb. 1970; m. Joyce Bair (b. 29 Oct. 1970).

11a Autumn Leah Hall, b. 8 Jan. 1994.

10b William Walter Hall, b. 16 Feb. 1973.

9d Dean Norman Sass, b. 20 Dec. 1950; m. 8 Feb. 1969 Rhonda Elaine Rohlman (b. 18 Sept. 1949).

10a Shannon Donnel Sass, b. 1 April 1975.
10b Steven Dean Sass, b. 24 Aug. 1976.

9e Marcy Jo Sass, b. 19 April 1963; m. Joseph Hurst (b. 26 Dec. 1964); live Temperance, Mich.

8b Hugh J. Defrees Jr., b. Jan. 1924 Alexandria, Va.; d. Aug. 1942 Solomon Islands; W.W. II on cruiser *Quincy.* (*Note:* This may be the only known member of this large Morris family who was lost in World War II.)

7e Eleanor Defrees, b. 1879 Indianapolis; d. 1879, infant.

6b Julia A. Morris Defrees, b. 20 Nov. 1848 Indianapolis; knew Pres. Lincoln; was in the Ford Theater when Lincoln was shot; m. 16 Dec. 1868 in Washington, James Anthony Sample of South Bend, Ind. (b. 1845; cashier U.S. Treasury, Wash., D.C.; pres. Wash. bank; d. 1917; was son of Mary McKnight [Defrees] and Andrew Russell Sample, grandson of Margaret Russell and John Sample, who was U.S. Army captain in War of 1812); Julia d. 1928 Wash.

7a Morris Defrees Sample, b. 19 May 1870 Wash.; engineer in Detroit; m. 20 Sept. 1902 Clinton, N.Y., Ada M. Hathaway (b. 1878 Clinton, N.Y.; d. 1947); d. 24 Dec. 1950 Eustice, Fla.

8a Jane Hathaway Sample, b. 1903.
8b James A. Sample Jr., b. 8 June 1905 Chicago, chief of issues, U.S. Treasury Dept., Wash., D.C.; m. 1933 Claire Walbridge.

9a James A. Sample III, b. 1935.

9b Sally Helen Sample, b. 1941.
9c Robert Walbridge Sample, b. 1942.

8c LeRoy Hathaway Sample, b. 20 March 1909 Chicago, m. 1935 Leslie M. Rutter, lived Mt. Clemens, Mich.

9a LeRoy H. Sample Jr., b. 1938.
9b Susan Jane Sample, b. 1939.

7b Mary Defrees Sample, b. 24 Oct. 1872, d. 27 Sept. 1873, infant.

7c Julia Defrees Sample, b. 3 Feb. 1876 Wash., m. 26 Oct. 1896 in Phila. Capt. Archibald Campbell (U.S. Army col. W.W. I, later brig. gen.; d. 15 Feb. 1959); ten children in twenty-one years; d. 29 Nov. 1950.

7d Elizabeth Morris "Bettie" Sample (also listed later at end of Samples where she really belongs but put here so she isn't "lost," because of the very long list of the ten Campbell children immediately below); b. 13 Jan. 1880 in Washington; m. Dr. Walter Allen Williams (b. 29 Jan. 1882 Columbus, Ga., U.S. Army surgeon); divorced; no issue.

Note: The following line of ten children all descend from 7c Julia Defrees Sample, just above.

8a Archibald Campbell Jr., b. 22 Nov. 1897 San Francisco; left Honolulu where his father was stationed when he was 14 to live with his paternal grandmother in Cold Spring, N.Y.; attended boarding school in New York State; W.W. I p.f.c.; advertising exec.; lived Cold-Spring-on-Hudson, N.Y.; m. 10 Nov. 1939 Alice Saturnia Johnson (b. 21 Aug. 1910 N.Y.C.; d. Sept. 1994, Cold Spring, N.Y.); d. 20 Feb. 1980, Beacon, N.Y.).

9a Archibald Campbell III, b. 7 April 1944 Cold-Spring-on-Hudson, Vietnam War U.S. Army Intel.; m. Alice Romano; lives Cold-Spring-on-Hudson.

9b Alice Alworth Campbell, b. 17 July 1941 N.Y.C., m. Renato Romano (b. Italy); writer, translator, exec. film distribution company, lives Los Angeles, Calif.

10a Robert Campbell Romano, b. 12 Oct. 1972 Rome, Italy.

10b Val Campbell Romano, b. 26 Jan. 1974, Rome.

8b Elizabeth Morris Campbell, b. 4 Sept. 1898 Los Gatos, Calif.; lived Washington, D.C., and Alexandria, Va., during her childhood and youth; became very close to her grandmother, the friend of Lincoln; during W.W. I was a nurse's assistant; after the war became a trained nurse; m. 1 May 1926 Wash., D.C., Walter Allan Galt; no issue; d. 26 Oct. 1994, Alexandria, Va., age 94.

8c Mary Douglas Campbell, b. 6 May 1900; d. 20 June 1900, San Diego, infant.

8d Allan Campbell, b. 1 Oct. 1902 N.Y.C., grad. Am. Institute of Banking, N.Y.C.; W.W. II U.S. Army colonel, three years in China; 1st m. 1940, one child; div.; 2nd m. 5 June 1952 Margaret Ruble (b. 21 April 1917 Lexington, Va.); d. 23 April 1989 in Fla., age 86. Margaret lives in Largo, Fla.

9a Allan Campbell Jr., grad. U. Southern Florida; grad. Stetson School of Law; asst. district attorney for 18th Judicial Circuit; m. Rhea Aza; two children are hers only; live Lake Mary, Fla.

8e John "Jack" Campbell, b. 10 May 1904 St. Louis, Mo.; grad. Colgate U.; W.W. II U.S. Army colonel; m. Margaret "Peggy" Sinclair (b. 18 July 1913 Wash.; when widowed, m. Charles Wade, now deceased; lives Kailua, Hawaii); John d. 30 May 1978 in Hawaii.

9a John Campbell Jr., b. 10 Oct. 1933 Ft. Totten, N.Y.; grad. U. of Calif. and U.C. Law School; m. 7 Jan. 1968 Karin Maurinals (b. 14 Jan. [?] Riga, Latvia); adopted son; live Hawaii.

9b Douglas Campbell, b. 3 Jan. 1938 Passaic, N.J.; d. 18 Oct. 1961, airplane accident.

9c Mary Margaret Campbell, b. 8 Feb. 1941 Patterson, N.J.; grad. jr. col.; teacher, lives Tacoma, Wash.; m. ——.

10a Mark D. Campbell, b. 20 Oct. 1961 in Washington.

9d Ann Elizabeth Campbell, b. 5 Nov. 1942 Passaic, N.J.; grad. jr. col.; m. 1 Sept. 1962 Paul Osborn

(b. 6 April 1939 California); div.; teacher, lives Kona, Hawaii.

10a Joelie Osborn, b. 16 June 1963, California.
10b Paul Osborn Jr., b. 17 May 1965, California.
10c John C. Osborn, b. 31 Aug. 1966, California.

9e Catherine Gordon Campbell, b. 9 Oct. 1946 Passaic, N.J.; grad. jr. col.; m. 5 April 1966 J. Roger Allen (b. 26 May 1944, Pa.); live Rollins, Mont.

10a Jeffrey R. Allen, b. 5 Feb. 1968 Hawaii.
10b Leah E. Allen, b. 29 Jan. 1971.
10c Ryan J. Allen, b. 2 July 1977.

8f Gordon Campbell, b. 1 Oct. 1905 Wash.; grad. 1926 U.S. Naval Academy, Annapolis; W.W. II U.S. Navy capt., U.S.N., retired; administrative asst. in a manufacturing company which makes navigation and aviation equipment; corresp. sec. for Class '26 USNA; m. 27 April 1933 Addo Shafer (b. 20 July 1908 Austin, Tex.); live Durham, N.C.

9a Jayne Campbell, b. 22 Feb. 1934 Annapolis, Md.; travel agent Ft. Lauderdale, Fla.; 1st m. Robert J. Darnell, three children; div.; 2nd m. James Nance, one child; 3rd m. Donald H. Byal (d. 29 Jan. 1977); no issue.

10a Diane L. Darnell, b. 6 March 1951; m. David Gerhardt.
10b Michael R. Darnell, b. May 1954; m. Cindy Winans.

11a Lindsey Elizabeth Darnell, b. 15 May 1986.
11b Alyssa Michelle Darnell, b. 29 May 1989.

10b Collin C. Darnell, b. 30 Oct. 1955.
10c James N. Nance, b. 4 March 1963.

8g Julie Defrees Campbell (seventh child of Julia Defrees Sample and Archibald Campbell), b. 1 June 1908 Flushing, L.I., N.Y.; grad. Spence School; newspaper woman; author of more than thirty books; in *Who's Who in America, Who's Who in the South and East, Who's Who in the World;* and *The Social Register;* m.

30 March 1933, N.Y.C., Charles Tatham Jr. (b. 21 Aug. 1905 N.Y.C., grad. 1928 Harvard; public utility analyst; v. pres. Bache & Co., N.Y.C.; d. 17 Sept. 1973 Ossining, N.Y.); lives Alexandria, Va.

9a Charles "Chuck" Tatham III, b. 15 Aug. 1936 N.Y.C.; grad. West Chester Com. Col., engineer; professional dog-show photographer; m. 10 Oct. 1960 Keene, N.H., Gail Brusse (b. 26 Aug. 1938 Tarrytown, N.Y.); div.; 2nd m. 11 Sept. 1982 Sandra —— ; he lives Munsonville, N.H.

    10a Tracy D. Tatham, b. 15 Aug. 1962 Keene, N.H.; lives Unionville, Pa.

9b Campbell Tatham, b. 5 July 1940 N.Y.C.; grad. Hotchkiss School; B.A. Amherst Col.; M.A. NYU; Ph.D. U.Wis.-Milwaukee; prof. Eng., U.Wis.; 1st m. 28 Dec. 1963 Susan Masland (b. 19 April 1941 Coral Gables, Fla.); four children; 2nd m. 14 Aug. 1974 Kathleen Dale (b. 15 March 1945 Stafford, Kans.), one child; 3rd m. 21 June 1980 Lynne Schumann (b. 10 Feb. 1949 Milwaukee), two children.

    10a Gregory Campbell Tatham, b. 19 Aug. 1966 Madison, Wis.

    10b Anne Comfort Tatham, b. 20 Dec. 1969, Milwaukee, Wis.

    10c Holly Susan Tatham, b. 9 Dec. 1971, twin, Milwaukee.

    10d Rebecca Masland Tatham, b. 9 Dec. 1971, twin, Milwaukee.

    10e Jessica Morgan Dale, b. 27 Aug. 1977 Milwaukee (hers).

    10f Benjamin Arthur Tatham, b. 11 Sept. 1983, Milwaukee.

    10g Jocelynn Margaret Tatham, b. 5 Nov. 1984, Milwaukee.

8h Donald Campbell, b. 12 Dec. 1914 Honolulu; grad. Fordham U. and Cornell Med. Col.; colonel U.S. Army Med. Corps 1941-68, capt. W.W. II, Korea and Vietnam, awarded Legion of Merit, March 1968; U.S.

Army retired; m. 15 March 1941 Bette L. Campbell (b. 13 Dec. 1920 N.Y.C.), live San Antonio, Tex.

9a Donald Campbell III, b. 3 Dec. 1943 Carlisle, Pa., grad. West Point; capt. Artillery Vietnam War; capt. U.S. Army, El Paso, Tex.; m. Mary Jo Valentz (b. 25 July 1946 Baltimore, Md.); div.; 2nd m.; one child.

> 10a Mary Elizabeth Campbell, b. 19 Dec. 1969 El Paso, Tex.
> 10b Donald Campbell IV, b. 6 March 1972 Wiesbaden, Germany.
> 10c Rosita Maria Campbell, b. 8 April 1979 El Paso, Tex.

9b Gordon Campbell, b. 9 March 1947 Wash.; grad. Texas A&M; U.S. Army Vietnam War; commercial real estate, Bedford, Tex.; 1st m. 24 May 1970 Pamela Thorpe (b. 29 Sept. 1948 Minneapolis, Minn.); 2 children; div.; 2nd m ——; one child.

> 10a Tamara Lynn Campbell, b. 7 May 1971, Nuremberg, Germany.
> 10b Bethany Jo Campbell, b. 26 Aug. 1973, Nuremberg, Germany.
> 10c Jeffrey Gordon Campbell, b. 12 Feb. 1984, Dallas, Tex.

9c Allan Campbell, b. 6 Aug. 1949 Munich, Germany; attended Texas A&M; U.S. Army, Vietnam War; IBM service representative; m. 19 July 1975 Lorelei L. Sherrell (b. 18 July 1952 Detroit); live San Antonio, Tex.

> 10a Christopher Allan Campbell, b. 29 Aug. 1980 San Antonio, Tex.
> 10b Heather Mitchell Campbell, b. 10 Feb. 1983 San Antonio, Tex.

9d Bruce Campbell, b. 13 Sept. 1950 Munich, Germany; grad. West Point; Vietnam War; nuclear engineer Colorado Springs, Colo.; m. 19 Aug. 1978 Catherine Fry, San Antonio, Tex.

        10a Caroline Campbell, b. 15 Oct. 1980, Tacoma, Wash.

        10b Sarah Campbell, b. 10 Aug. 1985, twin, Colorado Springs.

        10c Laura Campbell, b. 10 Aug. 1985, twin, Colorado Springs.

    9e Colin Campbell, b. 29 April 1953, Wash.; grad. U. of Colo.; lt. U.S. Air Force; m. 11 Sept. 1976 Margaret R. Saunders (b. 14 March 1957 San Antonio, Tex.); three children; div.; 2nd m. 12 Dec. 1990 San Antonio, Ann Lambert; no issue.

        10a Cameron Campbell, b. 4 Nov. 1981, San Antonio.

        10b Colin Trenton Campbell, b. 6 Sept. 1983, San Antonio.

        10c Stuart Campbell, b. 28 Feb. 1985, San Antonio.

    9f Stuart Campbell, b. 3 Jan. 1955 Fort Riley, Kans.; grad. Stephen F. Austin State U.; urban planner; m. 27 July 1991 Ogden, Utah, Kathryn Bertilson.

        10a Theodore Scott Campbell, b. 11 March 1993, Wenatchee, Wash.

8i Charmian Campbell, b. 22 March 1917 Savannah, Ga.; member, Colonial Dames; 1st m. 20 Aug. 1938 Henry MacDonald (b. 24 Jan. 1898 Pa., d. 24 Jan. 1956), three children; 2nd m. 2 May 1958 Sidney A. Trundle (b. 22 Jan. 1908, Baltimore, Md.; grad. Georgetown U., Rutgers School of Banking, Fordham Law School; banker; d. 9 March 1981, Baltimore); one child; lives New York City.

    9a Catherine MacDonald, b. 22 Oct. 1940 N.Y.C., grad. Sarah Lawrence Col., post-grad. Julliard School of Music and Columbia Univ., N.Y.C.; composer for theater music; resident composer for the Vivian Beaumont Theater in Lincoln Center, N.Y.C.; recently with the Shakespeare Theatre at the Folger Theatre, Washington, D.C.; the Lansburgh Theater, Washington, where she wrote the score for their first production and received a Helen

Hayes Award; and the Carter Barron Theater, Washington; has worked with some of the finest directors and actors in the U.S.; lives Alstead, N.H., and New York City.

9b Gerald MacDonald, b. 12 Sept. 1942 N.Y.C.; inventor, builder; lives San Rafael, Calif.

9c Joseph MacDonald, b. 19 Oct. 1947 N.Y.C.; lives Sag Harbor, N.Y.

9d Charles Trundle, b. 8 March 1959 N.Y.C.; grad. U. New Mexico; m. 20 June 1992 Ann McCurry; live Corpus Christi, Tex.

10a Jennifer Trundle, b. 26 Oct. 1994.

8j Mary Margaret Campbell (tenth child of Julia Defrees Sample and Archibald Campbell), b. 11 Nov. 1918 Savannah, Ga;, m. in New York 17 Sept. 1941 Richard Fairfield Humphreys (b. New Hampshire 5 Oct. 1916, grad. Princeton U.; lt. U.S. Navy W.W. II; executive in pharmaceuticals; d. 26 Nov. 1974); she lives Watertown, Mass.

9a Julie Defrees Humphreys, b. 29 July 1943 N.Y.C.; grad. Finch Col.; m. 25 Nov. 1972 Dr. Andre Vasu; div.; lives Cambridge, Mass.

7d Elizabeth Morris "Bettie" Sample (second listing is deliberate, as explained far above the Campbells), b. 13 Jan. 1880 Wash., D.C.; m. Dr. Walter Allen Williams (b. 29 Jan. 1882 Columbus, Ga., U.S. Army surgeon); div.; no issue.

6c Amanda Morris Defrees (third child of Elizabeth Morris and John Defrees), b. 10 April 1852.

6d John Dougherty Defrees Jr., b. 6 March 1855, twin; m. Anna Fisher; div.; no issue; lived Washington, D.C.; d. 1924, Washington.

6e Anthony Colfax Defrees (fifth child of Bettie Morris and John Defrees), b. 6 Mar 1855, twin; d. 5 April 1903 Berkeley Springs, W.Va.; unmarried.

6f Thomas Morris Defrees, named for his uncle, General Thomas A. Morris; m. Lydia "Nellie" Bradley Defrees, widow of oldest brother, 6a Morris Morris Defrees.

5h William Little Morris, eighth child of Morris and Rachael Morris, b. 3 March 1828; m. 20 Feb. 1850 Ann E. Morrison; one child; d. 21 Feb. 1853 Indianapolis; bur. Crown Hill.

5i Nicholas McCarty Morris, ninth and last child of Morris and Rachael Morris, b. 12 March 1830; d. 12 Oct. 1830, infant; bur. Crown Hill.

Simon McCarty of early Indianapolis is mentioned twice, once in the hemp-raising and -processing business on his bayou on Pogue's Run. This was probably the Mr. McCarty who must have been a close friend of Rachael and Morris; the time is right. In the next generation, Thomas B. McCarty bought the Morris House Hotel from Morris's son, General Thomas Morris, who built it across from the new Union Station. The McCartys are mentioned four times in B. R. Sulgrove's *History of Indianapolis and Marion County*.

Generation 4: Daniel Cushman Morris
Third Child of Morris I and Sarah Cushman Morris

Generations: 1st, John Morris I of Wales; 2nd, Richard Morris of America; 3rd, Morris Morris I and Sarah Cushman of Virginia.

Sources: *Cushman Genealogy and General History;* Anne Wilson Allen, 11829 172nd Ave., NE, Redmond, WA 98052-2223; Edna Mae Morris Montgomery, Box 522, Cloverdale, IN 46120; Mary Ann Piper, 2469 Wayfarer Court, Chapel Hill, NC 27514; all three descendants of Daniel Morris; Frances Gibson Poulos, 8748 Gibson Lane, Potter Valley, CA 95469, descendant of Preston Morris.

4c Daniel Cushman Morris, b. 14 April 1788 Bryan Station, Fayette Co., Ky. This is stated on his tombstone in Cloverdale, Ind.; his first cradle was a sugar trough; m. 25 April 1811 Bourbon Co., Ky. Anna Minnick (Meenack) (Bourbon Co. Rec.) (b. 2 April 1854; came to Kentucky with her daughter's families, the Harts and McDowells, in 1854. Dayse Whitecotton, her granddaughter, said Anna was "Pennsylvania Dutch" and "a perfect lady, good looking, with hazel eyes and black hair that stayed that way. She wore a black silk riding habit when she rode into Paris, Ky., on her pacing horse." She died 24 July 1854 Greenfield, Dade Co., Mo.). Daniel owned many acres in Bourbon Co., Ky., moved to Nicholas Co., Ky., then to Cloverdale, Ind.; d. 21 April 1852 Cloverdale, Putnam Co., Ind., of "lung fever" at 64, recorded in the Hart family Bible, owned in 1988 by Catherine Morris's great-granddaughter, Bess Hopkins, of St. Joseph, Mo.; four children:

5a Morris (Maurice) Robinett Morris, "Mod" b. c. 1812, lived with his sister, Catherine Morris Hart, on his brother-in-law's farm in Ralls Co., Mo., after the Civil War; d. single c. age 77 c. 1890 in Ralls Co., Mo.; bur. Norton Cem.
5b Dulcimer Morris, b. 26 July 1819; m. Thomas Lane (b. Kentucky); lived Cloverdale, Ind.

    6a Thomas Lane Jr., lived Cloverdale, Ind.
    6b John C. Lane, b. 1851; m. 1921 Anna Cooper; lived Arkansas and Cloverdale, Ind.
    6c Ella Lane, m. Simpson McCoy of Cloverdale; lived Salina, Kans.
    6d Carrie Lane, m. Joel McCoy; lived Cloverdale.
    6e Joseph Lane, b. 1854; m. Nora DeVore (b. 1861; d. 1922), lived Cloverdale.
    6f Elizabeth Lane, b. 1839; m. Robert McMains, lived Cloverdale, d. 13 Feb. 1906.

5c Thomas B. Morris, b. 1820; m. Julia A. Young (b. 1878; d. 13 July 1878); d. 16 April 1881.

    6a Eliza Jane Morris, d. 1879.
    6b Elizabeth C. Morris, d. 1882.
    6c Alma G. Morris
    6d James A. Morris
    6e John P. Morris
    6f Fannie A. Morris
    6g George D. Morris, d. Muncie, Ind.

        7a Earl Morris of Muncie, Ind.

    6h William Franklin Morris

        7a Clara Morris, m. —— Vandersmith, lived Orland Park, Ind.
        7b Olive Morris, m. —— Denova.

    6i Ella Morris, m. —— Treuesdel, d. Cloverdale, Ind.

5d Catherine Elizabeth Morris, b. 22 Oct. 1822, Nicholas Co., Ky.; m. 12 Sept. 1839, Nicholas Co., Richard Lindsey Hart (b. 21 June 1815, Bath Co., Ky., son of Mary Jane Pearson and William Hart). Following their marriage, they rode on horseback from

Kentucky to their new home in Cloverdale, Ind., where he had a general store. Unfortunate Richard went on bond for a friend, eventually was required to pay $3,000, and therefore lost his store. This caused a move to Caldwell Co., Mo., in 1854, where land was being opened up.

The following incidents reveal some of the difficulties of living before and during the Civil War. A surveyor like his forebears, Richard Hart surveyed and laid out the town of Breckenridge, Mo., north of the Mason-Dixon Line, where sympathies proved to be with the North. Here misfortune struck again, when he was followed home from a meeting by men who beat him severely and left him to die. A kind neighbor discovered his riderless horse and rescued him.

Catherine (Morris) and Richard Hart, believing in the Confederate cause (as did the Wilsons), finally moved further south in Missouri, from Breckenridge to Ralls County, and farmed near Center. Here, all the wooden buildings were made of logs from their own land. Catherine's brother, Morris Robinett Morris, who remained single, lived with them. Richard affiliated with the Masonic Lodge and died at age 84 after a taxing life of hard work.

During this war-time period, Catherine proved to be a heroine. She learned of a plot to kill her daughter's father-in-law, Eli Wilson, so she bravely rode horseback forty miles to warn him. (Those Morris women were not only long-lived but also very stalwart, in spite of their hard lives.) Sleeping in haystacks, Eli did escape to family in Illinois by using horses furnished him along the way. After the war, Eli Wilson returned to his 1500-acre farm in Missouri, formerly well-stocked, to find only one blind mare left. In despair, he went to Arizona, remarried, and died there. Such were the fortunes of war.

After the death of her husband, Catherine moved on down to Whitesboro, Texas, to live with family and died at 57, having reared eight children.

6a Mary Ann Hart, b. 9 June 1840, Cloverdale, Putnam Co., Ind. 1st m. 25 June 1856 at Breckenridge, Andrew Henderson Wilson (1831-1868, son of Eli, above) in a double ceremony with her young aunt, 5g Almanza Palmyra Morris, sister of Catherine Morris Hart, above.

Adventurous Andy Wilson went to California during the Gold Rush, luckily found gold, came home with $3,000 in his pockets, first taking a boat to Panama where he rode a horse across the isthmus, then boarded a boat for New Orleans and another up the Mississippi River. Because he was under age, half of what was left of his $3,000 went to his father (a father's own rule?). With the rest, Andy bought a cook for his mother and a farm for himself in Gentry Co., Mo. He then studied medicine under Dr. Mac Wilson while attending Rush Medical College in Chicago for six months. With that little background he practiced medicine! Then Andy went to fight with the Confederate army in a unit called "The South Tommies." While cleaning his gun, he accidentally shot off his thumb and forefinger, making him exempt from the war. After that he was a farmer and teamster and took "freight strings" to Mexico for the government. He and Mary Ann moved to Bentonville, Ark., where he died of pneumonia at age 37 on 19 July 1868. Mary Ann went with her children to live with her parents near Spalding Springs, Ralls Co., Mo., where she earned her living as a milliner. She died at age 83 on 21 Nov. 1923 in Paris, Mo. She had reared two children: Zora and Mortimer.

> 7a Zora Almanza Wilson, b. 4 Feb. 1858 Daviess Co., Mo.; teacher; m. 18 May 1878, Albany, Mo., James Henry Whitecotton (b. 1854 Ralls Co., Mo.; lawyer; d. 1944 Paris, Mo., age 90; was Missouri state senator 1927-29); d. 24 July 1954 Paris, Mo., age 95.
>
>> 8a Dayse Mary Whitecotton, b. 28 Oct. 1880 Albany, Mo.; attended Ward Belmont College in Kansas City; became a genealogist; m. 7 Oct. 1906 David Milton Proctor (b. 2 April 1881 Ralls Co., Mo.; attended Columbia U.; wrote the book *Pay Day* for the Alfred Landon presidential campaign; d. 1995 Kansas City; attorney and city counselor for Kansas City); d. 20 Feb. 1972, Kansas City, Mo., age 91; bur. Walnut Grove Cem., Paris, Mo.
>>
>>> 9a David M. Proctor Jr., b. 10 Jan. 1909 Kansas City, Mo.; 1st m. Evalyn Layson; 2nd m. 9 Nov. 1932 Kansas City, Mary Jane Dodge; attorney in Kansas City, Mo.; two children; div.
>>>
>>>> 10a David Milton Proctor III, b. 4 Feb. 1936 Kansas City; m. Britt Benjamisson.

10b Virginia Dodge Proctor, b. 14 July 1933, Kansas City; m. William Young.

    11a Terry Young
    11b Susan Young
    11c David Young

9b Zora Wilson Proctor, b. 18 Aug. 1913, Kansas City; m. 1935 Richard Currie Montague (b. 28 June 1911; d. 17 Jan. 1984 Norfolk, Va.).

10a John Currie Montague, b. 25 April 1942 Salisbury, N.C.; m. 1965 Doris Suetta Smithe, div.

    11a Richard Allen Montague, b. 16 June 1968, Florida.
    11b Charles Strother Montague, b. 31 May 1972, North Carolina.

10b Richard Proctor Montague, b. 10 Aug. 1954 Norfolk, Va.; 1st m. 3 Jan. 1976 Marsha Elizabeth Blackwell, one child; div.; 2nd m. 7 Nov. 1985 Jamie Ewell (b. 1957).

    11a Courtney Proctor Montague, b. 1980.

9c Elizabeth Ellen Proctor, b. 6 June 1919 Kansas City; m. 1940 Robert Jenks.

10a Susan Hamilton Jenks, b. 1942 Kansas City, Mo.; m. 1966 Gerald Liamsden ?.
10b Ellen Proctor Jenks, b. 1944 Kansas City; m. 1967 Dennis Shoemaker.

    11a Beth Park Shoemaker, b. 1979.
    11b David Howard Shoemaker, b. 1982.

10c Mary Elizabeth Jenks, b. 1948.
10d Sarah L. Jenks, b. 1955.

8b Andrew Tilden Whitecotton, b. 25 Nov. 1883; m. 24 June 1924 Lola Alverson; no issue; d. 1949; bur. Walnut Grove Cem.

8c Elizabeth Morris Whitecotton, b. 20 Oct. 1888 Paris, Mo.; no issue; d. 1962 Paris, Mo.; bur. Walnut Grove.

8d James Henry Whitecotton Jr., b. 8 Aug. 1893; m. Florence Deaver, no issue; d. 12 Dec. 1918 Moberly, Mo.; bur. Walnut Grove Cem.

7b Mortimer Hart Wilson, b. 12 Sept. 1864, Red River Co., Texas; m. 25 Jan. 1885, Albany, Gentry Co., Mo., Lillie Jane Holloway (b. 27 April 1869 Leavenworth, Kans.; livery stable owner, real estate salesman; d. 16 Sept. 1928, Hannibal, Mo.; bur. Mt. Olivet Cem.); d. 13 Sept. 1935, Hannibal, Marion Co., Mo.

8a George Andrew Wilson, b. 28 Sept. 1886, Albany, Mo. As a boy he helped with the horses in his father's livery stable and drove people in their rented rigs. He taught school right out of high school, then attended William Jewell College, as he wished to become an attorney. Finances prevented this so he became a salesman of newspaper advertising and insurance. 1st, Lola Mae Heffner (b. 1 July 1894 Rush Co., Ind.; d. 16 July 1984 Ripley Co., Ind.), one son; m. 17 Feb. 1913, Table Rock, Pawnee Co., Nebr., Frances Hudnall Hales (b. 6 Aug. 1886, Paces, Halifax Co., Va. After high school she taught in an eight-grade school three miles from home, so her father bought her a shotgun for protection. She saved enough to go to State Teachers College in Nebraska, then taught in the Omaha public schools and later in private Brownell Hall, continuing to take credit courses all her life. Divorced, Frances Hales worked in a store in order to send her daughter to college. She d. 25 Aug. 1949 Seattle, Wash.); two children.

George then m. c. 1942 Denver, Colo., Marjorie Beer (b. 8 Feb. 1902, Ill., prob. Abingdon; school librarian; d. 31 March 1977, Denver, Colo.); no issue. George became a Master Mason in 1920. Both he and Marjorie were Unitarians. While she was driving their car it was hit by a train which killed George instantly; he d. 12 Jan. 1964, Mesa, Maricopa Co., Ariz.

9a Carl Lee Heck, b. 9 July 1912 Newcastle, Ind. (lived with his grandmother and step-grandfather, so was given their name as his surname); grad. Dayton U. and Juris Doctor from law school in Cincinnati; educator and teacher in Cincinnati schools, mem.

Methodist Church; officer in Army Air Corps in W.W. II and in 1950, Korea and Va.; 1st m. 31 Dec. 1934 Richmond, Ind., Constance Botting (b. 29 Sept. 1912 Narberth, Pa., d. of cancer 6 Feb. 1970 Cincinnati, Ohio); three children; 2nd m. 28 July 1973 Mary Scott Birdsong, no issue.

10a Carl Lee Heck Jr., b. 3 June 1936 Dayton, Ohio; processing engineer; m. 18 Feb. 1956 Roberta Nemec (b. 5 Aug. 1938 Dayton, Ohio); d. 5 Jan. 1987 Jackson, Mich.; four children, all born in Dayton:

11a Carl Steven Heck, b. 27 July 1956.
11b Susan Frances Heck, b. 13 Nov. 1959.
11c Michael James Heck, b. 22 Sept. 1961.
11d David Allen Heck, b. 12 Dec. 1963.

10b Joan Frances Heck, b. 30 Sept. 1940; nurse; m. 24 Nov. 1962, Dayton, John A. Morris (b. 10 Oct. 1941; teacher industrial arts, Cincinnati); divorced.

11a Dean Mathew Morris, b. 23 July 1963, Dayton; m. 1982 Lori Surges; div.
11b Scott Andrew Morris, b. 8 Aug. 1964, Hamilton, Ohio; divorced.
11c Amy Catherine Morris, b. 7 April 1968, Miami, Ohio; registered nurse.

10c James Peyton Heck, b. 3 April 1942 Dayton; 1st m. 17 July 1965 Hatboro, Pa., Linda Ann Heacock (b. 27 May 1944 Hatboro, Pa.); two children; 2nd m. 23 July 1977 Lee Kauffman (art director); one child.

11a Elizabeth Botting Heck, b. 14 Nov. 1966, Detroit, Mich.
11b Annie Heck, b. 26 Jan. 1970, Detroit.
11c Rebecca Heck, b. 13 May 1983, Richmond, Va.

9b George Hales Wilson, b. 31 July 1914, Omaha, Nebr.; grad. Illinois Institute of Technology; registered professional engineer in Missouri; in *Who's Who in*

America for the Soc. of Heating, Refrig., and Air Conditioning Engineers; loved river life; had a summer home on the banks of the Mississippi. A radio buff, he listened to the river pilots from his home. Later, entering the construction business, he supervised the building of schools, hospitals, and commercial buildings. Married 8 June 1940 Hannibal, Mo., Elizabeth Katherine Schultz (b. 1913, grad. Culver-Stockton in Canton, Mo.; M.A. from U. of Minnesota; elem. teacher and asst. principal in Hannibal, Mo.; deaconess and elder of First Christian Ch.; pres. of CYF, of Delta Kappa Gamma, of local Amer. Assoc. of Univ. Women; 50-year mem. of the Order of the Eastern Star; d. of Lou Gehrig's disease 18 Nov. 1993 at Arlington Heights, Ill.) George d. of lung cancer 25 Aug. 1949.

>10a Anne Ellen Wilson, b. 1943; grad. Drake U. and M.A. from National-Lewis Col., Evanston, Ill.; teacher, school Internet coordinator, mem. district learning lab; 2nd m. Mark "Casey" Pasieka (b. Poland, owns a machine shop in Chicago); live Arlington Heights, Ill.
>
>>11a Helena Beth Pasieka, b. 1978.
>>11b Bryan Wilson Pasieka, twin, b. 1979.
>>11c Jeffrey Carey Pasieka, twin, b. 1979.

9c Anne Wilson, b. 31 Oct. 1918 Omaha, Douglas Co., Nebr.; attended Carleton College, Minn. The Depression prevented finishing so she worked for an insurance company and United Airlines, took a government drafting course (W.W. II years) and then was employed by the Boeing Co. both to work and go to engineering classes; obtained a realtor's license; became a genealogist; m. in Unitarian Church 8 Sept. 1945 in Seattle, King Co., Wash., Arthur Donald Allen (b. Aug. 1916, attended engineering school U. of Wash., Seattle; in the National Guard; then in the U.S. Army, Coast Artillery; exempted from active service to work for Boeing on a project in England; retired as a principal aircraft engineer); live Redmond, Wash.

10a Roger Donald Allen, b. 21 Nov. 1947, Seattle; Vietnam War helicopter pilot, then flew in the jungles of Panama and Colombia; attended Northrup Institute of Technology, Calif.; Green River and Lake Washington Com. Colleges, excelling in welding; four-year apprenticeship at the U.S. Bremerton Shipyards; sent to Spain; now in Army Corps of Engineers; enjoys hunting, scuba diving and mountain climbing.

10b Timothy Arthur Allen, b. 23 Sept. 1956, enlisted in the U.S. Army for three years; four-year electrical apprenticeship course at N. Seattle Com. Col.; works for Boeing Aircraft as electrician for construction and maintenance; m. 29 Aug. 1981, Carnation, Wash., Tracy Ann Anderson (b. North Bend, Wash., 30 July 1958); three children, all born in Bellevue, Wash.

11a Aaron Malcolm Allen, b. 24 Jan. 1982.
11b Michael Jerome Allen, b. 15 Sept. 1984.
11c Eric Ryan Allen, b. 6 July 1988.

10c Susan Elizabeth Allen, b. 11 Dec. 1959 Seattle; grad. Central Wash. U., Ellensburg, Wash.; accomplished seamstress, mgr. of bridal shop, reservations and ticket agent with Northwest Airlines; worked at a bank in Bellevue; 1st m. in Bellevue 5 May 1982 Jon Bergsland Waude (b. King Co., Wash.); div.; no issue; 2nd m. 6 June 1987 Paul James Valley (b. 18 Dec. 1960 Flint, Mich.; grad. Central Wash. U.; M.S. in the science of finance, Seattle U.; store manager); two children, born in Bellevue.

11a Katherine Elizabeth Valley, b. Jun 1990.
11b Alaura Anne Valley, b. 22 Feb. 1995.

8b Zora Myrton Wilson, b. 28 June 1889, Goss, Mo.; attended Cincinnati Conservatory of Music; m. 7 Nov. 1913 St. Louis, Mo., Clarence O. Hanes (b. 9 Aug. 1889; exec. sec. Chamber of Commerce, Jefferson

City, Mo.; d. 16 Dec. 1962 Jefferson City, Mo.); d. 18 March 1953 Jefferson City.

9a John Wilson Hanes, b. Washington, Pa., 26 Sept. 1918; never married; d. 20 July 1958, Alton, Ill.

9b Clarence O. Hanes Jr., b. 24 July 1920 Steubenville, Ohio; grad. U. of Missouri; commercial real estate salesman; m. 22 May 1948 Red Bud, Ill., Luella Ahnefeld; no issue; d. St. Louis, Mo.

8c Cleo Mary Wilson, b. 19 March 1895, Strother, Ralls Co., Mo.; grad. U. of Nebraska; during W.W. II in Quartermaster and Personnel Depts. of U.S. Gov't, then newspaper, kindergarten teacher and principal; m. 5 June 1925 St. Louis, Mo., Dr. Virgil Martin Campbell (b. 2 March 1895 Bowling Green, Mo.; grad. Washington U., D.D.S.; dentist, elder emeritus Christian Ch., W.W. I veteran, master Hannibal Lodge, high priest Royal Arch Masons, officer Amer. Legion and Lions Club; d. 1 Sept. 1968, Hannibal, Mo., bur. Bowling Green Cem., Mo.); no issue; d. 4 April 1979 Hannibal, Mo., bur. Bowling Green Cem.

8d James Mortimer Wilson, b. 2 Oct. 1897 New London, Mo.; grad. Missouri School of Mines, Rolla, Mo.; civil engineer for Illinois State Highway Dept.; m. 1934 Marie Earle; div.; d. 3 Jan. 1959, Pawnee, Ill.

9a James Mortimer Wilson Jr., b. 26 Jan. 1942; m. 1 Aug. 1964 Kathryn Ann Beirman; div.

10a Bret Wilson, b. 1966.
10b Bart Wilson, b. 1969; div.; m. Ruth ——.
10c Brandon Troy Wilson, b. 1972.

8e Morris Duke Wilson, b. 20 July 1900 New London, Mo.; manager shoe store in Hannibal; m. 8 Feb. 1925 Shelbyville, Mo., to Ola Beatrice Hammond (b. 23 Sept. 1903 Shelby Co., Mo.; circuit clerk and recorder of Shelby Co., pres. of Shelby Historical Assoc., chrm. of Shelbyville Salvation Army for 15 years; d. 5 Feb. 1993 Columbia, Mo.); div.; d. 27 Aug. 1951 Miami, Fla.; bur. Mt. Olivet Cem., Hannibal, Mo.

9a Morris Duke Wilson Jr., b. 25 Nov. 1925, Hannibal, Mo.; Ph.D. in education; supt. schools Des Moines, Iowa; dir. of evaluation, research, and testing; now consultant; m. 30 April 1960 Elizabeth "Lisa" High.

10a Martin Duke Wilson, b. 1960; grad. U. Iowa, attending Indiana U. studying voice to be an opera singer.

10b Patrick High Wilson, b. 1967; grad. U. Iowa.

6a Mary Ann Hart (continued from far above here, following marriage to Andrew Wilson and above descendants); 2nd m. 12 Dec. 1872 William Lane Graves (b. 23 March 1845 Ralls Co., Mo., son of Nancy Utterback and William Henry Graves; physician; d. 12 Dec. 1876 Albany, Gentry Co., Mo., where he owned a 200-acre farm); two children:

7c Berta Graves, b. 1875; d. 1891 (age 17).

7d Frances Laura Graves, b. 17 Jan. 1877 Spaulding Springs, Mo.; m. 27 March 1907, Paris, Mo., to Dr. Martin Stapleton Bodine (b. 27 Feb. 1876, M.D. from U. of Louisville); d. 13 April 1970 Indianapolis.

8a Martin Stapleton Bodine Jr., b. 19 Oct. 1908 Paris, Mo.; 1st m. Josephine Brandon, two daughters; 2nd m. Jacqueline Thompson, no issue; d. 14 March 1981.

9a Ann Brandon Bodine, b. 28 Nov. 1943 Jefferson City, Mo.; 1st m. James Barry, deceased; 2nd m. Thomas Barrale; lives Newhall, Iowa (1988); two children, born in Jefferson City.

10a Shannon Barry Barrale, b. 11 Jan. 1968.
10b Courtney Barry Barrale, b. 28 April 1971.

9b Elizabeth Graves Bodine, b. 31 March 1946 Jefferson City; m. Robert Mitchell; lives in Texas (1988); two children, born in Houston.

10a Laura Elizabeth Mitchell, b. 19 March 1973.
10b Leanne Marie Mitchell, b. 26 Jan. 1976.

9c Mary Ann Bodine, b. 22 July 1910 Paris, Mo.; m. 2 Aug. 1946 Indianapolis, Robert Lawrence Piper (b.

21 Sept. 1904 Cherokee Co., Kans.; newspaper man).

10a Ann Hart Piper, b. 25 May 1947 Indianapolis; grad. Wellesley Col.; Ph.D.; associate prof. of biochemistry and biophysics; m. 12 June 1969 Bruce Wayne Erickson (b. 19 Oct. 1942 New Haven, Conn.; Ph.D. Harvard; prof. of chemistry at U.N.C.).

11a Evan Lawrence Erickson, b. 7 June 1979 Westwood, N.J.
11b Ryan Bodine Erickson, b. 1 July 1982, Hanover, N.H.

6a Mary Ann Hart (2nd continuance, following Andrew Wilson and William L. Graves); 3rd m. after 1924 to —— Alexander, no issue; lived with dau. Frances L. Graves Bodine until her death; d. 21 Nov. 1923 Paris, Monroe Co., Mo.; bur. Walnut Grove Cem., Paris.

6b Benjamin Arnold Hart, b. 3 Sept. 1842 Cloverdale, Ind.; Confederate captain, one of the last survivors at Vicksburg; lived in Texas; 1st m. in Missouri Ellen Hearn (b. 11 Sept. 1849 Fannin Co., Texas); four children; 2nd m. aft. 19 Feb. 1882 Rose —— ; one child; d. 19 April 1887 on the Chisholm Trail; bur. Duncan, Okla.

7a Ed Hart, b. 1869; banker in Okmulgee, Okla.; m. Agnes Miller.

8a Florence Hart, m. —— McInturf.

7b Bud Hart, b. 1872 Texas; m. 1927 Muskogee, Okla., May Lindsay of Kentucky; d. near Bozeman, Mont.

8a Virginia L. Hart, m. C. A. S. Davison; lives 1976 Anaconda, Mont.
8b Richard Lindsay Hart, m. Luella —— ; lives Bozeman, Mont.
8c Elizabeth Hart, b. c. 1900.

7c William Hart, b. c. 1876.
7d Claude Hart, b. c. 1878 Texas; lived Muskogee, Okla.; d. Oklahoma.
7e Harry Hart (son of 2nd wife).

6c Thomas Austin Hart, b. 10 Feb. 1845, Cloverdale, Ind.; m. 20 Feb. 1866 Ralls Co., Mo., Mehethalem Ellen (or Ellea) Rosser (b. 4 Jan. 1847 Ralls Co., Mo.; d. 20 Sept. 1915); inducted into Missouri militia 1862 in St. Louis; d. 1925 Ralls Co., Mo.

7a Richard Rosser Hart, b. 17 Sept. 1871, Ralls Co., Mo.; m. Laura Ann Davis (b. 9 May 1872 Flint, Pike Co., Ill.); surveyor and farmer.

8a Mary Elizabeth Hart, b. 14 May 1898 Ralls Co., Mo., seamstress; m. 5 June 1913 Ralls Co. Ronnie M. Gaskill; machinist; d. 15 April 1972 Quincy, Ill.

9a Morris Hart Gaskill, b. 8 Jan. 1915, New London, Mo.; accountant; m. 13 Feb. 1937, Ellington, Mo., Golda Lou Christian (b. 9 March 1914 Leeper, Mo.).

10a Linda Kay Gaskill, b. 14 July 1940, Ellington; m. 9 July 1860, Ellington, Herman Troy Barnes (b. 8 Aug. 1936, Redford, Mo.).

11a Linda Kay Barnes, b. 8 July 1965, Poplar Bluff, Mo.

10b Morris Edward Gaskill, b. 16 May 1942, Ellington, Mo.

9b Thomas Emory Gaskill, b. 27 Dec. 1917 New London, Mo.; d. 7 Aug. 1940 Hannibal, Mo.

9c Harold R. Gaskill, b. 24 Dec. 1920 Hannibal; m. 2 Oct. 1943 Quincy, Ill., Jean Trower, (b. 25 July 1923 Quincy).

10a Carol Ann Gaskill, b. 14 April 1945, Quincy; m. June 1967, Quincy, John Franklin Scott (b. 31 March 1939).

11a David John Scott, b. 13 March 1967; d. 1968.
11b John Franklin Scott Jr., b. 22 Oct. 1968.
11c Rebekah Lynn Scott, b. 15 April 1970.
11d Stephen Mark Scott, b. 13 May 1971.

10b Harold Richard Gaskill, b. 19 Jan. 1947.

10c Ronald Joe Gaskill, b. 4 Feb. 1950, Quincy; m. 18 Jan. 1969 Pamela Sue Schultz (b. 7 Jan. 1949, Bowen, Ill.).

11a Amy Jo Gaskill, b. 29 Aug. 1969.
11b Andrea Beth Gaskill, b. 1 April 1973.

10d Mary Ellen Gaskill, b. 20 March 1954.
10e David Kent Gaskill, b. 23 Sept. 1956.

9d Glen Edward Gaskill Sr., b. 9 Dec. 1922, Hannibal, Mo.; radio engineer; m. 20 May 1945, Quincy, Charlotte Julia Clara Cramm (b. 15 April 1923; teacher); live Madison, Wis. (1981).

10a Glen Edward Gaskill Jr., b. 22 March 1946, Quincy, Ill.; realtor; 1st m. Cheryl Ann Marie Heuvel; 2nd m. 20 Oct. 1978, Madison, Wis., Diane Elizabeth Wheeler (b. 20 July 1948, Bryn Mawr, Pa.; registered nurse).

11a Tiffany Ann Gaskill, b. 22 Aug. 1980, Madison, Wis.

10b Charlotte Christi Gaskill, b. 21 Sept. 1954, Madison; m. 20 Aug. 1977, Madison, Ronald Brian Trower (b. 30 June 1953, Troy, Mo.; utility engineer).

11a Keith Edward Trower, b. 22 June 1979, Madison.
11b Jeffrey Nathan Trower, b. 24 Aug. 1982, Janesville, Wis.

10c Gregory Scott Gaskill, b. 23 Jan. 1961.

9e Imogene Gaskill, twin, b. 24 Jan. 1927, Hannibal, Mo.; d. 30 Oct. 1927, Hannibal.
9f Erma Dean Gaskill, twin, b. 24 Jan. 1927; registered nurse; 1st m. 3 July 1943, Quincy, Ill., Harold L. Dillinger (registered nurse); 2nd m. 17 Nov. 1955, Quincy, James Alvin Saxbury, b. 1 July 1922).

10a Donna Sue Dillinger, b. 15 Dec. 1946, Quincy; d. 23 Dec. 1946, Quincy.

10b Mary Susanne Dillinger, b. 5 April 1950, Kansas City, Mo.; m. 25 Nov. 1967, Louisiana, Pike Co., Mo., Robert Wayne England.

11a Donna Dean England, b. 7 Oct. 1968.
11b Debra Susanne England, b. 25 July 1971.

9g Ronald Max Gaskill, b. 25 Nov. 1930; m. 29 Feb. 1960, Parkland, Md., Ursala H. Willkomm.

10a Marlies Ursala Gaskill, b. 16 Aug. 1966.
10b Ronald Max Gaskill Jr., b. 22 March 1968.

8b Lulu Mae Hart, b. 15 April 1903, Ralls Co., Mo.; m. 17 May 1924 George D. Howald (b. 10 Nov. 1924; d. 30 March 1979; farmer); d. 11 Jan. 1979, Ralls Co., Mo.

9a Annie Josephine Howald, m. Woodward Clark.

10a Dewey Lee Clark
10b Frank Faye Clark
10c Belinda Clark

9b Georgia Mae Howald, m. Kenneth Gibbs.

10a David Gibbs
10b Bonnie Gibbs

9c Richard D. Howald, m. Gloria Loraine Sanderson.

10a Jessie D. Howald
10b Joyce Howald
10c Richard Franklin Howald
10d Joseph Grant Howald
10e Robert Victor Howald
10f Lora Jean Howald
10g Dennis Lee Howald
10h Vincent Stackey Howald

8c Ida Marie Hart, b. 1910 Ralls Co., Mo.; m. William Rissmiller, farmer.

7b Elizabeth Hart, m. —— Hendricks.
7c Thomas B. Hart, d. Center, Mo.

7d Mame Austin Hart, b. 2 Oct. 1876, Ralls Co., Mo.; m. Dr. Robert Armsted Norton (b. 3 Oct. 1871, Huntsville, Mo.); d. Jasper Co., Mo.

6d William Theodore "Thee" Hart, b. 20 Feb. 1849 Cloverdale, Ind.; m. 1886 in Decatur, Texas, Adelia Hardwick (b. Decatur, Texas; d. 21 April 1824, Pauls Valley, Okla.; reared the four sons of Ben Hart, her brother-in-law who d. on the Chisholm Trail). William took herds from Decatur and Abilene, Texas, up the Chisholm Trail to Kansas eighteen times; d. Pauls Valley, Okla.

7a Richard Hugh Hart, b. 14 Jan. 1891, Okla.; m. 4 June 1916 in Paoli, Okla., Hazel Elizabeth Prater; no issue.

7b Nell Hart, b. 9 Oct. 1892; m. Carson D. Willis; d. 18 Feb. 1955.

8a Marion Willis
8b William Henderson Willis

9a William Henderson Willis Jr.

7c Walter Lauren Hart, b. Oklahoma; m. Charlotte Blackwell.

8a Jack Hart, b. Pauls Valley, Okla., attended VMI, Va.; grad. The Citadel; in W.W. II six years; drilling business for oil and gas; m. Mary Wirt (member DAR).

9a Noel Blake Hart, B.S. Mills Col., law school U.Okla.; attorney; m. —— LeCrone (clinical psychologist), live Waco, Texas.

10a Adam LeCrone
10b Andrew LeCrone
10c Noel Elizabeth LeCrone

9b Junia Ann Hart, m. —— VanHorn, attorney; live Houston, Texas.

10a Travis Howerton VanHorn
10b Gavin Page VanHorn
10c Derek VanHorn

9c Dr. Frank Laurin Hart, grad. Yale and Okla.U., internal medicine; in foreign service stationed Jakarta, Indonesia, caring for embassy personnel in New

Zealand and Sydney, Australia; m. Paula Prescott of Boston, Mass.

8a Walter Dean Hart, b. Pauls Valley, Okla.; attended VMI, Va.; grad. Okla.U. and Okla.U. Law; m. Lucille Antoinette Germaine Greiner of N.Dak. (grad. N.D.U.).

    9a Walter Dean Hart Jr., tank commander Vietnam War; m. Armelle Parker; lives Pauls Valley, Okla.; lawyer.
    9b Charlotte Clara Hart; m. James Riorden.
    9c Anastasia Germaine Hart; m. Douglas Shirley.
    9d Lucinda Antoinette Hart; m. Phil Kennon; live Oklahoma City.
    9e Laura Beth Hart, m. Anthony J. Powell.
    9f Simone Bernice Hart, m. Gerard Gustin; live Paris, France.

7d James Theodore Hart, b. 21 June 1902; no issue.

6e Frances Rebecca Hart, b. 9 July 1852 Albany, Mo.; m. 1874 Ralls Co., Mo., Samuel Graham; d. 1903 Albany, Mo.

7a May Graham, m. O. Hopkins.

    8a Elizabeth Hopkins, m. Leo Johnson.

        9a Elizabeth Johnson, m. Paul Hoppe.

            10a Paul Hoppe Jr., m. Barbara Rosing.

                11a Christian Paul Hoppe

            10b Elizabeth Hoppe.

7b Earl Graham, m. Rae E. Brown.

    8a Dr. Richard Graham, heads hospital in Hot Springs, Ark.; 1st m. Sue Darneal of Richmond, Mo.; four children; 2nd m. Joyce Knight.

        9a Samuel Darneal Graham
        9b Katherine Ann Graham
        9c William Richard Graham
        9d Suzanne Rae Graham

7c Georgia Anna Graham, b. 1889; d. young.

7d Katherine Graham
7e Son

6f George Morris Hart, b. Breckenridge 27 June 1855; farmer; Civil War cavalryman with Quantrill, who burned down Lawrence, Kans.; m. 5 Nov. 1891 Ralls Co., Mo., Ruth Ann Coontz (b. 9 April 1864 Center, Mo.; d. 19 Dec. 1949); d. 5 Jan. 1940 on Chisholm Trail while making a cattle drive from Texas; bur. Duncan, Okla.

7a Mary Bell Hart, b. 20 Sept. 1900; m. 17 May 1927 Thomas J. Glendinning (b. 4 Dec. 1900 Marion Co.); no issue; reared four foster children; d. 31 Aug. 1978; bur. Norton Cem.

7b Morris V. Hart, b. 30 Jan. 1898; farmer and auditor; 1st m. Margaret Hulse, two children; 2nd m. 23 March 1946 St. Frances, Ark., to Bessie Catherine Bess *(sic)*.

8a Wallace E. Morris Hart, b. 12 May 1923 Ralls Co., Mo.; m. 16 June 1944 Scott AFB, St. Clair Co., Ill., Alene M. Lynes (b. 7 Dec. 1921 Boone Co.).

9a Jack E. Hart, b. 14 Jan. 1946 Cole Co.; m. 25 April 1970 Karen Kay Walter (b. 5 Sept. 1949 Mercer Co., Ohio).

10a Christine Marie Hart
10b Cary Edward Hart
10c Cherie Kay Hart

8b Margaret June Hart, b. 8 Oct. 1925 Ralls Co., Mo.; m. Ernest Vandiver.

9a Karen George Vandiver, m. Darrell Hedges.

10a Brian Hedges
10b Diana Hedges

9b Sharon George Vandiver, m. Anthony Rigoli.

10a Jason Rigoli

9c Jeffrey Vandiver, m. Sheila Lewis.

10a Jeremy Vandiver

6g Dulcimer May Hart, b. 19 May 1858; d. 8 July 1864, age six.

- 6h Richard Lindsey Hart Jr., b. 17 Sept. 1866; gunfighter with horse and rope, went to Alaska during gold rush; returning, the ship sank so he had to remove his belt full of gold so he wouldn't sink; went to Yakima Valley to start raising Delicious apples; became wealthy; m. 27 Feb. 1904 in Zillah, Yakima Co., Wash., Lura E. Macy, lived Yakima, Wash.; Mason in Texas c. 1880; re-affiliated Ralls Co., Mo., 1891; lived Yakima; d. 19 July 1899.

5e Albert Famous Morris (son of David Cushman Morris, *not* son of Morris Morris I but named for him—his uncle), b. 19 Feb. 1828, Cloverdale, Ind., m. Celinda Ann Hart (b. 28 Sept. 1829, Bath Co., Ky., dau. of Joyce [Jewett] and Thos. Hart [b. 1802]; d. 16 June 1898, Cloverdale, Ind.). She was the niece of Richard Lindsey Hart (see 5d above), who m. Catherine Elizabeth Morris, who was a sister of Albert Famous Morris (5e herein); so a sister and brother married an uncle and a niece. Albert Famous Morris d. 23 Sept. 1878.

- 6a Unnamed twin, b. 4 June 1855 Cloverdale.
- 6b Joyce Ann Morris, b. 4 Jun 1855, twin, Cloverdale; m. James Young Davis (b. 28 Nov. 1852; d. 20 July 1912 Arkansas City, Kans., bur. same).
  - 7a Albert Davis, b. 20 Dec. 1882; m. 28 Aug. 1909 Rosetta Johnson.
  - 7b Robert Morris Davis, b. 29 June 1884; m. Gloria Kenniwell; d. 25 Feb. 1935.
  - 7c Edith Joyce Davis, b. 29 Oct. 1887 on farm near Arkansas City, Kans.; unmarried; physical ed. and health teacher in high school and community col. 1915-1957; alive and mentally sharp in 1988 at age 101, living in same house in Arkansas City since six months old.
- 6c Thomas Hart Morris, b. 22 Aug. 1852 Cloverdale; 1st m. bef. 1892 Belle Mugg (b. 1867, d. 1898); two children; 2nd m. 8 April 1901 Sadie Catherine Dickenson (b. 1864, d. 1950); three children; d. 22 Oct. 1938, bur. Cloverdale Cem.
  - 7a Albert Gale Morris, b. 30 July 1892, Cloverdale; m. 23 Oct. 1920 Anna Elizabeth Raikes (b. 1897 Pitnam Co., Ind., d. Aug. 1985 Columbus, Ind., bur. Cloverdale); lived Seymour, Ind.; d. 2 Aug. 1983 Columbus, Ind., bur. Cloverdale.

8a Alice Jane Morris, b. 16 July 1921; d. 8 Aug. 1928, bur. Cloverdale.
8b Albert Gene Morris, b. 1925; d. 1925, bur. Cloverdale.
8c Phyllis Katheryn Morris, b. 11 Feb. 1929; m. 21 June 1953 Charles Francis Roemmel (b. 9 June 1927); live Columbus, Ind.

    9a Steven Morris Roemmel, b. 2 Oct. 1955; m. 2 June 1979 Kathy Alane Mundy (b. 30 March 1957).
    9b Sharon Lynn Roemmel, b. 3 Feb. 1957; m. 11 June 1983 Denny Dumas (b. 22 Sept. 1947).
    9c Janet Sue Roemmel, b. 22 May 1958; m. 22 Nov. 1986 Roy Donald Adams (b. 22 Feb. 1951).

7b Lena Morris, b. 29 Dec. 1894; d. 20 July 1906, bur. Cloverdale Cem.
7c Mary Mabel Morris, b. 4 Aug. 1902; lived Cloverdale, Ind.
7d Albert Francis Morris, b. 28 Dec. 1903; d. 14 Oct. 1924, bur. Cloverdale Cem.
7e Edna Mae Morris, b. 4 Aug. 1906; grad. from and also M.S. at IU; teacher; m. 19 Aug. 1931 Forrest Montgomery (b. 9 Nov. 1900; d. 28 Dec. 1970); lived Gosport, Ind.

    8a John David Montgomery, b. 30 Oct. 1938, Gosport, Ind.; grad. ISU; m. 21 July 1961 Terre Haute, Ind., to Mary Lou Came (b. 1939, Terre Haute, Ind.; grad ISU); dir. of institutional services at Ivy Tech, Indianapolis.

        9a Craig Montgomery, b. 1968, Indianapolis.
        9b Lori Montgomery, b. 1970, Indianapolis.

    8b Martha Lynette Montgomery, b. 4 Dec. 1940, Gosport, Ind.; grad. ISU; elem. teacher; m. 22 Aug. 1964 Jerry D. Leonard (b. 1939 Tenn.; grad. Ball State U., Ind.; manuf. industrial chemicals).

        9a Lee Ann Leonard, b. 13 Aug. 1972, Indianapolis.
        9b Amy Jo Leonard, b. 3 Sept. 1976, Indianapolis; d. Feb. 1984.

6b —— Morris, b. c. 1855 or '56.
6c Joyce Ann Morris, b. c. 1855 or '56; m. James Young Davis.

5f Samuel Morris.

5g Almanza Palmyra Morris, b. c. 1833 Nicholas Co., Ky.; m. 25 June 1856, Breckenridge, in a double ceremony with her niece, Mary Ann Hart (dau. of 6a Catherine Elizabeth Morris Hart) to William Trosper; d. 6 June 1857, Breckenridge, Mo.

5h Rebecca Ann Morris, b. 25 Jan. 1836, Nicholas Co., Ky.; m. 20 Nov. 1851 in Cloverdale, Ind., to Andrew McDowell; d. 6 June 185?.

> 6a Ora Ann McDowell, b. 3 Oct. 1852, m. 12 Oct. 1873 William Winfield Seibert.
>
>> 7a Elizabeth McDowell Seibert, b. 27 May 1876 Galesburg, Ill.
>
> 6b Lula M. McDowell, b. 26 Nov. 1855; m. Melvin L. Walker.
>
>> 7a Ora Zoe Walker, b. 6 Feb. 1880; m. 14 Aug. 1912 John Leo Roach; no issue.

Generation 4: Mary "Polly" Morris
Fourth Child of Morris I and Sarah Cushman Morris

Sources: Author; *Cushman Genealogy and General History;* Bettie Turney Greenup, P.O. Box 6, Paris, KY, descendant of Mary Morris; Frances Gibson Poulos, 8748 Gibson Lane, Potter Valley, CA 95469, descendant of Preston Morris.

4d Mary "Polly" Morris, b. 20 April 1791, Bourbon Co., Ky.; m. 16 Sept. 1810, Bourbon Co., Ky., to Ezekial McIntire of Nicholas Co., Ky. (d. 1822 Bourbon Co., Ky., intestate); John McIntire is mentioned three times in the will of Polly's father, Morris Morris I; mentioned once each are P. Turney (probably Peter, b. 1781) and R., possibly Rebecca, b. 1790, both children of Daniel; m. c. 1779 Turney; 2nd m. to —— Parks (mentioned in will of mother, Sarah Cushman Morris Forrest).

> 5a Sally McIntire, as orphans she and her sister Lucinda had as guardians their uncles John and Horatio Morris, attorney, and John Griffith, security, Sept. 5, 1831. (Order Bk. I, p. 514).
>
> 5b Lucinda McIntire, b. 7 Dec. 1814; 1st m. 15 July 1830, Bourbon Co., Ky., William Todd; 2nd m. 13 Oct. 1833 Amos Turney (b. 28 Dec. 1798; d. 22 Jan. 1877 or '79; bur. Paris, Ky., cem.; son

of Daniel Turney, b. 1740 or '50 Culpeper, Va.; d. 11 March 1845).

6a Mary Turney, b. 4 Nov. 1834, 1st m. —— Colville, four daus., no living issue; 2nd m. to Joseph Neely.

   7a Sam Turney Neely, m. Gertrude ——.

      8a Elizabeth W. Neely m. H. H. Temple.

         9a Stephen Temple

6b Sallie Turney, b. 1839; d. 1897; never married.

6c Betty Turney, b. 1840; m. 26 Nov. 1878 John Current (widower with three children); no issue; d. 1905.

6d Amos McIntire "Dick" Turney Jr., b. 1846; m. 10 Oct. 1871 Mary Elizabeth Mannen (of Mason Co. Ky., b. 1848; d. 23 Feb. 1927); d. 1918. Amos and brother Jesse, 6f below, were very close and were in business ventures together. Both were farmers in the business of breeding and racing horses. They bought a large lot in the Paris Cemetery where they, their spouses, and their children are buried (except Elizabeth Mannen Turney Winn, 7b below, dau. of 6f Jesse Turney).

   7a Jesse Turney (female), b. 8 Aug. 1879; m. Ezekiel Clay Arnold, no issue; d. 1949.

   7b Leslie Mannen Turney (female), b. 28 Dec. 1888 or 27 Dec. 1887; m. 20 Oct. 1909 Louis Taylor (b. 15 June 1886, d. 20 Dec. 1963); d. 20 April 1963.

      8a Amos Turney Taylor, b. 6 July 1912; m. 25 Sept. 1933 Elizabeth Emerson Roberts (b. 19 May 1916 Somerset, Ky.; d. 9 March 1985 Paris, Ky.).

         9a Mary Martin Taylor, b. 6 Jan. 1940; m. John Henry Letcher III (b. 18 July 1936).

            10a Charles Wesley Letcher II, b. 29 June 1962; m. 9 July 1983 Elizabeth Alice Kindall (b. 17 May 1963).

            10b John Henry Letcher IV, b. 27 July 1966.

         9b Betsy Turney Taylor, b. 27 July 1943 Paris, Ky.; 1st m. 16 May 1964 Barry Chalfaunt Tucker; 2nd m. 22 March 1986 Gerald S. Mayer; d. 2 July 1987 Paris, Ky.

10a Amy Elizabeth Tucker, b. 3 Feb. 1969.
10b Leslie Chalfaunt Tucker, b. 28 Jan. 1972.

6e Daniel E. Turney, b. 6 May 1837; m. Mary "Mollie" Mitchell (dau. of William W. Mitchell; d. 29 Dec. or Jan. 1867); six children; d. 27 March 1899.

7a Margaret Turney, m. Harry B. Clay.

8a Mary Clay
8b John Clay
8c Nell Clay

7b Lucille Turney, m. Frank Clay.

8a Frances Clay
8b Dau. —— Clay

7c Nellie Turney, m. Samuel Willis.

8a Margaret Willis, m. Vaughn Drake.

7d Edna Turney, m. Charles McMillan; no issue.

6f Jesse Turney, b. 1847, nephew of Jesse Turney, the husband of 4f Rebecca Morris; m. 16 Jan. 1878 Mary "Mollie" Hester Ewing (dau. of A. J. and Lydia Conner Ewing of Bath Co., Ky.; b. 6 Aug. 1857; d. 25 Feb. 1934); d. 18 Dec. 1928.

7a McClellan Ewing Turney, b. 3 Nov. 1878, m. 6 Aug. 1907 Bettie Brent Johnson (b. 20 Oct. 1882, d. Jan. 1972); d. 2 Nov. 1918 of influenza.

8a Jesse McClellan "Clell" Turney, b. 25 July 1909; 1st m. 9 May 1933 Greenwood, Ind., Helen Elizabeth Sheridan (of Rochester, Ind.; b. 27 July 1914; d. 28 March 1974); three children; 2nd m. April 1948 Jean Thompson (b. 11 Feb. 1916); one son.

9a Mary Ewing Turney, b. 31 July 1934; m. 27 Dec. 1957 Homer Allen Hail (of Pineville, Ky., b. 10 Nov. 1928).

10a Amy Winn Hail, b. 5 Dec. 1962, Lexington, Ky.; m. 22 July 1986 in Lexington to Christian Obering.

11a Shauna Ann Obering, b. Jan. 1987.

Genealogy, Section II ♦ 363

10b Ann Ewing Hail, b. 6 Aug. 1966.
10c Allen Turney Hail, b. 9 Aug. 1967.
10d Jesse McClellan Turney Hail, b. 2 Feb. 1968.

9b Bettie Sheridan Turney, b. 27 May 1936 Paris, Ky.; m. 24 June 1956 Calvin Pinkerton Greenup (b. 30 Sept. 1929 Frankfort, Ky.; retired 1988 from U.S. Postal Service).

10a Russell Lee Greenup, b. 11 Nov. 1957 Paris, Ky.; grad. Transylvania U. and U. Kentucky College of Law; attorney.
10b Elizabeth Mannen Greenup, b. 29 April 1962 Paris, Ky.; grad. Transylvania U. and U. of Kentucky, College of Dentistry; m. 28 Dec. 1991 James Curtis Faulkner.

11a Nathaniel James Faulkner, b. 15 Feb. 1995, Charlotte, N.C.

9c Robert Winn Turney, b. 15 Dec. 1939 Paris, Ky.; m. 25 Aug. 1962 Sally Ann Fluent (b. 17 Aug. 1939 Chicago); attorney.

10a John Barton Turney, b. 14 May 1965 Lexington, Ky.
10b Lori Winn Turney, b. 4 June 1968 Lexington.
10c Brooks Helm Turney, b. 1 Nov. 1971 Lexington.

9d Jesse McClellan Turney Jr., b. 2 Feb. 1958.

7b Elizabeth "Lizzie" Mannen Turney, b. 10 Dec. 1880; m. 1 June 1905 Judge Robert Hiner Winn (of Mt. Sterling, Ky., attorney; d. 17 May 1946; bur. Mt. Sterling); no issue; d. 4 May 1963; bur. Mt. Sterling.
7c Amos Ewing Turney, b. 28 Dec. 1886; m. 28 June 1911 Edna Earl Hinton (b. 28 Sept. 1887; farmed original Turney land; d. 4 Jan. 1981); d. 17 March 1979; no issue.
7d Andrew Jackson Ewing Turney, b. 4 June 1890; farmer; lived with family; d. single 29 May 1947.
7e Leslie Turney.

6g Henry Turney, b. 1842; m. Elizabeth Stitt; d. 1906; two children.

7a Alfred Turney, d. young.
7b Lucy Turney, m. Robert Tucker.

    8a Henry Tucker
    8b Gideon Tucker

6h Mathew "Mat" Turney, b 1836, m. Mary L. Goodman, two children, d. 1888.

> **Generation 4: John Morris**
> **Fifth Child of Morris I and Sarah Cushman Morris**

Sources: Author; *Cushman Genealogy and General History;* Frances Gibson Poulos, 8748 Gibson Lane, Potter Valley, CA 95469; Feather Davis, 5001 Wetheredsvale Road, Baltimore, MD 21207; Alice Wootton Horn, 101 Inwood Drive, Frankfort, KY 40601; John Graves Morris, 618 San Pedro SE, Albuquerque, NM 87108; Nancy Rorden, deceased. The last four persons are descendants of the John Morris below.

4e John Morris, b. 10 Feb. 1793 Paris, Ky.; m. three times; d. 22 Aug. 1870 or '67 or '71 at Millersburg, Ky.; buried there. Often referred to as "Captain John," merchant and captain on a Mississippi River boat, lived in Cane Ridge, Ky., active member of Cane Ridge Meeting. Farmer, owned at least ten slaves before his death. Guardian along with his lawyer brother Horatio for their orphan nieces Sally and Lucinda McIntire, daughters of Polly Morris. First marriage, wife's name unknown; two children (a and b, below); second marriage 4 or 21 Oct. 1827, "on the headwaters of Flat Lick in Bourbon," to widow Mrs. John Payne (Elizabeth "Eliza" Bowles, dau. of David Bowles Sr. [Deed Bk. X, p. 273]); 7 Feb. 1830 sale of 130 acres to brother Albert Morris for $2,000 in Bourbon Co. which had been willed to Eliza by her father (Bk. X, p.283); 17 Feb. 1830 sale of same land back to John Morris, to be given to children of Eliza Bowles Morris, Henry and Sallie Ann Morris, at John's death (Bk. X, p. 284); two children; then must have divorced because John's youngest brother, Beauford, m. Eliza Bowles Morris 24 Jan. 1830, Bourbon Co., and they had children. Third marriage of John, 13 March 1831, Bourbon Co., Ky., was to Katherine "Kitty" Turney (b. 1 April or 29 March 1803, Bourbon Co.; d. 25 March 1885 Bourbon Co.; seven children. Captain John had eleven children in all.

5a Perry W. Morris (child of 1st wife), b. 30 May 1823, m. Eliza Ann Horton, d. April 1843 (was said to have been a slave trader).

5b Elizabeth Morris (child of 1st wife), "Lizzie" was said to have gone to California with her husband, an alleged thief.

5c Morris Henry Morris (child of 2nd wife), m. Mary —— ; member of Cane Ridge Meeting (Bourbon Co. Deed Bk. K, p. 280): "It is ordered that Jno. Morris be appointed guardian of Morris H. Morris, orphan of Jno. Morris, deceased, who with Amos and Jesse Turney [brothers] his security entered bond of $500." Jesse Turney was husband of the orphan's aunt, either 4g Nancy Morris or 4f Rebecca Morris.

5d Sarah Ann "Sally" Morris, child of 2nd wife.

5e Lucinda Morris, b. c. 1832 (first child of 3rd wife, Katherine Turney); member of Cane Ridge Meeting; m. James Sconce.

    6a John Sconce
    6b Robert Sconce
    6c Sallie Sconce, m. —— Peak.

5f Susan A. Morris, m. Robert Soper.

    6a Claire Soper
    6b Catherine Soper

5g Nancy G. Morris, member of Cane Ridge Meeting; m. 21 Sept. 1854 John L. Soper (Bourbon Co. record).

    6a Louella Soper, m. J. M. Hughes.

        7a Leslie Hughes
        7b William Hughes

    6b William Soper.
    6c Katherine Soper, m. Dr. George Grimes; no issue.
    6d Sue Soper, m. John F. Young.

        7a Chester Young, m. Ruth Chandler.
        7b Nancy Young
        7c Katherine Young
        7d John Young

5h John Graves Morris, b. 25 April 1839 Bourbon Co., Ky.; m. 1 Aug. 1865 Robertson Co., Ky., Hepsibaugh Ricketts (b. 1 March 1846 Robertson, Ky., dau. or granddau. of Robert Ricketts of Maryland; d. 29 Nov. 1926 Lexington, Ky.). "He enlisted in the Kentucky Mounted Infantry in Prestonsburg, Ky., accompanied the [Orphan] Brigade on the Great Raid into Indiana and Ohio in July 1863, was captured 3 July 1863, sent to Camp Douglas (Chicago), Illinois. He escaped with twenty-five other men, made his way back to Tennessee and rejoined [General John Hunt] Morgan's command. The 'Morris Brothers' rode with Morgan's Raiders. John was captured again in Morgan's last action, was imprisoned in Camp Chase near Columbus, Ohio, released in June 1865 [at the end of the war]. He was wounded three times. Reportedly he was a drover of horses and was promoted 4th corporal in

1864." Source: Report of the Adjutant General, State of Kentucky, and *Confederate Veteran Magazine* [ceased pub. 1932]. A proud Confederate, he named his first son Robert E. Lee. He had vowed never to cut his hair until the war was over, so when he returned home he had long blonde curls around his shoulders and a beard to match. He saw "Hepsi" on a neighboring farm shaking a spinning wheel, vowed to "tame" her, and soon they were married. They lived together for fifty-three years, had twelve children, eleven of whom lived to old age. He died 10 Sept. 1918, Lexington, Ky.

Note: The descendants of 5h John Graves Morris, above, follow now in their right order. The genealogical lines of 5i, 5j, and 5k are far, far below here, to stay in consecutive order.

6a Robert E. Lee Morris, b. 27 April 1866; m. Myrtle Collins Allison; lived to be 100; d. c. 1965.

    7a Guy Edward Morris, m., had children.

    7b Hazel "Sazie" Graves Morris, b. 28 May 1897 near Blue Licks Spring, Ky.; 1st m. 12 Jan. 1924 Thomas Higgins (d. 1936?); 2nd m. William Claybrook Jacoby; lives in Versailles, Ky.; age 98 in 1989.

        8a Charles Volney Higgins, b. 23 June 1926; 1st m. ——, one child; 2nd m. Geneva McConnell (she adopted 10a); d. 1979; buried Paris, Ky.

            9a Sazie (real name) "Little Sazie" Higgins, b. 1965 Lexington, Ky.

    7c Bobby Morris (female; father Robert always wanted a boy), b. c. 1902 Hopkinsville, Ky.; 1st m. John Stuart; no issue; 2nd m. Robert Hamilton; no issue; d. 1950, buried Columbus, Ohio.

6b John Allen Morris, b. 14 Nov. 1867; m. Laura Strausbaugh.

    7a Walter Morris
    7b Lillian Morris
    7c John M. Morris
    7d Raymond Morris
    7e Louis M. Morris

6c Nancy Turney Morris, b. 10 Oct. 1869; 1st m. William Strausbaugh; had twins; 2nd m. —— Van Deren; no issue.

7a Allene Strausbaugh (twin), b. 25 March 1893; m. Darby W. Doyle.

7b Eugene F. Strausbaugh (twin); b. 25 March 1893; m. Mary Quisenbury.

6d Katherine "Kitty" Morris, b. 23 Nov. 1873 Millersburg, Ky.; journalist; m. 16 Oct. 1890 Aberdeen, Ohio, Albert Sidney Collins (b. 14 Nov. 1871 Mason Co., Ky.; d. 23 July 1897 Ewing, Ky.); 2nd m. James Irvine Dempsey (first station agent for Eastern Div. of L&N Railroad); d. 2 Nov. 1951 Frankfort, Ky.

7a Albert Marvin Collins, b. 21 Nov. 1891; m. Martha Snowden, no issue; d. 17 April 1949.

7b Clara Collins, b. 16 Oct. 1893 Ewing, Ky.; grad. Miller School of Business, Ohio; bookkeeper for a law firm; active in many patriotic organizations; m. 9 Nov. 1916 Lexington, Ky., Bailey Peyton Wootton (b. 20 May 1870 Muhlenberg Co., Ky.; pioneer lawyer instrumental in developing the town of Hazard, Ky.; attorney general of Kentucky 1931-36; director of state parks 1936; ran the Hazard newspaper; d. 16 April 1949 Frankfort. This was his 2nd marriage. Clara reared his son by his first marriage, Thomas Wootton, who d. 9 Oct. 1956, California); Clara d. 1 Oct. 1978 at Frankfort, Ky.

8a Katherine Jane "Kitty" Wootton, b. 3 Aug. 1917 Hazard, Ky.; 1st m. 18 Aug. 1939, Frankfort, William Harold Beck, one daughter; 2nd m. 23 July 1950 Fantley M. Smither; member Mayflower Society, DAR, Colonial Dames, and Daughters of Colonial Wars; two children.

9a Kitty Anne Beck, b. 26 May 1940; m. Don Velkley, no issue; live in Lebanon, Pa.

9b Fantley Wootton Smither, b. 25 June 1951 Frankfort; m. 9 Oct. 1979, Frankfort, Elizabeth Johnson.

10a Clay Smither, b. 19 Oct. 1980.
10b Mathew Smither, b. 28 Dec. 1983.

9c Rebecca Jane Smither, b. 12 Sept. 1953, Frankfort; m. 14 June 1975 William James (b. 27 Feb. 1953, Brunswick, Mo.).

10a Katherine Lindsey James, b. 2 Sept. 1977 Brunswick, Mo.
10b Evan James, b. 6 Dec. 1979 Brunswick.
10c Caroline James, b. 17 Jan. 1982 Brunswick.
10d Amanda James, b. 11 Jan. 1985 Brunswick.

8b Alice Rebecca Wootton, b. 30 March 1920 Hazard, Ky.; grad. U. of Ky.; lab asst. zoology dept., U. of Ky.; newspaper work; mem. Kentucky Mayflower Society, DAR, Colonial Dames, and Daughters of Colonial Wars; m. 17 March 1949 Frankfort, Ky., William Murray Horn (b. 26 Nov. 1914 Daviess Co., Ky.; worked for Nat. Distilleries, four years U.S. Navy, C.P.O. on Adm. Nimitz's staff in Waikiki, Hawaii; Kentucky House of Representatives 1950-4; general manager of a building supply company, church deacon, American Legion, board of State National Banks); live in Frankfort.

9a Claramargaret Horn, b. 26 Feb. 1953 Frankfort, named for both grandmothers; grad. Stetson Col., Florida; grad. Law School, U. Fla., Gainsville; attorney at law and counsel for Universal Studios; m. 2 Aug. 1975 Frankfort, Ky., Jere Tolleson Groover (b. 14 March 1952 Orlando, Fla.); div. Dec. 1991; 2nd m. 2 Oct. 1994 James McCabe (of Long Island, N.Y., architect); live Orlando, Fla.

10a Nathaniel Tolleson Groover, b. 28 March 1979, Orlando, Fla.

9b Rebecca Murray "Becca" Horn, b. 18 July 1954 Frankfort, Ky.; grad. Wesleyan College, Georgia; accountant for Western Kentucky Gas; adm. asst. to director of Owensboro, Ky., Community Theater Group; m. 11 Aug. 1984 Frankfort, John Michael Turner (b. 10 May 1956 Louisville, Ky.); divorced 1995.

10a Laura Frances Turner, b. 13 June 1988.

6e James Sconce Morris, b. 19 Dec. 1875 Blue Licks, Fleming Co., Ky.; building contractor and carpenter; 1st m. c. 1900-1902 Ethel Ball of Jefferson Co., Ky.; three children; 2nd m.

22 April 1916 Pearlie Ethel Turner (of Hazard, Perry Co., Ky., b. 14 July 1895 Lee Co., Va.; three children; d. 8 Jan. 1986, Lexington, Ky.); d. 10 April 1945 Lexington, Ky.

7a Margaret Morris, b. c. 1903; m. Robert Erd, two children.
7b Russell Morris, b. c. 1905; m. ——, lived in Indiana.
7c Catherine "Kitty" Morris, b. c. 1907; 1st m. ——; 2nd m. Chester Kopp of Louisville, Ky.; live Louisville.

    8a Catherine Jane Kopp, lived in Paris, France; d. c. 1970.

7d Enid Annette Morris, b. 22 Feb. 1917 Hazard, Ky.; m. 23 Dec. 1935 Joseph Hartley Durkin of Lexington, Ky.

    8a Paula Jo Durkin, b. 5 May 1939 Lexington; m. William Bader of Lexington.

        9a Julie Ann Bader, b. 19 Oct. 1959; m. Joseph Barclay Mulholland of Georgetown, Ky.

        10a Joseph Bradley Mulholland, b. June 1987.

7e James Hayden Morris, b. 12 July 1920 Hazard, Ky.; handsome model for advertisements, especially Vaseline hair tonic; 1st m. Blanche Walker; two children; 2nd m. Lorene Petersen of Florida; no issue; 3rd m. Myrene Friede of Florida; no issue; d. 20 Oct. 1980.

    8a Michael Graves Morris, b. 1946; name legally changed to Sims by adoption; m. ——.

    9a Amy Sims
    9b Chad Sims

    8b Paula Kay Morris, b. 29 June 1949; name legally changed to Sims; m.—— Redwine.

    9a Jennifer Redwine (twin)
    9b —— Redwine (twin)

7f John Graves Morris II, b. 23 Sept. 1925 Lexington; attended Geo. Wash. U., U. of Maryland, and U. of New Mexico; W.W. II, retired major U.S. Air Force; journalist; m. 12 Aug. 1947 Lexington, Ky., Marian Cary Miles (b. 15 May 1927 Richmond, Va.); divorced 1965; lives in Albuquerque, N.M.

8a John Graves Morris III, b. 24 Jan. 1956, Belleville, Ill.; grad. Arizona State 1988.
8b Rebecca Cary Morris, b. 25 June 1957, Tokyo, Japan; m. June 1981 Chippewa Falls, Wis., Jose Ferriz Munos of Granada, Spain.

9a Lyna Munos, b. 1982 (twin).
9b Mariana Munos, b. 1982 (twin).
9c Juan Miguel Munos, b. 1984.

8c Catherine Miles Morris, b. 27 July 1959, Tokyo, Japan.

6f Sallie Peak Morris, b. 3 Dec. 1878; m. W. T. Robinson; no issue; d. 1949, bur. Lexington, Ky.
6g Henrietta "Henri" Morris, b. 15 Nov. 1880; m. Charles B. Johnson; no issue; bur. Lexington.
6h Mitchell Morris, b. 1 July 1883; m. 6 May 1911 Gertrude Miller; d. 5 June 1941; lived Connorsville, Ind.

7a Gertrude Morris, m. —— .
7b Edward Morris, m. —— .
7c Dora Morris, m. —— .

6i Hugh Henry Morris, b. 15 April 1885; m. Elida Roberts, bur. Indianapolis.

7a Mary Morris, m. —— .
7b John Morris m. —— ; U.S Army.

6j Adelaide "Lady" Morris, b. 10 March 1887; m. Frank Warren; lived in St. Petersburg, Fla.; deceased.

7a Marjorie Warren, m. William Herring.
7b Jane Warren, m. —— Butler; lived in St. Petersburg, Fla.; deceased.
7c Cleora Warren

6k Susan Rebecca "Bess" Morris, b. 14 March 1889; m. H. R. Cox; lived with 7i Henrietta; d. c. 1965.

7a Duke Cox, died early.

5i William Amos Morris, b. 26 Dec. 1841, m. 18 Sept. 1866 Mary Jane "Molly" Snivens (b. 21 May 1843 Lexington, Ky.); in House of Representatives; surveyor, solicitor, farmer; lost farm having to pay all the debts of his fourth child, 6d "Billy"; lived Paris, Ky.

6a Dan Turney Morris, b. 19 Aug. 1867; trained and raced thoroughbred horses; lived in Paris and Lexington, Ky.; m. 1 June 1910 Ellen Vaughan Gividen (d. 19 Jan. 1952); d. 25 Aug. 1941.

   7a Margaret Ellen Morris, b. 1 April 1912 Lawrenceburg, Ky.; m. 13 June 1942 Albert Bryant Karsner (bred and sold horses, d. 22 Oct. 1972); lives Lexington, Ky.

      8a Nancy Ellen Karsner, b. 12 Dec. 1943 Lexington; m. 17 Jan. 1964 Versailles, Ky., Howard Florence; div. Oct. 1978; lives in Lexington.

         9a Howard Bryant Florence, b. 28 April 1967.
         9b James Mark Florence, b. 1 Jan. 1972.

      8b Mary Dan Karsner, b. 23 Oct. 1946 Lexington, Ky.; 1st m. 27 Oct. 1967 John Buford Penn III (d. 16 May 1974); 2nd m. 25 Nov. 1977 Versailles, Ky., Anthony Lloyd Raider (b. 28 Oct. 1943); no issue; lives in Versailles, Ky.

         9a Margaret Anissa Penn, b. 20 April 1970 Lexington.
         9b Edgar Duke Penn II, b. 10 July 1972 Lexington.

      8c Margaret Bryant "Pegi" Karsner, b. 15 Nov. 1950 Lexington; mem. DAR; m. 23 June 1972 John Michael Ivancevich; no issue; three stepchildren.

      8d Albert Creath Karsner, b. 31 Oct. 1957 Lexington.

6b Lulu "Loulie" Morris, b. 6 Feb. 1869; d. 1900 of tuberculosis; single.

6c Katherine (later Katheryne) Morris, b. 9 July 1871, Blue Licks Spring, Ky.; m. 11 Sept. 1901 Thomas Vaughn Chandler (b. 12 March 1869 Mount Olivet, Ky., teacher fourteen years in Robertson Co., Ky.; in 1901 House of Representatives—member of lower house of Federal Assembly, Robertson and Nicholas Counties; d. 15 Oct. 1909 Georgetown, Ky.); moved to Erie, Pa.; expert seamstress; in Mayflower Index of New Jersey; d. 3 Dec. 1954 Erie, Pa.; buried there.

   7a Morris Von Chandler, b. 1 Jan. 1903; d. 22 May 1903; buried Maysville, Ky.
   7b Nancy Katherine Chandler, b. 19 Jan. 1904 Charleston, W.Va.; m. 3 July 1928 Erie, Pa., Harold Louis Rorden (b.

27 Aug. 1900 The Dalles, Ore.; d. 27 July 1968 Nutley, N.J.; buried Willamette Nat. Cem., Portland, Ore.); in Mayflower Index of New Jersey; d. 19 Oct. 1989 in Portland; buried Willamette Nat. Cem., Portland.

8a Harold Reinhardt Rorden, b. 11 Aug. 1931 Pittsfield, Mass.; 1st m. 1953 Joyce Bryan; div. 1956; no issue; 2nd m. March 1964 Wake Island, Adele Costa; no issue; living Kent, Wash., 1988.

8b Nancy Katherine Rorden, b. 19 Oct. 1934 Barberton, Ohio; Dept. of Defense teacher, London, Morocco, Japan, 1990 asst. principal in Germany.

7c Mary Doris Chandler, b. 5 July 1905 Salem, Mass.; m. 22 Sept. 1934 Erie, Pa., Willis Feather Davis (b. 5 Nov. 1906 Terra Alta, W.Va.; grad. WVU, M.A. from MIT, also M.A. from Penn State U.; electrical engineer; active Mason; lived Erie, Pa.; d. 14 April 1985).

8a Charles Walton Davis II, b. 27 Oct. 1938 Erie, Pa.; U.S. Air Force, ret.; grad. Penn State U.; M.A. physics at Northeastern U., Boston; M.A. industrial management, Central Michigan University; m. 31 July 1965 Bedford, Mass., to Mary Elizabeth Powers (b. 13 July 1939 Watertown, Mass.); lives in Omaha, Nebr.; employed by Harris Corp.

9a Charles Walton Davis III, b. 29 April 1970 Dayton, Ohio.

9b Donna Jean Davis, b. 30 March 1973 Dayton.

8b Feather Ann Davis, b. 12 Jan. 1944 Erie, Pa.; grad. Penn State U.; M.A. and Ph.D. sociology at Vanderbilt U.; analyst for the U.S. Dept. of Health and Human Services, Baltimore, Md.; 2nd m. 13 May 1978 at Ft. Meade, Md., Michael David Willis (b. 1 July 1941 Mishawaka, Ind.; lawyer and computer systems specialist for Gould); no issue; three stepchildren and one adopted child.

9a Reena Katherine Willis-Davis, b. 16 Aug. 1982 Inchon, Korea, naturalized U.S. citizen 1986.

6d William Amos Morris Jr., b. 1876; m. Gertrude —— ; at least two children.

7a Dan Turney Morris
7b William Amos Morris Jr.

JGM: "There were two Daniel Turney Morrises, separated by a generation, alive and contemporary in 1866, children of brothers who were both sons of Captain John and Catharine Morris. There were two William Amos Morrises, alive c. 1870, also children of the same two brothers. William Amos Morris Jr., b. 1876, son of William Amos Morris, m. Gertrude —— and sired both Dan Turney Morris and William Amos Morris Jr. Thus we can herein account for four William Amos Morrises, three of whom were "Jr.," meaning their fathers were identically named. There were three Daniel Turney Morrises."

6e Thomas Gano Morris, b. 1879 Paris, Ky., m. Marie Rash, no issue; worked in a livery stable, then farmed; d. c. 1945.

5j Allen Gano Morris, m. Hattie Rodman.

6a Thomas Rodman Morris

5k Daniel Turney Morris. (His entire line was omitted from *Cushman Genealogy and General History*. His line, following, was copied from the family Bible of Daniel Turney Morris owned by Mrs. Robert Byrd [8b Catherine Ann Wimpy, several pages hence].) Born 23 July 1844 Cane Ridge, Ky.; began farming 1868 near Carlisle, Ky.; raised stock and ran a grist, saw, and shingle mill built 1876; in Confederate Army as a member of Giltner's Regiment, Morgan's command; mem. Christian Church at Blue Licks, Mason, and Democrat (source: William Henry Perrin's *History of Bourbon, Scott, Harrison, and Nicholas Counties, Kentucky*. Chicago: O. L. Baskin & Co., Hist. Pubs., 1882). Married 10 Sept. 1868 Sarah Kelly Anderson (b. 5 April 1850 Bangor, Ireland; d. 16 Dec. 1894); d. 5 Feb. 1913.

6a Infant son, b. and d. 27 May 1869.
6b William Amos Morris, b. 10 Nov. 1870; m. Molly Morgland 21 March 1894; d. c. 1903.

7a Guy Kenton Morris, b. 23 July 1895; d. 1956; single.
7b Hazel Morris, m. Jack Long; lived Frankfort, Ky.

8a Mary Catherine Long, m.; two children; lives Louisiana.
8b Helen Long, m. Dr. Williams; three children; lives Nicholasville.

8c Ivaleen Long
8d Elizabeth Sean Long

7c W. A. Morris

6c Sarah Catharine Morris, b. 17 June 1873; d. 18 April 1890.
6d Rebecca Anderson Morris, b. 8 March 1876; m. Bruce Ham; d. 31 Aug. 1930.

7a Alice Ham, m.—— Hunter, d. young.
7b Sarah Ham, m.—— Jackson; several children; d. 193-.
7c Dell Ham, m. —— Ogden, several children; lived Hickman, Ky.
7d Willie Kate Ham, d. young.
7e Dorothy Ham, m. —— McKinney; lived Covington, Ky.
7f Daniel Ham, m.; several children; d. 1941 or '2.
7g Gertrude Ham, m. —— Laughlin; no issue.
7h Nancy Ham, d. young.
7i Myrtle Ham, 1st m. —— Shea, two sons; 2nd m. —— Lockman; lived Cincinnati, Ohio.
7j Ida Bruce Ham, 1st m. —— Osborn; 2nd m. J. Daley.
7k Lena Smith Ham, m. A. Taul; two chidren; lived London, Ky.
7l John Ham, 1st m.; two children; 2nd m.; d. Dec. 1955.

6e James Robinson Morris, b. 22 Jan. 1873; m. Lillie G. Pender (b. 28 Oct. 1869; d. 26 Oct. 1949); d. 4 July 1953.

7a Sarah Rebecca Morris, b. 3 Sept. 1904; m. 25 Nov. 1950 John W. Broome (d. Feb. 1989); lives Hopkinsville, Ky.
7b James Pender Morris, b. 22 June 1908; m. 8 Nov. 1953 Ruth Lorentz; lived Riverside.

6f Nancy Turney Morris, b. 19 Jan. 1886; m. Edwin Boyd.

7a Daughter

6g Mary Elizabeth Morris, b. 19 Jan. 1886; m. Jarred F. Boyd.

7a Edwine Morris Boyd (female), b. 22 May 1908; m. 17 Oct. 1927 Cecil Jeffords.

8a Martha Ann Jeffords, b. 1 Nov. 1931, m. 9 March 1957 Robert Vickers.

8b Jerry Jeffords, b. 5 Sept. 1940; m. Ann —— ; D.D. Vanderbilt U.; United Methodist minister; lives Huntingdon, Tenn.

9a Jerri Ann Jeffords, b. 9 Feb. 1957 Paducah, Ky.; m. 26 Dec. 1983 Colin Rule; lives Mayfield, Ky.

10a Mathew Boyd Rule, b. 29 July 1988.
10b, c, d Stepchildren: Steven, Shannon, and Christy Rule.

9b Jonathan Lee Jeffords, b. 20 July 1964 Paducah, Ky.; grad. Vanderbilt Divinity Sch.; United Methodist minister for Clopton-Macedonia churches; m. Kristy Lynn Williams (b. 6 Dec. 1966); lives Brighton, Tenn.

9c James Eric Jeffords, b. 17 March 1970; grad. Lambuth U., Jackson, Tenn.; minister.

7b Catherine Ann Byrd, b. 15 July 1913; m. 21 Feb. 1934 John Wimpy; in 1992 owned Turney Bible.

8a Catherine Ann Wimpy, b. 7 June 1936; m. Aug. 1957 Robert Byrd.

6h John Kelly Morris, b. 12 April 1888; m. Mary Roach, 29 Aug. 1957.

7a Marguerite Louise Morris, b. 20 Aug. 1913; m. Thomas W. Baker.

Generation 4: Rebecca Morris
Sixth Child of Morris I and Sarah Cushman Morris

Sources: Author; *Cushman Genealogy and General History,* by Alvah W. Burt; Bettie Turney Greenup, a descendant of Mary Morris; Frances Gibson Poulos, 8748 Gibson Lane, Potter Valley, CA.

4f Rebecca Morris, b. 17 Oct. 1774; 1st m. 5 Feb. 1812 Jesse Turney (according to Burt, p. 236; some family members think this is an error, see 5g Nancy, below, 3rd m. for Jesse Turney; perhaps Rebecca was only m. to Parker); 2nd m. to Henry Parker. A listing as "Rebecca Morris" is recorded as a member of the Cane Ridge Meeting, Paris, Ky., in 1848 and 1860; d. 1860.

Generation 4: Nancy Morris
Seventh Child of Morris I and Sarah Cushman Morris

Sources: Same as for Rebecca Morris, sixth child, above.

4g Nancy Morris (omitted from Burt's book, p. 227), b. 24 Oct. 1796; 1st m. 12 Dec. 1815 Thomas Bowles; one known child; 2nd m. 20 Oct. 1824 John Thomas; 3rd m. Bourbon Co., Ky., Jesse Turney; lived near Paris, Ky. (Turney family history shows her married only to Turney.) He was the uncle of another Jesse Turney who was sixth child of Lucinda McIntire and Amos Turney. See line of Mary Morris. Did this Jesse Turney first marry Nancy's older sister Rebecca (above), or was that an error? We know there were three Jesse Turneys. Nancy Morris died 14 Sept. 1876, buried in old Turney graveyard on farm.

5a Nancy Bowles

> **Generation 4: Elizabeth Morris**
> **Eighth Child of Morris I and Sarah Cushman Morris**

Sources: Same as for Rebecca Morris, sixth child, above.

4h Elizabeth "Betsy" Morris, b. 10 Oct. 1798; m. 12 Dec. 1815 Bourbon Co., Ky., Samuel D. (or William) Brown; d. before 1835/6.

5a James H. Brown, b. 15 Oct. 1816.
5b Katherine Ann "Kitty" Brown, m. —— Tanner.
5c Rachel Brown, m. —— Bowles, lived Quincy, Ill.
5d Emily Brown, m. —— Coon (not in Burt's book).
5e Thomas H. Brown, b. 6 Dec. 1819 (not mentioned in suit as an heir of Elizabeth [Morris] Brown; death date not known.).

> **Generation 4: Horatio Morris**
> **Ninth Child of Morris I and Sarah Cushman Morris**

Sources: Author; Church of Jesus Christ of Latter Day Saints (Mormon); Robert Thomas, 303 S. Harrison Street, Papillion, NE 68046, descendant of Horatio Morris.

4i Horatio Morris, b. 12 Sept. 1800, Bourbon Co., Ky.; attorney in 1835; guardian with brother John Morris of orphan nieces Sally and Lucinda McIntire, whose mother was Mary "Polly" Morris McIntyre, sister of Horatio and John; mentioned 22 Jan. 1824 with several brothers in the sale by their brother Thomas Morris of a Negro boy, farm equipment, furniture, etc. as a mortgage for two years, ending: "Horatio has loaned $300 in silver ... and Horatio has become security for Thomas in replevy bonds." (Bourbon Co., Book R, p. 419.)

A year later, on 22 Jan. 1825, Bourbon Co.: "Thomas borrowed $500 from brothers Horatio, Preston, Alfred, and Beauford for all household and livestock, which Thomas may use in the meantime. Horatio [lawyer] will go his bond."

First married 16 July 1827 Bourbon Co., Ky., Polly Hughes (b. 7 Dec. 1810, dau. of Christiana Hughes, b. 1775, and George W. Hughes, d. 1833; Polly d. 5 Jan. 1832); three children; 2nd m. before July 1837 Malinda Fruit (b. 1819 in Missouri, sister of Lucinda Fruit, who was the third wife of Thomas Morris, Horatio's eldest brother; d. 1846); seven children; lived in Kentucky, Illinois, and

Iowa; moved west to Illinois to join brothers Beauford and Albert Morris; d. 16 Nov. 1881 Shenandoah, Iowa.

Children of Horatio and Polly Hughes Morris:
5a George Hughes Morris, b. 18 Nov. 1828 Bourbon Co., Ky., reared by stepmother after mother's death.
5b Adilizza Morris, b. 21 Feb. 1830.
5c Sara Ann Morris, b. 24 Nov. 1831, d. 12 Oct. —.

Seven children of Horatio and Malinda Fruit Morris:
5d Henry Alexander Morris, b. 1 July 1837 Bourbon Co., Ky.; m. 5 Sept. 1861 Warren Co., Ill., Mary Etta Watson (b. 11 Jan. 1842 Salem, N.Y.; d. 24 Aug. 1916 Aurora, Nebr.); lived Illinois, Iowa, and Nebraska; d. 29 April 1907 Aurora, Nebr., of cancer; bur. Aurora.

  6a Cora Morris, b. 1862 or '3, Illinois; d. age two-and-one-half, bef. 1866, Warren Co., Ill.
  6b Lou Allen Morris, b. 30 Nov. 1866 Warren Co., Ill.; 1st m. Cora A. Savery (b. 9 July 1869; d. 8 May 1899 Nebr.); three children; 2nd m. 15 Aug. 1906, Aurora, Nebr., Maysel Evelyn Hebb (b. 17 Feb. 1883 Vermont; d. 29 Oct. 1973 Lincoln, Nebr.); five children; d. 10 Nov. 1938, Lincoln, Nebr.

    7a Olive Dawn Morris, b. 7 Sept. 1891 Aurora, Nebr.; m. 9 June 1909 Harry Stewart.
    7b Infant son, d. at birth.
    7c Don Randall Morris, b. 6 Oct. 1908; m. 28 Dec. 1931 Grand Island, Nebr., Aileen Nicholas; d. 26 Sept. 1971 Omaha, Nebr.
    7d Howard Allen Morris, b. 2 March 1911 Aurora, Nebr.; m. 31 Jan. 1937 Denver, Colo., Erma Ryan; d. 11 June 1973 Atlanta, Ga.
    7e Erle C. Morris, b. 5 Aug. 1912 Aurora, Nebr.; m. 28 April 1924 Hutchinson, Kans., Melba Lynn.
    7f Evelyn Maysel Morris, b. 12 June 1914 Aurora, Nebr.; 1st m. 2 Dec. 1930, Nebraska, Harold Lee Thomas; three children; 2nd m. Dean Timm.

      8a Dorothy Lee Thomas, b. 18 Sept. 1931, Nebr.; m. 30 June 1951, Nebraska., Laurevle E. Osburn.
      8b Betty Eilene Thomas, b. 1 Sept. 1933, Nebr.; 1st m. 29 Nov. 1958 Robert Humphrel, Iowa; 2nd m. Gary Cook.

8c Robert K. Thomas, b. 22 Nov. 1936 Grand Island, Nebr.; m. 27 Sept. 1969 Papillion, Nebr., Karen Lee Giermann (b. 9 July 1943 Omaha, Nebr.).

9a Catherine Lynn Thomas, b. 17 Dec. 1971 Omaha, Nebr.
9b Catherine Lorene Thomas, b. 9 Dec. 1972 Omaha.

8d Nevada Janet Morris, b. 1 Dec. 1918 Aurora, Nebr.; m. Joseph Howard, Kansas.

6c Horatio Nelson Morris, b. 3 Sept. 1868 Warren Co., Ill.; m. Ida Eliza Black; d. 19 July 1930.
6d Henry Pearl Morris, b. 6 July 1873 Warren Co., Ill.; d. 9 Dec. 1898 Aurora, Ill.
6e Sarah Emma Morris, b. Nov. 1839 Ill.; m. 4 March 1858 Warren Co., Ill., Joseph Wheeler; d. c. 1910 Cuba, Crawford Co., Mo.

5f William Harry Morris, b. 1841 Ill.?
5g Horatio Morris Jr., b. 1843 Ill.; m. Malissa ——.

6a Dell Morris, b. 1875 Warren Co., Ill.
6b Jessie Morris, b. 1878 Warren Co., Ill.

5h Ann R. Morris, b. 1845 Ill.; m. William McMahill; d. 27 April 1984, bur. Rose Hill Cem., Shenandoah, Page Co., Iowa.
5i John A. Morris, b. 1848.

6a Son, "W." Morris, born out of wedlock; reared by John's mother, Malinda.

5j Frances Morris, b. 1868 or '9, Illinois; m. Robert Russell.

> **Generation 4: Preston Morris**
> **Tenth Child of Morris I and Sarah Cushman Morris**

Sources: Hazel Jean Morris Laws, 3226 Fairfield Rd., Olympia, WA 98501; Frances Gibson Poulos, Bramble Hedge Farm, 8748 Gibson Lane, Potter Valley, CA 95469; Janet Sparks, 16100 SW Sumac, Beaverton, OR 97007, all three descendants of Preston Morris; Anne Allen, 11829 172nd Avenue NE, Redmond, WA 98052; and *Powell History*, by James M. Powell, M.D., written 1922, updated 1977, available at LDS libraries.

4j Preston Morris, b. 7 Aug. 1802 Bourbon Co., near Paris, Ky., on Redemption Land given to his father Morris and grandfather Richard for their services in Monongalia Co. during the Revolution. Adventurous Preston left Kentucky, found and married Adaliza Miller 6 Aug. 1829 in Wash. Co., Mo. (b. 3 May 1813, Wash. Co.; d. 16 May 1845 Adams Co., Ill.). His younger brothers Beauford and Albert and, later, his oldest brother Horatio joined him in Illinois. Still later, in 1850, Preston left Missouri, taking his eight-year-old motherless son, Nathaniel, along to cross the plains to Oregon. He d. 28 Dec. 1869 in Linn Co., Ore.

On 22 Jan. 1824 Thomas sells to four brothers (including Preston) for $500 a Negro boy, farm equipment, and furniture as a mortgage for two years, etc. (Book R, p. 419).

5a Sarah Jane Morris, b. 19 Aug. 1830, Washington Co., Mo.; m. 31 Dec. 1848 Adams Co., Ill., Alley B. Griggs; d. 5 Sept. 1862; bur. Old Lebanon Cem., Linn Co., Ore.

5b Andrew Beauford Morris, b. 19 March 1832, Adams Co., Ill., or 17 April 1902, Quincy, Ill.; 1st m. 9 Jan. 1853 Linn Co., Ore. Martha E. Bensley; six children; 2nd m. 17 June 1876 Linn Co., Ore., Rebecca Crabtree Randel (b. 17 June 1876); six children; d. 7 April 1902, Linn Co., Ore.; bur. Riverside Cem., Linn Co.

6a Ida Morris, b. 3 Nov. 1865 Linn, Ore.; m. in Linn, Robert Wilson Nichols; eight children; d. 1 March 1938 Salem, Ore.

7a Chrystal Ann Nichols, b. 25 Dec. 1889 Harney Co., Ore.; 1st m. 3 Jan. 1908, Linn, Edward Lee Keebler (1884-1934; Lebanon city engineer, also owned Keebler Const. Co.); nine childen; 2nd m. Emil Christenson; 3rd m. Lester John Sparks; d. Lebanon, Ore., 25 Sept. 1980.

8a Arden Louise Keebler, b. 16 Oct. 1929, Lebanon, Ore.; m. in Lebanon 2 May 1948 Gerald Lee Sparks Larsen (b. 29 Aug. 1926 Albany, Ore., owned Mercury dealership; d. 8 Dec. 1970 of cancer).

9a Steven Ward Larsen, b. 24 April 1949 Lebanon (step-grandfather's surname); two children: Casey Larsen, m. — Kristi, and Vicki Larsen, m. — Deming, one child, Nicolette Deming, b. c. June 1952.

9b Janet Lee Larson Sparks (1953 legally changed her name to Sparks, her bloodline), b. 5 Dec. 1952 Albany, Ore., granddaughter of Lester Sparks (1926-1970) of Lebanon and Albany; grad. civil engineer; volunteer asst. school instructor, needlewoman and gardener; unmarried.

5c Catherine Morris, b. 1834 Adams Co., Ill.; m. 19 June 1851 Linn Co., Ore., William S. Claypool; d. c. 1854 Linn Co.

5d Clarence Lee Morris, b. 6 June 1837 Adams Co., Ill.; m. 27 Dec. 1857 Linn Co., Catherine Thomas; d. 1 Aug. 1911; bur. Kelly Cem., Wasco Co., Ore.

5e Josephine B. Morris, b. 30 June 1839 Adams Co., Ill.; m. 1 Nov. 1857 Linn Co., Arthur Marshall; d. 30 May 1911 Linn Co.

5f Nathaniel Miller Morris, b. 12 March 1842 Quincy, Adams Co., Ill.; m. 2 May 1862 Linn Co., Ore., Margaret Ann Propst (a Powell descendant, b. 25 Aug. 1845 Sugar Grove, Menard Co., Ill.; d. 31 July 1907 Grangeville, Idaho; 1st cousin of 5g Mary Ann Morris's husband, Henry Clay Powell; d. 31 July 1907, Grangeville). They were early pioneers in Oregon where they had six children, then moved on to Washington Territory to build a farm near Lone Pine, there twenty years, had six more children and moved on again to Grangeville, Idaho. Nathaniel d. 1 Aug. 1904, three years before Margaret, in Grangeville. Both were descended from a long line of pioneers, with "a spirit bred deep within them" (from a Washington State history).

6a Henry Rosencrans Morris, b. 2 March 1863 Scio, Linn Co., Ore. He is said to be named after Gen. William S. Rosencrans of the Union Army in the Civil War. (This is the very same Rosencrans who, under Gen. Thomas A. Morris, the author's great-grandfather, fought and won the very first land battles of the Civil War: the Battles of Philippi and Belington in western Virginia. Young Rosencrans was made a general later on; he is mentioned earlier in this book. So it seems that Preston's grandson, Rosencrans Morris, born in 1863, was named for the Union Gen. Rosencrans who fought under his own second-cousin-twice-removed, Gen. Thomas A. Morris, who was nearly fifty at the time of the battles. These distant cousins, descended from the two different Morris Morrises of this story, surely never knew this!) *The Powell Family* spells the name Rosencranse; his death certificate spells it Rosencranz; most historians spell it Rosencrans, as it is here. He died 30 Nov. 1847 in Battle Ground, Clark Co., Wash.

"Hank" grew up on Camus Prairie and was a life-long friend of the Nez Perce tribe of Indians and knew Chief Joseph. He was a blacksmith and gun repairman; could make or repair anything made of iron, wood, or leather. Hank moved from Oregon to Washington where he met and married 20 Jan. 1887 in Whitman Co., Wash., Cora Narcissis Fletcher (b. 19 Aug. 1869 in California, dau. of Alfred M. Fletcher and Nancy Day). Henry and Cora Morris were farmers, members of the Seventh Day Adventist Church, and reared four children.

The following story about Cora's grandfather has survived the years: Al Fletcher was an artist and painter, manufacturing his own paint and painting signs and murals in hotels, saloons, houses, and other buildings. The Fletchers, from Virginia, were staunch sympathizers of the Confederacy during the Civil War. Camp Babbitt, a Union camp, was near Visalia, Calif., where the Fletchers were living. Some of the town girls would stroll out to the camp in the evening. On one such occasion, Julia Brown waved a silk Confederate flag, made by her and Al Fletcher, over an officer's head. She was nearly put in the guardhouse and felt her life was in danger! The story remains today.

Now let us return to the four children of 6a Henry Rosencranz and Cora (Fletcher) Morris:

    7a Nancy Margaret Morris, b. 4 March 1888 Oakesdale, Wash.; m. 15 Sept. 1909 Milton, Ore., John Jacob Hash (b. 26 Aug. 1885 Clarissa, Minn.; d. 2 July 1973 Battle Ground, Wash.); d. 19 Dec. 1982 Portland, Ore.; bur. Vancouver, Wash.

        8a Gifford LeRoy Hash, b. 18 Dec. 1910 Nyssa, Ore.; attended Walla Walla Col.; joined the Navy; m. 4 Nov. 1935 Long Beach, Calif., Ruth Leota Evans (b. 22 Aug. 1910 Silver Springs, Colo.; d. 22 Feb. 1976); in California border patrol, then real estate.

            9a Linda Lee Hash b. 8 July 1938 Long Beach, Calif.; m. 30 May 1959 Reno, Nev., Ron Sanders; three children.

- 9b Dinah Lee Hash, b. 14 June 1943 Bellingham, Wash.; m. 13 Feb. 1959 Reno, Nev., Roy Ford; two children.
- 8b Corene Oletta Hash, b. 10 or 11 April 1913 Nyssa, Ore.; 1st m. 10 July 1933 Longview, Wash., Herbert Noonan; one daughter; 2nd m. 18 Nov. 1961 John C. Becker; lived Gresham, Ore.; d. 18 Nov. 1987 Portland, Ore.
    - 9a Denise Margalo Noonan, b. 10 April 1942; m. 7 March 1964 Joseph VanHaverbeke.
        - 10a Tiffany Jo VanHaverbeke, b. 13 Oct. 1964.
        - 10b Stephany Jo VanHaverbeke.
        - 10c Brittany Jo VanHaverbeke.
- 7b Henry Lee Morris, b. 7 Feb. 1890 Oakesdale, Wash.; m. 22 July 1912 Lillian Myrtle Sibley (b. 4 Feb. 1893 San Francisco, Calif.; d. 13 June 1972); d. 19 June 1967 Willits, Calif.
    - 8a Elizabeth Agnes Morris, b. 4 Dec. 1913 Nyssa, Ore.; m. 3 Dec. 1930 Burns, Ore., Joseph Byron Wilson (b. 6 July 1904 Lakeport, Calif.)
        - 9a Betty Ann Wilson, born and died 4 June 1935 Glen Eden, Calif.
        - 9b Marilynn Marie Wilson, b. 17 May 1936, Lakeport, Calif.; registered cosmetologist; m. 3 Dec. 1955 Sedro Wooley, Wash., Donald Alan Currie (b. 27 Jan. 1927 Sedro Wooley).
            - 10a Shawn Marie Currie, b. 18 Aug. 1956 Sedro Wooley, Wash.; writes poetry and music; m. 20 July 1973 Seattle, Wash., Michael Oliver Warren (b. 20 July 1953; U.S.N., musician); live San Diego, Calif.
                - 11a Gibson Oliver Currie, b. 23 Dec. 1973 Seattle.
            - 10b Erin Colleen Currie, b. 29 Jan. 1959 Seattle.
            - 10c Donald Alan Currie II, b. 10 Jan. 1961 Seattle.
            - 10d Kelly Kathleen Currie, b. 29 Sept. 1963; d. 3 April 1964; bur. Bothell, Wash.

10e Michael Kevin Currie, b. 14 Feb. 1965 Seattle.
10f Patrick Collin Currie, b. 20 March 1968 Seattle.

9c John "Jack" Clark, b. 10 Sept. 1942 Ukiah, Calif.; U.S. Coast Guard; m. 6 May 1967 Suzanne Biestel; live Italy and England.

10a Scott Christopher Clark, b. 22 Feb. 1969 in Seattle.
10b David Michael Clark, b. 28 Nov. 1972.

8b Jessie Margaret Morris, b. 18 Sept. 1916 Nyssa, Ore.; m. 11 Aug. 1934 Lakeport, Calif., Henry Bardelmier (b. 29 July 1913 Lakeport, Calif.; d. 29 June 1969); d. 12 April 1977.

9a Dorothy Louise Bardelmier, b. 26 July 1935 San Jose, Calif.; m. 11 Dec. 1954 Salinas, Calif., Arthur Wickham (b. 9 Jan. 1931 San Miguel, Calif.)

10a Stephen Reynolds Wickham, b. 25 March 1956 Santa Rosa, Calif.
10b Laura Lee Wickham, b. 16 June 1957.

9b Henry Bardelmier, b. 5 Sept. 1936 Kelseyville, Calif.; m. Carol —— .
9c Edward Bardelmier, b. 17 Jan. 1942 San Anselmo, Calif.; m. Lonnie —— .
9d Toni Jean Bardelmier, b. 9 Dec. 1944 San Jose, Calif.; m. 3 April 1965 Willits, Calif., Daniel R. Mueller (b. 14 June 1943 Renton, Wash.).

10a Troy Mueller, b. 13 July 1966 San Pablo, Calif.
10b Michael Mueller, b. 7 Aug. 1968 Casper, Wyo.
10c David Mueller, b. 5 June 1972 Casper, Wyo.

9e Fred Lee Bardelmier, b. 11 May 1947, San Jose, Calif.; m. 22 Nov. 1969 in San Jose, Sandra Lee Driedger (b. 4 Feb. 1951 San Jose).

10a Michael Henry Bardelmier, b. 5 Aug. 1970 San Jose, Calif.
10b Michelle Lee Bardelmier, b. 5 Oct. 1976 San Jose.

9f Paul Dean Bardelmier, b. 17 May 1956 Santa Rosa, Calif.; m. 9 Oct. 1973 Ukiah, Calif., Martha Jean Ables (b. 13 Aug. 1956 Livermore, Calif.).

10a Jason Paul Bardelmier, b. 7 Aug. 1974 Ukiah, Calif.

10b Jennifer Denise Bardelmier, b. 7 Feb. 1976 San Jose.

8c Cora Rosetta Morris (3rd child of Henry Lee Morris); b. 20 Sept. 1918 Battle Ground, Wash.; 1st m. 5 Nov. 1935 Potter Valley, Calif., Clarence Francis Gibson (b. 25 Dec. 1914, Ukiah, Mendocino, Calif.); four children; div. 1946; d. 30 March 1985.

9a Frances Marie Gibson, b. 7 Nov. 1936 Modesto, Stanislaus Co., Calif.; B.A. U.Fla., Gainsville; teacher, genealogist; life mem. Mayflower Soc., Calif., Pilgrim John Howland Soc., and Mendocino Co. Historical Soc.; member DAR; m. 28 Dec. 1955 Potter Valley, Calif., Dr. Paul William Poulos Jr., (b. 1 June 1933 Ukiah, Calif.; B.A. UC-Davis; D.V.M., Ph.D. in veterinary medicine, Royal Veterinary College, Stockholm; assoc. prof. of Radiology, U. of Utrecht, Netherlands; prof. and chairman, Dept. of Radiology and Pathology U.Fla.; exec. dir. and C.E.O. Institute of Genetic Disease Control in Animals; consulting practice in Davis, now in Potter Valley, Calif.; Phi Zeta Soc.; Royal Dutch Veterinary Med. Assoc. Award; silver medalion for continuing ed. of Dutch practitioners; in *Who's Who in the West*, *Who's Who in Science and Technology, 1985*; *Who's Who in Veterinary Science and Medicine, 1987-88*).

10a Paige Marie Poulos, b. 26 April 1958 Woodland, Calif.; attended UC-Davis; APR accreditation of Public Relations Soc. of America; pres. East Bay Chap. of Public Relations Soc. of Amer.; master lady of the vine in the Knights of the Vine; in *Who's Who of American Women*, *Who's Who in American Business Women*, *Who's Who in America*, *Strathmore's Who's*

Who, and *O'Dwyer's Directory of Public Relations Professionals;* wine editor of *Focus Magazine;* writes bi-monthly column in *Practical Winery and Vineyard Magazine;* m. 3 Feb. 1990 St. Helena, Calif., John Stuart Woolley (b. 29 Sept. 1947 Palo Alto, Calif.; B.A. Stanford U.; M.A. in humanities UC-San Francisco; M.A. in German lit UC-Berkeley; Fulbright fellowship at U. of Tuebingen, Germany; dir. of marketing and public relations of Wente Vineyards; volunteer and board dir. of organization for rehabilitation of abused children); live Berkeley, Calif.

10b Geoffrey Paul Poulos, b. 25 Aug. 1959 Woodland, Calif.; B.A. UC-Davis; manager of winery tasting San Martin, Calif. winery; owner Snap-on Tool distributorship; m. 30 Sept. 1989 in San Juan Bautista, Calif., Jody Bernadette Ferrais (b. 24 Feb. 1958 Castro Valley, Calif.); live Folsom, Calif.

    11a Jordan Bernadette Poulos, b. 24 Nov. 1990, Sacramento, Calif.

    11b Claire Marie Poulos, b. 13 March 1993 Greenbrae, Marin Co., Calif.

10c Gregory William Poulos, b. 8 Dec. 1960 Porterville, Calif.; B.A. UC-Davis; Juris Doctorate, Tulane U., New Orleans, 1987; attorney in San Francisco; bd. Pacific Admiralty seminar steering com.; m. 7 Aug. 1986, Davis, Cynthia Marie Crandall (b. 29 Nov. 1960 Ventura, Calif.; B.A. UC-Davis; M.F.A. in set design, Tulane; meritorious achievement award at Louisiana Col. Theatre Festival; set designer and prop. master); live San Rafael, Calif.

9b Marvin Everett Gibson I, b. 27 Jan. 1938 Willits, Calif.; U.S. Marines veteran; 1st m. 8 Feb. 1958 Joyce Fernandes; one child; div.; 2nd m. 18 Nov. 1961 Virginia City, Nev., Beverly Clark (b. 1 April 1932 Covelo, Calif.; two children; d. 20 Jan. 1967 Ukiah, Calif., automobile accident.

10a Michael Lee Gibson, b. 1 July 1959 San Diego, Calif.; d. 17 April 1983 in shooting accident in San Fernando Valley, Calif.
10b Janice Marie Gibson, b. 2 Aug. 1964 Ukiah, Calif.; m. unknown.

11a Tiffany ——, b. c. 1981 Ukiah, Calif.

10c Nelson Webb Gibson, b. 29 Sept. 1966 Ukiah, Calif.

11a Joshua Webb Gibson, b. 25 Jan. 1993.
11b Marvin Everett Gibson II, b. 1994, Ukiah.
11c Cheyanne Cherie Gibson, b. 23 Jan. 1995, Ukiah; d. 13 July 1995, Willits, Calif.

9c Gilbert Lee Gibson, b. 14 Jan. 1939 Willits, Calif., U.S. Marines veteran; electrician for Union Oil in Sonoma, Calif.; m. 4 Nov. 1962 Carson City, Nev., Lorna Claire Jones (b. 12 Sept. 1941 Oakland, Calif.); live Sonoma.

10a Julie Carol Gibson, b. 8 May 1964 Jacksonville, N.C;. live Sonoma.
10b Lee Morris Gibson, b. 11 April 1966 Sonoma; m. 22 Oct. 1987 Santa Rosa, Calif., Alissa Annette Nicander (b. 7 June 1969 Sonoma); live Sonoma.

11a James Lee Gibson, b. 7 Nov. 1991 Sonoma.
11b Jennifer Gibson, b. 21 Jan. 1993 Sonoma, d. 23 Sept. 1995 Butte Co., Calif.
11c Kaytlyn Gibson, b. 25 Aug. 1994 Vallejo, Calif.

10c Mike Dalton Gibson, b. 27 June 1968 Vallejo; m. 7 Oct. 1989, Sonoma, Addie Marie Nicander (b. 16 Jan. 1971); live Sonoma.

11a Stephen Michael Gibson, b. 28 Feb. 1990 Vallejo, Calif.
11b Brian Dalton Gibson, b. 28 Feb. 1990 Sonoma.
11c Sara Marie Gibson, b. 19 Sept. 1994 Vallejo.

10d James Allen Gibson, b. 2 Oct. 1969 Vallejo, Calif.; lives Sonoma.

10e John Thomas Gibson, b. 7 June 1972 Vallejo.

9d James Dalton Gibson, b. 9 Sept. 1940 Potter Valley, Calif.; 1st m. 31 Oct. 1959 Sharon Ann Burdine; three daughters; div. 1964; 2nd m. 20 Sept. 1964 Sandra Lee McGuire (b. Spokane, Wash.); one dau.; div.; 3rd m. 19 June 1981 Vancouver, B.C., Canada, Marina Linda Soares Oram (b. 20 Jan. 1948 Napa, Calif.); one child, hers, adopted (10e, below); live Kelseyville, Calif.

10a Kimberly Ann Gibson, b. 9 May 1960 Sonoma; m. —— White of Redwood City, Calif.; div.

11a Melissa Angelica White, b. 28 Dec. 1981, San Francisco, Calif.

11b Christina Marie White, b. 12 Nov. 1986, Palo Alto, Calif.

10b Renee Lynn Gibson, b. 23 Aug. 1961 Sonoma; m. 16 Dec. 1989 San Carlos, Scott Bradley Rourk.

11a Shauna Rae Rourk, b. 20 Dec. 1989 Palo Alto.

10c Sandra Kay Gibson, b. 7 March 1964 Sonoma; m. 10 April 1983 San Mateo, Calif., Paul Adelmo Catena (b. 9 Dec. 1962 San Francisco).

11a Paul Adelmo Catena Jr., b. 21 Sept. 1983 Redwood City, Calif.

11b Jennifer Christina Catena, b. 15 May 1987 San Mateo, Calif.

10d Barbara Gail Gibson, b. 20 April 1965 Sonoma; m. 4 June 1983 Gilbert Harold Compher (b. 15 Nov. 1964 Medford, Ore.).

11a Tabitha Dawn Compher, b. 27 Oct. 1983 Medford, Ore.

11b Damiann Lee Compher, b. 18 June 1990 Medford.

10e Shane Lawrence Oram, child of 3rd wife of 9d J. D. Gibson, b. 1975 Vallejo; adopted by J. D. Gibson.

8d Richard Alvin Morris (4th child of Henry Lee Morris); b. 17 Dec. 1920 Plush, Ore.; in California Div. of Forestry; m. 28 Sept. 1938 Willits. Calif., Frances Lenora Rains (b. 25 Dec. 1919 Live Oak, Calif.).

9a Lillian Lenora Morris, b. 10 June 1939 O'Brien, Ore.; 1st m. William. A. Postlewait Jr.; five children; 2nd m. 12 July 1964 Reno, Nev., William Arnold Gordon; two children.

10a Michelle Lee Postlewait, b. 21 June 1958 Willits; m. 27 Jan. 1976 Klamath Falls, Ore., Raymundo B. Briones (b. 29 Oct. 1954).

11a Amanda Rose Briones, b. 3 July 1973 Hollis, Okla.
11b Antoinette Marie Briones, b. 1 July 1976, Ore.

10b William Andrew Postlewait, b. 20 Dec. 1959 Lawton, Okla.
10c Patti Lorraine Postlewait, b. 2 Dec. 1960 Fortuna, Calif.
10d Barbara Jean Postlewait, b. 25 April 1962 Eureka, Calif.
10e Tina Marie Postlewait, b. 23 Aug. 1963 Eureka, Calif.
10f Greta Kay Gordon, b. 24 Feb. 1965 Arcata, Calif.
10g Janet Lynn Gordon, b. 26 March 1968 Arcata.

9b Jessie Margaret Morris, b. 22 Feb. 1941 Susanville, Calif.; 1st m. Ernest Cate, four children; 2nd m. William Randell Whitney, one child; 3rd m. Edward N. Brenzel, no issue; 4th m. 10 March 1971 John William Tucker, one child.

10a Richard LeRoy Cate, b. 6 July 1957 Willits, Calif.
10b Eugene Robert Cate, b. 9 Oct. 1959 Fortuna, Calif.

10c Michael Paul Cate, b. 25 Dec. 1960 Fortuna, Calif.; d. 31 Jan. 1961.
10d Sandra Yvonne Cate, b. 14 Aug. 1962.
10e Debra Ann Whitney, b. 10 Oct. 1965 Eureka, Calif.
10f Clint Tucker, b. 8 Dec. 1966 Paso Robles, Calif.

9c Gloria May Morris, b. 9 May 1942 Susanville, Calif.; 1st m. 1962, California, R. L. Gibbs; five children (see *Powell Family*); 2nd m. 1969, Nevada, S. H. Stevens; two children (see *Powell Family*).
9d Barbara Jean Morris, b. 30 Aug. 1943 Susanville, Calif.; 1st m. 1962 Ronald Lee Carpenter, two children *(Powell Family)*; 2nd m. 13 July 1968 Andalusia, Ala., Jerald Emmitt Miller (b. 17 July 1947 Fla.); two children *(Powell Family)*.

7c Bessie MayBelle Morris (3rd child of 6a Henry Rosencrans Morris), b. 8 Sept. 1894 Oaksdale, Wash.; registered nurse W.W. I; m. 14 Sept. 1916 Portland, Ore., Oggie Iver Nelson (b. 24 May 1890 Sleepy Eye, Minn.; d. 31 Dec. 1960 Portland); d. 1 Nov. 1988 Redding, Calif.

8a Gordon James Nelson, b. 17 Oct. 1923 Portland; dentist; m. 1947 Enid M. Benson; three children (see *Powell Family*).
8b James L. McMillan (adopted); b. 7 March 1924 Princeton, Wash.; doctor; three children (see *Powell Family*).

7d Sylvester Osmer Morris (4th child of Henry Rosencrans Morris); b. 12 April 1898 Nez Perce, Lewis Co., Idaho, in the cabin of a Nez Perce Indian named Eli; U.S. Army W.W. I in France; m. 15 June 1920 Vancouver, Wash., Jessie Leona Mickey (b. 26 July 1901 Battleground, Clark Co., Wash., 1st dau. of John A. Mickey, railroad foreman, and Maud Holman, who was in an all-female section gang of that railroad during W.W. I; teacher; d. 16 June 1985 Walla Walla, Wash.). They celebrated their 65th wedding anniversary. When they were first married, they spent summers as lookouts for the Forest Service on Red Mountain. Sylvester Morris was a commercial artist in Portland, an asst. postmaster in College Place, chief of volunteer fire dept., and member of the school board and the Presbyterian Church. He wrote the poignant "Emigrant Woman," republished in this book at the end of Chapter IV. Sylvester d. 26 Jan. 1987 Dayton, Wash.; bur. Odd Fellows, Walla Walla, Wash.

8a Margery Joyce Morris, b. 7 March 1923 Portland, Ore.; assoc. degree in counseling, drug and alcohol counselor, retired; 1st m. 27 Feb. 1943 Seattle, Wash., William Richard Ickes (b. 5 Nov. 1921 Elyria, Ohio; W.W. II gunner's mate 1st class, U.S. Navy on USS *Tennessee* at Pearl Harbor; owner of tool and dyemaking company; d. 18 Aug. 1982 South Amherst, Ohio); four children; div. 1976; 2nd m. 12 May 1978 to Bud Stafford (b. 29 March 1927, foreman and guide for a dude ranch); no issue.

9a Mary Ann Ickes, b. 25 Oct. 1943 Elyria, Ohio; m. 29 Dec. 1961 Sherrill Wayne Hudson (b. 26 Feb. 1943; B.S. Ashland Col., Ohio; valedictorian; managing partner of accounting firm in Latin America and Florida; chrm. Miami Chamber of Commerce; in 1991 dined with the Queen of England and several U.S. presidents on the queen's royal yacht); homemaker and world traveler; active members Church of Christ; live Miami, Fla.

10a Richard Wayne Hudson, b. 2 Nov. 1962, Ashland, Ohio; grad. Fla.U., M.A. English education; sportswriter and English teacher in Homestead, Fla.; m. 3 Dec. 1983 Dayton, Ohio, Linda Carol Jones; divorced.

11a Brook Ann Hudson, b. 30 May 1984.

10b Michael Wayne Hudson, b. 17 Jan. 1964 Ashland, Ohio; A.B. in computer science David Lipscomb Col., Nashville; certified actuary in Atlanta; m. 9 June 1984 Nashville, Tenn., Regina Kaye Sullivan; divorced; 2nd m. 11 July 1992 Beth Howley.

10c Robert Wayne Hudson, b. 13 Sept. 1967 Xenia, Ohio; grad. U. Tenn.; Juris Doctor U. Miami Law School; attorney in Miami.

9b William Richard Ickes Jr., b. 17 Jan. 1951 Elyria, Ohio, m. 26 June 1972 Vermilion, Ohio, Lori Kaye Balogh; divorced; a flint knapper in Tucson, Ariz.

9c John Henry Ickes, b. 10 March 1954, South Amherst, Ohio; 1st m. 13 July 1972 Edmonton, Alberta, Canada, Beverly Lucile Trottier; divorced; 2nd m. Carol Wortman; drives school bus in Kooskia, Idaho.

> 10a Cody John Ickes, b. 10 Aug. 1980.

9d Timothy Wayne Ickes, b. 18 Dec. 1958, South Amherst, Ohio; grad. Lewis and Clark Col., Lewiston, Idaho, assoc. degree in bus. mngm.; m. 17 Aug. 1976 Nancy Stewart, two chil.; divorced; 2nd m. 14 Jan. 1985 Renee Hamrich; 3rd m. Dena Jennings; live in Phoenix, Ariz.

> 10a Travis Ickes, b. 7 April 1975; student at Okla. Christian Col.
>
> 10b Melanie Joyce Ickes, b. 3 March 1978, lives with Aunt Mary Ann in Miami.

8b Carol Leona Morris, b. 1 June 1926 Portland, Ore.; B.A. cum laude Washington State U.; civilian and information officer U.S. Military Govt. in Japan 1948-51; child welfare social worker for Wash. State; dir. volunteer services, Harrington Mem. Hosp. in Sturbridge, Mass., twenty-two years; retired 1988; member Mass. Mayflower Society, DAR, AAUW; m. 16 Aug. 1952 Santa Maria, Calif., Richard Paul Reardon (b. 15 May 1931 Cambridge, Mass.; B.A. Whitman Col.; M.Ed. Worcester State Col.; 1st lt. U.S. Army Korean War; received Purple Heart; teacher and guidance counselor twenty-two years, Northbridge, Mass.; d. 30 Sept. 1993).

> 9a Catherine Jean Reardon, b. 25 Aug. 1953 Richland, Wash.; B.A. cum laude Worcester State Col.; former customer service rep.; homemaker; m. 7 April 1984 Sturbridge, Mass., David M. Nalewajk (b. 3 March 1955).
>
> > 10a James Reardon Nalewajk, b. 3 Feb. 1985.

10b Jessica Lee Nalewajk, b. 21 Aug. 1987.

9b Gail Marie Reardon, b. 29 July 1956 Walla Walla, Wash.; B.A. magna cum laude U. Mass.; former teacher; homemaker; m. 8 Nov. 1980 Webster, Mass., Ronald Jay Alden (b. 2 Dec. 1955).

10a Michael Richard Alden, b. 29 Oct. 1982 Dudley, Mass.
10b Steven James Alden, b. 27 Aug. 1984.
10c Timothy Jay Alden, b. 8 July 1988.

9c Maurine Anne Reardon, b. 24 Jan. 1959 Walla Walla (retained maiden name); grad. U. Mass.; group pension administrator; m. 20 June 1981 Webster, Mass., Thomas Reinzo (b. 21 July 1952; grad. U.Mass.; d. 9 May 1994 Phoenix, Ariz.); no issue.

9d Jennifer Margaret Reardon, b. 18 Dec. 1963 Webster, Mass.; B.S. summa cum laude Nichols Col.; systems consultant; m. 9 June 1984, Dudley, Mass., Derek Scott Speed (b. 1962; grad. Worcester Polytechnic Inst. with distinction).

10a Amanda Leigh Speed, stillborn 3 June 1990.
10b Katherine Elizabeth Speed, b. 4 July 1991.
10c Megan Laura Speed, b. 14 April 1994.

8c Hazel Jean Morris, b. 3 Oct. 1930 Portland, Multnomah Co., Ore.; B.A. Washington State U.; airline school, reservations for Northwest and TWA; teacher, librarian in charge of genealogy dept.; retired 1992; active in Olympia Gen. Soc., Wash. State Gen. Soc., Dau. of the Pioneers of Washington; mem. DAR; m. 29 Aug. 1954, Walla Walla, Keith Raymond Laws (b. 12 Aug. 1929, Yakima, Wash.; U.S. Navy submarine, Pearl Harbor and New Hebrides; B.A. U. of Wash.; Ed. Cert. and Ph.D. Eastern Wash. State; U.Mass. Amer. Grad School of Internat. Mng.; M.A. in international marketing; taught in Alaska, California, and Washington; prof., Central Wash. U.; national evaluator for national media conventions; won the Kettering Foundation's IDEA 1970-74; won New Media Award from Encyclopedia Britannica for five Pacific Northwest states; 1980 Fulbright prof. to Israel and met with Indira Gandhi; 1982 Fulbright prof. to Israel and had tea with the president of Israel; retired 1985; state pres. Washington Soc. Sons of American Revolution; member at large Sons of Union Veterans of the Civil War). A trip to Wales took them to Castle Madoc, the Powell family's residence. Nothing remains, but the Powells were remembered.

9a Victoria Ivy Laws, b. 5 May 1959, Los Angeles, Calif.; d. 5 July 1964 Twisp, Okanogan Co., Wash., of accidental drowning; bur. Greenwood Cem., Spokane, Wash.

9b Donald Robert James Laws, b. 28 Oct. 1960, Seattle; B.A. Wash. State U. in hotel and restaurant management; employed by Boston Market Corp.; m. 14 Sept. 1985 Covina, Calif., to Christina Fela Rangel (dau. of Rick Rangel and Karen Mae Hayes; b. 14 Sept. 1966 Covina, Calif.; attended Cerritos Com. Col.; former bank teller; homemaker).

10a Victoria Celia Laws, b. 31 Dec. 1985 Long Beach, Calif.

10b Mathew Shane Laws, b. 30 May 1991 San Bernardino, Calif.

10c Timothy Ryan Keith Laws, b. 8 May 1993, Upland, Calif.

8d Robert Lee Morris, b. 13 June 1932, Walla Walla, Wash.; grad. Whitman Col. bus. admin.; former cost control executive Boeing Co., retired; m. 1 Oct. 1950 Walla Walla, Patricia Ann Cosgrove (b. 30 Aug. 1933 Lawrence, Kans.); eight children.

9a Carol Ann Morris, b. 13 April 1951 Walla Walla; mgr. Manassas Animal Hospital in Manassas, Va.; m. 14 Nov. 1970 Huntsville, Ala., William L. Swift, one child; 2nd m. 1975 Neil Soifer, no issue; 3rd m. 16 Aug. 1978 Dr. John Michael Todd (B.S. Louisiana State U., Baton Rouge; D.V.M. Iowa State U., Ames; surgery residency Ames; major, U.S. Army; owner Stafford Animal Hospital in Stafford, Va.; three children.

10a Robert Christopher Swift, b. 26 May 1972 New Orleans, La.

10b Michael David Todd, b. 9 Nov. 1982 Manassas, Va.

10c Alexander Eric Todd, b. 31 Jan. 1985.

9b Kathleen "Kathy" Lee Morris, b. 25 July 1952, Walla Walla, Wash.; R.N.; charge nurse in neonatal center of Eggleston Hospital, Atlanta, Ga.; m. 6 Sept. 1974 Arnold Thatcher (U.S. Army, Vietnam War; purchasing agent for Building Material Supply in Tucker, Ga.)

10a Brittany Marie Lee Thatcher, b. 3 Sept. 1983; adopted.

10b Patrick Clay Thatcher, b. 28 Dec. 1987, own biological child.

10c Catelin Lee Thatcher, b. 23 July 1992; own biological child.

9c Mary Susan Morris, b. 4 Feb. 1954, Walla Walla; registered nurse, nursing supervisor of emergency room Northside Hospital, Atlanta, Ga.

10a Mathew Robert Morris, b. 8 Sept. 1978.

9d Robert Steven Morris, b. 26 April 1955, Walla Walla; exec. v. p., chief operating officer, and bd. of directors Friedman Jewelers, Savannah, Ga., third largest chain in the U.S.; 1st m. 1 Sept. 1973 Angela Shumate; two chil.; div.; 2nd m. 5 Oct. 1984 Toni Lynn Huggins (homemaker); one child.

10a Wendy Leigh Morris, b. 27 April 1974, Atlanta.

10b Melissa Lynn Morris, b. 12 May 1978.

10c Candace Ann Morris, b. 2 Dec. 1991.

9e Judith Lynn Morris, b. 18 July 1957, Walla Walla; gymnastics coach at Georgia Gymnastics Academy in Lawrenceville, Ga.; coach of the year for the state of Georgia; m. 8 Feb. 1975, Stone Mountain, Ga., Gary Prestigiacomo (B.A. U. of Wisconsin; customer rep., All Tel Inc. in Norcross, Ga.).

10a Kelly Nichols Prestigiacomo, b. 18 July 1978 Atlanta, Ga.
10b Kara Lynn Prestigiacomo, b. 21 Sept. 1982, twin.
10c Krista Lee Prestigiacomo, b. 21 Sept. 1982, twin.

9f Nancy Jean Morris, b. 24 Aug. 1959 Seattle, Wash.; student at Calhoun Col., Decatur, Ga., dean's list and president's list.

10a Ian James Donlin, b. 2 Jan. 1989.

9g Richard "Rick" Allen Morris, twin, b. 26 Nov. 1961, Seattle; B.S. Rutgers U., New Brunswick, N.J.; captain U.S. Army Operations, Fort Myer, Va.; manager Kimberly-Clark in Neenah, Wis.; m. 11 Jan. 1986 Vicki Lynn Haynes (B.A. Mary Washington Col., Va.; homemaker).

10a Taylor Martin Morris, b. 24 May 1990.
10b Evan Robert Morris, b. 28 Jan. 1992.

9h Thomas Edward Morris, twin, b. 26 Nov. 1961 Seattle; B.S. Rutgers U., New Brunswick, N.J.; Northeastern U., Boston; captain U.S. Army; district manager Pfizer Pharmaceuticals in Hartford, Conn.; m. 11 June 1984 Ramsey, N.J., Lisa Diane Asta (homemaker).

10a Steffani Allyse Morris, b. 26 July 1990.
10b Erica Lindsay Morris, b. 3 July 1992.

Note: The people listed *before* this point, back to 6f Nathaniel Miller Morris, are *all* descendants of him and also of 6a Henry Rosencrans Morris. Thus follows 6b through 6l, the remaining eleven children of Nathaniel Miller Morris.

6b Manuel Clayton Morris (2nd child of Nathaniel Miller Morris), b. 25 Nov. 1865 Albany, Ore.; farmer; m. 4 Feb. 1890 Farmington, Wash., Mrs. Armina (Simmons) Cooper; d. 11 April 1949.

6c Martha Josephine Morris (3rd child of Nathaniel Miller Morris), b. 17 Nov. 1867 Linn Co., Ore.; d. 25 Jan. 1868.

6d Anthony Preston Morris, b. 22 Jan. 1869 Linn Co., Ore.; farmer; lived Kamiah, Idaho; d. 13 Jan. 1944.

6e Eva Malinda Morris, b. 23 Sept. 1870 Scio, Ore.; m. 6 Nov. 1887 Oakesdale, Wash., Jeffrey Martin Baskett (b. 13 Sept. 1869); lived on the Nez Perce Indian Reservation in Idaho; d. 1 Aug. 1944.

    7a Lura Gertrude Baskett, b. 30 Jan. 1892, Tekoa, Wash.; m. 25 Nov. 1911 DeForrest Harding, Nez Perce, Idaho; four children (see *Powell Family*); d. 13 Oct. 1976.

    7b Leslie Arthur Baskett, b. 10 Oct. 1893; m. 13 June 1918 Mamie Espya Stellman; three children (see *Powell Family*); d. 19 Sept. 1959.

    7c Callie Anne Baskett, b. 9 May 1897 Grangeville, Idaho; m. 8 March 1925 Lewiston, Idaho, James Roy Cox; one dau.; d. 11 July 1982 Spokane, Wash.

    7d Mary Hazel Baskett, b. 26 March 1899 Grangeville, Idaho, m. 20 June 1918 Nez Perce, Idaho, Clarence Bliss Eastman; three chil.; d. 8 March 1966 Garden Grove, Calif.

    7e Herschel Nathaniel Baskett, b. 30 July 1904 Winona, Idaho; m. 10 June 1928 Nez Perce, Idaho, Velma E. Reinhardt; three children.

6f John Wesley Morris (sixth child of Nathaniel Miller Morris); b. 12 Jan. 1872 Linn Co., Ore.; d. 1 Feb. 1901. (See *Powell Family*.)

6g Clarence Lee Morris, b. 16 May 1874 Farmington, Wash.; m. 8 Jan. 1899 Nettie Terwhilegar (b. 10 March 1878 Cherokee, Iowa); lived Kamiah, Idaho; d. 7 April 1978 Winona, Idaho.

    7a L. G. Sylvanis Morris, b. 14 Feb. 1900; 1st m. 21 Jan. 1922 Margaret Delilah Reed; five children (see *Powell Family*); 2nd m. 4 Aug. 1966 Ethel Bowles; d. 27 July 1974.

    7b Charles Thomas Morris, b. 9 Aug. 1905 Greencreek, Idaho; m. 12 March 1929 Nez Perce, Idaho, Dollie Mae Mathews; three children (see *Powell Family*); live Alaska.

    7c Mary Violet Morris, b. 20 Feb. 1907 Greencreek, Idaho; m. 3 Aug. 1927 Oral Lewis Young; four children (see *Powell Family*); d. Sept. 1975 Kamiah, Idaho.

    7d Elmo Melvin Morris, b. 10 Sept. 1910 Greencreek, Idaho; m. 25 May 1934 Gladys Marie Mathews; three children (see *Powell Family*).

6h Minnie Mae Morris (eighth child of Nathaniel M. Morris), b. 29 Oct. 1878 Farmington, Wash.; m. 18 Dec. 1895 Gilliam T. Mattox (b. 7 Aug. 1870; farmer); d. 9 Jan. 1952 Winona, Idaho.

6i James Nathaniel Morris, b. 2 March 1880 Oakesdale, Wash.; farmer; m. 23 Jan. 1904 Winona, Idaho, Ella Pfannebecker (b. 25 June 1883 Spencer, Iowa); lived Winona, Mo., where her parents settled on a farm in 1898; six children; after the children were grown, James and Ella both attended high school; d. 28 June 1950.

 7a Fred Miller Morris, b. 18 Oct. 1904 Greencreek, Idaho; m. 22 Sept. 1946 Spokane, Wash., Margaret Stockton; one daughter (see *Powell Family*).

 7b Margaret Hannah Morris, b. 17 Nov. 1905 Winona, Idaho; m. 3 July 1937 Sunnyside, Wash., Joseph Robert Prewitt.

 7c Blanche Lucile Morris, b. 8 Oct. 1907 Winona, Idaho; m. — Hersman.

 7d Arthur James Morris, b. 28 Jan. 1909 Winona, Idaho; m. — —; one son (see *Powell Family*); d. 26 Jan. 1954.

 7e Clyde Nathaniel Morris, b. 28 Oct. 1911 Winona, Idaho; d. 31 July 1938.

 7f Dorothy Winnifred Morris, b. 10 Sept. 1919; m. 20 Sept. 1947 Ernest Eugene Nimnicht; one child (see *Powell Family*).

6j Thomas Jerome Morris, b. 23 Sept. 1881 Farmington, Wash.; m. 4 July 1915 Marguerite Stewart; d. 31 Oct. 1935, Portland.

6k Albert Joseph Morris, b. 20 Jan. 1882 Farmington; m. 4 Oct. 1904 Cora Sapp (b. 8 March 1887); lived Winona, Idaho; d. 19 Dec. 1965 Grangeville, Idaho. At birth he was named Marcus Whitman Morris, but when five years old his parents changed his name to Albert Joseph Morris. Both names are used in the will of his grandfather, Nathaniel Morris.

 7a John W. Morris, b. 8 Aug. 1905 Grangeville, Idaho; m. 11 May 1940 Mary Elizabeth Miller; five children (see *Powell Family*).

 7b Ralph J. Morris, b. 28 Dec. 1907; m. 23 Dec. 1928 Alberta Henderson; divorced.

6l Lucinda Adaliza Morris (twelfth child of Nathaniel Miller Morris); b. 30 July 1885 or 6, Whitman Co., Wash.; d. 19 Dec. 1898.

5g Mary Ann Morris (seventh child of Preston Morris); b. 12 Feb. 1845 Quincy, Ill.; m. 1 May 1862 Linn Co., Ore., Henry Clay Powell (first cousin of wife of 5f Nathaniel Miller Morris); eight children; d. 9 March 1928 Linn Co., Ore. (see *Powell Family).*

Generation 4: Albert Famous Morris I
Eleventh Child of Morris I and Sarah Cushman Morris

Sources: Author; Anne Wilson Allen, 11829 172nd Avenue N.E., Redmond, WA 98052-2223; *Cushman Genealogy and General History,* by A. W. Burt.

4k Albert Famous Morris I, b. 4 Dec. 1804, Kentucky; m. 4 Jan. 1831 Mary Summers (b. Kentucky); ten children, all born in Illinois; 22 Jan. 1824 included with several brothers in sale by their brother Thomas Morris of a Negro boy, farm equipment, etc.; in 1840 census; 1850 census, farmer in Adams Co., Ill.; 1860 census, farmer near Page City, Warren Co., Ill.; d. 1869 in Oregon.

5a William Morris, b. c. 1833, farmer.
5b (Daughter) Morris, b. c. 1835.
5c John Morris, b. c. 1836, farmer, m. Maria (b. Illinois).
5d Mary Morris, b. c. 1837.
5e Thomas Morris, b. c. 1838.
5f Oscar Morris, b. c. 1841.
5g Albert H. Morris, b. c. 1843.
5h Hiram Morris, b. c. 1846.
5i Sarah Morris, b. c. 1858.
5j Seath Morris, b. c. 1859.

Note: Albert Famous Morris II must not be confused with Albert I, above. Albert II was Albert I's nephew, b. 1804, son of Daniel Cushman Morris.

Genealogy, Section II ♦ 401

| Generation 4: Beauford Scott Morris
Twelfth Child of Morris I and Sarah Cushman Morris |

Sources: Author; Anne Wilson Allen, 11829 172nd Avenue NE, Redmond, WA 98052-2223; Melba Kuntzelman, P.O. Box 10121, Eugene, OR 97440; Agnes Nygren, Route 2, Box 23, Newman Grove, NE 68758; and Rodney Gay Walker, 1545 Maddux Drive, Redwood City, CA 94061.

4l Beauford Scott Morris, twelfth and last child of Morris and Sarah Cushman Morris; b. 10 June 1807 Bourbon Co., Ky.; 1st m. 23 July 1830, Bourbon Co., Elizabeth "Eliza" Bowles (b. 1810, Bourbon Co., Ky.; four children; d. near Quincy, Ill., in childbirth of fourth child, Beauford Jr., in August 1836 at age 27, or she died of lockjaw from a rusty nail [Bowles family record]); settled in Peyson, Ill. (Beauford's older brother John Morris, b. 1793, was m. 2nd to widow Mrs. John Payne, formerly Elizabeth Bowles, and had two children by her in Kentucky. She was living in 1831 on Cane Ridge, Ky., so Beauford must have been Eliza's third husband.) Beauford's 2nd m. was to Jane Dobson (b. 16 Feb. 1838, Adams Co., Ill.); nine children, only four listed here; d. 16 April 1849 Hazel Green, Wis., or Aug. 1837 in Adams Co., Ill.

5a Jesse Warren Morris, b. 1830, m. 6 Sept. 1849 Mary A. Martin.

   6a Mary Morris, b. c. 1850.

5b Benjamin Franklin Morris, b. 1833 Adams Co., Ill.

5c George Albert Morris, b. 1835 Adams Co., Ill.

5d Beauford Scott Morris Jr., b. 16 Feb. 1837, Dodgerville, Iowa Co., Wis.; also in 1900 census; in 1850 Illinois census, a "Bluford" Morris, age 14, is listed as a laborer living with Thomas Tate (farmer) and America Bowles Tate (maternal aunt), in Ellington, now part of Quincy, Adams Co., Ill.; apparently his family was broken up; many of Beauford's relatives now live in Adams County; m. 22 Aug. 1861, Dodgerville, Wis., Sarah A. Persons (thought to be McPherson originally; b. Wisconsin 17 March 1839); came west c. 1872 to Creston, Platte Co., Nebr., in an "immigrant wagon to homestead," then to a farm near Akron, Nebr.; served in Union army, Co. A, 10th Illinois Cavalry in

Civil War, discharged 1867; mem. GAR; worked for railroad, teamster, jobber, fishing and hunting expert; d. 21 April 1904, Missoula, Mont.; ten children.

6a John E. Morris, b. June 1862 Wisconsin; m. Mary —— .
6b Thomas Morris, b. c. 1863, Wisconsin; d. age 16.
6c Laura Ann Morris, b. 2 July 1868 Stevens Co., Wis.; came with parents across the country in a covered wagon at age three; m. 30 April or 1 May 1892, Creston, Nebr., Mervin Daniel Kuntzelman of Columbus (b. 10 July 1868 Kanakee Co., Ill.; sportsman; close friend of two white leaders of Pawnee Scouts during Indian uprisings; knew William Cody, better known as Buffalo Bill; d. Casper, Wyo., 17 Jan. 1952); belonged to Episcopal Church after marriage; lived Wisconsin and Nebraska; 1872 operated Albion House Hotel, Albion, Nebr.; cook, seamstress, and gardener; made quilts and reared five children; later farmed on the Bonanza near Albion, Boone Co., Nebr.; d. 21 Nov. 1958, Casper, Wyo.

7a Hazel Drucilla Kuntzelman, b. 16 Dec. 1894; 1st m. Walter Smith; four children: Darrel, lived Elmira, Ore., had five sons; Shirley m. —— Young; Virginia m. —— Mannelin; and Walter Jr.; 2nd m. 12 July 1929 Arthur Coakes, two children: Robert, deceased, and Charles Jr.; Hazel d. 24 March 1981.

7b Rex Lafayette Kuntzelman, b. 3 May 1897 Columbus, Nebr.; m. 9 May 1921, Albion, Nebr., Margaret Louise Hayes (b. 17 July 1901, Loretto, Boone Co., Nebr.; d. 15 Jan. 1991); farmer; U.S. Navy, W.W. I; four children; d. 3 July 1932 of a rare skin disease in Lincoln, Nebr. Widow Margaret m. June 1943 Gay Beauford Kuntzelman (7c, below), brother of first husband.

8a Agnes Ann Kuntzelman, b. Boone Co. 9 Feb. 1921, attended college, teacher; m. in Newman Grove, Nebr., 6 Feb. 1942, Alden Nygren (rec'd Pioneer Farm award for farm-in-family 100 years; school board and board of home for aged, choir soloist); live on farm near Albion.

9a Lawrence John "Larry" Nygren, b. Norbolk, Nebr., 25 Jan. 1943, grad. U. of Nebr.; M.A. U. of Colo.; U.S. Air Force twenty-one years; major, retired; Germany, Vietnam; Bronze Star, Silver Star; Mc-

Donnell-Douglas Co.; employed UC-Irvine; m. 1967 in Enid, Okla., Katherine Gerhardt (b. 22 Nov. 1945 Salsburg, Austria); divorced.

> 10a Heather Nygren, b. 11 Jan. 1968, Lincoln, Nebr.; part-time television actress and commercial model in Hollywood.
> 10b Matt Nygren, b. 24 Oct. 1970, Sacramento, Calif.
> 10c Aaron Nygren, b. 7 May 1973, Rapid City, S.Dak.

9b James Alden "Jim" Nygren, b. 3 May 1937, Columbus, Nebr.; U.S. National Guard; asst. engineer at packing company; construction, maintenance; company awards; m. Columbus, Nebr., 1970 Delores Kucera (b. 16 Aug. 1947, West Point, Nebr.).

> 10a Bryan James Nygren, b. Spencer, Iowa, 29 May 1971.
> 10b Jason Eric Nygren, b. Columbus, Nebr., 28 July 1973.

9c Ronald Richard "Ron" Nygren, b. Columbus, Nebr. 16 Nov. 1949; attended U. Nebr.; U.S. Army; farmer; m. in South Dakota Jody Snyder (b. 14 Aug. 1956, California); live Albion, Nebr.

> 10a Inez Nygren, b. 12 Aug., Genoa, Nebr.
> 10b Yancey Nygren, triplet, b. 11 May 1976, Grand Island, Nebr.
> 10c Brandy Nygren, triplet, b. 11 May 1976.
> 10d Melissa Nygren, triplet, b. 11 May 1976.
> 10e Caleb Nygren, b. 6 Feb. 1981, Albion, Nebr.

9d Julia Ann "Julie" Nygren, b. 8 Feb. 1956, Newman Grove, Nebr.; grad. Lincoln School of Commerce; works for auditing and income tax service; m. in Lincoln, Nebr., 9 May 1983 Kelvin Roehrs (b. 15 Nov. 1956 Hampton, Nebr.).

> 10a Whitney Roehrs, b. 30 Dec. 1985 Lincoln.
> 10b Nicole Roehrs, b. 17 Aug. 1990 Lincoln.

8b James Moffat "Jim" Kuntzelman, b. 5 Feb. 1925, Albion, Nebr.; U.S. Navy; 1st m. Sylvia Middaugh Teft; no issue; 2nd m. Delores Robinson Casey.

9a Douglas Kuntzelman
9b Gary Kuntzelman

8c Paul Rex Kuntzelman, b. 24 Nov. 1929, Loretto, Nebr.; m. 17 Oct. 1954 in Chadron, Nebr., Melba Anne Payne (b. 13 May 1936 in Stuart, Nebr.; writer); U.S. Marines; live Eugene, Oregon.

9a Stephanie Gay Kuntzelman, b. 8 Oct. 1955; community liaison director YWCA; Girl Scout leader; m. 8 Aug. 1975 Timothy Torczon.

10a Craig Lee Torczon, b. 22 Feb. 1978.
10b Jennifer Renee Torczon, b. 28 Sept. 1980.
10c Brett Joseph Torczon, b. 29 Aug. 1983, lives Hastings, Nebr.

9b Terry Michael Kuntzelman, b. 10 May 1958; m. Nov. 1979, Columbus, Nebr., Hazel Ann Kosch; d. 8 Jan. 1988.

10a Alicia Ann Kuntzelman, born and died 1979.
10b Christopher Michael Jaixen, b. 5 Nov. 1980.
10c Sean Paul Jaixen, b. 3 Nov. 1984. (Both boys adopted by maternal aunt, Joyce Kosh Jaixen.)

9c Lori Katherine Kuntzelman, b. 18 Dec. 1960; 1st m. 2 Jan. 1980 Todd Francke Muhle; 2nd m. March 1994, Grand Island, Nebr., Richard Radke Jr.; live Grand Island.

10a Jason Paul Muhle, b. 28 Oct. 1981.
10b Justin Allan Muhle, b. 4 Dec. 1985.

8d Rex Lafayette Kuntzelman Jr., b. 7 Oct. 1932; farmer, outdoorsman, hunter; served in U.S. Army Occupational Forces in Germany after W.W. II; m. Violet Starkey; Boone Co. A.S.C.S office manager; state area supervisor; live Fremont, Nebr.

9a Merle Kuntzelman
9b Eldon Kuntzelman, m., has children, lives Kansas.

9c Kristal Kuntzelman

7c Gay Beauford Kuntzelman, b. Columbus, Nebr., 13 Feb. 1899; farmer, outdoorsman, hunter; m. 9 June 1943 Margaret Louise Hayes Kuntzelman, widow of oldest brother, 7b Rex L. Kuntzelman Sr.; Gay died 11 Dec. 1976; no issue.

7d Lorena Rose Kuntzelman, b. Florence, Nebr., 2 Dec. 1904; m. 10 Sept. 1924 Harold Hinze (d. 18 Feb. 1966 Albion); no issue; d. 5 June 1990.

7e Florence Clara Kuntzelman, b. 30 March 1907, Columbus, Nebr.; 1st m. Orval Keith Walker (b. 5 May 1907, Maywood, Nebr.; d. 26 Jan. 1978 Casper, Wyo.); three children; 2nd m. Marlin B. Rogers (b. 8 Jan. 1915; d. 22 June 1990, Casper, Wyo.); no issue; live in California.

   8a Carla Roseann Walker, b. 27 April 1934, Haxtun, Colo.; m. James Kenneth Wollard; live San Marino, Calif.

      9a David Lee Wollard, b. 17 July 1953, Casper, Wyo.
      9b Michael James Wollard, b. 13 Sept. 1955, Casper.

   8b Larry Keith Walker, b. 20 April 1941, Scottsbluff, Nebr.; m. 1 July 1962 Evelyn Dean Hoyle (b. 5 Dec. 1943); live Gilroy, Calif.

      9a Lorrie Kay Walker, b. 24 Dec. 1962.
      9b Christina Louise Walker, b. 10 Feb. 1966.
      9c Alanna Liane Walker, b. 30 Sept. 1978.

   8c Rodney Gay Walker, b. 9 Jan. 1943, Scottsbluff, Nebr.; m. 18 Feb. 1962, Casper, Wyo., Sue Ann Schrock (b. 10 Feb. 1944, Ft. Wayne, Ind.); live Redwood City, Calif.

      9a Cameron Scott Walker, b. 15 July 1964, Los Gatos, Calif.; m. 3 Aug. 1991 Barbara Jean Pollock.
      9b Shannon Lynn Walker, b. 17 April 1969, Redwood City, Calif.; m. 27 June 1992 Mark Kendall Weiss.

6d Henry Morris, b. 1869 Stevens, Wis.; fireman; m. Grace L. Belknap.

6e Mary F. Morris, b. 1871, Wis.; m. Frank Connelly of Lindsay, Nebr.; four children: Iza, David, Marjorie, and Morris. Marjorie's daughter is a nun and teacher.

6f Clara Faye Morris, b. 3 Sept. 1872, Creston, Nebr.; artist; m. Sherman Dixon; two sons and one daughter; lived Humphrey, Nebr.; d. 24 Aug. 1966.

6g George Wallace Morris, b. 4 July 1874, Creston, Nebr.; train engineer.

6h Eliza D. Morris, b. Creston, Nebr., 7 Feb. 1876.

6i William Isaac Morris, b. 17 Dec. 1877, Creston, Platte Co., Nebr.; engineer; m. Mary Bernadette Cunningham (b. 10 Aug. 1881 Akron, Nebr.; d. April 1965 Washtenaw, Mich.), d. April 1954 Albion, Boone Co., Nebr.; seven children.

    7a Viola Morris, b. 28 Nov. 1904 Albion, Boone Co., Nebr.; m. 21 Jan. 1929; d. 17 March 1981 Dexter, Washtenaw, Mich.

    7b George Morris, b. 4 Aug. 1906 Albion, Nebr., m. Gerda Bygland; d. Feb. 1987, Carmel, Calif.

        8a Dr. Robert Morris, lives Carmel, Calif.
        8b Sharyn Morris, m. —— Richards, lives Bothel, Wash.

    7c William Morris, b. 15 March 1908 Albion, Nebr.; d. April 1974 Santa Barbara, Calif.

    7d John Morris, b. 2 Dec. 1910 Albion, Nebr., d. Santa Barbara, Calif.

    7e Clifford Morris, b. 20 Feb. 1913 Albion, Nebr.; m. 20 May 1939 Seattle, Wash., Olive Lillian Dougherty (b. 6 March 1914 Hartland, Wis.); d. near Mesa, Ariz.

        8a Daniel C. Morris, b. 16 Dec. 1944.
        8b Joy Ann Morris, b. 9 March 1946.

    7f Thomas Morris, b. 8 June 1915 Albion, Nebr., m. in Albion, Nebr., d. Dec. 1968, San Diego, Calif.

    7g Joseph Morris, b. 24 March 1920 Spalding, Greeley Co., Nebr.; d. Ann Arbor, Washtenaw, Mich., or Albion, Nebr., killed by a train.

6j Rachel K. Morris, tenth child of Beauford Scott Morris Jr.; b. Creston, Platte Co., Nebr., 30 Dec. 1883; lived Montana.

INDEX
Genealogy, Section II

Note: Married women are indexed by maiden and married name(s).

Ables, Martha Jean, 386
Adams
   Denise Gay, 322
   Douglas Bruce, 323
   Janet Sue (Roemmel), 359
   Julia Anne, 323
   Martha Morris, 323
   Mary Culbertson, 323
   Mary Stewart Carey (Haines), 322
   Nancy Gay (Gould), 323
   Pamela H. (Wakeman), 323
   Reily Gibson, 322
   Reily Morris, 323
   Roy Donald, 359
   Ruth Carey, 322
Ahnefeld, Luella, 349
Alden, Gail Marie (Reardon), 394
Alden, Michael Richard, 394
Alden, Ronald Jay, 394
Alden, Steven James, 394
Alden, Timothy Jay, 394
Alexander, ——, 351
Alexander, Mary Ann (Hart), 351
Allen
   Aaron Malcolm, 348
   Anne (Wilson), 347
   Arthur Donald, 347
   Catherine Gordon (Campbell), 335
   Eric Ryan, 348
   Jeffrey R., 335
   Leah E., 335
   Michael Jerome, 348
   Roger, 335
   Roger Donald, 348
   Ryan J., 335
   Susan Elizabeth, 348
   Timothy Arthur, 348
   Tracy Ann (Anderson), 348
Allison, Myrtle, 367
Alverson, Lola, 344
Ames, Nancy, 321
Anderson, Sarah Kelly, 374
Anderson, Tracy Ann, 348
Anton, Ingrid, 316
Appell
   Charles Wilbur, 309
   Christopher Anthony, 309
   Genevive Marjorie, 309
   Joseph Patrick, 309
   Marjorie Isabelle (Greer), 309
   Mark Andrew, 309
   Ruth Elizabeth, 309
Arnold, Alexandra (Morris), 311
Arnold, Ezekiel Clay, 361
Arnold, Jesse (Turney), 361
Arnold, Stephen Ross, 311
Asta, Lisa Diane, 397
Aza, Rhea, 334
Bader, Julie Ann, 370
Bader, Paula Jo (Durkin), 370

Bader, William, 370
Bair, Joyce, 332
Baker, Marguerite Louise (Morris), 376
Baker, Thomas W., 376
Ball, Ethel, 369
Balogh, Lori Kaye, 393
Bardelmier
   Carol (——), 385
   Dorothy Louise, 385
   Edward, 385
   Fred Lee, 385
   Henry, 385
   Jason Paul, 386
   Jennifer Denise, 386
   Jessie Margaret (Morris), 385
   Lonnie (——), 385
   Martha Jean (Ables), 386
   Michael Henry, 385
   Michelle Lee, 385
   Paul Dean, 386
   Sandra Lee (Driedger), 385
   Toni Jean, 385
Barnes, Herman Troy, 352
Barnes, Linda Kay, 352
Barnes, Linda Kay (Gaskill), 352
Barrale, Ann Brandon (Bodine) (Barry), 350
Barrale, Courtney Barry, 350
Barrale, Shannon Barry, 350
Barrale, Thomas, 350
Barry, Ann Brandon (Bodine), 350
Barry, James, 350
Baskett
   Callie Anne, 398
   Eva Malinda (Morris), 398
   Herschel Nathaniel, 398
   Jeffrey Martin, 398
   Leslie Arthur, 398
   Lura Gertrude, 398
   Mamie Espya (Stellman), 398
   Mary Hazel, 398
   Velma E. (Reinhardt), 398
Beattie, Catherine Morris (Brown), 322
Beattie, Thomas Tyler, 322
Beck, Katherine Jane (Wootton), 368
Beck, Kitty Anne, 368
Beck, William Harold, 368
Becker, Corene Oletta (Hash) (Noonan), 384
Becker, John C., 384
Beer, Marjorie, 345
Beirman, Kathryn Ann, 349
Belknap, Grace L., 405
Benjamisson, Britt, 343
Bensley, Martha E., 381
Benson, Enid M., 391
Berry, Katherine, 315
Bertilson, Kathryn, 338
Bess, Bessie Catherine, 357
Biestel, Suzanne, 385
Birdsong, Mary Scott, 346
Bjorklund, Ann Ashley (Mothershead), 328
Bjorklund, Ashley Elizabeth, 329
Bjorklund, Peter B., 329
Bjorklund, Peter Burton, Jr., 329
Black, Ida Eliza, 380
Blackwell, Charlotte, 355
Blackwell, Marsha Elizabeth, 344
Bodine, Ann Brandon, 350
Bodine, Elizabeth Graves, 350
Bodine, Frances Laura (Graves), 350
Bodine, Jacqueline (Thompson), 350
Bodine, Josephine (Brandon), 350
Bodine, Martin Stapleton, Jr., 350

Bodine, Martin Stapleton, Dr., 350
Bodine, Mary Ann, 350
Bond, Margaret Mary, 315
Bonzi, Alice Maria, 329
Botting, Constance, 346
Boullé, Robert Patrick, 319
Boullé, Tracy Morris (O'Brien), 319
Bowen, Robert and Delilah, 306
Bowles
    David, Sr., 365
    Elizabeth, 365, 401
    Ethel, 398
    Nancy, 377
    Nancy (Morris), 377
    Rachel (Brown), 378
    Thomas, 377
Boyd, Edwin, 375
Boyd, Edwine Morris, 376
Boyd, Jarred F., 375
Boyd, Mary Elizabeth (Morris), 375
Boyd, Nancy Turney (Morris), 375
Brackenbush, Carlotta, 326
Bradley, John H., 330
Bradley, Lydia Ellen, 330
Brandon, Josephine, 350
Brenzel, Edward N., 390
Brenzel, Jessie Margaret (Morris) (Cate) (Whitney), 390
Briones, Amanda Rose, 390
Briones, Antoinette Marie, 390
Briones, Michelle Lee (Postlewait), 390
Briones, Raymundo B., 390
Broome, John W., 375
Broome, Sarah Rebecca (Morris), 375
Brown
    Anne Maxwell (Miller), 322
    Catherine Morris, 322
    Catherine (Morris), 321
    Elizabeth, 378
    Emily, 378
    Estelle (Johnston), 322
    George, Jr., 321
    George, Commander, 321
    Hugh, 322
    James H., 378
    John Morris, 322
    Katherine, 327
    Katherine Ann, 378
    Rachel, 378
    Rae E., 356
    Samuel D. (or William), 378
    Sarah Elizabeth, 322
    Thomas H., 378
    William J., 321
Browning, Douglas E., 323
Browning, Julia Anne (Adams), 323
Brusse, Gail, 336
Bryan, Joyce, 373
Burdine, Sharon Ann, 389
Burr
    David (Shields?) Eugene, 326
    David August, 326
    David Augustus, 326
    Desdemona Augustine, 326
    Helen Merritt, 326
    Julia Mary Morris (Mothershead), 326
    Leland M., Jr., 326
    Leland Mothershead, 326
    Ruth Cooley (Merritt), 326
    Ruth Winifred, 326
Burt, Ruth, 326
Butler, —, 371
Butler, Jane (Warren), 371
Byal, Donald H., 335
Byall, Jayne (Campbell) (Darnell) (Nance), 335

Bygland, Gerda, 406
Byrd, Catherine Ann, 376
Byrd, Robert, 376
Came, Mary Lou, 359
Campbell
    Addo (Shafer), 335
    Alice (Romano), 333
    Alice Alworth, 333
    Alice Saturnia (Johnson), 333
    Allan, 334, 337
    Allan Jr., 334
    Ann (Lambert), 338
    Ann Elizabeth, 334
    Archibald III, 333
    Archibald Jr., 333
    Archibald, Capt., 333
    Bethany Jo, 337
    Bette L., 337
    Bruce, 337
    Cameron, 338
    Caroline, 338
    Catherine (Fry), 337
    Catherine Gordon, 335
    Charmian, 338
    Christopher Allan, 337
    Cleo Mary (Wilson), 349
    Colin, 338
    Colin Trenton, 338
    Donald, 336
    Donald III, 337
    Donald IV, 337
    Douglas, 334
    Elizabeth Morris, 333
    Gordon, 335, 337
    Heather Mitchell, 337
    Jayne, 335
    Jeffrey Gordon, 337
    John, 334
    John, Jr., 334
    Julia Defrees (Sample), 333
    Julie Defrees, 335
    Karin (Maurinals), 334
    Kathryn (Bertilson), 338
    Laura, 338
    Lorelei L. (Sherrell), 337
    Margaret (Ruble), 334
    Margaret R. (Saunders), 338
    Margaret (Sinclair), 334
    Mark D., 334
    Mary Douglas, 334
    Mary Elizabeth, 337
    Mary Jo (Valentz), 337
    Mary Margaret, 334, 339
    Pamela (Thorpe), 337
    Rhea (Aza), 334
    Rosita Maria, 337
    Sarah, 338
    Stuart, 338
    Tamara Lynn, 337
    Theodore Scott, 338
    Virgil Martin, Dr., 349
Carey, Ruth Newman, 322
Carpenter, Barbara Jean (Morris), 391
Carpenter, Ronald Lee, 391
Casey, Delores Robinson, 404
Cate, Ernest, 390
Cate, Eugene Robert, 390
Cate, Jessie Margaret (Morris), 390
Cate, Michael Paul, 391
Cate, Richard LeRoy, 390
Cate, Sandra Yvonne, 391
Catena, Jennifer Christina, 389
Catena, Paul Adelmo, 389
Catena, Paul Adelmo, Jr., 389
Catena, Sandra Kay (Gibson), 389
Chambers, Eleanora I. (Morris), 320
Chambers, John M., 320
Chandler, Katherine/Katheryne (Morris), 372
Chandler, Mary Doris, 373

Chandler, Morris Von, 372
Chandler, Nancy Katherine, 372
Chandler, Ruth, 366
Chandler, Thomas Vaughn, 372
Chism, ——, 317
Chism, Estelle Patricia (Morris), 317
Christenson, Chrystal Ann (Nichols) (Keebler), 381
Christenson, Emil, 381
Christian, Golda Lou, 352
Christman, Sue Ann, 315
Cieslwicz, Jackie, 331
Clark
    Annie Josephine (Howald), 354
    Belinda, 354
    Beverly, 387
    David Michael, 385
    Dewey Lee, 354
    Frank Faye, 354
    John, 385
    Scott Christopher, 385
    Suzanne (Biestel), 385
    Woodward, 354
Clay
    Dau. ——, 362
    Frances, 362
    Frank, 362
    Harry B., 362
    John, 362
    Lucille (Turney), 362
    Margaret (Turney), 362
    Mary, 362
    Nell, 362
Claypool, Catherine (Morris), 382
Claypool, William S., 382
Coakes, Arthur, 402
Coakes, Charles, Jr., 402
Coakes, Robert, 402
Coakes, Hazel Drucilla (Kuntzelman), 402
Cody, William "Buffalo Bill," 402
Collins, Albert Marvin, 368
Collins, Albert Sidney, 368
Collins, Clara, 368
Collins, Katherine (Morris), 368
Collins, Martha (Snowden), 368
Colville, ——, 361
Colville, Mary (Turney), 361
Compher, Barbara Gail (Gibson), 389
Compher, Damiann Lee, 390
Compher, Gilbert Harold, 389
Compher, Tabitha Dawn, 389
Connelly, David, 406
Connelly, Frank, 406
Connelly, Iza, 406
Connelly, Marjorie, 406
Connelly, Mary F. (Morris), 406
Connelly, Morris, 406
Cook, Betty Eilene (Thomas), 379
Cook, Gary, 379
Coon, ——, 378
Coon, Emily (Brown), 378
Coontz, Ruth Ann, 357
Cooper, Anna, 341
Cooper, Mrs. Armina (Simmons), 397
Corwin, Desdemona, 311
Corwin, Desdemona (Morris), 311
Corwin, Richard Mortimer, 311
Cosgrove, Patricia Ann, 395
Costa, Adele, 373
Cox, Callie Anne (Baskett), 398
Cox, Duke, 371
Cox, H. R., 371
Cox, James Roy, 398

Cox, Susan Rebecca (Morris), 371
Cramm, Charlotte Julia Clara, 353
Crandall, Cynthia Marie, 387
Cranston, Julia, 331
Crawford, Ora Henri, 321
Crossett. Elizabeth Ashley, 328
Cunningham, Mary Bernadette, 406
Current, Betty (Turney), 361
Current, John, 361
Currie
    Donald Alan, 384
    Donald Alan II, 384
    Erin Colleen, 384
    Gibson Oliver, 384
    Kelly Kathleen, 385
    Michael Kevin, 385
    Patrick Collin, 385
    Shawn Marie, 384
    Marilynn Marie (Wilson), 384
Curtis, Rosemary, 331
Cushman, Sarah, 305
Cushman, Thomas VI, 305
Daggett, Catherine Frost, 325
Dale, Jessica Morgan, 336
Dale, Kathleen, 336
Daley, Ida Bruce (Ham), 375
Daley, J., 375
Darneal, Sue, 356
Darnell
    Alyssa Michelle, 335
    Cindy (Winans), 335
    Collin C., 335
    Diane L., 335
    Jayne (Campbell), 335
    Lindsey Elizabeth, 335
    Michael R., 335
    Robert J., 335
Davis
    Albert, 358
    Charles Walton II, 373
    Charles Walton III, 373
    Donna Jean, 373
    Edith Joyce, 358
    Feather Ann, 373
    Gloria (Kenniwell), 358
    James Young, 358, 359
    Joyce Ann (Morris), 358, 359
    Laura Ann, 352
    Mary Doris (Chandler), 373
    Mary Elizabeth (Powers), 373
    Robert Morris, 358
    Rosetta (Johnson), 358
    Willis Feather, 373
Davison, C. A. S., 351
Davison, Virginia L. (Hart), 351
de Zaba, Marie, 310
Deaver, Florence, 345
Defrees
    Amanda Morris, 339
    Anna (Fisher), 339
    Anthony Colfax, 339
    Beatrice Fay (Johnson), 331
    Bradley C., 331
    Eleanor, 332
    Elizabeth Mitchell (Morris), 330
    Elizabeth Morris, 331
    Ethel (Held), 331
    Frederick Bradley, 331
    Hugh J., Jr., 332
    Hugh Jackson, 331
    John Dougherty, 330
    John Dougherty, Jr., 339
    Julia A. Morris, 332
    Lou Ellen, 331
    Lydia (Bradley), 339
    Lydia Ellen (Bradley), 330
    Lydia Ellen, 331
    Mary McKnight, 332
    Morris Morris, 330
    Thomas Morris, 339

Delgado, Desdemona Corwin (Morris), 310
Delgado, Louis Sherwood, 310
Delgado, Sherwood, 310
Dell, Benjamin R., 308
Dell, Lena, 308
Dell, Mary Campbell, 308
Deming, ——, 381
Deming, Nicolette, 381
Deming, Vicki (Larsen), 381
Dempsey, James Irvine, 368
Dempsey, Katherine (Morris) (Collins), 368
Denova, ——, 341
Denova, Olive (Morris), 341
DeVore, Nora, 341
Dickenson, Sadie Catherine, 358
Dillinger, Donna Sue, 353
Dillinger, Erma Dean (Gaskill), 353
Dillinger, Harold L., 353
Dillinger, Mary Susanne, 354
Dixon, Clara Faye (Morris), 406
Dixon, Sherman, 406
Dobson, Jane, 401
Dodge, Mary Jane, 343
Donlin, Ian James, 397
Dougherty, Olive Lillian, 406
Doyle, Allene (Strausbaugh), 368
Doyle, Darby W., 368
Drake, Margaret (Willis), 362
Drake, Vaughn, 362
Driedger, Sandra Lee, 385
Dumas, Denny, 359
Dumas, Sharon Lynn (Roemmel), 359
Durkin, Enid Annette (Morris), 370
Durkin, Joseph Hartley, 370
Durkin, Paula Jo, 370
Earle, Marie, 349
Eastman, Clarence Bliss, 398

Eastman, Mary Hazel (Baskett), 398
England, Debra Susanne, 354
England, Donna Dean, 354
England, Mary Susanne (Dillinger), 354
England, Robert Wayne, 354
Erd, Margaret (Morris), 370
Erd, Robert, 370
Erickson, Bruce Wayne, 351
Erickson, Evan Lawrence, 351
Erickson, Ryan Bodine, 351
Evans, Ruth Leota, 383
Ewell, Jamie, 344
Ewing, A. J., 362
Ewing, Lydia Conner, 362
Ewing, Mary Hester, 362
Falls, Emilie Adele, 330
Farnsworth, Estelle Patricia (Morris), 317
Farnsworth, John, 317
Faulkner, Elizabeth Mannen (Greenup), 363
Faulkner, James Curtis, 363
Faulkner, Nathaniel James, 363
Fernandes, Joyce, 387
Ferrais, Jody Bernadette, 387
Fisher, Anna, 339
Flanagan, Anna Hamilton (Smalley), 318
Flanagan, Christopoher John, 318
Fletcher, Alfred M., 383
Fletcher, Cora Narcissis, 383
Fletcher, Nancy Day, 383
Florence, Howard, 372
Florence, Howard Bryant, 372
Florence, James Mark, 372
Florence, Nancy Ellen (Karsner), 372
Fluent, Sally Ann, 363
Ford, Dinah Lee (Hash), 384

Ford, Roy, 384
Forrest, Sarah Cushman Morris, 360
Frazee, Mary, 305
Friede, Myrene, 370
Friley, Charles Edward, Jr, 315
Friley, Mary Louise (Morris), 315
Friley, Michael Gage, 316
Friley, Sherrie (Gage), 316
Friley, Susan Dawn, 315
Friley, Timothy John, 316
Friley, William Arthur, 316
Fruit, Lucinda, 305
Fruit, Malinda, 305, 378
Fry, Catherine, 337
Gage, Sherrie, 316
Galt, Elizabeth Morris (Campbell), 334
Galt, Walter Allan, 334
Gandhi, Indira, 395
Gaskill
   Amy Jo, 353
   Andrea Beth, 353
   Carol Ann, 352
   Charlotte Christi, 353
   Charlotte Julia Clara (Cramm), 353
   Cheryl Ann Marie (Heuvel), 353
   David Kent, 353
   Diane Elizabeth (Wheeler), 353
   Erma Dean, 353
   Glen Edward, Jr., 353
   Glen Edward, Sr., 353
   Golda Lou (Christian), 352
   Gregory Scott, 353
   Harold R., 352
   Harold Richard, 352
   Imogene, 353
   Jean (Trower), 352
   Linda Kay, 352
   Marlies Ursala, 354
   Mary Elizabeth (Hart), 352
   Mary Ellen, 353
   Morris Edward, 352
   Morris Hart, 352
   Pamela Sue (Schultz), 353
   Ronald Joe, 353
   Ronald Max, 354
   Ronald Max, Jr., 354
   Ronnie M., 352
   Thomas Emory, 352
   Tiffany Ann, 353
   Ursala H. (Willkomm), 354
Gerhardt, David, 335
Gerhardt, Diane L. (Darnell), 335
Gerhardt, Katherine, 403
Gibben, Ethel, 314
Gibbs, Bonnie, 354
Gibbs, David, 354
Gibbs, Georgia Mae (Howald), 354
Gibbs, Gloria May (Morris), 391
Gibbs, Kenneth, 354
Gibbs, R. L., 391
Gibson
   Addie Marie (Nicander), 388
   Alissa Annette (Nicander), 388
   Barbara Gail, 389
   Beverly (Clark), 387
   Brian Dalton, 388
   Cheyanne Cherie, 388
   Clarence Francis, 386
   Cora Rosetta (Morris), 386
   Frances Marie, 386
   Gilbert Lee, 388
   J. D., 390
   James Allen, 389
   James Dalton, 389
   James Lee, 388

Index, Genealogy, Section II ♦ 415

Janice Marie, 388
Jennifer, 388
John Thomas, 389
Joshua Webb, 388
Joyce (Fernandes), 387
Julie Carol, 388
Kaytlyn, 388
Kimberly Ann, 389
Lee Morris, 388
Lorna Claire (Jones), 388
Marina Linda Soares (Oram), 389
Marvin Everett, 388
Marvin Everett I, 387
Marvin Everett II, 388
Michael Lee, 388
Mike Dalton, 388
Nelson Webb, 388
Renee Lynn, 389
Sandra Kay, 389
Sandra Lee (McGuire), 389
Sara Marie, 389
Sharon Ann (Burdine), 389
Stephen Michael, 388
Tiffany ——, 388
Giermann, Karen Lee, 380
Gividen, Ellen Vaughan, 372
Glendinning, Mary Bell (Hart), 357
Glendinning, Thomas J., 357
Goodale, Estelle Jane, 314
Goodman, Mary L., 364
Gordon, Greta Kay, 390
Gordon, Janet Lynn, 390
Gordon, Lillian Lenora (Morris) (Postelwait), 390
Gordon, William Arnold, 390
Gould, Nancy Gay, 323
Graham
  Dr. Richard, 356
  Earl, 356
  Frances Rebecca (Hart), 356

  Georgia Anna, 356
  Joyce (Knight), 356
  Katherine, 357
  Katherine Ann, 356
  May, 356
  Rae E. (Brown), 356
  Samuel, 356
  Samuel Darneal, 356
  Sue (Darneal), 356
  Suzanne Rae, 357
  William Richard, 356
Grase, Jennifer, 311
Graves, Berta, 350
Graves, Frances Laura, 350
Graves, Mary Ann (Hart), 350
Graves, Nancy (Utterback), 350
Graves, William Henry, 350
Graves, William Lane, 350
Greenup, Bettie Sheridan (Turney), 363
Greenup, Calvin Pinkerton, 363
Greenup, Elizabeth Mannen, 363
Greenup, Russell Lee, 363
Greer
  Austin Morris, 309
  Desdemona Morris, 309
  George Bates, 308
  George Bates II, 308
  George Bates III, 308
  George Morris, 308
  Gregory Patrick, 308
  Ida (Northrup), 309
  Isabell Elizabeth (McCarthy), 308
  Joseph, 308
  Josephine B. (Morris), 308
  Lena (Dell), 308
  Louis Morris, 309
  Mabel Adele (Seymour), 309
  Marjorie Isabelle, 309
  Mary Janice, 308
  Mary Patricia (Sarbach), 308

Mary Sharon, 308
Michael Daly, 308
Theodore Morris, 308, 309
Greiner, Lucille Antoinette Germaine, 356
Griffith, John, 360
Griggs, Alley B., 381
Griggs, Sarah Jane (Morris), 381
Grimes, George, Dr., 366
Grimes, Katherine (Soper), 366
Groover, Claramargaret (Horn), 369
Groover, Jere Tolleson, 369
Groover, Nathaniel Tolleson, 369
Gustin, Gerard, 356
Gustin, Simone Bernice (Hart), 356
Hail, Allen Turney, 363
Hail, Amy Winn, 362
Hail, Ann Ewing, 363
Hail, Homer Allen, 362
Hail, Jesse McClellan Turney, 363
Hail, Mary Ewing (Turney), 362
Haines, Barbara Carey, 323
Haines, Charles Farquar, 322
Haines, John Morris, 322
Haines, Mary Stewart Carey, 322
Haines, Nancy Maria (Morris), 322
Haines, Ruth Newman (Carey), 322
Hales, Frances Hudnall, 345
Hall, Autumn Leah, 332
Hall, Carol Anne (Sass), 332
Hall, Frederick Ernest, 332
Hall, Frederick Ernest, Jr., 332
Hall, Joyce (Bair), 332
Hall, William Walter, 332
Ham
—— (Osborn), 375
Alice, 375
Bruce, 375
Daniel, 375
Dell, 375
Dorothy, 375
Gertrude, 375
Ida Bruce, 375
John, 375
Lena Smith, 375
Myrtle, 375
Nancy, 375
Rebecca Anderson (Morris), 375
Sarah, 375
Sarah Catherine (Morris), 375
Willie Kate, 375
Hamilton, Bobby (Morris), 367
Hamilton, Robert, 367
Hammond, Ola Beatrice, 349
Hamrich, Renee, 393
Hanes, Clarence O., 348
Hanes, Clarence O., Jr., 349
Hanes, John Wilson, 349
Hanes, Luella (Ahnefeld), 349
Hanes, Zora Myrton (Wilson), 348
Harding, DeForrest, 398
Harding, Lura Gertrude (Baskett), 398
Hardwick, Adelia, 355
Haren, Michael, 316
Haren, Susan Marie (Krofcheck), 316
Harrison, Benjamin, 326
Harrison, Pres. Benjamin, 313
Hart
Adelia (Hardwick), 355
Agnes (Miller), 351
Alene M. (Lynes), 357
Anastasia Germaine, 356
Armelle (Parker), 356
Ben, 355
Benjamin Arnold, 351

Bessie Catherine (Bess), 357
Bud, 351
Cary Edward, 357
Catherine Elizabeth (Morris), 341
Celinda Ann, 358
Charlotte (Blackwell), 355
Charlotte Clara, 356
Cherie Kay, 357
Christine Marie, 357
Claude, 351
Dulcimer May, 357
Ed, 351
Elizabeth, 351, 354
Ellen (Hearn), 351
Florence, 351
Frances Rebecca, 356
Frank Laurin, Dr., 355
George Morris, 357
Harry, 351
Hazel Elizabeth (Prater), 355
Ida Marie, 354
Jack, 355
Jack E., 357
James Theodore, 356
Joyce (Jewett), 358
Junia Ann, 355
Karen Kay (Walter), 357
Laura Ann (Davis), 352
Laura Beth, 356
Lucille Antoinette Germaine (Greiner), 356
Lucinda Antoinette, 356
Luella (——), 351
Lulu Mae, 354
Lura E. (Macy), 358
Mame Austin, 355
Margaret (Hulse), 357
Margaret June, 357
Mary (Wirt), 355
Mary Ann, 342, 350, 351
Mary Bell, 357
Mary Elizabeth, 352
Mary Jane Pearson, 341
May (Lindsay), 351
Mehethalem Ellen (Rosser), 352
Morris V., 357
Nell, 355
Noel Blake, 355
Paula (Prescott), 356
Richard Hugh, 355
Richard Lindsay, 351
Richard Lindsey, 341, 358
Richard Lindsey, Jr., 358
Richard Rosser, 352
Rose ——, 351
Ruth Ann (Coontz), 357
Simone Bernice, 356
Thomas Austin, 352
Thomas B., 354
Thos., 358
Virginia L., 351
Wallace E. Morris, 357
Walter Dean, 356
Walter Dean, Jr., 356
Walter Lauren, 355
William, 341, 351
William Theodore, 355
Hash, Corene Oletta, 384
Hash, Dinah Lee, 384
Hash, Gifford LeRoy, 383
Hash, John Jacob, 383
Hash, Linda Lee, 383
Hash, Nancy Margaret (Morris), 383
Hash, Ruth Leota (Evans), 383
Hathaway, Ada M., 332
Haworth, James Harrison, 316
Haworth, Leah Ashley, 316
Haworth, Susan Dawn (Friley), 316
Hayes, Karen Mae, 395
Hayes, Margaret Louise, 402

Hayes, Pres., 330
Haynes, Vicki Lynn, 397
Heacock, Linda Ann, 346
Hearn, Ellen, 351
Hebb, Maysel Evelyn, 379
Heck
    Annie, 346
    Carl Lee, 345
    Carl Lee, Jr., 346
    Carl Steven, 346
    Constance (Botting), 346
    David Allen, 346
    Elizabeth Botting, 346
    James Peyton, 346
    Joan Frances, 346
    Lee (Kauffman), 346
    Linda Ann (Heacock), 346
    Mary Scott (Birdsong), 346
    Michael James, 346
    Rebecca, 346
    Roberta (Nemec), 346
    Susan Frances, 346
Hedges, Brian, 357
Hedges, Darrell, 357
Hedges, Diana, 358
Hedges, Karen George (Vandiver), 357
Heffner, Diane Frazier, 328
Heffner, Lola Mae, 345
Held, Ethel, 331
Henderson, Alberta, 399
Hendricks, ——, 354
Hendricks, Elizabeth (Hart), 354
Herring, Marjorie (Warren), 371
Herring, William, 371
Hersman, ——, 399
Hersman, Blanche Lucile (Morris), 399
Herst, Sarah, 321
Heuvel, Cheryl Ann Marie, 353
Higgins, Charles Volney, 367

Higgins, Geneva (McConnell), 367
Higgins, Hazel Graves (Morris), 367
Higgins, Sazie, 367
Higgins, Thomas, 367
High, Elizabeth, 350
Hinton, Edna Earl, 363
Hinze, Harold, 405
Hinze, Lorena Rose (Kuntzelman), 405
Holloway, Lillie Jane, 345
Holman, Maud, 391
Hopkins, Bess, 341
Hopkins, Elizabeth, 356
Hopkins, May (Graham), 356
Hopkins, O., 356
Hoppe, Barbara (Rosing), 356
Hoppe, Christian Paul, 356
Hoppe, Elizabeth, 356
Hoppe, Elizabeth (Johnson), 356
Hoppe, Paul, 356
Hoppe, Paul, Jr., 356
Horn, Alice Rebecca (Wootton), 369
Horn, Claramargaret, 369
Horn, Rebecca Murray, 369
Horn, William Murray, 369
Horton, Eliza Ann, 365
Howald
    Annie Josephine, 354
    Dennis Lee, 354
    George D., 354
    Georgia Mae, 354
    Gloria Loraine (Sanderson), 354
    Jessie D., 354
    Joseph Grant, 354
    Joyce, 354
    Lora Jean, 354
    Lulu Mae (Hart), 354
    Richard D., 354

Richard Franklin, 354
Robert Victor, 354
Vincent Stackey, 354
Howard, Joseph, 380
Howard, Nevada Janet (Morris), 380
Howley, Beth, 392
Hoyle, Evelyn Dean, 405
Hudson, Beth (Howley), 392
Hudson, Brook Ann, 392
Hudson, Linda Carol (Jones), 392
Hudson, Mary Ann (Ickes), 392
Hudson, Michael Wayne, 392
Hudson, Regina Kaye (Sullivan), 392
Hudson, Richard Wayne, 392
Hudson, Robert Wayne, 392
Hudson, Sherrill Wayne, 392
Huggins, Toni Lynn, 396
Hughes
    Christiana, 378
    George W., 378
    J. M., 366
    Leslie, 366
    Louella (Soper), 366
    Polly, 378
    William, 366
Hulse, Margaret, 357
Humes, Mary Miller (Wildhack), 314
Humphrel, Betty Eilene (Thomas), 379
Humphrel, Robert, 379
Humphreys, Julie Defrees, 339
Humphreys, Mary Margaret (Campbell), 339
Humphreys, Richard Fairfield, 339
Hunter, ——, 375
Hunter, Alice (Ham), 375
Hurst, Joseph, 332
Hurst, Marcy Jo (Sass), 332
Ickes
    Beverly Lucile (Trottier), 393
    Carol (Wortman), 393
    Cody John, 393
    Dena (Jennings), 393
    John Henry, 393
    Lori Kaye (Balogh), 393
    Margery Joyce (Morris), 392
    Mary Ann, 392
    Melanie Joyce, 393
    Nancy (Stewart), 393
    Renee (Hamrich), 393
    Timothy Wayne, 393
    Travis, 393
    William Richard, 392
    William Richard, Jr., 393
Irwin, Elizabeth Rachel, 313
Ivancevich, John Michael, 372
Ivancevich, Margaret Bryant (Karsner), 372
Jackson, ——, 375
Jackson, Mary French, 324
Jackson, Sarah (Ham), 375
Jacoby, Hazel Graves (Morris), 367
Jacoby, William Claybrook, 367
Jaixen, Christopher Michael, 404
Jaixen, Joyce Kosh, 404
Jaixen, Sean Paul, 404
James, Amanda, 369
James, Caroline, 369
James, Evan, 369
James, Katherine Lindsey, 369
James, Rebecca Jane (Smither), 368
James, William, 368
Jeffords
    Ann (——), 376
    Cecil, 376
    Edwine Morris (Boyd), 376
    James Eric, 376

Jerri Ann, 376
Jerry, 376
Jonathan Lee, 376
Kristy Lynn (Williams), 376
Martha Ann, 375
Jenks, Elizabeth Ellen (Proctor), 344
Jenks, Ellen Proctor, 344
Jenks, Mary Elizabeth, 344
Jenks, Robert, 344
Jenks, Sarah L., 344
Jenks, Susan Hamilton, 344
Jennings, Dena, 393
Jewett, Joyce, 358
Johnson
  Alice Saturnia, 333
  Beatrice Fay, 331
  Bettie Brent, 362
  Charles B., 371
  Elizabeth, 356, 368
  Elizabeth (Hopkins), 356
  Henrietta (Morris), 371
  Leo, 356
  Rosetta, 358
Johnston, Estelle, 322
Jones, Linda Carol, 392
Jones, Lorna Claire, 388
Joseph, Chief, 383
Karsner, Albert Bryant, 372
Karsner, Albert Creath, 372
Karsner, Margaret Bryant, 372
Karsner, Margaret Ellen (Morris), 372
Karsner, Mary Dan, 372
Karsner, Nancy Ellen, 372
Kauffman, Lee, 346
Keebler, Arden Louise, 381
Keebler, Chrystal Ann (Nichols), 381
Keebler, Edward Lee, 381
Kennedy, Emma, 321
Kenniwell, Gloria, 358

Kennon, Lucinda Antoinette (Hart), 356
Kennon, Phil, 356
Kindall, Elizabeth Alice, 361
Knight, Joyce, 356
Kopp, Catherine (Morris), 370
Kopp, Catherine Jane, 370
Kopp, Chester, 370
Kosch, Hazel Ann, 404
Krauss, Eleanor Carey, 325
Krauss, John Landers, 325
Krauss, Lisette Susanna, 317
Krofcheck, Debora Ann, 317
Krofcheck, Joseph, 316
Krofcheck, Julia Lynn, 317
Krofcheck, Laurine (Morris), 316
Krofcheck, Susan Marie, 316
Kruse, Anne Elizabeth, 328
Kruse, Katharine (Mothershead) (Lecy), 328
Kruse, Katharine Marie, 328
Kruse, Richard, 328
Kucera, Delores, 403
Kuntzelman
  Agnes Ann, 402
  Alicia Ann, 404
  Delores Robinson (Casey), 404
  Douglas, 404
  Eldon, 404
  Florence Clara, 405
  Gary, 404
  Gay Beauford, 402, 405
  Hazel Ann (Kosch), 404
  Hazel Drucilla, 402
  James Moffat, 404
  Kristal, 405
  Laura Ann (Morris), 402
  Lorena Rose, 405
  Lori Katherine, 404
  Margaret Louise (Hayes), 402, 405

Melba Anne (Payne), 404
Merle, 404
Mervin Daniel, 402
Paul Rex, 404
Rex L., Sr., 405
Rex Lafayette, 402
Rex Lafayette, Jr., 404
Stephanie Gay, 404
Sylvia Middaugh (Teft), 404
Terry Michael, 404
Violet (Starkey), 404
Lambert, Ann, 338
Landon, Alfred, 343
Lane
   Anna (Cooper), 341
   Carrie, 341
   Dulcimer (Morris), 341
   Elizabeth, 341
   Ella, 341
   John C., 341
   Joseph, 341
   Nora (DeVore), 341
   Thomas, 341
   Thomas, Jr., 341
Larsen, —— Kristi, 381
Larsen, Arden Louise (Keebler), 381
Larsen, Casey, 381
Larsen, Gerald Lee Sparks, 381
Larsen, Steven Ward, 381
Larsen, Vicki, 381
Laughlin, ——, 375
Laughlin, Gertrude (Ham), 375
Laws
   Christina Fela (Rangel), 395
   Donald Robert James, 395
   Hazel Jean (Morris), 394
   Keith Raymond, 394
   Mathew Shane, 395
   Timothy Ryan Keith, 395
   Victoria Celia, 395
   Victoria Ivy, 395

Layson, Evalyn, 343
LeCrone, ——, 356
LeCrone, Adam, 355
LeCrone, Andrew, 355
LeCrone, Noel Blake (Hart), 355
LeCrone, Noel Elizabeth, 355
Lecy, Katharine (Mothershead) (Kruse), 328
Lecy, Mathew Wilson, 328
Lecy, Stanley, 328
Leonard, Amy Jo, 359
Leonard, Jerry D., 359
Leonard, Lee Ann, 359
Leonard, Martha Lynette (Montgomery), 359
Letcher, Charles Wesley II, 361
Letcher, Elizabeth Alice (Kindall), 361
Letcher, John Henry III, 361
Letcher, John Henry IV, 361
Letcher, Mary Martin (Taylor), 361
Lewis, Sheila, 357
Liamsden, Gerald, 344
Liamsden, Susan Hamilton (Jenks), 344
Lichnor, Desdemona Augustine (Burr), 326
Lichnor, John S., 326
Liese, Alvina, 313
Lietaert, Janet A., 331
Lincoln, Abraham, 330
Lindsay, May, 351
Linsmith, Denise Gay (Adams), 322
Linsmith, Douglas Franz, 322
Linsmith, Eleanor Adams, 323
Linsmith, Miles Howard, 323
Linsmith, Ruth Carey (Adams), 322
Linsmith, Scott Culbertson, 323
Linsmith, Stewart May, 322

Lizarraga, Domingo Gregory, 311
Lizarraga, Manuel, 311
Lizzaraga Alexandra (Morris), 311
Lockman, ——, 375
Lockman, Myrtle (Ham) (Shea), 375
Long, Elizabeth Sean, 375
Long, Hazel (Morris), 374
Long, Helen, 374
Long, Ivaleen, 374
Long, Jack, 374
Long, Mary Catherine, 374
Loomis, Lois, 310
Lorentz, Ruth, 375
Lundquist, Sabrina, 311
Lundquist, Stephen, 310
Lundquist, Desdemona (Morris), 310
Lusch, Carlotta (Mothershead), 326
Lusch, Henry Bernard, 326
Luthin, Melinda Marie, 328
Lynes, Alene M., 357
Lynn, Melba, 379
MacDaniel, Lucie, 314
MacDonald, Catherine, 338
MacDonald, Charmian (Campbell), 338
MacDonald, Gerald, 339
MacDonald, Henry, 338
MacDonald, Joseph, 339
Mackay, Carol, 319
Macy, Lura E., 358
Mannelin, Virginia (Smith), 402
Mannen, Mary Elizabeth, 361
Marshall, Arthur, 382
Marshall, Josephine B. (Morris), 382
Masland, Susan, 336
Mathews, Dollie Mae, 398

Mathews, Gladys Marie, 398
Mattox, Gilliam T., 399
Mattox, Minnie Mae (Morris), 399
Maurinals, Karin, 334
Mayer, Betsy Turney (Taylor) (Tucker), 361
Mayer, Gerald S., 361
Mayer, Lucie, 314
McCabe, Claramargaret (Horn) (Groover), 369
McCabe, James, 369
McCarthy, Isabell Elizabeth, 308
McCarthy, Michael Joseph, 308
McCarthy, Nannie Patrick, 308
McCarty, Simon, 340
McCarty, Thomas B., 340
McConnell, Geneva, 367
McCoy, Carrie (Lane), 341
McCoy, Ella (Lane), 341
McCoy, Joel, 341
McCoy, Simpson, 341
McCurry, Ann, 339
McDonnell, Catherine Hunter, 329
McDowell, Andrew, 360
McDowell, Lula M., 360
McDowell, Ora Ann, 360
McDowell, Rebecca Ann (Morris), 360
McGuire, Sandra Lee, 389
McIntire, Ezekial, 360
McIntire, John, 360
McIntire, Lucinda, 360, 365
McIntire, Mary (Morris), 360
McIntire, Sally, 360, 365
McInturf, ——, 351
McInturf, Florence (Hart), 351
McIntyre, Frances, 330
McKee
  Donald Morris, 314
  John Douglas, 314

Josephine, 314
Josephine Goodale (Morris), 314
Kathryn, 314
Kenneth Morris, 314
Lucie (Mayer), 314
Robert G., 314
McKinney, —, 375
McKinney, Dorothy (Ham), 375
McMahill, Ann R. (Morris), 380
McMahill, William, 380
McMains, Elizabeth (Lane), 341
McMains, Robert, 341
McMillan, Charles, 362
McMillan, Edna (Turney), 362
McMillan, James L., 391
Meriwether, Thomas, 326
Merritt, Ruth Cooley, 326
Mertz
    Andrew Mackay, 320
    Anne Estelle (Morris), 318
    Carol (Mackay), 319
    David Allerton, 320
    Deborah Elizabeth (Smith), 320
    Elizabeth Morris, 319
    Gregory Morris, 320
    Jonathan Frederick, 320
    Peter Tyler, 320
    Susanne Day, 318
    Theodore Morris, 320
    Walter Day, 318
    Walter Day III, 320
    Walter Day, Jr., 319
Metropole, Christienne Elene, 311
Metropole, Desdemona (Morris), 310
Metropole, James, 310
Mickey, Jessie Leona, 391
Mickey, John A., 391
Mickey, Maud (Holman), 391

Miles, Marian Cary, 370
Miller, Adaliza, 381
Miller, Agnes, 351
Miller, Anne Maxwell, 322
Miller, Barbara Jean (Morris) (Carpenter), 391
Miller, Gertrude, 371
Miller, Jerald Emmitt, 391
Miller, Mary Elizabeth, 399
Minnick/Meenack, Anna, 340
Mitchell, Elizabeth Graves (Bodine), 350
Mitchell, Laura Elizabeth, 350
Mitchell, Leanne Marie, 350
Mitchell, Mary "Mollie," 362
Mitchell, Robert, 350
Mitchell, William W., 362
Montague
    Charles Strother, 344
    Courtney Proctor, 344
    Doris Suetta (Smithe), 344
    Jamie (Ewell), 344
    John Currie, 344
    Marsha Elizabeth (Blackwell), 344
    Richard Allen, 344
    Richard Currie, 344
    Richard Proctor, 344
    Zora Wilson (Proctor), 344
Montgomery, Craig, 359
Montgomery, Edna Mae (Morris), 359
Montgomery, Forrest, 359
Montgomery, John David, 359
Montgomery, Lori, 359
Montgomery, Martha Lynette, 359
Montgomery, Mary Lou (Came), 359
Morgan, General John Hunt, 366
Morgland, Molly, 374

Morris
  Abigail C. (Thayer), 312
  Adaliza (Miller), 381
  Adelaide, 371
  Adilizza, 379
  Aileen (Nicholas), 379
  Albert F., 306
  Albert Famous, 358
  Albert Famous I, 400
  Albert Francis, 359
  Albert Gale, 358
  Albert Gene, 359
  Albert H., 400
  Albert Joseph, 399
  Alberta (Henderson), 399
  Alexandra, 311
  Alice Jane, 359
  Allen Gano, 374
  Alma G., 341
  Almanza Palmyra, 342, 360
  Amanda Melvina, 325
  Amy Catherine, 346
  Andrew Beauford, 381
  Andrew Seymour, 315
  Angela (Shumate), 396
  Ann E. (Morrison), 340
  Ann R., 380
  Anna, 310
  Anna (Minnick/Meenack), 340
  Anna Elizabeth (Raikes), 358
  Anne Estelle, 318
  Anne Maxwell (Miller), 322
  Anthony Preston, 398
  Antoinette, 316
  Armina (Simmons) (Cooper), 397
  Arthur James, 399
  Austin W., 307
  Austin W., Jr., 312
  Barbara Jean, 391
  Beauford Scott, 401
  Beauford Scott, Jr., 401
  Belle (Mugg), 358
  Benjamin Franklin, 401
  Bessie MayBelle, 391
  Blanche (Walker), 370
  Blanche Lucile, 399
  Bobby, 367
  Candace Ann, 396
  Carol Ann, 395
  Carol Leona, 393
  Caroline, 312
  Catherine, 321, 370, 382
  Catherine (Thomas), 382
  Catherine Elizabeth, 341, 358
  Catherine Miles, 371
  Celinda Anne (Hart), 358
  Charles Goodman, 321
  Charles Thomas, 398
  Clara, 341
  Clara Faye, 406
  Clarence Lee, 382, 398
  Clifford, 406
  Clyde Nathaniel, 399
  Cora, 379
  Cora A. (Savery), 379
  Cora (Sapp), 399
  Cora Narcissis (Fletcher), 383
  Cora Rosetta, 386
  Dan Turney, 372, 374
  Daniel C., 406
  Daniel Cushman, 340
  Daniel Turney, 374
  (Daughter), 400
  David Corwine, 325
  Dean Mathew, 346
  Debora Ann (Krofcheck), 317
  Dell, 380
  Desdemona Corwin, 310
  Desdemona H., 311
  Desdemona Marie, 310
  Deseriee, 316
  Dollie Mae (Mathews), 398
  Don Randall, 379

Donald Seymour, 314
Donna Antoinette (Piva), 317
Dora, 371
Dorothy Winnifred, 399
Dulcimer, 341
Earl, 341
Edna Mae, 359
Edward, 371
Edwin Talbot, 305
Eileen Mae (Spoon), 315
Eleanor, 305
Eleanor (Roberts), 305
Eleanor I., 320
Elida (Roberts), 371
Eliza Ann (Horton), 365
Eliza D., 406
Eliza Jane, 341
Elizabeth, 365, 378
Elizabeth "Eliza" (Bowles) (Morris), 401
Elizabeth (Bowles) (Payne) (Morris), 365
Elizabeth Agnes, 384
Elizabeth C., 341
Elizabeth Mitchell, 330
Elizabeth Rachel (Irwin), 313
Ella, 341
Ella (Pfannebecker), 399
Ellen Vaughan (Gividen), 372
Elmo Melvin, 398
Emma (Kennedy), 321
Enid Annette, 370
Erica Lindsay, 397
Erle C., 379
Erma (Ryan), 379
Estelle Jane (Goodale), 314
Estelle Patricia, 317
Ethel (Ball), 369
Ethel (Bowles), 398
Ethel (Gibben), 314
Eva Malinda, 398
Evan Robert, 397

Evelyn Maysel, 379
Fannie A., 341
Frances, 380
Frances Lenora (Rains), 390
Fred Miller, 399
Frederick Davis, 320
Gabrielle, 308
Gail (Simpson), 316
Geoffrey McKay, 311
George, 406
George Albert, 401
George D., 341
George Hughes, 379
George Wallace, 406
Gerda (Bygland), 406
Gertrude, 371
Gertrude (——), 373
Gertrude (Miller), 371
Gladys, 321
Gladys Marie (Mathews), 398
Gloria May, 391
Grace L. (Belknap), 405
Guy Edward, 367
Guy Kenton, 374
Harold Chambers, 314
Harry, 313
Hattie (Rodman), 374
Hazel, 374
Hazel Graves, 367
Hazel Jean, 394
Helen I., 313
Henrietta, 371
Henry, 365, 405
Henry Alexander, 379
Henry Lee, 384
Henry Pearl, 380
Henry Rosencrans, 382
Hepsibaugh (Ricketts), 366
Hiram, 400
Horace McKay, 311
Horatio, 305, 361, 378
Horatio, Jr., 380

Horatio Nelson, 380
Howard Allen, 379
Hugh Henry, 371
Hyrum Bowles, Sr., 305
Ida, 381
Ida Eliza (Black), 380
Ingrid (Anton), 316
James A., 341
James Hayden, 370
James Nathaniel, 399
James Pender, 375
James Robinson, 375
James Sconce, 369
James Wiles, 321
Jane (Dobson), 401
Jane Maria (Peppard), 307
Jennifer (Grase), 311
Jesse Warren, 401
Jessie, 380
Jessie Leona (Mickey), 391
Jessie Margaret, 385, 390
Jno., 365
Joan Frances (Heck), 346
John, 313, 371, 400, 406
John A., 346, 380
John Allen, 367
John D., 321
John D. III, 321
John D., Jr., 321
John E., 402
John Graves, 366
John Graves II, 370
John Graves III, 371
John I, 307
John II, 305
John Irwin, 313
John Kelly, 376
John M., 367
John of Wales, 305
John P., 341
John Peck, 322
John Preston, 306

John W., 399
John Wesley, 398
John, Capt., 365
Jonathan King, 311
Joseph, 406
Josephine B., 308, 382
Josephine Goodale, 314
Joy Ann, 406
Joyce Ann, 358, 359
Judith Ann, 317
Judith Lynn, 396
Julia A. (Young), 341
Julia Ann, 330
Juliet Ann (Nold), 321
Kate (Tousey), 312
Katherine, 368
Katherine (Berry), 315
Katherine/Katheryne, 372
Katherine (Turney), 365
Kathleen Lee, 396
Kenneth Archbell, 310
Kevin, 316
L. G. Sylvanis, 398
Laura, 305
Laura (Strausbaugh), 367
Laura Ann, 402
Laurine Mae, 316
Leland Burnette, 310
Leland Burnette II, 311
Lena, 359
Lillian, 367
Lillian (Dougherty), 406
Lillian (Nowlin), 315
Lillian Lenora, 390
Lillian Myrtle (Sibley), 384
Lillie G. (Pender), 375
Lisa Diane (Asta), 397
Lisette Susanna (Krauss), 317
Lois (Loomis), 310
Lorene (Petersen), 370
Lori (Surges), 346
Lou Allen, 379

Louis M., 367
Louis Thompson, 309
Louis Thompson, Jr., 309
Lucie (MacDaniel), 314
Lucinda, 366
Lucinda (Fruit), 305
Lucinda Adaliza, 400
Lulu, 372
Malinda (Fruit), 378
Malissa, 380
Manuel Clayton, 397
Marcus Whitman, 399
Margaret, 370
Margaret (Smith), 314
Margaret (Stockton), 399
Margaret Ann (Propst), 382
Margaret Delilah (Reed), 398
Margaret Ellen, 372
Margaret Hannah, 399
Margaret Mary (Bond), 315
Margery Joyce, 392
Marguerite (Stewart), 399
Marguerite Louise, 376
Maria (——), 400
Marian Cary (Miles), 370
Marie (de Zaba), 310
Marie (Rash), 374
Martha A. McKinley (Wiles), 321
Martha E. (Bensley), 381
Martha Josephine, 398
Mary, 305, 360, 371, 400, 401
Mary (——), 403
Mary (——), 365
Mary (Roach), 376
Mary (Summers), 400
Mary A. (Martin), 401
Mary Ann, 400
Mary Bernadette (Cunningham), 406
Mary Elizabeth, 375

Mary Elizabeth (Miller), 399
Mary Etta (Watson), 379
Mary F., 406
Mary Jane (Snivens), 371
Mary Louise, 315
Mary Mabel, 359
Mary Miller (Wildhack) (Humes), 314
Mary Susan, 396
Mary Violet, 398
Mathew Robert, 396
Maude Courtney (Staub), 321
Maysel Evelyn (Hebb), 379
Melba (Lynn), 379
Melissa Lynn, 396
Michael Dennis, 317
Michael G. II, 317
Michael Graves Sims, 370
Michelle Denise, 317
Milton, 308, 312
Milton Aspden, 321
Minnie Mae, 399
Mitchell, 371
Molly (Morgland), 374
Molly (Patterson), 314
Morris, 314, 321
Morris Chester, 314
Morris Henry, 365
Morris I, 305, 360
Morris II, 307
Morris/Maurice Robinett, 341
Myrene (Friede), 370
Myrtle Collins (Allison), 367
Nancy, 377
Nancy Beauford, 305
Nancy G., 366
Nancy Jean, 397
Nancy Margaret, 383
Nancy Maria, 322
Nancy Turney, 367, 375
Nathaniel, 398
Nathaniel Miller, 382

Nettie (Terwhilegar), 398
Nevada Janet, 380
Nicholas McCarty, 340
Noah Noble, 312
Olive, 341
Olive Dawn, 379
Olive Lillian (Dougherty), 406
Ora Henri (Crawford), 321
Oscar, 400
Patricia Ann (Cosgrove), 395
Paula Kay, 370
Pearlie Ethel (Turner), 370
Perry W., 365
Phyllis Katheryn, 359
Polly, 365
Polly (Hughes), 378
Preston, 306, 381
Rachael (Morris), 307
Rachel K., 406
Ralph J., 399
Raymond, 367
Rebecca, 305, 377
Rebecca Anderson, 375
Rebecca Ann, 306, 360
Rebecca Cary, 371
Rebecca Crabtree (Randel), 381
Richard, 305
Richard Allen, 397
Richard Alvin, 390
Robert E. Lee, 367
Robert Lee, 395
Robert Steven, 396
Robert, Dr., 406
Russell, 370
Ruth (Lorentz), 375
Sadie Catherine (Dickenson), 358
Sallie Peak, 371
Sally Ann, 365
Samuel, 360
Sara Ann, 379

Sarah, 400
Sarah A. (Persons), 401
Sarah Ann, 366
Sarah Catharine, 375
Sarah Emma, 380
Sarah (Herst), 321
Sarah Jane, 381
Sarah Kelly (Anderson), 374
Sarah Rebecca, 375
Scott Andrew, 346
Seath, 400
Sharyn, 406
Sophia (Talbot), 305
Stanley Sherwood, 315
Stanley Sherwood III (b. 1942), 316
Stanley Sherwood III (b. and d. 1936), 316
Stanley Sherwood, Jr., 315
Steffani Allyse, 397
Stephen Michael, 317
Steven William, 315
Sue Ann (Christman), 315
Susan A., 366
Susan Frances (Reece), 309
Susan Rebecca, 371
Sylvester Osmer, 391
Tallitha Thomas, 305
Taylor Martin, 397
Theodore Hatfield, 317
Theodore Hatfield, Jr., 320
Theodore W., 311
Thomas, 305, 400, 402, 406
Thomas A., Gen., 382
Thomas Armstrong, 313
Thomas B., 341
Thomas Edward, 397
Thomas Gano, 374
Thomas Hart, 358
Thomas Jerome, 399
Thomas O'Neil, 313
Thomas Rodman, 374

Thomas, Gen., 340
Toni Lynn (Huggins), 396
Vicki Lynn (Haynes), 397
Viola, 406
W., 380
W. A., 375
Walter, 367
Wendy Leigh, 396
William, 400, 406
William Amos, 371, 374
William Amos, Jr., 373
William Franklin, 341
William Harry, 380
William Isaac, 406
William Little, 340
William Patterson, 314
Morrison, Ann E., 340
Mothershead
  Alice Maria (Bonzi), 329
  Alvin Morris, 326
  Alvina (Liese), 313
  Amanda Melvina (Morris), 325
  Amanda Morris, 326
  Ann Ashley, 328
  Anna Stockton (Owen), 327
  Bennet F., Dr., 312
  Bessie Owen, 327
  Carlotta, 326
  Carlotta (Brackenbush), 326
  Caroline (Morris), 312
  Desdemona Morris, 313
  Diane Frazier (Heffner), 328
  Elizabeth Ashley (Crossett), 328
  Ethel (Warner), 328
  Fabricus McCalla, 312
  Irene, 327
  John Leland III, 328
  John Leland IV, 328
  John Leland, Jr., 327
  John Leland V, 328
  John Leland VI, 328
  John T., Dr., 325
  John Wilson, 327
  Julia, 327
  Julia Mary Morris, 326
  Katharine (Brown), 327
  Katherine, 328
  Katherine Bullard, 312
  Leland, 326
  Leland Morris, 313
  Maria, 329
  Maria Christy, 329
  Mary (——), 329
  Mary Duncan (Wilson), 327
  Melinda Marie (Luthin), 328
  Michael Anthony, 329
  Milton Morris, 313
  Morris Warner, 329
  Nathaniel, 312, 326
  Owen Morris, 327
  Pat (——), 329
  Ruth (Burt), 326
  Serene Threlkeld, 312
  Therese (Petkelis), 328
  Warner Bonzi, 329
  Wilson, 327
Mueller, Daniel R., 385
Mueller, David, 385
Mueller, Michael, 385
Mueller, Toni Jean (Bardelmier), 385
Mueller, Troy, 385
Mugg, Belle, 358
Muhle, Jason Paul, 404
Muhle, Justin Allan, 404
Muhle, Lori Katherine (Kuntzelman), 404
Muhle, Todd Francke, 404
Mulholland, Joseph Barclay, 370
Mulholland, Joseph Bradley, 370
Mulholland, Julie Ann (Bader), 370

Mundy, Kathy Alane, 359
Munos, Jose Ferriz, 371
Munos, Juan Miguel, 371
Munos, Lyna, 371
Munos, Mariana, 371
Munos, Rebecca Cary (Morris), 371
Nalewajk, Catherine Jean (Reardon), 393
Nalewajk, David M., 393
Nalewajk, James Reardon, 393
Nalewajk, Jessica Lee, 394
Nance, James, 335
Nance, James N., 335
Nance, Jayne (Campbell) (Byal), 335
Neely, Elizabeth W., 361
Neely, Gertrude (——), 361
Neely, Joseph, 361
Neely, Mary (Turney) (Colville), 361
Neely, Sam Turney, 361
Nelson, Bessie MayBelle (Morris), 391
Nelson, Enid M. (Benson), 391
Nelson, Gordon James, 391
Nelson, Oggie Iver, 391
Nemec, Roberta, 346
Nesbitt, Samuel, 306
Nicander, Addie Marie, 388
Nicander, Alissa Annette, 388
Nicholas, Aileen, 379
Nichols, Chrystal Ann, 381
Nichols, Ida (Morris), 381
Nichols, Robert Wilson, 381
Nimnicht, Dorothy Winnifred (Morris), 399
Nimnicht, Ernest Eugene, 399
Noble, Dr., 312
Nold, Juliet Ann, 321
Noonan, Corene Oletta (Hash), 384
Noonan, Denise Margalo, 384
Noonan, Herbert, 384
Northrup, Ida, 309
Norton, Mame Austin (Hart), 355
Norton, Robert Armsted, Dr., 355
Nowlin, Lillian, 315
Nygren
   Aaron, 403
   Agnes Ann (Kuntzelman), 402
   Alden, 402
   Brandy, 403
   Bryan James, 403
   Caleb, 403
   Delores (Kucera), 403
   Heather, 403
   Inez, 403
   James Alden, 403
   Jason Eric, 403
   Jody (Snyder), 403
   Julia Ann, 403
   Katherine (Gerhardt), 403
   Lawrence, 402
   Matt, 403
   Melissa, 403
   Ronald Richard, 403
   Yancey, 403
O'Brien, Elizabeth Morris (Mertz), 319
O'Brien, Kathleen Becker, 319
O'Brien, Terrence Becker, 319
O'Brien, Tracy Morris, 319
Obering, Amy Winn (Hail), 362
Obering, Christian, 362
Obering, Shauna Ann, 362
Ogden, ——, 375
Ogden, Dell (Ham), 375
Oram, Marina Linda (Soares), 389
Oram, Shane Lawrence, 390
Osborn, ——, 375

Osborn, Ann Elizabeth
    (Campbell), 334
Osborn, Ida Bruce (Ham), 375
Osborn, Joelie, 335
Osborn, John C., 335
Osborn, Paul, 334
Osborn, Paul, Jr., 335
Osburn, Dorothy Lee (Thomas),
    379
Osburn, Laurevle E., 379
Owen, Anna Stockton, 327
Parker, Armelle, 356
Parker, Henry, 377
Parker, Mary, 305
Parker, Rebecca (Morris)
    (Turney), 377
Parks, ——, 361
Parks, Mary (Morris), 360
Pasieka, Anne Ellen (Wilson),
    347
Pasieka, Bryan Wilson, 347
Pasieka, Helena Beth, 347
Pasieka, Jeffrey Carey, 347
Pasieka, Mark, 347
Patterson, Molly, 314
Payne, Melba Anne, 404
Payne, Mrs. John (Elizabeth
    Bowles Morris), 365
Peak, ——, 366
Peak, Sallie (Sconce), 366
Pearson, Mary Jane, 341
Pender, Lillie G., 375
Penn, Edgar Duke II, 372
Penn, John Buford III, 372
Penn, Margaret Anissa, 372
Penn, Mary Dan (Karsner), 372
Peppard, Jane Maria, 307
Pershing, Gen., 328
Persons, Sarah A., 401
Petersen, Lorene, 370
Petkelis, Therese, 328
Pfannebecker, Ella, 399

Piper, Ann Hart, 351
Piper, Mary Ann (Bodine), 350
Piper, Robert Lawrence, 350
Piva, Donna Antoinette, 317
Polk, Pres., 321
Pollock, Barbara Jean, 405
Postlewait
    Barbara Jean, 390
    Lillian Lenora (Morris), 390
    Michelle Lee, 390
    Patti Lorraine, 390
    Tina Marie, 390
    William Andrew, 390
    William. A., Jr., 390
Poulos
    Claire Marie, 387
    Cynthia Marie (Crandall), 387
    Frances Marie (Gibson), 386
    Geoffrey Paul, 387
    Gregory William, 387
    Jody Bernadette (Ferrais), 387
    Jordan Bernadette, 387
    Paige Marie, 386
    Paul William, Jr., Dr., 386
Powell, Anthony J., 356
Powell, Henry Clay, 400
Powell, Laura Beth (Hart), 356
Powell, Mary Ann (Morris), 400
Powers, Mary Elizabeth, 373
Prater, Hazel Elizabeth, 355
Prescott, Paula, 356
Prestigiacomo, Gary, 396
Prestigiacomo, Judith Lynn
    (Morris), 396
Prestigiacomo, Kara Lynn, 397
Prestigiacomo, Kelly Nichols,
    397
Prestigiacomo, Krista Lee, 397
Prewitt, Joseph Robert, 399
Prewitt, Margaret Hannah
    (Morris), 399
Proctor, Britt (Benjamisson), 343

Proctor, David M., Jr., 343
Proctor, David Milton, 343
Proctor, David Milton III, 343
Proctor, Dayse Mary (Whitecotton), 343
Proctor, Elizabeth Ellen, 344
Proctor, Evalyn (Layson), 343
Proctor, Mary Jane (Dodge), 343
Proctor, Virginia Dodge, 344
Proctor, Zora Wilson, 344
Propst, Margaret Ann, 382
Queen of England, 392
Quisenbury, Mary, 368
Radke, Lori Katherine (Kuntzelman) (Muhle), 404
Radke, Richard, Jr., 404
Raider, Anthony Lloyd, 372
Raider, Mary Dan (Karsner), 372
Raikes, Anna Elizabeth, 358
Rains, Frances Lenora, 390
Randel, Rebecca Crabtree, 381
Rangel, Rick, 395
Rangel, Christina Fela, 395
Rash, Marie, 374
Reardon, Carol Leona (Morris), 393
Reardon, Catherine Jean, 393
Reardon, Gail Marie, 394
Reardon, Jennifer Margaret, 394
Reardon, Maurine Anne, 394
Reardon, Richard Paul, 393
Redwine, —, 370
Redwine, —, 370
Redwine, Jennifer, 370
Redwine, Paula Kay Morris (Sims), 370
Reece, Susan Frances, 309
Reed, Margaret Delilah, 398
Reinhardt, Velma E., 398
Reinzo, Maurine Anne (Reardon), 394
Reinzo, Thomas, 394

Richards, —, 406
Richards, Sharyn (Morris), 406
Ricketts, Hepsibaugh, 366
Ricketts, Robert, 366
Riggs, Nancy Beauford (Morris), 305
Riggs, John Lyle, 305
Rigoli, Anthony, 357
Rigoli, Jason, 357
Rigoli, Sharon George (Vandiver), 357
Riorden, Charlotte Clara (Hart), 356
Riorden, James, 356
Rissmiller, Ida Marie (Hart), 354
Rissmiller, William, 354
Roach, John Leo, 360
Roach, Mary, 376
Roach, Ora Zoe (Walker), 360
Roberts, Eleanor, 305
Roberts, Elida, 371
Roberts, Elizabeth Emerson, 361
Robinson, Sallie Peak (Morris), 371
Robinson, W. T., 371
Rodman, Hattie, 374
Roehrs, Julia Ann "Julie" (Nygren), 403
Roehrs, Kelvin, 403
Roehrs, Nicole, 403
Roehrs, Whitney, 404
Roemmel, Charles Francis, 359
Roemmel, Janet Sue, 359
Roemmel, Kathy Alane (Mundy), 359
Roemmel, Phyllis Katheryn (Morris), 359
Roemmel, Sharon Lynn, 359
Roemmel, Steven Morris, 359
Rogers
    Linda Lee (Walden), 329
    Andrei, 329

Brian Lee, 330
Catherine Hunter
  (McDonnell), 329
Christopher Buergin, 329
Emilie Adele (Falls), 330
Florence Clara (Kuntzelman)
  (Walker), 405
Kevin Bonzi, 330
Kevin Lee, 329
Kimberly Buergin, 330
Kyle Andrew, 330
Laura Lynn, 330
Maria (Mothershead), 329
Marlin B., 405
Matthew Marbury, 330
Michael Mothershead, 329
Peter McDonnell, 329
Steven Lee, 329
Rohlman, Rhonda Elaine, 332
Romano, Alice, 333
Romano, Alice Alworth
  (Campbell), 333
Romano, Renato, 333
Romano, Robert Campbell, 333
Romano, Val Campbell, 333
Roosevelt, Pres. F. D., 310
Rorden, Adele Costa, 373
Rorden, Harold Louis, 373
Rorden, Harold Reinhardt, 373
Rorden, Joyce (Bryan), 373
Rorden, Nancy Katherine, 373
Rose, Kathleen Becker (O'Brien), 319
Rose, Robert Nelson, 319
Rosencrans, William S., Gen., 382
Rosing, Barbara, 356
Ross, Frances (McIntyre), 330
Ross, Julia Ann (Morris), 330
Ross, Morris Morris, 330
Ross, Norman, 330
Rosser, Mehethalem Ellen, 352

Rourk, Renee Lynn (Gibson), 389
Rourk, Scott Bradley, 389
Rourk, Shauna Rae, 389
Ruble, Margaret, 334
Rule, Christy, 376
Rule, Colin, 376
Rule, Jerri Ann (Jeffords), 376
Rule, Mathew Boyd, 376
Rule, Shannon, 376
Rule, Steven, 376
Rumsey, Barbara (Wallace), 324
Rumsey, Peter Connely, 324
Rumsey, Todd Connely, 324
Russell, Frances (Morris), 380
Russell, Margaret, 332
Russell, Robert, 380
Rutter, Leslie M., 333
Ryan, Erma, 379
Ryan, Russell, 331
Ryan, Tracey Lee (Soules), 331
Sample
  Ada M. (Hathaway), 332
  Andrew Russell, 332
  Claire (Walbridge), 332
  Elizabeth Morris, 333, 339
  James A. III, 332
  James A., Jr., 332
  James Anthony, 332
  Jane Hathaway, 332
  John, 332
  Julia A. Morris (Defrees), 332
  Julia Defrees, 333
  LeRoy H. Jr, 333
  LeRoy Hathaway, 333
  Leslie M. (Rutter), 333
  Mary Defrees, 333
  Morris Defrees, 332
  Robert Walbridge, 333
  Sally Helen, 333
  Susan Jane, 333
Sanders, Linda Lee (Hash), 383

Sanders, Ron, 383
Sanderson, Gloria Loraine, 354
Sandhagen, —, 329
Sandhagen, Dusty, 329
Sapp, Cora, 399
Sarbach, Mary Patricia, 308
Sass
    Carol Anne, 332
    Dale Lynn, 331
    Daniel Warren, 331
    David Norman, 331
    Dean Norman, 332
    Jacob Isaac, 331
    Janet A. (Lietaert), 331
    Kristy (Stachak), 331
    Lou Ellen (Defrees), 331
    Marcy Jo, 332
    Nancy Lee, 331
    Nicole Elizabeth, 331
    Norman C., 331
    Rhonda Elaine (Rohlman), 332
    Rosemary (Curtis), 331
    Shannon Donnel, 332
    Steven Dean, 332
    Tobis Thomas, 331
Saunders, Margaret R., 338
Savery, Cora A., 379
Saxbury, Erma Dean (Gaskill) (Dillinger), 353
Saxbury, James Alvin, 353
Schrock, Sue Ann, 405
Schultz, Elizabeth Katherine, 347
Schultz, Pamela Sue, 353
Schumann, Lynne, 336
Sconce, James, 366
Sconce, John, 366
Sconce, Lucinda (Morris), 366
Sconce, Robert, 366
Sconce, Sallie, 366
Scott, Carol Ann (Gaskill), 352
Scott, David John, 352
Scott, John Franklin, 352
Scott, John Franklin, Jr., 352
Scott, Rebekah Lynn, 352
Scott, Stephen Mark, 352
Seibert, Elizabeth McDowell, 360
Seibert, Ora Ann (McDowell), 360
Seibert, William Winfield, 360
Seymour, Mabel Adele, 309
Shafer, Addo, 335
Shea, —, 375
Shea, Myrtle (Ham), 375
Sheridan, Helen Elizabeth, 362
Sherrell, Lorelei L., 337
Shirley, Anastasia Germaine (Hart), 356
Shirley, Douglas, 356
Shoemaker, Beth Park, 344
Shoemaker, David Howard, 344
Shoemaker, Dennis, 344
Shoemaker, Ellen Proctor (Jenks), 344
Shumate, Angela, 396
Sibley, Lillian Myrtle, 384
Simmons, Armina (Cooper) (Morris), 397
Simpson, Gail, 316
Sims, Amy, 370
Sims, Chad, 370
Sims, Michael Graves Morris, 370
Sims, Paula Kay Morris, 370
Sinclair, Margaret, 334
Smalley, Anna Hamilton, 318
Smalley, James Lee, 318
Smalley, Martha Day, 318
Smalley, Sallie Morris, 318
Smalley, Susanne Day (Mertz), 318
Smith, Darrel, 402
Smith, Deborah Elizabeth, 320

Smith, Hazel Drucilla
  (Kuntzelman), 402
Smith, Margaret, 314
Smith, Shirley, 402
Smith, Virginia, 402
Smith, Walter, 402
Smith, Walter, Jr., 402
Smithe, Doris Suetta, 344
Smither, Clay, 368
Smither, Elizabeth (Johnson),
  368
Smither, Fantley M., 368
Smither, Fantley Wootton, 368
Smither, Katherine Jane
  (Wootton) (Beck), 368
Smither, Mathew, 368
Smither, Rebecca Jane, 369
Snivens, Mary Jane, 371
Snowden, Martha, 368
Snyder, Jody, 403
Soifer, Carol Ann (Morris)
  (Swift), 395
Soifer, Neil, 395
Sold, —, 313
Soper
  Catherine, 366
  Claire, 366
  Katherine, 366
  John L., 366
  Louella, 366
  Nancy G. (Morris), 366
  Robert, 366
  Sue, 366
  Susan A. (Morris), 366
  William, 366
Soules
  Ashley Rose, 331
  Darren Thomas, 331
  Jackie (Cieslwicz), 331
  Julia (Cranston), 331
  Justin Thomas, 331
  Megan Lynn, 331

Nancy Lee (Sass), 331
Thomas Christopher, 331
Thomas Christopher, Jr., 331
Tracey Lee, 331
Sparks, Janet Lee Larson, 381
Sparks, Chrystal Ann (Nichols)
  (Keebler) (Christenson), 381
Sparks, Lester, 382
Sparks, Lester John, 381
Speed, Amanda Leigh, 394
Speed, Derek Scott, 394
Speed, Katherine Elizabeth, 394
Speed, Megan Laura, 394
Speed, Jennifer Margaret
  (Reardon), 394
Spoon, Eileen Mae, 315
Stachak, Kristy, 331
Stafford, Bud, 392
Stafford, Margery Joyce
  (Morris), 392
Starkey, Violet, 404
Staub, Maude Courtney, 321
Stellman, Mamie Espya, 398
Stevens, Gloria May (Morris)
  (Gibbs), 391
Stevens, S. H., 391
Stewart, Harry, 379
Stewart, Marguerite, 399
Stewart, Nancy, 393
Stewart, Olive Dawn (Morris),
  379
Stitt, Elizabeth, 363
Stockton, Margaret, 399
Strausbaugh, Allene, 368
Strausbaugh, Eugene F., 368
Strausbaugh, Laura, 367
Strausbaugh, Mary (Quisenbury),
  368
Strausbaugh, Nancy Turney
  (Morris), 367
Strausbaugh, William, 367
Stuart, Bobby (Morris), 367

Stuart, John, 367
Sullivan, Regina Kaye, 392
Summers, Mary, 400
Surges, Lori, 346
Sweeney, Laura Lynn (Rogers), 330
Sweeney, Stuart Howard, 330
Sweeney, James Grayson, 330
Swift, Carol Ann (Morris), 395
Swift, Robert Christopher, 396
Swift, William L., 395
Talbot, Sophia, 305
Tanner, ——, 378
Tanner, Katherine Ann (Brown), 378
Tarkington, Booth, 322
Tate, America Bowles, 401
Tate, Thomas, 401
Tatham
    Anne Comfort, 336
    Benjamin Arthur, 336
    Campbell, 336
    Charles III, 336
    Charles, Jr., 336
    Gail (Brusse), 336
    Gregory Campbell, 336
    Holly Susan, 336
    Jocelynn Margaret, 336
    Julie Defrees (Campbell), 335
    Kathleen (Dale), 336
    Lynne (Schumann), 336
    Rebecca Masland, 336
    Sandra ——, 336
    Susan (Masland), 336
    Tracy D., 336
Taul, A., 375
Taul, Lena Smith (Ham), 375
Taylor, Amos Turney, 361
Taylor, Betsy Turney, 361
Taylor, Elizabeth Emerson (Roberts), 361
Taylor, Leslie Mannen (Turney), 361
Taylor, Louis, 361
Taylor, Mary Martin, 361
Teft, Sylvia Middaugh, 404
Temple, Elizabeth W. (Neely), 361
Temple, H. H., 361
Temple, Stephen, 361
Terwhilegar, Nettie, 398
Thatcher, Arnold, 396
Thatcher, Brittany Marie Lee, 396
Thatcher, Catelin Lee, 396
Thatcher, Kathleen Lee (Morris), 396
Thatcher, Patrick Clay, 396
Thayer, Abigail C., 312
Thomas
    Betty Eilene, 379
    Catherine, 382
    Catherine Lorene, 380
    Catherine Lynn, 380
    Dorothy Lee, 379
    Evelyn Maysel (Morris), 379
    Harold Lee, 379
    John, 377
    Karen Lee (Giermann), 380
    Nancy (Morris), 377
    Robert K., 380
Thompson, Jacqueline, 350
Thompson, Jean, 362
Thorpe, Pamela, 337
Timm, Dean, 379
Timm, Evelyn Maysel (Morris) (Thomas), 379
Todd, Alexander Eric, 396
Todd, Benjamin, 306
Todd, Carol Ann (Morris) (Swift) (Soifer), 395
Todd, Dr. John Michael, 395
Todd, Lucinda (McIntire), 360

Todd, Michael David, 396
Todd, William, 360
Topping, —, 317
Topping, Estelle Patricia, 317
Torczon, Brett Joseph, 404
Torczon, Craig Lee, 404
Torczon, Jennifer Renee, 404
Torczon, Stephanie Gay
  (Kuntzelman), 404
Torczon, Timothy, 404
Tousey, Geo., 312
Tousey, Kate, 312
Treuesdel, —, 341
Treuesdel, Ella (Morris), 341
Trosper, Almanza Palmyra
  (Morris), 360
Trosper, William, 360
Trottier, Beverly Lucile, 393
Trower, Charlotte Christi
  (Gaskill), 353
Trower, Jean, 352
Trower, Jeffrey Nathan, 353
Trower, Keith Edward, 353
Trower, Ronald Brian, 353
Troy, Eleanor Adams (Linsmith), 323
Troy, Stephen Patrick, 323
Trundle, Ann (McCurry), 339
Trundle, Charles, 339
Trundle, Charmian (Campbell)
  (MacDonald), 338
Trundle, Jennifer, 339
Trundle, Sidney A., 338
Tucker, Amy Elizabeth, 362
Tucker, Barry Chalfaunt, 361
Tucker, Betsy Turney (Taylor), 361
Tucker, Clint, 391
Tucker, Gideon, 364
Tucker, Henry, 364

Tucker, Jessie Margaret (Morris)
  (Cate) (Whitney) (Brenzel), 390
Tucker, John William, 390
Tucker, Leslie Chalfaunt, 362
Tucker, Lucy (Turney), 364
Tucker, Robert, 364
Turner, John Michael, 369
Turner, Laura Frances, 369
Turner, Pearlie Ethel, 370
Turner, Rebecca Murray (Horn), 369
Turney
  —, 360
  Alfred, 364
  Amos, 360, 365
  Amos Ewing, 363
  Amos McIntire, Jr., 361
  Andrew Jackson Ewing, 363
  Bettie Brent (Johnson), 362
  Bettie Sheridan, 363
  Betty, 361
  Brooks Helm, 363
  Daniel E., 362
  Edna, 362
  Edna Earl (Hinton), 363
  Elizabeth (Stitt), 363
  Elizabeth Mannen, 363
  Helen Elizabeth (Sheridan), 362
  Henry, 363
  Jean (Thompson), 362
  Jesse, 361, 362, 363, 365, 377
  Jesse McClellan, 362
  Jesse McClellan, Jr., 363
  John Barton, 363
  Katherine, 365
  Leslie, 363
  Leslie Mannen, 361
  Lori Winn, 363
  Lucille, 362

Lucinda (McIntire) (Todd), 360
Lucy, 364
Margaret, 362
Mary, 361
Mary Clay, 362
Mary Elizabeth (Mannen), 361
Mary (Ewing), 362
Mary L. (Goodman), 364
Mary (Mitchell), 362
Mathew, 364
McClellan Ewing, 362
Nancy (Morris), 377
Nellie, 362
P., 360
R., 360
Rebecca (Morris), 377
Robert Winn, 363
Sallie, 361
Sally Ann (Fluent), 363
Utterback, Nancy, 350
Valentz, Mary Jo, 337
Valley, Alaura Anne, 348
Valley, Katherine Elizabeth, 348
Valley, Paul James, 348
Valley, Susan Elizabeth (Allen) (Waude), 348
Van Deren, ——, 367
Van Deren, Nancy Turney (Morris) (Strausbaugh), 367
Vandersmith, ——, 341
Vandiver, Ernest, 357
Vandiver, Jeffrey, 357
Vandiver, Jeremy, 357
Vandiver, Karen George, 357
Vandiver, Margaret June (Hart), 357
Vandiver, Sharon George, 357
Vandiver, Sheila (Lewis), 357
VanHaverbeke, Brittany Jo, 384
VanHaverbeke, Denise Margalo (Noonan), 384
VanHaverbeke, Joseph, 384
VanHaverbeke, Stephany Jo, 384
VanHaverbeke, Tiffany Jo, 384
VanHorn, ——, 355
VanHorn, Derek, 355
VanHorn, Gavin Page, 355
VanHorn, Junia Ann (Hart), 355
VanHorn, Travis Howerton, 355
Vasu, Dr. Andre, 339
Vasu, Julie Defrees (Humphreys), 339
Velkley, Don, 368
Velkley, Kitty Anne (Beck), 368
Vickers, Martha Ann (Jeffords), 375
Vickers, Robert, 375
Wade, Charles, 334
Wade, Margaret (Sinclair) (Campbell), 334
Wakeman, Pamela H., 323
Walbridge, Claire, 332
Walden, Linda Lee, 329
Walker
  Alanna Liane, 405
  Blanche, 370
  Cameron Scott, 405
  Carla Roseann, 405
  Christina Louise, 405
  Evelyn Dean (Hoyle), 405
  Florence Clara (Kuntzelman), 405
  Larry Keith, 405
  Lorrie Kay, 405
  Lula M. (McDowell), 360
  Melvin L., 360
  Ora Zoe, 360
  Orval Keith, 405
  Rodney Gay, 405
  Shannon Lynn, 405
  Sue Ann (Schrock), 405
Wallace
  Ann Morris (Werbe), 324

Barbara, 324
Barbara Stewart, 325
Corwin, 311
Desdemona Morris (Corwin), 311
Harriet Marie, 313
Harry Mothershead, 312
James Walter, 312
Katherine Bullard (Mothershead), 312
Leland Morris, 313
Michael Lee, 324
Michael Stewart, 324
Mrs. A. W., 324
Rose Katherine, 313
Timothy, 324
Walter E., 311
Walter, Karen Kay, 357
Warner, Ethel, 328
Warner, Ezra J., 328
Warren, Adelaide (Morris), 371
Warren, Cleora, 371
Warren, Frank, 371
Warren, Jane, 371
Warren, Marjorie, 371
Warren, Michael Oliver, 384
Warren, Shawn Marie (Currie), 384
Watson, Mary Etta, 379
Waude, Jon Bergsland, 348
Waude, Susan Elizabeth (Allen), 348
Weiss, Mark Kendall, 405
Weiss, Shannon Lynn (Walker), 405
Werbe
  Ann Morris, 324
  Barbara Carey (Haines), 323
  Catherine Chandler, 325
  Catherine Frost (Daggett), 325
  Daniel Stewart, 324
  Eleanor Carey, 325
  Elizabeth French, 324
  Mary French (Jackson), 324
  Thomas C. III, 324
  Thomas Chandler, Jr, 323
Wheeler, Diane Eliz., 353
Wheeler, Joseph, 380
Wheeler, Sara Emma (Morris), 380
White, ——, 389
White, Christina Marie, 389
White, Kimberly Ann (Gibson), 389
White, Melissa Angelica, 389
Whitecotton, Andrew Tilden, 344
Whitecotton, Dayse, 340
Whitecotton, Dayse Mary, 343
Whitecotton, Elizabeth Morris, 344
Whitecotton, Florence (Deaver), 345
Whitecotton, James Henry, 343
Whitecotton, James Henry, Jr., 345
Whitecotton, Lola (Alverson), 344
Whitecotton, Zora Almanza (Wilson), 343
Whitney, Debra Ann, 391
Whitney, Jessie Margaret (Morris) (Cate), 390
Whitney, Willian Randell, 390
Wickham, Arthur, 385
Wickham, Dorothy Louise (Bardelmier), 385
Wickham, Laura Lee, 385
Wickham, Stephen Reynolds, 385
Wiles, Martha A. McKinley, 321
Wiles, Nancy (Ames), 321
Wiles, William McKinley, 321
Willliams, Dr., 374

Williams, Elizabeth Morris
   (Sample), 333
Williams, Helen (Long), 374
Williams, James, 306
Williams, Kristy Lynn, 376
Williams, Walter Allen, Dr.,
   333, 339
Willis
   Carson D., 355
   Feather Ann (Davis), 373
   Margaret, 362
   Marion, 355
   Michael David, 373
   Nell (Hart), 355
   Nellie (Turney), 362
   Samuel, 362
   William Henderson, 355
   William Henderson, Jr., 355
Willis-Davis, Reena Katherine,
   373
Willkomm, Ursala H., 354
Wilson
   Andrew Henderson, 342
   Anne, 347
   Anne Ellen, 347
   Bart, 349
   Betty Ann, 384
   Brandon Troy, 349
   Bret, 349
   Cleo Mary, 349
   Eli, 342
   Elizabeth (High), 350
   Elizabeth Agnes (Morris), 384
   Elizabeth Katherine (Schultz),
     347
   Frances Hudnall (Hales), 345
   George Andrew, 345
   George Hales, 346
   James Mortimer, 349
   James Mortimer, Jr., 349
   Joseph Byron, 384
   Kathryn Ann (Beirman), 349
   Lillie Jane (Holloway), 345
   Mac, Dr., 343
   Marie (Earle), 349
   Marilynn Marie, 384
   Marjorie (Beer), 345
   Martin Duke, 350
   Mary Ann (Hart), 342, 350
   Mary Duncan, 327
   Morris Duke, 349
   Morris Duke, Jr., 350
   Mortimer Hart, 345
   Ola Beatrice (Hammond), 349
   Patrick High, 350
   Ruth (——), 349
   Zora Almanza, 343
   Zora Myrton, 348
Wimpy, Catherine Ann, 376
Wimpy, Catherine Ann (Byrd),
   376
Wimpy, John, 376
Winans, Cindy, 335
Winn, Elizabeth Mannen
   (Turney), 363
Winn, Judge Robert Hiner, 363
Wirt, Mary, 355
Wollard, Carla Roseann
   (Walker), 405
Wollard, David Lee, 405
Wollard, James Kenneth, 405
Woolard, Michael James, 405
Woolley, John Stuart, 387
Woolley, Paige Marie (Poulos),
   386
Wootton, Alice Rebecca, 369
Wootton, Bailey Peyton, 368
Wootton, Clara (Collins), 368
Wootton, Katherine Jane, 368
Wootton, Thomas, 368
Wortman, Carol, 393
Young
   Chester, 366
   David, 344

John, 366
John F., 366
Julia A., 341
Katherine, 366
Mary Violet (Morris), 398
Nancy, 366
Oral Lewis, 398
Ruth (Chandler), 366
Shirley (Smith), 402
Sue (Soper), 366
Susan, 344
Terry, 344
Virginia Dodge (Proctor), 344
William, 344

The "Morris Family Tree"

Allied Families: Cushman, Frazee, Friends, Robinett, Spurgeon, Worley, Worral

BRIEF ACCOUNTS OF THESE FAMILIES are given here because they were connected with our Morrises through intermarriage or as neighbors, thereby contributing in important ways, especially in the early days, to this family's welfare and survival.

The Cushman Family

A COMPLETE LISTING of this family and much information about the Pilgrims and the *Mayflower* is in *Cushman Genealogy and Family History*, published in 1942 by Alvah Burt. This is out of print but available in a few libraries and on microfilm in libraries of the Latter Day Saints. There are some errors, which is always unavoidable but true of any large genealogy. Many Morrises and Frazees are in it.

Very briefly, the Cushman story is one of pioneering and migration.

Having lived in England for many generations, then in Holland for perhaps twelve years because of Separatist religious beliefs, Robert Cushman brought his young son Thomas to Massachusetts in 1620 on the *Fortune*. But Robert did not remain there long, as he was on business missions for Plymouth Colony. Son Thomas, who was left in the care of William Bradford, grew up in Bradford's home under his tutelage.

Here in Plymouth the Cushmans started a family line; consequently, all Cushmans in America are descended from Robert and Thomas. The first Thomas Cushman in America (Thomas II on the *Mayflower* Relationships chart) married in Massachusetts Mary Allerton, daughter of Isaac and Mary Allerton; all three Allertons came from London to America on the *Mayflower*. Thomas Cushman III married Ruth Howland, also in Massachusetts. Their son, Thomas IV, married a girl from Connecticut, and their son, Thomas V, was born there. He and *his* son, Thomas VI, went west to claim land in the newly-opened northwest Virginia. That son, Thomas VI, married Mary Frazee from New Jersey. But he, born in Connecticut, traversed the long distance back to his birth state to fight in the Revolution with his brother Isaac and comrades. He was a private. After the war was over Thomas VI and wife Mary Frazee returned to their new wilderness land where their daughter Sarah was born in Monongalia Co., Va., in 1786. She married Morris Morris I, son of Richard of Welsh descent.

Isaac Cushman, born 1752 in Essex County, N.J., was in James Dougherty's Pennsylvania Company during 1775, 1776, 1777, and 1778, stationed part of the time as a spy at Fort Morris on Little Sandy Creek. His land in Pennsylvania adjoined brother Thomas's in Virginia. State boundaries were questionable at that time.

This pattern of moving reveals the migration south and then to the new West of several members of the Cushman family. Listed below is only the main part of the Cushman genealogy which concerns the Morris family.

Generations:

1 Thomas Cushman I, born in Kent County, England, married Elynor Hubbard.

2 Robert Cushman, born in Kent County, England, baptized 9 Feb. 1577, married 31 July 1606 Sarah Reeder. He was a wool comber and deacon in Leyden, Holland; remained there temporarily to be governor for those who could not come on the *Mayflower* because of lack of space; arrived in America 8 Nov. 1621 on the second ship, the *Fortune,* with his young son, Thomas.

3 Thomas Cushman II, born before 8 Feb. 1607-8 in Canterbury, Kent County, England; came to America on the *Fortune* in 1621 with his father; lived with Governor Bradford; married c. 1636 Mary Allerton, a *Mayflower* passenger (as were her parents, Isaac and Mary Allerton). Thomas II was ruling elder in 1649 after Governor Bradford's death. He died 10-11 Dec. 1691, at Plymouth, Mass.

4 Thomas Cushman III, born 16 Dec. 1637 at Plymouth, Mass., first married 17 Nov. 1664 Ruth Howland. Had three children. Second marriage 16 Oct. 1679 to Abigail Fuller, by whom he had four children. He died 23 Aug. 1726 at Plympton, Mass., age 89 wanting a month.

5 Thomas Cushman IV, third child of Thomas and Ruth above, born 18 May 1670, Plymouth; married Sarah Strong (daughter of Jedidiah and Freedom [Woodward] Strong, born Coventry, Conn., c. 1674; died 25 Dec. 1726, Lebanon, Conn.). Six children. He died 9 Jan. 1726/7, Lebanon, Conn.

Allied Families ♦ 445

6 Thomas Cushman V, born c. 1705, probably Lebanon, Essex Co., Conn.; married 1727 at New London, Conn., Mary —— (b. Coventry, Conn.); second marriage 17 Jan. 1764 at New Providence, N.J., to Susanna Johnson (d. Elizabeth, N.J.).

7 Thomas Cushman VI (six Thomas Cushmans in a row in our line!), born 19 Dec. 1739, Lebanon, Conn.; married 5 Jan. 1764 at New Providence, N.J., Mary Frazee (daughter of Ephraim Frazee of Monongalia Co., Va., born 3 April 1744); second married —— Abbott); private in Revolution. He was shot by father-in-law, mistaken for an Indian, died in Kentucky after 1787.

8 Sarah Cushman, born 10 Sept. 1766, Monongalia Co., Va.; married c. 1781/2 Morris Morris I (born 12 Feb. 1761, Monongalia Co., Va., son of Richard Morris; died 17 May 1809). Second marriage 1780 to Graham Forrest of Harrison Co., Ky. Sarah died 10 Jan. 1842.

The Frazee Family

MEMBERS OF THE FRAZEE FAMILY intermarried with the Morris and Cushman families quite a lot. (See Intermarriage chart.) Because some members of the Frazee generations one through five are our ancestors, they are listed here. Only partial information is given here after the marriage of 5g Mary Frazee, born 1744, to Thomas Cushman VI, to show migration and Morris relationships. Details are available in the Frazee genealogy, *Ancestral Lines of the Doniphan, Frazee, and Hamilton Families* by Frances Frazee Hamilton, published in 1928. Also see *The Frazee-Frazeur Family History* by Dean R. Frazeur Jr., 1985, which covers a somewhat different line. There is much Frazee information in the *Cushman Genealogy and General History* by Alvah Burt, 1942. See the Bibliography for publication details of these three books.

* * * * *

There was a very early settlement of Frazees and a few Spurgeons in the northwestern corner of Maryland called "Blooming Rose," at Frazee's Ridge very close to the larger settlement of Friends, called "Friendsville." Today, this is a town with a museum, a library, and a librarian well informed about the historic Swedish family of Friends and their friends.

The name Frazee is from the French word *fraiseur,* which means frizzled hair. Fraze, Frazer, and Frazier are all derivatives used by the same family in America. The Frazees possibly were French Huguenots who fled from France to England when the Protestants were driven from France by the Catholics at the time of the Bartholomew Massacre, or they may have been Walloons from the Netherlands. There appears to be no definite proof of either of these theories. An attempted compilation of "our" line follows:

Generations:

1 Ephraim (or Samuel) Frazer or Frazee had two, three, or four sons who emigrated to a grant of land from the English Crown and were among the founders of Elizabethtown, N.J., in 1665/6, the year after New Jersey was granted to Carteret.

    2a Samuel Frazee, died between 1675 and 1726 in New Jersey.
    2b —
    2c —
    2d Joseph Ephraim Frazee, born c. 1640 at Elizabethtown, N.J., one of the "Eighty Associates of Elizabethtown in 1664"; Revolution; is listed for non-military service in Monongalia Co., Va. (*West Virginia Ancestors* by A. W. Reddy, Baltimore: 1930). The oldest-found document mentions Joseph 19 Feb. 1665. Name of first wife unknown. Second marriage of Joseph Ephraim Frazee, in Elizabethtown, N.J., to Mary Osborn (born c. 1661, of Newbury, Mass.), lived Rahway, Union Co., N.J., five children; died Jan. 1715.

        3a Elisha Frazee, born c. 1570 Woodbridge, Glouster, N.J.; married Sarah ——; died 27 Sept., Woodbridge, N.J.

            4a Ephraim Frazee, Jr., *grandson* of 2d Joseph Ephraim Frazee, born c. 1703 Elizabethtown, N.J., member Scotch Plains, N.J., church in 1747; married three times; died 1776. Had eighteen children spanning forty-one years: nine children by his first wife, Rebecca Cutler (born c. 1797 in Westmoreland Co., Pa.); two by the second wife, name unknown; and seven by the third wife, Anna Squire Maxfield (LDS record). A record exists of his bragging in church in Monongalia County of siring eighteen children.

Allied Families ♦ 447

The nine children by Rebecca Cutler:
5a Miriam Frazee, b. 29 March 1729, Westmoreland Co., Pa.; nine children.
5b Martha Frazee, b. 6 April 1731.
5c Ephraim Frazee Jr., b. 25 Jan. 1733, soldier in the Revolution from Borough of Elizabeth, N. J.; 1772 returned to Westmoreland, Pa.; held land in Virginia adjoining land of sister 5g Mary Frazee on 15 Oct. 1783 (record book Monongalia Co., Va.); taxed 1785 in Monongalia Co., Va.
5d David Frazee, b. 9 Oct. 1737, one of earliest settlers c. 1760 of Westmoreland Co., southeast of Pittsburgh, Pa.; one of the earliest in Preston Co., Va.; in 1769 on Sandy Creek adjoining brother-in-law Thomas Cushman; in census of 1782 for Monongalia Co., Va.
5e Rachel Frazee, b. 1 Nov. 1739, Westmoreland Co., Pa., d. Jun. 1748.
5f Hannah Frazee, b. 25 Jan. 1742, Westmoreland Co., m. David Sayre.
5g Mary Frazee, b. 3 April 1744, Westmoreland Co., m. 5 Jan. 1764 at New Providence, N.J. (recorded in Minute Book, First Presbyterian Church), Thomas Cushman (b. 19 Dec. 1739 at Lebanon, Conn.; private from New Jersey in Revolution (DAR record); d. after 11 April 1787); three children; see *Cushman Genealogy.*
5h Elizabeth Frazee, b. 13 Jan. 1747, m. 1768 James Cole.
5i Jeremiah Frazee, b. 7 March 1749, moved from New Jersey to Shellysport, Garrett Co., Md., settled on Frazee's Ridge, Md.; six children.

The two children of Ephraim Frazee Jr. by second wife, name unknown:
5j Thurman Frazee, b. 20 March 1752, Westmoreland Co., Pa.; moved to Ohio; 1st m. Anna Edwards (b. 1755), six or nine children; d. 19 April 1844 at Frazee's Ridge, Md.
5k Samuel Frazee, b. Nov. 1753, N.J.; a scout at age 21; in 1774 at Battle of Point Pleasant under General Lewis; with Daniel Boone in 1778 in Kentucky; 1782 census in Monongalia Co.; m. 1787 Rebecca Jacobs of Virginia (1769-1837); 1800 census Mason Co., Ky.; d. 1849 in Kentucky.

6a Rebecca Frazee
6b Hannah Frazee, d. Nov. 1849, Mason Co., Ky., age 96.
6c Ephraim Frazee
6d Jacob Frazee
6e Louis Frazee
6f Hiram Frazee
6g Joseph Frazee, b. 1794, Mason Co., Ky.; 1st m. Mary Ann Coburn; three children.

    7a Anderson Frazee, b. 1827, Kentucky.
    7b Samuel Frazee, b. 19 April 1831; 1st m. Corburnetta Dewees (1837-1912); d. 17 Sept. 1897.

        8a Maria Defrees Frazee, b. April 1858; 1st m. 17 Oct. 1891 Charles Gates (d. 1892); 2nd m. Henry Lindsey Browning (d. 1923).

            9a Netta Dewees Browning, m. George Pittman.

            10a Georgianna Browning Pittman, b. 1918.
            10b Sylvia Browning Pittman, b. 1921.

    7c — Frazee

Note: Maria Frazee Browning (8a above), who wrote the letter and genealogical chart for Mrs. Thomas O'Neil Morris in 1930 (in text of *Migration* story), descends from 5k Samuel Frazee, his son 6g Joseph Frazee, and his son 7b Samuel Frazee, all directly above. They are shown here because Maria Frazee Browning and descendants lived in Indianapolis.

    6h Joseph Frazee (cont'd from above): 2nd m. 22 April 1834 Ann Cushman (b. 12 Oct. 1798, d. 11 Aug. 1851; dau. of David and Dorcas Morris Cushman; see *Cushman Genealogy*); four children.

        7d Daughter, died young.
        7e Joseph T. Frazee, b. 1836, Kentucky; named for father.
        7f John Morris Frazee, b. 1837, Kentucky; named for grandfather, a medical doctor; m. Eliza Lusk; lived Maysville, Ky.

  8a Anna C. Frazee, m. Posey Dixon Ball; is listed in *Mayflower Index*.

  9a Frances Dixon Ball

  8b Frances L. Frazee, m. Henry Lloyd; is listed in *Mayflower Index*.

  9a Henry Lloyd Jr.

 7g David Cushman Frazee, b. 17 Sept. 1842, Kentucky; named for maternal grandfather; Confederate Army; lived Maysville and Lexington, Ky.; m. Maria Lee.

  8a Jennie Lee Frazee, died young.

The seven children by third wife, Anna Squire Maxwell:
5l Anna "Nancy" Frazee, b. 19 Oct. 1757.
5m Deborah Frazee, b. 12 May 1760, d. 7 April 1800, m. Isaac Cushman, brother of the Thomas Cushman who m. 5g Mary Frazee. Mary and Deborah were half-sisters.
5n Ephraim Frazee Jr. (second Ephraim by same father, see 5c, above), b. 3 Jul. 1762.
5o Squier *[sic]* Frazee, b. 22 July 1764, moved to Kentucky with mother and twin brothers Aaron and Moses in 1784 to join his half-brother Samuel; m. in Kentucky Priscilla Forman (b. 1778); in 1800 census, Mason Co., Ky.; seven children.
5p Sarah "Sally" Frazee, b. 10 Dec. 1766.
5q Moses Frazee, b. 8 Sept. 1770 (twin of 5r Aaron, below); carpenter; m. Elizabeth Morris (dau. of John Morris and sister of Morris Morris II, who m. Rachael); moved to Kentucky 1784; in 1800 census of Mason Co., Ky.; later went to Indianapolis. (See Morris genealogy.)

  6a Alfred Frazee
  6b Dorcas Frazee, d. young.
  6c Polly Frazee, m. —— Poe (probably the son of pioneer Dr. Poe who came to Indianapolis in 1821); three sons.
  6d Phoebe Frazee, m. —— Adamsen, had children.

6e John M. Frazee, nephew of Morris Morris and Rachael, lived Indianapolis after 1821, unmarried; mentioned in Jacob P. Dunn's *Greater Indianapolis*, p. 9, and in Chapter VI of this book.

5r Aaron Frazee, b. 8 Sept. 1770, twin of 5q Moses, moved with him to Kentucky in 1784; m. Eleanor ———; in 1800 census Mason Co., Ky., d. 1841; eight children, including Ira, James, Ellen, Richard, and Squier Frazee, who begot Demia, Rachel, and Samuel Frazee.

The Friend Family

SWEDES ORIGINALLY CAME to America in 1638, landing at what is now Wilmington, Delaware. A family with the surname Friend came from Sweden just a bit later than the earliest immigrants and settled near Philadelphia. One of the original sons built bridges over Ridley and Crum Creeks in the 1680s, the area of the Robinetts and Worleys. Another son went to "Augusta"—anywhere west of the coastal settlements. One John Friend, in 1748, sold land to Richard Morris in "Swedeland," near Emmitsburg, Maryland, land which John Friend had already patented in 1741. The Friends made a settlement in Maryland which they called Friendsville, on the very western border of Maryland not far east of the Sandy Creek area of Virginia. They, too, used Fort Morris on occasion. Many members of the Frazee family and a few Spurgeons also settled in or near Friendsville.

The records of history have shown us that families and friends usually migrated together. So we can find the Morrises, can follow their migrations by finding the names of their friends. The wanderlust and moving were "catching," although there were nearly always some who remained settled. Our Morris men were always among the earlier explorers and movers, which may be why they are not recorded more often. An even earlier pioneer was Daniel Boone, who generally was ready to move on soon after the Morrises had arrived. Their mutual times on the frontiers often overlapped, but not for long; however, they surely knew each other.

The Friends were somewhat the exception in this migration pattern, for a large group of that family never did go further west but stayed in Friendsville in far-western Maryland to make it the large town it is today.

Located there are a library with a knowledgeable librarian, and a Friends museum.

The Robinett Family

THE SOURCE FOR THIS FAMILY is *Allen Robinett and His Descendants in America,* privately published in 1967 by James M. Robinett. (See the Bibliography for publication data.) In 1990, Feather Davis made excerpts from the Robinett family book at the Genealogy Room of the Allegheny Community College in Cumberland, Maryland. The following information is from these excerpts.

The Robinett origin was probably from the French Huguenots. A 1563 family Bible still exists.

1 Allen Robinett I, born about 1632 in England, died 5 Jan. 1694, married about 1653 Margaret Symm in the parish of Michall Queenheth (d. before 1694). They arrived in Philadelphia with William Penn in 1682, bringing four children and three servants. They lived briefly in Upland (Chester), Pa., on Ridge Creek near Peter Worral. Then they bought 250 acres from William Penn in Upper Providence, Chester Co. (now Delaware Co.), Pa. The Worley property was adjacent. Allen Robinett also bought a lot in Philadelphia at Eighth and Walnut Streets which at the time was worthless (probably too far out). Later on, inherited by son Samuel, it was valuable. In 1689, Allen was arraigned for writing papers abusive to the king's servant. The Robinetts were probably not Quakers.

    2a Allen Robinett II died early. Upon his death he sent sons Joseph II and Allen III to live with their uncle and aunt, Joseph I and Sarah Robinett, in Northeast, Maryland.

        3a Joseph Robinett II was deputy keeper of the House of Correction in 1735 under Nathan Worley; 1st m. 1730 Barbara Cullin of Chester; 2nd m. —— Carter; was in Chester, Pa., in 1766.

            4a James, probably born before 1713, Upper Providence Township, Chester County, Pa., m. by 1734/5 to Ann ——, owned land in Adams Co. (now York Co.), Pa. Both are buried in Huntington Friends Meeting House, Adams Co., Pa. (*Note:* County seat is Gettysburg, very close to Emmitsburg, Md., near Swedeland, where Richard Morris bought land in 1748 from John Friend.) Seven children: Allen IV; Samuel; a girl who married Alexander Brandon of York Co., Pa. (commissioner of the revenue, colonel of the 104th Regiment of the state militia, went to Monongalia County in 1777, died 1813); one son went to Ontario, Canada; and Joseph Robinett III, born 1751, who emigrated to Monongalia County, then to Kentucky, having married Rachel Morris, daughter of Richard Morris.

3b Sarah Robinett, married —— Bond; married —— Carter.
3c Allen Robinett III, b. c. 1703 in Maryland, lived with his uncle and aunt, Joseph I and Sarah Robinett, and with his uncle, —— Carter (above 3a, 2nd husband of other aunt, Barbara Cullin Robinett), in Cecil Co., Md.; in 1718, carpenter-builder. Married Lydia Derrick (b. 1712, d. 1768), died 1759 Marcus Hook, Pa.; six children, all born in Marcus Hook: Prudence, b. 1731; Allen IV, b. 1735, moved to Wilmington, Del.; Joseph III, b. 1738; Rachel, b. 1742; David, b. 1745; and Lydia, b. 1750, m. Adam Grubb.

2b Samuel Robinett, m. Mary Taylor, inherited homestead and a Philadelphia lot.
2c Susannah Robinett, m. Robert Ward, had a daughter, Elizabeth.
2d Sarah Robinett, m. 1694 Richard Bond, inherited property and a slave.
2e Joseph Robinett I, m. Sarah ——, lived in Northeast, Md., reared Joseph II and Allen III, sons of his older brother, Allen II.

Robinetts were found in Frederick Co., Md., in 1748, the year the county was organized.

In 1782, James, John, and Joseph Robinett all signed the petition concerning the division of Virginia and Pennsylvania.

Quite a few Robinetts remained in Oldtown, Maryland. Some did not move westward as did the other families of Morris, Spurgeon, Frazee, Worley, Worral, Friend, Greathouse, and Hogue during their migration in the latter 1700s. The name George Robinett appears today on a Maryland state marker as one of four men who in 1791 surveyed the old Braddock Road from Hancock to Fort Cumberland—the first wagon road where before were only horse trails.

Allied Families ♦ 453

The Spurgeon Family

THERE EXISTS a privately typed, sixteen-page "Spurgeon Family History" by Barbara Ahart, written in 1990, which is available in the Maryland Historical Society. A bit of information is in Alvah Burt's *Cushman Genealogy and General History,* published in 1942, and a little more in *Allen Robinett and His Descendants,* published in 1967 by James M. Robinett in Beaumont, Texas, available through the Latter Day Saints libraries. A good descriptive autobiography by Meshach Browning, a Spurgeon nephew who often mentions the Spurgeons, is *Forty-four Years in the Life of a Hunter,* reprinted in 1985 by Appalachian Background, Inc., of Oakland, Md.

*   *   *   *   *

The earliest known Spurgeon was a London laborer named James Spurgeon (1700-1790) of Whitechapel, Middlesex, who was imprisoned at Newgate where the conditions were deplorable, ravaged with plague and pestilence. He had burgled clothing from a spinster's house. Very fortunately, in 1719 James was sentenced to be transported to America and was sold as an indentured servant to pay for the cost of his transportation to the port of Oxford, Md. By 1733 James had paid his indenture in Baltimore County and was a landowner at Monocacy Hundred in north-central Maryland. He lived in the Antietam Creek area and at one time owned about 600 acres in Maryland and Pennsylvania. A 1736 map shows two "Spurgeants" on opposite sides of the Potomac River where the great wagon road, previously called Packhorse Ford, crossed the river just beyond Antietam Creek at Shepherdstown. James was on the first petit jury in Frederick in 1749.

About 1875 he sold most of his land to live in Monongalia County, Va., near his sons who had moved there earlier. James and Susanna were only a mile from their good friend Richard Morris at Sandy Creek Glades. They had at least ten children. On Spurgeon's land at a crossroads one of the earliest surveys was made, for a meeting house, the first community church and school of the Sandy Creek Glades, serving the neighborhood of three states, as did the fort on Richard Morris's land. Their properties were right up in the corner where three states come together. James was described as a wise, kind, good man by his nephew, Meshach Browning, who lived with him for a year.

William Spurgeon, born in 1740 in Prince George's County, Md., married Priscilla Robinett, went to Sandy Creek Glades in 1777/8, and lived on Little Sandy in 1785. He was next to Samuel Robinett and a neighbor of Joseph Robinett (State Enumeration of Inhabitants for 1782). In 1761, James Spurgeon Sr. was taxed with four tithables. In the same year, James Jr., William and Jonathan Spurgeon were taxed with one tithable each, listed after Richard Morris. By 1872 Jeremiah, James, and William Spurgeon had signed the petition concerning the division of Virginia and Pennsylvania. The old records contain many Spurgeons.

One very exciting event which happened to this household in September 1784 was that George Washington and his nephew Bushrod asked for lodging and spent the night in the Spurgeon home. The purpose of their trip across the Allegheny tableland was to visit land which George Washington owned and to learn if there was a possible route for a canal from the headwaters of the Potomac River to those of the Cheat River by way of the Monogahela River to Fort Pitt. This is all described in Washington's diary.

Another event which should be mentioned is the marriage of Samuel Spurgeon to Catherine Morris, the youngest of the three daughters of Richard Morris. Samuel was not a child of the original James so must have been one of his many grandchildren. In the 1782 census, there are five in his household, implying a marriage for Samuel about 1775 and three children (by then), as their only daughter "died young," as did so many children then.

Very many Spurgeons, as well as Robinetts and Morrises, are recorded in Maryland and especially in the Glades of (West) Virginia, with intermarriage a natural occurrence among neighbors.

The Worley Family

WHEN WILLIAM PENN AND HIS PARTY arrived in America in 1682, the Worleys already held property in the Philadelphia area. Allen Robinett, who came with Penn, bought land adjacent to the Worley land.

Ezekial Worley, a blacksmith and sickle maker, moved from Philadelphia to the Sandy Creek Glades and became a neighbor of the Morrises by 1770.

Anthony and Joshua Worley, who moved on to Ohio, were also in Monongalia County in 1770. Later, Anthony migrated to Hazleton, south of Sandy Glades, and built a corn husker.

Joseph Robinett, a grandson of Allen Robinett II, worked under Nathan Worley in 1735 back in Pennsylvania. Then Nathan, also a sickle maker, and Bruce Worley left Philadelphia for Sandy Creek Glades in 1776.

The next year, 1777, Nathan Worley (Wirley) was killed by Indians at Dunkard Bottom, near Statler's Fort in Monongalia County, Va.

Sources: *History of Preston County, West Virginia,* Vol. I, by Oren F. Morton; and *Monongahela: The River and the Regions,* by Richard T. Wiley. See the Bibliography for publication data.

The Worral Family

THE WORRALS, also neighbors of the Morrises and also among the earliest settlers in the Sandy Creek area, are enumerated in lists of Philadelphia Quakers associated with William Penn. A Richard Worral lived a few blocks north of Penn on Second Street, in Philadelphia. Penn lived on Front Street, as did William Penn Jr. (map of 1684). A Peter Worral lived on Crum Creek (map of Chester County, Pa.).

In 1782, Samuel, Samuel Jr., and Anthony (Autern) signed that same petition concerning the division of Virginia and Pennsylvania, which must have been a heated issue that bothered most of the populace.

No records have been found of intermarriage between the Worral or the Worley families and the early Morris families.

The "Morris Family Tree"

GENERAL BIBLIOGRAPHY

Note: Additional references may be found following Chapters II and III, and in the selected bibliography following Chapter X.

Adjutant General's Office. Trenton, N.J.
Ahart, Barbara. *Spurgeon Family History*. Unpublished manuscript, 1990.
Allen, Irvin G. *Historic Oldtown, Maryland*. Parsons, W.Va.: McLain Printing Co., 1983.
Ambler, Charles Henry. "West Virginia History." *Encyclopaedia Britannica*. Vol. 23. Chicago: Encyclopaedia Britannica Co., 1957.
Annapolis Hall of Records. Maryland State Archives. Court Proceeding Files. Land Records. Index. Patents. Judgments. Wills.
Army and Navy Journal. New York. 10 June 1899.
Author's File. Anne Morris Mertz, 726 Loveville Road #904, Hockessin, Delaware 19707-1513.
Bergon, Frank. *The Journals of Lewis and Clark*. New York: Viking Penguin, 1989.
Biographical Directory of the Indiana General Assembly, 1816-1899. Vol. 1. Indianapolis: Select Committee on the Centennial History of the Indiana General Assembly in Cooperation with the Indiana Historical Bureau, 1980.
Bode, Carl. *Maryland: A Bicentennial History*. New York: W. W. Norton, 1976.
Bourbon County, Kentucky, Records. Deed Book. Marriage Register 2:14.
Browning, Edward Franklin. *Genealogy of the Brownings in America from 1621 to 1908*. Filmed by Salt Lake City, Utah, 1965 0381773 RN0374041. Newburgh, N.Y.: Journal Print, 1908 (?).
Burke, John. *The Castle in Medieval England*. Totawa, N.J., 1978.
Burt, Alvah Walford. *Cushman Genealogy and General History*. Greenfield, Ind.: Wm. Mitchell Printing Co., 1942. A. W. Burt, 3031 Temple Ave., Westwood, Cincinnati, OH.
Cane Ridge Meeting House Museum, Paris, Ky.
Castles and Historic Places. Wales Tourist Board. Llangolen, Wales: Dobson & Crother, 1978.

Chalkley, Lyman. *Records of West Augusta County, Virginia.* Stanton, Va., n.d.
Chance, Hilda. *Index of Ten Mile Country and Its Pioneer Families: Genealogical History of Upper Monongahela Valley.* Liberty, Pa.: Hilda Chance, n.d.
Clarke, Charles G. *The Men of the Lewis and Clark Expedition.* Glendale, Calif.: Arthur H. Clark & Co., 1970.
Corbit, William F. "Welsh Emigration to Pennsylvania; An Old Charter Party." *Emigrants to Pennsylvania,* Michael Tepper, author. Baltimore: Genealogical Pub. Co., 1975. Reprint 1992. A consolidation of ship passenger lists from *Pennsylvania Magazine of History and Biography.*
Core, Earl L. *The Monongahela Story: A Bicentennial History.* Vol. 1. Parsons, W.Va.: McLain Printing Co., 1974, 1984.
Craig, Peter S. *The Family of Neils Larson Friend.* Unpublished manuscript, 1988.
———. *West Virginia.* Parsons, W.Va.: McLain Printing Co.
Crown Hill Cemetery. P.O. Box 188349, Indianapolis, IN.
Crumrine, Boyd, ed. *History of Washington County, Pennsylvania.* Philadelphia: L. H. Everts, 1882.
Dalton, Pamela. *In Britain.* London: March 1985.
Davis, Feather Ann. Notes. 5001 Wetherdsvale Road, Baltimore, MD 21207.
Davis, Julia A. *Shenandoah, Daughter of the Stars.* Baton Rouge: Louisiana State University Press. Printer and Binder, Topan Printing Co., Inc., 1994.
Dern, John P. "The Upper Potomac in 1736." *Western Maryland Genealogy.* Vol. 2. Middletown, Md.: Catoctin Press, 1986.
DeVoto, Bernard, ed. *The Journals of Lewis and Clark.* Boston: Houghton Mifflin, 1953.
Doddridge, Joseph, Rev. Dr. "Memoir." *Notes on the Settlement and the Indian Wars of the Western Parts of Virginia and Pennsylvania from the Year 1763 until the Year 1783 Including Together with a View of the State of Society and Manners of the First Settlers of That Country.* Parsons, W.Va.: McLain Printing Co., special edition, 1989.
Draper, Lyman C. Manuscript-interview in Madison, Wis. MSS 13 CC. Louisville, Ky.: *The Filson Club Quarterly.* Collection in Church History, Baptist, Mays Lick.
Dunn, Jacob Piatt. *Indiana and Indianans.* Chicago and New York: American Historical Society, 1919.
"Early Bourbon Families." Kentucky Archives. Morgantown, W.Va.

Eckert, Allan W. *The Frontiersmen.* Boston and Toronto: Little Brown, 1967.
——. *Wilderness Empire.* Boston and Toronto: Little Brown, 1969.
Ellis, Franklin. *History of Fayette County, Pennsylvania.* Philadelphia: L. H. Everts, 1872.
Encyclopedia Britannica. Vol. 23. Chicago: Encyclopaedia Britannica Co., 1957.
Evening Bulletin. Philadelphia: 2 December 1944.
Filby, P. William, ed., with Mary K. Meyer. *Passenger and Immigration Lists Index.* Vol. 2. Detroit, Mich.: Gale Research Co.
Fischer, David Hackett. *Albion's Seed.* New York and Oxford: Oxford University Press, 1989.
Frazeur, Dean R., Jr. *The Frazee-Frazeur Family History.* Richmond, Va.: privately published, 1985.
Frederick County, Maryland, Historical Society.
Friend Family History Museum, Friendsville, Pa.
Ganoe, William Addleman. *The History of the United States Army.* Ashton, Md.: Eric Lundberg, rev. ed., 1964.
Greathouse, Jack Murray. *A Partial History of the Greathouse Family.* Fayetteville, Ark.: Washington County Historical Society.
Greer, George Bates, Jr. *Greer Family History.* (printed) Denver, Colo.
Haines, Nancy. Files. In possession of Reily Adams, 663 Forest Boulevard., Indianapolis, IN 46240.
Hamilton, Frances F. *Ancestral Lines of Doniphan, Frazee, Hamilton.* Greenfield, Ind.: Wm. Mitchell Printing Co., 1928.
Hardin, Bayless E. "Dr. Preston W. Brown, 1775-1826: His Family and Descendants," *Genealogies of Kentucky Families.* Louisville: *The Filson Club Quarterly.*
Haw, James. "Patronage, Politics, and Ideology, 1753-1762." *Maryland Historical Magazine.* Baltimore: Maryland Historical Society, Fall 1990.
Heads of Families in Virginia (Taxpayers List), 1782.
Hedstrom, Elizabeth E. "Scenes from the Indian Wars." *National Parks Magazine.* Washington, D.C.: National Parks and Conservation Association, 1776 Mass. Ave., N.W., January/February 1995.
Heitman, Francis Bernard. *Historical Register of Officers of the Continental Army, April 1775 to 1863.* Harrisburg, Pa.: Historical and Museum Commission, 1977.
——. *Historical Register and Dictionary of the United States Army.* Vol. 1. Washington, D.C.: Government Printing Office, 1903.
Hinton, John. "A New Map of the Province of Maryland in North America." *Universal Magazine, 1780.* Maryland HR G 1213-60.

Holiday, John H. *Indianapolis and the Civil War.* Indianapolis: E. J. Hecker, 1911.
Holy Bible. The Book of Joel. Chapter 2, verse 28.
Honolulu Star Bulletin. Honolulu, Hawaii, 4 April 1935.
Howard, William Willard. "The City of Indianapolis." Supplement in *Harper's Weekly.* New York: Harper, 11 August 1888.
Hoye, Charles E. "The Cuppett Family." *Maryland Mountain Democrat.* Oakland, Md., 1935.
———. *Pioneer Families of Garrett County, West Virginia.* Compiled by Garrett County Historical Society. Parsons, W.Va.: McLain Printing Co., 1988.
Hyman, Max R. *Indianapolis, An Outline History and Description of the Hoosier Capital.* Published in Commemoration of the Centennial Celebration of Indiana at Indianapolis, October Two to Fifteen. Indianapolis: Max R. Hyman, 1916.
Indiana Freemason. Franklin, Ind.: Grand Lodge Free and Accepted Masons of Indiana, November 1965.
Indianapolis News. 6 June 1906; 10 March 1909.
International Genealogical Index (IGI). Microfiche. Salt Lake City, Utah.
Iowerth, Peate. *The Welsh Home.* No publication data.
Irving, Washington. "English Writers in America." *The Sketch Book.* Chicago: Great Books Foundation, 1963.
James, Alfred P. *The Ohio Company: Its Inner History.* Pittsburgh: University of Pittsburgh Press, 1959.
Johnston, Ross B., compiler. *West Virginia Estate Settlements.* Baltimore: Genealogical Publishing Co., 1898.
Ka Hoku o Red Hill. Honolulu: 13 December 1941.
Kenny, Hamill. *West Virginia Place Names.* Piedmont, W.Va.: The Place Name Press, 1945.
Kentucky Ancestors. Brides' Index. Bourbon County, Ky.
Kentucky Citizen. Paris, Ky.: H. E. Brooks, 10 July 1945.
Kentucky General Records. NSDAR Library, 1776 D St., N.W., Washington, DC 20006-5392. Bible Listings. 1934-39.
Kercheval, Samuel. *A History of the Valley of Virginia, 1883.* Strasburg, Va.: Shenandoah Publishing House, 4th ed., 1925.
Knight, Jeremy K. *Chepstow Castle.* Cardiff, Wales: Welsh Historic Monuments, Brunel House, 2 Fitzalan Road, Cardiff CF2 IUY, 1986.
Lavender, David Sievert. *The Way to the Western Sea.* New York: Harper & Row, 1988.

General Bibliography ♦ 461

Leckey, Howard L. *The Ten Mile Country and Its Pioneer Families: A Genealogical History of the Upper Monongahela Valley with Surname Index, 1892-1951.* Waynesburg, Pa.: Waynesburg Republican, 1950. Reprint, Apollo, Pa.: Closson Press, 1993.
Logan's History of Indianapolis from 1818. No publication data. The author possesses only thirteen pages of this old book.
Map. "Philadelphia as William Penn Knew It—1684." Philadelphia: Program Committee for Commemoration of Penn's First Arrival in America, 1933.
Marriage Bonds Filed in Monongalia County. Compiled from DAR Magazines, typewritten copy, 1937. Morgantown, W.Va., Archives.
Mayflower Story. Plymouth, Mass.: General Society of Mayflower Descendants, November 1933.
Mertz, Anne Morris. Author's File. 726 Loveville Road #904, Hockessin, Delaware 19707-1513.
Moise, Elizabeth A. "Daniel Boone: First Hero of the Frontier." *National Geographic.* Washington, D.C.: National Geographic Society, December 1985.
Monongalia County Clerk Records. Book 2, pp. 8, 36, 129, 168.
Monongalia County Court Records. Env. 114D, Sept. 1800.
Monongalia County Deeds. OS 2:347.
Montgomery, Thomas Lynch. *Pennsylvania Archives.* Vol. 2. Harrisburg: Harrisburg Publishing Co., State Printer, 1906.
Morris Bros. Pub. *The Morris Family and Its Coats of Arms.* New York: DeVilliers, 854 W. 34th St., New York, N.Y.
Morris-Butler House Museum. "Abstract to Deed." Indianapolis: Historic Landmarks Foundation of Indiana, n.d.
Morris, Jan. *The Matter of Wales.* Oxford: University Press, Walton Street, Oxford 2 6DP, 1984.
Morris, John Graves. Notes. 618 San Pedro, SE, Albuquerque, N.Mex., 87108.
Morton, Oren F. *History of Preston County, West Virginia.* Kingswood, W.Va.: Journal Publishing Co., 1914.
National Archives. Washington, D.C.
National Geographic. Vol. 1. Washington, D.C.: National Geographic Society, July 1983.
National Society Daughters of the American Revolution Library, 1776 D Street, N.W., Washington, D.C. 20006-5392.
National Trust for Historic Preservation. 1976.
Nicholas, Anna. *Indiana.* Indianapolis: privately printed, n.d.
Nicholas County, Ky., Record Office.

Old Northside Historic District Preservation Plan 3. Indianapolis: Indianapolis Historic Preservation Commission, 1979.

Olsen, Evelyn Guard. *Indian Blood.* Parsons, W.Va.: McLain Printing Co., 1967.

Oman, Charles W. C. *British Castles.* New York: Dover Publications, Inc., copyright 1989.

Peat, Wilbur D. *Pioneer Painters of Indiana.* Indianapolis: Art Association of Indianapolis, 1954.

Peck, David W. *The Greer Case, a True Court Drama.* New York: Simon & Schuster, 1955. Reprint 1963.

Pennsylvania Archives. Harrisburg, Pa.

Peppliers, John S., Allen Chambers, and Nancy B. Schwartz. "What Style Is It? Part III." Washington, D.C.: Historic Preservation, n.d.

Perks, John Clifford. *Chepstow Castle.* London: Her Majesty's Stationery Office, 1978.

Powell, James Madison, M.D., Monmouth, Oregon. *Powell History.* Portland, Ore.: 1922. Second edition, 1977, includes 1929 Appendage by Dr. Powell. Current update compiled by Virginia McKechnie. Portland, Ore.: Design Printing, Inc. Church of Jesus Christ of Latter Day Saints, Salt Lake City, Utah, microfilm 1036375, item 3.

Purdue University Alumni Records. Lafayette, Ind.

Quinsbury, Anderson Chenault. *Revolutionary Soldiers in Kentucky.* Baltimore: Genealogical Publishing Co., 1896. Reissued 1947.

Reddy, A. W. *West Virginia Ancestors.* Baltimore, Md.: 1930.

———. *West Virginia Revolutionary Ancestors.* Washington, D.C.: Model Printing Co., 1930.

Reif, Rita. *Treasure Rooms of America's Mansions, Manors, and Houses.* New York: Country Beautiful Corp. and Coward-McCann, Inc., 1970.

Rensselaer Polytechnic Institute. *Alumni Records, Class of 1870.* Troy, N.Y.

Rice, Millard Milburn. *This Was the Life: Excerpts from the Judgement Records 1748-1765.* Baltimore: Genealogical Publishing Co., 1984.

Robinett, James M. *Allen Robinett and His Descendants in America. Part I, Allen Robinett.* Manuscript, 2 vols. Privately published by the author, 4875 Regina Lane, Beaumont, Tex.: 1 October 1967. Available through the Baltimore Historical Society and Latter Day Saints libraries.

Rocky Gap State Park. Tourism and Public Relations, Allegany County. Cumberland, Md.: Commercial Press Printing Co., 1990.

Ryan, Barbara Milligan. *The Relationship Between Women and Victorian Interiors, 1850-1890: With Specific Reference to the Morris-Butler House.* Bloomington: Indiana University, 1994.
Saturday Evening Post. "They Cover the Waterfront." Philadelphia: 31 July 1943; 18 August 1943.
Scharff, John Thomas. *History of Western Maryland.* Philadelphia: L. H. Everts, 1900. Reprint 1983.
———. *History of Western Maryland From the Earliest Period to the Present Day.* Baltimore: Regional Pub. Co., 1882. Reprint, Hatboro, Pa.: Tradition Press, 1967.
Schaun, George, and Virginia Schaun. *Boundaries.* Annapolis, Md.: Greenburg Publications, n.d.
"Science and Invention." *Literary Digest.* New York: 23 March 1935.
Schlissel, Lillian. *Women's Diaries of the Westward Journey.* New York: Schoken Books, Inc., 1982.
Schrader, Christian. *Indianapolis Remembered: Christian Schrader's Sketches of Indianapolis.* Indianapolis: Indiana Historical Bureau, 1987.
Schreiner-Yantis, Nettie, and Florence Speakman Love. *Personal Property Tax Lists for the Years 1786, 1787 (Partial), and 1788 for Monongalia County, Virginia.* Springfield, Va.: Genealogical Books in Print, 1987.
Seaver, J. Montgomery. *Morris Family Records.* Philadelphia: American Historical-Genealogical Society, 1924.
Shepherd, Rebecca, compiler. *A Biographical Directory of the Indiana General Assembly, 1816-1899.* Vol. 1. Indianapolis: Select Committee of the Centennial History of the Indiana General Assembly, 1980.
Sheppard, Walter Lee, Jr., compiler. *Passengers and Ships Prior to 1684.* Baltimore: Genealogical Publishing Co., 1970.
Smith, Bradford. *Bradford of Plymouth.* Philadelphia and New York: J. B. Lippincott, 1951.
Spofford, Ernest. *Armorial Families of America.* Philadelphia: Bailey Banks and Biddle, 1929.
Spooner, Walter W. *Historic Families of America.* Vol. 3. New York: Historic Families Publishing Assoc., 1907.
Stille, Charles J. *Major General Anthony Wayne and the Pennsylvania Line in the Continental Army.* Port Washington, N.Y.: Kennikat Press, 1893. Reprint 1968.
Stillwell, John M. *Historical and Genealogical Miscellaney, Early Settlers of New Jersey and Their Descendants.* Vol. 4. Baltimore: Baltimore General Publishing Co., 1970.

Stoddard, Frank R. *The Truth About the Pilgrims.* New York: New York Society of Mayflower Descendants, 1952.
Suburban and Wayne Times. Wayne, Pa.: 23 April 1937.
Sulgrove, B. R. *History of Indianapolis and Marion County, Indiana.* Philadelphia: L. H. Everts & Co., 1884. Evansville: Unigraphic, 1878. Reprint 1974.
Temple Index Bureau (TIB). Salt Lake City, Utah: Latter Day Saints.
Time Magazine. New York: Time, Inc., 27 July 1962.
Tracey, Grace L., and John P. Dern. *Pioneers of Old Monocacy: Early Settlement of Frederick County, Maryland, 1721-1743.* Baltimore: Genealogical Publishing Co., 1987.
Trussel, John B. B., Jr. *The Pennsylvania Line, Regimental Organization and Operations, 1776-1783.* Harrisburg: Historical and Museum Commission, 1977.
University of West Virginia Library. Morgantown, W.Va.
U.S. Bureau of the Census, Bourbon County, Kentucky, 1800.
Vassar College Alumnae Records. Poughkeepsie, N.Y.
Veech, James. *Monongahela of Old: Historical Sketches of Southwestern Pennsylvania to the Year 1800.* Pittsburgh: Clearfield Co. Reprints and remainders, 1858 and 1892. Reprint, Baltimore: Genealogical Pub. Co., 1975.
Virginia Genealogist, The. Vol. 17. Bowie, Md.: Heritage Books, 1973.
Virginia Land Grants. Master Index. University of West Virginia Library, Morgantown, W.Va.
Virginia Taxpayers List (Heads of Families). 1782.
Virkus, Frederick A., ed. *Abridged Compendium of American Genealogy.* 7 vols. Chicago: The Virkus Co., 1925-1943.
Western Maryland Genealogy. Vol. 2. Middletown, Md.: Catactin Press, 1986.
West Virginia Archives. State Dept. of Culture and History, Charleston, W.Va. Maps. Auditor's Land Grants.
West Virginia History. Charleston, W.Va.: State Dept. of Culture and History, 1939.
Who's Who in America. Chicago: American Historical Society, 1919. New publisher: Chicago: Marquis Who's Who, Inc.
Who's Who in America. Vol. 2, 39th edition. Chicago: Marquis Who's Who, Inc., 1976-1977.
Wiley, Richard T. *Monongahela: The River and the Regions.* Butler, Pa.: Ziegler Co., 1937.
Williams, Edward, alias Iolo Morganwg. Wales: Ref. 13115b.

Willison, Hilary F. *History of the Pioneer Settlers of Flintstone, 1908.* Reprint of his memoirs. 1st ed. publisher, Albert L. Feldstein. Cumberland, Md.: Sir Speedy Printing Center, 1986.

Wishard, Elizabeth Moreland, *William Henry Wishard, A Doctor of the Old School.* Indianapolis: The Hollenback Press, 1920.

And it came to pass that after a time the writer was forgotten, but the work lived.

— Olive Schreiner

About the Author

Anne Morris Mertz is the sixth- and fifth-generation descendant, respectively, of the two Morris Morrises of this book. She is a graduate of Randolph-Macon Woman's College, Lynchburg, Virginia, and has two daughters, two sons, and eleven grandchildren.

She was selected for Marquis' *Who's Who of American Women* and elected to the National League of American Pen Women. A former governor of the Society of Mayflower Descendants in the State of Delaware, she is active in the Delaware Genealogical Society, the Delaware Historical Society, and the National Society of the Colonial Dames in America in the State of Delaware. Her researched historical and travel articles have been published in international journals, magazines, and newspapers.

Mrs. Mertz resides with her husband, Walter Day Mertz, in Hockessin, Delaware.

Notes

Notes

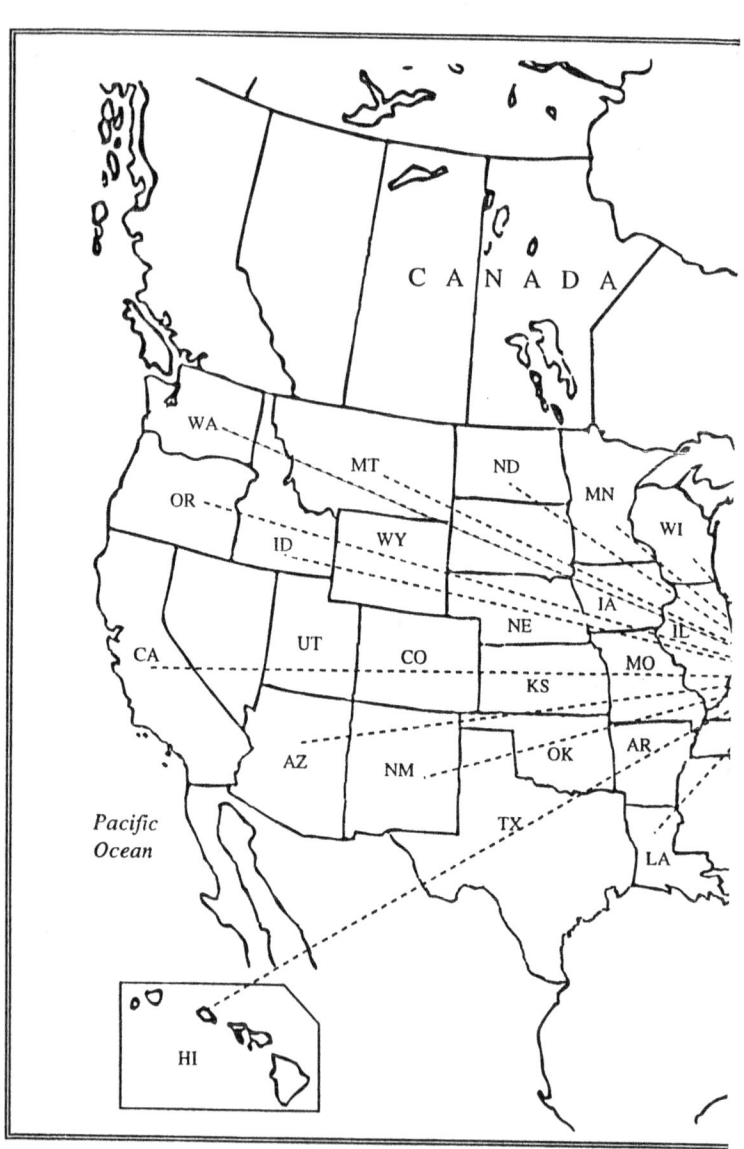

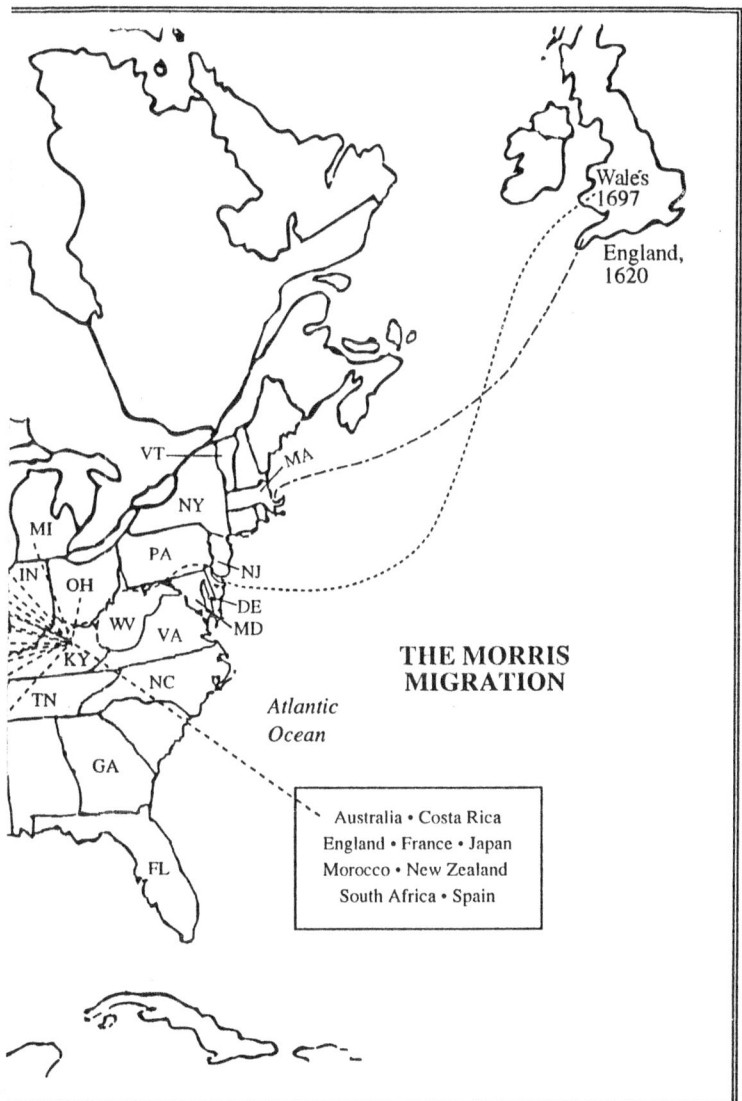

www.ingramcontent.com/pod-product-compliance
Lightning Source LLC
Chambersburg PA
CBHW071221230426
43668CB00011B/1260